D1394931

Good Housekeeping

COOK'S
YEAR

Good Housekeeping
COOK'S
YEAR

THE ULTIMATE GUIDE TO COOKING
THROUGH THE SEASONS
WITH OVER 500 RECIPES

BCA

LONDON   NEW YORK   SYDNEY   TORONTO

This edition published 1995 by BCA
by arrangement with Ebury Press

CN 1949

Copyright © 1995 Random House UK Limited or the National
Magazine Company Limited

All rights reserved. No part of this publication may be
reproduced, stored in a retrieval system, or transmitted in any form
or by any means, electronic, mechanical, photocopying, recording or
otherwise, without the prior permission of the copyright owners.

The expression GOOD HOUSEKEEPING as used in
the title of this book is the trade mark of the National Magazine
Company Limited and The Hearst Corporation, registered in the
United Kingdom and USA, and other principal countries of the
world, and is the absolute property of the National Magazine
Company Limited and The Hearst Corporation.
The use of this trade mark other than with the express
permission of The National Magazine Company Limited or The
Hearst Corporation is strictly prohibited.

Managing Editor: Julia Canning
Design: Sara Kidd, Jerry Goldie

Contributing authors: Jacqueline Clark, Joanna Farrow,
Louise Pickford, Janet Smith, Louise Steele
Contributing editors: Helen Southall, Donna Wood
Additional editorial research and assistance: Hilary Bird,
Fiona Hunter, Sara Lewis
Recipe testing: Emma-Lee Gow, Patricia Stone

Special photography: Karl Adamson, Graham Kirk
Photographic styling: Helen Payne
Food for photography: Louise Pickford
Colour illustrations: Madeleine David

Printed and bound in Spain by Printer Barcelona

FOREWORD

A superb guide to cooking from spring through to winter, *Good Housekeeping Cook's Year* includes over 500 double-tested recipes that make the most of fresh foods. An Ingredients Through The Seasons chapter gives guidance on buying and preparing produce, and an introduction to each season is packed with ideas for using seasonal ingredients – from soft fruits in summer to game in autumn. We have also included a range of original craft ideas, such as decorated pumpkins and a Christmas marzipan tree, so you can make a special occasion even more memorable.

The book includes all the unique features which make Good Housekeeping recipes so reliable and easy to use. All the dishes have been double-tested in the kitchens of the Good Housekeeping Institute and each recipe has a calorie count, preparation and cooking times and freezing instructions, plus symbols so that you can tell at a glance whether a recipe is low-calorie or extra-quick. In addition, a colour picture index, with every recipe in the book illustrated in colour and organized according to course rather than season, means you can find the perfect choice for every meal.

Moyra Fraser
Cookery Editor, *Good Housekeeping*

COOKERY NOTES
- Both metric and imperial measures are given for the recipes. Follow either metric or imperial throughout as they are not interchangeable.
- All spoon measures are level unless otherwise stated. Sets of measuring spoons are available in metric and imperial for accurate measurements of small quantities.
- Ovens should be preheated to the temperature specified. Grills should also be preheated. The cooking times given in the recipes assume that this has been done.
- Where a stage is specified in brackets under freezing, the dish should be frozen at the end of that stage.
- Size 2 eggs should be used except where otherwise specified.
- Use freshly ground black pepper unless otherwise specified.
- Use fresh rather than dried herbs unless dried herbs are suggested in the recipe.

AT-A-GLANCE SYMBOLS

✳ The recipe can be frozen.

☺ The recipe can be prepared and cooked in 30 minutes or under.

♡ The recipe is under 350 calories per portion for main courses and under 200 calories for starters, accompaniments and desserts.

CONTENTS

COLOUR INDEX

In this Colour Index you will find a photograph of every recipe in the book, plus the following information:
- a brief description of the dish
- the number of servings
- page on which recipe appears
- useful, at-a-glance symbols

SYMBOLS
❋ Freeze-ahead
☺ Recipe can be prepared and cooked in 30 minutes or under
♡ Under 350 cals per portion for main courses; under 200 cals for starters, accompaniments and desserts

USING THE COLOUR INDEX
Where a photograph of the finished dish does not appear next to a recipe, you will find a reference to a page in the Colour Index. Just turn to the page number indicated and you will see a photograph of the dish.

Asparagus Soup
Delicately flavoured creamy smooth soup topped with almonds and parsley.

SERVES 4 . PAGE 102 . ❋

Creamy Carrot and Celeriac Soup
Velvety smooth carrot and celeriac soup with a hint of orange and soy.

SERVES 6 . PAGE 321 . ♡ . ❋

Lettuce and Sorrel Soup
Delicately flavoured soup, garnished with Parmesan and served hot.

SERVES 4 . PAGE 175 . ❋

Parsnip and Apple Soup
Creamy, smooth soup bursting with distinctive autumnal flavours.

SERVES 6 . PAGE 246 . ♡ . ❋

Broccoli and Watercress Soup
Deliciously smooth, deep green soup, full of fresh flavour.

SERVES 6 . PAGE 103 . ❋

Jerusalem Artichoke and Parmesan Soup
Lightly curried, creamy soup.

SERVES 6 . PAGE 320 . ♡ . ❋

Garlic and Onion Soup
A rich onion soup, highlighted with a mellow garlic taste.

SERVES 6 . PAGE 247 . ♡ . ❋

Spiced Dal Soup
Coarsely textured split pea soup spiced with cumin and chillies.

SERVES 4-6 . PAGE 321 . ♡ . ❋

Bouillabaisse
Mediterranean-style chunky seafood soup with saffron and garlic.

SERVES 6 . PAGE 246

Thai Chicken Soup
Chunky chicken soup spiced with chilli, ginger and coconut.

SERVES 4 . PAGE 102 . ◔ . ❋

Chilled Tomato and Vodka Soup
Wonderfully refreshing and very low in calories, perfect for a hot day.

SERVES 6 . PAGE 174 . ♡

Chilled Avocado and Lime Soup
Elegant soup with a velvety smooth texture and just a hint of lime.

SERVES 4 . PAGE 174

Pâté de Campagne
Coarse pork pâté, speckled with black olives and layered with bacon.

SERVES 10-12 . PAGE 104 . ❋

Chicken Liver and Pistachio Pâté
This tasty pâté is made with butter and low fat cheese for a lighter texture.

SERVES 8-10 . PAGE 248 . ❋

Peppered Mackerel and Apple Mousses
Individual mousses served with slices of apple and horseradish sauce.

SERVES 6 . PAGE 249 . ❋

Spicy Crab Dip
Perfect partnered with crudités and a
glass of white wine, alfresco style.

SERVES 4 . PAGE 176 . ♡

Nutty Chicken Bites, Smoked Salmon Roulade, Nan Bread with Spicy Prawns.
Three delicious canapés - tiny chicken kebabs with satay-style sauce; delicate
smoked salmon and cheese rolls; little curried prawn bites.

MAKES 60-70 . PAGE 322/323

Little Spanish Savouries
Irresistible hot cheesy pastries topped
with anchovies, olives and pesto.

MAKES 24 . PAGE 322 . ✳

Corn Scones with Avocado
Bite-sized scones with tasty toppings
- ideal for serving with drinks.

MAKES 30 . PAGE 104 . ✳

Courgette and Pesto Rounds
Colourful layers of tomato, courgette
and basil baked in the oven.

SERVES 6 . PAGE 178 . ♡ . ⏱

Vegetable Samosas
Deep-fried crispy parcels of spicy vegetables - an Indian speciality.

MAKES 24 . PAGE 324 . ✳

Potato Pancakes with Smoked Salmon
Warming pancakes with a topping.

MAKES 6 . PAGE 251 . ✳

Carpaccio of Salmon
Deliciously light, wafer thin slices of
salmon in a lime and chive dressing.

SERVES 10 . PAGE 325 . ♡ . ⏱

**Soy-glazed Chicken Livers with
Chinese Leaves**
Chicken livers on shredded pak choi.

SERVES 4 . PAGE 106

Bruschetta
Full of Mediterranean flavour, this
hot tasty starter is quick to make.

SERVES 6 . PAGE 176 . ⏱

**Skewered Tiger Prawns with
Parma Ham**
Grilled kebabs - an easy starter.

SERVES 4 . PAGE 177 . ♡

Deep-fried Whitebait with Hot Sauce
Crispy fried whitebait served with a
fiery paprika and chilli sauce.

SERVES 4 . PAGE 105

Grilled Pears with Stilton
An amazingly quick to make savoury
pear starter.

SERVES 4 . PAGE 250 . ⏱

Golden Stuffed Mushrooms
Bite-sized mushrooms filled with
bacon, cashews, garlic and parsley.

SERVES 4 . PAGE 251 . ⏱

11

Bulghur Wheat Salad with Dried Fruit
Deliciously tangy salad speckled with
figs, apricots, peaches and herbs.

SERVES 4-6 . PAGE 250

**Warm Seafood Salad with
Toasted Polenta**
Delicious haddock and prawn starter.

SERVES 6 . PAGE 249

Toasted Bacon and Goats' Cheese Salad
Crisp bacon coating concealing a melting soft cheese centre, perfect with salad.

SERVES 6 . PAGE 107

**Spinach, Bacon and
Roquefort Salad**
A fresh-tasting French starter.

SERVES 8 . PAGE 178 . ⏱

**Grapefruit and Chicory Salad
with Prawns**
A refreshing salad starter.

SERVES 4 . PAGE 107 . ♡ . ⏱

Mango and Prawn Salads
New twist to an old favourite, with
mango and fromage frais added.

SERVES 4 . PAGE 179 . ♡ . ⏱

Cucumber and Strawberry Salad
Refreshing mix of summer ingredients complement each other beautifully.

SERVES 4 . PAGE 179 . ♡

Grilled Pepper and Aubergine Salad
Contrasting salad of black aubergine
slices and red pepper with garlic.

SERVES 4 . PAGE 325 . ♡ . ⏱

**Cod Fillet Wrapped in Filo Pastry
with Rocket**
Crisp parcels of tasty fish.

SERVES 6 . PAGE 109 . ♡ . ❄ .

Cod Cutlets Provençale
Robust flavours and bright colours
characterize this French dish.

SERVES 4 . PAGE 110 . ♡

**Pan-fried Cod with Chanterelle
Mushrooms**
Seared cod on a crisp bread croûte.

SERVES 4 . PAGE 253

Cod in Orange and Cider Sauce
Deliciously tangy and colourful, this
fish dish is very easy to prepare.

SERVES 4 . PAGE 326 . ♡ . ❄

Fish Plaki with Root Vegetables
Tasty Greek-style dish flavoured with
lemon, white wine and thyme.

SERVES 4 . PAGE 326 . ♡ . ❄

Roasted Fish with Garlic-herb Crumbs
Buttery baked white fish steaks
sprinkled with crisp garlicky crumbs.

SERVES 6 . PAGE 111

Haddock and Corn Chowder
This hearty main meal soup is packed
with fish and vegetables.

SERVES 4 . PAGE 254

Kedgeree with Lentils
Lentils and lime add a new twist to
the traditional kedgeree.

SERVES 6 . PAGE 327 . ♡

Thai Grilled Caramelized Fish
Rolled plaice fillets on a bed of salad
leaves served with a hot chilli sauce.

SERVES 4 . PAGE 254

Plaice with Grapes
Plaice fillets poached in wine and herbs, with a surprise grape filling.

SERVES 4 . PAGE 255 . ♡

Fish with Lemon and Ginger
Spicy marinated sole fillets stuffed with coriander, in a creamy saffron sauce.

SERVES 6 . PAGE 328 . ♡

Lemon Sole with Spinach Hollandaise
Melt-in-the-mouth grilled sole, served with a tangy lime and spinach sauce.

SERVES 4 . PAGE 328

Whiting in Soured Cream
Grilled whiting bathed in a cheesy cream sauce - simplicity itself.

SERVES 2 . PAGE 110 . ⊕

Grilled Halibut with Stir-fried Vegetables
Stylish and speedy combination.

SERVES 4 . PAGE 184 . ♡ . ⊕

Pan-roasted Monkfish with Sweet Potatoes and Onions
Stuffed monkfish all-in-one meal.

SERVES 4 . PAGE 256

Light Monkfish and Prawn Sauté
Quick-and-easy combination of seafood and vegetables.

SERVES 4 . PAGE 112 . ♡ . ⊕

Normandy Skate with Caper Sauce
A more unusual but very successful way of serving skate.

SERVES 4 . PAGE 329 . ♡ . ⊕

Red Mullet with Spinach and Bacon
This colourful treatment traps in the
full flavour of the fish.

SERVES 4 . PAGE 111

Pan-fried Mullet with Citrus and Basil
Marinated fish fillets served in a
tangy orange and lemon sauce.

SERVES 4 . PAGE 257

Spiced Barbecued Salmon
Melt-in-the-mouth salmon fillet with
a crisp and spicy skin.

SERVES 6 . PAGE 180 . ♡ . ◷

**Baked Salmon with Walnut
Oil and Herbs**
Marinated salmon with a rich sauce.

SERVES 4 . PAGE 180

Roast Salmon with a Peanut Crust
Nutty topped salmon fillets served
with ginger and chilli butter.

SERVES 4 . PAGE 257 . ◷ . ❄

Roast Salmon in Mustard Butter
Simplicity itself - thick slices of hot
buttery salmon on a bed of crisp salad.

SERVES 6 . PAGE 330 . ◷

Salmon Pie with Parmesan Crust
Freeze ahead this luxurious fish pie
for effortless Christmas entertaining.

SERVES 8 . PAGE 330 . ❄

Smoked Salmon Fishcakes
These upmarket fishcakes are an
excellent freezer standby.

SERVES 12 . PAGE 331 . ❄

Salmon Trout with Herb Sauce
A decorated whole fish makes a
splendid centrepiece.

SERVES 4 . PAGE 181

15

Poached Trout with Fennel
Buttery baked trout on a bed of
thinly sliced fennel and potato.

SERVES 2 . PAGE 108

**Tuna Steaks with Parmesan
Basil Butter**
Grilled tuna with flavoured butter.

SERVES 6 . PAGE 182

Trout with Dill and Horseradish Mayonnaise
Poached trout served with mayonnaise,
mixed with dill, horseradish and apple.

SERVES 4 . PAGE 108

Grilled Sardines with Tomato Sauce
Herby spiked sardines, grilled and
served with a garlicky tomato sauce.

SERVES 4 . PAGE 182 . ♡

Oatmeal Crusted Herrings
Traditional Scottish recipe updated
and flavoured with lemon and dill.

SERVES 4 . PAGE 112 . ⏱

Coconut Fish Pilau
Colourful rice dish enhanced with
nuts, curry paste and prawns.

SERVES 4 . PAGE 114

Paella with Peppers
Packed with pieces of fish and peppers, delicately flavoured with saffron.

SERVES 6 . PAGE 114

Spiced Fish Kebabs with Avocado Salsa
The salsa offsets the spicy fish perfectly.

SERVES 4-6 . PAGE 183

Fresh Seafood Stew
Chunky Mediterranean fish stew gently cooked with wine and herbs.

SERVES 6 . PAGE 185 . ♡

Creamy Fish and Pumpkin Pie
Break through the crisp filo topping to reveal a delicious chunky fish filling.

SERVES 4 . PAGE 252

Fisherman's Pie
Chunky pieces of fish cooked in tomato sauce, topped with potato.

SERVES 4 . PAGE 252 . ❋

Winter Fish Stew
Hearty Mediterranean-style fish stew, perfect for informal entertaining.

SERVES 8 . PAGE 332

Chillied Mediterranean Prawns
Quick and spicy luxury prawn dish, ideal for a romantic dinner for two.

SERVES 2 . PAGE 185 . ♡ . ⏱

Charred Scallops with Fennel and Pernod
Fast and flavourful scallop dish.

SERVES 4 . PAGE 259 . ⏱

Warm Scallop and Basil Salad
Sautéed scallops tossed in walnut oil and served on a bed of salad leaves.

SERVES 6 . PAGE 186 . ⏱

***Steamed Mussels in Saffron Cream
Sauce***
Mussels bathed in a wine sauce.
SERVES 4-6 . PAGE 115

Mussels in Tomato Sauce
Shelled mussels in a chunky tomato
sauce flavoured with oregano.
SERVES 4 . PAGE 258 . ♡ . ◔

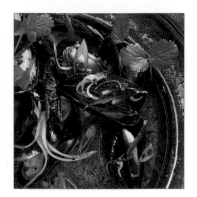

***Mussels with Ginger, Chilli and
Coriander***
An exotic blend of spicy flavours.
SERVES 2 . PAGE 333 . ♡ . ◔

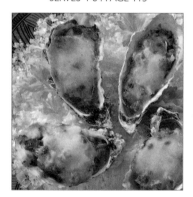

Oysters au Gratin
Stretch a dozen oysters by topping with
bacon, artichokes and mozzarella.
SERVES 4-6 . PAGE 333 . ♡ . ◔

Dressed Crab
Classically decorated crab always
makes an impressive centrepiece.
SERVES 2-3 . PAGE 187 . ♡

Grilled Lobster
Simply grilling with butter brings out
the true taste of this prized shellfish.
SERVES 4 . PAGE 186 . ♡ . ◔

Mixed Seafood Gratin
Rich seafood cocktail coated in a
cheese sauce, topped with tortillas.
SERVES 4 . PAGE 113 . ◔

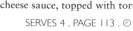

Mixed Seafood Salad
Colourful, chunky main meal salad
served with warm crusty bread.
SERVES 6 . PAGE 187

Seafood Risotto
Mixed flavourful seafood combined
with creamy rice.
SERVES 4 . PAGE 258

French Roast Chicken
Succulent tarragon roast chicken
served with garlic-flavoured gravy.

SERVES 4 . PAGE 120

Roasted Pecan Chicken
Creamy goats' cheese and ground
pecans transform a roast chicken.

SERVES 4 . PAGE 336

**Chicken Breasts with Spinach
and Ricotta**
Spinach-wrapped chicken with cheese.

SERVES 4 . PAGE 117

**Chicken Breasts with Apples
and Thyme**
Apple-flavoured roasted chicken.

SERVES 4 . PAGE 262 . ♡

**Herb Marinated Chicken with Spring
Vegetables in a Warm Dressing**
Herby oven-baked chicken breasts.

SERVES 4 . PAGE 118

Poached Chicken in Watercress Sauce
Chicken wrapped in Parma ham, served
in a creamy watercress sauce.

SERVES 4 . PAGE 188 . ♡ . ⏱

Sweet Gingered Chicken
Sticky soy and ginger glazed chicken
breasts roasted with aubergine.

SERVES 6 . PAGE 338

**Garlic Chicken with Roast
Pepper Purée**
Colourful peppers adorn baked chicken.

SERVES 6 . PAGE 263

Chicken in Smoky Bacon Sauce
Quick chicken dish with bacon,
apples and crème fraîche

SERVES 4 . PAGE 337 . ♡ . ⏱

19

Spring Chicken Fricassee
Stuffed chicken breasts, pan-fried in a creamy vermouth sauce.

SERVES 4 . PAGE 119

Spicy Coconut Chicken
Pan-fried chicken simmered with Thai spices, tomatoes and creamed coconut.

SERVES 6 . PAGE 261 ♡

Oriental Chicken Parcels
Orange-marinated chicken, baked in foil to seal in the flavour.

SERVES 4 . PAGE 261 . ♡

Savoury Crumbed Chicken
Crispy baked chicken thighs - delicious spring meal served hot or cold.

SERVES 4-6 . PAGE 116

Southern Fried Chicken with Corn Fritters
American-style golden chicken.

SERVES 4-6 . PAGE 262

Cheesy Chicken and Bacon Rolls
Prepare these tasty rolls ahead, then bake just before serving.

SERVES 4 . PAGE 191 . ✳

Lime-peppered Chicken
Marinated chicken kebabs with a chilli
dipping sauce, ideal for barbecues.

SERVES 6 . PAGE 189 . ♡

Stir-fried Chicken with Courgettes
Thin strips of chicken quickly fried
and tossed in sherry and soy sauce.

SERVES 4 . PAGE 188 . ♡ . ⏱

Hot Red Jungle Curry
Colourful Thai-style chicken curry
with fragrant Kaffir lime leaves.

SERVES 4 . PAGE 116 . ♡ . ⏱

Chicken and Apple Casserole
Hearty chicken casserole packed with
vegetables, lentils and apples.

SERVES 4 . PAGE 260

Country Chicken Casserole
Slow-cooked chicken pieces flavoured
with bacon, mushrooms and wine.

SERVES 4 . PAGE 119 . ❄

Chicken Hotpot with Leeks
Potato-topped chicken hotpot with a
creamy sauce.

SERVES 4 . PAGE 337 . ♡

Marinated Chicken with Prunes
The prunes and wine add a rich
mellow flavour to this wintery dish.

SERVES 4 . PAGE 339

Winter Chicken
Colourful chicken casserole packed
with wintery vegetables.

SERVES 4 . PAGE 338 . ♡

**Smoked Chicken with Cucumber
and Mango**
Bright salad with unusual dressing.

SERVES 6 . PAGE 192

21

Warm Asparagus and Chicken Salad
Hot sliced chicken and asparagus with
a tomato, olive and caper dressing.

SERVES 4 . PAGE 120 . ☺

Chicken with Spiced Wheat
Lightly curried pieces of grilled chicken
make up this main meal salad.

SERVES 6 . PAGE 190 . ♡

Grilled Chicken Salad
Tomato and olive encrusted chicken,
sliced and tossed in a crunchy salad.

SERVES 4 . PAGE 192 . ♡

Mediterranean Chicken
Bursting with flavour, this tightly-
packed loaf is great for picnics.

SERVES 6 . PAGE 191

**Cinnamon Roast Poussin with
Couscous**
An unusual dish featuring pistachios.

SERVES 4 . PAGE 121

**Lemon and Ginger Poussin with
Onions**
Poussins on a bed of onions.

SERVES 6 . PAGE 122

Mustard-roasted Turkey
Full of flavour, this mustard-glazed
turkey is perfect for Christmas.

SERVES 8 . PAGE 334

Oriental Turkey
A tasty alternative to the traditional
Christmas roast turkey.

SERVES 6 . PAGE 334 . ❊

Turkey, Apricot and Hazelnut Pilaff
Use up the turkey leftovers in this
delicious Middle-Eastern rice dish.

SERVES 4 . PAGE 335

22

Pan-fried Turkey with Lemon
Crunchy hazelnut coated escalopes
with a lemon and tarragon sauce.

SERVES 4 . PAGE 123 . ◔

Roast Duckling with Sherry Vinegar
Slices of roast duck on a colourful
bed of glazed winter vegetables.

SERVES 6 . PAGE 341

Guinea Fowl with Rocket Sauce and Spring Vegetables
Braised with wine and served with a rich creamy rocket sauce.

SERVES 6 . PAGE 122

Duckling Breasts with Armagnac
Marinated in Armagnac and herbs
for an exquisite flavour.

SERVES 6 . PAGE 341 . ♡

***Crispy Chinese Duck with Oriental
Vegetables***
Sliced duck on piquant vegetables.

SERVES 6 . PAGE 342 . ◔

Warm Duck Salad
Low in calories, this upmarket salad
is great for summer entertaining.

SERVES 8 . PAGE 193 . ♡

23

Goose with Prune Stuffing
A traditional alternative to turkey at
Christmas.

SERVES 10 . PAGE 340

**Pot-roasted Pheasant with Red
Cabbage**
A classic combination of flavours.

SERVES 4 . PAGE 267

**French Roast Pheasant with Grapes
and Nuts**
An unusual way to serve pheasant.

SERVES 6 . PAGE 266

Christmas Pheasant
Casseroled pheasant flavoured with
Madeira, chestnuts and cranberries.

SERVES 6 . PAGE 342 . ✻

Casserole of Grouse with Red Wine
Slow-cooked grouse in a rich wine,
celery and shallot sauce.

SERVES 4 . PAGE 266 . ♡ . ✻

Quails on Gnocchi with Cream Sauce
Roasted quail on a circle of potato
gnocchi, served with a creamy sauce.

SERVES 6 . PAGE 343

Country-style Rabbit Casserole
Sautéed rabbit, flamed in brandy and
slowly cooked with tomatoes and wine.

SERVES 6 . PAGE 264 . ♡ . ✻

**Pan-fried Venison with
Blueberry Sauce**
Rich venison with a tangy sauce.

SERVES 6 . PAGE 264 . ♡ . ⏱ . ✻

Raised Game Pie
This impressive pie encases a richly
flavoured mixture of game.

SERVES 8-10 . PAGE 265 . ✻

Spiced Rib of Beef
Always an impressive roast, here the fat is spread with spiced butter.

SERVES 6 . PAGE 344

Grilled Steaks with Shallots and Wine
Quickly grilled beef steaks served with a rich buttery wine sauce.

SERVES 4 . PAGE 268 . ◔

Beef Medallions with Stilton Mousse
Pan-fried fillet steaks topped with a creamy Stilton and chicken mousse.

SERVES 6 . PAGE 345 . ◔

Pizzaiola Steak
Flash-fried steak with a summery basil and tomato sauce.

SERVES 4 . PAGE 195 . ♡ . ◔

Beef Rendang
Melt-in-the-mouth beef cooked in a Thai spice paste with coconut.

SERVES 6 . PAGE 268 . ✳

Rich Beef Daube
A delicious make-ahead casserole for easy entertaining.

SERVES 6 . PAGE 124 . ✳

Country Beef with Barley
Beef slowly cooked with barley, root vegetables, wine and orange.

SERVES 4 . PAGE 269 . ♡ . ✳

Festive Beef Casserole
Rich spicy beef and venison casserole, flavoured with orange and sherry.

SERVES 8 . PAGE 345 . ♡ . ✳

Steak and Kidney Pudding
Traditional dish of slow-cooked steak and kidney encased in suet pastry.

SERVES 6 . PAGE 346 . ✳

Classic Oxtail Casserole
This warming, traditional casserole is packed with wintery vegetables.

SERVES 6 . PAGE 346 . ✽

Italian Meatloaf
A hearty, wholesome dish, just right for large family gatherings.

SERVES 8 . PAGE 125 . ✽

Babotee
Spicy South African meat loaf topped with a cheesy turmeric custard.

SERVES 4 . PAGE 347

Spicy Burgers
Lightly spiced burgers flavoured with parsley and coriander, served in pittas.

SERVES 4 . PAGE 125 . ♡ . ⏲ . ✽

Middle Eastern Meat Skewers
Spiced beef sausages pressed onto skewers, served with a minty sauce.

SERVES 6 . PAGE 194 . ✽

Roast Lamb with a Creamy Fennel Sauce
Split racks of lamb roasted quickly.

SERVES 6 . PAGE 126

Sesame Beef Salad
Hot strips of marinated beef, served with celery, onion and cucumber for a light main course dish.

SERVES 6 . PAGE 195 . ♡

Boned and Stuffed Shoulder of Lamb
Dried fruit adds a wonderful flavour to this favourite roast.

SERVES 6 . PAGE 127

***Roast Eye Fillet of Lamb with
Candied Lemons***
Marinated lamb with lemon.

SERVES 8 . PAGE 126

***Honeyed Leg of Lamb with Winter
Vegetables***
Lamb roasted with root vegetables.

SERVES 4 . PAGE 348

***Tomato-crusted Lamb with Summer
Vegetables***
Rack of lamb with summer flavours.

SERVES 6 . PAGE 196

Lamb Chops with Leeks and Lentils
Orange marinated lamb chops served
on a bed of red lentils and leeks.

SERVES 4 . PAGE 271

Lamb Steaks in Herby Tomato Sauce
Baked lamb on a bed of herby
tomatoes and topped with lemon.

SERVES 4 . PAGE 128

Minted Lamb Escalopes
Lamb marinated with yogurt, mint,
lemon and garlic for added flavour.

SERVES 4 . PAGE 196 . ♡

Spiced Lamb Hot Pot
Cinnamon spiced lamb cooked slowly
with potato, red pepper and barley.

SERVES 6 . PAGE 271 . ✳

Spicy Lamb Casserole
Chunky pieces of lean lamb, lightly
spiced with ginger, cumin and paprika.

SERVES 6 . PAGE 128 . ✳

Fruity Lamb Casserole with Spices
Marinated lamb, gently casseroled
with dried fruit, saffron and sherry.

SERVES 8 . PAGE 348 . ✳

Moussaka
Greek minced lamb topped with fried
aubergines and a cheese sauce.

SERVES 6 . PAGE 129 . ✳

**Moroccan Lamb Pie with Spinach
and Sultanas**
Spicy mince with spinach in filo.

SERVES 4 . PAGE 270 . ✳

Lamb and Lentil Bake
Aromatic mince and raisin mixture
baked in golden layers of pastry.

SERVES 4 . PAGE 349 . ✳

Autumn Spiced Kidneys
Delicious combination of sautéed kidneys, mushrooms and double cream.

SERVES 4 . PAGE 272 . ⊘

Kidneys in Sherry Sauce
Garlicky lambs' kidneys pan-fried in olive oil and sherry
provide a rich Spanish-style main dish.

SERVES 4 . PAGE 130

Sautéed Liver with Orange and Sage
Quick to cook, pan-fried liver with
fresh sage, tangy orange rind and juice.

SERVES 4 . PAGE 350 . ♡ . ⊘

Roast Pork with Apple Gravy
Garlic and rosemary marinated roast
pork with a delicious cider gravy.

SERVES 6 . PAGE 131

**Herby Rack of Pork with Roast
Vegetables**
Pork roasted on a bed of vegetables.

SERVES 6 . PAGE 351

Pork Loin Stuffed with Figs
Transform the Sunday joint with this
easy-to-make stuffing.

SERVES 4 . PAGE 274

**Peppered Garlic Pork with
Crème Fraîche**
Stuffed fillet with a creamy sauce.

SERVES 6 . PAGE 197 . ♡

Pork Chops with Rhubarb Chutney
Grilled pork chops topped with a
quick-to-make rhubarb chutney.

SERVES 4 . PAGE 132 . ⏱

Grilled Pork with Spiced Butter
Grilled pork chops spread with mustard butter, served with a cider sauce.

SERVES 4 . PAGE 272 . ⏱

**Braised Pork Chops with
Plums and Ginger**
Pork and ginger plums with yogurt.

SERVES 4 . PAGE 273 . ✳

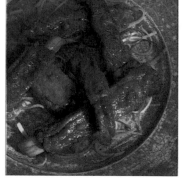

Chinese-style Spare Ribs
Pork ribs flavoured with five-spice
powder, ginger and soy sauce.

SERVES 4-6 . PAGE 199 . ♡

Pork and Lemon Brochettes
Marinated cubes of pork and lemon
slices, threaded onto skewers.

SERVES 2 . PAGE 132

Homemade Sausages with Rocket Pesto
Coarse pork sausages to barbecue.

SERVES 6 . PAGE 199 . ✳

Spanish Pork and Bean Casserole
Slowly cooked gammon joint with white beans, chorizo and black pudding.

SERVES 6-8 . PAGE 274

Harvest Pork Casserole
Rich mellow-tasting casserole of pork, parsnips and apples.

SERVES 4-6 . PAGE 275 . ✳

Stir-fried Pork
Strips of pork, Chinese vegetables and rice make up this bumper stir-fry.

SERVES 4 . PAGE 130 . ♡

Maple-glazed Gammon with Papaya Salsa
Sweet gammon with tangy fruit salsa.

SERVES 10 -12 . PAGE 198

Braised Ham with Madeira
This Madeira-glazed ham joint is perfect for large Christmas gatherings.

SERVES 12-16 . PAGE 350 . ✳

Mushroom and Ham Risotto
Quick spring supper dish, perfect for informal gatherings.

SERVES 4 . PAGE 133 . ⏱

Saltimbocca
Buttery fried veal escalopes and Parma ham, with sage and wine.

SERVES 6 . PAGE 133 . ♡

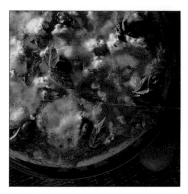

Four Cheese Pizza
Pizza base topped with mozzarella,
Dolcelatta, ricotta and Parmesan.

SERVES 6 . PAGE 134 . ♡ . ❋

Feta and Oregano Tarts
Individual tomato tarts flavoured
with feta, oregano and cream.

SERVES 4 . PAGE 201 . ❋

Asparagus and Red Onion Tart
This delicious tart makes a little
asparagus go a long way.

SERVES 8 . PAGE 135 . ❋

Stilton, Walnut and Bacon Flan
Crisp walnut pastry with a creamy
bacon, celery and Stilton filling.

SERVES 4-6 . PAGE 352 . ❋

Melting Cheese and Ham Parcel
Wonderful combination of melting
cheese, ham and crisp pastry.

SERVES 4 . PAGE 278

**Deep-fried Camembert with
Rhubarb Sauce**
Melting cheese in crisp coating.

SERVES 4 . PAGE 134

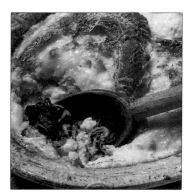

Golden Cheese and Spinach Pudding
Savoury version of bread and butter
pudding makes a tasty supper dish.

SERVES 4 . PAGE 352

Aubergine and Pepper Parmigiana
Oven-baked layers of grilled peppers,
aubergines, tomatoes and cheese.

SERVES 6 . PAGE 279 . ❋

Goats' Cheese Puffs
Rather like a double cooked cheese
soufflé, coated with chopped nuts.

SERVES 8 . PAGE 137 . ♡

Chick-pea and Parsnip Soufflés
Individual soufflés lightly spiced with curry powder.

SERVES 4 . PAGE 278 . ♡

Eggs in Poppadom Baskets
Unusual poppadom baskets richly filled with quails' eggs and hollandaise.

SERVES 6 . PAGE 137

Poached Eggs on Smoked Haddock
Smoked haddock with a poached egg, croûtons and hot caper dressing.

SERVES 4 . PAGE 136 .

Poached Eggs on Toasted Bacon Baguette
All-in-one supper dish.

SERVES 4 . PAGE 277 . ⏱

Vegetable Egg Nests
Individual rings of summer vegetables, filled with poached eggs.

SERVES 4 . PAGE 200 . ♡ . ⏱

Courgette and Bacon Frittata
Jumbo omelette flavoured with courgettes, bacon and herbs.

SERVES 4 . PAGE 200 . ♡ . ⏱

Caramelized Onion and Gruyère Frittata
An omelette with a difference!

SERVES 4 . PAGE 276 . ♡

Stuffed Thai Omelette
Folded omelette enclosing a gingered pork filling.

SERVES 2 . PAGE 276 . ⏱

Sweet Potato and Leek Tortilla
Thick sweet potato and leek omelette - delicious hot, cut into wedges.

SERVES 4 . PAGE 353 . ⏱

Seafood Lasagne
Always popular for informal entertaining or fork suppers.

SERVES 6 . PAGE 138

Spaghetti with Clams
Baby clams, wine, garlic and parsley
feature in this classic pasta dish.

SERVES 4-6 . PAGE 354 . ⏱

Italian Seafood Pasta Salad
Attractive salad bursting with
seafood, perfect for a light lunch.

SERVES 6 . PAGE 202

**Seafood Spaghetti with Pepper and
Almond Sauce**
Vibrant red sauce to top pasta.

SERVES 4 . PAGE 280 . ♡

Pasta with Tuna and Olive Sauce
Easy store-cupboard supper, richly
flavoured with fish and olives.

SERVES 4 . PAGE 354

Pad Thai Noodles
This is one of Thailand's favourite
noodle dishes.

SERVES 4 . PAGE 357 . ⏱

Thai Chicken Noodle Salad
Colourful main meal salad with all
the tastes of the East.

SERVES 6 . PAGE 203

Noodles with Meatballs and Shallots
Noodles tossed with pesto and shallots and served with meatballs.

SERVES 4 . PAGE 280 . ♡

Gingered Chicken and Noodles
Thai-style noodles flavoured with
ginger, curry paste and coconut.

SERVES 4 . PAGE 139 . ♡ . ⏱

33

Pastitsio
Spicy minced lamb and pasta topped
with a cheese sauce - a Greek classic.

SERVES 4 . PAGE 281 . ✽

Chilli Pork with Noodles
Chillied pork cooked with
noodles,broccoli and yellow pepper.

SERVES 4 . PAGE 139 . ♡ . ⏱

Pasta in Sweet Pepper Sauce
Finely chopped red peppers and salami flavour this easy-to-make sauce.

SERVES 4 . PAGE 203 . ✽

Pumpkin Ravioli with Herbs
Tasty parcels filled with pumpkin, Parmesan, prosciutto and basil.

SERVES 4 . PAGE 283 . ✽

**Linguine with Parma Ham and Sun-
dried Tomatoes**
Creamy pasta with crisp ham.

SERVES 4 . PAGE 355

Creamy Pasta Bake
This luxurious version of macaroni
cheese is flavoured with Gruyère.

SERVES 4 . PAGE 356

Roasted Vegetable and Pasta Gratin
This colourful and tasty pasta dish is
great for feeding a crowd.

SERVES 8 . PAGE 356 . ✽

Crespoline
Spinach stuffed cannelloni on a tomato base, topped with a light sauce.

SERVES 4 . PAGE 141 . ♡

Pasta Primavera
Ribbon pasta perfectly offsets the
spring vegetables in this colourful dish.

SERVES 4-6 . PAGE 140

Classic Tomato Sauce
This tomato and basil pasta sauce
can be made in batches and frozen.

SERVES 4 . PAGE 140 . ♡ . ❄

Pasta with Walnut and Basil Sauce
Homemade tomato pesto-style sauce,
added to cream and walnuts.

SERVES 4 . PAGE 202 . ⏱

Crunchy Courgette Pasta
Lightly chillied courgette, red pepper
and tomato sauce on a bed of pasta.

SERVES 4 . PAGE 204 . ♡ . ⏱

**Pasta with Grilled Asparagus and
Broad Beans**
Pasta with summery flavours.

SERVES 4 . PAGE 205 . ⏱

Tomato and Mozzarella Noodles
Choose tomatoes with lots of flavour
for this quick summery supper dish.

SERVES 4 . PAGE 204 . ⏱

**Japanese Noodles with Pak Choi
and Mooli**
Soft noodles with a vegetable sauce.

SERVES 4 . PAGE 282 . ♡

Calabrian Pasta
Garlic-flavoured breadcrumbs and pine nuts, tossed with
broccoli, top this pasta dish.

SERVES 4-6 . PAGE 283 . ⏱

35

Vegetable Strudel
Cut through the crisp filo layers to
the hearty mix of vegetables inside.

SERVES 6 . PAGE 144 . ❋

**Leek Pancakes with Watercress
Sauce**
Stuffed pancakes baked in sauce.

MAKES 8 . PAGE 145 . ♡

Vegetable Pithivier
Attractive layered vegetable pie,
served in thick slices.

SERVES 6 . PAGE 206

Tomato and Gruyère Pie
Open pie made unusually with green
tomatoes, gruyère and mayonnaise.

SERVES 4 . PAGE 207

Quick Tomato and Garlic Pizza
Thin crispy base topped with tomatoes,
olives, garlic, herbs and feta cheese.

SERVES 2 . PAGE 284

Crusty Mediterranean Parcels
Puff pastry encases a rich vegetable
filling with a cheesy topping.

SERVES 8 . PAGE 359 . ❋

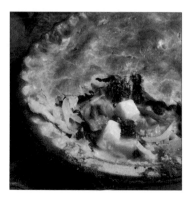

**Vegetable Cheese Pie with
Potato Crust**
Colourful pie with unusual topping.

SERVES 4 . PAGE 285 . ❋

Mixed Mushroom Parcels
Crisp filo purses with a tasty wild
mushroom and rice filling.

SERVES 6 . PAGE 286

Gnocchi with Red Pesto
Delicious red pesto sauce served with
potato gnocchi - a tasty combination.

SERVES 4-6 . PAGE 286

Summer Couscous
Herby trio of mint, coriander and parsley flavour this tasty salad.

SERVES 6 . PAGE 207 . ♡ . ⊕

Summer Risotto
Colourful mixture of bright green vegetables, tomatoes and wild rice.

SERVES 4 . PAGE 208 . ♡ . ⊕

Vegetable Biryani
Basmati rice mixed with Indian spices, carrots and cauliflower.

SERVES 4 . PAGE 360

Turkish Aubergines
Chilled tomato stuffed aubergines, flavoured with allspice and parsley.

SERVES 6 . PAGE 208

Couscous-filled Aubergines with a Coriander Dressing
Tasty stuffed aubergines bursting with minty couscous, apricots and pine nuts for a satisfying vegetarian dish.

SERVES 4 . PAGE 142 . ♡

Catalan Red Peppers
Chilled red peppers with a rice stuffing, tossed in a garlicky dressing.

SERVES 4 . PAGE 145 . ♡

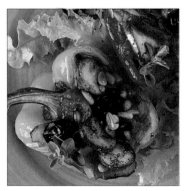

Stuffed Peppers with Pine Nuts
Vegetarian feast served with a tasty tomato sauce.

SERVES 4 . PAGE 206 . ♡

Baked Cabbage with Fruited Bulghur Wheat Stuffing
Tasty, stuffed cabbage parcels.

SERVES 4 . PAGE 360

Filled Baked Potatoes
Baked potatoes topped with two
delicious vegetarian fillings.

SERVES 8 . PAGE 287

Baked Vegetables with a Spicy Sauce
Roasted Mediterranean vegetables served with a chillied passata sauce.

SERVES 4-6 . PAGE 284

Broccoli and Cheese Timbale
Hot cheesy broccoli mould turned
out and served with a tomato sauce.

SERVES 6 . PAGE 142 . ♡

**Vegetable Kebabs with Mango Sauce
and Tropical Rice**
Colourful kebabs with tangy sauce.

SERVES 4 . PAGE 209

**Stir-fried Spring Vegetables with
Cashews**
Easy stir-fry to serve with noodles.

SERVES 4 . PAGE 143 . ♡ . ◷

**Mixed Vegetables and Tofu in
Coconut Sauce**
Quick Oriental-style supper dish.

SERVES 4 . PAGE 358

Vegetable Stew with Rouille
Mixed vegetable and bean stew,
served with a fiery pepper sauce.

SERVES 4 . PAGE 358

Spiced Vegetable Tagine
This fiery North African stew is
traditionally served with couscous.

SERVES 4 . PAGE 361 . ❊

Spring Green Sauté
Quickly fried shreds of garlicky
spring greens sprinkled with pine nuts.

SERVES 6 . PAGE 146 . ♡ . ⊙

Crispy Chinese Greens
Crisply-fried spring green shreds,
with a Chinese touch.

SERVES 4 . PAGE 146 . ⊙

Cauliflower in Curry Sauce
Cauliflower fried with spices, then
simmered with tomatoes.

SERVES 4 . PAGE 291 . ⊙

Red Cabbage with Pine Nuts
Sautéed red cabbage flavoured with
ginger, balsamic vinegar and pine nuts.

SERVES 8 . PAGE 362 . ♡

Chestnut and Sprout Sauté
A classic combination and the perfect
accompaniment for roast turkey.

SERVES 8 . PAGE 363

Citrus Leeks with Sugar Snap Peas
Bright green leeks and peas tossed in
a tangy mustard dressing.

SERVES 6 . PAGE 363 . ♡ . ⊙

***Broad Beans in Herbed Lemon
Cream***
Creamy dish of baby broad beans.

SERVES 4-6 . PAGE 210

***Sweet and Hot Green Beans
with Peanuts***
Stir-fried green beans in a fiery sauce.

SERVES 4-6 . PAGE 366 . ♡ . ⊙

Spicy Mushrooms
Hot and spicy mushroom and
aubergine dish.

SERVES 6 . PAGE 366 . ♡

Carrots in Spiced Dressing
Buttery young carrots tossed with
spices, honey and almonds.

SERVES 4 . PAGE 147 . ♡ . ⏱

Mixed Onion Casserole with Juniper
Different types of onion baked slowly
for a wonderfully mellow flavour.

SERVES 4 . PAGE 288

Marrow with Tomato and Onion
Chunky cubes of marrow simmered
in a garlic tomato sauce.

SERVES 4-6 . PAGE 288 . ♡

Spiced Pumpkin Fritters
Sliced pumpkin fried in an Indian
spiced batter until crisp.

SERVES 4 . PAGE 289 . ⏱

Squash with Nutty Gingered Crumbs
Soft cubes of squash coated in buttery
fried crumbs, ginger and pine nuts.

SERVES 4 . PAGE 290 . ⏱

Parsnip and Carrot au Gratin
Smooth parsnip and carrot purée
topped with breadcrumbs.

SERVES 4-6 . PAGE 290 . ♡

Parsnips in a Lime Glaze
The piquant, fresh taste of lime is
perfect with sweet parsnips.

SERVES 4 . PAGE 364 . ⏱

Swede and Orange Purée
Creamy smooth swede purée with
just a hint of orange.

SERVES 4 . PAGE 291 . ♡ . ❄

Aromatic Swede and Carrots
Stem ginger and mustard seeds
provide fragrant flavour.

SERVES 4 . PAGE 365 . ♡

**New Potatoes with Creamy
Mint Butter**
Sautéed new potatoes with herbs.

SERVES 4 . PAGE 146 . ⏱

Potato and Celeriac Galette
Buttery layers of sliced potato and
celeriac, oven-baked until golden.

SERVES 4 . PAGE 365 . ♡

Golden Potatoes
Crisp, golden jacket roast potatoes,
spiked with garlic and rosemary.

SERVES 6 . PAGE 365

Vegetable and Apple Stir-fry
Quickly fried vegetables flavoured
with chopped apple and cashew nuts.

SERVES 4 . PAGE 293 . ⏱

Stir-fried Summer Vegetables
Make the most of summer vegetables
in this colourful stir-fry.

SERVES 4-6 . PAGE 212 . ♡ . ⏱

Vegetable Medley
Carrot sticks, baby sweetcorn and
asparagus cooked with lemon.

SERVES 4 . PAGE 148 . ♡ . ⏱

**Roasted Tomatoes, Peppers and
Courgettes**
Full of Mediterranean flavour.

SERVES 4 . PAGE 213

Pan-fried Tomatoes
Serve this tasty salad with ciabatta
bread and goats' cheese.

SERVES 4 . PAGE 211 . ⏱

Baked Artichokes
Artichokes baked with olive oil and
served with lemon and parsley.

SERVES 6 . PAGE 211 . ♡

41

Okra with Apricots
Gently simmered okra with orange juice, tomatoes and sweet shreds of apricot.
SERVES 4 . PAGE 211

Buckwheat and Lentil Pilaff
Spiced lentils, nutty buckwheat and crispy bacon make up this pilaff.
SERVES 8 . PAGE 367

Mixed Herb Salad
Serve this pretty salad between courses to refresh the palate.
SERVES 4 . PAGE 214 . ♡ . ⏲

Mixed Leaf, Orange and Strawberry Salad
A tangy and colourful salad.
SERVES 6 . PAGE 214 . ♡ . ⏲

Cucumber and Watercress Salad
A cool, quick-to-make salad with chopped nuts for added texture.
SERVES 6 . PAGE 215 . ♡ . ⏲

Tomato and Red Onion Salad
Use a mixture of different tomatoes in this vibrant summer salad.
SERVES 6 . PAGE 214 . ♡ . ⏲

Leeks and Asparagus in Vinaigrette
Bright green vegetables tossed in a mustard dressing, topped with eggs.
SERVES 6 . PAGE 148 . ⏲

Artichoke and Asparagus Salad
Wonderful combination of flavours which improve with marinating.
SERVES 6 . PAGE 216 . ♡

Minted Vegetable Salad
A light fresh accompaniment to
barbecued meat or salmon.

SERVES 6 . PAGE 217 . ♡ . ⊘

Grated Baby Beetroot Salad
Young uncooked beetroot, grated and
tossed in horseradish dressing.

SERVES 4-6 . PAGE 149 . ⊘

New Potato and Dill Salad
Baby new potatoes tossed in a
yogurt and dill dressing.

SERVES 6 . PAGE 213 . ⊘

Spiced Coleslaw with Pecans
Fine shreds of cabbage tossed in a
spicy mayonnaise dressing.

SERVES 4 . PAGE 292

Winter salad
Crisp coleslaw-style salad with a
tangy lemon and yogurt dressing.

SERVES 4 . PAGE 367 . ⊘

Feta Cheese and Olive Salad
Refreshing Greek-style mix of
cucumber, tomatoes, olives and feta.

SERVES 2 . PAGE 215 . ⊘

Avocado and Chick-pea Salad
A feast of flavours and textures,
topped with a light dressing.

SERVES 4 . PAGE 216 . ⊘

Wild Mushroom and Lentil Salad
Sautéed mushrooms and bacon
served on crisp sprouting lentils.

SERVES 4 . PAGE 292 . ♡ . ⊘

Warm Chinese Salad
Spicy stir-fried vegetables and
bamboo shoots on a bed of lettuce.

SERVES 4 . PAGE 149 . ♡ . ⊘

Berry Compote
Sweet summer currants and strawberries served in a delicious syrup.

SERVES 6 . PAGE 218 . ♡ . ⏱

Summer Pudding
This sublime British pudding captures
berry fruits in a thin bread casing.

SERVES 6-8 . PAGE 220 . ♡ . ❉

Strawberry Mille Feuilles
Melt-in-the mouth pastry layers with
creamy crème pâtissière and fruit.

SERVES 6-8 . PAGE 218 . ❉

Raspberry Fool
Swirls of fresh raspberry purée
combined with tangy fromage frais.

SERVES 4 . PAGE 220 . ♡

Gooseberry Mousse
A delicate tasting dessert of puréed
gooseberries and yogurt.

SERVES 4 . PAGE 221 . ♡

Cherry Brûlées
Crack through the brittle topping to
velvety custard and boozy cherries.

SERVES 8 . PAGE 221

Poached Apricots
Halved apricots lightly poached in a
spiced wine and cinnamon syrup.

SERVES 6 . PAGE 222 . ♡

Grilled Peaches with Chocolate and Marzipan
An unusual hot peach dessert.

SERVES 4 . PAGE 223 . ⏱

Poached Pears with Apricots
Lightly poached pears and dried
apricots with Grand Marnier.

SERVES 4 . PAGE 297 . ♡ . ⏱

Crispy Pear Clafoutis
Sliced pears baked in a deliciously
crisp and golden batter.

SERVES 6 . PAGE 297

Plum Custard Bake
Melt-in-the-mouth plums in a light
custard, drizzled with warm honey.

SERVES 6 . PAGE 296 . ♡

Bramley Apples with Ginger
Baked apples, stuffed with a delicious
ginger filling.

SERVES 4 . PAGE 294

Flambéed Pineapple
Oven-baked pineapple wedges flamed
with brandy just before serving.

SERVES 4 . PAGE 155 . ♡

Passion Fruit and Mango Soufflé
Be a little exotic with this wonderfully
light, fruity soufflé.

SERVES 10 . PAGE 373 . ❋

Clementines in Brandy
Quick, refreshing dessert, perfect for
unexpected visitors.

SERVES 6 . PAGE 374 . ♡ . ◷

Fragrant Fruit Salad
A divine concoction of exotic fruits,
producing a tantalizing fragrance.

SERVES 6 . PAGE 155 . ♡

*Pineapple and Date Salad with
Kumquats*
An exotic fruit salad steeped in tea.

SERVES 6 . PAGE 374

*Apple and Blackberry Upside-down
Pudding*
Autumnal fruit tops light sponge.

SERVES 8 . PAGE 296 . ❋

Rhubarb and Cinnamon Cobbler
Delicious buttery pastry surrounds
cinnamon spiced rhubarb.

SERVES 4 . PAGE 150 . ❄

Banoffi Fudge Pie
Wonderfully indulgent layers of
banana, fudge, cream and caramel.

SERVES 6 . PAGE 150

Light Christmas Puddings
Weight-watchers will love this lighter
festive pudding.

SERVES 8 . PAGE 368 . ❄

Sticky Fudge and Walnut Pudding
Moist walnut and date pudding
served with a rich fudge sauce.

SERVES 6 . PAGE 369

Bread and Butter Pudding with Prunes
A luxurious version of this well loved
English pudding.

SERVES 6 . PAGE 368

Gooey Chocolate Pudding
A chocolate treat - moist rich sponge
with a dark saucy layer.

SERVES 4 . PAGE 370

Honey-toasted Rice
Creamy rice pudding, sprinkled with
almonds and drizzled with honey.

SERVES 4 . PAGE 299

Raisin and Orange Custard Tart
Rich buttery pastry case filled with
custard and orange-soaked raisins.

SERVES 8 . PAGE 371

Apple and Fig Strudel
Sliced apples and moist figs flavoured
with lemon and encircled in filo.

SERVES 6 . PAGE 294 . ♡ . ❄

Almond Tarte Tatin
Melt-in-the-mouth almond pastry topped with caramelized apples.

SERVES 6 . PAGE 295

Higgledy-piggledy Apple Tart
Buttery filo case filled with honeyed mascarpone and caramelized apples.

SERVES 6 . PAGE 152

Apple and Walnut Filo Pie
Crisp golden layers of filo pastry conceal the generous nutty apple filling.

SERVES 6 . PAGE 370

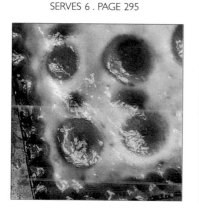

Golden Nectarine Tart
Rich tart filled with nectarines and a creamy nutmeg and brandy custard.

SERVES 8 . PAGE 222 . ✽

Lime Meringue Pies
Individual pies filled with a tangy lime sauce and topped with meringue.

SERVES 6 . PAGE 151

Whisky Mocha Flan
Heart-shaped flan coated with chocolate, filled with coffee custard.

SERVES 6-8 . PAGE 153

Chocolate Truffle Cake
This rich, dense chocolate dessert is ideal for parties.

SERVES 16 . PAGE 298 . ✽

White Chocolate Torte
Wonderfully decadent creamy chocolate dessert with chocolate stars.

SERVES 12 . PAGE 372 . ✽

Easter Cheesecake
Baked cheesecake with a surprise pear layer. Decorated with primroses.

SERVES 8 . PAGE 152 . ✽

Strawberry Cheesecake
Baked lemon cheesecake on an oaty
base, topped with strawberries.

SERVES 8 . PAGE 219 . ✻

***Saffron Meringues with Blueberry
Sauce***
Fruity sauce tops crispy meringue.

SERVES 6 . PAGE 298 . ✻

Chocolate Chestnut Meringues
Chocolate meringues filled with
chestnut cream.

SERVES 6 . PAGE 373 . ✻

Crêpes with Orange Ice
Hot lacy pancakes filled with orange
ice cream and flamed with liqueur.

SERVES 6 . PAGE 154 . ✻

Frozen Strawberry Ice
A lightweight ice, this pretty dessert
is perfect for hot balmy days.

SERVES 6 . PAGE 224 . ♡ . ✻

***Iced Orange and Lemon Terrine with
Burnt Sugar Sauce***
Citrus ice cream with rich sauce.

SERVES 6 . PAGE 224 . ✻

Melon Ice
Tiny balls of refreshing melon ice
cream with marinated melon.

SERVES 6-8 . PAGE 225 . ✻

Lime and Cranberry Ice
Refresh those festive palates with this
tangy ice cream.

SERVES 8 . PAGE 375 . ✻

Vanilla Ice with Espresso
The perfect instant dessert, hot
espresso tops cool ice cream.

SERVES 6 . PAGE 375 . ⏱

The Ultimate Chocolate Cake
Wonderfully rich chocolate cake
coated in a creamy chocolate icing.

MAKES 25 . PAGE 156 . ❊

Crumbly Apple and Cheese Cake
Moist, crumbly fruit cake with a
surprise layer of Caerphilly cheese.

MAKES 10 SLICES . PAGE 300 . ❊

Cinnamon Coffee Cake
Spicy layered cake flavoured with
soured cream, perfect with coffee.

MAKES 8 SLICES . PAGE 300 . ❊

Ginger Cake
This moist dark ginger cake improves
with keeping.

MAKES 25 SLICES . PAGE 301 . ♡ . ❊

**Almond, Chocolate and Sweet
Potato Loaf**
A moist cake with sweet potato.

MAKES 8-10 SLICES . PAGE 301 . ❊

Walnut Torte
Nutty walnut cake flavoured with
orange and ricotta cheese.

MAKES 8-10 SLICES . PAGE 156

**Lemon Sponge with Kirsch and
Fresh Currants**
Delicious syrup-soaked sponge cake.

SERVES 8-10 . PAGE 226 . ♡ . ❊

Chocolate Roulade
Everyone's favourite, soft moist chocolate sponge
encircling whipped cream.

SERVES 6-8 . PAGE 227 . ❊

Simnel Cake
Spiced fruit cake layered with marzipan and traditionally decorated.

SERVES 20 . PAGE 157 . ✽

Rich Christmas Cake
The fruit for this traditional cake is soaked in rum for extra flavour.

SERVES 12-16 . PAGE 376

Stollen
Rich, fruity yeast bread with a marzipan filling.

SERVES 10 . PAGE 377 . ✽

Bûche de Noël
Chestnut filled Swiss roll, decorated with a rich chocolate butter cream.

SERVES 8-10 . PAGE 378 . ✽

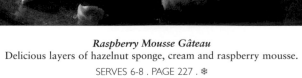

Hazelnut Vacherin with Apricots
Spirals of hazelnut meringue filled with fresh apricots and cream.

SERVES 6 . PAGE 228

Raspberry Mousse Gâteau
Delicious layers of hazelnut sponge, cream and raspberry mousse.

SERVES 6-8 . PAGE 227 . ✽

Sticky Orange Flapjacks
This sticky tea-time bake is a great
favourite with all ages.

MAKES 18 . PAGE 303 . ✳

Honey and Yogurt Muffins
Wonderfully craggy, easy to make,
American-style muffins.

MAKES 12 . PAGE 302 . ♡ . ◔ . ✳

Berry Scones
These moist crumbly scones are made with blackberries.

MAKES 16 . PAGE 302 . ♡ . ◔ . ✳

Mince Pies
No need for special tins for these
festive fruit pies.

MAKES 24 . PAGE 377 . ✳

Mini Hot Cross Buns
Spicy buns speckled with currants
and marked with pastry crosses.

MAKES 25 . PAGE 158 . ✳

Almond Squares
A version of almond Bakewell tart,
topped with toasted flaked almonds.

MAKES 12 . PAGE 159 . ✳

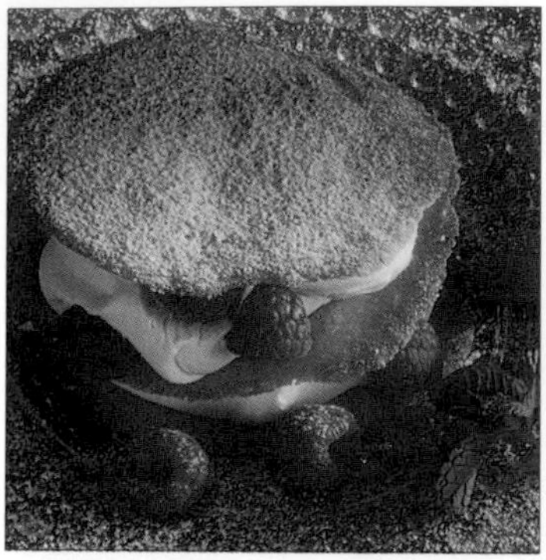

Honey Wafers
Wafer-thin sponge rounds, delicious served layered with cream and fruit.
MAKES 24 . PAGE 229 . ❄

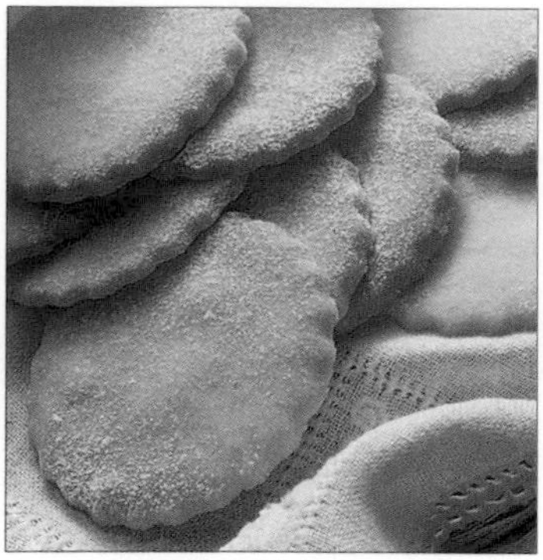

Orange Flower Biscuits
Crisp, buttery biscuits, delicately flavoured with orange flower water.
MAKES 20-24 . PAGE 229

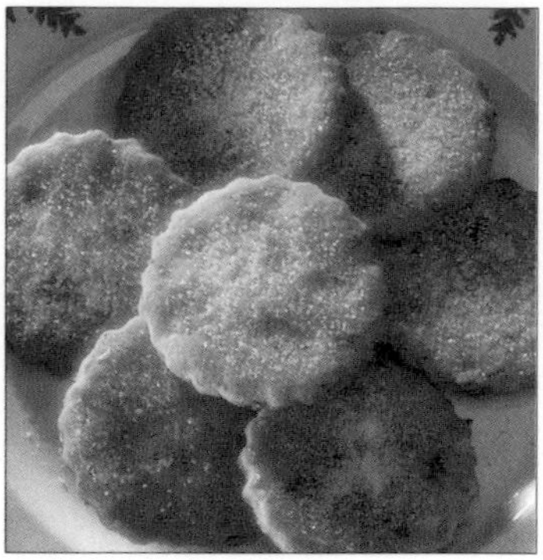

Easter Biscuits
Spiced currant biscuits flavoured with brandy and mixed peel.
MAKES 30 . PAGE 158 . ❄

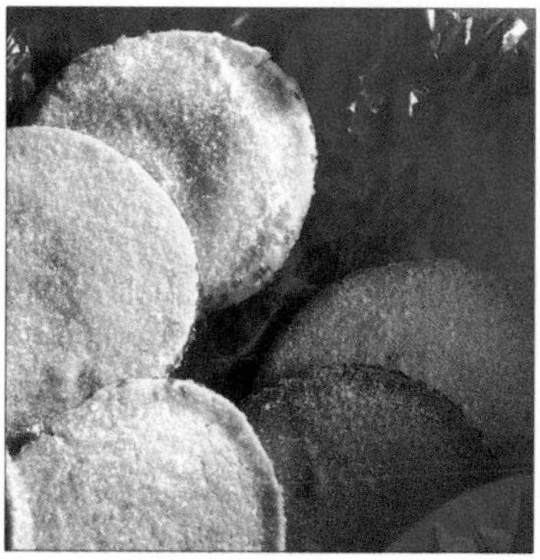

Shortbread
Home-made buttery shortbread makes an ideal Christmas gift.
MAKES 24-36 . PAGE 379

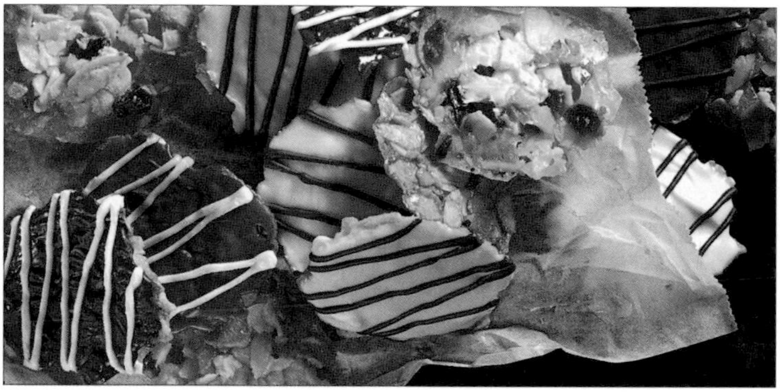

Florentines
Dainty Italian fruit and nut biscuits coated with chocolate.
MAKES 30 . PAGE 378

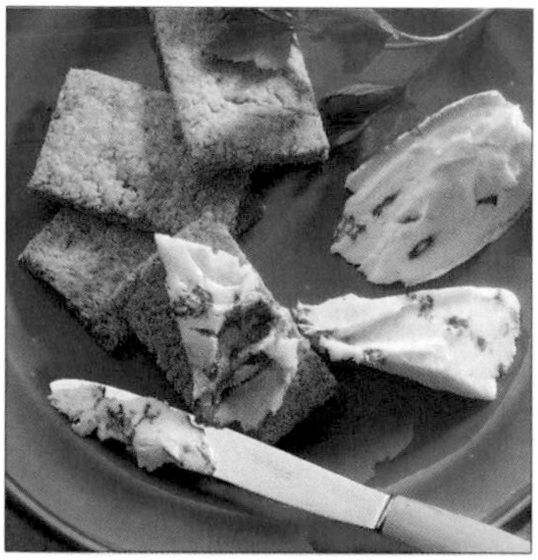

Oat and Sesame Biscuits
These crisp wholemeal biscuits are delicious with blue cheese.
MAKES 50 . PAGE 304 . ♡ . ❄

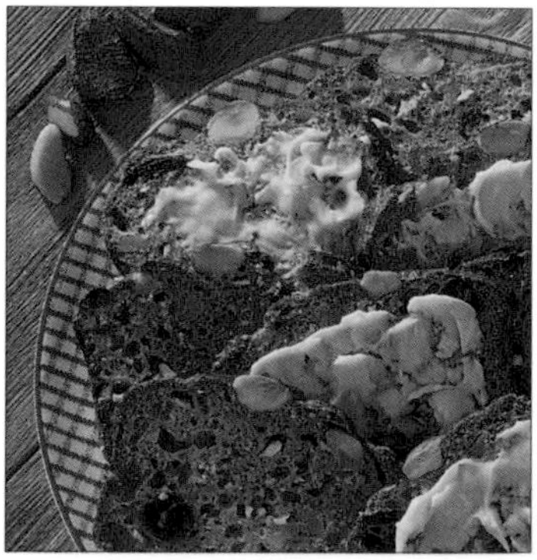

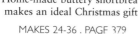

Cottage Cheese and Brazil Nut Teabread
This nutty loaf is virtually fat free.
MAKES 12 SLICES . PAGE 304 . ♡ . ❄

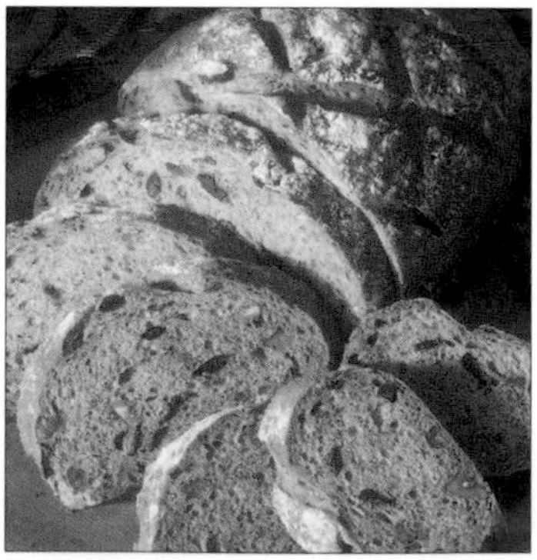

Olive and Walnut Bread
Serve warm and thickly sliced for a taste of the Mediterranean.
MAKES 2 LOAVES . PAGE 305 . ♡ . ❄

Chocolate Eggs
For Easter - one large egg, or 4 small solid eggs.

MAKES 1 OR 4 EGGS . PAGE 161

Chocolate Colettes with Frosted Flowers
Creamy-filled dark chocolate cases.

MAKES 16 . PAGE 160

Summer Pickle
Piquant vegetables, herbs and spices - ideal with cold meats or cheese.

MAKES 450 G (1 LB) . PAGE 230

Sweetcorn Relish
Colourful American-style preserve, good with cold roast meats or burgers.

MAKES 2.3 KG (5 1B) . PAGE 307

Cranberry and Roast Shallot Chutney
Ideal accompaniment to cold turkey.

MAKES 900 G (2 LB) . PAGE 380

Damson Chutney
Mellow-tasting chutney captures all the tastes of autumn.

MAKES 1.8 KG (4 LB) . PAGE 307

Apple and Mint Jelly
Clear, golden jelly, flecked with fragrant chopped mint.

PAGE 306

Marrow and Apricot Jam
A good way to use and preserve gluts of marrow.

MAKES 2.3 KG (5 LB) . PAGE 306

Berry Jam
A cream tea just wouldn't be complete without this favourite jam.

MAKES 1.8 KG (4 LB) . PAGE 230

Apricot Jam
Delicious golden coloured jam, the
ideal breakfast choice.

MAKES 3 KG (6½ LB) . PAGE 230

Tangerine Jelly Marmalade
Crystal clear marmalade, textured
with fine tangerine shreds.

MAKES 2.3 KG (5 LB) . PAGE 381

Seville Orange Marmalade
The purist's marmalade with its
classic bitter-sweet taste.

MAKES 4.5 KG (10 LB) . PAGE 381

Brandy-soaked Cherries
Capture the best of the cherry crop in
this boozy preserve.

MAKES 450 G (1 LB) . PAGE 231

Apricot Mincemeat
An easy-to-make preserve for the
festive season.

MAKES 1.8 KG (4 LB) . PAGE 380

Summer Punch
Refreshingly cool and bubbly, ideal
for entertaining.

SERVES 18-20 . PAGE 232

Mangoade
Refreshingly non-alcoholic cocktail,
ideal for any time of day.

SERVES 4-6 . PAGE 232

Apricot Flip, Tropical Fruit Crush
Two fruity and refreshing drinks for
summer days.

SERVES 2 OR 8-10 . PAGE 232/233

Redcurrant Rum
Wonderfully decadent pale pink
liqueur made with redcurrants.

SERVES 16 . PAGE 233

INGREDIENTS THROUGH THE SEASONS

MEAT

We are constantly being told to cut down on our consumption of red meat, but as a good source of protein, B vitamins and minerals such as iron and zinc, it can still contribute to a healthy diet. Always choose the leaner cuts, and trim off most of the visible fat before cooking.

Buying

When buying meat it should always smell fresh with no signs of greying; meat cuts should be neatly trimmed. Check date stamps on all packaged food and ensure that it is well sealed; frozen meat should be quite solid when bought.

Always ask the butcher for help as he should be able to advise on the meat of the moment and the best way to cook it. Conservation- and organic-grade meat is becoming more readily available and this meat is thought to have a superior flavour.

Storing

All meat should be stored in the refrigerator. Unwrap it as soon as you get it home, then place on a clean plate and cover loosely with foil or clingfilm. Position on the bottom shelf in the refrigerator so that no juices can drip onto other foods. Minced meat, veal and offal are best eaten within two days; chops, steaks and larger joints within three days. Lean meat keeps better than fatty cuts as the fat can turn rancid. When calculating amounts to buy, allow about 125-225 g (4-8 oz) chops, cutlets, steaks per person or, for roasting, allow 350 g (12 oz) meat on the bone per person.

All meat can be frozen, although offal does toughen slightly. Wrap meat carefully for freezing and store for about 6 months.

Roasting Meat

Use only the best-quality joints, such as leg or shoulder of lamb or sirloin or topside of beef. Allow about 225 g (8 oz) boned and rolled meat per person or 350 g (12 oz) meat on the bone.

First weigh the meat and calculate the cooking time (see chart on page 59). If the joint is quite fatty, lightly slash the surface, then place it fat-side up on a wire rack over a roasting tin; baste frequently with the juices that run off the meat during cooking. For leaner cuts of meat first heat a little oil or dripping in the roasting tin and use this to baste. For crisp pork crackling first lightly rub the skin with oil and salt and do not baste the joint at all

during cooking. To test if the meat is cooked, push a meat thermometer into the thickest part to check the internal temperature – see meat roasting chart on page 59. Alternatively, push a fine skewer into the middle of the joint – if the juices run clear the meat is cooked.

BEEF

Beef should be a good clear colour; bright red doesn't necessarily indicate freshness as the colour will quickly darken on exposure to air. The fat should be creamy white except for some specialist breeds of Jersey or Guernsey where it is yellower. All beef should have small flecks (marbling) of fat running through the flesh. This helps to tenderize the meat during cooking.

Sirloin Ideal for roasting, this joint is sold on the bone or boned and rolled.

Topside A very lean roasting or braising cut, often sold with fat tied around. Thin slices are sold for making beef olives.

Rib An excellent roasting joint sold on the bone or boned and rolled.

Fillet The prime beef cut; sold whole to roast, or sliced for steaks.

Silverside A lean boneless joint which is best pot-roasted as it can be dry if oven roasted. It is also sold salted for boiling; when raw this looks grey but turns pink during cooking.

Brisket Sold on the bone or boned and rolled, it is best pot-roasted or braised as it can be tough. It can be bought salted for boiling.

Steaks All steaks can be quickly cooked by grilling or stir-frying; the slightly coarser steaks, such as rump, can be marinated first.

ENTRECOTE Cut from between the ribs, although a slice cut from the sirloin or rump is sometimes sold by this name.

FILLET The centre or eye of the fillet is considered the best. Chateaubriand is a thick slice taken from the middle and it can weigh up to 350 g (12 oz). A tournedos is a small round of fillet steak, about 125 g (4 oz) in weight. A *filet mignon tournedos* is a small round, about 75 g (3 oz), cut from the end of the fillet.

SIRLOIN A porterhouse steak is cut from the thick end of the sirloin and can weigh as much as 700 g (1½ lb). When cooked on the bone, it is known as a T-bone steak. A minute steak is a very thin steak from the upper part of the sirloin.

RUMP Sold in a variety of thicknesses, this tender cut is taken from the hind quarter.

FLASH FRY Cut from the thick flank topside or silverside, these steaks are beaten and passed between spiked rollers to tenderize them.

Chuck and blade steak Usually sliced or cubed for braising or stewing.

Thick flank (top rump) A lean boneless cut for pot-roasting and braising or for flash fry steaks.

Thin flank Used for braising and mince.

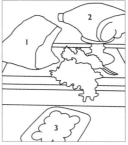

1 *Rib of beef*
2 *Cooked ham*
3 *Lamb noisettes*

57

Neck and clod Used for stewing or mince.

Shin and leg Very lean meat which needs slow moist cooking to tenderize it.

Ox kidney This has a strong flavour and needs long slow cooking to tenderize it – ideal for steak and kidney pie.

Ox tongue Weighing about 1.8-3 kg (4-6½ lb), this is usually boiled and then pressed to serve cold.

Ox liver Strongly flavoured, ox liver can be simmered in casseroles or minced for pâtés.

Oxtail One oxtail weighs about 1.4 kg (3 lb) and will serve 3 people. Sold jointed it needs long slow cooking to tenderize.

Tripe Tripe is the stomach lining from the ox. The smooth first stomach is known as 'blanket', the second 'honeycomb' and the third 'thick seam'. All should be thick, firm and white and there is no difference in taste. Tripe is sold bleached (dressed) and partly boiled.

VEAL

Veal comes from calves; the palest meat, which is thought to be the best, comes from milk-fed calves. As the animals get older the diet is supplemented by grass and the meat darkens. It is a very tender meat requiring little cooking.

Leg The prime cut, sold thinly sliced as fillets or escalopes for frying or grilling.

Fillet Sold in a piece for roasting or pot-roasting. Cook carefully as it quickly dries out.

Osso buco or knuckle Cut from the shin with meat and bone attached, this is used for casseroles or the Italian speciality, Osso Buco. Allow about 225 g (8 oz) per person and remember that the marrow in the bones is a delicacy.

Loin Sold boned and rolled for roasting or pot-roasting, or as cutlets and chops for grilling.

Breast A cheaper cut, usually boned, stuffed and rolled for roasting.

Pie veal Diced veal for casseroles or pies.

Calf's liver The most expensive and delicate liver sold. Cook quickly by grilling or frying to keep it tender.

Calf's kidneys A delicacy, but rarely seen today.

LAMB

Home-produced lamb is best in the spring but with New Zealand imports, lamb is available all the year round. The fat should look crisp and white with the lean meat firm and pinky brown. The bones should be pinkish white. All the flesh is quite tender but some cuts are best casseroled.

Leg This is an excellent roasting joint, sold whole, divided into fillet end or shank end, or boned and rolled. After boning, it can be 'butterflied' – spread flat for grilling or barbecuing. Leg steaks are suitable for grilling, frying or barbecuing.

Shoulder Sold whole, halved or boned and rolled for roasting or braising. Chops or steaks are also available for grilling or braising.

Loin The whole loin consists of both chump and loin chops. It can be simply roasted or first boned, stuffed and rolled. Alternatively, it can be divided into loin end and chump end chops – both ideal for grilling or frying. Loin steaks are loin chops with the bone removed.

Saddle of lamb A large roasting joint for special occasions, consisting of the whole loin from both sides of the animal. It is sometimes sold sliced into Butterfly or Barnsley chops.

Fillet of lamb A very lean, tender cut of lamb taken from the loin. It can be roasted, or sliced for stir-frying.

Rack of lamb Sometimes known as best end of neck, this is a whole roasting joint consisting of about 7 cutlets. Always ask the butcher to chine (cut through) the backbone to make carving easier. Two trimmed racks of lamb are tied together to form a Guard of Honour or a Crown Roast.

Lamb cutlets These are cut from the rack of lamb and are ideal for grilling or frying.

Lamb noisettes These small rounds of meat are cut from a boned, rolled and tied rack of lamb. Perfect for grilling, frying and barbecuing.

Scrag and middleneck These are the traditional cuts for Lancashire Hot Pot and Irish Stew; they are sold on the bone. The 'eye' of meat from the neck is sometimes removed and sold as neck fillet for grilling or stir-frying.

Breast of lamb This is the cheapest cut of lamb and very fatty too. It is usually sold boned, rolled and stuffed for roasting or pot-roasting. The breast can also be cut into riblets for grilling.

Lamb's liver Sold sliced, this should be cooked for the minimum of time to keep it tender. It can be grilled, fried or gently casseroled.

Lamb's kidneys These should be quickly cooked to keep them tender, either fry or skewer and grill.

Lamb's heart Whole hearts can be stuffed and braised or casseroled; serve one per person.

Sweetbreads These come from the thyrus gland. They are sold in pairs and are considered to be a delicacy. They are first simmered and then often crumbed for frying.

Lamb's tongue Weighing about 225 g (8 oz), this needs gentle simmering or casseroling to tenderize.

PORK

Pork should have a thin even layer of white fat and, where appropriate, a thin elastic skin. All pork should be well cooked; never serve it underdone.

Leg This large roasting cut is usually sold divided into the fillet end and the knuckle (shank) end and is sometimes boned and rolled. It can also be sliced into steaks and escalopes for grilling and frying.

Loin This can be roasted on or off the bone and has a good covering of 'crackling'. It is also sold divided into chops, sometimes with the kidneys attached, and as steaks where the bone has been removed. Both chops and steaks can be grilled, fried or casseroled.

Shoulder Sometimes known as hand and spring, this joint can be roasted, or cubed for casseroling. It can also be sliced into steaks for grilling.

Tenderloin or fillet This tender lean cut looks like a thin beef fillet and can be roasted whole. Alternatively, cut it into thin slices to stir-fry, or cubes to grill as kebabs. Escalopes are thin batted-out slices of tenderloin (or sometimes leg).

Spare ribs These are sometimes sold as barbecue ribs, Chinese-style ribs or American-cut ribs and are cut from the belly or the ribs. They can be bought as a whole rack which needs to be divided before cooking.

Neck end Boned and rolled for roasting, or cut into meaty spare rib chops for grilling or frying.

Belly This is a fatty cut which is either sold boned and rolled to roast or cut into slices for grilling or casseroling. It is often minced to add to pâtés.

Pig's liver This has a strong flavour and is used primarily for pâtés and terrines.

Pig's kidneys Strongly flavoured, these can be halved and grilled or fried.

BACON, GAMMON AND HAM

Bacon is simply cured fresh pork. Gammon is the name given to whole hind legs cut from a side of bacon after curing. Ham is the hind leg of a pig cut from the whole carcass, then cured and matured separately, but nowadays cooked gammon is often described as ham.

There are several different methods of curing pork which give different flavours to the bacon. The pork is injected with a brine solution which colours, flavours and preserves the flesh. After curing some bacon is smoked. Unsmoked bacon is known as 'green', 'pale' or 'plain' bacon. Bacon sold in vacuum packs as 'sweet', 'mild' or 'tender cure' has had sugar added to the curing brine. Vacuum-packed bacon will remain moist until opened; once opened, wrap in foil or store in a plastic container in the refrigerator for up to two weeks. Bacon which is sold sliced and unpacked (loose) should be refrigerated for not more than a week.

Prime back bacon Very lean and usually sold as rashers or boneless chops for grilling or frying.

Prime streaky bacon Fattier than back bacon, it can be bought sliced for grilling or frying, or as a whole joint to boil.

Middle or throughcut Back and streaky rashers sold in one piece – use for grilling or frying.

Gammon This can be bought whole, halved or as smaller cuts known as middle, corner or hock. These can be boiled, braised or baked. Gammon steaks and rashers are boneless and suitable for grilling or frying.

Ham Usually sold cooked but if raw can be boiled or baked (roasted). Some of the best-known cures are York where the meat is pale with a mild, delicate flavour and sweet-tasting honey-roast.

Raw hams Several hams are produced especially for eating raw. The best known are Italian Parma ham, French Bayonne and Spanish Serrano.

MEAT ROASTING CHART

MEAT	COOKING TIME AT 180°C (350°F) MARK 4	INTERNAL TEMP.
BEEF		
Rare	20 mins per 450 g (1 lb) plus 20 mins	60°C (140°F)
Medium	25 mins per 450 g (1 lb) plus 25 mins	70°C (160°F)
Well done	30 mins per 450 g (1 lb) plus 30 mins	80°C (175°F)
VEAL		
Well done	25 mins per 450 g (1 lb) plus 25 mins	70°C (160°F)
LAMB		
Medium	25 mins per 450 g (1 lb) plus 25 mins	70-75°C (160-170°F)
Well done	30 mins per 450 g (1 lb) plus 30 mins	75-80°C (170-175°F)
PORK		
Well done	35 mins per 450 g (1 lb) plus 35 mins	80-85°C (175-180°F)

POULTRY AND GAME

Poultry is the name given to all domesticated birds bred for the table; that is chickens, turkeys, ducks, geese and guinea fowl.

Buying

The ever-increasing range of poultry available today can be confusing for the consumer. Generally, free-range and corn-fed birds are more expensive and have the best and strongest flavour whilst standard fresh and frozen birds are much blander and sometimes drier too.

Buy poultry from a reliable source only where you can be sure the turnover is quick or the freezer facilities adequate. Carefully check date stamps and never buy anything with damaged packaging. All poultry should smell fresh and have moist, unbroken skin without any dark patches; ducks should have an unbroken light-coloured skin.

Storing

All poultry, raw and frozen, must be handled carefully as it contains low levels of salmonella and campylobacter, the bacteria responsible for food poisoning. Given the right conditions these bacteria can multiply, but if poultry is stored and cooked correctly they pose no threat.

In warm weather bring poultry home in a cool bag with a freezer block. Immediately unwrap fresh poultry, remove giblets and place both on separate plates. Cover loosely and refrigerate.

Frozen poultry should be placed in the freezer until required. To thaw, place on a plate, pierce the wrappings and thaw at cool room temperature overnight. Once thawed, cover and refrigerate, cooking the poultry within a day. Never refreeze poultry once thawed unless first cooked and cooled.

Never handle raw and cooked poultry at the same time or use the same knife for cutting.

Always cook poultry thoroughly. To test if cooked, pierce the thickest part of the leg with a skewer – if the juices run clear it is cooked; if not return to the oven for a little longer.

Nutrition

Nutritionally, poultry is an excellent food. It is a good source of protein and turkey, chicken and guinea fowl are very low in fat, especially if the skin is trimmed away. Duck and goose are very fatty and must be roasted on a rack to drain off fat.

CHICKEN

Oven-ready chickens These can be chilled or frozen and range in weight from 1.4-3.2 kg (3-7 lb). Allow at least 350 g (12 oz) per person. They can be roasted, poached, casseroled or barbecued.

Corn-fed chickens Available fresh or frozen, these have a distinctive yellow colour due to their diet of maize. Use as for oven-ready chickens.

Poussins These are 4-6 week old chickens weighing 450-575 g (1-1¼ lb). They are very tender and can be roasted, casseroled, split and grilled or barbecued. One poussin serves 1-2 people.

Spring chickens These are 12-week old chickens weighing about 1.1 (2½ lb). Cook as for oven-ready chickens. One bird serves 2-3 people.

Boiling fowl These are rarely seen today but are delicious. They are older, tougher birds weighing 2.3-3.2 kg (5-7 lb), which need long slow casseroling to tenderize them.

Chicken pieces (portions) Chicken can now be bought cut into many different pieces including legs (drumsticks), thighs (with or without bone), wings, halves and breasts (with or without skin and bone). The darker meat cuts – the legs, thighs and wings – are usually best casseroled whilst the tender breast meat can be fried or grilled. When the breasts are skinned and flattened they are known as escalopes; with the wingbone attached they are known as supremes. Allow about 150 g (5 oz) boned chicken per person, about 225 g (8 oz) per person when on the bone.

Chicken livers These can be simply stir-fried and served on toast or salad, or processed into rich pâtés.

GUINEA FOWL

Guinea fowl has a slightly more gamey flavour than chicken and usually weighs about 1.4 kg (3 lb), sufficient to feed 4 people. Cook as for oven-

1 *Corn-fed chicken*
2 *Brace of pheasant*
3 *Duckling*
4 *Poussins*

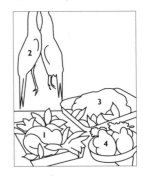

ready chickens but remember that the flesh can be dry, so use plenty of fat when roasting.

TURKEY

Turkey is available all year round, either whole, as a boned roast, or cut into portions.

Oven-ready turkey Can be bought fresh or frozen, ranging from 2.3-13.5 kg (5-30 lb) in weight. Look out for free-range turkeys and for ready-basted varieties where a little vegetable oil, butter or stock has been added to keep the meat moist during cooking. Whole turkeys, turkey breast joints and drumsticks are best roasted (see chart).

Turkey pieces (portions) Turkey breast fillets (escalopes) or steaks are ideal for grilling or frying. Alternatively, buy diced meat for casséroles. Some supermarkets also sell minced turkey.

Roast turkey

• *Thawing* Always ensure that turkey is thoroughly thawed before roasting.

• *Stuffing* Stuff the neck end only to ensure that heat penetrates to the centre of the bird.

• *Cooking* Weigh the stuffed bird and calculate the cooking time to be ready 20 minutes before carving. Spread with butter and season. Wrap loosely in foil, place in a roasting tin and cook at 180°C (350°F) mark 4. Fold back foil 45 minutes before end of cooking time. Baste occasionally.

• *Testing* Insert a fine skewer into a thigh. If the juices run clear it is cooked.

TURKEY ROASTING CHART

OVEN-READY WEIGHT	COOKING FOIL WRAPPED	WITHOUT FOIL
550 g-1.4 kg (1¼-3 lb)	1¾-2 hr	1½-1¾ hr
1.4-2.3 kg (3-5 lb)	2-2½ hr	1¾-2 hr
2.3-3.6 kg (5-8 lb)	2½-3½ hr	2-2½ hr
3.6-5 kg (8-11 lb)	3½-4 hr	2½-3¼ hr
5-6.8 kg (11-15 lb)	4-5 hr	3¼-3¾ hr
6.8-9 kg (15-20 lb)	5-5½ hr	3¾-4¼ hr
9-11.3 kg (20-25 lb)	not recom.	4¼-4¾ hr
11.3-13.5 kg (25-30 lb)	not recom.	4¾-5½ hr

DUCK

Ducklings are sold fresh or frozen, all year round. They can be bought whole for roasting, as portions for casseroling or as breasts for roasting, grilling and frying. Strictly speaking a duckling is about 8 weeks old – after that it is a duck. Allow a minimum of 450 g (1 lb) duck per person when roasting.

GOOSE

Goose is a very fatty bird so you will need to allow at least 700 g (1½ lb) per person. Avoid any with deep yellow fat as this indicates an old bird.

GAME

The term game refers to wild animals or birds which have been hunted for food. Wild game is protected by law and can only be hunted at certain times of the year but hare, rabbit and wood pigeon can be hunted at any time. Most game needs hanging to develop its flavour – supermarket game is usually fairly mild to suit all tastes whilst game from butcher shops can be strong. Young birds are best roasted, older ones should be casseroled.

Pheasant Season Oct 1st to Feb 1st. The hen pheasant is smaller than the cock pheasant and has more tender flesh. A brace of pheasants serves 4-5.

Partridge Season Oct 1st to Feb 1st. Serve one per person.

Grouse and ptarmigan Season Aug 12th to Dec 10th. A whole bird serves one person.

Quail This is now a protected species, so all quail available from shops are farmed. They are tiny birds so you could serve 2 per person. The flavour is quite mild. Either roast or split and grill.

Wild duck Season Sept 1st to Jan 31st. These have a rich almost fishy flavour. One bird serves 2.

Woodcock Season Oct 1st to Jan 31st. These are generally cooked whole (without drawing) with their heads intact. Serve one per person.

Wood pigeon Wild pigeon is best casseroled; farmed pigeon can be roasted.

Venison Wild venison usually has a stronger flavour than farmed varieties. The meat is very lean and benefits from marinating. The loin, saddle, fillet and leg can be roasted or braised. Chops, escalopes or medallions are delicious grilled or fried. Shoulder, neck and breast cuts are best for casseroles.

Rabbit and hare The flavour of rabbit and hare are very different. Rabbit can be quite mild, whilst hare is strong and gamey. Both hare and rabbit can be roasted, but are more usually casseroled. One small hare or one large jointed rabbit will serve 6.

FISH AND SHELLFISH

Fish is becoming more and more important in our diet as the nutritional benefits are being understood. It's high in protein, vitamins and minerals yet low in fat and carbohydrate. Where fat is present in the oil-rich fish, such as mackerel, herring and sardines, the oil is high in polyunsaturated fatty acids, in particular omega-3. These fatty acids have been shown to have a lowering effect on blood fats and so are helpful to protect against thrombosis. Most fish is quick to cook and easily digested.

Buying and Storing

Fish can be bought wet (fresh) or frozen. Always buy from a reputable source where you know the turnover is quick and do ask the fishmonger for advice. There are many new varieties of fish appearing on the counter and these can often be substituted in your favourite recipe. When really fresh, whole fish should have clear, bright eyes, bright red gills and a moist slippery skin with firm flesh. Fillets and steaks of fish should have a white translucent colour with no discolouration, and avoid any that look dry or shrivelled. With the exception of skate and shark, which do have a fishy smell, all fish should smell fresh. If you're buying pre-packed fish check the date stamp and ensure the wrapping isn't damaged. Frozen fish must be completely solid and not half thawed when you buy it.

Ideally fresh fish should be cooked and eaten on the day of purchase or stored for a maximum of a day. Rinse and dry the fish, then place on a plate, cover with clingfilm and refrigerate. (Follow the instructions on pre-packed fish.) Frozen fish will keep well for 2-3 months after which it begins to lose its flavour. Leave in its wrappings and thaw out in the refrigerator overnight. Never refreeze fish once thawed unless it has been cooked first in a made-up dish.

Preparing Fish

If you buy fish from a wet fish counter the fishmonger will always gut, fillet and skin it for you. If preparing fish yourself be guided by the shape: round fish such as cod, haddock and monkfish require different methods to the flat fish such as sole, plaice and skate.

Round fish First gut them – cut along the belly and pull out the innards, then rinse well. To fillet the fish, lay the fish on its side with the tail pointing towards you. Cut along the backbone from the head to tail, cutting right through to the backbone. Starting at the head end, insert the knife between the fillet and bones and gradually fillet the flesh away from the bones. Remove the fillet from the other side similarly. To skin the fish, lay each fillet skin-side down on a board. Grasp the tail end and gradually fillet by inserting the knife between the flesh and the skin and pushing the flesh away from the skin with the knife until the other end of the fillet is reached.

Herring and mackerel These small round fish are often cooked whole. To bone them, cut off the head, tail and fins and slit open the whole way along the underside. Place cut-side down on a board and press firmly along the backbone. Turn the fish over and ease out the backbone.

Flat fish To gut, make a small incision below the gills and pull the innards out. When cooking a whole fish remove the dark skin only. Make a small incision by the tail and ease up the dark skin. Salt your fingers, grasp hold of the skin and pull it firmly away from the flesh.

To prepare fillets don't skin the fish first. Lay the fish on a board with the tail towards you and using a flexible filleting knife cut straight down the backbone. Starting at the head end, gradually fillet and ease the flesh away from the bone. Remove second fillet similarly. Turn the fish over and remove two fillets from this side.

Cooking Fish

Fish lends itself to all methods of cooking – frying, grilling, baking, poaching, steaming. Whichever you choose, it should be quick as the delicate flavour and texture of fish is spoilt by overcooking. Oily fish are best grilled. White fish quickly dry out so they must be well basted during grilling or baking, or be coated in a batter for frying. Chunky pieces of a firm textured fish such as monkfish are perfect for casseroles. To check if fish is cooked insert a skewer into the thickest part of the flesh; it should begin to flake. Cooked flesh should look white or opaque, not translucent.

Deep frying An ideal method of cooking for fillets of firm fish, pieces of skate and small whole fish. All fish for deep frying should be coated in seasoned flour, batter or egg and breadcrumbs. Deep fry a few pieces at a time at 190°C (375°F) until

golden. Drain on absorbent kitchen paper. Fillets of fish usually take 4-5 minutes; whitebait about 1-2 minutes.

Shallow frying Ideal for fillets, steaks and small whole fish, such as sole, plaice, bass, mackerel, trout and skate. First coat the prepared fish with seasoned flour or egg and breadcrumbs. Fry in vegetable oil or a mixture of oil and butter, turning once. Drain on absorbent kitchen paper. Thin fillets take 1-2 minutes a side; larger fish up to 8-10 minutes a side. For stir-frying, coat strips of fish in flour and fry in a little oil for 2-3 minutes.

Grilling and barbecuing Especially good for oil-rich fish such as mackerel, sardines and trout. Slash the skin lightly before grilling. Fillets or steaks of cod, haddock, salmon, tuna and so on are delicious grilled but must be generously brushed with oil or butter to keep them moist. Turn all fish when grilling. For barbecuing, the fish can be placed inside a fish rack or threaded onto skewers.

Baking One of the best methods for whole fish but very successful too for steaks, fillets or cuts from large fish such as salmon, monkfish, cod, haddock and halibut. Wrap in foil or greaseproof paper with herbs and seasoning or place in a covered baking dish with water, wine, herbs and seasoning. Bake at 180°C (350°F) mark 4 for about 30-40 minutes for medium-sized whole fish; 15-20 minutes for fish steaks. (Check recipes for exact timings.) If the fish is to be served cold, leave to cool in the foil before unwrapping.

Poaching Here the fish is either partially or completely covered in a court bouillon (fish stock) and then simmered until it's just tender; the liquid must not boil rapidly or the fish will break up. Whole salmon are often cooked this way. Place in a large fish kettle, cover with water, wine and flavourings. Cover and bring very slowly to the boil. Simmer for 2-3 minutes. Take off the heat and allow to cool completely. Whatever the size of fish the method is the same; the larger the fish the greater volume of liquid required to cover it and therefore the longer it takes to come to the boil and cool down again, so cooking the fish right through. Fillets and steaks of fish such as haddock (including smoked haddock), monkfish and hake can be poached and the liquid used to make a light sauce.

Steaming This is a very gentle method of cooking fish. Wrap small whole fish, steaks or fillets in buttered foil or place between two buttered heatproof plates with a few flavourings. Place in a steamer or over a pan of simmering water for about 10 minutes for fillets; 15 minutes for steaks and a little longer for whole fish. Ideal for fillets of sole or plaice, salmon steaks and pieces of skate.

Microwaving Fish cooks very well in the microwave as it keeps very moist. Ideal for small whole fish, fillets and steaks such as cod, bass, haddock and mullet.

WHITE FISH

All white fish come from the sea and can be divided into two categories – flat species and round species. Those from a similar category are often interchangeable in recipes so check with your fishmonger. The following guide gives the best time to buy fresh fish but remember that many can be bought frozen all the year round.

Flat Species

Brill Season June to February. Firm slightly yellowish flesh. Flavour and texture resembles turbot. Sold whole or filleted. Bake, grill or fry.

Dab Season September to May. Bake, grill, fry or poach.

Halibut Season June to March. Regarded as one of the best flavoured fish, it is sold as fillets or steaks. Usually baked or grilled.

Plaice Season May to February. Sold whole or filleted. The flesh is quite delicate. Grill, poach, bake or fry.

Skate Season May to February. Only the wings are sold. The flesh is slightly pink. Grill, fry, poach or bake.

Dover sole Season May to February. A delicious delicately flavoured fish with fine yet firm texture. Ideal grilled whole or filleted to poach or fry.

Lemon sole Season May to March. A cheaper fish than Dover sole, the flesh is slightly more stringy with a milder flavour.

Turbot Season April to February. Firm white delicately flavoured flesh. A prized flat fish, it is usually cut into steaks. Grill or poach.

1 *Skate wing*
2 *Red snapper*
3 *Parrotfish*
4 *Mackerel*
5 *Sea bream*
6 *Sardines*
7 *Lemon sole*

Round Species

Bass Season August to March. Sold whole or in steaks or fillets. Whole fish can weigh up to 4.5 kg (10 lb). The flesh is delicate and slightly pink. Grill, fry, poach or bake.

Catfish (rockfish) Season February to July. Firm white flesh with a strong flavour. Sold as fillets or cutlets to grill, poach, fry or casserole.

Cod Season June to February. A large fish usually sold as fillets, steaks or cutlets. It can be grilled, fried, poached or baked and is good in pies.

Coley (Saithe coalfish) Season August to February. The flesh is pinkish grey, turning white when cooked. Best in pies.

Haddock Season May to February. Related to the cod, this fish also has firm white flesh. Sold as fillets, cutlets and steaks; good for any cooking method.

Hake Season June to March. From the cod family but with a closer flesh. Cook as for cod.

Huss (dogfish, rocksalmon) Season all year. Related to the shark family, the flesh is firm yet creamy in flavour. Excellent fried.

John Dory Season all year. Firm white flesh with a delicate flavour. Poach or bake whole, or fillet to grill, fry or bake.

Monkfish (anglerfish) Season all year. Only the tail is eaten served as fillets. The flesh is very firm making it ideal for casseroles. Bake, grill or poach.

Red mullet Season May to November. Sold whole, these may be grilled, fried or baked.

Sea bream (red and black) Season June to February. Firm, mild-flavoured flesh. Bake, poach, fry or grill.

Whiting Season June to February. Soft delicate flesh, often minced for quenelles. Poach, steam or shallow fry.

OILY FISH

In oily fish the oil is found throughout the flesh. This oil is thought to be beneficial to our health.

Anchovy Season June to December. These strong flavoured fish can be grilled but are more usually filleted and cured by salting and brining.

Herring Season May to December. A small delicately flavoured bony fish. Usually served whole for grilling, baking or frying, but they can also be filleted.

Mackerel Season all year. They have a strong distinctive flavour and cream-coloured flesh. Eat really fresh. Cook as for herrings.

Sardine (pilchard) Season January, February, April, November and December. Sardines are strictly speaking young pilchards but the name is also applied to the young of other fish (sprats and herrings for instance). Most are canned but when fresh they're best grilled or fried.

Salmon Season all year. Salmon spends some of its life in salt water and some in freshwater. It is extensively farmed and so available all the year round. The flesh is firm and rich. It can be bought whole or as steaks or fillets. Bake or poach whole fish; grill, fry or steam steaks and fillets.

Sprat Season October to March. Small members of the herring family, best grilled or fried.

Trout There are several different varieties.

SEA TROUT Best March to July. This is a freshwater trout which has spent a season or more at sea. Cook as for salmon.

RAINBOW TROUT Season all year. This trout spends all its life in freshwater and is widely farmed. Grill, poach or fry whole.

RIVER OR BROWN TROUT Best March to September. In scant supply but thought to have a superior flavour to rainbow trout. Grill, poach or fry.

Tuna Season all year. A very large firm-fleshed fish which is sold as steaks or cutlets. Grill, fry or bake.

Whitebait Season February to July. The fry or young of the herring or sprat. Usually deep-fried.

EXOTIC FISH

This group includes groupers, parrotfish, snappers and swordfish. These fish are imported from many different tropical regions. The varieties are changing constantly so ask your fishmonger for advice on cooking.

SMOKED FISH

Some fish are preserved or cured by salting or smoking. They can be hot or cold smoked. Cold smoking is done at relatively low temperatures and most cold smoked fish needs to be cooked before eating (kippers and smoked haddock for instance). The exception is smoked salmon; this is smoked for a long period so can be eaten raw. Hot smoking is done at a much higher temperature and the fish is ready to eat; smoked mackerel is an example.

1 *Clams*
2 *Tiger prawns*
3 *Scallops*
4 *Crab*
5 *Lobster*
6 *Mussels*
7 *Mediterranean prawns*

SHELLFISH

Shellfish can be divided into three types – crustaceans, molluscs and cephalopods. CRUSTACEANS, which include lobster, crabs, shrimps, prawns and freshwater crayfish, all have hard external shells or skeletons which are segmented, and legs to allow for movement. MOLLUSCS have a soft body and live inside a solid hard shell – cockles and winkles are a good example. Some have a pair of shells and are known as bivalves; these include oysters, mussels, clams and scallops. CEPHALOPODS – squid, octopus and cuttlefish – belong to the mollusc family but have no shells.

Buying and Storing

All shellfish are highly perishable and must be bought from a reliable source where turnover is quick. Frozen shellfish must be quite solid when you buy it. All shellfish should smell fresh – if prawns have a strong, almost chlorine-like smell they're past their best. Choose molluscs with tightly closed shells and no cracks or chips. Lobsters and crabs should feel heavy for their size. If possible, bring shellfish home in a cool bag with a freezer pack and refrigerate immediately. Ideally, eat on day of purchase.

Lobsters The king of shellfish, lobsters are available all the year round, but best in the warmer months from April to October and November. Live lobsters are dark blue and turn red during cooking. A 450-700 g (1-1½ lb) lobster feeds two people.

Crawfish (spicy lobster/rock lobster) These resemble a lobster without the big claws. Best from April to October. Prepare and cook as for lobster. Allow about 450 g (1 lb) for two people.

Dublin Bay prawns (Norway lobsters, langoustine, scampi) These belong to the lobster family and their peeled tail meat is known as scampi. Cook gently to prevent them from toughening. Best April to November. Allow about 350-450 g (¾-1 lb) for two people.

Prawns and shrimps The term shrimp applies to the smallest shellfish and the larger ones are known as prawns. Just to confuse the issue, in America, what we know as prawns are called shrimps.

Over 100 different species of shrimp or prawn are caught around the world and many are farmed. There are the North Atlantic (cold water) prawns and pink and brown shrimps as well as warm water prawns from the Middle and Far East. We find jumbo Mediterranean prawns in the shops as well as Tiger Prawns from the Far East (the striped tail of the shell gives rise to the name). Prawns and shrimps are often bought cooked but if raw, cook gently by frying, grilling or poaching for a matter of minutes (see recipes) until just pink and opaque – overcooked prawns can be very tough. They are available all the year both fresh and frozen. Allow about 125 g (4 oz) shelled prawns per person; about 175 g (6 oz) per person with shells.

Crabs Crabs have a delicious mix of rich brown meat in the body cavity and delicate white meat in the legs and claws. They can be bought live or cooked. All crabs have a hard shell which they periodically shed to allow the crab to grow. While the new shells are forming they are quite soft and some species are eaten in this state, claws and all. Best April to December. A 900 g (2 lb) crab will serve 2-3 people.

Oysters These are highly prized the world over and all purists say they should be eaten raw, simply seasoned with black pepper and lemon juice. Oysters are extensively farmed, the main variety being the Pacific Oyster which has largely replaced the Trachmonal flat oyster. Available all year round. Allow 6-12 oysters each for a main course.

Mussels These are usually sold live but can be bought shelled and frozen. Best from September to March. Allow about 1.4 kg (3 lb) mussels for 4-6 people. Always ensure that mussels are alive before cooking; tap the shells smartly and they should snap shut. Any that remain open should be discarded.

Scallops The large scallop commonly seen in fishmongers is known as the King Scallop; the smaller species are known as Queen Scallops and the young Queen Scallops are known as Princess Scallops. They can be bought fresh or frozen, in or out of shells. Best from September to March. Allow about 175 g (6 oz) shelled scallops per person (usually 2-3 King Scallops). Cook very gently or they will toughen.

Clams Available all year round but best in the autumn. Cook as for mussels allowing a similar quantity.

Squid Best from May to October. Small squid are often known as Calamari. Squid can be tough but cooked properly are delicious. Buy ready prepared as they are quite messy to clean. You will need about 125 g (4 oz) per person prepared weight or 225 g (8 oz) per person raw weight.

Octopus Best from May to December. This needs long slow cooking to tenderize it.

Cockles Best from May to December. Usually sold cooked. Wash well to remove any sand.

Winkles Best from September to April. Usually sold cooked. Wash well to remove any sand.

VEGETABLES

It's hard to keep apace of the amazing array of vegetables available today. Old friends, such as carrots and cauliflower, come in new miniature guises whilst strange exotic specimens, such as eddoes or dasheen, parade on the supermarket shelf. There's also a small but increasing number of organic vegetables to be found. These are grown without the use of artificial fertilizers and pesticides – chemicals which some people think could be damaging to our health. The lack of treatment means that these vegetables are often gnarled or knobbly, but they are still expensive as production costs are high. Whatever we buy, vegetables are vital to our health. They provide valuable amounts of fibre, minerals and vitamins whilst being low in fat and cholesterol.

Buying and Storing

With imports, most vegetables are now available all year round with the exception of some roots. But look out for seasonal British varieties – they are at their best when young and tender. At this stage they haven't become tough and woody. The miniature vegetables now sold can look appealing but can be disappointing as some are so immature that they have little or no flavour.

All vegetables should be brightly coloured and be firm and fresh looking; leafy vegetables should never be limp. Avoid any vegetables with obvious wrinkles or blemishes. Potatoes should never have green patches as this means that toxins have begun to form under the skin.

To get the best nutritionally out of vegetables they should be eaten as soon as possible after picking or buying. If vegetables cannot be consumed immediately, they should be stored in a cool dark place, as light destroys the vitamin B and C content. Root vegetables, such as carrots and parsnips, can be placed in a wire rack or in the bottom of the refrigerator. Green or leafy vegetables and salad ingredients should always be refrigerated. It's best to first loosely wrap refrigerated vegetables in polythene bags – ensure that the bags are vented with holes to allow moisture to escape, otherwise the vegetables will sweat and rot in the bags. Onions, leeks and strong-smelling vegetables must always be wrapped to prevent their odours transferring to other vegetables. Root vegetables will keep for about a week, green vegetables for 3-4 days. Most vegetables freeze well but need blanching first.

Cooking

As soon as vegetables are peeled they begin to lose their vitamins, so where possible prepare at the last minute or, better still, eat the skins too. Vitamin C, which is present in so many vegetables, is water soluble and leaches out during cooking. When boiling vegetables use as little water as possible and after cooking reserve the liquid for soups and gravies. Alternatively steam, stir-fry, grill or bake vegetables. Whichever way, cook vegetables for the minimum of time; they should be crisp, not flabby. Test with the point of a sharp knife. For greatest nutrient content eat them raw.

ROOTS AND BULBS (TUBERS)

This is a group of vegetables which grow underground; the group includes such well-known vegetables as potatoes, carrots, swedes and parsnips as well as the lesser-known ones such as salsify or eddoes. Generally, these vegetables have thick skins which need scrubbing and sometimes peeling before cooking. Peel as thinly as possible as many of the nutrients are just under the skin. To boil, cut into chunks, place in cold salted water and bring to the boil. Cover and simmer until tender. This takes from 15-30 minutes but see individual recipes for more information. Nutritionally, they're a good source of fibre especially when the skins are eaten. Carrots and swedes in particular are a very good source of betacarotene, one of the antioxidant vitamins. Allow about 175-225 g (6-8 oz) root vegetables per person. Best in the winter months.

Artichoke (Jerusalem) Beige to brownish red in colour, these knobbly tubers have a nut-like taste. They are delicious in soups, purées and stir-fries but be warned, they do cause flatulence! Peel thinly and immediately place in water with lemon juice added as they do quickly discolour. If very knobbly peel after cooking.

Beetroot These reddish-purple vegetables can be grated to serve raw or cooked to serve hot or cold. When buying raw choose even-sized 'beets' with undamaged skins and stalks cut off about 5 cm (2 inches) above the root. If the beet is damaged at all it will 'bleed' during cooking. Boil until soft – this can take as long as 2 hours. Peel and serve hot or cold.

Carrots Choose firm carrots which are brightly coloured with smooth skins. Scrub tiny new carrots and leave whole. Pare the skins from older ones

and slice or cut into sticks. Boil or serve raw, either grated or as carrot sticks.

Celeriac Looking like a rough turnip this is sometimes known as turnip-rooted celery; it has a pronounced celery flavour. Peel thickly as the skin is very tough. Cut into matchsticks and blanch for salads or cut into chunks to boil. It discolours quickly so add lemon juice to the water.

Dasheen, eddo and taro These potato-like tubers have a sweet, nutty flavour and pasty consistency. They are members of the same family and used much in Asian and Caribbean cooking as a starchy alternative to potatoes. Peel wearing gloves as they can irritate the skin. Slice and boil as for potatoes.

Mooli These long, tapering white roots are of the same species as radish. They can be grated to serve raw, or peeled and boiled but are inclined to be watery. They have a fresh peppery taste.

Parsnips These whitish, tapering vegetables have a nutty, sweet flavour. Avoid ones with brown marks. Peel thinly; slice large old ones into quarters and remove central core. Boil, or blanch and sauté or roast with a meat joint.

Potatoes British new potatoes are available from late spring to mid-summer with the main crop (old) potatoes appearing around September and October. New potatoes should have thin flaky skins which are traditionally only washed, not peeled, before cooking. The skins of old potatoes are delicious and nutritious, too, but must be well scrubbed before cooking.

There is a huge variety of potatoes available in the shops and new types are constantly appearing. Ask advice from your greengrocer or read supermarket labels to find the best variety for your recipe. Here are a few suggestions:

FLOURY (for mashing, sautéeing and roasting) Maris Piper, Pentland Squire, Pentland Crown, Cara, Wilja, King Edward, Estima.

FIRM (for slicing and boiling whole) Marfona, Desirée, Pentland Javelin, Ulster Sceptre, Roman, Maris Bard, Arran Comet.

WAXY (for salads) Charlotte, Belle de Fontenay, Pink Fir Apple, Jersey Royal, Romano.

ALL PURPOSE Cara.

Salsify and scorzonera These are both members of the same family and have long carrot-like tapering roots with a delicate flavour. Salsify's skin is whitish, while scorzonera's is brownish black.

Swedes Heavy, coarse-skinned vegetables with an orange flesh. Peel thickly, then cut into chunks and boil or steam. Good puréed.

Sweet potatoes These are sweet and starchy but despite their name are not related to the potato. There are several different types – some with red skins and orange flesh, others with darker brown skins and creamy yellow flesh. It's best to boil or bake them in their skins as the flesh quickly discolours. Cook and use as for potatoes.

Turnips Small young turnips have a nutty slightly sweet taste which is stronger and slightly peppery as they grow older. Leave young ones unpeeled.

Yams These have a bland, starchy flavour, which goes well with spicy food. The skins are usually brown, bark-like and sometimes hairy. The flesh can be white, yellow or purple. Peel and boil as for potatoes, adding lemon juice to the water.

The onion family This family includes the familiar red, white, and Spanish onions as well as shallots, garlic, leeks and spring onions.

ONIONS Choose ones with thin papery skins and no blemishes. Spanish onions are strong, while white onions give a milder flavour to recipes. Use red onions and spring onions (which are available all year round) raw in salads; button onions in casseroles or for pickling.

SHALLOTS Used in French cookery, shallots have a milder flavour than onions, but can be expensive.

LEEKS Wash leeks carefully as they can be gritty. Trim, split open and rinse under running water removing any dark green leaves before cooking.

GARLIC The purple-skinned variety is considered the best. Choose plump, firm bulbs and look out for the new season garlic arriving in late spring. Garlic is usually peeled and sliced or crushed to add to recipes but can be baked in its skin.

PODS, PEAS AND BEANS

This group takes in the many varieties of bean, along with peas, mangetout, okra and sweetcorn.

Broad beans Choose young small tender pods. Slit open and pop out the beans. Boil for 8-10 minutes. Best May to July. Allow 125 g (4 oz) podded

1 *Red onions*
2 *Runner beans*
3 *King Edward potatoes*
4 *Desirée potatoes*
5 *New potatoes*
6 *Jerusalem artichokes*
7 *Savoy cabbage*
8 *New carrots*
9 *Celeriac*
10 *Shallots*

weight per person, 350 g (12 oz) in the pod.

French beans Top and tail and boil for about 5 minutes. Bobby beans are a fatter variety of French bean. Available all year round. Allow 125 g (4 oz) per person.

Runner beans Choose medium-sized light green beans. Top and tail and cut away the strings from either side, before cutting into chunks or lengths. Boil for about 5 minutes. Best July and August. Allow 175 g (6 oz) per person.

Mangetout and sugar snap peas These are eaten whole, pod and all; the fatter varieties are known as sugar snap peas. Choose small bright green pods, snap off the top and tail and if necessary trim away any strings. Boil or stir-fry both types for a minute or two. They are available all year. Allow 125 g (4 oz) per person.

Peas The season for buying peas in the pod is very short – June to July. Choose crisp well-filled pods with some air space between the peas. Split open, pop out the peas and boil for 5-10 minutes. Allow 125 g (4 oz) podded weight per person or 350 g (12 oz) in the pod.

Okra These are eaten whole. Choose small firm bright green pods. Trim off the tops and boil or sauté for about 5 minutes, no longer or the sticky fluid will leach out. Allow 125 g (4 oz) per person.

Sweetcorn Choose cobs with a pale green, tightly fitting husk and creamy coloured kernels. Once they turn gold some of the sweetness goes and the corn becomes tougher. Remove stems, leaves and silky fibres; boil for 10-15 minutes. Boil baby corn for a few minutes only or stir-fry. Best July to November. Allow one cob per person or 75 g (3 oz) baby sweetcorn.

GREENS

All these vegetables should be cooked in boiling salted water for the minimum of time to preserve their colour, texture and vitamins. Dark green leafy vegetables, such as spinach and cabbage, are a good source of betacarotene, vitamin C and some of the B vitamins, notably folic acid. Allow about 175 g (6 oz) per person except for spinach-type leaves where you'll need more.

Broccoli This is available most of the year with home grown sprouting broccoli on the shelves from February to May and Calabrese from June to November. Trim and divide into florets before boiling.

Brussel sprouts Choose even-sized, tight green buds and trim before cooking.

Cabbages Winter cabbages such as red, white and Savoy should feel solid and will keep for several days. Leafy spring greens and summer cabbages wilt more quickly.

Cauliflower Available all year. Choose cauliflowers with firm compact white or creamy white heads and bright-green leaves. Divide into florets before cooking. A medium cauliflower serves four.

Chicory (known as endive in France) Choose small heads with crisp white leaves; too much green indicates bitterness. They can be braised or more usually added to salads.

Chinese leaves This has a mild cabbage-like taste and is available all year. Serve raw in salads, lightly boiled for a minute or two or stir-fried.

Kale A member of the cabbage family with the curly variety the most common. This winter vegetable has a strong, sometimes bitter flavour. Cook as for cabbage.

Seakale beet Unrelated to spinach but the leaves are used similarly, while the stems are cooked like seakale.

Sorrel This has a distinctive, almost acidic flavour and is used in small quantities in sauces, soups or omelettes or as an addition to salads. Available in the summer months.

Spinach With imports, spinach is now available all year round. Home-grown varieties are best in spring and early summer. Trim off stalks, wash in several changes of water and drain. Use young leaves for salad; cook coarser leaves for a few minutes only in just the washing water that sticks to the leaves and drain well after boiling. Allow 25 g (1 oz) per head for salads; 350 g (12 oz) for cooking. Look out for bags of ready washed young spinach leaves in large supermarkets.

Swiss chard Related to seakale, the leaves are used like spinach, the stems as for seakale.

Vine leaves Sold fresh, canned or packed in brine. Blanch fresh leaves before use.

SALAD LEAVES

The array of salad leaves is never ending, either loose or prepacked. Look out for really fresh leaves, avoid those that are wilted or browning. Mix the leaves as you wish, allowing about 25 g (1 oz) per person. Store in a polythene bag in the refrigerator for 2-3 days. Wash and dry well before use. Choose from the familiar varieties of Cos (Romaine), Iceberg (Crisphead) and Little Gem, or the more exotic Oak Leaf (Feuille de Chêne) and frilly Lollo Rosso (red lollo) or Lollo Biondo (green lollo). Curly green endive or Frisée (known as chicorée frisée in France) and red Radicchio can be bitter so use in small quantities. Rocket is quite peppery and very expensive. Lambs lettuce, also known as corn salad or mâche has a mild delicate flavour. Use chicory, spinach and sorrel in salads too (see *Greens* page 72).

Watercress With its strong peppery taste watercress is perfect in salads or cooked in soups and sauces. Avoid buying when in flower.

Mustard and Cress Grown in small punnets, this is usually a mix of rape and cress, sometimes with mustard. Traditionally used in sandwiches. Snip straight from the box to use.

Flowers During the summer months use edible flowers such as pansies, chive flowers, nasturtiums, violas and dandelions in salads or to decorate starters or creamy desserts or cakes.

SHOOTS AND STEMS

This group includes tender delicacies such as asparagus and globe artichokes.

Asparagus Imported all year round. British asparagus is best in May. Choose even-sized stems; cut off woody ends. Stand upright in a large pan of boiling salted water so that the heads are out of the

water. Cover with foil and simmer for 8-10 minutes. Serve warm with butter. Allow 6-10 stems per person.

Beansprouts These are the sprouts of mung beans. Choose crisp creamy white sprouts with no sign of browning. Use within a day of purchase. Rinse and drain well before use. Serve raw or stir-fry for 1 minute. Allow about 75 g (3 oz) per person.

Celery Green celery is available all year round; white celery is available in the winter months. Choose celery with thick, firm unblemished sticks. Always refrigerate in a polythene bag. Separate the sticks, wash and serve raw, braise as a vegetable or add to casseroles. Allow 3-4 sticks per person.

Fennel Known as Florence fennel to distinguish it from the herb, it has a strong aniseed flavour. Choose white or pale-green bulbs; the darker ones

1 *Watercress* 2 *Radicchio*
3 *Oak leaf* 4 *Lollo rosso*
5 *Cos* 6 *Chicory* 7 *Frisée*
8 *Nasturtiums* 9 *Lambs lettuce* 10 *Baby spinach*

can be bitter. Trim root and stalk, slice to serve raw or quarter and boil for 15-20 minutes. Allow 175g (6 oz) per person.

Globe Artichokes These are members of the thistle family. Look for bright-green, tightly curled heads with no dry leaves. Trim stalks and leaf ends and boil for 30-40 minutes. Allow one per person. Best July and August.

Kohlrabi This has a mild turnip-like flavour. Buy when the size of a large golf ball and boil whole for 10-15 minutes. It can be served raw. Allow 175 g (6 oz) per person.

Seakale The delicately flavoured stalks are best steamed for 20-25 minutes. Allow 125-175 g (4-6 oz) per person.

VEGETABLE FRUITS

All these vegetables are strictly speaking the fruits of their plants and include a diverse range of foods – from squashes and aubergines to avocados and tomatoes. Pumpkins and peppers are an excellent source of betacarotene. Avocados are high in calories which come from their high fat content but this is mainly the 'healthy' monounsaturated fat, which is considered beneficial.

Aubergines (brinjal, eggplant) Look for firm aubergines with bright unwrinkled skins. Cook small ones whole; larger ones can be sliced. Available all year round. Allow 175-225 g (6-8 oz) per person.

Avocados Many varieties exist, from the brown knobbly skinned Hass to the smooth green-skinned Fuerte. When ripe all avocados should feel soft when gently pressed at the stalk end. To ripen, leave in a warm place (the airing cupboard is ideal) for a few days. Ripe fruit will keep in the refrigerator for 2-3 days.

Mushrooms These used to fit neatly into two categories; cultivated mushrooms such as button, cup and flat mushrooms which were mildly flavoured, versatile and available all year round at a reasonable price; and wild mushrooms which had wonderful flavours with exotic prices to match, and only appeared in the spring and autumn months. Now many of the 'wild' mushrooms such as oysters are in fact cultivated. You will also see chanterelles, morels, ceps and shiitakes appearing more widely on the supermarket or greengrocers shelf. Never eat wild mushrooms you have picked yourself without first consulting an expert or specialist book; some wild mushrooms can be very poisonous – even fatal.

Most mushrooms do not need peeling; simply dust off any dirt particles or quickly dip in and out of cold salted water. Cook for a minimum of time. Wild mushrooms can be bought dried; about 75 g (3 oz) dried reconstitutes to about 450 g (1 lb). Some supermarkets now provide paper sacks specially for storing mushrooms in optimum condition once you get them home.

The pepper family This is a huge family of vegetables including the mild sweet red, orange and yellow peppers to the extremely hot chillies. Choose peppers that look bright and shiny with unwrinkled skins. The sweeter peppers can be eaten raw, the more bitter green varieties are better cooked. Always cut core and seeds away from peppers. Tiny seeds may be left in chillies before cooking or eating for extra 'heat' as the seeds are the most pungent part. When handling chillies it is always advisable to wear rubber gloves as they can irritate the skin.

The squash family This vast family includes the summer squashes, such as courgette, cucumber, marrow, and patty pans, and the winter varieties, such as pumpkins, snake gourds and butternut squashes. With imports the seasons have become confused but generally the summer varieties need no peeling whilst winter types have a hard tough outer skin and large seeds, which must be cut away before cooking. (See individual recipes for further information.)

Tomatoes Available all year round with British varieties at their best in late summer. Generally, redness means ripeness but the yellow cherry tomatoes are probably the sweetest of all. Buy tomatoes with fresh, bright tight skins and no blemishes. Their uses are interchangeable but try sweet cherry tomatoes in salads; large beef or marmande tomatoes for stuffing and strongly flavoured plum tomatoes for sauces, or in robust Italian dishes such as spaghetti Bolognese or lasagne.

1 *Asparagus*
2 *Aubergines*
3 *Globe artichokes*
4 *Fresh green chillies*
5 *Patty pans*
6 *Dried red chillies*
7 *Chanterelle mushrooms*
8 *Fennel*
9 *Plum tomatoes*

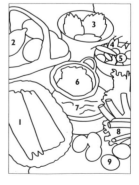

FRUIT AND NUTS

Fruit tastes wonderful and is good for our health too, being a valuable source of fibre, vitamins and minerals yet generally quite low in calories. Consumption used to be governed by seasons but now most types of fruit are available all year round, winging their way to this country from every corner of the earth. Yet there is still nothing better than British soft fruits fresh from the field in the summer months or crisp apples and pears straight from the orchards in autumn.

Exotic tropical varieties swell the fruit bowl year round with mangoes, papayas (pawpaws) and figs being almost commonplace on supermarket shelves these days.

Buying

All fruits should look bright and healthy with no signs of drying or decaying. The hard fruits such as apples should be free of blemishes and bruises with tight, never shrivelled, skins. Soft summer fruits like strawberries and raspberries should be well coloured, not pale and anaemic, plump and juicy with no mould.

Most fruits will eventually ripen at home if left in a warm place, but those that are picked too young and completely green will never do so. Make sure that fragrant fruits such as melons, pineapples or peaches have a slightly sweet smell when buying them. This means that the ripening process has started. Press the firmer fruits lightly at the stem end which should feel soft if ripening has begun.

Storing

Once home, pick over all fruits, particularly berry fruits that are prone to mould, and throw out any that are damaged. Place soft fruits on plates, cover loosely and refrigerate; they are best eaten within a day or two. Store all ripe fruit in the refrigerator to keep it at its best; tightly wrap melons or pineapples to prevent their strong aromas tainting other foods. Unripe fruit should be left at room temperature or even put into the airing cupboard to hasten ripening. Always wash fruit well just before eating.

Freezing

Most fruits can be frozen, but because of their high water content they lose their structure after thawing and so are best slightly stewed or poached before freezing. The soft, summer fruits can be frozen raw; raspberries and currants are reasonably satisfactory frozen whole but strawberries thaw into a pulpy mass and are best puréed before freezing.

SOFT FRUITS

These are perishable and should be eaten as close to the day of purchase as possible, the exceptions being rhubarb and cranberries. All these fruits are quite tart and need a little sweetening to bring out their best flavour. Allow about 125-175 g (4-6 oz) soft fruits per person (more of rhubarb as it cooks down to very little).

Bilberries Also known as whortleberries or huckleberries, these small dark-blue berries grow on open moorland in late summer. They can be eaten raw but are quite acid and are better lightly stewed with sugar. Remove the stalks from the berries before eating.

Blackberries Cultivated varieties tend to be larger and sweeter than wild hedgerow berries which appear in late July, August and September. Plump, deep purple-black berries are best. Pull out the stalk and hull before use. Eat raw or cooked in pies, crumbles and so on.

Blueberries These belong to the same family as the bilberry but are plumper and sweeter and are now widely grown commercially. Eat raw or use in compotes or as cheesecake toppings.

Boysenberries A hybrid most closely resembling a blackberry. Use in the same way.

Cranberries Available fresh in the winter months, these hard, robust berries have a very tart flavour. Best known when cooked into cranberry sauce to accompany turkey. Their high pectin content also makes them ideal for jams and jellies. They keep well, for two weeks or more, in the refrigerator.

1 *Blueberries* 2 *Strawberries*
3 *Cherries* 4 *Angelino plums*
5 *Cranberries* 6 *Russet apples* 7 *Bramley apples*
8 *Laxton Superb apples*
9 *Cox's apples* 10 *Rossi pears* 11 *Conference pears*
12 *Redcurrants*
13 *Raspberries*

Currants Home-grown varieties appear in July and August with imports arriving infrequently during the year at exorbitant prices. Black and red currants are the most common; both are sharp and quite acidic and are better cooked. White currants are rarer but sweeter too and can be eaten raw. Use a fork to strip currants off their stems before cooking. Delicious in summer puddings, pies and compotes, redcurrants make a perfect jelly to serve with poultry, too.

Elderberries Growing wild in abundance in the autumn months, these small purple berries are most commonly used in home-made wines and preserves. Use a fork to strip the berries off the stems before cooking.

Gooseberries Available mainly in June, July and August, the bright-green cooking berries have a very tart flavour with a mass of edible seeds. Dessert gooseberries are paler, sometimes a purple/russet colour and a little sweeter; they can be eaten raw but are an acquired taste. Strip off the tops and tails before cooking (this is unnecessary for jellies or fools when the fruit is strained). Use in pies, sauces or preserves.

Loganberries A hybrid of a blackberry and a raspberry. Use in the same way.

Mulberries Similar in flavour to blackberries but sweeter and juicier; best eaten raw.

Raspberries To many people the best of the soft fruits to eat raw. Home-grown varieties are available in June and July with another crop in late autumn. Pull out stalks, hull before use and sweeten to taste.

Rhubarb Strictly speaking this is a vegetable as it is the stem of a plant. Forced rhubarb is available in early spring with main-crop rhubarb appearing right through the summer months. It has a strong tart flavour but makes delicious pies, crumbles and fools. Never eat the leaves as they are poisonous and trim away any coarse strings from the stems before cooking.

Strawberries Available all year round but nothing compares with freshly picked home-grown varieties. They are best in the mid-summer months. Choose well ripened red berries; ones with large patches of green or white will be tart and unappetising. Pull or cut out the stalk or hull before use. Look out for miniature wild strawberries (*fraises des bois*); they're very expensive but do have a unique flavour and make an attractive decoration on creamy desserts.

Tayberries A hybrid of loganberry and blackberry – use similarly.

ORCHARD FRUITS

These include the familiar autumn fruits such as the firm-fleshed pears and apples and the softer plums, as well as nectarines, peaches, apricots and cherries which are best in the mid-summer months. All are supplemented by imports and all home-grown varieties are very susceptible to weather. If it's warm and sunny they become sweet and ripe, if it's cold and wet the flavour is never quite the same. The softer fruits are very perishable and need careful handling and storage; once ripe refrigerate until required. The colour deepens as the softer fruits ripen and they should be soft to touch at the stalk end.

Apples British apples are the best, especially in the late summer and autumn months. Shops are beginning to stock some of the old traditional dessert varieties such as Egremont Russets, James Grieve and Blenheim Orange, to supplement supplies of new season's Cox's Orange Pippins, Worcester Pearmains and Red Delicious. In the new year one can be forgiven for moving on to imported varieties which come from the southern hemisphere – once apples have been stored for several months they do begin to lose their crispness and flavour.

Cooking apples are tarter than dessert varieties, with Bramley Seedling being the favourite. Crab apples are so small that they're only suitable for cooking and straining for preserves. Apples have excellent pectin content so they're often added to jams and jellies to help them set.

Apricots Choose firm unwrinkled fruit with a deep colour. Eat when just soft; under-ripe they're hard and sour, over-ripe they're meaty and tasteless. Eat raw, skin and all, or poach lightly.

Cherries Varying in colour from white through to deep purple, generally the darker they are the sweeter they are. There are two distinct varieties – the sweet ones such as Napoleon Bigarreau or Merton Heart, which are best eaten raw, and the sour varieties such as Morellos, which lend themselves to cooking. All cherries are very perishable and should ideally be eaten on the day of purchase.

Damsons These have a wonderful sweet/sharp flavour but because of their large stones and small amount of flesh have lost popularity. Best stewed.

Greengages A small green plum which turns slightly golden when ripe.

Nectarines A smooth-skinned variety of peach with white-yellow or pinkish red flesh. The flesh is sweet and juicy. Eat raw or use for desserts.

Peaches These can be 'freestone', with a stone that readily separates from the flesh, or 'clingstone' where the flesh and stone cling together. White flesh peaches have the best flavour.

Pears Most pears can be eaten raw or gently poached. The Comice was always thought to be the sweetest and the best but now many varieties are snapping at its heels, especially the Williams, both the red and creamy coloured varieties.

Plums These appear in every shape and size, from the wonderful Victoria plum to the huge purple Friars. All can be eaten raw or cooked.

CITRUS FRUITS

These are imported, with most varieties now available all year round. All citrus fruits are rich in vitamin C and many varieties can be simply peeled and eaten raw. They are useful in cooking too – the grated rind adds flavour to cakes and biscuits, while the juice is a perfect ingredient for marinades as it helps to break down tough fibres in meat or poultry. Choose fruits that look bright and feel heavy for their size. Most varieties should have slightly roughened tight skins, with the exception of ugli fruit and easy peelers where the skin is loose, almost shrivelled-looking. Citrus fruits keep well, especially in the refrigerator, but they do lose some of their nutritional value with prolonged storage.

Easy peelers This is an ever-increasing group of citrus fruits. As their name implies they all have loose easy-to-peel skins – some are seedless. Generically they're known as tangerines or mandarins; satsumas, mineolas, clementines and clansellinas are just some within the group. But growers are constantly experimenting to find the ultimate sweet, seedless variety so always ask your greengrocer for advice and carefully read supermarket labels too.

Grapefruit The pink-skinned and ruby red grapefruits are gradually gaining in popularity. They're sweeter than the yellow-skinned varieties with attractive coloured flesh, but tend to be more expensive.

Kumquats Looking like a citrus fruit, these are strictly speaking not a member of the citrus family. They can be eaten raw, skin and all, or preserved or sliced into casseroles and compotes. They are quite tart. Green limequats are also available.

Lemons An essential ingredient for every cook, adding flavour and sharpness to recipes. Those with a deep yellow colour are the ripest and best to use, especially for marmalades.

Limes Used extensively in Eastern cooking, limes add a wonderful tangy hue to recipes. They can be used in place of lemons.

Oranges Eating varieties such as Navels and Valencias are available year round. The bitter Seville orange, essential to orange marmalade, is generally only available in January.

Pomelos Looking like a giant grapefruit, this fruit has sweet slightly dry flesh with a very thick peel and pith. Use as for grapefruit.

Ugli fruit A hybrid of the orange, tangerine and grapefruit with a loose baggy skin and sweet flesh. Eat raw.

TROPICAL FRUITS

Hardly a week goes by without some new weird and wonderful tropical fruit arriving in this country to tempt our tastebuds. These are a few; ask greengrocers for preparation and serving advice as new varieties appear.

Bananas Rich in carbohydrate and most vitamins. Choose ones with unmarked green-to-yellow skins. As the banana ripens the skins turn brown then black. Never store bananas in the refrigerator. Apple bananas – tiny bananas with the vaguest hint of apple flavouring – and red-skinned bananas with a slightly mealie taste are also available.

Cape gooseberries (Chinese lantern or physalis) Exotic lantern-shaped fruits with a papery skin enclosing a small yellowish berry when ripe. No relation to our gooseberries but with a similar sharp fragrant flavour. Eat raw.

Custard apples (cherimoya) The fruit of annona trees. They include the cherimoya, sugar apple and soursop. Best known is the cherimoya with a rough green skin and sweet white flesh containing a mass of inedible seeds. Eat raw.

Dates Fresh dates should be plump and shiny with golden brown skins. Medjool dates are the most highly prized.

Figs Varying in colour from green through to black or purple, the skin, flesh and seeds can all be eaten. Fresh ripe figs should be soft to the touch and have a bloom on the skin. They don't keep well and should be eaten soon after purchase.

Guavas Choose firm unblemished fruit; cut in half and peel to reveal the sweet aromatic flesh with edible seeds. They have a high vitamin C content and can be eaten raw or cooked.

Lychees, rambutans and longans Belonging to the same family these fruits all have soft white fragrant flesh, best eaten raw or poached in a light syrup. Avoid fruit with shrivelled dry skins and discard the stones.

Mangoes It's quite impossible to give an accurate buying guide for mangoes as so many varieties are

now available; some green and firm, others soft and yellow-orange when ripe. Ask your greengrocer for advice. All varieties have one thing in common – they have the most delicious fragrant, almost peachy flavour. Peel and eat raw or add to pies and mousses.

Mangosteens Unrelated to the mango this fruit has juicy, sweet flavoured, creamy white flesh. Cut the top third off and eat the flesh with a spoon.

Papayas (pawpaws) When ripe papayas have a yellow skin containing a delicate, slightly perfumed pinky orange flesh. Halve, scoop out the seeds (they can be eaten but they're strong and peppery) and serve simply with lime juice. Do not eat the skins. The fruit contains papain, an enzyme which is a great meat tenderizer but which prevents gelatine setting.

Persimmons (sharon fruit) Looking like large swollen tomatoes, true persimmons can be very bitter until really soft and ripe. Sharon fruit are a much sweeter seedless variety and can be eaten skin and all.

Pineapples A ripe pineapple is usually golden yellow with a sweet smell and leaves that can be easily pulled from the crown. Fresh pineapple also contains the enzyme papain which prevents gelatine setting.

Pomegranates Buy fruits with hard undamaged skins and scoop out the seeds and juice to eat raw or to add to fruit salads.

Prickly pears The fruit of cactus which when ripe are a deep orange colour. They are covered with prickly hairs so always wear rubber gloves when handling and peeling them. The sweet and juicy flesh is best sliced and served raw with lime juice.

Star fruit (carambola) With yellow or green waxy skins and juicy flesh these are frequently used sliced as attractive star-shaped garnishes. The flavour is bland.

Tamarillos (tree tomatoes) Very acidic even when ripe, tamarillos should be stewed with sugar. The skins must be peeled but the seeds are edible.

VINE FRUIT

Melons These should feel heavy for their size and most are fragrant smelling when ripe. Serve chilled with small melons simply cut in half; larger ones cut into wedges and the seeds scooped out.

CANTELOUPE A greeny yellow grooved skin encases orange-yellow peach-flavoured flesh.

CHARENTAIS A type of cantaloupe with perhaps the best flavour.

GALIA Less fragrant than cantaloupe but very sweet when ripe. The nettled skin turns from green to yellow as it ripens.

HONEYDEW Bright-yellow skin enclosing a mildly flavoured juicy melon.

OGEN Pale-green, lightly striped skin encloses sweet juicy flesh.

WATERMELON Appears in all sorts of guises, oblong or round, green, yellow or almost purple skinned. But the flesh is always bright red with a mass of black inedible seeds. They're refreshing but very bland.

Granadillas A large yellow-skinned member of the passion fruit family, with a milder flavour.

Grapes Choose plump unbruised fruit with no signs of mould. Seedless grapes such as the white Thompson Seedless or Red Flame Seedless are the most popular table grapes today. But the large seeded variety, Muscat, is still regarded as the king of grapes with its wonderful sweet fragrant flavour and light golden skin.

Kiwi (Chinese gooseberry) Now commonplace in this country, kiwi fruit are best simply cut in half and eaten with a teaspoon. They contain valuable amounts of vitamin C, but they also prevent gelatine setting so never use in mousses.

Passion fruit When ripe these should look purple and wrinkled. The hard skins are halved to reveal fragrant sweet juicy flesh with edible black seeds. Eat with a teaspoon or use to flavour drinks and desserts.

NUTS

A nut is a seed or fruit with an edible kernel which is found inside a hard shell. Nuts are a good source of protein and carbohydrate, but being high in fat, they're high in calories too. The best time to buy is the late autumn when new season nuts are appearing. They can be bought in their shells, or shelled and then processed further into halves, flakes, chopped (nibbed) pieces and finely ground. Some

1 *Pomegranates*
2 *Papayas* 3 *Limequats*
4 *Kumquats* 5 *Muscat grapes*
6 *Pomelo* 7 *Apple bananas*
8 *Limes* 9 *Charentais melon*
10 *Clementines* 11 *Galia melon* 12 *Pink grapefruit*
13 *Lemons* 14 *Persimmons*
15 *Figs* 16 *Lychees*

nuts can be bought 'green' (fresh) but they're usually dried for longer storage.

Nuts in shells should feel heavy for their size with no signs of mould; they'll keep in a cool dry place for about three months. Shelled and processed nuts once out of their packaging lose their flavour quickly and become rancid-smelling and tasting. Check date stamps carefully on packaging and always taste the nut before adding to a recipe; you'll soon know if it's rancid! Once opened, store nuts in an airtight container for a few weeks only, or better still freeze until required.

Nuts can be lightly toasted (by grilling or baking) to enhance the flavour. To crack nuts in shells you'll need a strong pair of nut crackers. Gently squeeze the shell until it splits and the nut can be eased out; too much pressure will result in a pulped nut.

Look out for exotic nut oils such as walnut – small amounts add wonderful flavour to dressings.

Almonds These are the seeds of a tree belonging to the peach family. There are both bitter and sweet almonds; the former are never eaten raw but used mainly for making essences or oils. Sweet almonds can be bought with their brown skins on or blanched (skinned). To remove the skins, cover the nuts with boiling water for about 1 minute, then drain and pop out of their skins. Dry on absorbent kitchen paper. Use almond essence sparingly as it can be very powerful.

*Brazil nut*s Large oval creamy coloured nuts mainly eaten raw or in confectionery.

Cashew nuts Highly prized nuts with a delicate sweet flavour, but expensive too. Usually sold as snacks, plain, salted or toasted, often with strange coatings. They can be cooked too, frequently appearing on Chinese and Indian menus.

Chestnuts Fruits of the sweet chestnut tree not the horse chestnut, they can be eaten freshly roasted or more usually are found cooked and canned whole or in a purée. Some purées are highly sweetened so check the label carefully before adding the purée to a recipe. Chestnuts in shells have a short shelf life as they're not dried at all. To peel them, nick the skins with a pointed knife, boil for about 5 minutes, drain and remove the outer and inner skin whilst warm. Chestnuts are rarely eaten raw. Simmer for about 30 minutes in stock or water.

Coconuts Their strong rich flavour is either loved or hated. They can be bought whole, desiccated (finely grated), flaked or in block or powder form. The desiccated variety is normally used in baking, whilst block or powder coconut is let down with water to make a creamy coconut milk used frequently in savoury recipes. Coconut milk is available in cans too; don't confuse it with the clear liquid, often called coconut milk, which is found inside fresh coconuts. Freshly picked coconuts, rarely seen here, have green almost soft shells whilst mature nuts are covered with the more familiar hard brown fibrous shell. To open a coconut first puncture two of the eyes with a hammer and screwdriver and drain out the liquid. Hammer around the circumference to crack the shell; separate halves and scrape the flesh out with a sharp knife. Grate to use.

Hazelnuts, filberts and cobnuts All are fruits of different varieties of the hazel tree. The nuts are sweet and used frequently in baking. To remove the brown skins, toast in a hot oven for about 10 minutes until golden; place inside a tea towel and rub off the skins.

Macadamias Wonderful creamy soft-textured nuts, best eaten raw or lightly toasted.

Peanuts (ground nuts, monkey nuts) Strictly speaking these are not nuts at all but a type of underground bean. Extremely versatile, peanuts are full of protein, though high in calories. They lend themselves to snacks in every shape and form. They are also ground into peanut butter and used in cooking, in Satay sauce for example.

Pecan nuts Similar looking but sweeter flavoured than walnuts, they are interchangeable in recipes. Used frequently in American cookery where they are also known as hickory nuts.

Pine nuts (pine kernels) Used extensively in Mediterranean cookery these small expensive nuts have a mild creamy flavour and go rancid very fast. They are the fruits of the stone pine.

Pistachio nuts When ripe the shell splits to reveal a small purple-coated, bright-green nut. Used mainly for their decorative appeal, they're delicious eaten raw or salted. To remove the purple skin blanch as for almonds.

Walnuts Used mainly in cooking, their slight bitterness perfectly complements sweet recipes.

SPICES AND HERBS

SPICES

Spices are the dried parts of aromatic plants, including fruits, bark, seeds, roots and flower buds, which are sold whole or ground. Whole spices keep their flavour best; grind them at the last moment either in a pestle and mortar or a coffee grinder (keep for spices only). Buy spices in small quantities and store in airtight containers in a cool, dry, dark place, for a year at the most. All ground spices need cooking to release their flavour.

Allspice (Jamaican pepper) Not to be confused with mixed spice, this is a member of the pepper family. Mainly used in savoury recipes it has a flavour of cinnamon, cloves and nutmeg with a hint of pepper.

Aniseed Strong flavour used mainly in cakes.

Caraway Pronounced aniseed flavour, seen much in strong casserole recipes, cakes and pastries.

Cardamom Either green, brown or black pods can be split open to reveal a clutch of tiny aromatic seeds. Use the pods whole or for a more intense flavour take out the seeds and grind or use these whole, discarding the pods. Cardamom is the traditional spice in Middle Eastern coffee and in sweet Indian desserts. The green pods are considered the best; also available ground.

Cayenne pepper Fiery hot pepper from the capsicum family. Always sold ground.

Chilli powder This must be bought with care! Sometimes it is pure ground chillies which are fiery hot, other times it is a blend of spices, including chilli, cumin, garlic and oregano which can be very mild. Always read the list of ingredients on the jar.

Chinese five-spice powder A powerful aniseed

1 *Pink peppercorns* 2 *Cardamom pods* 3 *Root ginger* 4 *Coriander seeds* 5 *Cayenne pepper* 6 *Ground turmeric* 7 *White mustard seeds* 8 *Cinnamon sticks* 9 *Root turmeric* 10 *Cumin seeds* 11 *Black peppercorns* 12 *Saffron* 13 *Nutmeg*

flavour is predominant in this blend of anise, cassia, fennel seed, star anise and cloves, often detected in Far Eastern cookery. Use sparingly.

Cinnamon The bark (sticks) are used to flavour casseroles and punches whilst the ground version is more commonly found in cakes, pastries and desserts. It has a distinctive aromatic flavour.

Cloves Use sparingly as they're very pungent. Use whole to decorate baked hams and flavour mulled wine and savoury recipes; use ground in cakes.

Coriander A mild slightly sweet spice with a hint of citrus, essential to all curry recipes.

Cumin Available as seeds or ground, this is another spice essential to Asian cookery. It has a mild, almost nutty flavour.

Curry powder A commercial blend of spices, including cumin, coriander and chilli, it is sold in various strengths.

Fenugreek Harsh, pungent seeds used in curry powder.

Garam masala A mild mixture of spices used in savoury recipes.

Ginger Available fresh, dried and ground, ginger has a strong fiery taste, especially when dried.

Juniper Sold only in berry form. The berries should be crushed to release their fresh aroma.

Mace The thin orange outer covering of nutmeg.

Mustard seeds Can be black, brown or white. The black ones give aroma, the white ones strength.

Nutmeg A distinctive spice with a wonderful sweet flavour. Best freshly grated from a whole nutmeg.

Paprika Sold ground, this is a member of the capsicum family. It comes in mild and hot forms but isn't fiery like chilli. Used in goulash recipes. It keeps poorly so buy little and often.

Peppercorns Fruits of the vine pepper, sold dried or pickled in brine. Available black, white, green or pink. Black peppercorns are the strongest.

Saffron The dried stigmas of a crocus, sold whole or ground. It's very expensive, but a tiny amount gives a rich aromatic flavour and yellow colour.

Star anise Attractive star-shaped spice tasting strongly of aniseed.

Tamarind The dried pulp from the pods of the tamarind tree with a strong bitter/sour taste.

Turmeric A bright-yellow spice with a slightly bitter flavour which colours and stains everything it touches – food, fingers, wooden spoons, worktops! Usually bought ground; sometimes in root form.

Vanilla The dried pods of an orchid, these are sold whole or in a liquid essence form. The pods give a far superior flavour to recipes and should be split open to reveal the black seeds before use.

HERBS

Herbs add a wonderful fragrance and life to recipes. They can be used fresh or dried. The fresh varieties generally having a much more subtle flavour. If chopping herbs, it is best to do this at the last minute, as once bruised they soon lose their pungency; large soft-leaved herbs such as basil should be torn not chopped. Remember to add strong herbs at the beginning of cooking time, and stir mild ones in at the end, so that their delicate flavour is not killed in the cooking.

Buying and Storing

Fresh herbs should look brightly coloured, fresh and never withered. Refrigerate in polythene bags and use as soon as possible. To revive, stand the cut stems in a jug or bowl of water and tent inside a polythene bag. Before use, wash herbs well, drain and spin or pat dry before chopping. The coarse spiky herbs like rosemary must be stripped off their woody stems before chopping; finer varieties like chervil can be chopped stems and all. Freeze chopped herbs in small quantities to add to casseroles and stews.

Dried herbs don't keep indefinitely – buy in small quantities, store in a cool dark place and use within about six months. As a rule, you need about one-third the amount specified for fresh herbs if substituting dried.

Anjelica The stem is sold candied but the leaves can be used as a vegetable or herb.

Balm (lemon balm) Strong lemon smell and taste.

Basil Both sweet and purple varieties have a pungent flavour and aroma. Basil is the main ingredient of pesto sauce and is used extensively in Mediterranean cookery. Wonderful with tomatoes.

Bay A strong spicy flavour, especially when dried. The traditional herb for a bouquet garni. Use whole or lightly crushed.

Borage Both leaves and blue flowers have a hint of a cucumber taste. Only use tiny leaves; the larger ones are too hairy. Add flowers to drinks.

Chervil A delicate, mildly aniseed flavour, chervil is good with fish and salads.

Chives Mild onion flavour; best added at the last minute. Often used in sauces.

Coriander (cilantro) A strong aromatic herb similar in appearance to flat-leaf parsley. Used in large quantities in Indian, Chinese and Thai cookery.

Dill Known as dill weed when dried, it has a mild sweet aniseed flavour. Especially good with fish.

Fennel Fine feathery aniseed-flavoured leaves; ideal with oily fish.

1 *Basil* 2 *Lavender*
3 *Oregano* 4 *Flat-leaf parsley*
5 *Tarragon* 6 *Rosemary*
7 *Mint* 8 *Coriander*
9 *Sage* 10 *Dill* 11 *Lemon
grass* 12 *Chives*

Kaffir lime Aromatic lime leaves frequently used in Thai cookery.

Lavender Use sparingly as it is very powerful. Good in cakes and bakes or to flavour meat.

Lemon grass Available fresh, dried and preserved in jars, this has a distinct fragrant lemon flavour. Frequently used in Eastern cookery. The long thin fresh stems can be added whole or sliced to flavour stir-fries and casseroles.

Lovage The strong sharp peppery taste is often used to liven up plain potato dishes.

Marjoram A strong powerful herb, the traditional ingredient of pizza toppings, and widely used in Italian cookery.

Mint There are many different varieties with varying flavours, applemint, peppermint and spearmint to name a few. Dried versions are disappointing.

Mixed herbs A mixture of dried herbs usually parsley, sage, thyme, marjoram and tarragon.

Oregano Related to marjoram but stronger.

Parsley Too frequently only used as a garnish, parsley has a mild fresh taste, the flat-leaf type being stronger than the curly variety. Great in sauces or stuffings or with fish and ham.

Rosemary A strong pungent, spiky herb – use in moderation either whole or finely chopped. The traditional flavouring for roast lamb.

Sage A strong, almost musty flavour, associated with pork and chicken.

Savory Both summer and winter savory have a similar spicy flavour, resembling thyme. Use in bean recipes, salads, soups and casseroles.

Tarragon Always use French not Russian tarragon, as it is infinitely superior. Tarragon has a powerful sharp flavour with a hint of aniseed. Ideal with egg and chicken dishes.

Thyme There are many varieties of thyme, all of which have a strong aromatic flavour, sometimes with a hint of lemon. Good with chicken and game.

RICE, GRAINS AND PULSES

RICE

Rice appears in many shapes and guises, brown and white, long grain and round grain, par-cooked, prefluffed, frozen – the ways are endless. Whatever you buy, rice is extremely nutritious, especially the brown varieties where some of the outer bran layer remains. Rice contains no fat and is therefore relatively low in calories too.

Preparing and Cooking

Most rice bought today is prepacked and shouldn't need washing, but if you do buy it loose, give it a good rinse. Boiling rice is a contentious business. Some people like to cook it by the absorption method, but the following way is the most fool-proof. Simply add rice to a large pan of boiling salted water and boil for about 10-12 minutes for white varieties, 35-40 minutes for brown varieties; or until a grain pressed between the fingers just begins to relent. Drain the rice and immediately pour over boiling water from the kettle. Serve straight away. Always check rice packets for indi-vidual timings or specific instructions.

Types of Rice

Long-grain The type most used for plain boiling as the rice cooks to a dry fluffy consistency. The best known are Basmati (deliciously fragrant); Patna and Carolina (American long-grain rice).
Short-grain The short grains are very absorbent and used mainly in milk puddings.
Arborio rice This is actually a long-grain rice but very absorbent and used primarily in Italian risot-tos. It's rich and creamy.
Glutinous rice A very starchy rice which swells and sticks together as it cooks. Much used in Chinese cookery.
Flaked rice Processed rice which makes delicious creamy puddings.
Ground rice and rice flour The former is slightly coarser than the latter, both used in baking.
Wild rice Not actually a rice at all but the seed of an aquatic grass. It has a sweet nutty flavour.

GRAINS

Grains such as wheat, barley, corn, oats and rye are the edible seeds of different grasses. Familiar in their ground form as flour, many grains can also be bought cracked, flaked or further processed to mix into cereals, to top puddings or to simply serve as an accompaniment. All grains are good sources of vitamins and fibre. Store in airtight containers in a cool dry place and use within six months.

Unusual Grains

Buckwheat Sold as a grain but actually the seeds of a plant related to rhubarb. It has quite a strong flavour and can be bought toasted.
Bulghur, burgul or bulgar wheat This is wheat which has been cooked, dried and cracked. It has a mild nutty taste. Some finer varieties simply need soaking, coarser varieties require a short boil. The traditional ingredient of Tabouleh.
Couscous This is a pre-cooked grain processed from semolina. It can be soaked for salads or soaked and steamed to serve hot.
Polenta Italian yellow cornmeal which forms the basis of the traditional baked savoury dish of the same name.
Pearl barley The husked polished barley grain used in soups and stews.

PULSES

The term pulse covers all the various beans, peas and lentils which have been preserved by drying. Pulses are an important source of protein, carbo-hydrate and fibre, especially in a vegetarian diet.

Pulses should be stored in airtight containers in a cool dark place. They keep well, but after six months their skins toughen and they take increas-ingly longer to cook.

Before Cooking

With the exception of lentils and split peas, all pulses should be soaked overnight in a large bowl of cold water. The following morning, drain the soaked pulses then bring to the boil in fresh water

1 *Arborio rice* 2 *Wild rice*
3 *Brown long-grain rice*
4 *Flageolet beans* 5 *Chick-peas* 6 *Buckwheat* 7 *Polenta*
8 *Black-eyed beans* 9 *Split yellow peas* 10 *Mung beans*
11 *Soya beans* 12 *Couscous*
13 *Borlotti beans* 14 *Green lentils* 15 *Brown lentils*

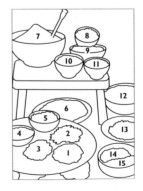

and boil rapidly for 10 minutes to destroy any toxins present. Although fast-boiling is not strictly necessary for all types of pulse, it does them no harm and saves the problem of remembering which ones require the treatment. After fast-boiling, lower the heat, cover and simmer for the required time until tender.

Cooking Dried Pulses

The flavour can be subtly enhanced by adding a couple of bay leaves or garlic cloves, or an onion studded with a few cloves, to the cooking water. The cooking time varies depending on the age of the pulse and the length of soaking time, but as a general guide lentils and split peas take 30-60 min-utes, while beans - such as black-eyed beans, borlotti beans, butter beans, cannellini beans, flageolet beans and mung beans – take 1-1½ hours. Exceptions are chick-peas which take 1½-2 hours, and soya beans which need 3-4 hours cooking time. Add salt approximately 15 minutes before the end of the cooking time. Salt added at the beginning of cooking tends to toughen the skins. Pulses also cook well in the pressure cooker. Once cooked, they can be refrigerated for a few days or frozen.

The weight of dried beans more or less doubles during cooking, so if a recipe calls for 400 g (14 oz) canned beans you'll only need to boil 200 g (7 oz) dried beans.

PASTA

Pasta now appears in every shape and form from spindly thin spaghetti to large bulbous pasta shells in a rainbow of colours, either fresh or dried. The best is made from 100 per cent durum wheat; look for 'pasta di semola di grano duro' on the packet.

Storing

Dried pasta will keep for months in an unopened packet but once the packet is opened the pasta will become brittle. Egg-flavoured pasta (*pasta all'uovo*) keeps less well. Fresh pasta should be covered and refrigerated for not more than a day; it freezes well and may be cooked from frozen.

Cooking

Allow about 50-75 g (2-3 oz) dried pasta per person, 125-150 g (4-5 oz) fresh. Bring a very large pan of salted water to the boil, allowing about 2-3 litres (3½ - 5¼ pints) water to every 450 g (1 lb) pasta. Add pasta to pan, slowly curling in spaghetti as it softens. Add a dash of oil, bring back to the boil and cook for time stated on packet, stirring occasionally. Fresh pasta cooks more quickly than dried, usually taking 2-3 minutes only. To test pasta, remove a small piece and bite into it. It should be just firm (*al dente*). Drain and serve immediately.

PASTA SHAPES

Just a few of the shapes available today –
Capellini – fine spaghetti
Cappelletti – small stuffed pasta shapes
Conchiglie – shells
Farfalle – pasta bows
Fettuccini – thin ribbon-like pasta sold curled into bird's nest shapes
Fusilli – a sort of spiral spaghetti
Linguine – flat ribbon pasta
Pappardelle – wide ribbon pasta with a wavy edge
Penne – thinnish pasta tubes cut diagonally
Rigatoni – short, ridged tubular pasta
Tortelloni – slightly larger stuffed pasta shapes
Vermicelli – very fine spaghetti

Oriental Noodles Available in Chinese and oriental stores and some supermarkets, the range of these grow daily. They're made from the staple grain of their country hence rice noodles (rice vermicelli) and cellophane noodles, the translucent noodles usually made from mung beans. Many Chinese noodles contain eggs. Cook noodles as instructed on the packet.

I *Vermicelli* 2 *Egg noodles*
3 *Tortellini* 4 *Rice noodles*
5 *Farfalle* 6 *Lasagne*
7 *Conchiglie* 8 *Tagliatelle*
9 *Penne* 10 *Fusilli*
11 *Conchiglie*

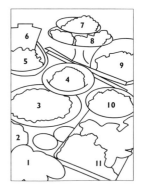

DAIRY FOODS

CHEESE

Cheese is a wonderfully tasty and versatile food which can be eaten raw or added to a multitude of recipes. It is an excellent source of protein and calcium but because of its relatively high fat content should be eaten in moderation as part of a balanced diet. Look out for the lower fat and reduced fat cheeses which can significantly reduce the fat and calorie intake.

Cheese falls roughly into four categories –

Hard cheese Produced by removing as much of the whey as possible, this group includes cheeses such as Parmesan and Pecorino.

Semi-hard cheese Again made by removing a certain amount of whey before moulding and ripening, this group includes traditional favourites such as Cheddar (from the strong-flavoured, mature English farmhouse type to the milder-tasting varieties), Gruyère (honeycombed with holes, ideal for fondues), Double Gloucester (orange-yellow in colour with a crumbly texture), Edam (wax coated, lower in fat) and Stilton (famous English cheese with blue mould veining).

Soft ripened cheese Included in this group are the mould-ripened cheeses, such as Brie and Camembert, as well as the blue-veined cheeses, such as Danish Blue.

Soft fresh cheese A myriad of soft cheeses are available today, ranging from rich cream cheese (such as Mascarpone) to low fat, skimmed milk soft cheese (such as fromage frais, quark and cottage cheese). Most are made from cow's milk, but there is also a wide range of goat's milk cheeses available.

It is worth noting that soft cheese described as 'full fat soft cheese' is not the same as the higher fat 'cream cheese'. Full fat means that the cheese must contain at least 20 per cent milk fat. Cream cheese is made from cream rather than milk and can contain at least 45 per cent fat. At the other end of the scale, skimmed milk soft cheese contains less than 2 per cent fat.

Vegetarian cheeses made with non-animal rennet are now available in all these categories. Most cheeses from a similar group are interchangeable in recipes.

Buying and Storing Cheese

Hard cheeses should have no signs of drying or cracking and when pre-packaged should never be sweating inside the wrappings. Soft ripened cheeses should be just soft to the touch and never have an ammonia smell which indicates that they've gone over the top. Fresh cheeses should always smell fresh and show no signs of browning around the edges. Always check date stamps on cheeses and buy in reasonable quantities; soft cheeses in particular don't have a long shelf life.

Wrap cheeses in greaseproof paper or foil – take special care with goat's cheeses or their strong aroma will penetrate other foods – and refrigerate or store in a cool larder. Leave all cheeses at room temperature for at least 30 minutes before serving.

It is important to remember that if a semi-hard cheese is overheated it will separate and go stringy. Always melt cheese gently and when adding it to a sauce, do not allow it to boil. Bear in mind that well-matured cheese gives the best flavour; if using a mild Cheddar, add a little mustard for extra flavour – adding an extra quantity of mild cheese will not give a greater depth of flavour.

Cheddar and Gruyère are often used in baking while Lancashire, Cheshire or Leicester are good for toasting. For pizzas mozzarella is ideal, while crumbly cheeses, such as Feta and Roquefort, are perfect in salads and dressings. Freshly grated Parmesan is popular for serving with pasta or for topping bakes. Skimmed milk soft cheeses are useful for reducing fat intake.

Following recent outbreaks of listeriosis, soft mould-ripened cheeses such as Brie, Camembert and blue-veined soft cheeses such as Danish Blue should not be eaten by pregnant women or by people with decreased resistance to infection.

EGGS

Eggs, like cheese, are another tasty versatile food rich in protein but because of their relatively high cholesterol content we are advised to keep our consumption to 3-4 per week. Most eggs are battery produced although there are increasing numbers of barn and free-range eggs where the chickens have more freedom.

Hen eggs These are the most commonly eaten and are graded from size 1-7; size 1 being the largest.

Quail eggs Used mainly for garnishing dishes, these tiny eggs take two minutes to soft boil, a little longer to hard boil.

Duck, goose and turkey eggs Not widely available, these must be thoroughly cooked as they are more susceptible to salmonella; never serve raw.

Buying and Storing Eggs

Always buy from a reputable source and check date stamps; some eggs are now stamped with the day they were laid. Never buy cracked eggs. Store pointed-side down in the refrigerator or a cool place and use within two weeks or follow advice on the box. If you have any doubts about the age of an egg, place it in a bowl of cold water; if it floats it will be old and possibly bad. Dirty eggs should be rinsed just before cooking. Do not store ingredients which include raw eggs, such as mayonnaise, for more than three days.

Eggs are susceptible to salmonella – for most of us this does not create any great risk. But the very young, the elderly, the sick, pregnant women and those with immune deficiency diseases should not eat raw or lightly cooked eggs.

CREAM

Cream is classified by its fat content and in order to whip successfully it must have a minimum of 35 per cent fat. Some of the very thick double creams need to be let down with a little single cream before whipping. This is necessary in order to prevent them from turning to butter in the process.

Clotted cream Traditionally the cream is scooped off large shallow dishes of milk then scalded so that the cream develops a rich yellow wrinkled crust. Simply spoon straight from the tub (55 per cent fat).

Soured cream A commercially soured single cream, not the same as single cream which has simply gone sour (18 per cent fat).

Smetana Another commercially soured cream of Russian origin. It's lower in fat than soured cream (6-12 per cent fat).

Crème fraîche This is a cream treated after pasteurization with a bacteria culture which thickens it but doesn't sour it. Much used in French cookery and now becoming more widely available in our shops (35 per cent fat).

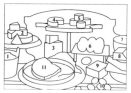

1 *Crème fraîche* 2 *Camembert*
3 *Blue Shropshire* 4 *Epoisses*
5 *French goats' cheese*
6 *Free-range hen eggs*
7 *Mascarpone* 8 *Gruyère*
9 *Parmesan* 10 *Quail eggs*
11 *Vacherin*

Spring

New stirrings of life herald the arrival of spring and, in the kitchen, the cook welcomes the season's fresh, new produce with open arms. Colourful young vegetables are the hallmark of spring cooking, and delicacies such as asparagus and new potatoes are firmly back on the menu for entertaining. The season's new lamb provides the perfect main course for Easter get-togethers, while traditional pursuits such as decorating eggs are enjoyable pastimes for all the family during this season of promise.

SOUPS AND STARTERS

Thai Chicken Soup
(page 102)

Asparagus Soup
(page 102)

Broccoli and Watercress Soup
(page 103)

Pâté de Campagne
(page 104)

Corn Scones with Avocado
(page 104)

Deep-fried Whitebait with
Hot sauce
(page 105)

Soy-glazed Chicken Livers with
Chinese Leaves
(page 106)

Toasted Bacon and
Goats' Cheese Salad
(page 107)

Grapefruit and Chicory Salad
with Prawns
(page 107)

FISH AND SHELLFISH

Poached Trout with Fennel
(page 108)

Trout with Dill and Horseradish
Mayonnaise
(page 108)

Cod Fillet Wrapped in Filo Pastry
with Rocket
(page 109)

Cod Cutlets Provençale
(page 110)

Whiting in Soured Cream
(page 110)

Roasted Fish with Garlic-herb
Crumbs
(page 111)

Red Mullet with Spinach and
Bacon
(page 111)

Oatmeal Crusted Herrings
(page 112)

Light Monkfish and Prawn Sauté
(page 112)

Mixed Seafood Gratin
(page 113)

Paella with Peppers
(page 114)

Coconut Fish Pilau
(page 114)

Steamed Mussels in Saffron
Cream Sauce
(page 115)

POULTRY AND GAME

Savoury Crumbed Chicken
(page 116)

Hot Red Jungle Curry
(page 116)

Chicken Breasts with Spinach and
Ricotta
(page 117)

Herb Marinated Chicken with
Spring Vegetables in a Warm
Dressing
(page 118)

Spring Chicken Fricassée
(page 119)

Country Chicken Casserole
(page 119)

Warm Asparagus and Chicken
Salad
(page 120)

French Roast Chicken
(page 120)

Cinnamon Roast Poussin with
Couscous
(page 121)

Lemon and Ginger Poussins with
Onions
(page 122)

Guinea Fowl with Rocket Sauce
and Spring Vegetables
(page 122)

Pan-fried Turkey with Lemon and
Hazelnuts
(page 123)

MEAT

Rich Beef Daube
(page 124)

Italian Meatloaf
(page 125)

Spicy Burgers
(page 125)

Roast Lamb with a Creamy
Fennel Sauce
(page 126)

Roast Eye Fillet of Lamb with
Candied Lemons
(page 126)

Boned and Stuffed Shoulder
of Lamb
(page 127)

Lamb Steaks in Herby
Tomato Sauce
(page 128)

Spicy Lamb Casserole
(page 128)

Moussaka
(page 129)

Kidneys in Sherry Sauce
(page 130)

Stir-fried Pork
(page 130)

Roast Pork with Apple Gravy
(page 131)

Pork Chops with Rhubarb
Chutney
(page 132)

Pork and Lemon Brochettes
(page 132)

Mushroom and Ham Risotto
(page 133)

Saltimbocca
(page 133)

CHEESE AND EGGS

Four-cheese Pizza
(page 134)

Deep-fried Camembert with
Rhubarb Sauce
(page 134)

Asparagus and Red Onion Tart
(page 135)

Poached Eggs on Smoked
Haddock with Hot Caper
Dressing
(page 136)

Eggs in Poppadom Baskets
(page 137)

Goats' Cheese Puffs
(page 137)

PASTA AND NOODLES

Seafood Lasagne
(page 138)

Chilli Pork with Noodles
(page 139)

Pasta Primavera
(page 140)

Gingered Chicken and Noodles
(page 139)

Classic Tomato Sauce
(page 140)

Crespoline
(page 141)

VEGETARIAN DISHES

Broccoli and Cheese Timbale
with Tomato Sauce
(page 142)

Stir-fried Spring Vegetables with
Cashews
(page 143)

Leek Pancakes with Watercress
Sauce
(page 145)

Couscous-filled Aubergines with
a Coriander Dressing
(page 142)

Vegetable Strudel
(page 144)

Catalan Red Peppers
(page 145)

VEGETABLES AND SALADS

New Potatoes with Creamy
Mint Butter
(page 146)

Carrots in Spiced Dressing
(page 147)

Warm Chinese Salad
(page 149)

Spring Green Sauté
(page 146)

Vegetable Medley
(page 148)

Grated Baby Beetroot Salad
(page 149)

Crispy Chinese Greens
(page 146)

Leeks and Asparagus in
Vinaigrette
(page 148)

DESSERTS

Rhubarb and Cinnamon Cobbler
(page 150)

Higgledy-piggledy Apple Tart
(page 152)

Crêpes with Orange Ice
(page 154)

Banoffi Fudge Pie
(page 150)

Easter Cheesecake
(page 152)

Fragrant Fruit Salad
(page 155)

Lime Meringue Pies
(page 151)

Whisky Mocha Flan
(page 153)

Flambéed Pineapple
(page 155)

BAKING

The Ultimate Chocolate Cake
(page 156)

Simnel Cake
(page 157)

Easter Biscuits
(page 158)

Walnut Torte
(page 156)

Mini Hot Cross Buns
(page 158)

Almond Squares
(page 159)

CONFECTIONERY

Chocolate Colettes with Frosted
Flowers
(page 160)

Chocolate Easter Egg
(page 161)

Solid Chocolate Eggs
(page 161)

The sight of the first green tips of spring bulbs pushing their way up into the cool spring air brings a strange excitement and sense of expectancy. The winter is over and long-awaited lighter fresh foods are on their way to the shops and markets.

SPRING LAMB

A symbol of renewal and rebirth from ancient times, lamb has always featured on festive Easter menus. The flavour of lamb depends largely on the diet and habitat of the animal. British spring lamb is fed for the main part on grass, producing a delicate meat that is pale and tender with a fine grain and white crumbly fat. It is at its most delicious cooked very plainly - roast or grilled - to rosy pinkness and served with a creamy gratin of potatoes and fresh spring vegetables. Allow the lamb to rest for at least 10 minutes before carving to relax the meat and disperse the pink juices.

A variety of lean cuts of lamb are increasingly on sale in supermarkets and good butchers and make really good quick meals, such as kebabs, stir-fries and grills.

• Mint sauce is the sauce traditionally served with lamb. To make this classic accompaniment, chop a small bunch of mint leaves and place in a bowl with 10 ml (2 tsp) caster sugar. Pour over 15 ml (1 tbsp) boiling water and stir to dissolve the sugar. Add 30 ml (2 tbsp) wine vinegar and leave to steep for at least 1 hour before serving. Mint and apple jelly (see page 306) is also good with lamb.

Cooking Tips

• Try brushing steaks and chops with mint and apple jelly before grilling for a delicious glaze.
• A simple glaze of one part Dijon or wholegrain mustard mixed with two parts soy sauce and a little crushed garlic produces succulent results. Brush liberally over a lamb joint before roasting and baste frequently, or brush over small cuts before grilling.
• For a sweet spicy flavour, mix a little ginger into some honey and use to baste lamb. This will also give a lovely glaze.

RIVER FISH

The trout fishing season starts in mid-spring and if you are lucky enough to be given wild brown trout, freshly-caught from the river, cook the cleaned fish by a simple method so that you can fully appreciate the delicate flavour of the whitish flesh. Grilling or sautéeing in butter is ideal.

Rainbow trout is the farmed equivalent of brown trout and is available all year round. Salmon trout, sometimes called sea trout, appears in March, and is generally smaller than salmon. The flesh is firm and moist, with a very delicate flavour. Generally slightly cheaper than salmon, it is really worth buying for a special occasion. It can be cooked the same way as salmon, but do not overpower the flavour with strong-tasting sauces.

NEW VEGETABLES

As the season for hearty winter vegetables comes to an end, the first spring vegetables make a welcome appearance. Lightly cooked and simply tossed in butter with a sprinkling of spice or herbs, these fresh vegetables give a lift to any meat, poultry or fish dish.

Quick Vegetable Tips

• Cook the first fresh sweet peas with a little mint and toss tiny sweet baby carrots in butter with a touch of ginger to make the ideal accompaniments to spring lamb.
• Young turnips sautéed in honey or brown sugar and a dash of soy sauce also go well with the lamb.
• Lightly boiled spring greens tossed in olive oil and lemon juice provide a healthy, tangy side dish.
• Purple-sprouting broccoli has a sweet fresh flavour which is delicious in oriental dishes
• Try eating young broad beans straight from the pod with a chunk of fresh Parmesan and slices of prosciutto.
• New potatoes are a real spring treat, especially Jersey Royals with their flaky skin and creamy taste. Make the most of their flavour by tossing the boiled potatoes in butter and black pepper.
• Asparagus is one of the delicacies of late spring. The best way to cook asparagus is to stand the stems upright in a deep saucepan, cover the tips with a cap of foil and simmer gently for about 8 minutes until tender. This way the stalks are poached while the tips are gently steamed, retaining their delicate texture.

PANCAKE DAY

You know that Spring is just around the corner when pancake day arrives! Mark the day by having a complete meal devoted to pancakes, both sweet and savoury (see page 145 for the basic quantities and cooking method).
• For Indian-style pancakes, replace the plain flour with chick pea (gram) flour and add 10 ml (2 tsp) ground cumin, 1.25 ml (¹/₄ tsp) ground turmeric and 1.25 ml (¹/₄ tsp) mild chilli powder. Use half milk and water for the liquid. Fry slightly thicker

Decorated chocolate eggs – the perfect Easter gifts.

than normal and fill with roughly mashed potato, chopped coriander and spring onions.

• Fill chive pancakes with 350 g (12 oz) cooked smoked haddock, mixed with 2 chopped hard-boiled eggs and 300 ml (10 fl oz) white sauce made with soured cream and flavoured with chives.

• Cover rolled pancakes with a tomato sauce, sprinkle generously with cheese and grill until bubbling.

• For chocolate pancakes, replace 30 ml (2 tbsp) plain flour with sifted cocoa powder and sweeten the batter with icing sugar or maple syrup. Fill with sliced banana which has been fried in butter and brown sugar and laced with rum.

• Or simply serve plain pancakes with a generous squeeze of lemon juice and a sprinkling of caster sugar - irresistible!

EASTER FESTIVITIES

Easter is a time for giving and receiving chocolate eggs – try making your own hollow eggs (see page 161) and decorating them with edible shapes for that special Easter gift.

• Simulate the fabulous eggs of the Russian royal jeweller, Fabergé, by sticking small, jewel-like sweets to the egg, attaching them with either a dab of royal icing or melted chocolate.

• Sugar-frosted edible flowers make delicate decorations. Choose from cowslips, daisies, sweet violets, grape hyacinths, pansies, primroses and rose buds. To frost petals and leaves, paint with beaten egg white and sprinkle with caster sugar. Shake off the excess sugar and leave to dry on greaseproof paper.

• Make fondant flowers with coloured ready-made fondant. To mould, dip your fingers in cornflour and shape petals to resemble a chosen bloom. Curve petals with a paint brush or modelling tool. Draw veins on leaves and dry over a pencil to form a curve. Attach leaves and flowers to chocolate eggs with dabs of royal icing or melted chocolate.

• Fill eggs with tiny foil-wrapped chocolate eggs, sugar-coated eggs, truffles, coloured marzipan eggs or chocolate coins.

97

EASTER EGGS

Dyeing eggs is a time-honoured tradition at Easter time. Children love to join in masking up and colouring eggs. Hen eggs take up the dye well but the shells are rarely white these days, which can affect the colour of the dyed eggs; duck eggs are white but don't take the dye as easily. Red, yellow and pink dyes are used here as they go well with the natural brown colours of hen egg shells.

Dye a whole clutch of eggs to fill a basket or bowl for an eye-catching Easter display. For a temporary decoration, at breakfast time for example, use hard-boiled eggs but if the eggs are to be kept for any length of time remove the contents first – prick the shell at either end, then blow out the raw egg. Wash before dyeing.

You will need:
Assortment of hen, duck or goose eggs, hard-boiled or blown clean
String
Rubber bands
Stick-on spot, ring or star labels
Onion skins
Food colourings
Saucepan
Vegetable oil

1 To mask off different patterns, wrap string or rubber bands around some eggs. Stick shaped labels onto others.

3 Remove the eggs from the dye and dry them. Remove masking material. Rub on vegetable oil to give a shine.

2 Mix a bowl of water and food colouring. Gently lower in the eggs and swirl them round. Leave for 30 minutes, moving frequently.

4 For a natural dye, wrap onion skins around the eggs. Fix them in place with rubber bands. Cook gently in boiling water for 15 minutes.

GREEN-AND-WHITE TABLE CENTREPIECE

A fresh, pretty bowlful of flowers is a perfect focal point for a sophisticated table setting. Here a vivid green-and-white colour scheme reflects the freshness of the season to perfection.

The mixture of growing hyacinths and cut flowers is chosen to last a long time. As the cut flowers fade the hyacinths continue to bloom, scenting the room with the fragrance of spring. Moss makes a good background for the arrangement and helps to support the cut stems in the shallow container.

You will need:
White spring flowers, such as chincherinchees, tulips, ranunculus, *Ornithogolum arabicum*
Green flowers, such as spray chrysanthemums, euphorbia
Scissors
String
Fresh moss
Large shallow bowl
3 white hyacinths with bulbs

1 Make up small posies of fresh flowers, using all one kind of bloom or mixtures of different types. Tie them with string and cut the stems off quite short.
2 Soak the moss in water. Put a little water into the bowl. Stand the hyacinth bulbs in the bowl and pack moss around them, leaving the top of the bulbs clear of the moss. Cover the rest of the bowl with more moss.

3 Tuck some of the bunches of flowers into the bowl, leaving plenty of moss showing. Top the moss up with water as required. Here there are six small bunches mixed with three hyacinths.
4 If desired, display a few more posies of different heights in individual tumblers around the large bowl or at place settings on the table.

BISCUIT TREE

Making sweet Easter biscuits is an age-old custom. Traditionally, the dough is enriched with eggs and dried fruit; this simpler version has a delicious spicy flavour. The dough can be cut into many shapes with novelty biscuit cutters. For hanging the biscuits with a loop of ribbon, cut a hole in the dough before baking.

Hang the biscuits on a bare twiggy branch with little spring flower wreaths for a christening, or chocolate eggs at Easter time. Use dried flowers instead of fresh ones to make sure the display lasts over the Easter weekend.

1 Sift the flour, spices and baking powder into a bowl. Rub in the butter. In a small saucepan, heat together the sugar and milk. Cool, then stir into the dry ingredients with the orange juice. Bind to a smooth dough and chill for 15 minutes.
2 Roll out the dough on a lightly floured surface to a thickness of 6 mm (¼ inch). Stamp out shapes with the biscuit cutters, place on baking sheets and bake at 180°C (350°F) mark 4 for 12-15 minutes.

3 Cool the biscuits on a wire rack, then pipe designs with different coloured icings.
4 Wire together small posies of spring flowers, such as miniature narcissi.
5 Fill the pot with foam or plaster filler and push the branch into it.
6 Hang the iced biscuits from the twigs with ribbon. Tie the posies onto the twigs with ribbon. Tie on extra ribbon bows if desired.

You will need:
FOR THE BISCUITS:
125 g (4 oz) white plain flour
2.5 ml (½ tsp) ground mixed spice
5 ml (1 tsp) ground ginger
Pinch of baking powder
65 g (2½ oz) butter or margarine
50 g (2 oz) light muscovado sugar
15 ml (1 tbsp) milk
10 ml (2 tsp) orange juice
Rolling pin
Biscuit cutters
Baking sheets
Royal icing for decorating
Natural food colours
Piping bag and nozzle
FOR THE POSIES:
Florist's wire
Small bunches of spring flowers, such as miniature narcissi and violets
Twiggy branch
Flower pot
Florist's foam or plaster filler
Fine ribbons

SHELL-TOPPED BOXES

The next time you serve shellfish such as mussels, oysters, cockles and snails, clean and save their shells for decorating a range of accessories. Such plain, everyday shells can be livened up with unusual ones collected on a beach and a few artificial pearl beads. Be sure to clean any shells carefully before using them, otherwise they'll start to smell before long.

It's easy to stick shells onto glass, metal, wood or card with an electric glue gun. Use the shells to edge serving plates or bowls, or to top off storage boxes for use in a kitchen or bathroom.

You will need:
Assortment of shells, such as mussels, cockles, oysters, limpets, plus a few exotic specimens
Small stiff brush or household bleach
Metal boxes
White spirit
Electric glue gun or adhesive
Artificial pearl beads

1 Boil any fresh shells and scour with a stiff brush or soak in bleach overnight.

3 Glue a ring of mussel shells onto the lid of a box – let each shell dry before fixing the next.

2 Drain and dry the clean shells. Clean metal boxes with white spirit to remove any grease. Sort out all the shells and beads before you start decorating.

4 To finish the arrangement, stick a limpet shell in the centre and glue a pearl in its cup. For small boxes, glue a single large shell on the lid with a pearl in its opening.

THAI CHICKEN SOUP

PREPARATION TIME 10 minutes
COOKING TIME 20 minutes
FREEZING Suitable

🕐 ❄

SERVES 4   **265 CALS/SERVING**

- *125 g (4 oz) creamed coconut, chopped*
- *15 ml (1 tbsp) vegetable oil*
- *1 green chilli, deseeded and finely chopped*
- *2.5 cm (1 inch) piece fresh root ginger, peeled and finely chopped*
- *350 g (12 oz) skinless chicken breast, cut into chunks*
- *2 garlic cloves, peeled and crushed*
- *750 ml (1½ pints) chicken stock*
- *45 ml (3 tbsp) fresh lime juice (about 2 limes)*
- *about 90 ml (6 tbsp) chopped fresh coriander*
- *225 g (8 oz) mangetout, sliced*
- *salt and pepper*
- *chopped spring onions, to garnish*

1 Dissolve the chopped coconut in 300 ml (10 fl oz) boiling water.
2 Heat the oil in a non-stick saucepan, add the chilli, ginger, chicken and garlic and cook for 1-2 minutes.
3 Add the stock, coconut milk, lime juice and half the coriander. Bring to the boil. Cover and simmer for 15 minutes. Add the mangetout and cook for a further 5 minutes until the chicken is tender.
4 Add the remaining coriander and season to taste. Garnish with chopped spring onions.

ASPARAGUS SOUP

PREPARATION TIME 15 minutes
COOKING TIME 25 minutes
FREEZING Suitable
COLOUR INDEX Page 8

❄

SERVES 4   **260 CALS/SERVING**

- *125 g (4 oz) blanched almonds*
- *1.1 litres (2 pints) vegetable stock or water*
- *15 ml (1 tbsp) vegetable oil*
- *4 celery sticks, diced*
- *450 g (1 lb) asparagus, trimmed and chopped*
- *30 ml (2 tbsp) chopped fresh parsley*
- *45 ml (3 tbsp) single cream*
- *salt and pepper*
- *cream, toasted flaked almonds and parsley, to garnish*

1 Place the almonds and stock in a blender or food processor and grind until very smooth. Sieve the mixture, reserving the liquid, and discard the grains.
2 Heat the oil in a large saucepan and gently fry the celery for 5-6 minutes. Add the asparagus and cook for 5 minutes. Pour the stock over the top and add the parsley. Cover and simmer for 15 minutes.
3 Cool slightly, then purée in a blender or food processor until smooth. Return to the pan and stir in the cream. Heat gently. Season and garnish with cream, toasted almonds and parsley.

BROCCOLI AND WATERCRESS SOUP

PREPARATION TIME 10 minutes
COOKING TIME 30 minutes
FREEZING Suitable

✳

SERVES 6
- *225 g (8 oz) broccoli*
- *75 g (3 oz) butter*
- *2 leeks, trimmed and sliced*
- *1-2 garlic cloves, peeled and halved*
- *2 bunches watercress, trimmed*
- *25 g (1 oz) white plain flour*
- *600 ml (1 pint) chicken stock*

215 CALS/SERVING
- *salt and pepper*
- *450 ml (15 fl oz) milk*
- *150 ml (5 fl oz) single cream*
- *Parmesan cheese shavings, to garnish*
- *a little freshly grated nutmeg, to taste*

1 Divide the broccoli into florets and slice the stalks into even-sized pieces.
2 Melt the butter in a saucepan, add the broccoli florets and stalks and stir in the leeks and garlic. Cook gently for 5 minutes, stirring occasionally.
3 Add the watercress and cook for a further 3 minutes, stirring frequently. Stir in the flour and cook for 1 minute, then gradually add the stock and bring to the boil, stirring. Season with salt and pepper.
4 Cover and simmer gently for 20 minutes or until all the vegetables are tender and cooked through. Remove from the heat and allow to cool slightly.
5 Purée the soup in a blender or food processor. Return the mixture to the rinsed-out pan, check the seasoning, stir in the milk and cream, and heat through gently.
6 Serve the soup hot, sprinkled with shavings of Parmesan and a pinch of freshly grated nutmeg.

VARIATION This soup is also delicious served cold, in which case thin the consistency with extra milk and cream.

CORN SCONES WITH AVOCADO

PREPARATION TIME 40 minutes
COOKING TIME 7-8 minutes
FREEZING Suitable (stage 3)
COLOUR INDEX Page 10

✻

MAKES ABOUT 30
- *75 g (3 oz) white self-raising flour*
- *salt and pepper*
- *5 ml (1 tsp) baking powder*
- *25 g (1 oz) maize meal or fine semolina*
- *15 ml (1 tbsp) caster sugar*
- *25 g (1 oz) butter*
- *milk*

AVOCADO TOPPING
- *125 g (4 oz) full-fat soft cheese*

25 CALS/SERVING
- *1 avocado, roughly mashed*
- *1 hard-boiled egg, finely chopped*
- *15 ml (1 tbsp) lemon juice*
- *dash each of Worcestershire sauce and paprika*
- *175 g (6 oz) rindless lean bacon, grilled and crumbled*

1 Sift the flour with a pinch of salt and the baking powder into a bowl. Stir in the maize meal and caster sugar. Rub in the butter until the mixture resembles fine breadcrumbs.
2 Make a well in the centre and stir in enough milk to give a soft dough, about 45-60 ml (3-4 tbsp). Knead lightly, then roll out to 5 mm-1 cm (¼-½ inch) thickness. Cut into rounds using a 2.5 cm (1 inch) cutter. (Use a cap from a bottle if you do not have a cutter.) Place on a baking sheet and brush with milk.
3 Bake at 220°C (425°F) mark 7 for about 7-8 minutes or until risen and light golden. Leave to cool.
4 To make the avocado topping, mix the soft cheese with the avocado, hard-boiled egg, lemon juice, Worcestershire sauce and paprika. Season to taste and cover tightly.
5 Split the cold scones in half and spoon on the avocado topping. Sprinkle with crumbled bacon and serve.

VARIATION For a tangy mackerel topping, finely chop a few capers or gherkins and mix with 150 ml (5 fl oz) crème fraîche. Season to taste. Spread onto the halved scones. Top with flakes of smoked mackerel and garnish with chives.

PATE DE CAMPAGNE

PREPARATION TIME 20 minutes, plus chilling
COOKING TIME 2 hours
FREEZING Suitable

✻

SERVES 10-12
- *300 g (10 oz) rindless streaky bacon rashers*
- *450 g (1 lb) belly of pork*
- *300 g (10 oz) diced pie veal*
- *175 g (6 oz) lamb's liver*
- *1 onion, peeled*
- *1 garlic clove, peeled and crushed*

380-310 CALS/SERVING
- *50 g (2 oz) pitted black olives, chopped*
- *salt and pepper*
- *5 ml (1 tsp) chopped fresh sage*
- *30 ml (2 tbsp) olive oil*
- *15 ml (1 tbsp) lemon juice*
- *30 ml (2 tbsp) brandy*

1 Stretch the bacon, using the back of a knife. Finely mince the pork, veal, liver and onion. Mix with the remaining ingredients.
2 Layer the bacon and minced ingredients in a 1.1 litre (2 pint) terrine, topping with a layer of bacon rashers.
3 Cover with foil or a lid and place in a roasting tin, half-filled with boiling water. Cook at 170°C (325°F) mark 3 for about 2 hours.
4 Weight down the pâté and allow to cool, then refrigerate overnight. Leave at room temperature for 30 minutes before serving. Cut the pâté into slices and serve on individual plates.

DEEP-FRIED WHITEBAIT WITH HOT SAUCE

PREPARATION TIME 20 minutes
COOKING TIME About 15 minutes
FREEZING Not suitable

SERVES 4

- *60 ml (4 tbsp) white plain flour*
- *700 g (1½ lb) whitebait*
- *oil for deep-frying*
- *chopped parsley, to garnish*
- *paprika, for sprinkling*
- *lime or lemon wedges, to serve*

HOT SAUCE
- *25 g (1 oz) ground hazelnuts*
- *2-3 hot red chillies, stems removed*

790 CALS/SERVING

- *1 small onion, peeled and quartered*
- *3 garlic cloves, peeled*
- *1 ripe tomato, skinned*
- *15 ml (1 tbsp) mild paprika*
- *salt and pepper*
- *10 ml (2 tsp) balsamic or red wine vinegar*
- *about 60 ml (4 tbsp) virgin olive oil*

1 To make the sauce, first spread the hazelnuts in the grill pan and toast until golden brown, shaking the pan occasionally.

2 Put all the sauce ingredients, except the olive oil, in a food processor or blender and process until smooth. Add a little of the olive oil if the mixture gets stuck around the blades. With the machine running, gradually add the olive oil in a thin stream to make a fairly thick sauce. Season to taste.

3 Put the flour in a bowl and season generously. Add the whitebait and toss to coat in the flour.

4 Heat the oil in a deep-fat fryer to 190°C (380°F) or until a cube of stale bread dropped into the oil turns golden brown in about 30 seconds.

5 Deep-fry the fish in the hot oil in batches for about 3 minutes or until golden brown. Drain on crumpled absorbent kitchen paper and keep hot while cooking the remainder.

6 Serve garnished with chopped parsley and a sprinkling of paprika, and accompanied by lime wedges and the sauce.

VARIATION If you're short of time, serve the whitebait with a spiced mayonnaise instead of the hot sauce. Flavour some homemade or good bought mayonnaise with grated lime rind, chopped chilli and chopped basil to taste.

SOY-GLAZED CHICKEN LIVERS WITH CHINESE LEAVES

PREPARATION TIME 10 minutes, plus marinating
COOKING TIME 5 minutes
FREEZING Not suitable

SERVES 4   275 CALS/SERVING

- *30 ml (2 tbsp) dark soy sauce*
- *30 ml (2 tbsp) dry sherry*
- *1 garlic clove, peeled and crushed*
- *5 ml (1 tsp) grated fresh root ginger*
- *5 ml (1 tsp) sesame oil*
- *5 ml (1 tsp) clear honey*
- *1.25 ml (¼ tsp) Chinese five-spice powder*
- *350 g (12 oz) chicken livers, thawed if frozen*
- *50 g (2 oz) watercress*

- *125 g (4 oz) pak choi or Chinese cabbage, shredded*
- *15 ml (1 tbsp) coriander leaves*
- *15 ml (1 tbsp) sesame seeds, toasted*
DRESSING
- *30 ml (2 tbsp) groundnut oil*
- *10 ml (2 tsp) chilli oil*
- *30 ml (2 tbsp) lime juice*
- *15 ml (1 tbsp) rice or wine vinegar*
- *10 ml (2 tsp) caster sugar*
- *salt and pepper*

1 Combine the soy sauce, sherry, garlic, ginger, sesame oil, honey and five-spice powder together until well blended. Wash and dry the chicken livers, discarding any discoloured parts. Toss the livers in the soy mixture and transfer to a shallow dish. Cover and marinate for 2 hours.

2 Meanwhile, make the dressing. Place all the ingredients in a small bowl and whisk until blended. Set aside.

3 Transfer the chicken livers, with all the juices, to a foil-lined grill pan and grill as close to the heat as possible for 1-2 minutes on each side until browned and just cooked through.

4 Place the salad leaves and coriander in a large bowl, add the dressing and toss until evenly coated. Divide the salad between individual plates, spoon on the chicken livers with their juices and serve at once, scattered with the sesame seeds.

VARIATION If preferred, you can fry the chicken livers – heat 30 ml (2 tbsp) sunflower oil in a frying pan, add the livers and fry quickly to seal. Add the marinade juices to the pan and simmer gently for 3 minutes.

TOASTED BACON AND GOATS' CHEESE SALAD

PREPARATION TIME 30 minutes
COOKING TIME About 6 minutes
FREEZING Not suitable
COLOUR INDEX Page 12

SERVES 6   **320 CALS/SERVING**

- *about 350 g (12 oz) soft, rindless goats' cheese*
- *2 bunches chives, finely chopped*
- *salt and pepper*
- *about 350 g (12 oz) thin-cut, rindless streaky bacon*
- *25 g (1 oz) toasted walnut pieces*
- *60 ml (4 tbsp) walnut oil*
- *10 ml (2 tsp) balsamic or red-wine vinegar*
- *1.25 ml (¼ tsp) sugar*
- *75 g (3 oz) mixed green salad leaves or rocket*
- *toasted ciabatta, to serve*

1 With wet hands, shape the goats' cheese into six round patties.
2 Roll the patties in the chopped chives and season with black pepper only. Chill.
3 Stretch the rashers of bacon by running the back of a round-bladed knife along each piece. Carefully wrap each pattie in bacon, making sure all the cheese is hidden and the ends of bacon are tucked underneath the pattie (you will need 3-4 rashers per pattie). Cover and chill until required.
4 Roughly chop the walnuts and mix with the walnut oil, vinegar and sugar. Season to taste. Wash and dry the salad leaves.
5 Place the patties on a foil-lined grill pan and grill for about 6 minutes, until golden and crisp, turning once. (If a little cheese oozes out, scoop it onto the mixed salad leaves to serve.)
6 Toss the dressing with the mixed salad, arrange on six plates and top each one with a pattie. Serve immediately with ciabatta.

TIP
Goats' cheese is most often sold in 125 g (4 oz) packs - just slice in half horizontally.

GRAPEFRUIT AND CHICORY SALAD WITH PRAWNS

PREPARATION TIME 15 minutes
FREEZING Not suitable
♡ ⏱

SERVES 4   **110 CALS/SERVING**

- *2 grapefruit*
- *2 heads of chicory, washed and trimmed*
- *30 ml (2 tbsp) sunflower oil*
- *freshly ground black pepper*
- *12 cooked prawns with shells*
- *snipped fresh chives, to garnish*

1 Using a serrated knife, remove all the peel and pith from the grapefruit then, holding the grapefruit over a bowl to collect the juice, divide into segments, discarding the pips and as much of the membrane as possible. Put the segments in another bowl and reserve the grapefruit juice.
2 Slice one of the chicory heads widthways into thin slices and add to the grapefruit segments. Mix gently together then arrange on four plates with the whole leaves of the other chicory head.
3 Add the oil and pepper to the reserved grapefruit juice and whisk everything together until well blended.
4 Pour the dressing over the salads and arrange the prawns on top. Garnish with the chives.

POACHED TROUT WITH FENNEL

PREPARATION TIME 15 minutes
COOKING TIME 40 minutes
FREEZING Not suitable
COLOUR INDEX Page 16

SERVES 2

545 CALS/SERVING

- *1 small head fennel, about 175 g (6 oz) total weight*
- *350 g (12 oz) potatoes, peeled and thinly sliced*
- *1 bay leaf*
- *60 ml (4 tbsp) dry vermouth*
- *salt and pepper*
- *2 fresh gutted trout, each weighing about 225 g (8 oz)*
- *25 g (1 oz) butter or margarine*
- *lemon slices, to garnish*

1 Trim the green feathery tops from the fennel and reserve for the garnish. Slice the fennel thinly and scatter over the bottom of a shallow ovenproof dish.

2 Cover the fennel with the slices of potato and place the bay leaf on top. Pour the vermouth and 60 ml (4 tbsp) water over, then season to taste.

3 Place the prepared trout on top of the fennel and potato and dot with the butter.

4 Cover tightly with foil. Bake in the oven at 180°C (350°F) mark 4 for about 40 minutes.

5 Remove the foil to serve. Chop the reserved fennel tops finely, then sprinkle over the dish. Serve immediately, garnished with lemon slices.

TROUT WITH DILL AND HORSERADISH MAYONNAISE

PREPARATION TIME 10 minutes, plus cooling
COOKING TIME 20 minutes
FREEZING Not suitable
COLOUR INDEX Page 16

SERVES 4

560 CALS/SERVING

- *100 ml (3½ fl oz) white wine vinegar*
- *10 ml (2 tsp) black peppercorns*
- *10 ml (2 tsp) dill seeds (optional)*
- *3 bay leaves*
- *5 ml (1 tsp) salt*
- *4 fresh gutted trout, each weighing about 200 g (7 oz)*

MAYONNAISE
- *1 Bramley apple, weighing about 150 g (5 oz)*
- *150 ml (5 fl oz) mayonnaise*
- *45 ml (3 tbsp) chopped fresh dill leaves*
- *10 ml (2 tsp) grated horseradish or horseradish sauce*
- *Cos lettuce leaves, to serve*
- *dill sprigs, bay leaves and lime wedges, to garnish*

1 Fill a large roasting tin with boiling water. Add the wine vinegar, peppercorns, dill seeds if using, bay leaves and salt. Immerse the fish in the liquid and bring back to the boil. Turn off the heat and leave the fish undisturbed in the liquid for at least 20 minutes.

2 To make the mayonnaise, peel, quarter, core and slice the apple. Place in a small pan with 45 ml (3 tbsp) water. Cover and cook until the apple is softened to a purée. Beat until smooth and allow to cool, then mix with the mayonnaise, chopped dill and horseradish.

3 Lift the trout from the poaching liquor, remove the skin, and their heads if preferred. Lay each fish in a long lettuce leaf on a serving plate and spoon some of the dill and apple mayonnaise alongside. Garnish with dill sprigs, bay leaves and lime wedges.

COD FILLET WRAPPED IN FILO PASTRY WITH ROCKET

PREPARATION TIME 20 minutes
COOKING TIME 18-20 minutes
FREEZING Suitable (stage 2)
♡ ❄

SERVES 6

335 CALS/SERVING

- *6 thick cod fillets, each weighing about 125 g (4 oz)*
- *salt and pepper*
- *50 g (2 oz) rocket leaves, roughly chopped*
- *50 g (2 oz) ricotta cheese*
- *25 g (1 oz) freshly grated Parmesan cheese*
- *1 garlic clove, peeled and crushed*
- *30 ml (2 tbsp) chopped mixed herbs*
- *grated rind and juice of ½ lemon*
- *90 ml (6 tbsp) olive oil*
- *12 small sheets filo pastry*
- *beaten egg for brushing*
- *30 ml (2 tbsp) freshly grated Parmesan cheese*

1 Wash and dry the cod fillets and season well on both sides. Place the rocket in a blender with the ricotta, 25 g (1 oz) Parmesan, the garlic, herbs, lemon rind and juice and 30 ml (2 tbsp) olive oil. Purée until smooth and season to taste.

2 Take 1 sheet of pastry, brush with a little oil and top with a second sheet; brush with oil. Place 1 cod fillet in the middle of the pastry and spread over a sixth of the rocket paste. Wrap the pastry over and around the fish and press the edges together to seal. Place on a greased baking sheet, seam side down and repeat to make 6 parcels.

3 Brush all the parcels with a little more oil and bake at 220°C (425°F) mark 7 for 10 minutes. Brush with egg, then sprinkle with the grated Parmesan and bake for 8-10 minutes until the pastry is crisp and golden and a skewer inserted into the centre of the fish comes out hot.

TIP
Make sure you buy thick fillets of cod from the head end of the fish.

109

scatter the olives between them. Cover and cook gently for 6 minutes, then turn the fish cutlets over and continue cooking for a further 4-5 minutes until cooked.

5 Adjust the seasoning, tear the basil leaves over the dish and serve immediately, garnished with extra basil sprigs.

NOTE Ricard is the best-known brand of pastis. Pernod is similarly flavoured with anise and has the same effect in cooking.

VARIATION Use other white fish steaks – such as swordfish or haddock. If you have no aniseed-flavoured liqueur, fry a teaspoonful of fennel seeds with the onion.

COD CUTLETS PROVENCALE

PREPARATION TIME 10 minutes
COOKING TIME About 25 minutes
FREEZING Not suitable
♡

SERVES 4
- 4 cod cutlets, each weighing about 150 g (5 oz)
- 75 ml (5 tbsp) olive oil
- 1 Spanish onion, peeled and finely chopped
- 5 ml (1 tsp) dried oregano
- 3 garlic cloves, peeled and crushed

325 CALS/SERVING
- 400 g (14 oz) can plum tomatoes
- 15 ml (1 tbsp) tomato purée
- 10 ml (2 tsp) pastis, ouzo or other aniseed liqueur
- salt and pepper
- 12 small black olives
- 1-2 fresh basil sprigs
- extra basil sprigs, to garnish

1 Rinse the fish cutlets and pat dry with absorbent kitchen paper; set aside.
2 Heat the olive oil in a large shallow frying pan. Add the onion with the oregano and cook over a very low heat for 10 minutes, stirring frequently. Add the garlic to the pan and cook for a further 2-3 minutes until the onion is translucent and beginning to turn pale golden.
3 Add the tomatoes to the pan, mashing with a fork. Add the tomato purée, bring to the boil and stir in the liqueur. Season to taste.
4 Bury the fish cutlets in the tomato sauce and

WHITING IN SOURED CREAM

PREPARATION TIME 10 minutes
COOKING TIME 6 minutes
FREEZING Not suitable
COLOUR INDEX Page 14
⊘

SERVES 2
- 25 g (1 oz) butter
- 350 g (12 oz) whiting fillet, skinned
- salt and pepper
- 1 large firm tomato
- 30 ml (2 tbsp) chopped parsley and chives, mixed

620 CALS/SERVING
- 150 ml (5 fl oz) soured cream
- 75 g (3 oz) Gruyère cheese, grated
- herb sprigs, to garnish

1 Choose a shallow serving dish that fits under the grill and is just large enough to take the fish in a single layer. Put the butter in the dish and grill until melted.
2 Remove the dish from the grill and put in the fish. Turn the fish so it is buttered side up, then sprinkle with salt and pepper to taste. Grill for 2-3 minutes.
3 Meanwhile, chop the tomato finely, place in a bowl and combine with the herbs and soured cream. Add 40 g (1½ oz) of the cheese, salt and pepper to taste, and mix again.
4 When the fish has cooked for about 3 minutes, spoon the cream mixture on top. Sprinkle a little more cheese over and grill for a further 2 minutes until bubbling. Serve at once, garnished with sprigs of herbs.

ROASTED FISH WITH GARLIC-HERB CRUMBS

PREPARATION TIME 20 minutes
COOKING TIME 25 minutes
FREEZING Not suitable
COLOUR INDEX Page 13

SERVES 6 — 430 CALS/SERVING

- *900 g (2 lb) firm-textured, chunky white fish fillets, such as monkfish or cod*
- *salt and pepper*
- *15 ml (1 tbsp) chopped fresh thyme or 5 ml (1 tsp) dried*
- *juice of 1 lemon*
- *175 g (6 oz) butter, plus a knob for finishing*
- *300 g (10 oz) baby courgettes, thickly sliced*
- *3 garlic cloves, peeled and crushed*
- *125 g (4 oz) fresh brown breadcrumbs*
- *60 ml (4 tbsp) chopped fresh parsley and basil*
- *6 plum tomatoes, about 700 g (1½ lb), thickly sliced*
- *lemon wedges, to garnish*

1 Trim the fish fillets of any skin and membrane, cut into large steaks and place in a single layer in a non-stick roasting tin. Season with pepper and thyme and sprinkle with the lemon juice.
2 Melt 125 g (4 oz) butter and pour over the fish. Cover with foil and cook at 220°C (425°F) mark 7 for 10-15 minutes.
3 Meanwhile, cook the courgettes in boiling, salted water for 4-5 minutes or until just tender. Drain well. Melt 50 g (2 oz) butter in a frying pan, then add the garlic and breadcrumbs. Fry until golden brown, stirring occasionally. Take off the heat, add the herbs and season well. Set aside.
4 Uncover the fish and scatter the courgettes and tomatoes around it. Season well and baste the vegetables with the fish juices. Cook, uncovered, for a further 10 minutes. Reheat the garlic crumbs with a knob of butter and sprinkle over the fish to serve. Garnish with lemon wedges.

NOTE Monkfish takes about 5-10 minutes longer to cook then flakier fish, such as haddock.

RED MULLET WITH SPINACH AND BACON

PREPARATION TIME 30 minutes
COOKING TIME 8 minutes
FREEZING Not suitable

SERVES 4 — 440 CALS/SERVING

- *4 red mullet, scaled, cleaned and heads removed*
- *salt and pepper*
- *16 small fresh spinach leaves*
- *1 garlic clove, peeled and crushed*
- *60 ml (4 tbsp) chopped fresh parsley*
- *75 ml (5 tbsp) olive oil*
- *4 streaky bacon rashers*
- *coriander or flat-leaf parsley sprigs and lemon rind strips, to garnish*

1 Rinse the fish in cold water and pat dry with absorbent kitchen paper. Season to taste.
2 Finely shred 8 of the spinach leaves and place in a small bowl. Add the garlic, parsley and 15 ml (1 tbsp) olive oil and mix well, then use to stuff the fish.
3 Stretch the bacon rashers with the back of a knife and wrap one around each fish, interleaving 2 of the remaining spinach leaves into each.
4 Heat the remaining oil in a large frying pan, add the fish and fry for about 4 minutes on each side until the fish is cooked and the bacon is golden brown. Serve at once, garnished with coriander or flat-leaf parsley sprigs and lemon rind strips.

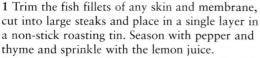

cucumber half crosswise into 1 cm (½ inch) slices. Cut the lettuce crosswise into slices of about the same thickness.

4 Grill the herrings, coated side up, for 4-5 minutes.

5 Meanwhile, melt the butter in a frying pan and add the lemon juice. Add the cucumber and lettuce and cook, stirring, until the lettuce wilts. Add the chopped dill and season with salt and pepper.

6 Transfer the grilled herrings to warmed serving plates and spoon the wilted lettuce and cucumber alongside. Garnish with dill to serve.

LIGHT MONKFISH AND PRAWN SAUTE

PREPARATION TIME 15 minutes
COOKING TIME 15 minutes
FREEZING Not suitable
COLOUR INDEX Page 14

♡ ☉

SERVES 4

230 CALS/SERVING

- 30 ml (2 tbsp) vegetable oil
- 450 g (1 lb) monkfish fillet, skinned and cut into chunks
- 1 bunch spring onions, sliced
- 1 garlic clove, peeled and chopped
- 2.5 cm (1 inch) piece fresh root ginger, peeled and finely chopped

- 300 g (10 oz) leeks, trimmed and sliced
- 1 red pepper, deseeded and roughly chopped
- 125 g (4 oz) cooked peeled prawns
- 15 ml (1 tbsp) hoisin sauce
- 15 ml (1 tbsp) light soy sauce
- 15 ml (1 tbsp) dry sherry
- black pepper

1 Heat the oil in a large non-stick frying pan and sauté the monkfish for 2-3 minutes. Remove using a slotted spoon. Add the onions, garlic and ginger to the pan and sauté for 2 minutes or until beginning to soften. Add the leeks and pepper and sauté for a further 10 minutes, stirring, until softened.

2 Return the monkfish to the pan with the prawns, hoisin sauce, soy sauce and sherry. Season with plenty of black pepper (the soy sauce is fairly salty). Cook for 30 seconds-1 minute, stirring. Serve at once.

OATMEAL CRUSTED HERRINGS

PREPARATION TIME 10 minutes
COOKING TIME 5-6 minutes
FREEZING Not suitable

☉

SERVES 4

700 CALS/SERVING

- 4 herrings, gutted and filleted, heads removed, each weighing about 225 g (8 oz)
- 15 ml (1 tbsp) olive oil
- 45-60 ml (3-4 tbsp) pinhead oatmeal
- 5 ml (1 tsp) dill seed

- finely grated rind and juice of 1 lemon
- salt and pepper
- ½ cucumber
- 1 Little Gem lettuce
- 50 g (2 oz) butter
- 30 ml (2 tbsp) finely chopped fresh dill leaves
- dill sprigs, to garnish

1 Rinse the herrings and pat dry with absorbent kitchen paper, then smear the fleshy surface of each fillet with olive oil. Line a grill rack with foil and arrange the fish flesh-side up on it.

2 Mix the oatmeal with the dill seed, grated lemon rind, and salt and pepper, then sprinkle the mixture evenly over the herring fillets. Pat down lightly to give a good coating.

3 Peel the cucumber, halve it lengthways and scoop out the seeds with a teaspoon. Cut each

MIXED SEAFOOD GRATIN

PREPARATION TIME 10 minutes
COOKING TIME 20 minutes
FREEZING Not suitable

🕐

SERVES 4
- *50 g (2 oz) butter*
- *50 g (2 oz) onion, peeled and roughly chopped*
- *2 garlic cloves, peeled and crushed*
- *15 ml (1 tbsp) white plain flour*
- *125 ml (4 fl oz) white wine*
- *50 ml (2 fl oz) milk*
- *225 g (8 oz) cod or haddock fillet, skinned and cut into cubes*
- *150 ml (5 fl oz) double cream*

800 CALS/SERVING
- *175 g (6 oz) Emmental cheese, grated*
- *225 g (8 oz) packet cooked mixed seafood*
- *125 g (4 oz) watercress, finely chopped*
- *salt and pepper*
- *50 g (2 oz) fresh breadcrumbs*
- *125 g (4 oz) plain tortilla chips, crumbled*

1 Melt the butter in a large saucepan, add the onion and garlic and sauté for 2-3 minutes. Add the flour and cook, stirring, for 1 minute. Pour in the wine and milk, and bring to the boil, stirring all the time.

2 Add the cod and simmer for 5-6 minutes. Add the cream and take off the heat.

3 Add 125 g (4 oz) grated cheese, the mixed seafood and watercress to the sauce. Season to taste. Place over a gentle heat and bring up to simmering point. Immediately, spoon into a shallow, ovenproof dish.

4 Mix the breadcrumbs, remaining cheese and tortilla chips together. Sprinkle over the fish then grill until golden and bubbling.

PAELLA WITH PEPPERS

PREPARATION TIME 15 minutes
COOKING TIME About 25 minutes
FREEZING Not suitable

SERVES 6

- 15-30 ml (1-2 tbsp) vegetable oil
- 175 g (6 oz) onion, peeled and thinly sliced
- 1 small red pepper, deseeded and chopped
- 1 small green pepper, deseeded and chopped
- 1 small yellow pepper, deseeded and chopped
- 225 g (8 oz) chicken breast fillet, chopped
- 300 g (10 oz) long-grain white rice
- 600 ml (1 pint) chicken stock

365 CALS/SERVING

- 225 g (8 oz) ripe tomatoes, skinned, deseeded and chopped
- finely grated rind and juice of 1 lemon
- pinch of saffron strands
- 350 g (12 oz) fish fillet, skinned and chopped
- salt and pepper
- 225 g (8 oz) packet cooked mixed seafood
- 125 g (4 oz) frozen peas
- lemon wedges and fresh parsley, to garnish

1 Heat the oil in a large sauté pan or flameproof casserole and fry the onion and peppers for 3-4 minutes until softened.
2 Using a slotted spoon, remove the vegetables, then add the chicken and the rice, with a little more oil if necessary. Cook, stirring, for 1-2 minutes.
3 Return the vegetables to the pan with the stock, tomatoes, lemon rind and juice and a pinch of

saffron. Bring to the boil and boil for 1 minute, then reduce the heat and add the fish. Season to taste.
4 Cover and simmer for about 15 minutes, or until the rice is almost tender, adding more stock if necessary (there should be little free liquid).
5 Stir the mixed seafood and peas into the rice. Cover the pan tightly and cook for a further 2-3 minutes or until all the fish is heated through. Adjust the seasoning, garnish and serve immediately.

COCONUT FISH PILAU

PREPARATION TIME 10 minutes
COOKING TIME 30 minutes
FREEZING Not suitable
COLOUR INDEX Page 16

SERVES 4

- 15 ml (1 tbsp) vegetable oil
- 125 g (4 oz) onion, peeled and roughly chopped
- 1 garlic clove, peeled and crushed
- 15 ml (1 tbsp) Thai green curry paste or Indian curry paste
- 225 g (8 oz) Thai fragrant rice or basmati rice
- 600 ml (1 pint) fish stock
- 150 ml (5 fl oz) coconut milk

375 CALS/SERVING

- 175 g (6 oz) cod fillet, skinned and cut into bite-sized pieces
- 125 g (4 oz) sugar snap peas, blanched
- 125 g (4 oz) cooked, peeled tiger prawns
- 25 g (1 oz) toasted almonds
- 15 ml (1 tbsp) lemon juice
- salt and pepper
- chopped fresh coriander, to garnish

1 Heat the oil in a large, non-stick frying pan and fry the onion and garlic for 4-5 minutes or until golden. Stir in the curry paste and cook, stirring, for 1-2 minutes.
2 Add the rice, stock and coconut milk. Bring to the boil. Cover and simmer gently for about 15 minutes, stirring occasionally with a fork.
3 When the rice is tender and all the liquid has been absorbed, add the cod. Cook for a further 3-5 minutes or until the fish is cooked through.
4 Stir in the sugar snap peas, prawns, almonds and lemon juice. Season. Heat through for about 1 minute then serve immediately, garnished with coriander.

STEAMED MUSSELS IN SAFFRON CREAM SAUCE

PREPARATION TIME 15 minutes
COOKING TIME 30 minutes
FREEZING Not suitable

SERVES 4-6

400-265 CALS/SERVING

- *1.4 kg (3 lb) fresh mussels*
- *25 g (1 oz) butter*
- *60 ml (4 tbsp) olive oil*
- *6 shallots, peeled and chopped*
- *3 garlic cloves, peeled and chopped*
- *2 leeks, trimmed and thinly sliced*
- *150 ml (5 fl oz) fish stock*
- *200 ml (7 fl oz) dry white wine*
- *good pinch of saffron strands*
- *150 ml (5 fl oz) single cream*
- *salt and pepper*
- *3 strips of lemon rind*
- *several coriander stalks*
- *30-45 ml (2-3 tbsp) mixed chopped fresh tarragon and coriander*
- *shredded leek to garnish (optional)*

1 Scrub the mussels and pull off the coarse threads (beards) from the side of the shells. Thoroughly rinse.

2 Heat the butter and half the oil in a frying pan and gently fry the shallots, garlic and leeks for 10 minutes, stirring occasionally.

3 Add the stock, 150 ml (5 fl oz) wine and the saffron, bring to the boil, then cover and simmer gently for 10 minutes. Cool slightly and purée in a blender or food processor. Transfer the sauce to a saucepan and add the cream. Reheat gently and season with salt and pepper.

4 Place the mussels in a large saucepan with the strips of lemon rind, coriander stalks, 45 ml (3 tbsp) water and remaining wine. Bring to the boil, cover and steam over a moderate heat for about 5 minutes or until the mussels have opened; shake the pan frequently during cooking.

5 Remove from the heat and discard any mussels that remain closed. Place the mussels in 4 or 6 warmed serving dishes. Strain the juices in the saucepan and add to the sauce. Heat through and pour over the mussels.

6 Scatter chopped herbs and shredded leek over the mussels and serve at once.

VARIATION Use onions rather than the leeks, if preferred. Although the mussels look attractive served in their shells, you may serve them 'shell-less' in the saffron flavoured liquor, if wished.

115

SAVOURY CRUMBED CHICKEN

PREPARATION TIME 10 minutes
COOKING TIME 45 minutes
FREEZING Not suitable

SERVES 4-6

480-320 CALS/SERVING

- *90 ml (6 tbsp) mayonnaise*
- *125 g (4 oz) spring onions, chopped*
- *45 ml (3 tbsp) chopped fresh thyme*
- *salt and pepper*
- *12 skinless chicken thighs, about 1.4 kg (3 lb) total weight, with bone*
- *75 g (3 oz) dry white breadcrumbs*
- *50 g (2 oz) butter, melted*
- *fresh thyme sprigs, to garnish*

1 Mix together the mayonnaise, spring onions, thyme and seasoning. Spread over the chicken, then roll in the breadcrumbs.
2 Place in a single layer in an ovenproof dish. Spoon over the butter.
3 Cook at 200°C (400°F) mark 6 for 45 minutes. Serve immediately or drain and serve cold, garnished with thyme.

HOT RED JUNGLE CURRY

PREPARATION TIME 10 minutes
COOKING TIME 15 minutes
FREEZING Not suitable
COLOUR INDEX Page 21
♡ ⏲

SERVES 4

200 CALS/SERVING

- *15 ml (1 tbsp) vegetable oil*
- *350 g (12 oz) skinless chicken breast fillet, cut into strips*
- *30 ml (2 tbsp) red curry paste*
- *125 g (4 oz) aubergine, cut into bite-sized pieces*
- *125 g (4 oz) baby sweetcorn, halved lengthways*
- *75 g (3 oz) green beans*
- *75 g (3 oz) button or brown-cap mushrooms, halved if necessary*
- *2-3 Kaffir lime leaves (optional)*
- *450 ml (15 fl oz) chicken stock*
- *2.5 cm (1 inch) piece fresh root ginger, peeled and finely sliced*
- *30 ml (2 tbsp) fish sauce*
- *grated rind of ½ lime*
- *5 ml (1 tsp) tomato purée*
- *15 ml (1 tbsp) soft brown sugar*
- *pared lime rind, to garnish*

1 Heat the oil in a wok or large sauté pan. Add the chicken and cook, stirring, for 5 minutes or until the chicken turns golden brown.
2 Stir in the red curry paste and cook for a further minute. Add the vegetables and lime leaves, if using, and stir until coated in the red curry paste.
3 Add all the remaining ingredients and bring to the boil. Simmer gently for 10-12 minutes or until the chicken and vegetables are just tender. Serve immediately, garnished with pared lime rind.

VARIATION Add a drained 227 g (8 oz) can of bamboo shoots with the other vegetables in stage 2 for extra texture.

CHICKEN BREASTS WITH SPINACH AND RICOTTA

PREPARATION TIME 30 minutes
COOKING TIME 35-45 minutes
FREEZING Not suitable

SERVES 4

- *4 skinless chicken breast fillets*
- *50 g (2 oz) frozen chopped spinach, thawed*
- *175 g (6 oz) ricotta cheese*
- *60 ml (4 tbsp) freshly grated Parmesan cheese*
- *freshly grated nutmeg*

400 CALS/SERVING

- *salt and pepper*
- *8 large fresh spinach leaves*
- *150 ml (5 fl oz) dry white wine*
- *300 ml (10 fl oz) chicken stock*
- *50 g (2 oz) butter, chilled and diced*

1 Using a sharp knife, make a deep horizontal slit in each chicken breast through the thicker side, to make a pocket.

2 Squeeze the moisture out of the thawed spinach, then place in a bowl. Add the ricotta, Parmesan and plenty of nutmeg, salt and pepper. Mix well, then spoon the filling evenly into the chicken pockets.

3 Bring a saucepan of salted water to the boil and add the spinach leaves. Immediately remove with a slotted spoon and plunge into a bowl of cold water to set the colour and prevent further cooking. Wrap two spinach leaves around each chicken breast. Tie with thin cotton string to secure.

4 Lay the chicken breasts in a wide shallow pan or flameproof casserole and pour in the wine and stock. Bring to the boil, lower the heat, cover and simmer gently for 30-40 minutes until cooked. Remove from the pan with a slotted spoon and keep warm.

5 Boil the cooking liquid rapidly until reduced by half. Take off the heat and whisk in the diced butter. Adjust the seasoning.

6 To serve, slice the chicken breasts and arrange on warmed serving plates with a little sauce. Serve the remaining sauce separately.

VARIATION Another type of curd cheese or soft cream cheese can be used in place of the ricotta.

HERB MARINATED CHICKEN WITH SPRING VEGETABLES IN A WARM DRESSING

PREPARATION TIME 20 minutes, plus marinating
COOKING TIME 50-55 minutes
FREEZING Not suitable

SERVES 4

- 60 ml (4 tbsp) extra-virgin olive oil
- 25 g (1 oz) chopped mixed spring herbs
- 1 garlic clove, peeled and crushed
- 4 spring onions, chopped
- 60 ml (4 tbsp) dry white wine
- 4 large chicken breast fillets, with skin, each weighing about 150 g (5 oz)
- 225 g (8 oz) baby new potatoes, scrubbed and halved if large

510 CALS/SERVING

- 175 g (6 oz) baby carrots, scrubbed
- 175 g (6 oz) mangetout, trimmed

DRESSING

- 30 ml (2 tbsp) extra-virgin olive oil
- 15 ml (1 tbsp) balsamic vinegar
- 4 ripe tomatoes, skinned, deseeded and diced
- 10 ml (2 tsp) sun-dried tomato paste
- salt and pepper

1 Heat 45 ml (3 tbsp) oil in a small frying pan, add the herbs, garlic and spring onions and heat gently for 3 minutes. Do not allow the oil to get too hot and burn the herbs. Set aside until cold, then stir in the wine.

2 Wash and dry the chicken. Place in a shallow baking dish and pour over the cooled herb marinade. Cover and leave to marinate for 4 hours or overnight. Remove the chicken 1 hour before cooking.

3 Briskly fry the chicken breasts in the remaining oil for a few minutes to brown the skin.

4 Place the chicken in an ovenproof dish, cover with foil and bake in the oven at 180°C (350°F) mark 4 for 40-45 minutes.

5 Meanwhile, cook the potatoes in lightly salted boiling water for 10-12 minutes until just cooked, adding the carrots after 6 minutes and the mangetout after 8 minutes. Drain the vegetables and keep warm.

6 Remove the chicken from the oven, and strain off the cooking juices, reserving 30 ml (2 tbsp). Keep the chicken warm.

7 Place the dressing ingredients and reserved chicken juices in a small pan, heat gently until just boiling, then remove from the heat. Arrange the vegetables on serving plates, top with the chicken and spoon over the dressing. Serve at once.

SPRING CHICKEN FRICASSEE

PREPARATION TIME 20 minutes
COOKING TIME 35 minutes
FREEZING Not suitable
COLOUR INDEX Page 20

SERVES 4 · **650 CALS/SERVING**

- 225 g (8 oz) cauliflower florets
- 225 g (8 oz) broccoli florets
- salt and pepper
- 225 g (8 oz) full-fat soft cheese with garlic and herbs
- 8 chicken breast fillets with skin, about 800 g (1¾ lb) total weight
- 15 ml (1 tbsp) white plain flour
- about 30 ml (2 tbsp) vegetable oil
- 225 g (8 oz) baby carrots, cut into fingers
- 225 g (8 oz) button onions, peeled and halved
- 100 ml (3½ fl oz) dry vermouth
- 300 ml (10 fl oz) chicken stock
- 30 ml (2 tbsp) chopped fresh tarragon or 2.5 ml (½ tsp) dried
- 1 garlic clove, peeled and crushed
- 60 ml (4 tbsp) single cream
- carrot tops, to garnish

1 Blanch the cauliflower and broccoli in salted water for 1-2 minutes only, then drain.
2 Push a little of the soft cheese underneath the skin of each chicken breast and tuck the ends of the breast under to form small, neat rounds. Toss in the flour.
3 Heat the oil in a shallow flameproof casserole. Brown the chicken pieces a few at a time, adding more oil as necessary. Remove with a slotted spoon. Add the carrots and onions to the casserole and brown lightly.
4 Return the chicken to the pan and pour in the vermouth and stock. Bring to the boil, stirring in the tarragon, garlic and seasoning.
5 Cover tightly and simmer gently for about 10 minutes. Stir in the cauliflower and broccoli and cook for another 10 minutes or until the chicken is cooked through.
6 Stir in the cream and simmer for 1-2 minutes. Adjust the seasoning and serve garnished with carrot tops. Accompany with rice.

COUNTRY CHICKEN CASSEROLE

PREPARATION TIME 10 minutes
COOKING TIME 1½ hours
FREEZING Suitable
COLOUR INDEX Page 21
❄

SERVES 4 · **405 CALS/SERVING**

- about 30 ml (2 tbsp) vegetable oil
- 175 g (6 oz) lightly smoked streaky bacon, roughly chopped
- 4 chicken quarters, about 700 g (1½ lb) total weight
- 225 g (8 oz) button onions, peeled and halved if large
- 1 garlic clove, peeled and crushed
- 225 g (8 oz) brown-cap mushrooms, thickly sliced
- 20 g (¾ oz) white plain flour
- 300 ml (10 fl oz) chicken stock
- 300 ml (10 fl oz) white wine
- salt and pepper

1 Gently heat the oil in a large, shallow, flameproof casserole. Add the bacon and fry until golden. Drain on absorbent kitchen paper. Brown the chicken, adding a little more oil if necessary. Drain on absorbent kitchen paper.
2 Sauté the onions and garlic for 2-3 minutes, then add the mushrooms for a further 2 minutes. Stir in the flour until smooth.
3 Off the heat, stir in the stock and wine and season generously. Bring to the boil and replace the bacon and chicken. Cover and cook at 170°C (325°F) mark 3 for 1¼ hours or until tender.

WARM ASPARAGUS AND CHICKEN SALAD

PREPARATION TIME 15 minutes
COOKING TIME 10 minutes
FREEZING Not suitable
🕒

SERVES 4

- *2 large chicken breast fillets, skinned*
- *225 g (8 oz) thin asparagus, trimmed*
- *slivers of fresh Parmesan cheese, to garnish*
DRESSING
- *about 120 ml (8 tbsp) virgin olive oil*
- *20 ml (1½ tbsp) red or white wine vinegar*
- *2 sun-dried tomatoes, finely chopped*

420 CALS/SERVING

- *15 ml (1 tbsp) capers, finely chopped*
- *about 8 pitted black olives, finely chopped*
- *1 small garlic clove, peeled and finely chopped*
- *large pinch of sugar*
- *salt and pepper*

1 To make the dressing, whisk 105 ml (7 tbsp) of the olive oil with the wine vinegar to make a thick dressing. Stir in the rest of the dressing ingredients, seasoning to taste with pepper and a little salt.

2 Beat the chicken breasts between two sheets of clingfilm to flatten thoroughly. Heat a heavy-based ridged frying pan or griddle pan and brush with olive oil. Cook the chicken for 3-4 minutes on each side until golden on the outside and cooked right through. Cut into neat serving pieces and set aside.

3 Meanwhile, tie the asparagus in a bundle with string. Bring a 7.5 cm (3 inch) depth of salted water to the boil in a small saucepan. Stand the bundle of asparagus in the pan, tips uppermost, and cover with a piece of foil. Cook for 5 minutes or until the asparagus is just tender. Drain thoroughly.

4 Arrange the asparagus and chicken on individual plates. Pour on the dressing and scatter with Parmesan. Serve while still warm.

NOTE This refreshing, warm salad makes an ideal light lunch dish, served with garlic bread. For a more substantial dinner party main course, double up the quantities.

FRENCH ROAST CHICKEN

PREPARATION TIME 10 minutes
COOKING TIME About 1¼-1½ hours
FREEZING Not suitable
COLOUR INDEX Page 19

SERVES 4

- *1.4 kg (3 lb) roasting chicken, with giblets*
- *1 carrot, peeled*
- *1 onion, peeled*
- *1 bouquet garni*
- *140 g (4½ oz) butter*
- *2 fresh tarragon sprigs*

470 CALS/SERVING

- *½ lemon*
- *6 garlic cloves*
- *salt and pepper*
- *10 ml (2 tsp) white plain flour*

1 Remove the giblets from the chicken and put them in a saucepan with the carrot, onion, bouquet garni and 600 ml (1 pint) water. Bring to the boil, then cover and simmer for 1 hour while the chicken is cooking.

2 Melt 125 g (4 oz) of the butter. Put the tarragon and lemon inside the chicken. Lay the bird on its side on a rack in a roasting tin. Brush the uppermost side with butter. Roast in the oven at 200°C (400°F) mark 6 for 20 minutes. Turn the

chicken onto the other side, brush with more butter and roast for a further 20 minutes.

3 Turn the chicken again so that the breast is uppermost. Brush with more butter. Scatter the garlic cloves in the base of the roasting tin. Cook the chicken for a further 40 minutes, or until the juices run clear when pierced with a skewer. Rest the chicken for 10 minutes.

4 To make the gravy, skim off excess fat from the roasting tin. Lift out the garlic cloves, remove the skins and return to the tin; mash with a fork. Strain the giblet stock into the pan and bring to the boil.

5 Blend together the remaining butter and the flour. Whisk a small piece at a time into the gravy. Simmer for a few minutes, whisking. Season to taste. Serve the chicken accompanied by the gravy.

CINNAMON ROAST POUSSIN WITH COUSCOUS

PREPARATION TIME 30 minutes
COOKING TIME 50-55 minutes
FREEZING Not suitable

SERVES 4

720 CALS/SERVING

- 250 g (9 oz) couscous
- 4 small spatch-cocked poussins, each weighing about 400 g (14 oz)
- 5 ml (1 tsp) ground turmeric
- 5 ml (1 tsp) ground cinnamon
- 125 g (4 oz) butter
- salt and pepper
- about 60 ml (4 tbsp) clear honey
- large pinch of saffron strands
- 2 onions, peeled and sliced
- 1 garlic clove, peeled and chopped
- 50 g (2 oz) pistachio nuts
- grated rind and juice of 1 lemon
- chopped parsley, to garnish
- lemon wedges, to serve

1 Put the couscous in a bowl and pour over 350 ml (12 fl oz) cold water. Leave to soak for about 15 minutes or until all of the water has been absorbed.

2 Place the poussins in two roasting tins. Sprinkle with the turmeric and cinnamon. Melt 40 g (1½ oz) of the butter and brush over the poussins. Season with salt and pepper. Roast in the oven at 200°C (400°F) mark 6 for 20 minutes. Reduce the temperature to 190°C (375°F) mark 5 and cook for a further 15 minutes. Brush with a little honey and cook for 15-20 minutes more or until cooked right through.

3 Meanwhile, add the saffron to a little boiling water, then mix with the soaked couscous. Spoon into a large muslin-lined metal sieve and steam over a pan of boiling water for about 35 minutes or until the grains are light and fluffy.

4 Remove the poussins from the roasting tins; cover with foil and keep warm. Tip all the juices into one pan, add the onions and garlic and cook quickly over a high heat until browned and softened. Add the nuts, lemon rind and juice and the remaining butter. Add the couscous and mix carefully with a fork. Season with salt and pepper.

5 Pile the couscous onto a large serving platter. Put the poussins on top and garnish with chopped parsley and lemon wedges.

NOTE For extra flavour, serve with Harissa sauce which is available in cans from larger supermarkets and delicatessens.

LEMON AND GINGER POUSSINS WITH ONIONS

PREPARATION TIME 15 minutes, plus marinating
COOKING TIME 45 minutes
FREEZING Not suitable
COLOUR INDEX Page 22

SERVES 6

555 CALS/SERVING

- grated rind and juice of 6 lemons
- 5 cm (2 inch) piece fresh root ginger, peeled and finely chopped
- 120 ml (8 tbsp) clear honey
- 150 ml (5 fl oz) vegetable oil
- 1 stalk lemon grass, split (optional)
- salt and pepper
- 3 oven-ready poussins, each weighing about 450 g (1 lb)
- 900 g (2 lb) onions, peeled and sliced
- 75 g (3 oz) soft light brown sugar
- slices of lemon, to garnish

1 Whisk together the lemon rind and juice, ginger, honey and oil. Add the split lemon grass if using. Season with salt and pepper. Halve the poussins lengthways and place in a non-metallic dish. Pour over the marinade, cover and refrigerate for at least 12 hours.

2 Place the poussins with half the marinade in a roasting tin, discard the lemon grass. Bake at 200°C (400°F) mark 6 for 45 minutes or until tender, basting occasionally.

3 Meanwhile, heat the remaining marinade in a sauté pan. Add the onions and sugar and bring to the boil, then simmer for about 35 minutes, stirring occasionally, until the onions soften and caramelize.

4 Lift the poussins into a serving dish, cover and keep warm. Bubble down the cooking juices to reduce them.

5 Serve the poussins on a bed of onions with the juices spooned over, and top with lemon slices.

GUINEA FOWL WITH ROCKET SAUCE AND SPRING VEGETABLES

PREPARATION TIME 20 minutes
COOKING TIME 1¼-1½ hours
FREEZING Not suitable
COLOUR INDEX Page 23

SERVES 6

515 CALS/SERVING

- 75 g (3 oz) butter
- 30 ml (2 tbsp) olive oil
- 2 guinea fowl
- 450 g (1 lb) very small new potatoes, scrubbed
- 2 garlic cloves, peeled
- 300 ml (10 fl oz) dry white wine
- 8 baby leeks, about 125 g (4 oz) total weight
- 225 g (8 oz) small new carrots
- 125 g (4 oz) broad beans, skinned
- 125 g (4 oz) peas
- 50 g (2 oz) rocket leaves
- 150 ml (5 fl oz) double cream
- salt and pepper
- chervil, to garnish

1 Heat 50 g (2 oz) of the butter with the oil in a large frying pan and cook the guinea fowl until browned. Arrange the potatoes and garlic in a casserole. Put the guinea fowl on top. Pour in the wine and 450 ml (15 fl oz) water.

2 Cover with a tight-fitting lid and cook at 200°C (400°F) mark 6 for 45 minutes. Add the leeks, carrots, broad beans and peas. Re-cover and cook for 30-45 minutes until the guinea fowl are cooked.

3 Remove the guinea fowl and vegetables from the casserole and keep warm. Skim off any excess fat from the cooking liquid, then pour into a measuring jug. Make up to 600 ml (1 pint) with stock or water if necessary. Put in a food processor with the rocket and cooked garlic cloves and process until smooth. Put the purée in the casserole.

4 Reheat the rocket purée, add the cream and season with salt and pepper to taste. Bring to the boil, then gradually whisk in the remaining butter a little at a time to make a thin, shiny sauce.

5 Carve the guinea fowl and serve with the vegetables and sauce.

VARIATIONS Replace the rocket with sorrel, but halve the quantity. Alternatively, make the sauce with watercress.

PAN-FRIED TURKEY WITH LEMON AND HAZELNUTS

PREPARATION TIME 15 minutes
COOKING TIME About 10 minutes
FREEZING Not suitable

SERVES 4

- 8 turkey escalopes, each weighing about 75 g (3 oz)
- 2 eggs, beaten
- 175 g (6 oz) finely chopped hazelnuts
- 75 g (3 oz) butter
- lemon wedges, to garnish

SAUCE

- 125 ml (4 fl oz) dry white wine

790 CALS/SERVING

- 30 ml (2 tbsp) lemon juice
- 15 ml (1 tbsp) chopped fresh tarragon or parsley
- salt and pepper
- 75 g (3 oz) butter, diced

1 Place the turkey escalopes between two sheets of greaseproof paper, and beat with a rolling pin, until about half the original thickness.
2 Dip the escalopes in the beaten egg, then press into the hazelnuts, coating all sides.
3 Heat the butter in a large frying pan until foaming, add the turkey and fry for about 1½ minutes on each side, until golden brown. Remove from the pan and keep warm.
4 To make the sauce, add the wine to the hot pan and boil rapidly until reduced by half. Add the lemon juice and tarragon and season to taste. Remove from the heat and gradually whisk in the diced butter to thicken the sauce slightly. Adjust the seasoning and pour over the turkey. Serve immediately, garnished with lemon wedges.

NOTE Turkey escalopes are sold in larger supermarkets; if unavailable, use thin slices of breast meat.

RICH BEEF DAUBE

PREPARATION TIME 15 minutes
COOKING TIME 2½ hours
FREEZING Suitable
❋

SERVES 6

- *900 g (2 lb) stewing steak, cut into 2.5 cm (1 inch) cubes*
- *salt and pepper*
- *30 ml (2 tbsp) olive oil*
- *45 ml (3 tbsp) plain flour*
- *2 garlic cloves, peeled and crushed*
- *2.5 cm (1 inch) piece fresh root ginger, peeled and chopped*
- *125 g (4 oz) sun-dried tomatoes, chopped*
- *45 ml (3 tbsp) chopped fresh mixed oregano, marjoram, thyme or 10 ml (2 tsp) dried mixed herbs*

600 CALS/SERVING

- *50 g (2 oz) dried wild mushrooms, such as porcini, soaked in 150 ml (5 fl oz) water*
- *300 ml (10 fl oz) red wine*
- *300 ml (10 fl oz) beef stock*
- *2 oranges*
- *225 g (8 oz) shallots or button onions, peeled*
- *15 ml (1 tbsp) caster sugar*
- *400 g (14 oz) can flageolet or borlotti beans, drained and rinsed*
- *125 g (4 oz) black olives, pitted*
- *50 g (2 oz) basil leaves, chopped*

1 Season the meat well with black pepper. Heat the oil in a large flameproof casserole and brown the meat in batches over a brisk heat.

2 Return all the meat to the casserole and stir in the flour, garlic, ginger, sun-dried tomatoes and herbs. Cook, stirring, for 1 minute.

3 Add the wild mushrooms with soaking liquid, wine, stock, pared rind of 1 orange and about 125 ml (4 fl oz) orange juice, shallots and sugar. Bring to the boil, then cover and cook at 170°C (325°F) mark 3 for about 2 hours or until tender.

4 Remove from the oven and add the beans and olives. Return to the oven for 15-20 minutes. Season to taste. Before serving, stir in the basil.

TIP

To remove skins from shallots, pour over boiling water to cover; leave for 5-10 minutes. Drain and remove the skin (it should easily peel away). To prevent shallots from falling apart, leave the root ends intact.

ITALIAN MEATLOAF

PREPARATION TIME 20 minutes
COOKING TIME 1 hour
FREEZING Suitable (stage 4)
Freeze crumb mixture separately
COLOUR INDEX Page 26

❄

SERVES 8

- *vegetable oil*
- *125 g (4 oz) chorizo or Italian sausage, finely diced*
- *175 g (6 oz) red onion, peeled and finely diced*
- *450 g (1 lb) lean minced beef*
- *2 garlic cloves, peeled and crushed*
- *75 ml (5 tbsp) chopped fresh parsley*
- *150 g (5 oz) fresh white breadcrumbs*

420 CALS/SERVING

- *2 eggs and 1 egg yolk*
- *150 ml (5 fl oz) passata*
- *salt and pepper*
- *75 g (3 oz) Cheddar cheese, grated*
- *50 g (2 oz) Roquefort cheese or any other soft blue cheese, crumbled*
- *150 ml (5 fl oz) single cream*
- *125 g (4 oz) sliced white bread, crusts removed, diced*

1 Mark a rectangle measuring 43 x 35.5 cm (17 x 14 inches) on a piece of foil and brush with oil.
2 Add the sausage and onion to the mince with the garlic, 60 ml (4 tbsp) parsley, 125 g (4 oz) breadcrumbs, the whole eggs, passata and seasoning. Knead well until the mixture is quite smooth. Spread over the foil, leaving a 2.5 cm (1 inch) border.
3 Mix the Cheddar cheese into the crumbled Roquefort. Set aside 25 g (1 oz) cheese and mix with the remaining 25 g (1 oz) breadcrumbs and 15 ml (1 tbsp) parsley for the topping.
4 Bring the cream to the boil and pour over the bread. Add the Cheddar and Roquefort and the egg yolk, and beat with a fork until well mixed. Spread over the meat. Roll up from the shorter side, using the foil as an aid. Place seam-side down on a lightly oiled non-stick, edged baking sheet or roasting tin; remove foil.
5 Bake at 180°C (350°F) mark 4 for about 1 hour. Sprinkle the reserved cheese and crumb mixture over the top and return to the oven for about a further 15 minutes or until the topping is well browned. Allow the meatloaf to sit for 5 minutes before cutting into thick slices, then serve immediately.

SPICY BURGERS

PREPARATION TIME 15 minutes
COOKING TIME 10 minutes
FREEZING Suitable (stage 1)

♡ ⏱ ❄

SERVES 4

- *3 spring onions, chopped*
- *450 g (1 lb) lean minced beef*
- *1 garlic clove, peeled and crushed*
- *15 ml (1 tbsp) ground coriander*
- *15 ml (1 tbsp) ground cumin*
- *1 egg, beaten*
- *30 ml (2 tbsp) chopped fresh parsley*

230 CALS/SERVING

- *30 ml (2 tbsp) chopped fresh coriander*
- *15 ml (1 tbsp) Tabasco or chilli sauce*
- *salt and pepper*
- *vegetable oil for brushing*
- *pitta bread, fried onions, roast peppers, cucumber slices and mint leaves, to serve*

1 Mix together the first ten ingredients, beating well. Divide into 8 burgers.
2 Brush lightly with oil and grill or fry for about 5 minutes on each side or until cooked through. Serve in pitta bread with fried onions, roast peppers, cucumber slices and mint leaves.

ROAST LAMB WITH A CREAMY FENNEL SAUCE

PREPARATION TIME 20 minutes
COOKING TIME 25-30 minutes
FREEZING Not suitable
COLOUR INDEX Page 26

SERVES 6

- *2 racks of lamb, each weighing about 575 g (1¼ lb), prepared weight*
- *salt and pepper*
- *olive oil, to drizzle*
- *700 g (1½ lb) Florence fennel*
- *5 ml (1 tsp) fennel seeds*

365 CALS/SERVING

- *40 g (1½ oz) butter*
- *300 ml (10 fl oz) lamb or beef stock*
- *90 ml (6 tbsp) double cream*
- *rosemary sprigs, to garnish (optional)*

1 Trim the lamb of any excess fat and divide each rack into three. Season the lamb and place in a roasting tin. Drizzle with olive oil.
2 Roast the lamb at 200°C (400°F) mark 6 for about 25 minutes for medium rare, about 30 minutes for well done.
3 Meanwhile, trim the feathery tops from the fennel and reserve for garnishing. Slice the fennel, discarding the core. Crush the fennel seeds with the end of a rolling pin.
4 Melt the butter in a frying pan, add the fennel slices and fennel seeds and fry gently for about 10 minutes until the fennel has softened. Add the stock, bring to the boil and simmer gently for 2 minutes. Stir in the cream and simmer until beginning to thicken.
5 Chop the reserved fennel tops, then sprinkle over the lamb. Serve, garnished with rosemary if wished, and accompanied by the sauce.

ROAST EYE FILLET OF LAMB WITH CANDIED LEMONS

PREPARATION TIME 15 minutes, plus marinating
COOKING TIME 35 minutes
FREEZING Not suitable
COLOUR INDEX Page 27

SERVES 8

- *4 small, thin-skinned lemons*
- *3 fillets of lamb, about 1.4 kg (3 lb) total weight*
- *sprigs of fresh thyme, rosemary and bay leaves, to garnish*

MARINADE

- *30 ml (2 tbsp) chopped fresh rosemary*

425 CALS/SERVING

- *2 bay leaves*
- *2 garlic cloves, peeled and crushed*
- *2.5 cm (1 inch) piece fresh root ginger, peeled and thinly sliced*
- *150 ml (5 fl oz) clear honey*
- *75 ml (5 tbsp) vegetable oil*
- *salt and pepper*

1 Mix together all the marinade ingredients. Add the strained juice of 2 of the lemons. Place the remaining 2 lemons in a small saucepan and cover with cold water. Bring to the boil, cover and simmer for 7-10 minutes or until just beginning to soften. Cool and cut into thickish slices, discarding any pips.
2 Place the lamb fillets in a shallow, non-metallic dish, add the lemon slices and the marinade, cover and leave in the refrigerator overnight.
3 Remove the lamb from the marinade and place in a shallow roasting tin. Roast at 220°C (425°F) mark 7 for 20-25 minutes. This produces a medium rare roast.
4 About 5 minutes before the end of cooking time, bring the marinade and lemon slices to the boil in a small saucepan. Simmer, stirring occasionally for about 5 minutes or until syrupy. Carefully add any pan juices from the lamb. Adjust the seasoning.
5 Serve the lamb thickly sliced with the candied lemon slices. Pour over the remaining honey sauce and garnish with sprigs of fresh thyme, rosemary and bay leaves.

BONED AND STUFFED SHOULDER
OF LAMB

PREPARATION TIME 20 minutes
COOKING TIME 1¾ hours
FREEZING Not suitable

SERVES 6

- *2 large slices white bread, crusts removed*
- *few sprigs fresh thyme*
- *few sprigs fresh parsley*
- *50 g (2 oz) shelled pistachio nuts*
- *175 g (6 oz) no-soak pitted prunes*
- *50 g (2 oz) no-soak dried apricots*
- *50 g (2 oz) butter*

600 CALS/SERVING

- *225 g (8 oz) onion, peeled and finely chopped*
- *1.25 ml (¼ tsp) freshly grated nutmeg*
- *salt and pepper*
- *1.4 kg (3 lb) boned shoulder or leg of lamb*
- *150 ml (5 fl oz) red wine*
- *fresh herbs, to garnish*

1 Place the bread, the leaves from the thyme and parsley and the nuts in a food processor and blend for about 1 minute or until finely chopped. Transfer to a bowl. Put 50 g (2 oz) prunes into the processor – reserve the remainder – with the apricots and finely chop. Stir into the crumb mixture.

2 Melt the butter in a small saucepan and sauté the onion until soft and transparent, stirring occasionally. Stir into the crumb mixture with the nutmeg and seasoning. Mix well and cool.

3 Unroll the shoulder of lamb. Spoon the stuffing into the lamb, roll up again and tie at regular intervals – don't worry if a little of the stuffing begins to ooze out.

4 Place the lamb in a dry roasting tin and cook at 200°C (400°F) mark 6 for about 1½ hours, basting occasionally, until the meat is golden and the juices run pale pink when it is pierced with a skewer. Allow an extra 10-15 minutes if you prefer lamb well done. Place the lamb on a heated serving dish, cover and keep warm.

5 Drain off most of the fat from the roasting tin, then add the wine with 300 ml (10 fl oz) water. Bring to the boil, scraping all sediment off the base of the pan. Strain into a small saucepan. Add the reserved prunes and simmer for about 5 minutes. Adjust the seasoning and serve with the sliced lamb. Garnish with fresh herbs.

minutes or until well reduced. Stir in the herb mixture and adjust the seasoning. Place the lamb steaks on top. Bring back to the boil.
4 Cover and bake at 170°C (325°F) mark 3 for about 40 minutes or until the lamb is tender.
5 Meanwhile, crush the remaining garlic clove and mix together with the lime and lemon rind. Sprinkle over the steaks. Cover and cook for a further 10 minutes. Adjust the seasoning before serving.

SPICY LAMB CASSEROLE

PREPARATION TIME 20 minutes
COOKING TIME 1¾ hours
FREEZING Suitable
COLOUR INDEX Page 27
❄

LAMB STEAKS IN HERBY TOMATO SAUCE

PREPARATION TIME 10 minutes
COOKING TIME 1 hour
FREEZING Not suitable

SERVES 4

390 CALS/SERVING

- 12 sprigs fresh mixed herbs, such as oregano, parsley, rosemary
- 3 garlic cloves, peeled
- 30 ml (2 tbsp) olive oil
- 4 lamb steaks, each weighing about 175 g (6 oz)
- 225 g (8 oz) onion, peeled and finely chopped
- 400 g (14 oz) can chopped tomatoes
- 30 ml (2 tbsp) white wine
- 7.5 ml (1½ tsp) sugar
- salt and pepper
- grated rind of 1 lime and 1 lemon

1 Strip the herbs off their stalks and place the leaves in a food processor with two of the garlic cloves. Blend until roughly chopped.
2 Heat the oil in a flameproof casserole that has a tight-fitting lid. Brown the steaks on both sides. Using slotted spoons, remove from the pan.
3 Add the onion to the pan and sauté until soft and beginning to brown. Stir in the tomatoes, white wine and sugar. Simmer, uncovered, for 3-4

SERVES 6

490 CALS/SERVING

- 30-45 ml (2-3 tbsp) vegetable oil
- 1.4 kg (3 lb) diced lamb
- 175 g (6 oz) onion, peeled and sliced
- 2 red peppers, deseeded and sliced
- 7.5 cm (3 inch) piece fresh root ginger, peeled and finely sliced
- 1 small red chilli, deseeded and finely chopped
- 10 ml (2 tsp) mild curry powder
- 5 ml (1 tsp) ground cumin
- 5 ml (1 tsp) ground paprika
- 30 ml (2 tbsp) white plain flour
- 600 ml (1 pint) chicken stock
- 75 g (3 oz) creamed block coconut, coarsely grated
- salt and pepper

1 Heat 30 ml (2 tbsp) oil in a large flameproof casserole. Brown the lamb in batches, adding a little more oil if necessary. Remove from the casserole, using slotted spoons.
2 Add the onion, peppers, ginger and chilli to the casserole with a little more oil if necessary. Sauté for 2-3 minutes or until beginning to soften, stirring occasionally.
3 Mix the spices and flour into the casserole and continue cooking for a further 1-2 minutes, stirring all the time. Return the lamb to the casserole, then add the stock, coconut and seasoning. Bring to the boil, stirring well to mix.
4 Cover the casserole and cook at 170°C (325°F) mark 3 for about 1½ hours or until the lamb is tender. Skim and adjust the seasoning.

MOUSSAKA

PREPARATION TIME 30 minutes
COOKING TIME 1½ hours
FREEZING Suitable (stage 4)

❊

SERVES 6

490 CALS/SERVING

- *45 ml (3 tbsp) vegetable oil*
- *175 g (6 oz) onion, peeled and chopped*
- *450 g (1 lb) lean minced lamb*
- *400 g (14 oz) can chopped tomatoes*
- *1.25 ml (¼ tsp) ground cinnamon*
- *5 ml (1 tsp) dried oregano*
- *salt and pepper*
- *900 g (2 lb) aubergines, sliced*
- *75 g (3 oz) butter*
- *75 g (3 oz) white plain flour*
- *568 ml (1 pint) warm milk*
- *25 g (1 oz) grated Parmesan cheese*
- *1 egg yolk*
- *30 ml (2 tbsp) fresh breadcrumbs*

1 Heat 30 ml (2 tbsp) oil in a large, heavy-based frying pan, and fry the onion until soft. Stir in the meat and fry until it changes colour. Add the next 3 ingredients, then season to taste. Cover and cook for 20 minutes or until all liquid has evaporated.

2 Brush the aubergine slices with oil and grill until golden on both sides. Drain on absorbent kitchen paper and season.

3 Melt the butter in a saucepan, stir in the flour, remove from the heat and whisk in the milk. Return to the heat and keep whisking for about 3-4 minutes or until it forms a thick sauce. Remove from the heat, cool slightly, then beat in half the cheese and the egg yolk. Season to taste.

4 Place the seasoned aubergines in a 2.8 litre (5 pint) shallow, ovenproof dish. Spread the meat mixture on top and cover with the sauce. Sprinkle over the remaining cheese and the breadcrumbs.

5 Cook at 180°C (350°F) mark 4 for about 1 hour or until golden.

VARIATION This classic Greek dish is also delicious made with lean minced beef instead of lamb.

KIDNEYS IN SHERRY SAUCE

PREPARATION TIME 15 minutes
COOKING TIME About 25 minutes
FREEZING Not suitable
COLOUR INDEX Page 28

SERVES 4   445 CALS/SERVING
- *16 lambs' kidneys,*   - *45 ml (3 tbsp) white*
  about 900 g (2 lb)   *plain flour*
  total weight   - *350 ml (12 fl oz) dry*
- *salt and pepper*   *sherry*
- *30 ml (2 tbsp) olive*   - *350 ml (12 fl oz)*
  oil   *beef stock*
- *2 onions, peeled and*   - *chopped fresh*
  finely chopped   *parsley, to garnish*
- *2 garlic cloves,*
  peeled and crushed
- *30 ml (2 tbsp)*
  chopped fresh
  parsley

1 Cut the kidneys in half. Remove the cores and
fat, then cut each in half again. Sprinkle with salt
and pepper.
2 Heat the oil in a large frying pan and fry the
kidneys over a high heat for 1 minute. Transfer to
a warm dish. Using the same pan, add the onion,
garlic and parsley and gently fry until soft. Stir in
the flour and cook for 1 minute. Add the sherry
and stock, stirring continuously until thickened
and smooth. Cover and simmer gently for 10
minutes.
3 Return the kidneys to the pan and simmer for a
further 5-10 minutes. Serve hot, garnished with
chopped parsley.

TIP
Be careful not to overcook the kidneys or they
will become tough. The insides should be just
pale pink. If you prefer a smooth sauce, sieve
the sauce before returning the kidneys to the
pan in stage 3.

STIR-FRIED PORK

PREPARATION TIME 15 minutes, plus marinating
COOKING TIME 20 minutes
FREEZING Not suitable
COLOUR INDEX Page 30
♡

SERVES 4   130 CALS/SERVING
- *350 g (12 oz) pork*   - *125 g (4 oz) baby*
  fillet, cut into 2.5 cm   *sweetcorn, halved*
  (1 inch) strips   *lengthways*
- *2 garlic cloves,*   - *125 g (4 oz) Chinese*
  peeled and crushed   *leaves, roughly*
- *10 ml (2 tsp) light*   *chopped*
  soy sauce   - *50 g (2 oz)*
- *10 ml (2 tsp) dry*   *beansprouts*
  sherry   - *4 spring onions,*
- *10 ml (2 tsp)*   *roughly chopped*
  demerara sugar   - *60 ml (4 tbsp)*
- *2.5 ml (½ tsp)*   *chopped fresh*
  Chinese five-spice   *coriander*
  powder   - *salt and pepper*
- *125 g (4 oz) Basmati*   - *coriander sprigs, to*
  rice   *garnish*
- *15 ml (1 tbsp)*
  sesame oil
- *125 g (4 oz) red*
  pepper, deseeded and
  cut into strips

1 Mix together the pork, garlic, soy sauce, sherry,
sugar and five-spice powder. Cover and leave to
marinate in the refrigerator for at least 30 minutes
or overnight.
2 Cook the rice in boiling water for 10-12
minutes. Drain and rinse in cold water.
3 Heat the oil in a large, heavy-based frying pan
or wok until smoking. Remove the pork from the
marinade and stir-fry in batches for 1-2 minutes or
until pale golden.
4 Add the red pepper, baby corn and Chinese
leaves to the pan and stir-fry for 1-2 minutes.
Return the pork with the rice and marinade and
stir-fry for about 4 minutes. Stir in the
beansprouts, spring onions and coriander, and
season to taste. Garnish with sprigs of coriander
and serve.

ROAST PORK WITH APPLE GRAVY

PREPARATION TIME 15 minutes, plus marinating
COOKING TIME 1½-1¾ hours
FREEZING Not suitable

SERVES 6

- 4 garlic cloves, peeled and finely chopped
- 5 long sprigs rosemary, finely chopped
- about 90 ml (6 tbsp) olive oil
- rock salt and pepper
- 1.7-1.8 kg (3½-4 lb) boneless leg, loin or shoulder of pork

515 CALS/SERVING

GRAVY

- 1 shallot, peeled and finely chopped
- 1 small eating apple, peeled, cored and finely chopped
- 600 ml (1 pint) unsweetened apple juice
- 300 ml (10 fl oz) dry cider
- ½ onion stock cube

1 Mix the garlic and rosemary with 30 ml (2 tbsp) olive oil to form a very rough paste. Season.

2 Place the meat, rind-side down, in a non-metallic dish. Spread the garlic paste all over the meat (not the rind). Cover and refrigerate for about 6 hours or overnight.

3 Place the pork in a roasting tin, rind-side up. Score the rind, then pour about 45 ml (3 tbsp) olive oil over. Rub rock salt into the rind. Cook at 230°C (450°F) mark 8 for 15 minutes, then reduce the heat to 200°C (400°F) mark 6 for 25 minutes per 450 g (1 lb), basting occasionally.

4 Meanwhile, sauté the shallot and apple in about 15 ml (1 tbsp) olive oil for about 3 minutes until beginning to soften. Pour in the apple juice, cider and 600 ml (1 pint) stock made with the half stock cube. Bring to the boil and boil rapidly for about 15 minutes to reduce by half. Remove from the heat.

5 Place the meat on a serving dish. Keep warm, uncovered. Pour away excess fat from the tin, then add the gravy mixture. Bring to the boil, scraping any sediment from the bottom. Season. Serve the meat, thickly sliced, with the gravy.

131

PORK CHOPS WITH RHUBARB CHUTNEY

PREPARATION TIME 10 minutes
COOKING TIME 20 minutes
FREEZING Not suitable

SERVES 4

- salt and pepper
- 4 pork chops, each weighing about 175 g (6 oz)
- 15 ml (1 tbsp) ground cumin
- flat-leaf parsley, to garnish

RHUBARB CHUTNEY

- 75 g (3 oz) caster sugar
- 75 ml (3 fl oz) cider vinegar
- 1 cm (½ inch) piece fresh root ginger, peeled and finely chopped

530 CALS/SERVING

- 40 g (1½ oz) red onion, peeled and chopped
- 350 g (12 oz) rhubarb, roughly chopped
- 1 garlic clove, peeled and chopped
- 1.25 ml (¼ tsp) each ground cinnamon and ground cloves
- 75 g (3 oz) raisins

1 First make the chutney. Place the sugar and vinegar in a heavy-based saucepan over a low heat. Add all the remaining chutney ingredients. Bring to the boil, then simmer for 5 minutes.
2 Meanwhile, season the chops and sprinkle with cumin. Grill for 5 minutes on one side, turn and spread about 30 ml (2 tbsp) of chutney over the other side. Grill for a further 5 minutes. Serve, garnished with flat-leaf parsley.

PORK AND LEMON BROCHETTES

PREPARATION TIME 15 minutes, plus marinating
COOKING TIME 12 minutes
FREEZING Not suitable
COLOUR INDEX Page 29

SERVES 2

- 350-450 g (12-16 oz) pork fillet
- 30 ml (2 tbsp) lemon juice
- 30 ml (2 tbsp) olive or vegetable oil
- 5 ml (1 tsp) paprika
- 2.5 ml (½ tsp) dried oregano

390 CALS/SERVING

- 2.5 ml (½ tsp) cayenne pepper
- 1.25 ml (¼ tsp) ground cumin
- 1.25 ml (¼ tsp) ground coriander
- salt and pepper
- slices of lemon, halved

1 Trim the pork of any fat or gristle and cut into 2 cm (¾ inch) cubes.
2 In a bowl, mix together the lemon juice, oil, paprika, oregano, cayenne, cumin, coriander and salt and pepper to taste. Add the cubed pork and mix well to coat. Cover and leave to marinate in the refrigerator for at least 1 hour.
3 Thread the pork cubes onto kebab skewers, alternating with the lemon slices. Cook under a hot grill for about 12 minutes, turning the brochettes occasionally to ensure even cooking. Baste occasionally during cooking with any remaining marinade.

VARIATION Make with lamb fillet or boneless chicken breast instead of pork.

MUSHROOM AND HAM RISOTTO

PREPARATION TIME 5 minutes
COOKING TIME 25 minutes
FREEZING Not suitable
COLOUR INDEX Page 30

🕐

SERVES 4   **445 CALS/SERVING**

- *350 g (12 oz) cooked ham*
- *50 g (2 oz) butter*
- *125 g (4 oz) onion, peeled and finely chopped*
- *1 bay leaf*
- *2 garlic cloves, peeled*
- *pinch of saffron strands*
- *225 g (8 oz) Arborio (risotto) rice*
- *150 ml (5 fl oz) dry white wine*
- *750 ml (1¼ pints) chicken stock*
- *15 g (½ oz) dried porcini mushrooms*
- *salt and pepper*
- *pared Cheddar cheese, to garnish*

1 Cut the ham into bite-sized pieces.
2 Melt the butter in a large saucepan. Add the onion, bay leaf and whole garlic cloves. Fry, stirring, for 4-5 minutes or until the onion is soft but not coloured.
3 Stir in the saffron, rice, wine, stock and mushrooms and season with salt and pepper. Bring to the boil, then simmer gently for 15 minutes.
4 Add the ham and continue cooking for 5 minutes or until most of the liquid has been absorbed and the rice is tender, stirring frequently. Add a little more stock if necessary. Adjust the seasoning and garnish with cheese.

NOTE Dried wild mushrooms are now available in most large supermarkets and delicatessens. If they're not available, jars of sliced mushrooms in oil make an excellent alternative.

SALTIMBOCCA

PREPARATION TIME 20 minutes
COOKING TIME 15 minutes
FREEZING Not suitable

♡

SERVES 6   **240 CALS/SERVING**

- *6 veal escalopes, each weighing about 75 g (3 oz)*
- *150 g (5 oz), about 6 slices, Parma ham or prosciutto*
- *about 12 sage leaves*
- *25 g (1 oz) white plain flour*
- *50 g (2 oz) unsalted butter*
- *150 ml (5 fl oz) white wine*
- *black pepper*

1 If necessary, pound the veal escalopes gently with a rolling pin until they are about 3 mm (⅛ inch) thick. If they are too large for the frying pan, cut them in half.
2 Lay a slice of Parma ham on each escalope and place a sage leaf on top. Fix in place with a wooden cocktail stick.
3 Dip each escalope in the flour and dust off any excess. Melt a knob of butter in a frying pan and when it is foaming, quickly fry the escalopes in batches for about 1 minute on each side or until lightly golden. Cover and keep warm in a low oven. Melt a little more butter for each batch.
4 Add the wine to the pan and loosen any sediment from the bottom, using a wooden spoon. Bring to a simmer, add the escalopes, and cook in wine for 2 minutes or until tender, then transfer to a serving dish. Season with black pepper. Serve immediately.

133

FOUR-CHEESE PIZZA

PREPARATION TIME 30 minutes, plus rising
COOKING TIME 40-50 minutes
FREEZING Suitable
COLOUR INDEX Page 31
♡ ✳

SERVES 6

- *5 ml (1 tsp) sugar*
- *5 ml (1 tsp) dried yeast*
- *125 g (4 oz) white plain flour*
- *125 g (4 oz) strong white plain flour*
- *5 ml (1 tsp) salt*
- *10 ml (2 tsp) olive oil*
- *400 g (14 oz) can chopped tomatoes*
- *5 ml (1 tsp) dried oregano*
- *15 ml (1 tbsp) tomato purée*
- *black pepper*

300 CALS/SERVING

CHEESE TOPPING

- *125 g (4 oz) mozzarella cheese, thinly sliced*
- *50 g (2 oz) Dolcelatte cheese, chopped*
- *125 g (4 oz) ricotta cheese, crumbled*
- *30 ml (2 tbsp) freshly grated Parmesan cheese*
- *a few olives*
- *fresh basil leaves, to garnish*

1 To make the dough, dissolve the sugar in 150 ml (5 fl oz) tepid water. Sprinkle over the yeast. Leave in a warm place for 15 minutes or until frothy.
2 Mix the flours and salt in a bowl. Add the yeast liquid and oil. Mix to a soft dough. Turn the dough onto a floured surface and knead for 5 minutes. Return the dough to the bowl and cover. Leave to rise in a warm place for 30 minutes or until doubled in size.
3 Place the tomatoes, oregano and tomato purée in a saucepan, adding pepper to taste, and bring to the boil. Reduce the heat and simmer, uncovered, for 15-20 minutes or until thick and pulpy. Remove from the heat and leave to cool.
4 Quickly knead the risen dough, then roll out to a 25 cm (10 inch) round and place on a lightly greased baking tray. Fold up the edges of the dough slightly to form a rim.
5 Spread the sauce over the dough to within 1 cm (½ inch) of the edge. Arrange the cheeses evenly over the sauce. Finish with a topping of Parmesan cheese. Decorate with the olives.
6 Bake in the oven at 200°C (400°F) mark 6 for 25-30 minutes or until the cheese has melted and the dough is golden. Serve the pizza piping hot, garnished with basil leaves.

DEEP-FRIED CAMEMBERT WITH RHUBARB SAUCE

PREPARATION TIME 25 minutes
COOKING TIME About 15 minutes
FREEZING Not suitable
COLOUR INDEX Page 31

SERVES 4

- *8 Camembert cheese portions*
- *1 large egg (size 1)*
- *125 g (4 oz) fine fresh breadcrumbs*
- *sunflower oil, for deep-frying*
- *green salad leaves, to garnish*

510 CALS/SERVING

SAUCE

- *225 g (8 oz) rhubarb, trimmed and cut into pieces*
- *40 g (1½ oz) sugar*
- *1.25 ml (¼ tsp) ground ginger*
- *salt and pepper*

1 To make the sauce, place the rhubarb and sugar in a saucepan with 15 ml (1 tbsp) water. Cover the pan and cook over a low heat for 10 minutes until the rhubarb is very soft.
2 Remove the pan from the heat and blend the rhubarb and liquid in a food processor until smooth. Stir in the ginger and add salt and pepper to taste, then return to the pan and heat through gently.
3 Meanwhile, trim off the rind from the Camembert portions. Beat the egg with salt and pepper to taste and pour onto a large plate. Spread out the breadcrumbs on another plate. Dip the Camembert portions first in egg, then in breadcrumbs. Repeat the process, dipping them carefully a second time.
4 Heat the oil in a deep-fat fryer to 190°C (375°F). Fry the Camembert portions, four at a time, for about 2 minutes until crisp and golden. Drain on absorbent kitchen paper and serve at once with the sauce. Garnish with salad leaves.

ASPARAGUS AND RED ONION TART

PREPARATION TIME 40 minutes, plus chilling
COOKING TIME 50 minutes
FREEZING Suitable (stage 1)

❃

SERVES 8

- *Shortcrust Pastry,
  made with 225 g
  (8 oz) white plain
  flour (see page 383)*
- *FILLING*
- *225 g (8 oz) fresh
  asparagus, trimmed*
- *4 rashers smoked
  bacon, cut into strips*
- *1 red onion, peeled,
  halved and thinly
  sliced*
- *15 ml (1 tbsp) olive
  oil, if necessary*

400 CALS/SERVING

- *15 ml (1 tbsp)
  chopped fresh
  parsley*
- *finely grated rind of
  ½ lemon*
- *salt and pepper*
- *3 eggs*
- *150 ml (5 fl oz)
  single cream)*
- *150 ml (5 fl oz) milk*
- *50 g (2 oz) Cheddar
  cheese, grated*

1 Roll out the pastry on a lightly floured surface and use to line a 28 cm (11 inch) flan tin. Cover and chill for 30 minutes. Bake blind (see page 383) at 200°C (400°F) mark 6 for 15 minutes or until lightly coloured.

2 Meanwhile, make the filling. Cook the asparagus in a frying pan of boiling water for 8-12 minutes or until tender-crisp. Using a fish slice, remove the asparagus from the pan and place on double thickness absorbent kitchen paper to drain for several minutes.

3 In a dry frying pan, fry the bacon for 5 minutes until beginning to crisp. Add the onion to the pan and fry for a further 3 minutes, adding a little oil if necessary. Cut the asparagus spears into pieces, add to the pan and toss in the juices for 2 minutes. Spoon the mixture into the pastry case and sprinkle with parsley, lemon rind and salt and pepper to taste.

4 Whisk the eggs with the cream and milk and strain over the asparagus mixture. Sprinkle with the grated cheese. Carefully lift the asparagus tips to stand slightly proud of the cheese, then cook in the oven at 190°C (375°F) mark 5 for about 25 minutes or until the filling is set and lightly golden. Serve warm or cold.

VARIATION Omit the bacon, if wished, and add more asparagus or onion, as preferred.

135

POACHED EGGS ON SMOKED HADDOCK WITH HOT CAPER DRESSING

PREPARATION TIME 10 minutes, plus soaking
COOKING TIME 12-15 minutes
FREEZING Not suitable

SERVES 4   550 CALS/SERVING
- *50 g (2 oz) baby French capers in salt*
- *4 thick slices rustic bread*
- *oil for frying*
- *4 smoked haddock fillets, each weighing about 125 g (4 oz)*
- *600 ml (1 pint) fish stock or water*
- *4 eggs*
- *75 ml (3 fl oz) olive oil*
- *15 ml (1 tbsp) lemon juice*
- *15 ml (1 tbsp) balsamic vinegar*
- *salt and pepper*
- *125 g (4 oz) baby spinach leaves*

1 Wash the salted capers and place in a small bowl. Cover with cold water and set aside to soak for 30 minutes. Drain, wash well and pat dry.
2 Cut the bread into bite-sized pieces. Heat a shallow layer of oil in a large, non-stick frying pan. When hot, add the bread and stir-fry for 4-5 minutes until crisp and golden. Drain on absorbent kitchen paper and set aside.
3 Place the haddock in a small saucepan with the fish stock or water. Bring to the boil and poach gently for 4-5 minutes until the fish is firm and cooked through. Remove from the pan with a slotted spoon, cover with foil and keep warm.
4 Poach the eggs in the fish liquid for 3 minutes; 5 minutes for harder-set eggs.
5 Meanwhile, place the olive oil in a small saucepan, with the lemon juice, vinegar and capers. Season and heat until almost boiling.
6 Arrange the fish on individual plates. Top with an egg, garnish with spinach and croûtons, and pour over caper dressing. Serve at once.

TIP
French capers are small and come packed in salt, unlike the larger capers which are kept in brine. French capers have a firmer texture and superior flavour to the larger capers. They are available from good delicatessens – normal capers can be used instead, but should also be soaked to remove the brine flavour.

EGGS IN POPPADOM BASKETS

PREPARATION TIME 35 minutes
COOKING TIME 20-35 minutes
FREEZING Not suitable
COLOUR INDEX Page 32

SERVES 6 — 445 CALS/SERVING

- oil for deep frying
- 6 small spicy poppadoms
- 12 quails' eggs or 6 hens' eggs
- 75 g (3 oz) watercress, roughly chopped
- 1 bunch chives
- 225 g (8 oz) leeks, thickly sliced
- salt and pepper
- 225 ml (8 fl oz) ready-made hollandaise sauce
- juice of 1 lemon
- 30 ml (2 tbsp) wholegrain mustard

1 Deep-fry one poppadom for 2-3 seconds. Lift out of the oil, preferably using tongs, and place over a slim jar or can covered with foil. Immediately press a wider teacup over the poppadom to shape it into a basket. Work as fast as you can, as the poppadom will soon harden. Once set, drain the basket on absorbent kitchen paper. Repeat with the remaining poppadoms.
2 Cook the quails' eggs in boiling water for 3 minutes. (If using hens' eggs, boil for 10 minutes.) Cool, peel and halve the eggs (quarter the hens' eggs). Finely chop the chives, reserving a few to garnish.
3 Cook the leeks in boiling, salted water for 3-4 minutes or until just tender. Drain well.
4 In a saucepan, heat the hollandaise sauce, lemon juice and mustard. Stir constantly until just bubbling. Add the chopped chives and season well. Gently stir in the eggs and leeks. Simmer very gently for 1-2 minutes only – do not overheat or the eggs will become rubbery.
5 Place the baskets on a baking sheet. Divide the watercress among the poppadoms and spoon in the hot egg mixture. Grill immediately for a few seconds only or until golden and bubbling. Garnish with the reserved chives and serve immediately.

TIP
You can find ready-made hollandaise sauce in supermarkets. Or, use mayonnaise thinned to a thick coating consistency with single cream, but don't let the mixture boil or it may separate.

GOATS' CHEESE PUFFS

PREPARATION TIME 25 minutes
COOKING TIME 15-20 minutes
FREEZING Not suitable
COLOUR INDEX Page 31
♡

SERVES 8 — 95 CALS/PUFF

- 15 ml (1 tbsp) toasted hazelnuts, finely chopped
- 15 ml (1 tbsp) fresh white breadcrumbs
- 15 ml (1 tbsp) freshly grated Parmesan cheese
- 15 g ($^{1}/_{2}$ oz) butter or margarine
- 15 ml (1 tbsp) white plain flour
- 75 ml (5 tbsp) milk
- 1 egg yolk
- 125 g (4 oz) soft goats' cheese, crumbled
- salt and pepper
- 4 egg whites
- 2.5 ml ($^{1}/_{2}$ tsp) lemon juice
- vegetable oil, for greasing
- salad leaves and nut oil vinaigrette, to serve

1 Grease and base-line eight 150 ml (5 fl oz) ramekin dishes.
2 Mix the nuts with the breadcrumbs and Parmesan. Use to coat the ramekins, reserving some to sprinkle on the top.
3 Melt the butter in a small pan. Add the flour and cook for 1 minute, stirring constantly. Remove from the heat, and stir in the milk. Cook, stirring, over a moderate heat until the mixture forms a thick sauce.
4 Cool slightly, then beat in the egg yolk and goats' cheese. Season.
5 Whisk the egg whites with a pinch of salt and the lemon juice until they form stiff peaks. Using a large, metal spoon, fold the cheese mixture into the egg whites.
6 Divide among the dishes and top with the remaining crumb mixture. Place in a roasting tin, half fill with boiling water and bake at 190°C (375°F) mark 5 for 12-15 minutes.
7 Cool for 10 minutes, then turn out, remove the lining paper and invert onto an oiled baking tray. Return to the oven or place under a hot grill to brown. Serve with salad leaves, dressed with nut oil vinaigrette.

1 Place the haddock in a saucepan, then cover with water and half the wine. Add the flavouring ingredients, season and bring to the boil. Cover and simmer for 5 minutes, or until tender.

2 Lift the fish onto a plate and flake the flesh, discarding any bones. Strain the cooking juices and make up to 1 litre (1¾ pints) with water.

3 Cook the lasagne according to the packet instructions, stirring occasionally with a fork. Drain and immediately run cold water over the pasta. Spread on a clean tea towel and cover.

4 Melt 50 g (2 oz) of the butter in a saucepan and gently cook the leeks and garlic, covered, for about 10 minutes. Remove from the pan using a slotted spoon.

5 Melt the remaining butter. Add the flour and cook, stirring, for 1 minute. Off the heat, stir in the reserved 1 litre (1¾ pints) stock and remaining wine. Bring to the boil, stirring, and cook for 2 minutes. Off the heat, whisk in the cream, soured cream and dill. Season.

6 Spoon a little of the sauce into a 3 litre (5¼ pint) shallow ovenproof serving dish. Top with a layer of pasta, followed by the haddock, mixed seafood and leeks, and a little more sauce. Continue layering, finishing with the sauce. Scatter over the grated cheeses.

7 Cook in the oven at 200°C (400°F) mark 6 for 45-50 minutes. Cool slightly before serving, garnished with dill and lemon.

VARIATION *Vegetarian Lasagne* Replace the haddock and seafood with 450 g (1 lb) mixed mushrooms and the dill with 60 ml (4 tbsp) chopped fresh basil or 5 ml (1 tsp) dried. Increase the leeks to 700 g (1½ lb) and Cheddar or Gruyère cheese to 225 g (8 oz). Omit stages 1-2. Continue as in stages 3-4. Then sauté the sliced mushrooms in the remaining 75 g (3 oz) butter for 3-4 minutes; remove from the pan using slotted spoons. Make the sauce as in stage 5, adding more butter if necessary and using 700 ml (1¼ pints) vegetable stock and 300 ml (10 fl oz) white wine with the basil in place of dill. Whisk in 30 ml (2 tbsp) Dijon mustard. Complete as in stages 6-7, layering the mushrooms and some of the Cheddar or Gruyère in place of the fish.

SEAFOOD LASAGNE

PREPARATION TIME 25 minutes
COOKING TIME About 1¼ hours
FREEZING Not suitable

SERVES 6

- *450 g (1 lb) fresh haddock fillet, skinned*
- *300 ml (10 fl oz) white wine*
- *slices of carrot, onion and bay leaf for flavouring*
- *salt and pepper*
- *200 g (7 oz) dried spinach lasagne*
- *150 g (5 oz) butter or margarine*
- *450 g (1 lb) leeks, trimmed and thickly sliced*
- *1 garlic clove, peeled and crushed*
- *90 g (3½ oz) plain flour*

640 CALS/SERVING

- *150 ml (5 fl oz) single cream*
- *150 ml (5 fl oz) soured cream*
- *15 ml (1 tbsp) chopped fresh dill*
- *225 g (8 oz) packet cooked mixed seafood*
- *50 g (2 oz) Cheddar or Gruyère cheese, grated*
- *30 ml (2 tbsp) freshly grated Parmesan cheese*
- *fresh dill and lemon slices, to garnish*

GINGERED CHICKEN AND NOODLES

PREPARATION TIME 5 minutes
COOKING TIME 20-25 minutes
FREEZING Not suitable
COLOUR INDEX Page 33

♡ ◷

SERVES 4

310 CALS/SERVING

- *15 ml (1 tbsp) vegetable oil*
- *1 bunch spring onions, sliced*
- *2.5 cm (1 inch) piece fresh root ginger, peeled and grated*
- *1 garlic clove, peeled and crushed*
- *275 g (10 oz) skinless chicken breast fillet, cut into bite-sized pieces*
- *30 ml (2 tbsp) mild curry paste or 15 ml (1 tbsp) Thai hot curry paste*

- *300 ml (10 fl oz) coconut milk*
- *about 300 ml (10 fl oz) chicken stock*
- *salt and pepper*
- *125 g (4 oz) Chinese egg noodles*
- *10 ml (2 tsp) lemon or lime juice*

1 Heat the oil in a large, non-stick sauté pan and fry the spring onions, ginger and garlic until just beginning to soften. Add the chicken pieces and curry paste and cook for a further 3-4 minutes or until golden brown.
2 Stir in the coconut milk, stock and seasoning. Bring to the boil. Break the noodles in half and add to the pan. Cover and simmer for about 5-10 minutes or until the noodles are just tender, stirring occasionally. Add a little more stock if the mixture becomes too dry.
3 Add the lemon or lime juice, season to taste and serve immediately, stirring well to mix.

TIP
Coconut milk: use canned coconut milk or roughly chop a 50 g (2 oz) block of creamed coconut and make up to 300 ml (10 fl oz) with boiling water. Stir well to mix.

CHILLI PORK WITH NOODLES

PREPARATION TIME 10 minutes
COOKING TIME 15 minutes
FREEZING Not suitable

♡ ◷

SERVES 4

285 CALS/SERVING

- *30 ml (2 tbsp) vegetable oil*
- *350 g (12 oz) pork fillet, cut into thin slices*
- *1 yellow pepper, deseeded and cut into thin slices*
- *225 g (8 oz) broccoli, divided into small florets*
- *1 onion, peeled and roughly chopped*
- *2.5 ml (¹/₂ tsp) mild chilli powder or few drops Tabasco sauce*

- *5 ml (1 tsp) dried oregano or dried mixed herbs*
- *50 g (2 oz) rice noodles or dried pasta*
- *30 ml (2 tbsp) sherry or medium white wine*
- *450 ml (15 fl oz) beef stock*
- *15 ml (1 tbsp) soy sauce*
- *pepper*

1 Heat the oil in a large non-stick sauté pan or wok and brown the pork well for about 2-3 minutes. Remove with a slotted spoon and drain on absorbent kitchen paper. Add the yellow pepper, broccoli and onion. Stir in the chilli powder and herbs and sauté, stirring, for 1-2 minutes.
2 Mix in the pork, noodles, sherry, stock and soy sauce. Bring to the boil, cover and simmer for about 7 minutes or until all the ingredients are tender. Add pepper to taste and serve.

CLASSIC TOMATO SAUCE

PREPARATION TIME 10 minutes
COOKING TIME 40 minutes
FREEZING Suitable (stage 2)

♡ ❄

SERVES 4

- *15 ml (1 tbsp) olive oil*
- *75 g (3 oz) onion, peeled and diced*
- *75 g (3 oz) carrots, peeled and diced*
- *75 g (3 oz) celery, trimmed and diced*
- *1 garlic clove, peeled and crushed*
- *two 400 g (14 oz) cans chopped tomatoes*
- *30 ml (2 tbsp) tomato purée*

150 CALS/SERVING OF SAUCE (WITHOUT PASTA)

- *150 ml (5 fl oz) light stock*
- *125 ml (4 fl oz) red wine*
- *salt and pepper*
- *50 g (2 oz) sun-dried tomatoes, in olive oil, drained and finely chopped*
- *freshly pared Parmesan cheese, to serve*

1 Heat the olive oil in a large saucepan. Add the diced vegetables and garlic. Cook, stirring continuously, for 5 minutes or until beginning to soften but not colour.

2 Stir in the canned tomatoes, tomato purée, stock, wine and seasoning. Simmer, covered, for about 30 minutes, stirring occasionally. Purée in a food processor, then stir in the sun-dried tomatoes.

3 Adjust the seasoning and reheat to serve before tossing into hot pasta. Top with Parmesan.

PASTA PRIMAVERA

PREPARATION TIME 15 minutes
COOKING TIME 35-40 minutes
FREEZING Not suitable
COLOUR INDEX Page 35

SERVES 4-6

- *175 g (6 oz) fine asparagus*
- *125 g (4 oz) sugar snap peas, topped and tailed*
- *1 red pepper*
- *50 g (2 oz) butter*
- *1 small onion, peeled and chopped*
- *2 celery stalks, diced*
- *2 courgettes, diced*
- *225 g (8 oz) baby carrots*
- *6-8 spring onions, white parts only, diced*
- *400 g (14 oz) dried tagliatelle*

950-635 CALS/SERVING

- *300 ml (10 fl oz) double cream*
- *60 ml (4 tbsp) freshly grated Parmesan cheese*
- *salt and pepper*
- *15 ml (1 tbsp) vegetable oil*
- *20 ml (4 tsp) snipped chives*
- *20 ml (4 tsp) chopped fresh chervil*
- *20 ml (4 tsp) chopped fresh dill*

1 Halve the asparagus spears and cook in boiling salted water for 3-4 minutes, adding the sugar snaps after 2 minutes so that both are cooked until just tender. Drain and refresh with cold water, then drain again; set aside.

2 Using a potato peeler, thinly pare the skin from the red pepper and discard, along with the core and seeds. Dice the red pepper.

3 Melt the butter in a large frying pan. Add the onion and sauté for 7-8 minutes until soft and golden. Add the red pepper and celery and cook for 5 minutes. Stir in the courgettes, carrots and spring onions and cook for 12-15 minutes, stirring frequently, until the vegetables are tender and beginning to colour.

4 Cook the pasta in boiling salted water until just tender (*al dente*).

5 Meanwhile, stir the cream into the vegetables and bring to a gentle boil. Allow to bubble, stirring frequently, for a few minutes until it reduces by about one third. Stir in the asparagus and sugar snaps. Add the Parmesan and heat gently. Season to taste.

6 Drain the pasta thoroughly, toss with the oil and pour the sauce over. Sprinkle with the herbs, toss well and serve at once.

CRESPOLINE

PREPARATION TIME 20 minutes, plus standing
COOKING TIME 40-50 minutes
FREEZING Not suitable

♡

SERVES 4

- *225 g (8 oz) leaf spinach*
- *175 g (6 oz) ricotta cheese*
- *pinch of freshly grated nutmeg*
- *1 garlic clove, peeled and crushed*
- *8 dried pasta cannelloni tubes, about 75 g (3 oz) total weight*
- *300 ml (10 fl oz) Classic Tomato Sauce (see left) or passata*

345 CALS/SERVING

PARMESAN SAUCE

- *40 g (1½ oz) butter or margarine*
- *25 g (1 oz) white plain flour*
- *450 ml (15 fl oz) milk*
- *40 g (1½ oz) freshly grated Parmesan cheese*
- *salt and pepper*

1 To make the Parmesan sauce, melt the butter in a small saucepan over a low heat. Stir in the flour and cook for a few seconds, stirring. Remove from the heat and gradually add the milk, whisking until smooth. Slowly bring to the boil, stirring. Simmer gently for 4-5 minutes, whisking again if necessary. Stir in the Parmesan cheese and season with salt and pepper.

2 Wash the spinach and cook in a large saucepan with just the water clinging to the leaves for 3-4 minutes or until wilted. Drain well, then cool and roughly chop.

3 Mix the spinach with the ricotta, nutmeg and garlic, and season with salt and pepper. Fill the pasta tubes with the mixture.

4 Pour the tomato sauce or passata into an ovenproof dish and place the stuffed cannelloni on top in a single layer. Pour the Parmesan sauce over the top. Leave to stand for 30 minutes.

5 Cook at 190°C (375°F) mark 5 for 30-40 minutes or until piping hot and golden brown.

NOTE Most cannelloni does not need any pre-cooking, but it is worth checking the packet instructions first.

If the cheese sauce gets too hot it may separate slightly around the edges, but it is still delicious.

BROCCOLI AND CHEESE TIMBALE WITH TOMATO SAUCE

PREPARATION TIME 25 minutes
COOKING TIME 1 hour 20 minutes
FREEZING Not suitable
COLOUR INDEX Page 38
♡

SERVES 6

142 CALS/SERVING

- 700 g (1½ lb) broccoli, cut into tiny florets
- 25 g (1 oz) butter or margarine
- 1 onion, peeled and finely chopped
- 300 ml (10 fl oz) milk
- 4 eggs
- 50 g (2 oz) mature Cheddar cheese, grated
- 50 g (2 oz) fresh white breadcrumbs
- salt and pepper
- fresh salad leaves, to garnish

TOMATO SAUCE
- 1 small onion, peeled
- 1 garlic clove, peeled
- 1 large fresh parsley sprig
- 400 g (14 oz) can chopped tomatoes
- 5 ml (1 tsp) tomato purée
- 2.5 ml (½ tsp) sugar

1 Cook the broccoli in boiling water for about 5 minutes until just soft. Drain well.
2 Melt the butter in a saucepan, add the onion and cook until softened. Stir in the milk.
3 In a large bowl, beat the eggs together, then stir in the onion mixture, the broccoli, cheese and breadcrumbs and season with salt and pepper.
4 Spoon the mixture into a lightly greased and base-lined 1.1 litre (2 pint) non-stick ring mould. Cover with foil and stand the mould in a roasting tin. Fill the tin with hot water to come halfway up the side of the mould. Bake in the oven at 180°C (350°F) mark 4 for about 1¼ hours until set.
5 Meanwhile, make the tomato sauce. Process the onion, garlic and parsley in a blender or food processor until finely chopped. Add the tomatoes with their juice, tomato purée, sugar and seasoning and work until smooth. Heat for 10-15 minutes until slightly reduced.
6 When the timbale is cooked, remove from the water and leave for 5 minutes. Loosen around the sides, then turn onto a flat dish. Serve with the sauce, garnished with salad leaves.

COUSCOUS-FILLED AUBERGINES WITH A CORIANDER DRESSING

PREPARATION TIME 30 minutes
COOKING TIME 35-45 minutes
FREEZING Not suitable
COLOUR INDEX Page 37
♡

SERVES 4

160 CALS/SERVING

- 2 small aubergines, each weighing about 250 g (9 oz)
- 30 ml (2 tbsp) lemon juice
- sea salt and pepper
- 50 g (2 oz) couscous
- 6 sun-dried tomatoes in oil, drained and chopped
- 25 g (1 oz) no-soak dried apricots, chopped
- 8 fresh mint sprigs, chopped
- 15 ml (1 tbsp) pine nuts, chopped
- 4 spring onions, chopped
- coriander sprigs, to garnish

CORIANDER DRESSING
- 150 ml (5 fl oz) low-fat bio yogurt
- 1 cm (½ inch) piece fresh root ginger, peeled and finely grated
- 1 garlic clove, peeled and crushed
- finely grated rind of 1 lime
- 30 ml (2 tbsp) chopped fresh coriander
- squeeze of lime juice

1 Cut the aubergines in half lengthways and score the cut sides deeply, without damaging the skins. Place, scored-side up, on a baking sheet. Rub in the lemon juice and sprinkle with a little sea salt. Bake in the oven at 200°C (400°F) mark 6 for 20-30 minutes until the flesh is soft and tender.
2 Meanwhile, put the couscous in a bowl and pour on 150 ml (5 fl oz) boiling water. Leave to soak while preparing the rest of the filling.
3 Mix together the sun-dried tomatoes, dried apricots, mint, pine nuts and spring onions. Season with salt and pepper.
4 Scoop the flesh out from the cooked aubergines and chop finely. Fork through the soaked couscous then add the chopped aubergine and sun-dried tomato mixture. Spoon into the aubergine shells. Return to the oven for 15 minutes.
5 Meanwhile, make the dressing. Mix the yogurt with the ginger, garlic, lime rind, coriander and lime juice to taste.
6 Serve the aubergines hot, garnished with coriander and topped with the dressing.

STIR-FRIED SPRING VEGETABLES
WITH CASHEWS

PREPARATION TIME 15 minutes
COOKING TIME 10 minutes
FREEZING Not suitable

♡ ⏲

SERVES 4
- *30 ml (2 tbsp) sunflower oil*
- *10 ml (2 tsp) sesame oil*
- *1 garlic clove, peeled and sliced*
- *5 ml (1 tsp) grated fresh root ginger*
- *175 g (6 oz) sprouting broccoli, cut into small florets*
- *2 small leeks, trimmed and sliced*
- *350 g (12 oz) spring greens, central core discarded and leaves thinly shredded*

195 CALS/SERVING
- *150 ml (5 fl oz) vegetable stock*
- *30 ml (2 tbsp) dark soy sauce*
- *5 ml (1 tsp) chilli sauce*
- *pinch of sugar*
- *25 g (1 oz) cashew nuts, toasted*
- *15 ml (1 tbsp) sesame seeds, toasted*
- *salt and pepper*

1 Heat the two oils in a wok or large frying pan. Add the garlic and ginger and fry gently for 30 seconds. Add the sprouting broccoli and stir-fry for 3 minutes.

2 Add the leeks and spring greens to the pan and continue to stir-fry for a further 2 minutes. Blend the stock, soy, chilli sauce and sugar together, add to the pan and cook over a low heat for 4-5 minutes until the vegetables are tender.

3 Stir in the cashew nuts and sesame seeds, season to taste and serve immediately.

NOTE Serve with noodles for a well-balanced vegetarian main course.

> *TIP*
> To toast the nuts, place them on a small baking sheet and cook in the oven at 200°C (400°F) mark 6 for 5-6 minutes until golden. Cook the sesame seeds for 3-4 minutes.

VEGETABLE STRUDEL

PREPARATION TIME 30 minutes, plus standing
COOKING TIME 35-45 minutes
FREEZING Suitable

✳

SERVES 6

- 150 g (5 oz) butter or margarine
- 30 ml (2 tbsp) olive oil
- 450 g (1 lb) waxy potatoes, such as Maris Bard or Wilja, peeled and diced
- 450 g (1 lb) carrots, peeled and diced
- 225 g (8 oz) leeks, trimmed and sliced
- 1 small bunch spring onions, chopped
- 450 g (1 lb) spring greens, thick stalks removed, shredded

515 CALS/SERVING

- 1 garlic clove, peeled and crushed
- 15 ml (1 tbsp) lemon juice
- 300 ml (10 fl oz) fromage frais
- ground mixed spice
- salt and pepper
- mild paprika
- 4 large sheets filo pastry
- 75 g (3 oz) ground almonds
- a few poppy seeds

1 Melt 50 g (2 oz) of the butter with half the olive oil in a large saucepan. Add the potatoes, carrots, leeks and spring onions and fry for 4-5 minutes, stirring all the time. Add 125 ml (4 fl oz) water, reduce the heat, cover and cook gently for 10-15

minutes. Leave to cool.

2 Meanwhile, heat 25 g (1 oz) butter with the remaining olive oil in a large frying pan, add the greens and garlic and stir-fry for 2-3 minutes or until softened. Do not overcook. Stir in the lemon juice and leave to cool.

3 Stir the fromage frais into the potato and leek mixture and season with a little mixed spice, salt, pepper and paprika.

4 Melt the remaining butter. Lay one sheet of filo pastry on a clean work surface and brush lightly with melted butter. Take a second sheet of pastry and place it so that it overlaps the first sheet to make a 45 cm (18 inch) square. Brush lightly with melted butter. Repeat with the remaining filo pastry to make a double thickness. Sprinkle the ground almonds evenly over the pastry.

5 Spoon half the potato mixture over the bottom quarter of the pastry, leaving a border around the edge. Top with the spring green mixture and the remaining potato.

6 Carefully fold the sides over the filling, then, starting from the filled end, roll the strudel up like a Swiss roll. Carefully transfer to a baking sheet, seam-side down. Brush with melted butter, sprinkle with poppy seeds and bake in the oven at 200°C (400°F) mark 6 for 20-25 minutes or until golden brown. Leave to stand for 5 minutes before serving.

LEEK PANCAKES WITH WATERCRESS SAUCE

PREPARATION TIME 20 minutes
COOKING TIME 40-45 minutes
FREEZING Not suitable
COLOUR INDEX Page 36
♡

MAKES 8   **200 CALS/SERVING**

- 125 g (4 oz) white plain flour
- 1 egg
- 300 ml (10 fl oz) milk
- salt and pepper
- 15 ml (1 tbsp) snipped fresh chives
- 15 ml (1 tbsp) vegetable oil
- 25 g (1 oz) butter or margarine
- 3 leeks, trimmed and cut into thin strips
- 125 g (4 oz) button mushrooms, wiped and sliced
- 30 ml (2 tbsp) chopped fresh parsley
- 15 ml (1 tbsp) chopped sunflower seeds
- 50 g (2 oz) Edam cheese, grated

WATERCRESS SAUCE
- 1 bunch of watercress, trimmed and chopped
- 10 ml (2 tsp) capers
- 30 ml (2 tbsp) olive oil
- 1 garlic clove, peeled and crushed
- grated rind and juice of 1/2 lemon
- about 45 ml (3 tbsp) vegetable stock

1 Put the flour into a bowl and make a well in the centre. Add the egg and half the milk and beat until smooth. Beat in the remaining milk, add salt and pepper to taste and the chives.
2 Lightly grease an 18 cm (7 inch) frying pan or crêpe pan with the vegetable oil, tilting the pan to coat the base and sides. Pour off any surplus oil that remains in the pan.
3 Pour in just enough batter to coat the base of the pan. Cook for 1-2 minutes or until the underside is light brown, then turn and cook the other side. Repeat to make eight pancakes.
4 Melt the butter in a heavy-based saucepan and cook the leeks for about 5 minutes or until soft. Add the mushrooms and cook for a further 2 minutes, then stir in the parsley, sunflower seeds and salt and pepper to taste.
5 Lay the pancakes out flat and divide the leek filling between them, then roll up. Arrange the pancakes in a single layer in a greased shallow ovenproof dish.

6 To make the sauce, purée the watercress, capers and half the olive oil in a blender or food processor until smooth. Gradually blend in the remaining oil, the garlic, lemon rind and juice. Add enough vegetable stock to give a smooth pouring consistency. Transfer to a saucepan and heat through gently.
7 Pour the sauce over the pancakes and sprinkle with the cheese. Bake in the oven at 190°C (375°F) mark 5 for 20 minutes or until heated through and golden.

NOTE The pancake batter can be made in a blender or food processor.

CATALAN RED PEPPERS

PREPARATION TIME 20 minutes, plus chilling
COOKING TIME 15-20 minutes
FREEZING Not suitable
COLOUR INDEX Page 37
♡

SERVES 4   **340 CALS/SERVING**

- 4 red peppers
- oil for brushing
- 175 g (6 oz) mixed long-grain and wild rice
- salt and pepper
- 8 tomatoes, skinned, quartered and deseeded
- 8 spring onions, chopped
- few pitted olives, chopped
- 30 ml (2 tbsp) capers
- 90 ml (6 tbsp) olive oil
- 30 ml (2 tbsp) white wine vinegar
- 1 large garlic clove, peeled and crushed

1 Put the peppers on a baking sheet and brush lightly with oil. Bake at 220°C (425°F) mark 7 for 15-20 minutes or until just tender. Cool, halve and remove the core and seeds. Pat dry with absorbent kitchen paper.
2 Meanwhile, cook the rice in boiling salted water according to the packet instructions or until tender. Drain and rinse under cold running water, then drain well again. Mix the tomatoes into the rice with the spring onions, olives and capers.
3 Whisk together the olive oil, vinegar and garlic, then season with salt and pepper. Stir into the rice mixture.
4 Pile the rice into the pepper halves and arrange on serving plates. Cover and chill for 30 minutes before serving.

NEW POTATOES WITH CREAMY MINT BUTTER

PREPARATION TIME 5 minutes
COOKING TIME 15 minutes
FREEZING Not suitable
🕐

SERVES 4

- 25 g (1 oz) butter, softened
- 10 ml (2 tsp) chopped fresh mint
- 575 g (1¼ lb) small new potatoes
- salt

240 CALS/SERVING

- 15 ml (1 tbsp) vegetable oil
- 45 ml (3 tbsp) crème fraîche or double cream
- mint sprigs, to garnish

1 Beat together the butter and mint. Spoon on to greaseproof paper and shape into a neat round. Chill.
2 Boil the potatoes in salted water until almost tender. Drain well.
3 Heat the oil in a large non-stick frying pan. Sauté the potatoes over a high heat until golden brown.
4 Lower the heat and add the crème fraîche and chilled mint butter. Garnish and serve immediately.

SPRING GREEN SAUTE

PREPARATION TIME 5 minutes
COOKING TIME 5 minutes
FREEZING Not suitable
COLOUR INDEX Page 39
♡ 🕐

SERVES 6

- 700 g (1½ lb) spring greens
- 30 ml (2 tbsp) olive oil
- 25 g (1 oz) butter
- 1 garlic clove, peeled and crushed

90 CALS/SERVING

- 15 ml (1 tbsp) lemon juice
- salt and pepper
- toasted pine nuts, to garnish

1 Coarsely shred the spring greens, discarding any thick stalks.
2 Heat the oil and butter in a large wok or sauté pan. Add the spring greens and garlic and stir-fry over a high heat for about 4-5 minutes until just tender. Add the lemon juice and season with salt and pepper.
3 Serve immediately, sprinkled with pine nuts.

CRISPY CHINESE GREENS

PREPARATION TIME 15 minutes
COOKING TIME 2 minutes
FREEZING Not suitable
COLOUR INDEX Page 39
🕐

SERVES 4

- 700 g (1½ lb) spring greens
- about 600 ml (1 pint) sunflower oil
- 7.5 ml (1½ tsp) caster sugar

540 CALS/SERVING

- salt
- 25 g (1 oz) natural roasted peanuts, halved

1 Discard the thick stems from the spring greens and wash the leaves. Dry thoroughly, then roll the leaves together tightly, a few at a time, and shred them very finely with a sharp knife. Spread out on absorbent kitchen paper and pat dry with more paper (the shreds must be completely dry before frying).
2 Heat the oil in a wok or large, deep pan until just smoking, then remove from the heat and add the spring greens. Stir well, return the pan to the

heat and fry for about 2 minutes, stirring.
3 Using a slotted spoon, carefully remove the fried greens to a plate lined with absorbent kitchen paper and drain for a few moments.
4 Turn the greens onto a warm plate and sprinkle with the sugar, salt to taste and nuts.

NOTE These crispy-fried shreds of spring greens make an excellent addition to a Chinese-style meal. The dish is particularly good served as a starter, accompanied by sesame prawn toasts and a crisp dry white wine.

VARIATION Use cashew nuts or sunflower seeds instead of the peanuts.

CARROTS IN SPICED DRESSING

PREPARATION TIME 5 minutes
COOKING TIME 5-7 minutes
FREEZING Not suitable

♡ ⏲

SERVES 4
- *450 g (1 lb) young carrots, scrubbed*
- *salt and pepper*
- *50 g (2 oz) butter or margarine*
- *25 g (1 oz) flaked almonds*
- *5 ml (1 tsp) ground cumin*

170 CALS/SERVING
- *10 ml (2 tsp) ground coriander*
- *5 ml (1 tsp) honey*
- *30 ml (2 tbsp) roughly chopped chives*
- *5 ml (1 tsp) lemon juice*

1 Steam the carrots or cook in boiling salted water for 4-5 minutes or until just tender. Drain.
2 Melt the butter or margarine in a large frying pan and stir in the almonds and spices. Cook, stirring, for 1-2 minutes or until the almonds are golden brown. Toss in the carrots, honey, chives and lemon juice. Stir over a high heat until well mixed, then season and serve.

VEGETABLE MEDLEY

PREPARATION TIME 10 minutes
COOKING TIME 11 minutes
FREEZING Not suitable
♡ ⏱

SERVES 4
- *225 g (8 oz) carrots, peeled and cut into strips*
- *grated rind of 1 lemon*
- *25 g (1 oz) butter or margarine*
- *15 ml (1 tbsp) sugar*
- *1 garlic clove, peeled and crushed*

90 CALS/SERVING
- *salt and pepper*
- *125 g (4 oz) baby sweetcorn*
- *125 g (4 oz) asparagus tips*
- *chopped fresh parsley, to garnish*

1 Place the carrots in a small saucepan with the lemon rind, butter, sugar, garlic and salt and pepper to taste. Just cover with cold water.
2 Bring to the boil, then cook over a moderate to high heat for 5 minutes. Add the corn and asparagus and cook for 5-6 minutes until the vegetables are tender and the liquid has evaporated. Shake the pan to prevent the vegetables from sticking.
3 Serve garnished with parsley.

LEEKS AND ASPARAGUS IN VINAIGRETTE

PREPARATION TIME 15 minutes
COOKING TIME 15 minutes
FREEZING Not suitable
COLOUR INDEX Page 42
⏱

SERVES 6
- *450 g (1 lb) small, tender leeks, cut into 7.5 cm (3 inch) lengths*
- *225 g (8 oz) thin asparagus, cut into 7.5 cm (3 inch) lengths*
- *salt and pepper*
- *6 quails' eggs or 2 hens' eggs*
- *1 egg yolk*

290 CALS/SERVING
- *15 ml (1 tbsp) Dijon mustard*
- *45 ml (3 tbsp) white wine vinegar*
- *25 ml (5 tsp) sugar*
- *150 ml (5 fl oz) olive oil*
- *30 ml (2 tbsp) caper berries*
- *30 ml (2 tbsp) flat-leaf parsley*

1 Cook the leeks and asparagus in boiling salted water for 1-2 minutes, then plunge into cold water.
2 Boil the quails' eggs for 1-2 minutes; the hens' eggs for 10 minutes. Peel and quarter.
3 Mix together the egg yolk, mustard, vinegar, and sugar; whisk in the oil. Season with salt and pepper.
4 Toss the asparagus and leeks in the dressing, then add the eggs, capers and parsley. Serve immediately.

NOTE This Spanish-style salad uses caper berries which are available, bottled, from larger supermarkets. However, if you have difficulty finding them, use normal capers instead.

WARM CHINESE SALAD

PREPARATION TIME 10 minutes
COOKING TIME 6 minutes
FREEZING Not suitable
COLOUR INDEX Page 43
♡ ⏱

SERVES 4

- *¼ small iceberg lettuce, shredded*
- *15 ml (1 tbsp) sesame or sunflower oil*
- *1 bunch of spring onions, cut into 1 cm (½ inch) pieces*
- *150 g (5 oz) mangetout, trimmed*
- *175 g (6 oz) baby sweetcorn*
- *225 g (8 oz) can sliced bamboo shoots or whole water chestnuts, drained*

85 CALS/SERVING

- *30 ml (2 tbsp) light soy sauce*
- *15 ml (1 tbsp) hoisin sauce*
- *1 small red chilli, deseeded and finely chopped*
- *pepper*

1 Arrange the lettuce on four individual plates.
2 Heat the oil in a wok or frying pan. Add the onions, mangetout and sweetcorn and stir-fry for 3 minutes, tossing all the time. Add the bamboo shoots or water chestnuts and stir-fry for 2 minutes.
3 Add the soy sauce, hoisin sauce, chilli and pepper. Stir well and boil for 1 minute. Spoon over the iceberg lettuce and serve.

GRATED BABY BEETROOT SALAD

PREPARATION TIME 30 minutes
FREEZING Not suitable
⏱

SERVES 4-6

- *450 g (1 lb) raw baby beetroot*
- *30 ml (2 tbsp) raspberry vinegar*
- *1.25 ml (¼ tsp) clear honey*
- *1 small garlic clove, peeled and crushed*
- *15 ml (1 tbsp) grated fresh horseradish*
- *5 ml (1 tsp) brown mustard seeds*

315-215 CALS/SERVING

- *75 ml (3 fl oz) walnut oil*
- *30 ml (2 tbsp) extra-virgin olive oil*
- *salt and pepper*
- *½ small red onion, peeled and thinly sliced*
- *30 ml (2 tbsp) chopped fresh chives*

1 Trim any roots from the beetroot, peel and set aside. In a small bowl, whisk together the vinegar, honey, garlic, horseradish and mustard seeds. Gradually whisk in the two oils until well blended. Season to taste.
2 Halve the beetroot if necessary and grate in a food processor. Transfer to a large bowl and stir in the dressing. Add the onion and chives and season to taste. Cover and chill for 1 hour. Return to room temperature before serving.

149

RHUBARB AND CINNAMON COBBLER

PREPARATION TIME 15 minutes
COOKING TIME 50 minutes
FREEZING Suitable
COLOUR INDEX Page 46

❀

SERVES 4

- *175 g (6 oz) white plain flour*
- *125 g (4 oz) butter*
- *150 g (5 oz) caster sugar*
- *700 g (1½ lb) rhubarb, trimmed and cut into bite-sized chunks*

565 CALS/SERVING

- *30 ml (2 tbsp) cornflour*
- *2.5 ml (½ tsp) ground cinnamon*
- *a little milk and sugar for glazing*
- *vanilla ice cream, to accompany*

1 Place the flour, butter and 25 g (1 oz) sugar in a food processor and blend until it has the texture of fine breadcrumbs. Add 45 ml (3 tbsp) cold water and blend until the pastry comes together to form a ball. If it is slightly sticky roll in some flour and chill for 20 minutes or until it is firm enough to handle.
2 Roll out the pastry into a large circle, making sure you leave the edges ragged and uneven. It should be large enough to line a 23 cm (9 inch) round, greased, ovenproof dish with sides at least 5 cm (2 inches) deep, and to allow the edge of the pastry to drape over the sides of the dish.
3 Toss the rhubarb in the remaining sugar, cornflour and cinnamon. Spoon into the dish. Bring the pastry edges up and over the fruit, leaving a gap in the centre to reveal the filling. Glaze with milk and sprinkle with sugar.
4 Place on a baking sheet and bake at 200°C (400°F) mark 6 for about 50 minutes or until the pastry is golden brown and the juice is bubbling up around the pastry. Serve hot with ice cream.

BANOFFI FUDGE PIE

PREPARATION TIME 30 minutes, plus chilling
COOKING TIME About 30 minutes
FREEZING Not suitable
COLOUR INDEX Page 46

SERVES 6

- *Shortcrust Pastry, made with 225 g (8 oz) white plain flour (see page 383)*
- *75 g (3 oz) butter*
- *50 g (2 oz) light soft brown sugar*
- *30 ml (2 tbsp) milk*

560 CALS/SERVING

- *218 g (8 oz) can condensed milk*
- *5 bananas*
- *300 ml (10 fl oz) double cream*
- *lemon juice*
- *50 g (2 oz) caster sugar*

1 Use the pastry to line a 23 cm (9 inch) round, 2.5 cm (1 inch) deep, loose-based flan tin and bake blind (see page 383) at 200°C (400°F) mark 6 for 15 minutes until light golden.
2 Meanwhile, place the butter and the brown sugar in a small, heavy-based saucepan. Heat gently until the butter melts and the sugar dissolves. Bring to the boil and bubble for 1 minute only, stirring frequently. Off the heat, add the milk and condensed milk, bring to the boil and bubble for 2 minutes only or until the mixture thickens to the consistency of a very thick sauce and turns golden. Stir constantly or the mixture will burn. Keep warm.
3 Meanwhile, thickly slice four of the bananas and place in the pastry case. Spoon the warm fudge thinly but evenly over the bananas to cover completely. Leave to cool, then chill for about 45 minutes until set.
4 Whisk the cream until it just holds its shape. Pile the cream in the centre of the pie. Refrigerate for at least 1 hour until chilled, so that the caramel sets immediately on it.
5 Slice the remaining banana and coat with lemon juice. Pile on top of the cream.
6 Place the caster sugar in a small, heavy-based saucepan. Heat gently until the sugar melts and turns a golden caramel colour. Cool for about 1 minute or until the caramel thickens and darkens slightly, then spoon over the banana. (The caramel will run through the cream.) Chill immediately to set. The pie will hold up in the refrigerator for 2-3 hours. Leave at room temperature for 30 minutes before serving.

LIME MERINGUE PIES

PREPARATION TIME 45 minutes, plus chilling
COOKING TIME 35 minutes
FREEZING Not suitable

SERVES 6   **480 CALS/SERVING**

- *Sweet Flan Pastry, made with 225 g (8 oz) white plain flour (see page 384)*
- *4-6 limes, depending on size*

- *250 g (9 oz) caster sugar*
- *45 ml (3 tbsp) cornflour*
- *3 eggs, separated*
- *25 g (1 oz) butter*

1 Roll out the pastry on a lightly floured surface and use to line 12 deep muffin tins, or six 7.5 cm (3 inch) base-measurement fluted flan tins. Chill for about 30 minutes. Bake blind (see page 383) at 200°C (400°F) mark 6 for 15 minutes until set and lightly browned.
2 Meanwhile, finely grate the rind of three limes and place in a saucepan with the juice from all the limes. You need at least 90 ml (6 tbsp). Add 200 ml (7 fl oz) water and 75 g (3 oz) sugar. Heat gently until the sugar dissolves.
3 Mix the cornflour to a smooth paste with 60 ml (4 tbsp) water. Off the heat, stir into the lime mixture, then bring to the boil, stirring all the time. Cook for 1-2 minutes, then remove from the heat. Leave to cool slightly, then beat in two egg yolks and the butter. Pour into the pastry cases.
4 Whisk the three egg whites until very stiff. Whisk in 75 g (3 oz) sugar, keeping the meringue very stiff. Fold in the remaining sugar. Spoon on top of the curd mixture. The meringue should be about 5 cm (2 inches) high. Rough up with a fork.
5 Bake the pies at 150°C (300°F) mark 2 for about 35 minutes, or until golden. Cool for 20-30 minutes, then remove from the tins and serve warm.

NOTE Serve with limes in caramel. Cut the rind and pith from 6 limes. Cut the flesh into 5 mm (¼ inch) slices and place in a heatproof serving dish. Gently heat 200 g (7 oz) sugar and 150 ml (5 fl oz) water in a pan until the sugar dissolves, then boil until the liquid turns a caramel colour. Immediately take off the heat and pour in 90 ml (3 fl oz) warm water. (Cover your hand as the caramel will splutter.) Return to the heat and warm gently, stirring occasionally, until evenly blended. Take off the heat and stir in some rum, then pour over the limes. Top with pieces of blanched lime rind if wished. Refrigerate for at least 3 hours. Bring to room temperature before serving.

HIGGLEDY-PIGGLEDY APPLE TART

PREPARATION TIME 25 minutes, plus chilling
COOKING TIME 25-30 minutes
FREEZING Not suitable

SERVES 6
- 125 g (4 oz) butter
- about 125 g (4 oz) filo pastry sheets
- 200 g (7 oz) low-fat soft cheese
- 125 g (4 oz) mascarpone cheese
- 2.5 ml (½ tsp) vanilla essence

345 CALS/SERVING
- 30 ml (2 tbsp) clear honey
- grated rind and juice of 1 large lemon
- 900 g (2 lb) Cox's eating apples

1 Melt 50 g (2 oz) of the butter and brush a little over the base and sides of a 23 cm (9 inch) loose-based, fluted flan tin. Line the tin with filo pastry, brushing lightly with butter between the layers. Overlap so there are no gaps. The pastry may fall over the edge of the tin, but this does not matter. Prick the base all over with a fork and bake at 200°C (400°F) mark 6 for 12-15 minutes or until crisp and golden.
2 Mix the soft cheese, mascarpone cheese, vanilla essence and 15 ml (1 tbsp) honey with the lemon rind and 15 ml (1 tbsp) juice in a small bowl. Cover and chill.
3 Peel the apples and cut into chunky slices. Melt the rest of the butter and fry the apples for about 3-4 minutes in two batches until translucent. Return all the apples to the pan. Pour the remaining honey and 30 ml (2 tbsp) lemon juice over. Fry at a high heat until the apples have caramelized and any excess syrup has evaporated.
4 With a palette knife, spread the cheese mixture evenly over the pastry base. Top the tart with the warm apples and serve.

EASTER CHEESECAKE

PREPARATION TIME 40 minutes, plus chilling
COOKING TIME 55-65 minutes
FREEZING Suitable (stage 4)
COLOUR INDEX Page 47

❈

SERVES 8
- 125 g (4 oz) butter
- 225 g (8 oz) white plain flour
- 45 ml (3 tbsp) caster sugar
- icing sugar for dusting
- crystallized primroses, to decorate

FILLING
- 400 g (14 oz) full fat soft cheese

570 CALS/SERVING
- 2 eggs, separated
- 2.5 ml (½ tsp) vanilla essence
- 200 ml (7 fl oz) double cream
- 150 ml (5 fl oz) soured cream
- 50 g (2 oz) caster sugar
- 1 ripe pear (optional)

1 Rub the butter into the flour with the caster sugar. Bind to a dough with about 60 ml (4 tbsp) water. Roll out and use to line a 21.5 cm (8½ inch) deep, fluted loose-bottomed flan tin. Chill for 15 minutes, then bake blind (see page 383) at 200°C (400°F) mark 6 for 20-25 minutes or until pale golden brown and cooked through.
2 Beat together the soft cheese, egg yolks and vanilla essence. Gradually beat in the creams until thoroughly combined.
3 Whisk the egg whites until they just hold their shape. Fold in 25 g (1 oz) caster sugar and continue whisking until stiff. Whisk in the remaining sugar. Fold into the cheese mixture.
4 Peel, core and thinly slice the pear into the prepared flan case, if using. Spoon over the cheese mixture. Place the tin on a baking sheet and bake at 220°C (425°F) mark 7 for 20 minutes. Reduce the oven temperature to 180°C (350°F) mark 4 for a further 35-40 minutes or until the cheesecake is golden and just set. Cool in tin.
5 Serve the cheesecake warm, dusted with icing sugar and decorated with crystallized primroses.

WHISKY MOCHA FLAN

PREPARATION TIME 1 hour, plus chilling
COOKING TIME 20 minutes
FREEZING Not suitable

SERVES 6-8
- *Pâte Sucrée, made with 225 g (8 oz) flour (see page 384)*
- *75 g (3 oz) plain chocolate*
FILLING
- *10 ml (2 tsp) powdered gelatine*
- *150 ml (5 fl oz) milk*
- *15 ml (1 tbsp) instant coffee granules*
- *3 egg yolks*

640-480 CALS/SERVING
- *15 ml (1 tbsp) caster sugar*
- *150 ml (5 fl oz) double cream*
TOPPING
- *200 ml (7 fl oz) double cream*
- *15-30 ml (1-2 tbsp) whisky*
- *15 ml (1 tbsp) caster sugar*
- *chocolate caraque, to decorate*

1 Roll out the pastry on a lightly floured surface and use to line a 23 cm (9 inch) heart-shaped tin. Bake blind (see page 383) at 200°C (400°F) mark 6 for 15 minutes, then remove the paper and beans, reduce the oven temperature to 190°C (375°F) mark 5 and bake for 5 minutes. Cool on a wire rack.
2 Melt the chocolate. Place the pastry case, upside-down, on a sheet of greaseproof paper. Using a pastry brush, brush half of the melted chocolate evenly all over the outside of the pastry case. Leave in a cool place until the chocolate sets. Turn the flan case over and brush the inside with the remaining chocolate. Leave in a cool place to set.
3 To make the filling, sprinkle the gelatine over 30 ml (2 tbsp) water in a small heatproof bowl and leave to soak for 2-3 minutes. Place the bowl over a saucepan of simmering water and stir until the gelatine has dissolved.
4 Put the milk and coffee granules into a small saucepan. Heat gently until the coffee dissolves completely and the milk comes almost to the boil. Very lightly whisk the egg yolks and sugar together in a heatproof bowl. Pour in the coffee-flavoured milk and mix well.
5 Place the bowl over a pan of hot water and cook the custard, stirring continuously, until thick enough to coat the back of the spoon. As soon as the custard thickens, strain it through a nylon sieve into a clean bowl. Stir in the dissolved gelatine. Leave the custard to cool, stirring

frequently to prevent a skin forming.
6 Whip the cream until it will just hold soft peaks, then gently fold it into the coffee custard. Place the chocolate-coated flan case on a flat serving plate and fill it with the coffee cream mixture. Chill until set.
7 To make the topping, whip the cream with the whisky and sugar until it will just hold soft peaks. Spread an even layer of cream over the top of the flan. Whip the remaining cream until thick enough to pipe and fill a piping bag fitted with a medium star nozzle. Pipe whirls of cream around the top of the flan, then decorate with chocolate caraque. Chill before serving.

TIP
To make chocolate caraque spread melted chocolate in a thin layer on a marble slab or clean, smooth work surface. When the chocolate is only just set, draw a fine-bladed knife across the chocolate at an angle of 45°.

CREPES WITH ORANGE ICE

PREPARATION TIME 30 minutes, plus freezing
COOKING TIME About 20 minutes
FREEZING Suitable, except sauce

❋

SERVES 6
- *125 g (4 oz) white plain flour*
- *pinch of salt*
- *2 eggs, beaten*
- *300 ml (10 fl oz) milk*
- *25 g (1 oz) butter, melted*
- *15 ml (1 tbsp) Grand Marnier*
ORANGE ICE CREAM
- *50 g (2 oz) sugar*
- *finely pared rind and juice of 1 orange*
- *225 g (8 oz) mascarpone cheese*

505 CALS/SERVING
- *200 g (7 oz) fromage frais*
- *30 ml (2 tbsp) Grand Marnier*
SAUCE
- *25 g (1 oz) unsalted butter*
- *50 g (2 oz) caster sugar*
- *juice of 2 oranges, strained*
- *juice of ½ lemon, strained*
- *30-45 ml (2-3 tbsp) Grand Marnier, warmed*

1 First make the ice cream. Put the sugar in a saucepan with 150 ml (5 fl oz) water and heat gently until the sugar has dissolved. Add the pared orange rind and boil rapidly until reduced by about half. Remove the orange rind with a slotted spoon, cut into strips and set aside. Add the orange juice to the syrup. Allow to cool.

2 Mix the mascarpone and fromage frais together in a bowl. Gradually work in the cooled orange syrup and liqueur. Turn into a freezerproof container, cover and freeze until firm, whisking occasionally during freezing. Transfer to the refrigerator to soften 30 minutes before serving.

3 To make the crêpe batter, place the flour, salt, eggs, milk, melted butter and Grand Marnier in a blender or food processor and work until smooth.

4 Heat a crêpe pan until very hot and wipe with a little oil. When a light haze forms, pour in just enough batter to thinly coat the base of the pan, tilting the pan to get an even coating. Cook over a fairly high heat until the upper surface looks set and the edges begin to curl. Turn the crêpe over and cook the other side. Transfer to a warmed plate and repeat to make 12 pancakes, interleaving the cooked ones with greaseproof paper.

5 To make the sauce, melt the butter in a large frying pan, add the sugar and heat gently until dissolved, then cook to a golden brown caramel. Carefully add the orange and lemon juices and stir until the caramel has dissolved.

6 To serve, place a spoonful or two of ice cream on each crêpe and fold to enclose the filling. Arrange the crêpes in the large frying pan and spoon the sauce over to warm them through. Sprinkle with the orange rind strips. Pour on the liqueur and set alight, shaking the pan gently. Serve immediately.

NOTE This is an ideal dinner party dish because most of the preparation can be done in advance; at the last minute you only need to assemble the dish, heat it through and flambé!

VARIATION Use any orange-flavoured liqueur instead of the Grand Marnier.

FRAGRANT FRUIT SALAD

PREPARATION TIME 20-30 minutes, plus chilling
FREEZING Not suitable
COLOUR INDEX Page 45

♡

SERVES 6
- *50 g (2 oz) caster sugar*
- *grated rind and juice of 1 lemon*
- *2 pieces of preserved stem ginger in syrup, finely chopped*
- *60 ml (4 tbsp) ginger wine*
- *700 g (1½ lb) lychees*

175 CALS/SERVING
- *3 ripe mangoes*
- *450 g (1 lb) fresh or canned pineapple in natural juice*
- *4 kiwi fruit*
- *50 g (2 oz) Cape gooseberries, to decorate*

1 Put the sugar in a pan with 150 ml (5 fl oz) water and the lemon rind and juice. Heat gently until the sugar dissolves, then bring to the boil and simmer for 1 minute. Remove from the heat.
2 Stir the ginger into the sugar syrup with the wine. Leave to cool while preparing the fruit.
3 Peel the lychees, cut in half and remove the shiny stones. Peel the mangoes and cut the flesh away from the stones. Cut the flesh into cubes.
4 If using fresh pineapple, peel, slice and remove the tough centre core from each slice. If using canned pineapple, drain well. Cut the pineapple slices into cubes. Peel and thinly slice the kiwi fruit. Cut the slices in half.
5 Place the fruit in a serving dish, pour over the syrup and toss lightly to mix. Cover with clingfilm and chill for several hours to allow the flavours to develop.
6 To decorate, peel back the calyx from each Cape gooseberry to form a 'flower'. Wipe the orange berry with a damp cloth. Arrange on top of he fruit salad to serve.

VARIATION Replace one mango with 1-2 oranges, according to size. Pare the rind thinly and set aside. Remove the pith and segment the fruit. Cut the rind into very thin strips, blanch in boiling water for 1 minute and use to decorate the fruit salad if wished, in place of the Cape gooseberries.

FLAMBEED PINEAPPLE

PREPARATION TIME 20 minutes
COOKING TIME 50 minutes
FREEZING Not suitable

♡

SERVES 4
- *1 pineapple, weighing about 900 g (2 lb)*
- *30 ml (2 tbsp) clear honey*

175 CALS/SERVING
- *125 ml (4 fl oz) brandy*
- *toasted flaked almonds, to decorate*
- *cream, to serve*

1 Trim about 1 cm (½ inch) from each end of the pineapple, reserving a few green leaves. Cut in quarters lengthways. Carefully trim the core away, then cut along the base of each quarter so that the flesh is separated from the skin. Cut the flesh in half lengthways, then four times across to give bite-sized pieces of pineapple.
2 Lay the pineapple shell and flesh in an ovenproof dish and spoon the honey over. Cook at 190°C (375°F) mark 5 for 45 minutes, basting occasionally.
3 When the pineapple is golden, remove from the oven. Gently heat the brandy in a small saucepan, then pour over the pineapple and ignite. Once the flames have died down, pour the cooking juice over. Decorate with toasted flaked almonds and the reserved green leaves. Serve the pineapple with cream.

THE ULTIMATE CHOCOLATE CAKE

PREPARATION TIME 15 minutes
COOKING TIME 1 hour 20 minutes
FREEZING Suitable (stage 5)
COL.OUR INDEX Page 49

✳

**MAKES ABOUT
25 SQUARES**

- 125 g (4 oz) white chocolate
- 125 g (4 oz) milk chocolate
- white vegetable fat for greasing
- 375 g (13 oz) plain chocolate
- 175 g (6 oz) butter, softened
- 175 g (6 oz) caster sugar

300 CALS/SQUARE

- 175 g (6 oz) ground almonds
- 6 eggs, separated
- 75 g (3 oz) fresh brown breadcrumbs
- 45 ml (3 tbsp) cocoa powder
- pinch of salt
- 150 ml (5 fl oz) double cream

1 Roughly chop the white and milk chocolate. Grease and base-line a 20 cm (8 inch) base-measurement square cake tin.
2 Break 225 g (8 oz) plain chocolate into a bowl and melt over a pan of gently simmering water; cool for 10 minutes.
3 Meanwhile, beat the butter and sugar until light and fluffy. Stir in the cooled melted chocolate with the almonds, egg yolks, breadcrumbs and cocoa.
4 Whisk the egg whites and salt to soft peaks. Fold into the chocolate mixture with the chopped chocolate.
5 Pour into the tin and bake at 180°C (350°F) mark 4 for about 1 hour 20 minutes, covering loosely with foil if necessary. Cool in the tin for 15 minutes before turning out onto a wire rack to finish cooling.
6 Place the remaining 150 g (5 oz) plain chocolate and cream in a bowl. Melt over a pan of gently simmering water, stirring occasionally. Cool for about 30 minutes or until slightly thickened. Pour over the cake to cover. Cool and cut up to serve.

NOTE The cut-up pieces of cake can be stored in an airtight container for up to 5 days.

WALNUT TORTE

PREPARATION TIME 25 minutes, plus cooling
COOKING TIME 30 minutes
FREEZING Not suitable
COLOUR INDEX Page 49

MAKES 8-10 SLICES

- 165 g (5½ oz) walnuts
- 150 g (5 oz) unsalted butter, softened
- 150 g (5 oz) caster sugar
- 5 eggs, separated
- grated rind of 1 orange
- 150 g (5 oz) ricotta cheese

530-425 CALS/SERVING

- 40 g (1½ oz) white plain flour
- 90 ml (6 tbsp) apricot jam
- 10 ml (2 tsp) orange juice
- 25 g (1 oz) plain chocolate

1 Grease and line the base of a 23 cm (9 inch) spring-release cake tin. Lightly toast the walnuts, allow to cool, then chop roughly. Reserve 40 g (1½ oz) for the decoration.
2 Cream the butter and 125 g (4 oz) of the sugar together in a bowl until pale and fluffy. Add the egg yolks, orange rind, ricotta cheese, flour and roughly chopped walnuts. Mix gently until evenly combined.
3 Put the egg whites into another large bowl and whisk until stiff but not dry. Gradually whisk in the remaining sugar. Fold a quarter into the cheese mixture to loosen it slightly, then fold in the remaining egg whites.
4 Turn into the prepared tin and gently level the surface. Bake at 190°C (375°F) mark 5 for about 30 minutes until risen and just firm. Remove from the oven and leave to cool in the tin.
5 Heat the apricot jam in a pan until melted, then press through a sieve into a bowl and stir in the orange juice to make a glaze. Brush half the apricot glaze around the sides of the cake. Using a palette knife, coat the sides of the cake with the reserved walnuts.
6 Brush the remaining apricot glaze over the top of the cake. Shave curls from the chocolate and scatter over the top of the cake to serve.

NOTE This gâteau can be made in advance and kept in the refrigerator for up to 2 days.

SIMNEL CAKE

PREPARATION TIME 40 minutes, plus cooling
COOKING TIME About 2½ hours
FREEZING Suitable (stage 6)

✳

SERVES 20

- *175 g (6 oz) butter or block margarine, softened*
- *175 g (6 oz) caster sugar*
- *3 eggs, lightly beaten*
- *225 g (8 oz) white plain flour*
- *pinch of salt*
- *2.5 ml (½ tsp) ground cinnamon*
- *2.5 ml (½ tsp) grated nutmeg*
- *125 g (4 oz) glacé cherries, washed, dried and cut into quarters*

345 CALS/SERVING

- *50 g (2 oz) chopped mixed peel*
- *250 g (9 oz) currants*
- *125 g (4 oz) sultanas*
- *finely grated rind of 1 lemon*
- *15-30 ml (1-2 tbsp) milk (if necessary)*
- *450 g (1 lb) white almond paste or marzipan*
- *1 egg white, lightly beaten*
- *ribbon and fresh or fondant flowers, to decorate*

1 Line and grease an 18 cm (7 inch) round cake tin. Cream the butter and sugar together until pale and fluffy. Gradually beat in the eggs.
2 Sift in the flour, salt and spices and fold into the mixture. Add all the fruit and the lemon rind, folding in to give a smooth dropping consistency. If too firm add 15-30 ml (1-2 tbsp) milk.
3 Divide the almond paste in half. Lightly dust a surface with icing sugar and roll out one half to a 16 cm (6½ inch) circle.
4 Spoon half of the cake mixture into the prepared tin. Place the round of almond paste on top and cover with the remaining cake mixture.
5 Tie a double thickness of brown paper around the outside of the tin. Bake at 150°C (300°F) mark 2 for about 2½ hours. When cooked the cake should be a rich brown colour, and firm to touch.
6 Cool in the tin for about 1 hour, then turn out and leave to cool completely on a wire rack.
7 Divide the remaining almond paste in two. Roll out one half to a 19 cm (7½ inch) circle and the rest into 11 small balls. Brush the top of the cake with egg white. Place the circle of almond paste on top, crimp the edges and, with a little egg white, fix the balls around the top edge of the cake.
8 Brush the almond paste with the remaining egg white and place under a hot grill for 1-2 minutes until the paste is well browned. Tie ribbon around the cake and decorate with flowers.

VARIATION Before grilling, apply a rope edging of almond paste around the top edge of the cake. When cool, cover the top of the cake with white glacé icing (see page 159).

with floured hands, knead for about 8-10 minutes
or until the dough is elastic and almost smooth.
Place in a large, lightly oiled bowl. Cover with
oiled clingfilm and leave in a warm place until
doubled in size; this usually takes 1½-2 hours.
3 Knock down the dough and knead lightly for
1-2 minutes. Divide the dough into about 25 equal-
sized pieces and knead each one into a small ball.
Place on buttered baking sheets, seam-side down,
and flatten slightly with the heel of your hand.
4 Roll out the pastry and cut into narrow strips.
Brush the buns with egg to glaze and top each one
with a pastry cross. Glaze again. Leave in a warm
place until doubled in size; about 30 minutes.
Bake at 190°C (375°F) mark 5 for 15-18 minutes
until they sound hollow when tapped. Cool on
wire racks.

MINI HOT CROSS BUNS

PREPARATION TIME 30 minutes, plus rising
COOKING TIME 15-18 minutes
FREEZING Suitable

❄

MAKES 25
- *15 g (½ oz) fresh
  yeast or 7 g sachet
  fast-action dried
  yeast*
- *about 175 ml (6 fl
  oz) tepid milk*
- *350 g (12 oz) strong
  white plain flour*
- *5 ml (1 tsp) salt*
- *5 ml (1 tsp) ground
  mixed spice*
- *5 ml (1 tsp) ground
  cinnamon*
- *5 ml (1 tsp) freshly
  grated nutmeg*

95 CALS/BUN
- *50 g (2 oz) butter*
- *finely grated rind of
  1 lemon*
- *25 g (1 oz) caster
  sugar*
- *75 g (3 oz) currants*
- *25 g (1 oz) chopped
  mixed peel*
- *1 egg, beaten*
- *75 g (3 oz) ready-
  made shortcrust
  pastry*
- *beaten egg, to glaze*

1 If using fresh yeast, blend with the milk. Sift the
flour, salt and spices into a bowl and rub in the
butter. Stir in the lemon rind, sugar, currants,
mixed peel and fast-action dried yeast if using.
Make a well in the centre; add yeast liquid or milk
and egg. Beat to form a soft dough, adding a little
more milk if necessary.
2 Turn out the dough onto a floured surface and,

EASTER BISCUITS

PREPARATION TIME 20 minutes
COOKING TIME 15 minutes
FREEZING Suitable
COLOUR INDEX Page 52

❄

MAKES 30
- *125 g (4 oz) butter,
  softened*
- *75 g (3 oz) caster
  sugar*
- *1 egg, separated*
- *200 g (7 oz) white
  plain flour*
- *pinch of salt*
- *2.5 ml (½ tsp)
  ground mixed spice*

65 CALS/BISCUIT
- *2.5 ml (½ tsp)
  ground cinnamon*
- *50 g (2 oz) currants*
- *15 ml (1 tbsp)
  chopped mixed peel*
- *15-30 ml (1-2 tbsp)
  brandy or milk*
- *caster sugar, for
  sprinkling*

1 Cream the butter and sugar together in a bowl
until pale and fluffy, then beat in the egg yolk. Sift
the flour, salt and spices together over the mixture.
Stir well, then add the fruit and mixed peel, with
enough brandy or milk to give a fairly soft dough.
2 Knead lightly on a lightly floured surface and
roll out to a 5 mm (¼ inch) thickness. Cut into 5
cm (2 inch) rounds using a fluted cutter. Place on
lightly greased baking sheets.
3 Bake at 200°C (400°F) mark 6 for 10 minutes,
then brush with the lightly beaten egg white and
sprinkle with a little caster sugar. Return to the
oven for a further 5 minutes, or until golden
brown. Transfer to wire racks to cool.

ALMOND SQUARES

PREPARATION TIME 25 minutes
COOKING TIME 35 minutes
FREEZING Suitable

❄

MAKES ABOUT 12	140 CALS/SERVING

- *Sweet Flan Pastry, made with 125 g (4 oz) white plain flour (see page 384).*
FILLING
- *45 ml (3 tbsp) raspberry jam*
- *1 egg white*

- *45 ml (3 tbsp) ground almonds*
- *50 g (2 oz) caster sugar*
- *few drops of almond flavouring*
- *45 ml (3 tbsp) flaked almonds*

1 Roll out the pastry on a lightly floured surface to an 18 cm (7 inch) square and use to line the base of a greased shallow 18 cm (7 inch) square cake tin. Spread the pastry with the jam, almost to the edges.
2 Whisk the egg white until stiff. Fold in the ground almonds, sugar and a few drops of almond flavouring. Spread the mixture over the jam on the pastry.

3 Sprinkle with flaked almonds and bake at 180°C (350°F) mark 4 for about 35 minutes until crisp and golden. Cool in the tin, then cut into squares to serve.

VARIATION *Glacé Icing Topping* For an indulgent treat, drizzle the top of the cooled baked mixture with glacé icing. To make the icing, simply sift 125 g (4 oz) icing sugar into a bowl, then gradually mix in 15 ml (1 tbsp) warm water until the icing is thick enough to coat the back of a spoon. If you would like to flavour the icing with orange or lemon, substitute 15 ml (1 tbsp) strained orange or lemon juice for the water.

159

CHOCOLATE COLETTES WITH
FROSTED FLOWERS

PREPARATION TIME 45 minutes, plus setting
COOKING TIME About 10 minutes
FREEZING Not suitable

MAKES ABOUT 16
- *125 g (4 oz) plain chocolate, broken into pieces*
- *small flower petals, such as violets and primroses*
- *1 egg white, lightly whisked*
- *caster sugar for sprinkling*

85 CALS/COLETTE
FILLING
- *50 g (2 oz) good quality white chocolate*
- *25 g (1 oz) butter*
- *10 ml (2 tsp) brandy*
- *60 ml (4 tbsp) double cream*

1 Arrange 16 double petit four cases on a baking sheet. Melt the plain chocolate in a heatproof bowl set over a pan of simmering water. Spoon a little into each paper case and, using a brush, spread evenly over the inside of each case, to coat completely. Chill until set. Re-melt the chocolate and repeat the process to make a thick chocolate shell.

2 To make the flower decoration, paint both sides of each petal with the lightly whisked egg white. Sprinkle both sides with caster sugar, shaking off the excess. Leave to dry. If necessary, sprinkle a second time with caster sugar to ensure they are evenly coated. Leave to dry completely.

3 To make the filling, melt the white chocolate with the butter and brandy. Remove from the heat and leave for about 10 minutes or until cool but not set.

4 Meanwhile, carefully peel away the paper from the set chocolate cases. Whisk the cream into the cooled white chocolate mixture and leave until thick enough to pipe. Spoon into a piping bag fitted with a small star nozzle and pipe into the chocolate cases.

5 Decorate the tops with frosted petals. Chill the colettes in the refrigerator for at least 1 hour before serving.

CHOCOLATE EASTER EGG

PREPARATION TIME 30 minutes, plus setting
COOKING TIME About 5 minutes
FREEZING Not suitable
COLOUR INDEX Page 53

**MAKES ONE 15 CM
(6 INCH) EGG**
- *300-325 g (10-11½ oz) plain, milk or white chocolate*
- *ready-made sweets, to fill*

2000 CALS/EGG
- *melted chocolate, to assemble*
- *ribbons and flowers, to decorate (optional)*

1 Using cotton wool, polish the insides of two 15 cm (6 inch) plastic Easter egg moulds. Place on a tray lined with non-stick baking parchment.
2 Melt the chocolate in a heatproof bowl set over a pan of simmering water. Remove from the heat and leave to cool slightly.
3 Using a large spoon, pour enough melted chocolate into each mould in turn to coat the sides. Tilt the moulds to coat completely.
4 Pour the excess chocolate back into the bowl. Invert the moulds on to the non-stick baking parchment and refrigerate briefly until set. Apply a second coat of chocolate and refrigerate again. Repeat once more, then return to the refrigerator and leave for 1 hour or until set. The eggs will crack if removed from the refrigerator too soon.
5 To turn out the chocolate egg halves, trim any excess chocolate from the outer edge of the moulds. Carefully pull each mould away from the chocolate around the edge to let air get in between the chocolate and the mould. Press firmly and the chocolate should slip out. Cover loosely and refrigerate.
6 To assemble the Easter egg, fill one half of the egg with sweets. Spread a little melted chocolate over the rims of the egg and, holding the remaining half in non-stick baking parchment, press it onto the melted chocolate to complete the egg. Refrigerate to set. Tie ribbon around the middle and decorate with flowers, if liked.

SOLID CHOCOLATE EGGS

PREPARATION TIME 1 hour, plus setting
COOKING TIME About 5 minutes
FREEZING Not suitable

MAKES 4
- *450 g (1 lb) plain, milk or white chocolate*

595 CALS/EGG
- *4 eggs*

1 With a needle, pierce a tiny hole in each end of one of the eggs and blow out the contents. Enlarge the hole in one end enough to take a small piping nozzle and wash out the shell with cold water. Leave to dry thoroughly while you blow the rest of the eggs. When they are dry, put a piece of sticky tape over the small hole in each egg so that it cannot leak.
2 Melt the chocolate in a heatproof bowl set over a pan of simmering water.
3 Spoon the melted chocolate into a nylon piping bag fitted with a small nozzle and pipe into the egg shells through the large holes. Swirl it round from time to time to remove any air bubbles. Leave the eggs overnight to set.
4 Carefully crack the eggs and peel off the shells.

VARIATION *Marbled Eggs* To make solid marbled Easter eggs, fill plastic egg moulds with alternate spoonfuls of melted plain and white chocolate. Tap on the work surface to remove any air bubbles, then leave to set. Unmould the egg halves and stick together with a little melted chocolate.

Summer

Summer is a wonderful time of year for any cook. Not only is there an abundance of glorious fresh produce to choose from, but there is also a wealth of opportunities for easy-going picnics. Food is fresh and light, but also full of the strong, fully-ripened flavours of the season. With summer fruit and fresh salad ingredients at their best, cooking can be simple and quick, allowing the quality of the ingredients to shine through.

SOUPS AND STARTERS

FISH AND SHELLFISH

POULTRY AND GAME

Stir-fried Chicken with
Courgettes
(page 188)

Poached Chicken in Watercress
Sauce
(page 188)

Lime-peppered Chicken
(page 189)

Chicken with Spiced Wheat
(page 190)

Mediterranean Chicken
(page 191)

Cheesy Chicken and Bacon Rolls
(page 191)

Grilled Chicken Salad
(page 192)

Smoked Chicken with Cucumber
and Mango
(page 192)

Warm Duck Salad
(page 193)

MEAT

Middle Eastern Meat Skewers
(page 194)

Sesame Beef Salad
(page 195)

Pizzaiola Steak
(page 195)

Tomato-crusted Lamb with
Summer Vegetables
(page 196)

Minted Lamb Escalopes
(page 196)

Peppered Garlic Pork with Crème
Fraîche
(page 197)

Maple-glazed Gammon with
Papaya Salsa
(page 198)

Homemade Sausages with Rocket
Pesto
(page 199)

Chinese-style Spare Ribs
(page 199)

CHEESE AND EGGS

Courgette and Bacon Frittata
(page 200)

Vegetable Egg Nests
(page 200)

Feta and Oregano Tarts
(page 201)

PASTA AND NOODLES

Italian Seafood Pasta Salad
(page 202)

Pasta with Walnut and Basil
Sauce
(page 202)

Thai Chicken Noodle Salad
(page 203)

Pasta in Sweet Pepper Sauce
(page 203)

Crunchy Courgette Pasta
(page 204)

Tomato and Mozzarella Noodles
(page 204)

Pasta with Grilled Asparagus and
Broad Beans
(page 205)

VEGETARIAN DISHES

Stuffed Peppers with Pine Nuts
(page 206)

Vegetable Pithivier
(page 206)

Tomato and Gruyère Pie
(page 207)

Summer Couscous
(page 207)

Summer Risotto
(page 208)

Turkish Aubergines
(page 208)

Vegetable Kebabs with Mango
Sauce and Tropical Rice
(page 209)

VEGETABLES AND SALADS

DESSERTS

BAKING

PRESERVES

DRINKS

'Summertime and the livin' is easy' goes the song - and how true! The abundance of fresh produce available during the summer months certainly makes cooking easier and the warmer weather inspires a more relaxed attitude to everyday eating and entertaining. This is the season of picnics, barbecues and holiday cooking, all of which should be fun, with the minimum of fuss and preparation.

SUMMER SALADS

The many different varieties of salad leaves now widely available make summer salads a joy to create. Go for different colour combinations and balance soft leaves with a crunchy texture, peppery leaves with sweet. Be brave and experiment!

Salad Combinations

• For a piquant salad, combine one radicchio with a bunch of watercress, a medium frisée, 50 g (2 oz) baby spinach, 50 g (2 oz) rocket and 250 g (9 oz) halved radishes. Fry some small bread croûtons and toss everything together with your favourite dressing.
• For a fruity fennel salad, toss together sliced fennel with orange and grapefruit segments and diced cucumber for added crunch.
• Add 'wild' foods such as sorrel, young dandelion leaves and nasturtium flowers, leaves and seeds.
• Combine traditional salad ingredients like cucumber, Cos or Webb's lettuce with crisply cooked vegetables such as beans, mangetouts,

A fresh salad of mixed leaves and crisp vegetables, tossed in a herb dressing, epitomizes summer eating.

asparagus, baby sweetcorn and broccoli.
• Add seeds - sesame, sunflower - for texture, and roughly chopped walnuts or peanuts for extra crunch.
• Cooked grains, such as couscous and mixed wild rice, make good bases for salads that can be prepared in advance.

Dressings

A good dressing will give any salad a lift. A classic vinaigrette is hard to beat and the basic recipe can be varied with different flavourings.

Basic vinaigrette Place 5 ml (1 tsp) Dijon mustard in a screw-top jar with 15 ml (1 tbsp) white wine vinegar, 45-60 ml (3-4 tbsp) olive oil, according to taste, and season with salt and pepper. Shake until well emulsified and use at once.
• For an Italian-style dressing, omit the mustard, add 5 ml (1 tsp) balsamic vinegar, 1 crushed garlic clove and 15 ml (1 tbsp) chopped fresh oregano or parsley.
• Use walnut or hazelnut oil instead of olive oil, but mix with a flavourless oil, such as groundnut or sunflower, to dilute the intensity.
• Use lemon or orange juice instead of vinegar, or try herb, spice or fruit vinegars.
• Try adding 5 ml (1 tsp) pesto sauce or sun-dried tomato paste for a Mediterranean touch. Alternatively, stir in chopped fresh herbs.

TOMATOES

Many different varieties of tomato are now appearing on the supermarket shelves – red and yellow cherry tomatoes, large beef tomatoes, oval Italian plum tomatoes, Provençal tomatoes to mention a few. Unfortunately, many of these are picked too early and as a result can be hard and lacking in flavour.

One way to ripen tomatoes is to set them on a sunny window sill for at least a week - you will notice that the colour deepens and that they become soft and sweet. Leaving the stalks on helps as well. Refrigerate the tomatoes once ripened, but eat quickly.

Here are a few ways to bring out the best in tomatoes.
• Mix 450 g (1 lb) cherry tomatoes with 60 ml (4 tbsp) olive oil, 2 crushed garlic cloves and salt and pepper. Toss to coat, then grill under a hot grill until charred. Serve hot or cold as a tasty accompaniment.
• Plum tomatoes are very firm and are particularly suitable for grilling and roasting as they tend not to

collapse too much.

• Add 4 diced tomatoes to 60 ml (4 tbsp) homemade pesto (see page 169) to make a wonderful light sauce for 350 g (12 oz) cooked pasta.

• Stir halved small tomatoes into hot pasta with a handful of rocket and some soft cheese for a quick summery snack.

• Make a salad using different shaped and coloured tomatoes, arranging the slices on a shallow platter. Spoon over a vinaigrette dressing made with a pinch of sugar and a little chopped mint to bring out the flavour.

• Fill ripe beef tomatoes with a mixture of couscous, toasted pine nuts and chopped roasted peppers for a vegetarian meal.

• Top thick Spanish omelettes with sliced tomatoes, cover with grated cheese and grill – this makes a great supper dish.

FRESH HERBS

Herbs are easy to grow - in the garden, on the patio or even on window sills - and can turn a simple summer dish into something quite memorable! Add chopped fresh herbs to mayonnaise, dressings, sauces and marinades to add extra flavour to meat, fish and vegetables, or use whole sprigs for pretty garnishes. Preserve the fresh flavours in the following ways.

Herb Oils and Vinegars

To capture the flavour of herbs for a short while try making herb oils and vinegars.

Herb oils Here are two simple methods.

• Wash and dry a large bunch of basil leaves and layer them in a flat dish. Cover with about 150 ml (5 fl oz) light olive oil, cover with a clean tea towel and leave in the sun for about 6 hours. Strain the oil into clean jars and keep refrigerated for up to 1 month.

• Blanch a large bunch of coriander, basil or mint leaves and refresh in iced water. Drain and pat dry on absorbent kitchen paper. Place in a blender with 150 ml (5 fl oz) light olive oil and blend until smooth. Pour into a jar and refrigerate overnight. Strain through two layers of muslin without pressing, then decant into clean bottles. Use the precious oil in dressings or just pour neat over salad.

Herb vinegars can be made in the same way as herb oil – or simply add your favourite fresh herb to a bottle of wine or cider vinegar and keep for at least a week.

Herb oils and fruit flavoured vinegars are very easy to make and will lend a subtle taste to salad dressings, sauces and marinades.

Freezing Herbs

A handy way to store chopped fresh herbs is to place them in ice-cube trays, top them with water and freeze. Pop an ice cube or two into a sauce or soup and allow to melt or use as an unusual garnish for chilled soup.

SALMON

Fresh salmon is a summmer favourite. The wild variety is a real treat, but the cheaper farmed version is still prized for its delicate flavour and attractive pink flesh. One of the great advantages of salmon is that it is easy to cook. A whole poached or baked salmon (see page 181) is ideal for a party, but cuts of salmon can provide quick summery dishes that will suit any occasion. Steaks and fillets are the quickest to cook and when marinated only need 30 minutes for the flavours to be absorbed. A large fillet coated with spices is excellent for barbecuing (see recipe page 180) or try brushing salmon steaks with a little soy sauce or teriyaki marinade and grill until charred, basting well.

• A delicate cucumber and dill sauce makes the perfect accompaniment to poached salmon. Peel, deseed and dice a cucumber. Melt 25 g (1 oz) butter, add the cucumber and cook for 2 minutes, then add 150 ml (5 fl oz) dry white wine and boil until all the liquid has disappeared. Stir in 45 ml (3 tbsp) chopped fresh dill or chervil and 60 ml (4 tbsp) crème fraîche, adjust the seasoning and serve at once.

SUMMER SHELLFISH

Fresh crab and crustacea, such as shrimps, langoustine (Dublin Bay prawns), lobster, winkles and so on, are wonderful at this time of year and make a great addition to a seafood platter. Buy the shellfish ready cooked for easy entertaining.

• For a summer seafood feast, present a crab to each guest or a platter of mixed crustacea on a bed of ice, together with crackers and lobster picks, a couple of herby or spicy dips, a few salads and lots of brown bread - and get cracking! Offer plenty of halved lemons for cleaning fingers afterwards.

• Frozen crabmeat is excellent for making the best peppery crab sandwiches - mix light and dark meat together with a little mayonnaise, some Tabasco and plenty of black pepper. Use generously to fill freshly sliced brown bread. Ideal for adding a special touch to picnic food.

SOFT SUMMER FRUITS

Strawberries, raspberries and the various currants are one of the great delights of summer. Delicately flavoured and deliciously juicy, these luscious fruits make wonderful, easy desserts.

• Summer Pudding (see recipe page 220) is a summer classic. A divine combination of mixed red fruit, this pudding is traditionally made with bread, but for a change, try using Madeira sponge instead. Sliced brioche is good too, as is thickly sliced Pannetone. Even a bought flan sponge works well, as the fruit really needs no embellishment. Serve with extra fruit juice and cream whisked with rosewater and a little grated orange rind to enhance the fruity flavours.

Strawberry Ideas

Turn 450 g (1 lb) strawberries into the following quick treats.

• Marinate the halved strawberries and segmented oranges in a couple of tablespoons of Cointreau for 20 minutes and serve with crème frâiche.

• Place whole berries in a bowl. Halve 2 passion fruit, scoop out the pulp and toss with the berries.

• Dip the tips of perfect strawberries into melted white, dark or milk chocolate. Leave on non-stick paper to harden and pile up on a dish decorated with flowers for that special dinner party dessert.

• Halve strawberries and grind over black pepper and a drizzle of balsamic or sherry vinegar - an explosion of flavour and very refreshing!

• Quickly sauté halved berries in butter, adding a little honey and balsamic vinegar and serve immediately with scoops of vanilla ice cream.

• Purée raspberries with a little sugar and kirsch, sieve and pour over halved strawberries.

• For handy sauces, purée strawberries and freeze in ice cube trays for quick thawing. Raspberry purée is a useful standby too.

Fruit Vinegars

It's always worth making jams and jellies from a glut of soft fruit, but why not try making your own fruit vinegars as well. Perfect for adding subtle flavouring to dressings and sauces, fruit vinegars are surprisingly easy to make. Simply place the fruit in a bowl and break it up slightly. For each 450 g (1 lb) soft fruit, pour in 600 ml (1 pint) red or white wine vinegar. Cover with a cloth and leave to stand for 3-4 days, stirring occasionally. Then strain through muslin, measure the vinegar and add 450 g (1 lb) sugar for each 600 ml (1 pint). Boil for 10 minutes then cool. Strain again, pour into bottles and seal with airtight and vinegar-proof tops.

BARBECUES

Barbecues are a great way of making the most of the long summer evenings and are perfect for easy, informal entertaining. Meat and fish, basted with tasty sauces and marinades, are popular barbecue fare, but the plentiful vegetables of summer are equally delicious cooked on the barbecue. Try these simple vegetable ideas for side dishes or a vegetarian feast.

• Slice red onions into 1 cm (1/2 inch) rounds and slide onto skewers. Barbecue on both sides, brushing with sweet chilli sauce.

• Remove the stem from the base of a large field mushroom, brush with olive oil, lemon juice, salt and pepper. Place on the grill stalk-side down for 1-2 minutes. Turn over and fill the cavity with garlic butter or pesto sauce. Heat for another 1-2 minutes.

• Cook whole ripe tomatoes over a low fire for 1-2 minutes, turning occasionally until soft and lightly charred.

• For minted aubergines, lightly fry 6 sliced garlic cloves in 15 ml (1 tbsp) olive oil. Add 180 ml (12 tbsp) wine vinegar and 60 ml (4 tbsp) sugar. Heat slowly until the sugar dissolves and reduce by half.

Add 90 ml (6 tbsp) roughly chopped fresh mint. Drizzle over 450 g (1 lb) sliced grilled aubergines. Serve hot or cold.

• Halve or quarter chicory or radicchio, leaving the core in place. Grill on a cool part of the barbecue, turning frequently until beginning to wilt, then drizzle with olive oil and reduced balsamic vinegar. (To make reduced vinegar, boil balsamic vinegar in a pan until reduced by half - keep in a jar and use sparingly.)

Finishing Touches

Marinades and accompanying dips and sauces can make all the difference to the flavour of barbecued food.

Watercress pesto Put 75 g (3 oz) soft goats' cheese in a blender or food processor with 25 g (1 oz) Gruyère cheese, 200 ml (7 fl oz) olive oil, 25 g (1 oz) pistachio nuts, 1 garlic clove, 2.5 ml ($^{1}/_{2}$ tsp) salt and 75 g (3 oz) watercress and blend until smooth. Serve with barbecued or grilled steak or fish, or spoon over baked potatoes.

Basil aioli Blend 175 ml (6 fl oz) olive oil with 125

Barbecue a selection of summer vegetables alongside succulent pieces of meat or fish to create a complete al fresco feast, full of delicious smoky flavours.

g (4 oz) fresh basil in a blender or food processor, then transfer to a jug. Blend 1 egg yolk with 15 ml (1 tbsp) white wine vinegar and half the basil oil. Blend together until thickening, then add 1 garlic clove and the remaining basil oil. Work for 30 seconds and season. Use as a dip for barbecued vegetables.

Spiced marinade Mix 150 ml (5 fl oz) soy sauce with 150 ml (5 fl oz) dry or medium sherry, 4 garlic cloves, 2.5 cm (1 inch) grated fresh ginger root, 30 ml (2 tbsp) clear honey, 2.5 ml ($^{1}/_{2}$ tsp) ground star anise and 30 ml (2 tbsp) chopped fresh coriander. Use for marinating lamb, chicken pieces or a whole salmon.

Sun-dried tomato butter Blend in a food processor 1 small bunch chives, 25 g (1 oz) pitted black olives, 30 ml (2 tbsp) sun-dried tomato paste, 225 g (8oz) softened unsalted butter, 1 garlic clove and black pepper. Use to top barbecued food.

169

HERB FRAME

The plentiful fresh herbs of summer have innumerable uses in the kitchen, but their delicate colouring and attractive aroma also make them ideal for decorative purposes. A rich harvest of herbs can be turned into a subtle, sweet-smelling display that will enhance any summer setting.

Here a simple wooden structure is covered with bunches of mixed herbs to create a fresh, leafy frame that will add a touch of natural colour and scent to a room. Hang or prop the frame against a plain wall for a simple, rustic look, or use the frame flat as part of a table setting - herb displays look particularly good set against crisp, white table linen and wrought iron candle holders.

You will need:
**Twelve 40 cm (16 inch) lengths
and four 10 cm (4 inch)
lengths of garden training
wood
Garden string
Scissors
Florist's wire on a reel
Large bunches of fresh
herbs, such as rosemary
sage, oregano, lavender
Ribbon with wire edging**

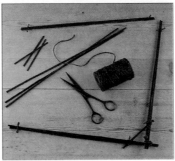

1 Bind together three 40 cm (16 inch) lengths of wood by tying with string 2.5 cm (1 inch) in from either end. Repeat with remaining 40 cm (16 inch) wood to make the four sides of the frame. Arrange into a square frame shape, overlapping the wood at the knots, then tie in place. To give extra support, attach a 10 cm (4 inch) length of wood across each corner.
2 Separate the herbs into sprigs and trim to 10-15 cm (4-6 inch) lengths. Tie into small bunches, using 4-6 mixed sprigs per bunch.

3 Lay one bunch along the wooden frame, positioning the stems at a slight angle. Bind the bunch in place with wire, winding it around two or three times. Do not cut the wire. Place another bunch on the frame at a different angle, close enough to cover the stems of first bunch. Bind as before.
4 Continue binding on bunches until the frame is completely covered in herbs. Finish with a ribbon bow.
5 Move the completed frame with care, as the structure is fairly delicate.

ROSE RIBBONS

Ribbons of rose buds are a wonderfully romantic idea, suited to the most glamorous occasions such as a wedding or a landmark anniversary. Threaded onto fine florist's wire, the rose buds can be used to spell out initials on the table. For a more flexible ribbon, use thread instead of wire - try looping this around the edge of a buffet table, catching it in places with a large rose.

Experiment with different flowers and buds. To save money, you can alternate roses with leaves and fresh flowers from the garden.

You will need:
Plenty of the smallest rose buds available
Fine florist's wire
Fine strong thread
Darning needle

1 For a wired rose 'ribbon', simply push a length of wire across the base of a bud or up through the bud and out at the top. Continue threading buds along the wire until the 'ribbon' is as long as required.

2 To form initials, trace out the letters on a piece of paper first, enlarging them from a pattern book if necessary. Bend the rose ribbon round the traced pattern then slide the paper out.
3 For a looser rose 'ribbon' string buds onto thread with a darning needle to form a long chain of roses.
4 Wrap the chain of rose buds around dishes, loop it along the edge of a table or twist it around glass stems.

MELON FLOWER BOWL

A carved melon bowl filled with brightly-coloured flowers is the perfect finishing touch for a summer table setting. Creating the decorative edge of the melon is easy, yet very effective, and the scooped-out shell makes an excellent holder. If wished, use the melon as part of the meal, perhaps as a starter filled with salad and topped with edible flowers, such as nasturtiums.

The sculptured look of this display can be enhanced by adding other carved fruit to the setting - for instance, the skin of a whole pomelo or other large citrus fruit can be given a dramatic pattern by simply carving into the rind with a zester or peeler.

You will need:
1 melon, such as ogen or
**   charentais**
Large sharp knife
Small sharp knife
Dessert spoon
Edible flowers and leaves, such
**   as geraniums**
Side plate

1 Using a large knife, cut a thin slice off the bottom of the melon so that it stands upright.

2 Using a small sharp knife, cut round the top third of the melon in a zig-zag pattern. Remove top from melon.

3 Scoop out the seeds from the centre of the melon with a dessert spoon.

4 Arrange stems of flowers and leaves in the scooped-out melon and stand on a small plate to create an attractive display.

ICED BOTTLES

Frosted bottles look spectacular encased in ice with flowers, leaves and fruits trapped in it. This attractive idea only works for bottles filled with spirits, such as schnapps and vodka, that have a low freezing point. However, strong empty bottles can also be packed in ice and used to serve drinks at a summer party or barbecue – a perfect way of keeping drinks cool! Stand the iced-up bottles on a tray or plate to catch the drips as they slowly melt.

Large milk containers with their tops cut off make ideal moulds in which to freeze the bottles. The containers and bottles take up a fair amount of space in the freezer, so make room in advance. Carefully build up the ice in layers to distribute the flowers and fruit evenly throughout. Spring water is less likely than tap water to freeze cloudy.

You will need:
Vodka, schnapps or flavoured
  vodka in strong bottles
Plastic milk containers for
  moulds
Spring water or tap water
Flowers, petals and leaves
Fruits, such as cherries,
  strawberries

1 Cut off the top of the plastic container horizontally and make space in the freezer to stand it upright. Pour 2.5 cm (1 inch) water into the base and place in the freezer until frozen solid.
2 Stand the bottle centrally in the container and add another 2.5 cm (1 inch) water. If the bottle moves around, wedge it with paper or wooden skewers near the top, above the water level. Place in the freezer again to freeze until the bottle is firmly anchored.

3 Arrange flowers, leaves and fruit around the bottle and pour in 10 cm (4 inches) water. Leave to freeze and continue building up in layers until the container is full.
4 When the last layer of water is frozen, take the container out of the freezer and plunge it briefly into a deep bowl or sinkful of hot water. The plastic container should slide off easily. Return the frozen bottle to the freezer until it is needed.

CHILLED TOMATO AND VODKA SOUP

PREPARATION TIME 10 minutes plus chilling
FREEZING Not suitable
COLOUR INDEX Page 9
♡

SERVES 6

- *125 g (4 oz) celery, trimmed and chopped*
- *1 red pepper, deseeded and chopped*
- *900 ml (1½ pints) tomato juice*
- *60 ml (4 tbsp) vodka*
- *45 ml (3 tbsp) chopped fresh coriander*

55 CALS/SERVING

- *60 ml (4 tbsp) Worcestershire sauce*
- *juice of 2 lemons, about 45 ml (3 tbsp)*
- *2.5 ml (½ tsp) chilli sauce*
- *salt and pepper*
- *3 garlic cloves, peeled and crushed*
- *crushed ice, to serve (optional)*

1 Mix the celery and pepper with the remaining ingredients in a large bowl.
2 Cover and chill for at least 1 hour. Serve over a little crushed ice, if wished.

CHILLED AVOCADO AND LIME SOUP

PREPARATION TIME 5-10 minutes, plus chilling
COOKING TIME 15-20 minutes
FREEZING Not suitable
COLOUR INDEX Page 9

SERVES 4

- *15 ml (1 tbsp) extra-virgin olive oil*
- *1 bunch spring onions, trimmed and sliced*
- *225 g (8 oz) potatoes, peeled and cubed*
- *900 ml (1½ pints) vegetable stock*

235 CALS/SERVING

- *1-2 limes*
- *2 ripe avocados*
- *salt and pepper*
- *90 ml (6 tbsp) very low-fat fromage frais*
- *snipped chives, to garnish*

1 Heat the oil in a large saucepan, add the spring onions and fry gently until softened.
2 Add the potato to the softened onions and fry, stirring, for 2 minutes. Add the stock and bring to the boil. Cover and simmer for 15-20 minutes.
3 Towards the end of the cooking time, remove a little zest from one of the limes, using a zester, and set aside for the garnish. Squeeze the juice from the lime. Halve, stone and peel the avocados, then chop roughly. Add the avocado to the soup with the lime juice. Taste and adjust the seasoning; add extra lime juice (from the other lime) if required.
4 Remove the soup from the heat, allow to cool slightly, then work until smooth in a blender or food processor. Add 30 ml (2 tbsp) fromage frais and stir to mix. Pour into soup bowls and chill for 3-4 hours. (The soup thickens as it is chilled.)
5 To serve, add a swirl of fromage frais and a squeeze of lime juice. Grind some black pepper on top and garnish with snipped chives and the lime zest. Serve with Melba Toast.

> *TIP*
> To make Melba Toast, cut 4-5 thin slices from a day-old loaf of wholemeal bread. Toast lightly on both sides. Quickly cut off the crusts and split each slice in two horizontally. Bake in a 180°C (350°F) mark 4 oven for 10-15 minutes until crisp and curled.

LETTUCE AND SORREL SOUP

PREPARATION TIME 15 minutes
COOKING TIME 20-25 minutes
FREEZING Suitable
❄

SERVES 4
- *60 ml (4 tbsp) extra-virgin olive oil*
- *6 spring onions, chopped*
- *1 garlic clove, peeled and crushed*
- *5 ml (1 tsp) chopped fresh thyme (lemon thyme preferably)*
- *50 g (2 oz) long-grain rice*
- *450 g (1 lb) cos lettuce, shredded*

205 CALS/SERVING
- *125 g (4 oz) sorrel, shredded*
- *1.2 litres (2 pints) vegetable stock*
- *30 ml (2 tbsp) chopped fresh chives*
- *pinch of grated nutmeg*
- *salt and pepper*
- *Parmesan cheese shavings, to garnish (optional)*

1 Heat 15 ml (1 tbsp) of the oil in a saucepan, add the spring onions, garlic and thyme and fry gently for 5 minutes until softened but not coloured. Add the rice and stir-fry for 1 minute.

2 Stir in the lettuce and the sorrel and pour in the stock. Bring to the boil, cover and simmer gently for 15 minutes until the rice is cooked.

3 Transfer to a blender or food processor, add the chives and nutmeg and purée until smooth. Return the soup to the pan, and heat through, whisking in the remaining oil and seasoning with salt and pepper. Serve hot, garnished with a little Parmesan.

VARIATIONS For a more substantial soup, omit the rice, reduce the lettuce to 225 g (8 oz) and add 225 g (8 oz) potatoes. If sorrel is not available, use spinach instead.

SPICY CRAB DIP

PREPARATION TIME 10 minutes, plus chilling
FREEZING Not suitable
♡

SERVES 4
- *225 g (8 oz) white crab meat, flaked*
- *225 g (8 oz) soft cheese*
- *45 ml (3 tbsp) canned pimiento, finely chopped .*
- *juice of ½ lemon*

135 CALS/SERVING
- *10 ml (2 tsp) Worcestershire sauce*
- *5 ml (1 tsp) anchovy essence*
- *1.25 ml (¼ tsp) cayenne pepper*
- *salt and pepper*
- *crudités, to serve*

1 Fold the crab meat into the soft cheese until evenly mixed.
2 Fold in the pimiento, then stir in the lemon juice, Worcestershire sauce, anchovy essence and cayenne and season with salt and pepper. Turn into a serving bowl and chill for at least 2 hours. Serve with crudités.

BRUSCHETTA

PREPARATION TIME 20 minutes
COOKING TIME 4 minutes
FREEZING Not suitable
COLOUR INDEX Page 11
🕐

SERVES 6
- *12 slices Italian bread (such as Ciabatta), about 2 cm (¾ inch) thick*
- *salt and pepper*
- *1-2 garlic cloves, peeled*
- *90 ml (6 tbsp) olive oil*
- *lemon rind and basil leaves, to garnish*
HERB AND LEMON TOPPING
- *15 ml (1 tbsp) each chopped fresh mint and parsley*
- *15 ml (1 tbsp) lemon juice*

300 CALS/SERVING
TOMATO TOPPING
- *3 plum or very ripe tomatoes, skinned, deseeded and diced*
- *15 ml (1 tbsp) pesto sauce*
- *30 ml (2 tbsp) chopped fresh basil*
TAPENADE TOPPING
- *45-60 ml (3-4 tbsp) tapenade (black olive paste)*
- *4 pitted black olives, shredded*

1 To make the toppings, mix together the ingredients in three small separate bowls and season each with salt and pepper to taste.
2 Toast both sides of the slices of bread until golden. Press the garlic cloves with the blade of a large knife to bruise them and rub over one side of each slice. Drizzle the toast with olive oil, then spoon each of the toppings onto four of the slices.
3 Drizzle the remaining olive oil on top and garnish the Herb and Lemon Topping with lemon rind and the Tomato Topping with basil leaves. Serve while still hot and crisp.

SKEWERED TIGER PRAWNS WITH PARMA HAM

PREPARATION TIME 20 minutes, plus marinating
COOKING TIME 4-6 minutes
FREEZING Not suitable
♡

SERVES 4
- *225 g (8 oz) raw tiger prawns*
- *65 g (2½ oz) sliced Parma ham*
- *coriander or flat-leaf parsley sprigs, to garnish*
MARINADE
- *1 shallot, peeled and finely chopped*
- *1 garlic clove, peeled and crushed*

200 CALS/SERVING
- *5 ml (1 tsp) wholegrain mustard*
- *1 small fresh red chilli, deseeded and very finely sliced*
- *15 ml (1 tbsp) olive oil*
- *juice of ½ lemon*
- *salt and pepper*

1 Peel the prawns, discarding the heads. Cut down the back of each prawn and remove the black intestinal vein. Wash and dry well. Thread the prawns onto 8 small bamboo skewers which have been previously soaked in warm water for 30 minutes.
2 Cut the Parma ham slices in half lengthways and wrap around the skewered prawns. Place the skewers in a glass or china dish and set aside.
3 Mix together the marinade ingredients and pour over the skewered prawns. Cover and marinate in the refrigerator for 1-2 hours, turning occasionally.
4 Drain the skewered prawns and place on a grill rack. Cook under a hot grill for 4-6 minutes, basting with the marinade and turning occasionally until the prawns are cooked and the ham is beginning to crisp and brown. Serve at once, garnished with coriander or parsley sprigs.

VARIATION Thread lemon wedges onto the skewers, in between the prawns.

177

SPINACH, BACON AND ROQUEFORT SALAD

PREPARATION TIME 15 minutes
COOKING TIME 10 minutes
FREEZING Not suitable

🕐

SERVES 8
- *8 slices French bread, cut on the diagonal into slices about 2.5 cm (1 inch) thick*
- *120 ml (8 tbsp) olive oil*
- *175 g (6 oz) streaky bacon or pancetta (Italian bacon), sliced very thinly*
- *50 g (2 oz) pine nuts*
- *60 ml (4 tbsp) sesame oil*

520 CALS/SERVING
- *30 ml (2 tbsp) red wine vinegar*
- *pepper*
- *125 g (4 oz) baby spinach, washed*
- *125 g (4 oz) Roquefort cheese, crumbled*
- *175 g (6 oz) black seedless grapes, halved*

1 Brush both sides of each slice of French bread with 60 ml (4 tbsp) of the olive oil. Place on a baking sheet. Halve or chop the bacon and place on a second baking sheet with the pine nuts. Cook at 230°C (450°F) mark 8 for about 10 minutes or until the bread slices are golden brown and the bacon is cooked, turning all the food halfway through.
2 Whisk the remaining 60 ml (4 tbsp) olive oil with the sesame oil, vinegar and pepper.
3 Pile the spinach, bacon, cheese, pine nuts and grapes on the croûtes. Pour on the dressing and toss well.

COURGETTE AND PESTO ROUNDS

PREPARATION TIME 20 minutes
COOKING TIME 10 minutes
FREEZING Not suitable
COLOUR INDEX Page 10

♡ 🕐

SERVES 6
- *225 g (8 oz) courgettes*
- *olive oil*
- *2 beefsteak tomatoes, about 450 g (1 lb) total weight*
- *30 ml (2 tbsp) red pesto sauce or tapenade (black olive paste)*

90 CALS/SERVING
- *large handful of fresh basil leaves*
- *salt and pepper*
- *50 g (2 oz) fresh Parmesan cheese*

1 Cut the courgettes diagonally into slices about 5 mm (¼ inch) thick. Lightly brush a non-stick frying pan with oil. Cook the courgette slices on both sides for about 5 minutes or until brown and tender.
2 Cut each tomato into 3 slices about 1 cm (½ inch) thick and place on a lightly oiled baking sheet. Spread 5 ml (1 tsp) of pesto or tapenade on top of each slice. Place 5 or 6 basil leaves in a circle on top of the pesto.
3 Place an overlapping circle of courgettes on the basil leaves. Season with salt and pepper.
4 Cook at 200°C (400°F) mark 6 for 10 minutes. Top with thinly pared Parmesan cheese. Serve immediately.

VARIATION *Courgette and Mozzarella Rounds*
This recipe works equally well with mozzarella cheese. Assemble the rounds as above but top each one with a thin slice of mozzarella at the end of stage 3 – you'll need about 75 g (3 oz). Cook as directed in the recipe above, then brown under a hot grill before serving.

CUCUMBER AND STRAWBERRY SALAD

PREPARATION TIME 40 minutes
FREEZING Not suitable
COLOUR INDEX Page 12
♡

SERVES 4

- ½ *cucumber*
- *salt and pepper*
- *225 g (8 oz) ripe strawberries*
- *2 fresh ripe figs, wiped*

130 CALS/SERVING

- *45 ml (3 tbsp) sunflower oil*
- *15 ml (1 tbsp) balsamic or wine vinegar*

1 Score the skin of the cucumber lengthways with the prongs of a fork. Slice the cucumber very thinly, then place on a plate and sprinkle with salt. Leave to stand for about 30 minutes to draw out the excess moisture.

2 Meanwhile, prepare the strawberries and figs. Reserve a few small strawberries for the garnish. Slice the remaining strawberries in half lengthways. Slice the figs into quarters lengthways.

3 To prepare the dressing, whisk together the oil, vinegar and pepper with a fork.

4 Drain the cucumber and pat dry with absorbent kitchen paper. Arrange the cucumber slices, quartered figs and halved strawberries on a serving plate. Sprinkle over the dressing, then garnish with the reserved whole strawberries. Serve as soon as possible.

TIP

The combination of sweet and sour in this salad is unusual, but most refreshing. Do not use malt vinegar as it is too strong. Balsamic vinegar is perfect, or you can use wine vinegar.

MANGO AND PRAWN SALADS

PREPARATION TIME 20 minutes
FREEZING Not suitable
♡ ⏲

SERVES 4

- *2 ripe mangoes*
- *225 g (8 oz) cooked, peeled prawns*
- *90 ml (6 tbsp) fromage frais*
- *30 ml (2 tbsp) mayonnaise*
- *grated rind of 1 lime*
- *10 ml (2 tsp) lime juice*

180 CALS/SERVING

- *5 ml (1 tsp) snipped fresh chives*
- *salt and pepper*
- *mixed salad leaves*
- *cooked prawns with their shells on*
- *slices of ripe mango, to garnish*

1 Slice each mango twice lengthways, either side of the stone. Cut the flesh in the segments lengthways and widthways without breaking the skin, then push the skin inside out to expose the cubes of flesh. Slice off and remove the flesh in neat cubes and put in a bowl. Peel the remaining centre sections and cut the flesh away from the stones into cubes. Add to the bowl.

2 Add the peeled prawns, fromage frais, mayonnaise, lime rind and juice, chives, salt and pepper, and mix together.

3 Arrange the mixture on a bed of salad leaves on individual serving plates. Serve garnished with the whole prawns and mango slices.

VARIATION *Melon and Prawn Salads* Replace the mango with a sweet-flavoured melon such as charentais.

SPICED BARBECUED SALMON

PREPARATION TIME 15 minutes
COOKING TIME 15 minutes
FREEZING Not suitable
COLOUR INDEX Page 15
♡ ⏲

SERVES 6

• *900 g (2 lb) salmon
fillet, with skin on
and scales removed*
• *6 cardamom pods*
• *5 ml (1 tsp) cumin
seeds*
• *5 ml (1 tsp)
coriander seeds*

295 CALS/SERVING

• *2.5 ml (½ tsp) black
peppercorns*
• *2.5 ml (½ tsp)
coarse salt*
• *30 ml (2 tbsp) olive
oil*

1 Remove any remaining salmon bones with
tweezers. Using a sharp knife, slash the skin side
into diamonds.
2 Remove the dark seeds from the cardamom
pods and discard the pods. Finely grind the seeds
with the cumin seeds, coriander seeds, peppercorns
and coarse salt in a grinder or with a pestle and
mortar.
3 Brush the salmon with the oil and press the
spices firmly onto the skin side. Place the salmon
in a fish griller and cook on the barbecue for 10-
15 minutes, turning halfway through, until brown
and crisp but just cooked on the inside.

VARIATIONS The fish can be cooked in the oven,
if wished. Place the salmon on an oiled baking
sheet and cook at 230°C (450°F) mark 8 for 10-
15 minutes.

For an unusual touch, dip a small bunch of
mixed herbs into a bowl of olive oil and brush
lightly over the fish as it cooks.

TIP
If you barbecue fish frequently it's a good idea
to invest in a fish grill, which encloses the fish
and makes it much easier to handle.

BAKED SALMON WITH WALNUT OIL AND HERBS

PREPARATION TIME 35 minutes, plus marinating
COOKING TIME 15-20 minutes
FREEZING Not suitable
COLOUR INDEX Page 15

SERVES 4

• *575 g (1¼ lb) salmon
fillet, skinned*
• *125 ml (4 fl oz)
white wine*
• *50 ml (2 fl oz)
walnut oil*
• *60 ml (4 tbsp)
chopped fresh mixed
herbs, such as parsley
and chives*
• *2 garlic cloves,
peeled and crushed*
• *large pinch of
paprika*

490 CALS/SERVING

• *salt and pepper*
• *4 sticks celery, cut
into matchsticks*
• *225 g (8 oz) young
turnips, peeled and
cut into matchsticks*
• *olive oil*
• *90 ml (6 tbsp)
double cream*
• *lime juice to taste*
• *cooked shrimps or
prawns, to garnish*

1 Cut the fillet into four even-size pieces and place
in a shallow non-metallic dish. Mix the wine,
walnut oil, herbs, garlic, paprika and seasoning.
Spoon the mixture over the fish, cover and chill in
the refrigerator for at least 4 hours or overnight,
turning occasionally.
2 Meanwhile, blanch the celery and turnips
together in boiling, salted water for 1 minute, then
drain under cold water to cool quickly.
3 Lightly oil a shallow ovenproof dish. Place the
celery and turnips in it in a single layer and season
well. Lift the salmon out of the marinade and
place on top of the vegetables. Reserve the
marinade.
4 Bake the salmon and vegetables at 220°C
(425°F) mark 7 for 15-20 minutes or until the fish
is cooked.
5 Meanwhile, place the marinade and the cream in
a small saucepan and boil until reduced by about
half. Off the heat, quickly whisk in the lime juice
to taste and season with salt and pepper.
6 To serve, arrange the salmon and vegetables on
individual serving plates. Spoon the sauce over the
top and garnish with shrimps or prawns.

SALMON TROUT WITH HERB SAUCE

PREPARATION TIME 25 minutes, plus cooling
COOKING TIME 40 minutes
FREEZING Not suitable

SERVES 4   **575 CALS/SERVING**

- 1 salmon or sea trout, about 900 g (2 lb), cleaned
- 45 ml (3 tbsp) lemon juice
- 50 g (2 oz) butter or margarine
- salt and pepper
- 1 bunch watercress, roughly chopped
- 125 g (4 oz) spinach leaves, roughly chopped

- 45 ml (3 tbsp) chopped fresh parsley
- 30 ml (2 tbsp) chopped fresh chervil
- 5 ml (1 tsp) chopped fresh dill
- 150 ml (5 fl oz) mayonnaise
- herb sprigs and lemon rind shapes, to garnish

1 Place the fish in the centre of a large piece of foil. Add 30 ml (2 tbsp) of the lemon juice, then dot with 25 g (1 oz) of the butter. Season with salt and pepper.

2 Seal the foil, weigh the fish and place on a baking sheet. Calculate the cooking time at 15 minutes per 450 g (1 lb), plus 10 minutes. Bake at 180°C (350°F) mark 4 until tender.

3 Remove the fish from the foil, reserving the cooking liquor, then carefully remove the skin while still warm. Place the fish on a serving dish and leave to cool.

4 To make the sauce, put the cooking liquor and the remaining 25 g (1 oz) butter in a saucepan and heat gently. Add the watercress, spinach, parsley, chervil and dill, then cook for 2-3 minutes or until softened.

5 Put the sauce in a blender or food processor and blend until smooth. Transfer to a bowl, add the remaining lemon juice and season to taste. Leave to cool, then fold in the mayonnaise. Turn into a small serving jug and refrigerate until required.

6 Garnish the fish decoratively with herbs and lemon rind shapes, and serve with the herb sauce.

TUNA STEAKS WITH PARMESAN BASIL BUTTER

PREPARATION TIME 20 minutes, plus marinating
COOKING TIME 12-15 minutes
FREEZING Not suitable
COLOUR INDEX Page 16

SERVES 6

500 CALS/SERVING

- *6 tuna steaks, cut 2 cm (³/4 inch) thick, each weighing about 175 g (6 oz)*
- *fresh herbs, to garnish*
  MARINADE
- *100 ml (3¹/2 fl oz) olive oil*
- *2 garlic cloves, peeled and crushed*
- *10 ml (2 tsp) balsamic or sherry vinegar*
- *30 ml (2 tbsp)*

- *chopped fresh mixed herbs, such as thyme and parsley*
- *salt and pepper*
  PARMESAN BASIL BUTTER
- *75 g (3 oz) unsalted butter, softened*
- *30 ml (2 tbsp) freshly grated Parmesan cheese*
- *5 ml (1 tsp) balsamic or sherry vinegar*
- *5-6 fresh basil leaves*

1 Rinse the steaks and pat dry on absorbent kitchen paper. Place in a shallow non-metallic dish.
2 Whisk together all the marinade ingredients and pour over the steaks. Turn to coat, cover and leave to marinate in the refrigerator for 3-4 hours or overnight.
3 To make the basil butter, beat the butter until soft and creamy. Beat in the Parmesan cheese, vinegar and pepper to taste. Finely shred the basil and stir it into the butter mixture. Spoon into a sausage shape on wet non-stick baking parchment and roll up neatly. Chill for at least 1 hour or until firm enough to slice.
4 Lift the steaks out of the marinade and place directly over the barbecue or under the grill. Cook for 12-15 minutes or until firm and tender, turning once and brushing occasionally with the marinade. The flesh will turn a lighter colour when cooked. Pierce the centre with the tip of a sharp knife to see if it is cooked in the middle.
5 Serve the steaks topped with slices of Parmesan basil butter and garnished with fresh herbs.

VARIATION Use salmon for this dish if fresh tuna is not available.

GRILLED SARDINES WITH TOMATO SAUCE

PREPARATION TIME 20 minutes
COOKING TIME About 20 minutes
FREEZING Not suitable
COLOUR INDEX Page 16
♡

SERVES 4

295 CALS/SERVING

- *16 small or 8 large sardines, cleaned*
- *30 ml (2 tbsp) olive oil*
- *few sprigs of thyme*
- *pepper*
- *juice of ¹/2 lemon*
- *lemon rind shreds, to garnish*
  TOMATO SAUCE
- *15 ml (1 tbsp) olive oil*

- *1 small onion, peeled and finely chopped*
- *1 garlic clove, peeled and finely chopped*
- *450 g (1 lb) ripe tomatoes, finely chopped*
- *15 ml (1 tbsp) chopped fresh parsley*
- *salt and pepper*

1 To make the tomato sauce, heat the oil in a frying pan, add the onion and garlic and fry gently until the onion is softened. Add the tomatoes and parsley, then season with salt and pepper to taste. Cook, uncovered, for 10-15 minutes until the tomatoes are just tender.
2 Meanwhile, score the fish with three or four diagonal cuts on each side. Brush with oil, and push a few sprigs of thyme into some of the cuts. Season with pepper and sprinkle with lemon juice.
3 Arrange the fish on a grill rack and grill for about 4 minutes on each side or until cooked, brushing frequently with the oil and juices.
4 Arrange the sardines on a platter, and pour over any juices from the grill pan. Garnish with lemon rind shreds, and serve with the tomato sauce.

NOTE The sardines can be barbecued, if wished. The sauce can be kept hot on the edge of the barbecue grid.

SPICED FISH KEBABS WITH
AVOCADO SALSA

PREPARATION TIME 15 minutes, plus marinating
COOKING TIME 6-8 minutes
FREEZING Not suitable

SERVES 4-6

- *700 g (1½ lb)
  monkfish fillets,
  skinned*
- *12 large raw tiger
  prawns*

MARINADE

- *2 garlic cloves,
  peeled and crushed*
- *5 ml (1 tsp) ground
  coriander*
- *5 ml (1 tsp) ground
  turmeric*
- *2.5 ml (½ tsp)
  ground cumin*
- *2.5 ml (½ tsp) sea
  salt*
- *2.5 ml (½ tsp) chilli
  powder*
- *1.25 ml (¼ tsp)
  ground cinnamon*

465-310 CALS/SERVING

- *juice of 1 lime*
- *15 ml (1 tbsp)
  tomato purée*
- *90 ml (6 tbsp) olive
  oil*

AVOCADO SALSA

- *1 small ripe avocado*
- *½ small red onion,
  peeled and finely
  chopped*
- *15 ml (1 tbsp) lime
  juice*
- *15 ml (1 tbsp)
  chopped fresh
  coriander*
- *1 garlic clove, peeled
  and crushed*
- *pinch of sugar*
- *salt and pepper*

1 Wash and dry the monkfish and cut into 12 large chunks. Peel the prawns, discarding the heads, then cut down the back of each prawn and remove the black intestinal vein. Wash and dry well. Thread the monkfish and prawns alternately onto 4 skewers. Set aside.

2 To make the marinade, combine all the ingredients in a small bowl. Brush the marinade over the kebabs, then transfer to a shallow non-metallic dish, cover and marinate overnight.

3 Remove the kebabs from the refrigerator at least 1 hour before cooking.

4 Just before cooking the kebabs, make the salsa. Stone, peel and dice the avocado, then mix with the onion, lime juice, coriander, garlic and sugar. Season to taste and set aside for 10 minutes.

5 Place the kebabs on an oiled grill pan and grill as close to the heat as possible for 6-8 minutes, turning and basting frequently with the marinade juices, until charred and cooked through. Serve immediately with the salsa.

VARIATION Use any firm fleshed fish for this dish, such as swordfish or tuna. Scallops also work well as an alternative to the prawns.

> *TIP*
> If using wooden skewers, soak them in water
> for 30 minutes before threading on the seafood.

GRILLED HALIBUT
WITH STIR-FRIED VEGETABLES

PREPARATION TIME 15 minutes
COOKING TIME 6-10 minutes
FREEZING Not suitable
♡ ⏲

SERVES 4
- *4 halibut steaks*
- *melted butter for basting*
- *15 ml (1 tbsp) oil*
- *25 g (1 oz) butter*
- *1 large courgette, cut into matchstick strips*
- *1 red pepper, deseeded and cut into matchstick strips*

280 CALS/SERVING
- *15 ml (1 tbsp) sun-dried tomato paste*
- *10 ml (2 tsp) chopped fresh thyme*
- *10 ml (2 tsp) chopped fresh tarragon or chervil*
- *salt and pepper*
- *tarragon or chervil sprigs, to garnish*

1 Brush the halibut steaks with a little melted butter and grill for about 3-5 minutes on each side or until cooked through.

2 Meanwhile, heat the oil and butter in a frying pan and stir-fry the courgette and pepper strips for about 2 minutes. Stir in the sun-dried tomato paste and chopped herbs, then season with salt and pepper.

3 Serve the halibut with the stir-fried vegetables, garnished with sprigs of herbs.

FRESH SEAFOOD STEW

PREPARATION TIME 30 minutes
COOKING TIME 40 minutes
FREEZING Not suitable
COLOUR INDEX Page 17
♡

SERVES 6

- *60 ml (4 tbsp) olive oil*
- *900 g (2 lb) onions, peeled and finely sliced*
- *450 g (1 lb) thick cod fillets, skinned and cut into 5 cm (2 inch) pieces*
- *225 g (8 oz) plaice fillets, skinned and quartered*
- *175 g (6 oz) peeled raw tiger prawns*
- *salt and pepper*
- *450 g (1 lb) plum tomatoes, skinned, deseeded and chopped*

335 CALS/SERVING

- *30 ml (2 tbsp) tomato purée*
- *60 ml (4 tbsp) chopped fresh parsley*
- *30 ml (2 tbsp) chopped fresh marjoram or oregano*
- *150 ml (5 fl oz) dry white wine*
- *225 g (8 oz) cooked mixed seafood*
- *oregano leaves, to garnish*

1 Heat half the oil in a large flameproof casserole and cook the onions over a low heat for 5 minutes until softened. Using a slotted spoon, lift out about half of the onions and set aside.
2 Spread the remainder evenly over the base of the casserole, then cover with half the fish and prawns – do not add any of the mixed seafood yet. Season well with salt and pepper to taste.
3 Cover with half of the tomatoes and the tomato purée, then repeat the layers. Sprinkle the herbs on top and pour the wine over. Drizzle the remaining oil on top and cook, uncovered, over a very low heat for about 30 minutes or until the liquid has thickened slightly. Stir in the mixed seafood and heat through for 3-5 minutes. Serve garnished with oregano leaves.

CHILLIED MEDITERRANEAN PRAWNS

PREPARATION TIME 10 minutes
COOKING TIME 5-10 minutes
FREEZING Not suitable
♡ ⏱

SERVES 2

- *15 ml (1 tbsp) olive oil*
- *1 garlic clove, peeled and crushed*
- *4 small tomatoes, skinned and chopped*
- *1 fresh medium chilli, deseeded and chopped*

235 CALS/SERVING

- *few drops of Tabasco sauce*
- *salt and pepper*
- *12 raw peeled tiger prawns*
- *slices of lemon, to garnish*

1 Heat the oil in a small frying pan and add the garlic, tomatoes, chilli, a few drops of Tabasco and salt and pepper. Cover and cook gently for about 5 minutes or until the tomatoes are reduced to a pulp.
2 Stir in the prawns and cook gently for about 3 minutes until the prawns are cooked. Garnish with lemon slices.

GRILLED LOBSTER

PREPARATION TIME 20 minutes
COOKING TIME 5 minutes
FREEZING Not suitable
♡ ⏱

SERVES 4

• *4 cooked lobsters,
each weighing
450-550 g (1-1¼ lb)*
• *salt and pepper*
• *50 g (2 oz) butter,
melted*

305 CALS/SERVING

• *lemon slices and
parsley sprigs, to
garnish*

1 Twist off the lobster claws and pincers. Crack
open the large claws using the back of a heavy
knife, being careful not to crush the meat inside.
2 Put the lobster, back upwards, on a flat surface
and using a sharp knife split the lobster cleanly in
two, piercing through the 'cross' at the centre of
the head.
3 Remove and discard the intestine which runs
through the centre of the tail, the stomach (which
lies near the head) and the spongy looking gills or
'dead man's fingers', which are inedible.
4 Sprinkle the flesh with salt and pepper to taste
and brush with melted butter. Cook under a
medium grill for about 5 minutes.
5 Transfer to a warmed platter. Add the claws and
garnish with lemon slices and parsley.

WARM SCALLOP AND BASIL SALAD

PREPARATION TIME 10 minutes
COOKING TIME 4-6 minutes
FREEZING Not suitable
COLOUR INDEX Page 17
⏱

SERVES 6

• *50 g (2 oz) drained
sun-dried tomatoes in
olive oil*
• *1 small bunch fresh
basil*
• *60 ml (4 tbsp)
walnut oil*
• *30 ml (2 tbsp) sherry
vinegar or red wine
vinegar*

355 CALS/SERVING

• *selection of salad
leaves, such as lollo
rosso, rocket, frisée
or lamb's tongue
lettuce*
• *60 ml (4 tbsp) olive
oil*
• *700 g (1½ lb)
scallops*
• *salt and pepper*

1 Roughly chop the dried tomatoes and the basil.
Whisk together the walnut oil and vinegar in a
bowl. Stir in the tomatoes and basil. Place the
salad leaves in a large bowl.
2 Heat the olive oil in a large sauté pan and sauté
the scallops in two batches until well browned –
about 2-3 minutes. Take care not to overcook.
3 Off the heat, return all the scallops to the pan.
Stir in the tomato and basil mixture, adjust the
seasoning and immediately pour over the salad
leaves. Toss and serve on individual salad plates.

DRESSED CRAB

PREPARATION TIME 1 hour
FREEZING Not suitable
COLOUR INDEX Page 18
♡

SERVES 2-3

- *1 cooked crab, about 900 g (2 lb)*
- *salt and pepper*
- *15 ml (1 tbsp) lemon juice*
- *30 ml (2 tbsp) fresh white breadcrumbs*

195-130 CALS/SERVING

- *1 egg, hard-boiled*
- *15 ml (1 tbsp) chopped fresh parsley*
- *frisée lettuce, to serve*

1 Twist off the legs and claws as close to the body as possible. Break each claw in half then crack with a rolling pin or hammer without crushing the flesh. If you are not using the legs for garnishing, break the shell on the legs with your hands. Using a slender skewer to get at any awkward bits, carefully extract the flesh.
2 Put the crab on its back with the tail flap pointing towards you. Holding the shell firmly, press the body section upwards with your thumbs and it should come away. If it won't move, use the point of a rigid knife to ease it away.
3 With a teaspoon, scoop out into a separate bowl the creamy brown meat and roe (if any) from the shell. Remove and discard the stomach bag which you will find between the eyes. (If this breaks make sure you remove all the greenish or grey-white matter.)
4 Pull away from the body and discard the inedible feathery gills or 'dead man's fingers'. Using a large heavy knife, cut the body in half. Using a skewer, remove the flesh from the tiny crevices.
5 Using two forks, flake all the white meat from the crab. Season and add 5 ml (1 tsp) lemon juice.
6 Pound the brown meat in a bowl with the breadcrumbs and remaining lemon juice. Season.
7 Using a small spoon, put the white meat in both ends of the cleaned crab shell, making sure that it is well piled up in the shell. Spoon the brown meat in a neat line down the centre between the two sections of white crab meat.
8 Chop the egg white and sieve the yolk. Hold a blunt knife between the white and brown crab meat, then carefully spoon lines of parsley, egg yolk and egg white across the crab, moving the knife as you go. Serve on a bed of frisée.

MIXED SEAFOOD SALAD

PREPARATION TIME 20 minutes, plus chilling
COOKING TIME About 25 minutes
FREEZING Not suitable
COLOUR INDEX Page 18

SERVES 6

- *150 ml (5 fl oz) dry white wine*
- *1 bay leaf*
- *few peppercorns*
- *1 parsley sprig*
- *½ small onion, peeled and sliced*
- *350 g (12 oz) raw tiger prawns, thawed if frozen*
- *700 g (1½ lb) haddock fillet, skinned and cut into 2.5 cm (1 inch) chunks*
- *75 g (3 oz) mangetout, trimmed*
- *salt and pepper*

455 CALS/SERVING

- *450 g (1 lb) cooked mussels*
- *1 red pepper, deseeded and cut into strips*
- *2 carrots, peeled and cut into strips*
- *50 g (2 oz) pitted black olives*
- *150 ml (5 fl oz) olive oil*
- *45 ml (3 tbsp) white wine vinegar*
- *1-2 garlic cloves, peeled and crushed*
- *45 ml (3 tbsp) chopped fresh parsley*

1 Put the wine in a saucepan with 150 ml (5 fl oz) water. Add the bay leaf, peppercorns, parsley sprig and sliced onion. Bring to the boil. Add the tiger prawns and simmer for 5 minutes or until they turn pink. Lift out with a slotted spoon. Leave to cool.
2 Add the haddock to the wine mixture and simmer gently for about 5 minutes until the fish is cooked. Remove with a slotted spoon. Leave to cool.
3 Bring the wine mixture back to the boil and boil vigorously until reduced to about a quarter of its original volume. Leave to cool.
4 Cook the mangetout in boiling salted water for about 3 minutes, then drain.
5 Carefully peel the prawns. Put them in a bowl with the haddock and mussels. Add the mangetout, red pepper, carrots and olives.
6 Whisk together the oil, vinegar, garlic and chopped parsley. Strain the wine reduction and add to the dressing. Season, then pour over the salad and mix gently. Chill the salad in the refrigerator for 2 hours before serving.

STIR-FRIED CHICKEN WITH COURGETTES

PREPARATION TIME 10 minutes
COOKING TIME 7-10 minutes FREEZING Not suitable
♡ ⏰

SERVES 4   **250 CALS/SERVING**
- *30 ml (2 tbsp) oil*
- *1 garlic clove, peeled and crushed*
- *450 g (1 lb) skinless chicken breast fillets, sliced into strips*
- *450 g (1 lb) courgettes, sliced*

- *1 red pepper, deseeded and cut into strips*
- *45 ml (3 tbsp) dry sherry*
- *15 ml (1 tbsp) light soy sauce*
- *pepper*

1 Heat the oil in a wok or a large frying pan and fry the garlic for 1 minute. Add the chicken and cook for 3-4 minutes, stirring continuously.
2 Add the courgettes and red pepper and continue to cook for 1-2 minutes, until the chicken is cooked and the vegetables are tender but still crisp.
3 Stir in the sherry and soy sauce and cook for 1 minute. Season to taste with pepper and serve.

POACHED CHICKEN IN WATERCRESS SAUCE

PREPARATION TIME 5 minutes
COOKING TIME 15 minutes
FREEZING Not suitable
COLOUR INDEX Page 19
♡ ⏰

SERVES 4   **215 CALS/SERVING**
- *4 skinless chicken breast fillets, each weighing about 125 g (4 oz)*
- *4 thin slices of Parma ham*
- *90 ml (6 tbsp) dry white wine*
- *50 ml (2 fl oz) chicken stock*

- *60 ml (4 tbsp) single cream*
- *90 ml (6 tbsp) chopped watercress*
- *ground black pepper*
- *flat-leaf parsley, to garnish*

1 Wrap each chicken breast in a slice of ham. Place in a saucepan just large enough to fit the chicken in one layer.
2 Pour the wine and stock over. Bring to the boil, cover and simmer for 10-12 minutes or until the chicken is tender. Remove to a serving dish.
3 Boil down the juices to about 75 ml (5 tbsp). Add the cream and bring to the boil. Remove from the heat and mix in the watercress. Season with pepper, pour over chicken and garnish.

TIP
To serve cold, complete to the end of stage 2, then cool and thickly slice. Fold the watercress into 60 ml (4 tbsp) low-calorie mayonnaise and serve with the chicken.

LIME-PEPPERED CHICKEN

PREPARATION TIME 15 minutes, plus marinating
COOKING TIME 10-12 minutes
FREEZING Not suitable

♡

SERVES 6

- *6 skinless chicken breast fillets*
- *2 small red or yellow chillies, thinly sliced*
- *10 ml (2 tsp) coarse-ground black peppercorns*
- *shredded rind and juice of 3 limes*
- *1 garlic clove, peeled and crushed*
- *30 ml (2 tbsp) clear honey*
- *small aubergines or wedges of courgette, onion or lemon, to finish*

350 CALS/SERVING

DIPPING SAUCE

- *60 ml (4 tbsp) mango chutney*
- *1 garlic clove, peeled and crushed*
- *1 green chilli, seeded*
- *2.5 cm (1 inch) piece fresh root ginger, peeled and grated*
- *10 ml (2 tsp) light soft brown sugar*
- *10 ml (2 tsp) white wine vinegar*
- *45 ml (3 tbsp) soy sauce*
- *few drops Tabasco*
- *90 ml (6 tbsp) oil*

1 Cut the chicken into bite-size pieces. Toss together the chicken, chillies and the next four ingredients. Cover and marinate in the refrigerator for at least 10 minutes.

2 Meanwhile, make the dipping sauce. Place all the ingredients in a food processor and blend for about 15 seconds or until well combined. Cover and refrigerate until required.

3 Thread the marinated chicken pieces onto metal or wooden skewers. Thread an aubergine half, a slice of courgette or a wedge of onion or lemon on to the end of each skewer.

4 Cook on the barbecue or under a hot grill for 10-12 minutes, turning frequently, basting with the reserved marinade. Serve immediately with the sauce for dipping.

NOTE Garnish the dip with a few small mixed chillies for added colour.

It's a good idea to wear rubber gloves when preparing chillies as they can irritate the skin. Remove the seeds to reduce the hotness.

CHICKEN WITH SPICED WHEAT

PREPARATION TIME 20 minutes, plus marinating and cooling
COOKING TIME 20-24 minutes
FREEZING Not suitable

♡

SERVES 6

- 15 ml (1 tbsp) mango chutney
- 15 ml (1 tbsp) mild curry paste
- 10 ml (2 tsp) ground turmeric
- 50 ml (2 fl oz) olive oil
- 4 skinless chicken breast fillets, 575 g (1¼ lb) total weight
- 30 ml (2 tbsp) white wine vinegar

337 CALS/SERVING

- 175 g (6 oz) bulghur wheat
- salt and pepper
- 30 ml (2 tbsp) snipped fresh chives
- 175 g (6 oz) cherry tomatoes
- 1 bunch spring onions, roughly chopped
- marjoram leaves, to garnish (optional)

1 Mix together the chutney, curry paste and turmeric. Stir in half the oil. Cut the chicken into bite-size pieces and toss into the mixture. Cover and marinate in the refrigerator for 30 minutes, or overnight.

2 Spread the chicken pieces over a foil-lined grill pan. Cook under a hot grill in batches for 10-12 minutes until the chicken is cooked through and golden brown. Transfer to a bowl with the pan juices and stir in the remaining oil and the vinegar. Leave to cool.

3 Meanwhile, place the bulghur wheat in a bowl and pour over enough boiling water to cover. Leave to soak for about 30 minutes until all of the water has been absorbed and the grains are soft. Stir once or twice and drain well. Season to taste. Stir in the chives.

4 Drain the oil mixture from the chicken and stir into the wheat. Spoon onto a platter.

5 Halve the tomatoes. Mix together with the spring onions and chicken and spoon over the wheat. Garnish with marjoram, if wished.

MEDITERRANEAN CHICKEN

PREPARATION TIME 40 minutes
COOKING TIME About 5 minutes
FREEZING Not suitable
COLOUR INDEX Page 22

SERVES 6

480 CALS/SERVING

- *225 g (8 oz) courgettes*
- *olive oil*
- *10 sun-dried tomatoes in olive oil, drained, about 75 g (3 oz) total weight*
- *salt and pepper*
- *75 g (3 oz) young spinach leaves*
- *400 g (14 oz) crusty loaf*
- *350 g (12 oz) cooked skinned chicken breast fillet, thinly sliced*
- *340 g (12 oz) jar peperonata*
- *10 pitted black olives, halved*
- *300 g (10 oz) mozzarella cheese, thinly sliced*
- *10 fresh basil leaves*

1 Thinly slice the courgettes lengthways, brush lightly with olive oil and grill on each side for 3-4 minutes or until golden brown; drain and cool. Slice the sun-dried tomatoes.
2 Bring a large saucepan of salted water to the boil. Blanch the spinach leaves in batches for 10 seconds, remove with a slotted spoon and plunge into cold water. Drain well.
3 Cut away and remove the base of the loaf, leaving a border of about 2.5 cm (1 inch). Reserve the base. Hollow out the loaf so that the walls are about 1 cm (½ inch) thick. (Use the leftover bread to make breadcrumbs and freeze for use later.)
4 Drizzle the inside of the loaf with about 30 ml (2 tbsp) olive oil. Layer up the chicken, spinach, courgettes, peperonata, olives, sun-dried tomatoes, mozzarella and basil leaves, pressing well into the loaf. Season between layers.
5 When the loaf is full, replace the base. Press into shape and wrap tightly in clingfilm. Chill for at least 2 hours, preferably overnight.
6 Leave the loaf at room temperature for 1 hour before cutting into slices to serve.

NOTE Peperonata is a colourful Italian mixture of peppers, onions and tomatoes in a little oil. You'll find it with the pasta sauces in the supermarket, and in delicatessens. There's no need to drain the mixture, as the juice adds extra flavour and texture to the loaf.

CHEESY CHICKEN AND BACON ROLLS

PREPARATION TIME 10 minutes
COOKING TIME 35 minutes
FREEZING Suitable (stage 2)
COLOUR INDEX Page 20

❄

SERVES 4

600 CALS/SERVING (WITHOUT DIP)

- *12 boneless, skinless chicken thighs, about 700 g (1½ lb) total weight*
- *30 ml (2 tbsp) wholegrain mustard*
- *125 g (4 oz) Gruyère cheese*
- *12 slices lightly smoked streaky bacon, about 250 g (9 oz)*
- *Garlic Dip, to serve (see Tip)*

1 Unroll each chicken thigh and spread the inside with mustard. Cut the cheese into 12 fat sticks and place on top of the mustard. Roll up the chicken.
2 Gently stretch the bacon with the back of a knife and wrap one piece tightly around each thigh. Secure with wooden satay sticks.
3 Place the chicken rolls in a non-stick roasting tin and bake at 190°C (375°F) mark 5 for 30-35 minutes or until cooked through and golden brown. Serve immediately with Garlic Dip.

VARIATION Other types of cheese can be used inside these chicken pieces. Try Cheddar or Emmental.

TIP
For an instant Garlic Dip just beat equal quantities of fromage frais and mayonnaise with a little crushed garlic. Top with crispy grilled bacon and black pepper.

GRILLED CHICKEN SALAD

PREPARATION TIME 15 minutes, plus cooling
COOKING TIME 30 minutes
FREEZING Not suitable
COLOUR INDEX Page 22
♡

SERVES 4	350 CALS/SERVING

- *175 g (6 oz) ripe tomatoes, halved*
- *30 ml (2 tbsp) tapenade (black olive paste)*
- *olive oil*
- *4 skinless chicken breast fillets, each weighing about 125 g (4 oz)*

DRESSING
- *1 shallot, peeled and finely chopped*
- *45 ml (3 tbsp) olive oil*
- *15 ml (1 tbsp) walnut oil*

- *20 ml (4 tsp) white wine vinegar*
- *30 ml (2 tbsp) single cream*
- *15 ml (1 tbsp) chopped fresh basil*
- *salt and pepper*
- *mixed salad, to serve, such as green leaves, cherry tomatoes, olives, onions and cooked globe artichoke hearts*

1 Grill the tomatoes skin-side up until black and charred. Purée in a blender or food processor with the olive paste and a little olive oil, if necessary, to give a thinnish paste.
2 Place the chicken skinned-side down on a foil-lined grill pan. Brush lightly with olive oil and grill for 7-8 minutes.
3 Turn the chicken skinned-side up and grill for 5 minutes. Spoon the tomato paste over the chicken and grill for a further 5-6 minutes or until the chicken is cooked through and the topping is well browned. Cool, cover, then refrigerate for at least 1 hour to firm up.
4 Meanwhile, make the dressing. Whisk the shallot with the olive oil, walnut oil, vinegar, cream, basil and salt and pepper to taste. Set aside.
5 Thickly slice the chicken and serve with a selection of salad ingredients. Spoon over the dressing.

SMOKED CHICKEN WITH CUCUMBER AND MANGO

PREPARATION TIME 45 minutes, plus chilling
FREEZING Not suitable
COLOUR INDEX Page 21

SERVES 6	370 CALS/SERVING

- *1.1 kg (2½ lb) smoked chicken*
- *1 small cucumber*
- *1 large, ripe mango*
- *grated rind and juice of 2 limes*
- *150 ml (5 fl oz) vegetable oil*

- *30 ml (2 tbsp) chopped fresh coriander*
- *1 bunch spring onions, trimmed and finely chopped*
- *salt and pepper*

1 Slice the chicken flesh into 5 cm (2 inch) pieces, discarding skin and bone. You should end up with about 700 g (1½ lb) chicken flesh.
2 Halve the cucumber lengthways and remove the seeds with a teaspoon. Slice on the diagonal, then leave to drain on absorbent kitchen paper for about 30 minutes.
3 Cut down either side of the mango stone. Cut away the flesh from the skin and place in a blender or food processor, with the grated lime rind and strained lime juice. Process until smooth. Keep the processor running and add the oil in a slow, steady stream.
4 Pour the mango dressing into a large bowl and mix in all the remaining ingredients, adding seasoning to taste. Cover and chill for up to a day before serving.

NOTE Smoked chicken is available from larger supermarkets. Alternatively, use 350 g (12 oz) smoked ham and 350 g (12 oz) cooked chicken.

WARM DUCK SALAD

PREPARATION TIME 20 minutes
COOKING TIME 15-20 minutes
FREEZING Not suitable

♡

SERVES 8

325 CALS/SERVING

- 8 boned duckling breasts, each weighing about 125 g (4 oz)
- 30 ml (2 tbsp) ground coriander
- 10 ml (2 tsp) ground ginger
- 10 ml (2 tsp) ground mace
- 1 garlic clove, peeled and crushed
- 75 ml (3 fl oz) fresh orange juice

- 75 ml (3 fl oz) olive oil
- salt and pepper
- 7.5 ml (1½ tsp) clear honey
- 15 ml (1 tbsp) red wine vinegar
- 7.5 ml (1½ tsp) Dijon mustard
- selection of mixed salad leaves, to line the dish
- about 20 pitted black olives

1 Remove the skin from the duck. Mix together the coriander, ginger, mace and garlic with 30 ml (2 tbsp) each of orange juice and oil. Season with salt and pepper.

2 Spread the spice mixture on both sides of the duck breasts and place in a shallow ovenproof dish. Roast at 200°C (400°F) mark 6 for 15-20 minutes until the duckling is tender and the top has browned.

3 Meanwhile, whisk together the honey, vinegar, mustard and remaining orange juice and oil. Season to taste. Wash the salad leaves, dry them and arrange on a shallow platter.

4 Lift the duck breasts out of the pan juices, slice neatly and arrange on the salad leaves. Scatter the olives over the top and spoon over the dressing.

VARIATION If wished, the duck can be cooked in advance and served cold.

MIDDLE EASTERN MEAT SKEWERS

PREPARATION TIME 25 minutes
COOKING TIME 15 minutes
FREEZING Suitable (stage 2)

❋

SERVES 6

- 900 g (2 lb) minced beef or lamb
- 2 onions, peeled and grated
- 30 ml (2 tbsp) ground cumin
- 15 ml (1 tbsp) coarsely ground coriander
- 90 ml (6 tbsp) finely chopped fresh parsley
- salt and pepper

415 CALS/SERVING

- olive oil
- paprika
- lemon wedges, to serve

MINTED YOGURT SAUCE

- 3 spring onions
- 300 ml (10 fl oz) natural yogurt
- 15 ml (1 tbsp) chopped fresh mint

1 Get your butcher to mince the meat three times, or chop it in a food processor until very fine. Knead it with the grated onion, cumin, coriander, 60 ml (4 tbsp) parsley and seasoning to make a smooth paste.

2 Take about 15-30 ml (1-2 tbsp) of the mixture and press a flat sausage shape onto the ends of wooden skewers. Brush them lightly with oil and sprinkle with a little paprika.

3 Grill about half the kebabs at a time under a high heat for about 5 minutes. Turn, sprinkle with more paprika and grill the second side until well browned all over. (Keep the exposed wooden sticks away from the heat.)

4 Keep the kebabs warm, loosely covered, until they are all cooked. Sprinkle with parsley.

5 Meanwhile, make the sauce. Chop the spring onions, reserving a few dark green shreds for garnish, and mix with the yogurt and mint. Serve with the kebabs and lemon wedges.

SESAME BEEF SALAD

PREPARATION TIME 20 minutes, plus marinating
COOKING TIME 15 minutes
FREEZING Not suitable
COLOUR INDEX Page 26
♡

SERVES 6

- *30 ml (2 tbsp) soy sauce*
- *30 ml (2 tbsp) Worcestershire sauce*
- *30 ml (2 tbsp) soft brown sugar*
- *10 ml (2 tsp) tomato purée*
- *5 ml (1 tsp) lemon juice*
- *15 ml (1 tbsp) white wine vinegar*

215 CALS/SERVING

- *20 ml (4 tsp) sesame seeds*
- *vegetable oil*
- *2 garlic cloves, peeled and crushed*
- *salt and pepper*
- *700 g (1½ lb) rump steak*
- *6 sticks celery*
- *1 bunch spring onions*
- *1 small cucumber*

1 Mix the first seven ingredients together in a bowl with 30 ml (2 tbsp) oil, the garlic and seasoning. Slice the steak into strips 5 mm (¼ inch) thick and 5 cm (2 inches) long. Stir the strips into the marinade. Cover and leave to marinate in the refrigerator for at least 3 hours, until ready to cook.
2 Cut the celery, spring onions and cucumber (discarding the seeds) into thin matchsticks. Refrigerate in a polythene bag until ready to use.
3 Heat a little oil in a large wok or non-stick frying pan until the oil begins to smoke. Lift the steak strips from the marinade and fry in small batches until they are well browned. Place them in a large bowl.
4 Add the rest of the marinade to the pan and reduce until it forms a syrup. Pour over the steak strips. Either stir all the vegetables in with the steak or serve separately.

TIP

This makes an excellent quick after-work meal as all the ingredients can be prepared at least 24 hours in advance and cooked at the last minute just before serving.

PIZZAIOLA STEAK

PREPARATION TIME 15 minutes
COOKING TIME 10 minutes
FREEZING Not suitable
♡ ⏲

SERVES 4

- *60 ml (4 tbsp) olive oil*
- *4 thin rump steaks*
- *2 garlic cloves, peeled and crushed*
- *salt and pepper*
- *450 g (1 lb) firm red tomatoes, skinned and chopped*

340 CALS/SERVING

- *45 ml (3 tbsp) chopped fresh basil*
- *15 ml (1 tbsp) chopped fresh parsley*
- *basil sprigs, to garnish*

1 Heat the oil in a large frying pan, add the steaks and fry quickly over a high heat for 2-3 minutes until browned on both sides. Add the garlic and salt and pepper to taste and fry for 30 seconds.
2 Add the tomatoes and herbs and cook for 3-5 minutes until the tomatoes are softened and the juices reduced. Adjust the seasoning and serve at once, garnished with basil sprigs.

TOMATO-CRUSTED LAMB WITH SUMMER VEGETABLES

PREPARATION TIME 20 minutes
COOKING TIME About 1 hour
FREEZING Not suitable
COLOUR INDEX Page 27

SERVES 6   550 CALS/SERVING

- 2 garlic cloves, peeled
- 100 ml (4 fl oz) olive oil
- 125 g (4 oz) sun-dried tomatoes
- 5 ml (1 tsp) chopped fresh thyme or 2.5 ml (½ tsp) dried thyme
- salt and pepper
- 2 racks of lamb (about 7 cutlets each), chinèd
- 450 g (1 lb) new potatoes, roughly chopped
- 450 g (1 lb) young carrots, peeled and roughly chopped
- 450 g (1 lb) summer squash, peeled and roughly chopped
- about 18 pitted black olives
- 1.25 ml (¼ tsp) fennel seeds
- juice of 1 lemon
- 5 ml (1 tsp) caster sugar
- chopped flat-leaf parsley, to garnish

1 In a blender or food processor, blend together the garlic, 30 ml (2 tbsp) of the olive oil, the tomatoes and thyme to a smooth paste. Season with salt and pepper. Trim the lamb of most of the fat and score at regular intervals. Press the tomato mixture firmly over the lamb to coat.
2 Blanch the potatoes in boiling, salted water for 1-2 minutes, then drain. Toss the potatoes, carrots and squash in a roasting tin with the olives, fennel seeds, lemon juice, sugar and remaining oil.
3 Roast the vegetables, uncovered, at 220°C (425°F) mark 7 for about 30 minutes or until just tender. Place the lamb on a rack over the vegetables and cook for about 25 minutes for medium rare, or about 30-35 minutes for well done. Cover the lamb loosely with foil if the crust starts to burn.
4 Remove the lamb from the oven and leave to rest in a warm place for 5 minutes before carving. Transfer the vegetables to a serving dish.
5 Carve the lamb into cutlets and serve with the vegetables. Pour any pan juices over the lamb. Garnish with chopped flat-leaf parsley.

MINTED LAMB ESCALOPES

PREPARATION TIME 10 minutes, plus marinating
COOKING TIME 6 minutes
FREEZING Not suitable
COLOUR INDEX Page 27
♡

SERVES 4   210 CALS/SERVING

- 90 ml (6 tbsp) Greek natural yogurt
- 1 garlic clove, peeled and crushed
- 60 ml (4 tbsp) chopped fresh mint
- 30 ml (2 tbsp) lemon juice
- 450 g (1 lb) lamb escalopes
- salt and pepper
- mint leaves, to garnish
- warm pitta bread and tomato and onion salad, to serve

1 Mix the yogurt, garlic, chopped mint, and lemon juice with the lamb. Season with salt and pepper. Place in a non-metallic dish, cover and marinate in the refrigerator for 2-3 hours.
2 Spread the lamb in a grill pan and grill for 3 minutes on each side or until golden brown.
3 Garnish with mint and serve immediately with some warm pitta bread and tomato and onion salad.

NOTE For this recipe, you need very thin lean escalopes cut from the leg. These are sold ready-prepared in some supermarkets; alternatively ask your butcher to prepare them for you.

VARIATION For spiced lamb escalopes, replace the mint with 5 ml (1 tsp) each ground cumin and turmeric, and 2.5 cm (1 inch) piece fresh root ginger, grated.

PEPPERED GARLIC PORK WITH CREME FRAICHE

PREPARATION TIME 30 minutes
COOKING TIME 40-45 minutes
FREEZING Not suitable
♡

SERVES 6

- *2 pork tenderloins, each weighing about 350 g (12 oz)*
- *salt*
- *60 ml (4 tbsp) olive oil*
- *8 shallots, peeled and chopped*
- *6 garlic cloves, peeled and chopped*
- *15 ml (1 tbsp) coarsely crushed green peppercorns*
- *30 ml (2 tbsp) mixed chopped fresh chives and parsley*

350 CALS/SERVING

- *25 g (1 oz) fresh white breadcrumbs*
- *30 ml (2 tbsp) beaten egg*
- *450 ml (15 fl oz) chicken stock*
- *150 ml (5 fl oz) medium dry white wine*
- *60 ml (4 tbsp) crème fraîche*

1 Trim the pork tenderloins and cut a lengthways slit about halfway into each one, then open out flat. Cover with a piece of clingfilm and beat with a meat mallet or rolling pin until the pork is a rectangular shape about 1 cm (½ inch) thick. Season with salt.

2 Heat half the oil in a saucepan, add the shallots and garlic and fry gently for 5 minutes. Remove from the heat and add the peppercorns, herbs and breadcrumbs. Mix well, then stir in the egg.

3 Press the mixture along the middle of each tenderloin. Close the pork and tie at regular intervals with fine string.

4 Heat the remaining oil in a frying pan, add the tenderloins, cutting in half if necessary to fit into the frying pan, and brown all over. Transfer to a roasting tin and drizzle with any juices in pan. Add 200 ml (7 fl oz) stock to the roasting tin.

5 Cook in the oven at 190°C (375°F) mark 5 for 30-35 minutes or until cooked through, basting frequently with the juices. Remove the pork tenderloins to a serving plate and keep warm.

6 Add the remaining stock and the wine to the roasting pan and boil rapidly until reduced by one-third. Add the crème fraîche and boil for 3 minutes until smooth and creamy.

7 Remove the string from the pork and cut the pork into neat slices. Serve hot with the sauce.

VARIATION For a richer flavour, add 75 g (3 oz) sliced mushrooms with the crème fraîche at stage 6 and boil for 3 minutes, stirring occasionally.

MAPLE-GLAZED GAMMON
WITH PAPAYA SALSA

PREPARATION TIME 20 minutes, plus cooling
COOKING TIME 2½ hours
FREEZING Not suitable

SERVES 10-12　　　　**415-350 CALS/SERVING**

- 2.3 kg (5 lb) piece
  smoked gammon
- 1 bay leaf
- few parsley stalks
- 30 ml (2 tbsp) maple
  syrup
- 10 ml (2 tsp)
  American mustard
- 40 g (1½ oz) soft
  brown sugar
PAPAYA SALSA
- 1 ripe papaya

- 3-4 spring onions,
  trimmed and finely
  chopped
- 1 fresh green chilli,
  deseeded and finely
  chopped
- 30-45 ml (2-3 tbsp)
  chopped fresh
  coriander
- juice of 1 lime
- salt

1 Place the gammon in a large saucepan, cover
with cold water and add the bay leaf and parsley
stalks. Bring slowly to the boil, reduce the heat,
cover and simmer gently for 2 hours.
2 Remove the gammon from the pan, allow to
cool slightly, then strip off the skin, leaving the
layer of fat on the joint.
3 Place the gammon joint in a roasting tin. Score
the fat into a diamond pattern, cutting through
the layer of fat each time, but taking care not to
cut into the flesh. Mix the maple syrup with the
mustard and sugar and spread over the scored fat.
4 Cook in the oven at 190°C (375°F) mark 5 for
20-30 minutes until the fat is glazed and golden
brown; baste frequently with the juices in tin.
Remove from the oven and leave to cool.
5 About 30 minutes before serving, prepare the
papaya salsa. Halve the papaya and scoop out the
seeds. Remove the peel and dice the flesh. Place in
a serving bowl. Add the remaining ingredients,
seasoning with salt to taste, and mix well.
6 Carve the gammon into slices and serve with the
papaya salsa.

VARIATION The boiled and glazed gammon joint
is also extremely good served hot with seasonal
vegetables, such as baby broad beans, peas or
green beans and buttered new potatoes.

HOMEMADE SAUSAGES WITH ROCKET PESTO

PREPARATION TIME 20 minutes, plus chilling
COOKING TIME 10-12 minutes
FREEZING Suitable (stage 2)
COLOUR INDEX Page 30
❄

SERVES 6

- *125 g (4 oz) rindless smoked streaky bacon, finely chopped*
- *450 g (1 lb) lean minced pork*
- *225 g (8 oz) pork sausagemeat*
- *1 small red chilli, deseeded and finely chopped*
- *2 garlic cloves, peeled and crushed*
- *25 g (1 oz) fresh white breadcrumbs*
- *salt and pepper*
- *1 egg plus 1 egg yolk*

495 CALS/SERVING
ROCKET PESTO

- *75 g (3 oz) goats' cheese or low-fat soft cheese*
- *25 g (1 oz) Gruyère or Emmental cheese, grated*
- *200 ml (7 fl oz) olive oil*
- *25 g (1 oz) shelled pistachio nuts*
- *1 garlic clove, peeled*
- *2.5 ml (½ tsp) salt*
- *75 g (3 oz) rocket leaves or watercress*

1 Mix together the bacon, minced pork, sausagemeat, chilli, garlic and breadcrumbs. Season with salt and pepper, then beat in the egg and egg yolk.
2 Shape the mixture into about 18 sausages. Cover and chill for at least 15 minutes and preferably overnight.
3 Cook the sausages on the barbecue for about 10-12 minutes or until cooked through.
4 To make the rocket pesto, blend all the ingredients in a blender or food processor until smooth.
5 Serve the sausages with the rocket pesto as a dip.

VARIATION To oven-cook the sausages, heat 60 ml (4 tbsp) olive oil in a large roasting tin on the hob. Add the sausages in batches and brown on all sides. Return the sausages to the tin and cook in the oven at 200°C (400°F) mark 6 for 20-25 minutes or until cooked through.

CHINESE-STYLE SPARE RIBS

PREPARATION TIME 5 minutes
COOKING TIME 60-70 minutes
FREEZING Not suitable
♡

SERVES 4-6

- *900 g (2 lb) lean pork ribs*
- *30 ml (2 tbsp) vegetable oil*
- *salt*
- *spring onion and orange rind strips, to garnish*
SAUCE
- *2.5 cm (1 inch) piece fresh root ginger, peeled and finely chopped*

295-195 CALS/SERVING

- *1 garlic clove, peeled and chopped*
- *60 ml (4 tbsp) clear honey*
- *30 ml (2 tbsp) dark soy sauce*
- *30 ml (2 tbsp) tomato ketchup*
- *2 good pinches of five-spice powder*
- *150 ml (5 fl oz) unsweetened orange juice*

1 Cut the ribs into smaller pieces, if wished. Heat the oil in a large frying pan, add the ribs and season well with salt. Fry the ribs over a moderate heat for about 10 minutes, turning frequently.
2 Mix together all the sauce ingredients and pour over the ribs. Cover the pan and cook gently for 50-60 minutes or until the meat is tender and the sauce is reduced to a sticky syrup, turning the ribs occasionally.
3 Arrange the ribs on a hot serving plate and garnish with spring onion and orange rind strips.

COURGETTE AND BACON FRITTATA

PREPARATION TIME 10 minutes
COOKING TIME 6-10 minutes
FREEZING Not suitable
♡ ⏲

SERVES 4

160 CALS/SERVING

- *15 ml (1 tbsp) vegetable oil*
- *450 g (1 lb) courgettes, thickly sliced*
- *125 g (4 oz) rindless smoked streaky bacon, chopped*
- *50 g (2 oz) onion, peeled and chopped*

- *30 ml (2 tbsp) chopped fresh thyme*
- *15 ml (1 tbsp) chopped fresh rosemary*
- *2 eggs*
- *salt and pepper*
- *chopped fresh herbs, to garnish*

1 Heat the oil in a non-stick 20-25 cm (8-10 inch) frying pan. Sauté the courgettes, bacon and onion together for 4-5 minutes, stirring continuously, until just beginning to soften and turn golden brown.
2 Whisk together the thyme, rosemary and eggs. Season with salt and pepper. Pour over the courgette mixture and leave to set over a low heat for 2-3 minutes. Serve immediately, cut into wedges and sprinkled with chopped fresh herbs.

VEGETABLE EGG NESTS

PREPARATION TIME 15 minutes
COOKING TIME 15 minutes
FREEZING Not suitable
COLOUR INDEX Page 32
♡ ⏲

SERVES 4

240 CALS/SERVING

- *450 g (1 lb) trimmed leeks, sliced*
- *550 g (1¼ lb) courgettes, sliced*
- *225 g (8 oz) asparagus tips*
- *125 g (4 oz) peas*
- *50 g (2 oz) low-fat spread*

- *30 ml (2 tbsp) chopped fresh parsley*
- *1 garlic clove, peeled and crushed*
- *salt and pepper*
- *4 eggs*
- *8 anchovy fillets*

1 Steam the leeks, courgettes and asparagus for about 12-15 minutes or until tender, adding the peas for the last 5 minutes of cooking time.
2 Meanwhile, mix together the low-fat spread, parsley and garlic. Season well.
3 Poach the eggs in gently simmering water for 4-5 minutes or until just set.
4 Divide the hot vegetables among four individual dishes. Make a well in the centre and place an egg in each. Season each egg with pepper and cross two anchovy fillets on top. Top the vegetables with a little herb mixture to serve.

NOTE Many people believe that brown eggs are more nutritious than white, but this is not the case – the only difference is the colour of the shell.

VARIATION Vary the vegetables according to what is available – steamed baby sweetcorn, baby carrots and small broccoli florets will also work well in this dish.

FETA AND OREGANO TARTS

PREPARATION TIME 20 minutes, plus chilling
COOKING TIME 45 minutes
FREEZING Suitable (stage 1)

✳

MAKES 6
- *Shortcrust Pastry, made with 225 g (8 oz) white plain flour (see page 383)*
- *300 g (10 oz) tomatoes, skinned*
- *175 g (6 oz) feta cheese, roughly chopped*

435 CALS/TART
- *45 ml (3 tbsp) chopped fresh oregano*
- *2 eggs, beaten*
- *150 ml (5 fl oz) single cream*
- *pepper*

1 Roll out the pastry and use to line six 9 cm (3½ inch) flan tins about 2.5 cm (1 inch) deep. Chill for about 30 minutes then bake the pastry blind (see page 383) for 20 minutes or until golden.
2 Cut each tomato into 6-8 pieces, discarding the seeds. Place the feta cheese in a bowl. Stir in the oregano, eggs and cream.
3 Fill each tart case with a little of the mixture to come to within 5 mm (¼ inch) of the top of the pastry. Arrange the tomato pieces over the top of each flan.
4 Bake at 180°C (350°F) mark 4 for about 25 minutes or until just set and beginning to brown. Cool for 10 minutes. Grind over pepper and serve.

NOTE These tarts can be made a day in advance. Store them in the refrigerator and serve at room temperature.

> *TIP*
> These individual tarts are ideal for picnics. Allow to cool completely and wrap each one in foil before packing in a rigid container.

5 When the pepper is cool, peel off the skin, rinse the pepper under cold water and pat dry with absorbent kitchen paper. Shred finely and add to the seafood with the pasta. Toss lightly to mix, garnish with flat-leaf parsley sprigs and serve.

PASTA WITH WALNUT AND BASIL SAUCE

PREPARATION TIME 15 minutes
COOKING TIME 12 minutes
FREEZING Not suitable
COLOUR INDEX Page 35

ITALIAN SEAFOOD PASTA SALAD

PREPARATION TIME 15 minutes, plus marinating
COOKING TIME 15-20 minutes
FREEZING Not suitable

SERVES 6
- 225 g (8 oz) dried pasta twists
- 1 small red pepper, quartered and deseeded
- two 225 g (8 oz) packets cooked mixed seafood
- 6 each black and green olives, pitted and quartered
- flat-leaf parsley sprigs, to garnish

440 CALS/SERVING
DRESSING
- 60 ml (4 tbsp) balsamic or white wine vinegar
- 150 ml (5 fl oz) olive oil
- 2 garlic cloves, peeled and crushed
- 45 ml (3 tbsp) chopped fresh parsley
- salt and pepper

1 Bring a large pan of salted water to the boil, add the pasta and cook for 10-12 minutes until just tender (*al dente*). Drain, rinse in cold water and drain again, then leave to cool.
2 Meanwhile, grill the pepper, skin-side up, for 5-8 minutes until the skin is blistering and beginning to blacken. Place the pepper quarters in a polythene bag, seal tightly and leave to cool.
3 Place the mixed seafood in a large bowl, add the olives and set aside.
4 To make the dressing, whisk together the vinegar, olive oil, garlic and parsley and season with salt and pepper. Pour over the seafood mixture and leave to marinate at room temperature for 20 minutes.

SERVES 4
- 2 large garlic cloves, peeled
- 40 g (1½ oz) fresh basil leaves (a large bunch)
- 50 g (2 oz) freshly grated Parmesan cheese
- 1 small tomato, skinned and deseeded
- 60 ml (4 tbsp) olive oil
- salt and pepper

480 CALS/SERVING
- 350 g (12 oz) fresh pasta or 225 g (8 oz) dried
- 45 ml (3 tbsp) single cream
- 50 g (2 oz) walnut pieces, chopped
- basil sprigs
- freshly grated Parmesan, to serve

1 Place the garlic, basil leaves, Parmesan cheese and tomato flesh in a blender or food processor and work to a smooth paste.
2 Gradually add the olive oil, drop by drop, as if making mayonnaise. Season the mixture with salt and pepper to taste.
3 Cook the pasta in plenty of boiling, salted water until it is just tender (*al dente*). Drain well. Toss in a warmed serving bowl with the cream, basil sauce and walnuts. Serve immediately with fresh basil sprigs and freshly grated Parmesan cheese.

THAI CHICKEN NOODLE SALAD

PREPARATION TIME 20 minutes, plus marinating
COOKING TIME 20 minutes
FREEZING Not suitable
COLOUR INDEX Page 33

SERVES 6

415 CALS/SERVING

- *450 g (1 lb) skinless chicken breast fillets, cut into thick strips*
- *5 ml (1 tsp) caster sugar*
- *2.5 ml (½ tsp) salt*
- *2.5 ml (½ tsp) pepper*
- *2.5 ml (½ tsp) ground ginger*
- *2.5 ml (½ tsp) English mustard powder*
- *2.5 ml (½ tsp) ground turmeric*
- *2.5 ml (½ tsp) medium curry powder*
- *60 ml (4 tbsp) olive oil*

- *350 g (12 oz) courgettes, sliced*
- *150 g (5 oz) mangetout, trimmed*
- *1 each red and yellow pepper, deseeded and cut into strips*
- *45 ml (3 tbsp) clear honey*
- *60 ml (4 tbsp) lemon juice*
- *2.5 cm (1 inch) piece fresh root ginger, peeled and chopped*
- *250 g (9 oz) medium egg noodles*
- *50 g (2 oz) salted cashew nuts*

1 Mix the chicken with the sugar and all the seasonings. Cover and chill overnight.
2 Heat half the oil in a frying pan, add the courgettes and sauté for 2-3 minutes. Remove with a slotted spoon and transfer to a large bowl. Add the mangetout and peppers to the pan and sauté for 2-3 minutes. Add to the courgettes.
3 Heat the remaining oil and sauté the chicken in batches until golden brown. Return all the chicken to the pan and stir in the honey, lemon juice and ginger. Cover and simmer for about 5 minutes or until the chicken is quite tender.
4 Meanwhile, cook the noodles according to the packet instructions. Drain and snip into smaller pieces. Mix with the chicken and vegetables. Season with salt and pepper to taste. Sprinkle with the nuts and serve warm or cold.

PASTA IN SWEET PEPPER SAUCE

PREPARATION TIME 10 minutes
COOKING TIME 45 minutes
FREEZING Suitable (stage 2 – before adding salami)

❉

SERVES 4

360 CALS/SERVING

- *15 ml (1 tbsp) oil*
- *450 g (1 lb) red peppers, deseeded and finely chopped*
- *225 g (8 oz) onion, peeled and finely chopped*
- *1 garlic clove, peeled and crushed*
- *400 g (14 oz) can chopped tomatoes*
- *600 ml (1 pint) stock*

- *salt and pepper*
- *225 g (8 oz) dried pasta*
- *50 g (2 oz) salami, roughly chopped*
- *25 g (1 oz) freshly grated Parmesan cheese*
- *60 ml (4 tbsp) chopped fresh basil, to garnish*

1 Heat the oil and sauté the peppers, onion and garlic for 5-7 minutes or until they begin to soften.
2 Stir in the tomatoes and stock. Cover and simmer gently for 25-30 minutes or until the peppers are soft. Uncover and boil until most of the liquid has evaporated. Adjust the seasoning and add the salami.
3 Meanwhile, cook the pasta in boiling, salted water until just tender (*al dente*). Drain. Serve with the sauce, sprinkled with Parmesan cheese and garnished with fresh basil.

seasoning. Bring to the boil and simmer for 2-3 minutes or until piping hot.
4 Spoon the sauce over the cooked pasta and serve immediately, sprinkled with the chopped parsley and Parmesan cheese.

TOMATO AND MOZZARELLA NOODLES

PREPARATION TIME 10 minutes
COOKING TIME 10 minutes
FREEZING Not suitable
COLOUR INDEX Page 35

CRUNCHY COURGETTE PASTA

PREPARATION TIME 15 minutes
COOKING TIME 15 minutes
FREEZING Not suitable

SERVES 4
- 225 g (8 oz) mozzarella cheese
- 450 g (1 lb) tomatoes, deseeded and roughly chopped
- grated rind of 1 lemon
- 45 ml (3 tbsp) balsamic vinegar

410 CALS/SERVING
- salt and pepper
- 225 g (8 oz) dried pasta noodles, such as pappardelle
- 15 ml (1 tbsp) olive oil
- 15 ml (1 tbsp) chopped fresh thyme

1 Dice the mozzarella cheese and set aside. Place the tomatoes in a saucepan with the lemon rind and balsamic vinegar and season with salt and pepper.
2 Meanwhile, cook the pasta in boiling, salted water until just tender (*al dente*). Drain well. Toss in the olive oil with the fresh thyme.
3 Warm the tomato mixture for 2-3 minutes and spoon it over the pasta. Top with mozzarella cheese and serve immediately.

VARIATION Try cubes of dolcelatta cheese instead of the mozzarella.
  If you like garlic, sauté 2 crushed garlic cloves in a little olive oil and add to the tomato mixture at stage 3.

SERVES 4
- 175 g (6 oz) dried pasta
- salt and pepper
- 15 ml (1 tbsp) vegetable oil
- 125 g (4 oz) onion, peeled and finely chopped
- 1 garlic clove, peeled and crushed
- 1.25 ml (¼ tsp) mild chilli powder
- 1 red pepper, halved and chopped

260 CALS/SERVING
- 225 g (8 oz) tomatoes, diced
- 225 g (8 oz) courgettes, diced
- 350 ml (12 fl oz) tomato juice
- 15 ml (1 tbsp) red wine vinegar
- 30 ml (2 tbsp) chopped fresh parsley
- 20 ml (4 tsp) freshly grated Parmesan cheese

1 Cook the pasta in boiling, salted water until just tender (*al dente*), then drain.
2 Meanwhile, heat the oil in a non-stick frying pan and cook the onion and garlic for about 3 minutes or until beginning to soften. Stir in the chilli powder and cook for a further minute.
3 Add the red pepper, tomatoes and courgettes to the frying pan and cook over a medium heat for about 5 minutes or until hot but still crunchy. Stir in the tomato juice and vinegar with plenty of

PASTA WITH GRILLED ASPARAGUS AND BROAD BEANS

PREPARATION TIME 20 minutes
COOKING TIME 12-15 minutes
FREEZING Not suitable

SERVES 4

665 CALS/SERVING

- 225 g (8 oz) shelled broad beans
- salt and pepper
- 350 g (12 oz) dried pasta
- 450 g (1 lb) asparagus, trimmed and halved crossways
- 90 ml (6 tbsp) extra-virgin olive oil
- 2 garlic cloves, peeled and crushed
- grated rind and juice of 1 lemon
- 45 ml (3 tbsp) chopped fresh mint
- 60 ml (4 tbsp) single cream
- 60 ml (4 tbsp) grated Pecorino or Parmesan cheese

1 Blanch the beans in a large saucepan of lightly salted water for 2 minutes, then strain the water into a clean pan and reserve. Refresh the beans under cold running water and carefully remove the hard outer skin. Reserve the beans.

2 Return the bean water to a rolling boil, add the pasta, return to the boil and cook for 10 minutes until just tender (*al dente*).

3 Meanwhile, place the asparagus on the grill pan, brush with a little oil and grill for 3-4 minutes on each side until charred and tender.

4 While the asparagus is cooking, heat 30 ml (2 tbsp) of the oil in a pan, add the garlic and lemon rind and fry gently for 3 minutes until almost golden. Add the beans, mint and cream and heat gently.

5 Drain the pasta and immediately toss with the remaining oil, transfer to a warmed bowl and stir in the asparagus and the bean sauce. Stir in the cheese and lemon juice, then season to taste. Serve at once.

VARIATION Fresh peas also combine well with asparagus and mint and can be used instead of the broad beans if wished.

STUFFED PEPPERS WITH PINE NUTS

PREPARATION TIME 20 minutes
COOKING TIME 30-35 minutes
FREEZING Not suitable
COLOUR INDEX Page 37
♡

SERVES 4

- 2 large orange or red peppers
- 2 large yellow peppers

FILLING

- 45 ml (3 tbsp) extra-virgin olive oil
- 1 large onion, peeled and finely chopped
- 2-3 garlic cloves, peeled and finely chopped
- 450 g (1 lb) tomatoes, skinned and roughly chopped
- 30 ml (2 tbsp) tomato purée

315 CALS SERVING

- 5 ml (1 tsp) light muscovado sugar
- salt and pepper
- 50 g (2 oz) mushrooms, thickly sliced
- 50 g (2 oz) pine nuts
- 15 ml (1 tbsp) fresh marjoram leaves, roughly torn
- 50 g (2 oz) black olives
- 25-50 g (1-2 oz) freshly grated Parmesan cheese

1 Halve the peppers lengthways, then remove the core and seeds. Place cut-side down on a baking sheet and roast at 200°C (400°F) mark 6 for 15 minutes, turning frequently.
2 Meanwhile, make the sauce. Heat 30 ml (2 tbsp) oil in a saucepan, add the onion and garlic and fry gently until softened and lightly coloured. Add the tomatoes, tomato purée, sugar, salt and pepper. Cook, uncovered, for 15-20 minutes until reduced to a thick sauce. Check the seasoning.
3 Heat the remaining 15 ml (1 tbsp) oil in a pan and sauté the mushroom slices until softened.
4 Place the peppers, cut-side up, in an ovenproof dish. Transfer two thirds of the tomato mixture to a bowl and stir in the mushrooms, nuts, marjoram and olives. Fill the peppers with the mixture and top with the grated Parmesan cheese. Bake in the oven for 15-20 minutes until thoroughly heated through.

NOTE Use any remaining sauce to make a tasty accompaniment. Spread thick slices of crusty bread with the tomato mixture and sprinkle with sesame seeds. Warm through in the oven.

VEGETABLE PITHIVIER

PREPARATION TIME 1 hour, plus cooling
COOKING TIME About 1½ hours
FREEZING Not suitable
COLOUR INDEX Page 36

SERVES 6

- 4 red peppers
- 50 g (2 oz) butter
- 125 g (4 oz) shallots, peeled and finely diced
- 125 g (4 oz) mushrooms, sliced
- 75 ml (3 fl oz) double cream or crème fraîche
- 15 ml (1 tbsp) Parmesan cheese

585 CALS/SERVING

- 225 g (8 oz) ricotta cheese
- salt and pepper
- 125 g (4 oz) goats' cheese
- 450 g (1 lb) fresh spinach, washed
- freshly grated nutmeg
- 450 g (1 lb) Puff Pastry (see page 383)
- 1 egg, beaten

1 Roast the peppers in the oven at 200°C (400°F) mark 6 for 30-40 minutes. Remove their skins and slice the flesh into strips.
2 Meanwhile, melt 40 g (1½ oz) of the butter in a frying pan, add the shallots and sauté until soft. Add the mushrooms to the pan and cook until the liquid has evaporated. Pour in the cream and allow to bubble until the mushrooms are just coated in the cream. Cool. Stir in the Parmesan and half the ricotta. Add salt and pepper.
3 Crumble the rest of the ricotta and the goats' cheese. Set aside.
4 Melt the remaining butter in a large saucepan. Add the spinach and sauté until the leaves wilt. Drain and press out any excess moisture; roughly chop. Season with salt, pepper and nutmeg.
5 Roll out 175 g (6 oz) of the pastry into a rectangle 15 x 30 cm (6 x 12 inch). Place on a baking sheet, prick with a fork and bake at 200°C (400°F) mark 6 for about 15 minutes. Cool.
6 Place the cooked pastry on a baking sheet. Top with the pepper strips, crumbled ricotta, goat's cheese then the spinach, making an indentation along the centre. Fill with the mushroom mixture.
7 Thinly roll out 225 g (8 oz) pastry, large enough to wrap around the filling with some to tuck under the base. Brush with egg. Use the remaining pastry and trimmings for a lattice pattern over the top. Glaze with egg and chill until ready to cook.
8 Bake at 220°C (425°F) mark 7 for about 35-40 minutes.

TOMATO AND GRUYERE PIE

PREPARATION TIME 15 minutes, plus pastry
COOKING TIME 40 minutes
FREEZING Not suitable
COLOUR INDEX Page 36

SERVES 4

- 30 ml (2 tbsp) vegetable oil
- 75 g (3 oz) onion, peeled and finely chopped
- 225 g (8 oz) firm, green tomatoes, thinly sliced
- 125 g (4 oz) Gruyère cheese, grated

580 CALS/SERVING

- 45 ml (3 tbsp) chopped fresh basil
- 90 ml (6 tbsp) mayonnaise
- salt and pepper
- 225 g (8 oz) Puff Pastry (see page 383)
- beaten egg, to glaze

1 Heat the oil in a frying pan and gently sauté the onion for 2-3 minutes. Add the tomatoes and cook for 3-4 minutes or until beginning to soften, stirring occasionally.
2 Transfer to a bowl and stir in the cheese, basil, mayonnaise and seasoning.
3 Thinly roll out the puff pastry, cut out a 25 cm (10 inch) round and place on a baking sheet. Spread the tomato mixture over the centre to within 1 cm (½ inch) of the edge. Brush the pastry edge with beaten egg.
4 Bake at 180°C (350°F) mark 4 for 30-35 minutes until golden. Serve the pie hot or warm.

SUMMER COUSCOUS

PREPARATION TIME 30 minutes
FREEZING Not suitable
♡ ⏱

SERVES 6

- 225 g (8 oz) couscous
- 6 spring onions, roughly chopped
- 3 tomatoes, diced
- 6 sun-dried tomatoes in oil, drained and chopped
- 125 g (4 oz) pitted black olives
- 30 ml (2 tbsp) chopped fresh mint

230 CALS/SERVING

- 15 ml (1 tbsp) each chopped fresh coriander and chopped fresh parsley
- 2-3 garlic cloves, peeled and crushed
- 45 ml (3 tbsp) olive oil
- juice of 1 lemon
- salt and pepper

1 Put the couscous in a large bowl and pour in 600 ml (1 pint) cold water. Leave to soak for 15-20 minutes or until all the liquid has been absorbed.
2 Mix all the remaining ingredients into the couscous with plenty of seasoning.

TIP
This dish can be prepared the day before, if wished. Cover and chill.

TURKISH AUBERGINES

PREPARATION TIME 15 minutes, plus chilling
COOKING TIME 1½ hours
FREEZING Not suitable
COLOUR INDEX Page 37

SERVES 6

- *6 small aubergines*
- *200 ml (7 fl oz) olive oil*
- *450 g (1 lb) onions, peeled and finely sliced*
- *3 garlic cloves, peeled and crushed*
- *400 g (14 oz) can tomatoes, drained, or 450 g (1 lb) fresh tomatoes, skinned and chopped*

365 CALS/SERVING

- *60 ml (4 tbsp) chopped fresh parsley*
- *3.75 ml (¾ tsp) ground allspice*
- *salt and pepper*
- *5 ml (1 tsp) sugar*
- *30 ml (2 tbsp) lemon juice*
- *fresh parsley, to garnish*

1 Halve the aubergines lengthways. Scoop out the flesh and reserve. Leave a substantial shell so that they do not disintegrate.
2 Heat 45 ml (3 tbsp) of the olive oil in a saucepan, add the onions and garlic and fry gently for about 15 minutes or until the onions are soft but not coloured. Add the tomatoes, reserved aubergine flesh, chopped parsley and allspice. Season with salt and pepper. Simmer gently for about 20 minutes or until the mixture has reduced.
3 Spoon the tomato mixture into the aubergine halves and place them side by side in a shallow ovenproof dish. They should fit quite closely together.
4 Mix the remaining oil with 150 ml (5 fl oz) water, the sugar and lemon juice. Season with salt and pepper. Pour the mixture around the aubergines, cover and cook in the oven at 150°C (300°F) mark 2 for about 1 hour or until tender.
5 When cooked, remove from the oven, uncover and leave to cool for 1 hour. Chill in the refrigerator for at least 2 hours before serving garnished with parsley.

SUMMER RISOTTO

PREPARATION TIME 5 minutes
COOKING TIME About 25 minutes
FREEZING Not suitable

♡ ⏱

SERVES 4

- *225 g (8 oz) mixed, wild long-grain rice*
- *350 ml (12 fl oz) vegetable stock*
- *15 ml (1 tbsp) oil (from sun-dried tomatoes, if using)*
- *1 garlic clove, peeled and crushed*
- *350 g (12 oz) tomatoes, diced*

350-375 CALS/SERVING

- *4 sun-dried tomatoes in oil, drained and diced (optional)*
- *700 g (1½ lb) mixed blanched French beans, broad beans, mangetout, peas and asparagus*
- *12 pitted black olives, halved*
- *salt and pepper*

1 Cook the rice in the stock for about 20 minutes or until all the liquid has been absorbed and the rice is tender.
2 Heat the oil in a large non-stick frying pan or wok. Add the garlic and cook, stirring for 1-2 minutes.
3 Add the tomatoes and rice. Cook, stirring, over a gentle heat for 3-4 minutes. Stir in the blanched vegetables and olives. Increase the heat and cook for 1 minute, stirring, until piping hot. Season well and serve immediately.

VEGETABLE KEBABS WITH MANGO SAUCE AND TROPICAL RICE

PREPARATION TIME 20 minutes
COOKING TIME 20-25 minutes
FREEZING Not suitable

SERVES 4

- *5 ml (1 tsp) sesame or sunflower oil*
- *1 small onion, peeled and very finely chopped*
- *1 garlic clove, peeled and finely chopped*
- *45 ml (3 tbsp) mango chutney*
- *45 ml (3 tbsp) tomato purée*
- *grated rind and juice of 1 lime*
- *150 ml (5 fl oz) natural yogurt*

386 CALS/SERVING

- *salt and pepper*
- *8 shallots or baby onions, peeled*
- *2 courgettes, trimmed*
- *225 g (8 oz) button mushrooms*
- *175 g (6 oz) baby sweetcorn*
- *225 g (8 oz) basmati or long-grain rice*
- *40 g (1½ oz) creamed coconut, diced*

1 Heat the oil in a non-stick saucepan, add the onion and garlic and cook for about 5 minutes until softened. Remove from the heat and stir in the mango chutney, tomato purée, half the lime juice and the yogurt. Season with salt and pepper.

2 Put the shallots in a saucepan of boiling water, return to the boil, then drain well. Cut the courgettes into 2.5 cm (1 inch) pieces. Thread the shallots, courgettes, mushrooms and sweetcorn alternately onto eight skewers.

3 Arrange the skewers on a foil-lined grill pan. Brush the kebabs with mango sauce and cook under a hot grill for 10-15 minutes, turning frequently, until golden brown.

4 Meanwhile, cook the rice for 10-12 minutes until cooked. Drain, then add the lime rind and remaining lime juice and the coconut. Stir until the coconut has melted.

5 Gently heat the remaining sauce but do not allow to boil. Pour into a serving bowl. Serve the kebabs with the tropical rice and mango sauce.

BROAD BEANS IN HERBED
LEMON CREAM

PREPARATION TIME 20 minutes
COOKING TIME About 20 minutes
FREEZING Not suitable

SERVES 4-6
- *50 g (2 oz) butter*
- *2 garlic cloves, peeled and chopped*
- *4 shallots, peeled and finely chopped*
- *450 g (1 lb) fresh baby broad beans, shelled*
- *150 ml (5 fl oz) vegetable stock*
- *200 ml (7 fl oz) double cream*

385-260 CALS/SERVING
- *30 ml (2 tbsp) chopped fresh chervil or chives*
- *30 ml (2 tbsp) chopped fresh parsley*
- *grated rind of 1 lemon*
- *salt and pepper*

1 Melt the butter in a saucepan, add the garlic and shallots and cook gently for 3 minutes. Stir in the beans and stock. Bring to the boil, cover and simmer gently for 12-15 minutes, until the beans are tender.
2 Strain, reserving the liquid. Place the cooking liquid in a blender or food processor with 90 ml (4 tbsp) beans and blend to a purée, gradually adding the cream to make a smooth sauce.
3 Return the mixture to the pan. Add the beans, herbs and lemon rind and season with salt and pepper to taste. Reheat gently and serve hot.

VARIATION Omit the lemon rind and sprinkle with crisp, crumbled bacon just before serving.

> *TIP*
> Tender, fresh baby broad beans are best for this dish, or use frozen baby beans and skin them, if necessary, before cooking.

OKRA WITH APRICOTS

PREPARATION TIME 10 minutes
COOKING TIME 35-40 minutes
FREEZING Not suitable
COLOUR INDEX Page 42

SERVES 4   250 CALS/SERVING
- *450 g (1 lb) small okra*
- *juice of ½ orange*
- *60 ml (4 tbsp) olive oil*
- *1 onion, peeled and thinly sliced*
- *400 g (14 oz) can tomatoes*
- *30 ml (2 tbsp) tomato purée*
- *125 g (4 oz) no-soak dried apricots, cut into thick shreds*
- *salt and pepper*
- *30 ml (2 tbsp) chopped fresh basil*
- *orange rind strips and orange slices, to garnish*

1 Place the okra in a bowl, pour over the orange juice, toss lightly and set aside.
2 Heat the oil in a large saucepan, add the onion and cook for 5 minutes until softened. Add the okra and orange juice, then add the tomatoes and break up slightly with a wooden spoon.
3 Stir in the tomato purée and the apricots and season with salt and pepper to taste. Cover the pan and cook gently for 30-35 minutes until the okra and apricots are tender and the sauce thickened.
4 Stir in the basil and serve hot, garnished with orange rind strips and orange slices.

BAKED ARTICHOKES

PREPARATION TIME 10 minutes
COOKING TIME 45-50 minutes
FREEZING Not suitable
COLOUR INDEX Page 41
♡

SERVES 6   110 CALS/SERVING
- *6 small globe artichokes*
- *salt and pepper*
- *90 ml (6 tbsp) extra-virgin olive oil*
- *lemon slices and chervil or parsley sprigs, to garnish*

1 Trim the artichoke stalks close to the base. Bring a large saucepan of salted water to the boil.
2 Add the artichokes. Simmer, covered, for 30

minutes or until you can pull away a base leaf easily.
3 Drain the artichokes and refresh under cold water, then halve them lengthways. With a small spoon, remove the 'hairy' choke.
4 Place the artichokes cut side uppermost on a baking sheet. Drizzle with olive oil and season with salt and pepper. Bake at 200°C (400°F) mark 6 for about 15-20 minutes. Serve garnished with lemon slices and herbs.

VARIATION The artichokes can be grilled instead of baked. Grill for 20 minutes, basting occasionally with olive oil.

PAN-FRIED TOMATOES

PREPARATION TIME 8 minutes
COOKING TIME 3 minutes
FREEZING Not suitable
COLOUR INDEX Page 41
🕐

SERVES 4   240 CALS/SERVING
- *450 g (1 lb) plum tomatoes, thickly sliced*
- *rock salt and pepper*
- *100 ml (3½ fl oz) olive oil*
- *2 garlic cloves, peeled and sliced*
- *30 ml (2 tbsp) capers, drained and rinsed*
- *30 ml (2 tbsp) chopped fresh parsley*

1 Season the tomatoes with salt and pepper.
2 Heat the olive oil with the garlic in a large sauté pan. Fry the tomatoes for 1 minute only on each side. Using draining spoons, remove to a shallow serving dish.
3 Add the capers and parsley to the pan. Heat for 1 minute, stirring, then pour the contents of the pan over the tomatoes. Serve at once.

TIP
This dish also makes a refreshing starter served warm or cold with toasted ciabatta bread and goats' cheese.

STIR-FRIED SUMMER VEGETABLES

PREPARATION TIME 15 minutes
COOKING TIME 5 minutes
FREEZING Not suitable

♡ ⏲

SERVES 4-6
- *30 ml (2 tbsp) sunflower oil*
- *2.5 cm (1 inch) piece fresh root ginger, peeled and finely chopped (optional)*
- *1 garlic clove, peeled and finely chopped*
- *175 g (6 oz) baby carrots, trimmed*
- *125 g (4 oz) baby French beans, topped and tailed*
- *175 g (6 oz) baby courgettes (with flowers, if possible), halved lengthways*
- *125 g (4 oz) mangetout or sugar snap peas*

195-130 CALS/SERVING
- *125 g (4 oz) baby sweetcorn, halved diagonally*
- *3-4 spring onions, shredded*
- *175 g (6 oz) bean sprouts, rinsed*
- *30 ml (2 tbsp) light soy sauce*
- *salt and pepper*
- *5-10 ml (1-2 tsp) sesame oil*
- *coriander sprigs, to garnish*
SAUCE
- *45 ml (3 tbsp) sherry*
- *45 ml (3 tbsp) light soy sauce*
- *5 ml (1 tsp) clear honey*

1 To make the sauce, simply mix the sherry, soy sauce and honey together in a small jug; set aside.
2 Heat the oil in a wok or large frying pan and add the ginger and garlic to flavour the oil. When the oil is very hot, add the carrots and French beans and fry, turning constantly, for 2-3 minutes.
3 Add the courgettes, mangetout or sugar snaps, sweetcorn, spring onions and bean sprouts, together with the soy sauce. Stir-fry for 2 minutes.
4 Taste and season with salt and pepper if necessary. Sprinkle with the sesame oil. Serve immediately, garnished with coriander sprigs and accompanied by the sauce.

VARIATION To serve the stir-fry as a main course, include rice noodles or egg noodles. Cook according to the packet instructions until almost tender. Drain. Add to the stir-fry and cook, turning constantly, for 1 minute. Serve immediately.

ROASTED TOMATOES, PEPPERS AND COURGETTES

PREPARATION TIME 10 minutes, plus cooling
COOKING TIME 45 minutes
FREEZING Not suitable
COLOUR INDEX Page 41

SERVES 4
- *225 g (8 oz) aubergine, cut into large chunks*
- *350 g (12 oz) courgettes, cut into large chunks*
- *1 red pepper, deseeded and cut into chunks*
- *1 yellow pepper, deseeded and cut into chunks*

215 CALS/SERVING
- *225 g (8 oz) tomatoes, halved*
- *6 garlic cloves, peeled*
- *75 ml (5 tbsp) olive oil*
- *rock salt and pepper*
- *1 lemon*

1 Place all the vegetables in a large roasting tin in a single layer. Sprinkle the olive oil over them and season generously with plenty of rock salt.
2 Roast at 200°C (400°F) mark 6 for about 45 minutes or until tender and well browned, turning once during cooking.
3 Cool for 30 minutes in the tin and then squeeze over lemon juice to taste and adjust the seasoning. Lift the vegetables onto serving plates or into one large bowl. Serve straight away or leave to cool.

TIP
For a delicious light lunch, serve the roasted vegetables with this toasted treat – thickly slice a crusty loaf and rub each slice with a garlic clove. Toast lightly on both sides. Spread the toast thickly on both sides with pesto sauce or tapenade (olive paste), then top with slices of mozzarella, Emmental or goats' cheese. Place the slices under the grill until the cheese just begins to melt.

NEW POTATO AND DILL SALAD

PREPARATION TIME 5 minutes
COOKING TIME 15 minutes
FREEZING Not suitable

SERVES 6
- *900 g (2 lb) baby new potatoes*
- *salt and pepper*
- *60 ml (4 tbsp) Greek natural yogurt*
- *60 ml (4 tbsp) mayonnaise*

215 CALS/SERVING
- *20 ml (1 tsp) wholegrain mustard*
- *5 ml (1 tsp) lemon juice*
- *60 ml (4 tbsp) chopped fresh dill or 2.5 ml (½ tsp) dried*

1 Scrub the new potatoes. Boil them in salted water for 10-15 minutes or until tender.
2 Meanwhile, mix the remaining ingredients together and season with salt and pepper.
3 Drain the potatoes and leave to cool for 5 minutes, then mix with the dressing while still warm. Serve warm or cover and chill.

VARIATION Turn this into an inexpensive supper dish by mixing in some smoked salmon scraps, available from fishmongers.

MIXED LEAF, ORANGE AND STRAWBERRY SALAD

PREPARATION TIME 20 minutes
FREEZING Not suitable
COLOUR INDEX Page 42
♡ ⏱

SERVES 6

150 CALS/SERVING

- *1 small frisée lettuce*
- *1 bunch watercress*
- *3 large oranges*
- *225 g (8 oz) strawberries*
- *1 large ripe avocado*
- *45 ml (3 tbsp) olive oil*
- *5 ml (1 tsp) white wine vinegar*
- *5 ml (1 tsp) Dijon mustard*
- *salt and pepper*

1 Wash and dry the frisée and watercress, removing any coarse or discoloured stalks or leaves. Tear into small pieces and place in a large serving bowl.
2 Peel the oranges and slice into the serving bowl. Wash, hull and slice the strawberries; halve, peel and slice the avocado and place both in the bowl.
3 To make the dressing, whisk together the olive oil, wine vinegar and Dijon mustard. Season with salt and pepper to taste. Pour the dressing over the prepared salad. Toss well and serve.

TOMATO AND RED ONION SALAD

PREPARATION TIME 10 minutes, plus marinating
FREEZING Not suitable
COLOUR INDEX Page 42
♡ ⏱

SERVES 6

120 CALS/SERVING

- *700 g (1½ lb) mixed tomatoes, halved*
- *1 large red onion, peeled and finely chopped*
- *60 ml (4 tbsp) olive oil*
- *20 ml (4 tsp) balsamic vinegar*
- *salt and pepper*

1 Combine the tomatoes and onion.
2 Whisk together the remaining ingredients and season with salt and pepper. Pour over the tomatoes, toss well and leave to marinate for at least 20 minutes before serving.

MIXED HERB SALAD

PREPARATION TIME 15 minutes
FREEZING Not suitable
♡ ⏱

SERVES 4

100 CALS/SERVING

- *selection of seasonal fresh herb leaves, such as rocket, sorrel, lamb's lettuce, dandelion, enough for 4 people*
- *handful of chervil sprigs*
- *handful of parsley sprigs*
- *a few flowers, such as sweet violets and marigolds, if available*
- *2.5 ml (½ tsp) dry mustard powder*
- *5 ml (1 tsp) clear honey*
- *30 ml (2 tbsp) lemon juice*
- *2.5 ml (½ tsp) paprika*
- *30 ml (2 tbsp) sunflower oil*
- *15 ml (1 tbsp) walnut oil*
- *salt and pepper*

1 Wash and drain the salad leaves. Gently pat dry with absorbent kitchen paper. Shred them roughly by hand. Place them in a serving bowl with the chervil and parsley sprigs. Scatter the flowers, if using, over the top. Cover tightly and refrigerate until ready to dress the salad.
2 Blend the mustard powder with the honey until smooth. Add the lemon juice, paprika, sunflower and walnut oils and seasoning. Mix well.
3 Dress the salad about 10 minutes before serving.

CUCUMBER AND WATERCRESS SALAD

PREPARATION TIME 10 minutes, plus chilling
FREEZING Not suitable
COLOUR INDEX Page 42
♡ ⏱

SERVES 6
- *30 ml (2 tbsp) white wine vinegar*
- *5 ml (1 tsp) sugar*
- *15 ml (1 tbsp) olive oil*
- *20 ml (4 tsp) lemon juice*
- *salt and pepper*
- *1 cucumber, weighing about 350 g (12 oz) and cut into matchsticks*

70 CALS/SERVING
- *small bunch spring onions, sliced*
- *25 g (1 oz) chopped walnuts*
- *1 bunch watercress, divided into sprigs*

1 Whisk together the vinegar, sugar, olive oil and lemon juice. Season with salt and pepper. Toss the cucumber and spring onions together in the dressing. Cover and refrigerate until required.
2 Just before serving, toss the cucumber and spring onions again. Sprinkle the walnuts over and surround with watercress sprigs.

> ### TIP
> This is a useful salad for preparing in advance and assembling at the last minute. Store the watercress sprigs in a polythene bag in the refrigerator.

FETA CHEESE AND OLIVE SALAD

PREPARATION TIME 15 minutes
FREEZING Not suitable
⏱

SERVES 2
- *225 g (8 oz) tomatoes*
- *½ large cucumber*
- *125 g (4 oz) feta cheese*
- *1 onion, peeled and thinly sliced*
- *50 g (2 oz) pitted black olives*
- *chopped fresh herbs, to garnish*

430 CALS/SERVING
DRESSING
- *45 ml (3 tbsp) olive oil*
- *15-30 ml (1-2 tbsp) lemon juice*
- *15-30 ml (1-2 tbsp) chopped fresh herbs*
- *pinch of sugar*
- *salt and pepper*
- *crusty bread, to accompany*

1 Whisk the dressing ingredients together in a jug or shake together in a screw-topped jar.
2 Cut the tomatoes into bite-sized chunks, discarding the cores. Cut the cucumber and feta cheese into bite-sized chunks.
3 Put the tomatoes, cucumber and onion in a large bowl, add the olives and toss the ingredients together with your hands. Pour over the dressing and toss gently to mix, then scatter the feta cheese over the top. Serve as soon as possible, garnished with chopped fresh herbs and accompanied with slices of crusty bread.

ARTICHOKE AND ASPARAGUS SALAD

PREPARATION TIME 25 minutes, plus marinating
COOKING TIME 30-45 minutes
FREEZING Not suitable
COLOUR INDEX Page 42

♡

SERVES 6

- *6 small, young or 3 large, firm artichokes*
- *salt and pepper*
- *350 g (12 oz) asparagus*
- *100 ml (3½ fl oz) olive oil*
- *30 ml (2 tbsp) orange juice*
- *30 ml (2 tbsp) chopped fresh herbs such as basil, lemon thyme and marjoram or 10 ml (2 tsp) dried*

200 CALS/SERVING

- *1 bunch radishes*
- *175 g (6 oz) mixed black and green olives, with stones*
- *fresh basil, to garnish (optional)*

1 If using small, young artichokes, trim each stalk to within 4 cm (1½ inches) of the head and plunge into a large saucepan of boiling, salted water. Cover and simmer for 20-25 minutes or until tender when the base is pierced with the tip of a sharp knife. If using large artichokes, break and pull off the stalks. Snip off the sharp tips of the leaves. Cook in a large pan of boiling, salted water for 35-45 minutes, weighing them down with a heatproof plate or small lid to keep them completely submerged. They are cooked when a central leaf can be pulled out easily.
2 Drain the artichokes and plunge into cold water, then drain and pat dry on absorbent kitchen paper. Leave to cool. When completely cold, quarter each large artichoke and, using a teaspoon, very carefully scoop out the hairy choke at the base.
3 Trim any tough or woody stalks from the asparagus, cut into 5 cm (2 inch) lengths and plunge into boiling, salted water for 8-10 minutes or until tender but still crisp. Plunge into cold water and drain.
4 In a large bowl, whisk together the olive oil, orange juice, chopped herbs and salt and pepper to taste. Add the cooked vegetables and toss well to coat.

5 Trim the radishes; halve or quarter, if necessary. Place the olives in a polythene bag and lightly 'crack' with a rolling pin. Add the radishes and olives to the vegetables and toss lightly. Cover and leave to marinate in the refrigerator for 4 hours or overnight. (The flavour is better the longer you leave it.)
6 Allow the salad to come to room temperature for about 2 hours. Serve garnished with extra basil sprigs, if wished.

AVOCADO AND CHICK-PEA SALAD

PREPARATION TIME 15 minutes
FREEZING Not suitable
COLOUR INDEX Page 43

🕐

SERVES 4

- *45 ml (3 tbsp) lemon juice*
- *50 g (2 oz) fromage frais*
- *125 ml (4 fl oz) milk*
- *30 ml (2 tbsp) chopped fresh chives or parsley*
- *salt and pepper*
- *1 avocado*
- *450 g (1 lb) fresh young spinach, finely shredded*

330 CALS/SERVING

- *125 g (4 oz) radicchio lettuce, finely shredded*
- *430 g (15 oz) can chick-peas, drained and rinsed*
- *1 slice of wholemeal bread, toasted and cubed*
- *2 eggs, hard-boiled and chopped*

1 To make the dressing, place 30 ml (2 tbsp) of the lemon juice, the fromage frais and milk in a bowl and whisk until smooth. Add the herbs and salt and pepper to taste. Set aside.
2 Peel the avocado, discard the stone and dice the flesh. Coat with the remaining lemon juice to prevent discoloration.
3 Mix together the spinach and radicchio leaves and arrange on a large serving platter. Scatter the avocado, chick-peas, toast cubes and eggs on top and sprinkle over a little paprika.
4 To serve, spoon a little of the dressing over the salad. Serve the remaining dressing separately.

MINTED VEGETABLE SALAD

PREPARATION TIME 20 minutes
COOKING TIME 4 minutes
FREEZING Not suitable
♡ ⏲

SERVES 6

- *45 ml (3 tbsp) chopped fresh mint*
- *50 ml (2 fl oz) olive oil*
- *30 ml (2 tbsp) white wine vinegar*
- *grated rind of 1 lemon*
- *5 ml (1 tsp) Dijon mustard*
- *5 ml (1 tsp) caster sugar*
- *225 g (8 oz) shelled fresh peas*

145 CALS/SERVING

- *175 g (6 oz) shelled broad beans*
- *salt and pepper*
- *225 g (8 oz) courgettes, thickly sliced*
- *175 g (6 oz) runner beans, trimmed and sliced*
- *1 bunch spring onions, finely chopped*
- *fresh mint leaves, to garnish*

1 Whisk together the mint, olive oil, vinegar, lemon rind, mustard and sugar, then set aside.
2 Place the peas and beans in a saucepan of boiling, salted water. Return to the boil, cook for 3 minutes, add the courgettes and runner beans and boil for a further 1 minute, or until just tender. Drain well, then refresh under cold water so that they retain their colour.
3 Toss the vegetables with the spring onions in the prepared mint dressing, adjust the seasoning and serve warm or cold, garnished with mint.

TIP
Don't toss the dressing in until the last minute or you'll find that the vegetables will lose their bright colour.

217

BERRY COMPOTE

PREPARATION TIME 15 minutes
COOKING TIME 5 minutes
FREEZING Not suitable
COLOUR INDEX Page 44
♡ ⏲

SERVES 6

- *50 g (2 oz) granulated sugar*
- *225 g (8 oz) blackcurrants, prepared*
- *450 g (1 lb) redcurrants, prepared*

95 CALS/SERVING

- *pared rind and juice of 1 orange*
- *30 ml (2 tbsp) clear honey*
- *350 g (12 oz) strawberries, hulled*

1 Dissolve the sugar in 150 ml (5 fl oz) water. Bring to the boil and bubble for 1 minute.
2 Add the prepared currants with the pared orange rind and simmer for about 1 minute only until the fruits are just beginning to soften. Immediately remove from the heat and pour into a heatproof bowl. Stir in the honey and leave to cool.
3 Mix in the strained orange juice, cover the bowl and chill well in the refrigerator.
4 Just before serving, thinly slice the strawberries and stir gently into the compote.

NOTE With 50 g (2 oz) sugar the compote will be quite tart – add more sugar to taste.

STRAWBERRY MILLE FEUILLES

PREPARATION TIME 1 hour, plus chilling and cooling
COOKING TIME 15 minutes
FREEZING Suitable for the pastry
COLOUR INDEX Page 44
❄

SERVES 6-8

- *225 g (8 oz) Puff Pastry (see page 383)*
- *50 g (2 oz) raspberries*
- *30 ml (2 tbsp) redcurrant jelly*
- *350 g (12 oz) strawberries, hulled and halved*
- *150 ml (5 fl oz) double cream, whipped*

425-320 CALS/SERVING

- *strawberry leaves, to decorate*

CREME PATISSIERE

- *300 ml (10 fl oz) milk*
- *1 vanilla pod, split*
- *3 egg yolks*
- *75 g (3 oz) caster sugar*
- *30 ml (2 tbsp) cornflour*
- *15 g (½ oz) butter*

1 Roll out the pastry to a 23 x 30 cm (9 x 12 inch) rectangle. Transfer to a dampened baking tray, prick the pastry all over with a fork and chill for 15 minutes. Bake at 220°C (425°F) mark 7 for 10-12 minutes until golden brown. Trim the edges, then cut widthways into three equal strips. Turn the strips over, return to the oven and bake for 5 minutes more. Cool on a wire rack.
2 To make the crème pâtissière, heat the milk with the vanilla pod in a heavy-based saucepan until almost boiling, then remove from the heat and leave to infuse for 30 minutes.
3 Whisk together the egg yolks and sugar until frothy, then whisk in the cornflour. Strain in the milk and whisk again. Return this mixture to the pan and cook over a low heat, stirring all the time, until boiling and thickened. Remove from the heat and beat in the butter. Cover the surface of the sauce with clingfilm and leave to cool.
4 Meanwhile, purée the raspberries in a blender and place in a saucepan with the redcurrant jelly. Place over a low heat and stir until the jelly has melted. Leave to cool, stirring occasionally, then stir in one third of the strawberries. When the crème pâtissière is cold, fold in the cream.
5 When ready to serve, spread the crème pâtissière over two strips of the pastry and carefully arrange half of the plain strawberries on top of each. Lay one strip on top of the other, then top with the final layer of pastry and spoon the fruit mixture on top. Decorate and serve at once.

STRAWBERRY CHEESECAKE

PREPARATION TIME 25 minutes, plus cooling
COOKING TIME 50 minutes
FREEZING Suitable (stage 3)

❋

SERVES 8

- *50 g (2 oz) butter or margarine*
- *75 g (3 oz) plain flour*
- *25 g (1 oz) porridge oats*
- *75 g (3 oz) caster sugar*
- *700 g (1½ lb) natural cottage cheese*
- *2 eggs*

245 CALS/SERVING

- *grated rind of 1 lemon*
- *60 ml (4 tbsp) natural yogurt*
- *225 g (8 oz) fresh strawberries, hulled*

1 Grease and base-line a 20 cm (8 inch) loose-based round cake tin. Put the fat in a saucepan and heat until melted, then stir in the flour, oats and 25 g (1 oz) of the sugar. Stir until well mixed, then press into the base of the cake tin. Bake at 180°C (350°F) mark 4 for 10 minutes.

2 Meanwhile, rub the cottage cheese through a sieve into a bowl. Beat the eggs, then beat into the cottage cheese. Add the lemon rind and the remaining 50 g (2 oz) caster sugar and mix well together.

3 Pour the mixture into the cake tin. Return to the oven and bake for 20 minutes. Spoon the yogurt over the cheesecake and bake for a further 20 minutes. Leave to cool in the tin for 3-4 hours.

4 When cold, carefully remove the cheesecake from the tin. Slice most of the strawberries and arrange, with the remaining whole berries, on top of the cheesecake before serving.

TIP
The texture of a cooked cheesecake almost seems to improve with standing. Make and cook the day before and store, undecorated, in the refrigerator overnight. Remove from the refrigerator an hour before serving, to allow the cheesecake to return to room temperature.

5 Cover the pudding with a saucer, that fits just inside the top of the pudding basin, then set a 2 kg (4 lb) weight on the saucer. Chill overnight.
6 To serve the pudding, invert onto a serving plate, spoon the reserved juice over the pudding and decorate with redcurrant sprigs and lemon balm or mint sprigs.

NOTE Choose a good quality close-textured large white loaf, preferably one-day old.

RASPBERRY FOOL

PREPARATION TIME 10 minutes, plus chilling
FREEZING Not suitable
COLOUR INDEX Page 44
♡

SERVES 4
95 CALS/SERVING
- *450 g (1 lb) raspberries*
- *25 g (1 oz) caster sugar*
- *300 ml (10 fl oz) very low-fat fromage frais*
- *raspberry leaves, to decorate (optional)*

1 Reserve a few raspberries for decoration. Put the rest with the sugar in a blender or food processor and process to form a purée.
2 Turn the raspberry purée into a bowl, then gently swirl in the fromage frais to make a marbled effect. Divide the mixture between 4 individual serving dishes.
3 Chill in the refrigerator for about 2 hours before serving. Serve decorated with the reserved raspberries and raspberry leaves, if wished.

NOTE Using low-fat fromage frais makes this delicious fool surprisingly light in calories.

VARIATIONS Strawberry fool can be made in exactly the same way as the above recipe, simply substituting strawberries for the raspberries. For a mixed soft fruit fool, use an equal weight of raspberries and strawberries. Don't forget to reserve a little of the fruit for decoration.

SUMMER PUDDING

PREPARATION TIME 35 minutes, plus chilling
COOKING TIME 5 minutes
FREEZING Suitable
♡ ❉

SERVES 6-8
180-135 CALS/SERVING
- *450 g (1 lb) raspberries*
- *225 g (8 oz) redcurrants, prepared*
- *225 g (8 oz) blackcurrants, prepared*
- *75 g (3 oz) caster sugar*
- *8 large slices white bread, 5 mm (¼ inch) thick*
- *redcurrant sprigs and lemon balm or mint leaves, to decorate*

1 Place the raspberries in a saucepan, with the red and black currants, sugar and 45 ml (3 tbsp) water. Bring to a gentle simmer over a low heat, then cook gently for 3-4 minutes until the juices begin to run. Set aside.
2 Remove the crusts from the bread slices, then cut a round of bread from one slice to fit the base of a 1.5 litre (2½ pint) pudding basin. Cut the remaining slices in half lengthways.
3 Arrange the bread slices around the side of the pudding basin, overlapping them slightly at the bottom, so they fit neatly and tightly together. Position the round of bread to cover the base.
4 Spoon 100 ml (3½ fl oz) of the fruit juice into a jug. Spoon the remaining fruit and its juice into the bread-lined basin. Cover completely with the remaining bread slices, trimming to fit.

CHERRY BRULEES

PREPARATION TIME 15 minutes, plus chilling
COOKING TIME 40-45 minutes
FREEZING Not suitable
COLOUR INDEX Page 44

SERVES 8

- *350 g (12 oz) fresh cherries*
- *15 ml (1 tbsp) kirsch*
- *4 egg yolks*
- *50 g (2 oz) caster sugar*

395 CALS/SERVING

- *450 ml (15 fl oz) double cream*
- *125 g (4 oz) granulated sugar*

1 Stone the cherries, reserving eight with stems for decoration. Pour the kirsch over the remaining pitted cherries.
2 Whisk together the egg yolks and caster sugar until they have thickened and lightened in colour. Pour in the cream, stirring. Place in a heavy-based saucepan. Cook over a low heat, stirring continuously, until the mixture thickens to the consistency of double cream. This will take about 10 minutes. Do not boil.
3 Divide the soaked cherries among 8 ramekins or heatproof cups. Strain over the custard mixture.
4 Bake at 150°C (300°F) mark 2 for 30-35 minutes or until very lightly set. Cool and refrigerate until firm.
5 Place the granulated sugar in a small, heavy-based saucepan. Heat gently until the sugar dissolves and turns a golden caramel colour. Place a reserved cherry on each ramekin. Pour a thin layer of the caramel over each one. Chill, uncovered, for about 1 hour but not more than 6 hours before serving.

TIP
Cherry stoners are available from all good kitchen equipment shops. This inexpensive tool not only saves time but removes the stone with very little damage.

GOOSEBERRY MOUSSE

PREPARATION TIME 25 minutes, plus setting
COOKING TIME 15 minutes
FREEZING Not suitable
♡

SERVES 4

- *15 ml (1 tbsp) powdered gelatine*
- *450 g (1 lb) gooseberries, trimmed*
- *50 g (2 oz) caster sugar*

130 CALS/SERVING

- *150 ml (5 fl oz) natural yogurt*
- *a few drops of green food colouring (optional)*
- *fresh mint sprigs, to decorate*

1 In a small bowl, sprinkle the gelatine over 60 ml (4 tbsp) cold water. Put the gooseberries in a saucepan with 30 ml (2 tbsp) water. Bring to the boil, reduce the heat, cover and simmer for 15 minutes until the fruit is tender. If very juicy, drain off the cooking liquid and reserve. Stir in the sponged gelatine and stir well. Cool slightly.
2 Put the gooseberries and sugar in a blender or food processor and process to form a purée.
3 Push the purée through a nylon sieve into a measuring jug to remove the seeds. If necessary, make up to 450 ml (15 fl oz) with reserved juice.
4 When the gooseberry mixture is beginning to set, fold in the yogurt. Add a few drops of green food colouring if wished.
5 Pour the mousse into 4 individual serving dishes or one large dish. Put in the refrigerator to set. Serve decorated with sprigs of fresh mint.

POACHED APRICOTS

PREPARATION TIME 10 minutes, plus chilling
COOKING TIME 10 minutes
FREEZING Not suitable
COLOUR INDEX Page 44

♡

SERVES 6

100 CALS/SERVING

- *18 apricots, about 700 g (1½ lb) total weight*
- *1 cinnamon stick*
- *50 g (2 oz) caster sugar*
- *300 ml (10 fl oz) white wine*
- *1 vanilla pod*
- *15 ml (1 tbsp) brandy*

1 Halve and stone the apricots, if wished.
2 Cut the cinnamon stick lengthways and place in a saucepan with the sugar, wine, vanilla pod and 225 ml (8 fl oz) water.
3 Heat gently until the sugar dissolves. Bring to the boil and bubble for 2-3 minutes. Add the apricots and brandy and reduce to gentle simmer. Poach the fruit for 5-6 minutes or until just tender.
4 Pour into a heatproof glass bowl and leave to cool completely. Cover and chill in the refrigerator before serving.

NOTE When chilling the dish, make sure that the apricots are covered in syrup so that they don't discolour.

> *TIP*
> This recipe makes plenty of syrup for the apricots; if you don't serve it all, freeze the remainder and use as a base for a fruit salad.

GOLDEN NECTARINE TART

PREPARATION TIME 20 minutes, plus cooling
COOKING TIME 1 hour 20 minutes
FREEZING Suitable (stage 2)
COLOUR INDEX Page 47

❄

SERVES 8

500 CALS/SERVING

PATE SUCREE

- *125 g (4 oz) butter*
- *225 g (8 oz) white plain flour*
- *125 g (4 oz) caster sugar*
- *1 whole egg plus 1 egg yolk, beaten together*

FILLING

- *15 g (½ oz) fresh white breadcrumbs*
- *6 ripe nectarines or peaches, about 700 g (1½ lb) total weight*

- *2 whole eggs plus 1 egg yolk*
- *200 ml (7 fl oz) double cream*
- *40 g (1½ oz) icing sugar*
- *30 ml (2 tbsp) brandy*
- *1.25 ml (¼ tsp) freshly grated nutmeg*
- *90 ml (6 tbsp) apricot jam*

1 Make the pâte sucrée following the instructions on page 384.
2 Roll out the pâte sucrée carefully and use to line a 2.5 cm (1 inch) deep, 27.5 x 19.5 cm (10¾ x 7¾ inch) loose-based flan tin. Bake blind (see page 383) until set and lightly browned, then leave to cool.
3 Scatter the breadcrumbs evenly over the pastry base. Halve and stone the nectarines and arrange cut side down in the flan case.
4 Whisk together the two eggs, egg yolk, double cream, icing sugar, brandy and nutmeg. Pour the mixture around the nectarines.
5 Bake at 180°C (350°F) mark 4 for about 50 minutes or until just set. Flash under a hot grill to brown, then set aside to cool.
6 Warm the jam with 15 ml (1 tbsp) water to make a glaze. Sieve, then brush the glaze over the flan. Leave to set. Store in a cool place until ready to serve – not more than 6 hours.

VARIATION For an alternative dessert with fewer calories (215 per serving), simply place the nectarines in a shallow ovenproof dish. Pour the whisked egg mixture over and bake as above. Peaches can also be used but remove the skin first as it can be tough when cooked.

GRILLED PEACHES WITH CHOCOLATE AND MARZIPAN

PREPARATION TIME 10 minutes
COOKING TIME 5 minutes
FREEZING Not suitable

⏱

SERVES 4

- *4 ripe peaches*
- *150 ml (5 fl oz) double cream*
- *125 g (4 oz) plain chocolate, broken into pieces*
- *1 lime*
- *50 g (2 oz) marzipan, chopped into small pieces*

445 CALS/SERVING

- *30 ml (2 tbsp) icing sugar*
- *pouring cream, to serve*
- *mint sprigs, to decorate*

1 Halve the peaches and remove the stones. Arrange the peaches, cut-side up, in a shallow flameproof dish.

2 Pour the cream into a saucepan. Bring just to the boil, then add the chocolate and stir until smooth.

3 Pare thin strips of rind from the lime using a citrus zester; set aside. Squeeze 10 ml (2 tsp) juice from the lime and add to the chocolate sauce. Sprinkle a further 10 ml (2 tsp) over the peaches.

4 Divide the marzipan between the peach halves. Drizzle a little of the chocolate sauce over the peaches and pour the remainder into the dish.

5 Sift the icing sugar over the peaches and grill for about 5 minutes until the peaches and marzipan are lightly coloured.

6 Transfer to warmed serving plates and scatter with the pared lime rind. Pour a little cream onto the sauce. Serve decorated with mint sprigs and accompanied by pouring cream.

VARIATION Use ripe nectarines or pears in place of the peaches. You may need to take a thin slice off the rounded sides of the pears so they sit flat.

about 3 minutes, until the sugar has dissolved. Do not stir. Increase the heat and cook for 5 minutes, until the sugar is a light caramel colour. Add the salt and, off the heat, stir in the cream. Chill for 3 hours or overnight.

5 Briefly dip the tin in hot water, then invert the terrine onto a serving plate. Remove the clingfilm and slice the terrine with a hot knife. Serve with the burnt sugar sauce and decorate with mandarin segments.

NOTE The young, the elderly, pregnant women and people with immune-deficiency diseases should not eat raw eggs, due to the possible risk of salmonella.

ICED ORANGE AND LEMON TERRINE WITH BURNT SUGAR SAUCE

PREPARATION TIME 25 minutes, plus chilling and freezing
COOKING TIME 8 minutes (sauce)
FREEZING Suitable (stage 3)
❄

SERVES 6
- 4 egg yolks
- 30 ml (2 tbsp) caster sugar
- 300 ml (10 fl oz) whipping cream
- finely grated rind and juice of 1 large orange
- finely grated rind and juice of 1 lemon

375 CALS/SERVING
- mandarin or orange segments, to decorate
SAUCE
- 125 g (4 oz) caster sugar
- juice of ½ lemon
- pinch of salt
- 150 ml (5 fl oz) single cream

1 Using an electric whisk, whisk together the egg yolks and sugar for 5 minutes or until pale and thick.
2 Lightly whip the cream until it just holds its shape. Fold it into the egg mixture, along with all the orange and lemon juice and rind. The mixture will become quite liquid.
3 Line a 1.1 litre (2 pint) terrine or loaf tin with clingfilm. Pour in the mixture and freeze for 3 hours or overnight.
4 To make the sauce, put the sugar, plus 100 ml (3½ fl oz) water and the lemon juice in a heavy-based saucepan. Place over a medium heat for

FROZEN STRAWBERRY ICE

PREPARATION TIME 10 minutes, plus freezing
FREEZING Suitable
COLOUR INDEX Page 48
♡ ❄

SERVES 6
- 450 g (1 lb) strawberries, hulled
- 150 ml (5 fl oz) low-fat or low-calorie ice cream, slightly softened
- 150 ml (5 fl oz) low-fat bio natural yogurt

110 CALS/SERVING
- 15 ml (1 tbsp) framboise or cassis liqueur
- 2 egg whites
- 2 oranges
- strawberry leaves, to decorate

1 In a blender or food processor, blend 225 g (8 oz) of the strawberries, the ice cream, yogurt and liqueur until smooth.
2 In a clean, dry bowl, whisk the egg whites until they just form soft peaks. Fold them into the strawberry mixture. Divide the mixture among 6 individual ramekins and freeze for at least 4 hours, or preferably overnight.
3 Slice the remaining strawberries into a bowl. Add the juice of the oranges, cover and marinate for about 1 hour.
4 To serve, dip the outside of the ramekins into warm water for a few seconds and turn out onto serving plates. Leave at room temperature for about 10 minutes to soften a little before serving with the marinated strawberries. Decorate with strawberry leaves.

MELON ICE

PREPARATION TIME 20 minutes, plus marinating and freezing

FREEZING Suitable (stage 3)

❄

SERVES 6-8

- 450 ml (16 fl oz) double cream
- 75 g (3 oz) caster sugar
- 700 g (1½ lb) ripe orange-fleshed melon, such as charentais or cantaloupe, halved and deseeded
- 250 ml (9 fl oz) sweet wine, such as Moscatel de Valencia, or a light sugar syrup

465-350 CALS/SERVING

- 1 ripe ogen or galia melon, halved and deseeded
- ginger biscuits, to serve
- fresh mint sprigs, to decorate

1 Gently heat the cream and sugar until the sugar dissolves, stirring, then set aside to cool.

2 Place the 700 g (1½ lb) melon flesh in a blender or food processor with half the wine. Blend until smooth, then sieve to remove any coarse fibres.

3 Mix the sweetened cream with the purée. Pour into a freezerproof container. Freeze for 2½-3 hours, then stir to break down any ice crystals. Repeat this process twice, then leave to freeze for at least 2 hours until firm.

4 Scoop out the ogen or galia melon flesh with a melon baller and place in serving bowls. Pour a little of the remaining wine over each serving. Marinate in the refrigerator for about 1 hour.

5 To serve, scoop the melon ice into balls and serve with the marinated melon and ginger biscuits. Decorate with mint sprigs.

TIP
Although any freezerproof container is suitable for holding water ices or ice creams, a shallow one speeds up the freezing process.

LEMON SPONGE WITH KIRSCH AND FRESH CURRANTS

PREPARATION TIME 25 minutes, plus cooling
COOKING TIME About 30 minutes
FREEZING Suitable (stage 4)
♡ ✳

SERVES 8-10

- *3 eggs*
- *125 g (4 oz) caster sugar*
- *finely grated rind of 1 lemon*
- *75 g (3 oz) plain flour*
- *25 g (1 oz) unsalted butter, melted*
- *125 g (4 oz) red-currants, prepared*

170-140 CALS/SERVING

- *125 g (4 oz) white-currants, prepared*
- *60 ml (4 tbsp) kirsch*
- *15 ml (1 tbsp) lemon juice*
- *icing sugar, for dusting*
- *sprigs of lemon balm or mint, to decorate, (optional)*

TIP
This delicious syrup-topped ring cake can double up as a summer dessert, served with crème fraîche.

1 Grease the base of a 1.7 litre (3 pint) ring tin. Dust the sides of the tin with flour, shaking out the excess.
2 Put the eggs, 75 g (3 oz) sugar and the lemon rind in a large heatproof bowl set over a pan of hot water. Whisk until pale and creamy and thick enough to leave a trail on the surface when the whisk is lifted.
3 Remove from the heat and whisk until cool. Sift half the flour over the mixture and fold in with a large metal spoon. Pour half the butter around the edge of the mixture and fold in. Gradually fold in the remaining butter and flour.
4 Pour into the prepared tin and bake at 190°C (375°F) mark 5 for about 25 minutes until just firm to the touch. Loosen the edges of the tin, then turn the sponge onto a wire rack to cool.
5 Dissolve the remaining sugar in 75 ml (3 fl oz) water in a small saucepan. Bring to the boil and boil for 1 minute. Add the red and white currants and simmer for 1 minute. Stir in the kirsch and lemon juice. Leave to cool. Place the sponge on a serving plate and pour over the currant syrup.
6 Just before serving, dust the sponge with icing sugar and decorate with sprigs of lemon balm or mint, if wished.

RASPBERRY MOUSSE GÂTEAU

PREPARATION TIME 1½ hours, plus chilling
COOKING TIME 30-35 minutes
FREEZING Suitable (stage 6)
COLOUR INDEX Page 50

❆

SERVES 6-8

- *175 g (6 oz) shelled hazelnuts*
- *4 eggs*
- *125 g (4 oz) light muscovado sugar*
- *125 g (4 oz) white plain flour*
- *2.5 ml (½ tsp) baking powder*
- *25 g (1 oz) butter, melted and cooled*

845-630 CALS/SERVING
FILLING
- *450 g (1 lb) raspberries*
- *1 egg, separated*
- *25 g (1 oz) caster sugar*
- *7.5 ml (1½ tsp) powdered gelatine*
- *450 ml (15 fl oz) double cream*
- *150 ml (5 fl oz) Greek-style yogurt*

1 Grease and base-line a 20 cm (8 inch) round cake tin. Spread out the hazelnuts on a baking sheet and grill until browned. Leave to cool, then roughly chop 25 g (1 oz) and set aside. Finely grind the remaining nuts.
2 Whisk the eggs and muscovado sugar in a large bowl over a saucepan of barely simmering water until the mixture is thick and pale and will hold a trail. Remove the bowl from the heat and whisk for a further 3 minutes. Sift the flour and baking powder together and fold into the mixture alternately with the ground hazelnuts and butter.
3 Spread the mixture in the prepared tin and bake at 180°C (350°F) mark 4 for 30-35 minutes until risen and firm to the touch. Turn out, remove the paper and cool on a wire rack.
4 To make the mousse filling, rub half the raspberries through a sieve. Whisk the egg yolk, sugar and raspberry purée in a large bowl over a pan of barely simmering water until the mixture is thick and foamy and will hold a trail. Remove the bowl from the heat and whisk until cold.
5 Sprinkle the gelatine over 30 ml (2 tbsp) water in a small heatproof bowl and leave to soak, then stand the bowl in a pan of hot water until the gelatine is dissolved. Whip 50 ml (2 fl oz) cream and fold into the raspberry mixture. Gently stir in the gelatine. Whisk the egg white until holding soft peaks, then fold into the mixture.
6 Line a 20 cm (8 inch) spring-release cake tin with clingfilm. Cut the hazelnut cake into three

rounds and trim to a 20 cm (8 inch) diameter. Place one sponge round in the base of the tin. Whip 150 ml (5 fl oz) cream and fold in the yogurt, then spread over the cake. Scatter over one third of the reserved raspberries and cover with a second sponge round. Spoon on the mousse, scatter over another third of the raspberries and cover with the remaining sponge. Press down gently. Chill for 2 hours or until set.
7 Transfer to a plate. Whip the remaining cream and spoon mounds onto the cake. Scatter raspberries and chopped nuts in the middle.

CHOCOLATE ROULADE

PREPARATION TIME 30 minutes, plus cooling
COOKING TIME 25 minutes
FREEZING Suitable (undecorated)
COLOUR INDEX Page 49

❆

SERVES 6-8

- *60 ml (4 tbsp) cocoa powder*
- *150 ml (5 fl oz) milk*
- *4 eggs, separated*
- *125 g (4 oz) caster sugar*
- *150 ml (5 fl oz) double cream*

330-250 CALS/SERVING
- *150 ml (5 fl oz) Greek yogurt*
- *strawberries and grated chocolate, to decorate*

1 Grease and line a 20 x 30 cm (8 x 12 inch) Swiss roll tin. Mix the cocoa powder and milk in a small saucepan and heat gently until the cocoa powder has dissolved. Leave to cool.
2 Whisk the egg yolks and sugar together until pale and fluffy. Whisk the cooled milk mixture into the egg yolk mixture.
3 Whisk the egg whites until stiff, then fold into the cocoa mixture. Spread the mixture evenly into the prepared tin and bake in the oven at 180°C (350°F) mark 4 for about 20 minutes until the sponge has risen and is just firm to the touch.
4 Turn out onto a sheet of greaseproof paper and cover with a warm, damp tea towel to prevent the sponge from drying out. Leave for 20 minutes.
5 Meanwhile, whip the cream until quite stiff, then stir in the yogurt. Spread over the sponge, reserving half for decorating, and then roll it up carefully. Do not roll it up too tightly and do not worry if it cracks slightly. Decorate with cream, strawberries and chocolate. Serve chilled.

then whisk in half of the caster sugar, one spoonful at a time. Whisk for about 30 seconds until holding quite stiff peaks, then fold in the remaining caster sugar. Carefully fold in the hazelnuts with the vanilla essence.

3 Spoon the mixture into a large piping bag fitted with a 5 mm (¼ inch) plain nozzle. Line 2 baking trays with non-stick baking parchment and draw a 23 cm (9 inch) circle on each.

4 Pipe the meringue in a spiral to make a complete round on each piece of paper.

5 Bake the meringue in the oven at 150°C (300°F) mark 2 for 40-45 minutes until dry and crisp. Leave to cool on the baking trays, then carefully peel off the paper.

6 While the meringues are cooling, place the granulated sugar in a saucepan with 150 ml (5 fl oz) water and place over a low heat. Stir until the sugar has dissolved, then add the apricots and lemon rind and simmer for 10 minutes until the apricots are just tender, yet still holding their shape.

7 Remove half of the apricots from the pan and set aside. Cook the rest for 5 minutes more until very soft, then drain (reserving the syrup) and push through a sieve to remove the skins. Allow to cool.

8 When ready to serve, spread half of the apricot purée over one meringue. Whip the cream to soft peak stage and carefully spread over the apricot purée. Arrange the reserved apricot halves on the cream, and place the remaining meringue round on top. Stir 45 ml (3 tbsp) of the reserved syrup into the remaining apricot purée and serve as a sauce with the vacherin. Decorate the vacherin with sprigs of mint and fresh apricots.

VARIATION If wished, the apricot purée can be folded into the whipped cream to make a simple fool filling.

HAZELNUT VACHERIN
WITH APRICOTS

PREPARATION TIME 35 minutes, plus cooling
COOKING TIME 55-65 minutes
FREEZING Not suitable

SERVES 6 **400 CALS/SERVING**

- 125 g (4 oz) hazelnuts
- 3 egg whites
- 175 g (6 oz) caster sugar
- 2.5 ml (½ tsp) vanilla essence
- 50 g (2 oz) granulated sugar

- 225 g (8 oz) fresh apricots, halved and stoned
- grated rind of 1 lemon
- 150 ml (5 fl oz) double cream
- mint sprigs and fresh apricots, to decorate

1 Spread out the hazelnuts on a baking tray and grill, shaking frequently, until browned. Leave to cool completely, then finely chop with a sharp knife. (Do not chop in the food processor as this will make the meringue too oily.)

2 Whisk the egg whites until holding soft peaks,

HONEY WAFERS

PREPARATION TIME 20 minutes, plus cooling
COOKING TIME 20-30 minutes
FREEZING Suitable
COLOUR INDEX Page 52

❋

MAKES 24

- *50 g (2 oz) unsalted butter (at room temperature)*
- *75 g (3 oz) icing sugar*
- *60 ml (4 tbsp) clear honey*

50 CALS/WAFER

- *75 g (3 oz) white plain flour*
- *5 ml (1 tsp) ground cinnamon*
- *1 egg white, lightly beaten*

1 Line 2 large baking sheets with non-stick baking parchment. Beat the butter until very soft, then beat in the icing sugar and honey. Sift together the flour and cinnamon and stir into the mixture with the egg white to make a smooth batter.
2 Drop 4-6 heaped teaspoonfuls of the mixture onto the baking sheets, spacing well apart, and spread out to 7.5 cm (3 inch) rounds with the back of the spoon.
3 Bake at 220°C (425°F) mark 7 for 5-7 minutes until golden, then carefully lift off the baking sheet with a palette knife and transfer to a wire rack to cool and crisp. Use the remaining mixture to make at least 24 wafers in all.

NOTE Don't overcrowd the baking sheets, when making the wafers. Spread them on the baking sheet, keeping them well-spaced apart, so they cook to an even golden colour. It is important that the baking parchment is flat and smooth, not creased, otherwise the wafers will form odd shapes.

VARIATIONS These crisp wafers can be layered with raspberries, cream and yogurt to make a delicious dessert. Whip 300 ml (10 fl oz) double cream until holding soft peaks. Fold in 150 ml (5 fl oz) Greek-style yogurt, 30 ml (2 tbsp) icing sugar, and 30 ml (2 tbsp) framboise or kirsch if liked. Layer up the wafers in threes, sandwiching them together with the cream and 350-450 g (12 oz-1lb) raspberries. Dust generously with icing sugar and serve at once, decorated with mint sprigs. Alternatively use 225 g (8 oz) strawberries, sliced, and 2 oranges, peeled and segmented, in place of the raspberries. Use Grand Marnier or other orange-flavoured liqueur rather than framboise.

ORANGE FLOWER BISCUITS

PREPARATION TIME 10 minutes, plus chilling
COOKING TIME 8 minutes
FREEZING Not suitable

MAKES 20-24

- *125 g (4 oz) white plain flour*
- *15 g (½ oz) cornflour*
- *100 g (3½ oz) firm, lightly salted butter, diced*

65 CALS/BISCUIT

- *50 g (2 oz) icing sugar*
- *20 ml (4 tsp) orange flower water*
- *icing sugar, for dusting*

1 Sift the flour and cornflour and place in a food processor. Add the butter and blend until combined. (Alternatively sift the flours into a bowl and rub in the butter.)
2 Add the icing sugar and orange flower water and blend until the mixture binds together. Knead lightly and chill for 30 minutes.
3 Thinly roll out the paste on a lightly floured surface and cut out rounds using a 6.5 cm (2½ inch) cutter, re-rolling trimmings to make more biscuits.
4 Place on a lightly greased baking sheet and bake at 200°C (400°F) mark 6 for about 8 minutes until beginning to colour around the edges.
5 Transfer to a wire rack and leave to cool. Dust generously with icing sugar to serve.

VARIATION Use rosewater instead of the orange flower water, or add the finely grated rind of 1 orange or lemon.

BERRY JAM

PREPARATION TIME 15 minutes
COOKING TIME 10 minutes
FREEZING Not suitable
COLOUR INDEX Page 53

MAKES ABOUT 1.8 KG
(4 LB)
• *1 kg (2¼ lb)
prepared strawberries*

35 CALS/15 ML (1 TBSP)
• *1 kg (2¼ lb)
preserving sugar*
• *knob of butter*

1 Place the strawberries in a 4.5 litre (8 pint) heavy-based saucepan. Crush with a wooden spoon, then add the preserving sugar and heat gently until the sugar dissolves.
2 Add the butter and bring to a full, rolling boil. Boil for 4 minutes, then pot and cover in the usual way (see page 385).

SUMMER PICKLE

PREPARATION TIME 25 minutes, plus marinating
COOKING TIME about 8 minutes
FREEZING Not suitable
COLOUR INDEX Page 53

MAKES 450 G (1 LB)
• *225 g (8 oz) each
celery, carrots,
cucumber, red
peppers and red
onions*
• *125 g (4 oz) each
green beans, baby
sweetcorn and button
mushrooms*
• *600 ml (1 pint)
distilled malt vinegar*
• *6 allspice berries*
• *6 black peppercorns*
• *1 mace blade*

15 CALS/15 ML (1 TBSP)
• *1 bay leaf*
• *2 cloves*
• *pinch of powdered
saffron or turmeric*
• *30 ml (2 tbsp)
chopped dill*
• *90 ml (6 tbsp) light
soft brown sugar*
• *salt and pepper*
• *125 g (4 oz) cherry
tomatoes*
• *90 ml (6 tbsp)
walnut oil*

1 Thickly slice the celery. Peel and thinly slice the carrots. Halve the cucumber lengthways and thickly slice. Deseed the peppers and cut into similar-sized pieces. Trim the onions, leaving the root intact, and cut into 8 'wedges' each. Top and tail the green beans and corn; trim the mushrooms.
2 Combine all the ingredients, except the cherry tomatoes and walnut oil, in a preserving pan or large saucepan. Bring to the boil and simmer,

APRICOT JAM

PREPARATION TIME 20 minutes
COOKING TIME About 40 minutes
FREEZING Not suitable

MAKES ABOUT 3 KG
(6½ LB)
• *1.8 kg (4 lb) apricots*
• *juice of 1 lemon*

40 CALS/15 ML (1 TBSP)
• *1.8 kg (4 lb)
preserving sugar*
• *knob of butter*

1 Halve the apricots and remove the stones. Crack a few of the apricot stones with a weight, nutcracker or mallet. Take out the kernels and blanch them in boiling water for 1 minute, then drain.
2 Put the apricots, lemon juice, apricot kernels and 450 ml (15 fl oz) water in a preserving pan and simmer for about 15 minutes or until the fruit is soft and the contents of the pan are well reduced.
3 Take the pan off the heat and add the sugar, stirring until it dissolves. Add the butter and boil rapidly for about 15 minutes or until setting point is reached (see page 385).
4 Remove any scum with a slotted spoon, then pot and cover in the usual way (see page 385).

stirring gently, for 5 minutes.

3 Stir in the cherry tomatoes and walnut oil, then transfer to a non-metallic bowl. Cool, cover with a plate and leave to marinate overnight.

4 Pot and cover in the usual way (see page 385).

BRANDY-SOAKED CHERRIES

PREPARATION TIME 15 minutes
COOKING TIME 10 minutes
FREEZING Not suitable

MAKES 450 G (1 LB)   35 CALS/25 G (1 OZ)
- *450 g (1 lb) cherries*   - *about 150 ml*
- *125 g (4 oz) sugar*   *(5 fl oz) brandy*
- *1 cinnamon stick*

1 Prick the whole cherries all over with a darning needle. Place the sugar in a saucepan with 150 ml (5 fl oz) water and heat gently until the sugar dissolves. Add the cherries and cinnamon stick and simmer very gently for 4-5 minutes.

2 Strain the cherries, reserving the liquid. Reheat the liquid with the brandy and boil for 3-4 minutes.

3 Place the cherries in a 600 ml (1 pint) sterilized jar and pour in the liquid until the cherries are completely covered. Cover with a lid or cork and store in the refrigerator for up to 2 months.

VARIATION Add a few orange or lemon slices to the jar, if wished.

231

MANGOADE

PREPARATION TIME 20 minutes, plus cooling
COLOUR INDEX Page 54

SERVES 4-6
- *450 g (1 lb) ripe mango flesh, coarsely chopped*
- *50 g (2 oz) sugar, or to taste*
- *450 ml (15 fl oz) sparkling mineral water*

150-100 CALS/SERVING
- *5 ml (1 tsp) grated orange rind*
- *450 ml (15 fl oz) orange juice*
- *ice cubes*
- *lime slices and rose petals, to decorate*

1 Purée most of the mango in a blender or food processor. Keep the rest on one side.
2 Combine the sugar, water and orange rind in a saucepan and heat, stirring, until the sugar dissolves. Cool, then add to the mango with the orange juice.
3 Serve on ice, in tall glasses, with the remaining mango and a slice of lime. Add a few rose petals, if wished, removing the white 'heels' first.

SUMMER PUNCH

PREPARATION TIME 5 minutes, plus chilling

SERVES 18-20
- *3 bottles medium white wine, chilled*
- *¾ bottle dry sherry*
- *60 ml (4 tbsp) Grand Marnier or orange liqueur*
- *two 1 litre (1¾ pint) bottles tonic water*

135-125 CALS/SERVING
- *crushed ice*
- *cucumber slices, apple slices and fresh mint sprigs, to decorate*

1 Mix the wine, sherry and liqueur in one or more jugs and chill for about 2 hours.
2 To serve, add the tonic and crushed ice. Decorate with the cucumber and apple slices and mint sprigs.

TIP
For a refreshing berry milkshake for two, place 400 g (14 oz) mixed soft fruits in a blender with 400 ml (14 fl oz) milk and purée until smooth. Sieve, then add sugar to taste. Chill well before serving.

APRICOT FLIP

PREPARATION TIME 20 minutes, plus chilling
COLOUR INDEX Page 54

SERVES 2
- *400 g (14 oz) can of apricots in natural juice, drained*
- *150 g (5 oz) apricot yogurt*

170 CALS/SERVING
- *10 ml (2 tsp) clear honey*
- *grated rind and juice of 2 oranges*

1 Purée the apricots in a blender or food processor until smooth.
2 Add the yogurt, honey and the juice from the oranges and purée for a further minute. Chill in the refrigerator.
3 Serve decorated with grated orange rind.

TROPICAL FRUIT CRUSH

PREPARATION TIME 15 minutes, plus chilling
COLOUR INDEX Page 54

SERVES 8-10

240-195 CALS/SERVING

- 600 ml (1 pint) orange juice, chilled
- 2.4 litres (4 pints) grape juice, chilled
- 1 litre (1¾ pints) tropical fruit juice, chilled
- 1.8 litres (3 pints) sparkling mineral water, chilled

- *selection of prepared fresh fruit, such as kiwi fruit, strawberries, lemon slices, raspberries and grapes*
- *ice cubes*
- *star fruit slices, to decorate (optional)*

1 Mix all the chilled liquids together in a large bowl just before you are ready to serve. Float all the prepared fruit on the top.
2 Ladle the drink into large wine glasses, and drop an ice cube or two into each glass. Decorate each glass with a slice of star fruit, if liked.

VARIATION If available, fresh fruit and basil leaves can be scattered over for decoration.

REDCURRANT RUM

PREPARATION TIME 30 minutes, plus standing and chilling

SERVES 16

200 CALS/SERVING

- *900 g (2 lb) redcurrants*
- *350 g (12 oz) caster sugar*
- *1 vanilla pod*

- *about 1 bottle white rum*
- *borage flowers, to decorate (optional)*

1 String and wash the redcurrants. Drain well.
2 Place them in a clean jar, add the sugar and vanilla pod. Top up with the rum.
3 Seal the jar with a rustproof lid and shake to mix. Leave in a cool, dark place for at least a week, and no longer than three months, shaking occasionally.
4 To use, remove the vanilla pod, chill the drink and serve straight or pour over ice and top up with sparkling mineral water. Decorate with borage flowers, if wished.

233

As autumn approaches, so orchards and hedgerows yield a glorious abundance of fresh fruit, providing delicious flavours for both sweet and savoury dishes. More hearty vegetables start coming into their own again and the style of cooking takes on a more mellow, warming tone, in tune with the changing weather of the season. Halloween and bonfire night are good excuses for casual gatherings, while the rich, russet hues of the falling leaves offer inspiring ideas for subtle table decorations.

SOUPS AND STARTERS

FISH AND SHELLFISH

POULTRY AND GAME

MEAT

CHEESE AND EGGS

PASTA AND NOODLES

VEGETARIAN DISHES

Baked Vegetables with a Spicy
Sauce
(page 284)

Quick Tomato and Garlic Pizza
(page 284)

Vegetable Cheese Pie with Potato
Crust
(page 285)

Mixed Mushroom Parcels
(page 286)

Gnocchi with Red Pesto
(page 286)

Filled Baked Potatoes
(page 287)

VEGETABLES AND SALADS

Marrow with Tomato and Onion
(page 288)

Mixed Onion Casserole with
Juniper
(page 288)

Spiced Pumpkin Fritters
(page 289)

Squash with Nutty Gingered
Crumbs
(page 290)

Parsnip and Carrot au Gratin
(page 290)

Cauliflower in Curry Sauce
(page 291)

Swede and Orange Purée
(page 291)

Wild Mushroom and Lentil Salad
(page 292)

Spiced Coleslaw with Pecans
(page 292)

Vegetable and Apple Stir-fry
(page 293)

DESSERTS

Apple and Fig Strudel
(page 294)

Bramley Apples with Ginger
(page 294)

Almond Tarte Tatin
(page 295)

Apple and Blackberry Upside-
down Pudding
(page 296)

Plum Custard Bake
(page 296)

Poached Pears with Apricots
(page 297)

Crispy Pear Clafoutis
(page 297)

Saffron Meringues with Blueberry
Sauce
(page 298)

Chocolate Truffle Cake
(page 298)

Honey-toasted Rice
(page 299)

BAKING

Cinnamon Coffee Cake
(page 300)

Crumbly Apple and Cheese Cake
(page 300)

Almond, Chocolate and Sweet
Potato Loaf
(page 301)

Ginger Cake
(page 301)

Honey and Yogurt Muffins
(page 302)

Berry Scones
(page 302)

Sticky Orange Flapjacks
(page 303)

Oat and Sesame Biscuits
(page 304)

Cottage Cheese and Brazil Nut
Teabread
(page 304)

Olive and Walnut Bread
(page 305)

PRESERVES

Apple and Mint Jelly
(page 306)

Marrow and Apricot Jam
(page 306)

Sweetcorn Relish
(page 307)

Damson Chutney
(page 307)

This is the golden mellow season of abundance. Now's the time to make the most of the cheap and plentiful fruit and vegetables available by turning to the traditional preserving methods. Delicious-tasting jams, chutneys and relishes (see recipes on pages 306-7) are an excellent way of storing abundant produce and will certainly bring cheer to drab winter days. There are some other age-old preserving skills which are also well worth reviving.

PICKLED FRUIT

Freshly picked fruits steeped in spiced sweet-sour syrups are perfect gifts for the Christmas festivities ahead and are marvellous to serve with cold meats as a change from chutney. Try this easy recipe for pickled pears.

Spiced pears For 900 g (2 lb) firm eating pears, gently cook the peeled, cored and quartered pears in water for 5 minutes, then drain. Pour 450 ml (15 fl oz) cider vinegar into a pan with 300 ml (10 fl oz) water, 450 g (1 lb) sugar, 1 cinnamon stick, 10 cloves and a small piece of root ginger. Heat gently, stirring, until the sugar has dissolved then boil for 5 minutes. Add the pears and cook until tender. Remove the pears and pack into sterilized jars. Pour the strained syrup over, then cover immedi-

Crisp and full of flavour, English apples are one of the great pleasures of autumn.

ately with airtight and vinegar-proof tops.

Plums, nectarines and peaches can be bottled in this way too.

PICKLED VEGETABLES

Crisp vegetables pickled in a clear, spiced vinegar are another autumn must. Pickled onions are a favourite.

Pickled onions Place 1.8 kg (4 lb) unskinned pickling onions in a large bowl. Dissolve 225 g (8 oz) salt in 2.3 litre (4 pints) water, pour over the onions and leave for 12 hours. Drain and skin the onions, then recover with the same amount of fresh brine. Leave for 24-36 hours. Meanwhile, make spiced vinegar. Add 25-50 g (1-2 oz) pickling spice to 1.1 litres (2 pints) distilled malt vinegar, bring to the boil, then infuse for 2 hours. Strain through muslin and cool. Drain the onions and rinse well, then pack into sterilized jars. Cover with the spiced vinegar. Top with vinegar-proof tops and leave for 3 months before using.

FRUIT LIQUEURS

Liqueurs made by infusing fruits in spirits for several months are surprisingly easy to make and are a wonderful way of using up ripe autumnal fruit. Damsons in particular can be turned into a warming drink for encroaching winter days.

Damson gin or vodka Using a needle stuck into a cork, prick 900 g (2 lb) damsons all over. Place in a large jar, pour over two 75 cl bottles gin or vodka and add 350 g (12 oz) granulated sugar. Close tightly and keep in a cool dark place for 2-3 months, gently shaking the jar from time to time. Strain and decant into clean bottles.

For an attractive and unusual gift, fill small clean sherry bottles with the liqueur, replace the corks or stoppers and dip the entire top of the bottle in melted sealing wax.

ORCHARD HARVEST

Orchard fruits are abundant at this time of year and can be used in all sorts of sweet and savoury dishes. Apples, pears and plums are particularly useful turned into purées – simply poach the fruit in a little water and sugar, then mash, blend or sieve as necessary.

• To ring the changes, combine apple and pear purée or plum and apple purée. Use as fillings for tarts or puff pastry turnovers. Or mix with thick double cream to make a luscious cake filling.

• Serve spiced purées with roast meats such as pork or duck, or stir a couple of spoonfuls into mashed

root vegetables, such as celeriac or turnip for interesting complementary flavours.

Preserve-making is a satisfying way of capturing the delicious flavours of autumnal fruit and vegetables.

Quick Fruit Ideas

• For an attractive side dish to serve with roast chicken or game, core small dessert apples and fill with a mixture of sautéed bacon and onion, creamy goats' cheese and a scattering of toasted pine nuts. Cook at 200°C (400°F) mark 6 for 20-25 minutes.

• To make a quick, tasty supper dish, brown pork loin chops in a little oil, then wrap in foil parcels with slices of red apple, chopped prunes, chopped herbs, a little apple juice and seasoning. Bake at 180 °C (350°F) mark 4 for 1 hour until tender.

• For an easy dinner party dessert, poach apple rings in a little red wine and cinnamon until tender, sweeten to taste with honey and sprinkle with toasted almonds. Serve with crème fraîche.

• Poach plums in fragrant Earl Grey tea to round off a meal.

• Try adding half a grated apple to a blue cheese and bacon flan.

GAME

Game birds are well worth trying as they are almost fat free and provide filling meals. Butcher's game will have been hung to give a full flavour; supermarket game will not have been hung for so long, resulting in a milder flavour. A wide variety of fresh and frozen game is now available from supermarkets. Birds such as partridge, wild duck, pigeon and pheasant can be plainly roasted, or you can simply remove the breast meat and pan-fry or grill it like chicken. Keep it slightly rare to ensure that it remains tender and juicy. Use the remaining carcasses to make rich stock or freeze raw to use later.

Venison is a good lean alternative to beef and can be substituted in any beef recipe. It gives a particular richness to a steak pie if you use half venison and half beef. The secret is to slowly casserole the tougher cuts so that they become meltingly soft.

239

More tender cuts can be quickly pan-fried with seasonal fruit to make a quick, flavourful meal. Butcher's venison is stronger, so it is wise to marinate it first in wine and vinegar. Discard the marinade and use fresh wine in the finished dish.

All game is good with a sharp fruit sauce as it cuts through the richness - venison with blueberries makes an easy dinner party dish with a difference (see page 264). For a classic way to serve a whole roast bird, quickly sauté the livers in butter, then spread on a fried bread croûte. Place the bird on top – the croûte absorbs the juices from the bird giving it a delicious flavour.

Game chips are a traditional accompaniment. To prepare, peel and cut potatoes into very thin slices, then deep-fry until golden.

Bread sauce is another classic partner to game, and is so easy to make. Stick a few cloves into a peeled onion and place in a pan with a bay leaf and 450 ml (15 fl oz) milk. Bring slowly to the boil, remove from the heat, cover and leave for 10 minutes to infuse. Remove the onion and add 75g (3 oz) fresh breadcrumbs. Season, cover and simmer gently for 10-15 minutes, stirring occasionally. Stir in 15 g (½ oz) butter and 30 ml (2 tbsp) single cream to finish.

ABUNDANT SHELLFISH

With the 'R' returning to the names of the month, this is a very good time for all shellfish, including oysters, mussels and scallops.

For informal, easy entertaining, a 'mussel feast' is hard to beat. Get your friends to help with the scrubbing of the mussels, then cook huge pots of Moules Marinière – for a simple version for 4-6, heat 50 g (2 oz) butter in a large stock pot. Add 2 chopped onions, 3 chopped shallots and 2 chopped garlic cloves and sauté for about 10 minutes until soft. Add 300 ml (10 fl oz) dry white wine and some fresh parsley stalks and bring to the boil. Add 2.6 kg (6 lb) cleaned mussels, cover and boil rapidly, shaking occasionally, for about 5 minutes or until the mussels have opened. Serve with the broth (discarding any unopened mussels). Accompany with lots of French bread and butter.

If you're feeling extravagant, start the feast with half a dozen fresh oysters for each person. Serve with a squeeze of lemon and black bread. Your fishmonger will open them for you, but eat them as soon as you get home to appreciate their fresh sea flavour.

White fish is also excellent at this time of the year, inspiring you to make sumptuous fish pies. A really good fish pie, made up in individual portions, can make excellent dinner party food. Try a combination of jumbo prawns, chunks of flaky white cod and even some smoked fish and sautéed leeks, enrobed in a creamy wine sauce and topped with the fluffiest potato mixed with a little Parmesan and saffron.

HALLOWEEN NIGHT

On the 31st October it's fun to throw a Halloween party, particularly for children who thoroughly enjoy the spooky atmosphere of Halloween night.

Pumpkins

Pumpkins are widely available at this time of year and no Halloween party is complete without a pumpkin lantern. To make a lantern, simply scoop out the flesh, carve a face in the skin and place a candle inside the shell. Don't discard the scooped-out flesh as this can be used to make warming party fare from hearty soup to the all-American pumpkin pie. Puréed pumpkin is particularly good mixed into a baked potato, while slices of pumpkin can be turned into tasty fritters (see page 289).

• To make pumpkin pie, steam 450 g (1 lb) pumpkin pieces between two plates over a pan of boiling water for 15-20 minutes, then drain and purée. Beat together 2 eggs and 125 g (4 oz) sugar, then stir into the pumpkin purée with 60 ml (4 tbsp) milk, 10 ml (2 tsp) ground cinnamon and a pinch each of grated nutmeg and ground ginger. Pour into a 20 cm (8 inch) flan tin lined with shortcrust pastry and bake at 220°C (425°F) mark 7 for 15 minutes, then reduce the oven temperature to 180°C (350°F) mark 4 and bake for a further 30 minutes or until set. Serve warm with cream.

Bewitching Food

Here are just a few more ideas for a Halloween get-together.

• Halve a butternut squash, remove the seeds, pour 30 ml (2 tbsp) maple syrup into the hollow and bake in the oven at 220°C (425°F) mark 7 for 25 minutes. The syrup caramelizes and tastes superb.

• Toffee apples are a must for children. To make the toffee coating for 6-8 apples, heat in a heavy-based saucepan 450 g (1 lb) demerara sugar, 50 g (2 oz) butter or margarine, 10 ml (2 tsp) vinegar, 150 ml (5 fl oz) water and 15 ml (1 tbsp) golden syrup until the sugar has dissolved. Bring to the boil, then brush the inside of the pan with water just above the level of the sugar syrup. Boil rapidly for 5 minutes until the temperature reaches 143°C

A must for every Halloween party; toffee apples, 'bandaged toes' and pumpkin pie.

(290° F) or when a little syrup dropped into cold water separates into hard but not brittle threads. Push sticks into the cores of the apples and dip into the toffee, twirling around for a few seconds. Leave to set on waxed paper.

• For an adult version - toffee apple tart - bake a pastry case, arrange chunks of sautéed apple in the base, pour over double cream and drizzle over toffee (see above).

• Make a Halloween cake by covering a favourite sandwich cake with green fondant icing or marzipan and top it with a pile of fondant-moulded creepy-crawlies.

• For 'horror hands' arrange sausages in a baking tray in the shape of a hand. Bake at 220°C (425°F) mark 7 for about 10 minutes until browned. Meanwhile, make pancake batter (see recipe page 145). Pour the batter into the hot tin around the sausages and bake for about 40 minutes. Serve with plenty of tomato ketchup!

• To make 'bandaged toes', wrap bacon around chipolatas or cocktail sausages and bake in the oven, basting with maple syrup or a little treacle.

• Give children going-home presents of black or dark purple sweets, wrapped in black crêpe or tissue and tied with black and red liquorice laces.

BONFIRE NIGHT

Following on sharply from Halloween comes Guy Fawkes night and fireworks parties. Nowadays it is much simpler to go to a communal display and return home for a warming supper. Soup is essential, and a hearty beef and vegetable stew (see page 269) can be kept gently cooking in the oven while you enjoy the fireworks.

• Hot garlic bread is the perfect accompaniment - cut a large French loaf into thick slices and beat 2 crushed garlic cloves into about 125 g (4 oz) butter. Spread the butter generously between the slices, wrap in foil and bake in a medium oven for about 15 minutes.

• For a simple but irresistible pudding, spread thick slices of sticky gingerbread with cream cheese mixed with preserved ginger and a sliced raw apple.

GILDED NUT STOPPERS

Gilded and glued to corks or stoppers, nuts in their shells add a decorative top-knot to vinaigrette bottles, decanters or bottles of wine or sherry. Choose whole, undamaged nuts, such as Brazils, pecans, walnuts, hazelnuts and almonds. An electric glue gun is quick, clean and simple to use, although you can use any strong adhesive to stick the nuts to the corks.

To gild the nuts here, bronze powder is mixed into a paint medium, following the manufacturer's instructions. For a shiny, bright-gold finish, use gold foil leaf or a gold wax polish that is simply rubbed on to the nut and polished with a soft cloth.

Bear in mind that painted corks should be used for decorative purposes only.

You will need:
Bronze powder
Paint medium
Assortment of nuts in their shells
Sandpaper
Electric glue gun or strong adhesive
Corks
Paint brush

1 Mix the bronze powder with a little medium to make a gold-coloured paint.

3 Glue a suitable-shaped nut to an appropriate-sized cork and leave to dry thoroughly.

2 Rub one side of each nut with sandpaper to key the surface before gluing it to the cork.

4 Gild the nut on top of the cork or just paint the cork and leave the nut natural.

DECORATED PUMPKINS AND SQUASHES

In the autumn, there is an abundance of pumpkins and squashes on sale at greengrocers and supermarkets. With their brilliant colours and shapes, they need little in the way of decoration to make an impact at a Halloween or fireworks party. Look at each pumpkin and decide how best to decorate it.

Hunt out large-headed brass nails or upholsterers' gimp tacks in ironmongers and haberdashery departments to push into the pumpkins like gold studs. Gold beads and shiny gold leaves from cake-decorating accessory shops can be fixed to the pumpkin with gold wire.

You will need:
Large or small orange-skinned pumpkins and squashes
Gold cord, string, braid or ribbon
Brass studs, large-headed tacks or nails
Fine, small-headed brass pins to attach braid
Gold paper leaves
Gold florist's wire
Gold beads

• Wrap a criss-cross of gold braid around a small pumpkin, or pin twirls of gold cord over the surface of a large one.

• For the simple studded designs, work out where to place the studs by eye. In more elaborate designs it is best to mark out regular positions with a felt tip pen before inserting the studs.

• String gold paper leaves onto short lengths of wire and push them into the pumpkin or tie them around the top.

• Thread a few beads onto lengths of string and drape them around the top of the pumpkin.

• For an impressive grouping, stack a few pumpkins together, with the larger ones at the base and one or two smaller ones balanced on top.

LEAF PRINTS

You can use dried and pressed newly fallen autumn leaves to print beautiful patterns onto fabric or paper. Choose leaves that have an interesting shape with a clear outline, or compound leaves with several small leaves on a single stem. Leaves with distinct veins, such as rose leaves, work very well.

Many different paints, such as acrylic, poster or water colours are suitable for printing on paper but for printing on fabrics, special colourfast, washable fabric paints are essential.

You will need:
Autumn leaves
Small pieces of thick card
Corks
Adhesive
Acrylic paint
Paint brush
Paper
Scissors
Ready-made napkins or fabric for making napkins
Absorbent cloth
Fabric paint

1 Press leaves flat and dry, then glue them onto small pieces of stiff card.

3 Brush a mounted leaf with acrylic paint. Press onto a scrap of paper to remove excess paint, then print. Cut around prints to make labels.

2 Glue a cork to the back of each leaf block to make it easier to hold.

4 For printing on fabric napkins, lay napkin out flat on soft, absorbent cloth. Print using special fabric paint.

FRUIT AND LEAVES BASKET

A glowing arrangement of richly coloured fruits nestling on a bed of dried bracken and fallen leaves in a basket captures all the glorious shades of autumn magnificiently. Positioned on a dresser or sideboard, this stunning display will bring a touch of warmth to any kitchen or dining-room setting.

Rosy apples and pears form the basis of this display, interspersed with more exotic fruits such as scarlet cranberries, black grapes and plums, blooming pomegranates, tamarillos and cape gooseberries (physalis). Mix the fruits as you wish.

You will need:
Oval basket
Foil or clingfilm
Crumpled paper, tissue or
** bubble wrap for packing**
Dried bracken and autumn
** leaves**
Red apples and pears
Black grapes
Plums
Cranberries
Tropical fruits, such as
** pomegranates, tamarillos,**
** cape gooseberries, small**
** pineapple**

1 Line the basket with foil or plastic and then fill the base with crumpled paper, tissue or bubble wrap.

2 Cover the lining with a layer of dried bracken, letting some stems spill over the rim of the basket.
3 Pile up layers of the larger fruit, working so that the display can be viewed either from all sides or from the front alone, depending on where the basket is to be positioned.
4 Drop the small fruits in between the large ones, being careful to vary the colours and textures of the fruits. Open out the papery cover of some of the cape gooseberries to expose the orange-coloured fruit within.
5 As a final touch, tuck some dried leaves in among the fruits to fill in any gaps.

BOUILLABAISSE

PREPARATION TIME 25 minutes, plus soaking
COOKING TIME 20-25 minutes
FREEZING Not suitable
COLOUR INDEX Page 9

SERVES 6   365 CALS/SERVING

- *900 g (2 lb) mixed fish and shellfish, such as monkfish, red mullet, John Dory, bass, prawns, cleaned*
- *few saffron strands*
- *150 ml (5 fl oz) olive oil*
- *2–3 onions, peeled and sliced*
- *1 celery stick, chopped*
- *225 g (8 oz) tomatoes, skinned and sliced*
- *2 garlic cloves, peeled and crushed*
- *1 bay leaf*
- *2.5 ml (½ tsp) dried thyme or fennel*
- *a few parsley sprigs*
- *finely shredded rind of ½ orange*
- *salt and pepper*
- *about 1.1 litres (2 pints) fish stock*
- *parsley sprigs, to garnish*

1 Skin and fillet the fish if necessary, then cut into fairly large, thick pieces. Remove the shellfish from their shells.
2 Put the saffron in a small bowl. Pour in 150 ml (5 fl oz) boiling water and leave to soak for 30 minutes.
3 Heat the oil in a large saucepan, add the onions and celery and fry gently for 5 minutes, until beginning to soften. Add the tomatoes to the pan with the garlic, herbs, orange rind and seasoning.
4 Arrange the fish in a layer over the vegetables, pour over the saffron liquid and just enough stock to cover the fish. Bring to the boil and simmer uncovered for about 8 minutes.
5 Add the shellfish and cook for a further 5–8 minutes, until the fish pieces are cooked but still hold their shape. Serve garnished with parsley.

NOTE Choose from the wealth of fish and shellfish available at this time of year to create your own version of this mediterranean-style chunky soup.

PARSNIP AND APPLE SOUP

PREPARATION TIME 15 minutes
COOKING TIME 45 minutes
FREEZING Suitable (stage 3)
COLOUR INDEX Page 8
♡ ✳

SERVES 6   175 CALS/SERVING

- *25 g (1 oz) butter or margarine*
- *700 g (1½ lb) parsnips, peeled and roughly chopped*
- *1 cooking apple, peeled and roughly chopped*
- *1.1 litres (2 pints) vegetable stock*
- *4 sage leaves or 2.5 ml (½ tsp) dried sage*
- *2 cloves*
- *150 ml (5 fl oz) single cream*
- *salt and pepper*
- *sage leaves or parsley and croûtons, to garnish*

1 Melt the butter in a large saucepan; add the parsnips and apple, cover and cook gently for 10 minutes, stirring occasionally.
2 Pour in the stock, and add the sage and cloves. Bring to the boil, cover, then simmer for 30 minutes or until the parsnips are very soft.
3 Remove the sage leaves and cloves; leave the soup to cool slightly, then purée in a blender or food processor.
4 Return the soup to the saucepan, add the cream and reheat gently. Season with salt and pepper. Serve hot, garnished with the sage or parsley and croûtons.

> **TIP**
> This autumnal soup freezes very well, so make a double quantity to save time. It's useful to freeze the soup in single or double portions in readiness for last-minute suppers. Add the cream when reheating.

GARLIC AND ONION SOUP

PREPARATION TIME 10 minutes
COOKING TIME 50 minutes
FREEZING Suitable (stage 2)

♡ ❊

SERVES 6
- *50 g (2 oz) butter*
- *450 g (1 lb) onions, peeled and thinly sliced*
- *8 large garlic cloves, peeled and thinly sliced*
- *30 ml (2 tbsp) white plain flour*

115 CALS/SERVING
- *2 litres (3½ pints) vegetable or chicken stock*
- *2 egg yolks*
- *15 ml (1 tbsp) red wine vinegar*
- *salt and pepper*

1 Melt the butter in a saucepan; add the onions and garlic and cook until golden.

2 Stir in the flour and cook for 1 minute. Remove from the heat and pour in the stock, then bring to the boil, stirring. Cover and simmer for about 30 minutes.

3 Beat the egg yolks with the vinegar. Mix with a little hot soup, then stir the egg yolks into the rest of the soup. Cook over a gentle heat, stirring until the soup thickens slightly. Do not boil. Season to taste. Serve in individual bowls.

TIP
A roast garlic garnish looks attractive and enhances the flavour of this soup. Leave the skins on three small garlic bulbs. Halve each one. Place on an oiled baking sheet. Roast at 170°C (325°F) mark 3 for about 45 minutes or until they are tender.

CHICKEN LIVER AND PISTACHIO PATE

PREPARATION TIME 20 minutes, plus overnight chilling
COOKING TIME 15 minutes
FREEZING Suitable

❋

SERVES 8-10

- *2 rashers of rindless streaky bacon, finely chopped*
- *about 225 g (8 oz) butter*
- *700 g (1½ lb) chicken livers, chopped*
- *1-2 garlic cloves, peeled and chopped*
- *large pinch of ground allspice*
- *125 g (4 oz) flat mushrooms, finely chopped*
- *1 onion, peeled and finely chopped*
- *200 g (7 oz) low-fat soft cheese*

435-350 CALS/SERVING

- *30 ml (2 tbsp) double cream*
- *40 g (1½ oz) shelled pistachio nuts, roughly chopped*
- *45 ml (3 tbsp) chopped mixed fresh parsley, chives and thyme*
- *salt and pepper*

TO GARNISH
- *parsley or other herb leaves*
- *few shelled pistachio nuts*

1 Place the bacon in a heavy-based frying pan and cook until lightly browned.

2 Add 50 g (2 oz) of the butter to the pan and heat until just melted. Add the livers to the pan with the garlic and allspice, and cook briskly over a high heat until the livers are sealed and browned on the outside but still a little pink (but not bloody) on the inside. Remove the bacon and livers from the pan with a slotted spoon and set aside.

3 Add the mushrooms and onion to the pan and cook gently until the onion is softened. Remove from the heat.

4 Transfer the livers and bacon to a blender or food processor. Add the onion and mushrooms, along with any butter remaining in the pan. Add the soft cheese and cream and work until smooth. Turn into a mixing bowl.

5 Fold the nuts and herbs into the pâté. Season with salt and pepper to taste. Spoon the pâté into small individual dishes and level the tops.

6 Melt the remaining butter in a small saucepan over a very low heat. Slowly pour into a jug, leaving the milky sediment behind. Slowly pour the clarified butter onto the pâtés to cover them completely. Immerse herbs and pistachios in the butter to garnish. Chill overnight to set.

VARIATION To make a milder pâté, increase the cream cheese to 400 g (14 oz).

PEPPERED MACKEREL AND APPLE MOUSSES

PREPARATION TIME 30 minutes, plus chilling
COOKING TIME 13-18 minutes
FREEZING Suitable (stage 3)
COLOUR INDEX Page 9

❄

SERVES 6

- *15 ml (1 tbsp) vegetable oil*
- *1 small onion, peeled and chopped*
- *225 g (8 oz) cooking apples, peeled and chopped*
- *4 peppered mackerel fillets*
- *30 ml (2 tbsp) creamed horseradish*
- *75 ml (5 tbsp) mayonnaise*

380 CALS/SERVING

- *60 ml (4 tbsp) lemon juice*
- *15 ml (1 tbsp) powdered gelatine*
- *salt and pepper*
- *3 red eating apples*
- *few sprigs of watercress or flat-leaf parsley*
- *45 ml (3 tbsp) low-fat natural yogurt*

1 Heat the oil in a saucepan, add the onion and cook gently until softened. Add the cooking apples, cover, and cook for 10-15 minutes or until the apple has softened. Leave to cool.
2 Flake the mackerel, and put into a blender or food processor with half the creamed horseradish and 30 ml (2 tbsp) mayonnaise. Blend for a minute. Add the onion and apple, and blend until smooth.
3 Put 15 ml (1 tbsp) lemon juice and 15 ml (1 tbsp) water in a small bowl. Sprinkle the gelatine over it and leave to soak for 5 minutes. Stand the bowl in a pan of simmering water and stir until dissolved, then stir into the mackerel and apple purée. Season with salt and pepper. Spoon the mixture into six greased 150 ml (5 fl oz) ramekin dishes. Chill for 2 hours until set.
4 Core and thinly slice the red apples and toss in 30 ml (2 tbsp) of the lemon juice. Arrange on six plates with the watercress or parsley.
5 Dip the mousses briefly in hot water, then unmould them onto the plates. Grind a little pepper over the top. Mix the yogurt with the remaining horseradish, mayonnaise and lemon juice. Season and serve with the mousses.

WARM SEAFOOD SALAD WITH TOASTED POLENTA

PREPARATION TIME 15 minutes, plus cooling
COOKING TIME 15 minutes
FREEZING Not suitable
COLOUR INDEX Page 12

SERVES 6

- *75 g (3 oz) polenta*
- *150 ml (5 fl oz) salad dressing*
- *1 garlic clove, peeled and crushed*
- *30 ml (2 tbsp) chopped fresh herbs*

285 CALS/SERVING

- *350 g (12 oz) smoked haddock fillet, thinly sliced*
- *175 g (6 oz) cooked, peeled prawns*

1 Make up the polenta according to packet instructions. Spoon onto a sheet of foil, cool slightly, then press into a rectangle about 1 cm (½ inch) thick. Leave to cool.
2 Whisk together the dressing, garlic and half of the herbs. Place the haddock and prawns in a single layer in a shallow, heatproof dish. Pour the dressing over. Cover and chill.
3 Cut the cooled polenta into 7.5 cm (3 inch) triangles. Grill for about 4 minutes on each side until golden.
4 Grill the fish for 1-2 minutes, basting, until the haddock turns opaque. Serve the polenta with the warm salad. Sprinkle the remaining herbs over.

> ***TIP***
> Polenta is coarse-grained, yellow cornmeal which is cooked in water to a thick paste. The quick-cook variety is suitable for this recipe. Look for it in supermarkets and Italian delicatessens.

1 Place the bulghur wheat in a large bowl and pour over 300 ml (10 fl oz) boiling water. Leave to soak for 30 minutes until the bulghur has softened, then drain off any excess water.
2 Peel the lemon, being careful to remove all the pith. Cut the flesh into segments, discarding the pips. Finely dice the flesh.
3 Combine the bulghur wheat with the lemon and the next seven ingredients. Cover and chill for 1 hour for the flavours to develop.
4 Remove the salad from the refrigerator and stir in the pine nuts, olives and plenty of seasoning. Serve at once.

GRILLED PEARS WITH STILTON

PREPARATION TIME 10 minutes
COOKING TIME 6-7 minutes
FREEZING Not suitable
COLOUR INDEX Page 11

🕐

SERVES 4
- *8 thick slices cut from a large baguette*
- *1 packet ready-washed watercress, trimmed*
- *2 large ripe pears, peeled, cored and sliced*

350 CALS/SERVING
- *225 g (8 oz) blue Stilton cheese*
- *freshly ground black pepper*

1 Toast the bread on both sides then transfer to a baking sheet that will hold the slices in a close single layer.
2 Cover with the watercress and place the pear slices on top. Slice the cheese and arrange over the pears.
3 Place under a hot grill until the cheese is just beginning to melt. Grind black pepper liberally over the top and serve at once.

VARIATION Substitute another blue cheese, such as Gorgonzola or Bleu d'Auvergne.

BULGHUR WHEAT SALAD WITH DRIED FRUIT AND PINE NUTS

PREPARATION TIME 15 minutes, plus soaking and chilling
FREEZING Not suitable

SERVES 4-6
- *225 g (8 oz) bulghur wheat*
- *1 lemon*
- *1 large onion, peeled and finely chopped*
- *4 ripe tomatoes, skinned and diced*
- *75 g (3 oz) dried fruit, such as figs, apricots and peaches, chopped*
- *60 ml (4 tbsp) chopped fresh coriander*

635–425 CALS/SERVING
- *30 ml (2 tbsp) chopped fresh mint*
- *125 ml (4 fl oz) extra-virgin olive oil*
- *5 ml (1 tsp) clear honey*
- *50 g (2 oz) pine nuts, toasted*
- *50 g (2 oz) pitted black olives*
- *salt and pepper*

TIP
To toast the pine nuts, place the nuts on a baking sheet and toast in the oven at 200°C (400°F) mark 6 for 6-8 minutes until golden.

POTATO PANCAKES WITH SMOKED SALMON

PREPARATION TIME 15 minutes, plus standing
COOKING TIME About 30 minutes
FREEZING Suitable (stage 5)
COLOUR INDEX Page 10

❋

MAKES 6
- 350 g (12 oz) potatoes, peeled
- salt and pepper
- 45 ml (3 tbsp) milk
- 2 whole eggs, 2 egg whites
- 45 ml (3 tbsp) single cream
- 45 ml (3 tbsp) white plain flour

340 CALS/SERVING
- oil for frying
- 175 g (6 oz) sliced smoked salmon
- 200 ml (7 fl oz) crème fraîche or soured cream
- 40 g (1½ oz) jar salmon roe
- fresh chives and lemon wedges, to garnish

1 Cook the potatoes in boiling, salted water for 20 minutes until tender. Drain and mash well.
2 Beat in the milk, whole eggs, cream and flour: season well.
3 Lightly whisk the egg whites and fold into the potato mixture. Cover, then leave in a cool place for about 1 hour.
4 Heat a little oil in a non-stick crêpe pan and spoon in about 75 ml (5 tbsp) of the pancake mixture. Cook for approximately 2-3 minutes, then carefully flip over and cook the underside for a further 2-3 minutes. Cook the remaining pancakes. You should have 6 in total.
5 Keep the pancakes hot in a low oven, layered with greaseproof paper and wrapped in foil.
6 To serve, arrange one pancake on individual plates and top with a slice of smoked salmon, a spoonful of crème fraîche and a little salmon roe. Garnish with fresh chives and lemon wedges.

GOLDEN STUFFED MUSHROOMS

PREPARATION TIME 10 minutes
COOKING TIME About 25 minutes
FREEZING Not suitable

🕐

SERVES 4
- 12 cup mushrooms
- about 60 ml (4 tbsp) olive oil
- 175 g (6 oz) rindless streaky bacon, roughly chopped
- 1 small onion, peeled and finely chopped
- 50 g (2 oz) salted cashews, chopped
- 2 garlic cloves, peeled and crushed

320 CALS/SERVING
- 75 g (3 oz) fresh white breadcrumbs
- 45 ml (3 tbsp) chopped fresh parsley
- 1 egg, beaten
- salt and pepper
- lemon slices and basil, to garnish

1 Roughly chop the mushroom stems; rinse and drain the mushroom caps.
2 Heat 30 ml (2 tbsp) oil in a medium-sized frying pan and stir-fry the bacon for 2-3 minutes. Add the onion, mushroom stems, cashews and garlic. Cook for a further 3-4 minutes. Remove from the heat.
3 Stir the breadcrumbs, parsley and beaten egg into the mushroom mixture. Add plenty of pepper but only a little salt. Leave to cool.
4 Place the mushroom caps on an oiled edged baking tray. Fill with the mushroom mixture. Drizzle with oil.
5 Bake at 220°C (425°F) mark 7 for 15-20 minutes or until tender and lightly browned. Serve garnished with lemon slices and basil.

FISHERMAN'S PIE

PREPARATION TIME 10 minutes
COOKING TIME 54 minutes
FREEZING Suitable
COLOUR INDEX Page 17

❊

SERVES 4   390 CALS/SERVING
- *50 g (2 oz) butter or margarine*
- *1 red pepper, deseeded and thinly sliced*
- *1 green pepper, deseeded and thinly sliced*
- *1 small onion, peeled and sliced*
- *salt and pepper*
- *125 g (4 oz) button mushrooms, halved*
- *500 ml (16 fl oz) tomato juice*
- *575 g (1¼ lb) cod fillet, skinned*
- *450 g (1 lb) potatoes, peeled and very thinly sliced*
- *50 g (2 oz) Edam cheese, grated*

1 Melt 25 g (1 oz) of the butter in a frying pan, add the peppers and onion and fry gently for 10 minutes or until soft but not coloured. Using a slotted spoon, transfer to a 2.4 litre (4 pint) ovenproof dish. Season well with salt and pepper.
2 Add the mushrooms to the juices in the frying pan and cook for 3-4 minutes, stirring frequently, until evenly coloured.
3 Pour the tomato juice evenly over the pepper and onion mixture in the dish.
4 Cut the fish into large cubes. Arrange the cubes on top of the tomato juice, pressing down gently into the juice. Top with the mushrooms. Season again with salt and pepper to taste.
5 Arrange the potato slices on top of the mushrooms. Melt the remaining butter and brush over the potatoes. Bake in the oven at 190°C (375°F) mark 5 for 25 minutes.
6 Sprinkle the grated cheese over the pie, return to the oven and bake for a further 15 minutes or until the cheese has melted and is bubbling. Serve the pie hot.

CREAMY FISH AND PUMPKIN PIE

PREPARATION TIME 10 minutes
COOKING TIME 30 minutes
FREEZING Not suitable
COLOUR INDEX Page 17

SERVES 4   395 CALS/SERVING
- *700 g (1½ lb) pumpkin or squash, peeled, deseeded and chopped*
- *salt and pepper*
- *350 g (12 oz) courgettes, roughly chopped*
- *450 g (1 lb) cod fillet, skinned and cut into large chunks*
- *125 ml (4 fl oz) milk*
- *3 peppercorns*
- *1 bay leaf*
- *30 ml (2 tbsp) butter or margarine*
- *45 ml (3 tbsp) white plain flour*
- *50 ml (2 fl oz) dry white wine*
- *75 g (3 oz) soft cheese with garlic and herbs*
- *30 ml (2 tbsp) chopped fresh tarragon or 5 ml (1 tsp) dried*
- *4 sheets filo pastry, about 50 g (2 oz) total weight*
- *15 ml (1 tbsp) melted butter or margarine*
- *15 ml (1 tbsp) sesame seeds*

1 Simmer the pumpkin in salted water for 5 minutes. Add the courgettes and simmer for a further 5 minutes or until just tender. Drain well.
2 Meanwhile, place the cod in a saucepan with the milk, peppercorns, bay leaf and 125 ml (4 fl oz) water and simmer for about 2 minutes until just tender. Drain well, reserving the cooking liquid.
3 Melt the butter in a saucepan, add the flour and cook gently for 1 minute, stirring. Remove from the heat and gradually stir in 275 ml (9 fl oz) reserved cooking liquid and the wine. Bring to the boil and cook, stirring, until the sauce thickens. Remove from the heat and stir in the cheese and tarragon. Season to taste.
4 Place the vegetables and fish in a 1.1 litre (2 pint) ovenproof dish. Spoon over the sauce. Crumple pastry on top and brush with melted butter. Sprinkle with sesame seeds.
5 Bake at 200°C (400°F) mark 6 for about 15 minutes until golden brown and piping hot.

PAN-FRIED COD WITH CHANTERELLE MUSHROOMS

PREPARATION TIME 20 minutes
COOKING TIME About 20 minutes
FREEZING Not suitable

SERVES 4

- 4 slices white bread
- 4 cod steaks, each weighing about 175 g (6 oz)
- 75 g (3 oz) butter
- 30 ml (2 tbsp) vegetable oil
- salt and pepper
- plain flour for dredging
- 4 spring onions, finely chopped

480 CALS/SERVING

- 225 g (8 oz) chanterelle mushrooms or mixed mushrooms
- 1 garlic clove, peeled and crushed
- 45 ml (3 tbsp) crème fraîche
- 30 ml (2 tbsp) chopped fresh chives

1 Remove the crusts from the bread and cut the slices into ovals, the same size as the cod steaks. Heat half the butter and the oil in a frying pan. Fry the bread slices on both sides until crisp and golden. Keep warm.

2 Season the cod, then coat with flour. Heat the remaining butter in the frying pan and fry the cod for about 5 minutes on each side until cooked through and lightly golden. Remove from the pan and keep warm.

3 Add the spring onions, mushrooms and garlic to the pan and sauté for 5 minutes until the juices are just beginning to escape from the mushrooms. Stir in the crème fraîche and heat through gently. Season and add half the chives.

4 Place a bread croûte on each plate, arrange a cod steak on top and spoon the mushroom mixture on top of the fish. Sprinkle with the remaining chives and serve at once.

NOTE Any other variety of wild mushroom can be used instead of chanterelles.

THAI GRILLED CARAMELIZED FISH

PREPARATION TIME 15 minutes, plus standing
COOKING TIME 30 minutes
FREEZING Not suitable

SERVES 4   375 CALS/SERVING

- 4 *whole plaice fillets,*
  skinned and halved
- 5 *ml (1 tsp) salt*
- *juice of 2 limes*
- 60-90 *ml (4-6 tbsp)*
  demerara sugar
- *salad leaves, lime*
  wedges and 5 ml
  (1 tsp) finely
  chopped red chilli,
  to garnish
SWEET AND SOUR
CHILLI SAUCE
- 400 *g (14 oz) red*
  peppers, deseeded
  and chopped

- 50 *g (2 oz) red*
  chillies, deseeded
  and chopped
- 2 *garlic cloves,*
  peeled and chopped
- 30 *ml (2 tbsp) olive*
  oil
- 60 *ml (4 tbsp) sugar*
- 90 *ml (6 tbsp)*
  distilled malt vinegar

1 First make the sauce. Place the peppers, chillies
and garlic in a blender or food processor with
30 ml (2 tbsp) water and blend until smooth.
2 Put the remaining ingredients in a saucepan and
add the chilli paste with 125 ml (4 fl oz) water.
Bring to the boil and simmer for about 20
minutes or until reduced by half.
3 Meanwhile, sprinkle each half-fillet with salt
and lime juice and roll up. Secure with wooden
cocktail sticks. Set aside for 30 minutes. Just
before grilling, rub fish all over with the sugar.

4 Cook under the grill for 4-5 minutes on each
side, or until cooked and caramelized. Remove
cocktail sticks.
5 Serve immediately on a bed of salad leaves and
garnished with lime wedges and chopped red
chilli, with the sweet and sour sauce poured over.

HADDOCK AND CORN CHOWDER

PREPARATION TIME 20 minutes
COOKING TIME About 20 minutes
FREEZING Not suitable
COLOUR INDEX Page 13

SERVES 4   430 CALS/SERVING

- 25-50 *g (1-2 oz)*
  butter or margarine
- 450 *g (1 lb) old*
  potatoes, peeled and
  diced
- 225 *g (8 oz) onion,*
  peeled and thinly
  sliced
- 2.5 *ml (⅟₂ tsp) chilli*
  powder
- 600 *ml (1 pint)*
  vegetable stock
- 600 *ml (1 pint) milk*
- *salt and pepper*

- 225 *g (8 oz) fresh*
  haddock fillet,
  skinned and broken
  into bite-sized pieces
- 225 *g (8 oz) smoked*
  haddock fillet,
  skinned and broken
  into bite-sized pieces
- 200 *g (7 oz) can*
  sweetcorn kernels
- 125 *g (4 oz) cooked*
  peeled prawns
- *chopped fresh*
  parsley

1 Heat the butter in a large saucepan and fry the
vegetables and the chilli powder for 2-3 minutes
until beginning to soften.
2 Pour in the stock and milk with a little
seasoning. Bring to the boil, then cover and
simmer for 10 minutes.
3 Add the haddock to the pan with the corn.
Return to the boil, then cover and simmer until
the potatoes are tender and the fish begins to flake
apart. Skim the surface as necessary.
4 Stir in the prawns with plenty of parsley. Adjust
the seasoning and serve at once.

VARIATION This hearty, meal-in-a-bowl chowder
is equally delicious made with other fish. You can
use cod or whiting, or fresh salmon if you are
feeling extravagant. For extra colour, sauté a
finely diced red pepper with the other vegetables.

PLAICE WITH GRAPES

PREPARATION TIME 30 minutes
COOKING TIME 25 minutes
FREEZING Not suitable

♡

SERVES 4

- 175 g (6 oz) green grapes, skinned, halved and deseeded
- 8 large plaice fillets, each weighing about 125 g (4 oz), skinned
- 125 ml (4 fl oz) dry white wine
- 125 ml (4 fl oz) fish stock
- 10 ml (2 tsp) finely chopped fresh basil or 5 ml (1 tsp) dried basil

270 CALS/SERVING

- 2-3 bay leaves
- 5 ml (1 tsp) cornflour
- 125 ml (4 fl oz) milk
- salt and pepper
- 30 ml (2 tbsp) Greek yogurt
- chopped fresh parsley, to garnish

1 Place 2-3 grape halves on the skinned side of each plaice fillet. Roll up from the narrow end, secure with cocktail sticks and arrange close together in a poaching pan or large saucepan.
2 Mix together the wine, stock, basil and bay leaves and pour over the fish. Bring to the boil, lower the heat, cover and poach gently for 10 minutes until the fish is cooked.
3 Using a slotted spoon, transfer the fish rolls to a serving dish, draining well. Remove the cocktail sticks if wished, and keep warm. Simmer the cooking liquid for about 10 minutes to reduce by half. Remove the bay leaves.
4 Blend the cornflour with the milk, then stir into the cooking liquid. Season and bring back to the boil, stirring continuously until slightly thickened. Simmer for a further 5 minutes to give a pouring consistency. Stir in the yogurt.
5 Add the remaining grapes. Pour the sauce over the fish rolls and sprinkle with parsley. Serve at once.

TIP
To make skinning grapes an easier task, nick each one with a sharp knife and cover with boiling water for 30 seconds. Then drain and peel away the skins.

255

PAN-ROASTED MONKFISH WITH SWEET POTATOES AND ONIONS

PREPARATION TIME 20 minutes
COOKING TIME 40-45 minutes
FREEZING Not suitable

SERVES 4
490 CALS/SERVING

- *700 g (1½ lb) monkfish tail, skinned*
- *50 g (2 oz) can anchovies in oil, drained and washed*
- *salt and pepper*
- *4 slices Parma ham*
- *juice of ½ lemon*
- *700 g (1½ lb) sweet potatoes, scrubbed*
- *2 red onions, peeled and cut into wedges*
- *12 whole garlic cloves, peeled*
- *2 sprigs rosemary*
- *60 ml (4 tbsp) olive oil*
- *225 g (8 oz) baby tomatoes*
- *tapenade (black olive paste), to serve*

TIP
If preferred, ask your fishmonger to fillet the fish for you.

1 Wash and dry the monkfish and, using a sharp knife, cut down each side of the bone and discard. Arrange the fillets back together and place the anchovy fillets in the gap left by the bone. Season with pepper.

2 Wrap the Parma ham around the fish and secure with cocktail sticks. Squeeze over the lemon juice and set aside.

3 Cut the potatoes into wedges and place in a large roasting pan with the onions, garlic and rosemary sprigs. Season well and stir in the olive oil. Transfer to the oven and roast at 230°C (450°F) mark 8 on the top shelf for 15 minutes.

4 Remove the pan from the oven and arrange the monkfish tail well down amongst the vegetables. Arrange the tomatoes on top of the vegetables, return to the oven and roast for a further 25-30 minutes until the fish is firm to the touch and the vegetables are tender.

5 Cover with foil and allow to rest for 5 minutes before slicing and serving the fish with the roasted vegetables and a little tapenade.

VARIATION For a Mediterranean flavour, spread olive paste along the centre of the fish with the anchovies and roast with red peppers, aubergines and courgettes as well as the garlic and onions.

ROAST SALMON WITH A PEANUT CRUST

PREPARATION TIME 5 minutes
COOKING TIME 20 minutes
FREEZING Suitable (stage 2)
COLOUR INDEX Page 15
🕐 ❄

SERVES 4   865 CALS/SERVING

- 1 red chilli, finely
  chopped
- 2.5 cm (1 inch) piece
  fresh root ginger,
  peeled and grated
- 175 g (6 oz) unsalted
  butter, softened
- 45 ml (3 tbsp)
  chopped fresh
  parsley
- finely grated rind of
  1 lime

- 75 g (3 oz) salted
  roasted peanuts
- 3-4 spring onions,
  trimmed and finely
  chopped
- 125 g (4 oz) fresh
  white breadcrumbs
- salt and pepper
- 4 salmon fillets,
  about 175 g (6 oz)
  each (skinned if
  wished)

1 Beat the red chilli and the ginger into the
unsalted butter with the fresh parsley and lime
rind. Roughly process the peanuts in a blender or
food processor.
2 Melt 50 g (2 oz) of the flavoured butter in a
frying pan, add the spring onions, peanuts and
breadcrumbs and fry until golden, stirring
continuously to prevent the breadcrumbs from
sticking together. Season to taste.
3 Arrange the salmon fillets, skin-side uppermost,
in a roasting tin. Spoon the fried breadcrumb
mixture on the top. Cook at 200°C (400°F) mark
6 for 10-15 minutes or until the salmon is just
cooked.
4 Melt the remaining flavoured butter and serve
with the roast salmon.

TIP

To save cooking time, make up a batch of the
spicy flavoured butter and the fried peanut and
breadcrumb topping, and freeze ahead. Both of
these mixtures can be used direct from the
freezer; just allow an extra 2-3 minutes cooking
time at stage 3.

PAN-FRIED RED MULLET WITH CITRUS AND BASIL

PREPARATION TIME 10 minutes, plus marinating
COOKING TIME 10 minutes
FREEZING Not suitable
COLOUR INDEX Page 15

SERVES 4   430 CALS/SERVING

- 4 red mullet, each
  about 225 g (8 oz),
  filleted
- 90 ml (6 tbsp) olive
  oil
- 10 peppercorns,
  crushed
- 2 oranges

- 1 lemon
- 30 ml (2 tbsp) plain
  flour
- salt and peppet
- 15 g (½ oz) butter
- 2 anchovies
- 15 g (½ oz)
  shredded fresh basil

1 Place the fish fillets in a shallow dish, in a single
layer. Drizzle over the olive oil and sprinkle with
the peppercorns. Peel one of the oranges,
removing all of the skin and white pith, then cut
into thin slices. Lay the orange slices over the fish.
Cover and leave to marinate in the refrigerator for
4 hours.
2 Halve the lemon. Remove the skin and white
pith from one half, then slice thinly. Squeeze the
juice from the other half and reserve.
3 Using a fish slice lift the fish out of the
marinade, reserving the marinade, and pat dry on
absorbent kitchen paper. Season with salt and
pepper, then dust lightly with flour.
4 Heat 45 ml (3 tbsp) of the marinade in a sauté
pan or frying pan. Add the red mullet fillets and
fry for 2 minutes on each side. Remove from the
pan and set aside; keep warm. Discard the oil
remaining in the pan.
5 Melt the butter in the pan with the remaining
marinade. Add the anchovies and crush until
dissolved. Add the juice of the remaining orange
and the reserved lemon juice. Season and cook
until slightly reduced. Lastly, stir in the shredded
basil.
6 Pour the citrus sauce over the fish and garnish
with the orange and lemon slices. Serve at once.

150 ml (5 fl oz) of the hot stock and cook, stirring constantly, until the liquid is absorbed by the rice. Continue adding stock in 150 ml (5 fl oz) quantities until you have used half of it. This should take about 10 minutes and the rice should be about half cooked.

3 Stir in the seafood and cook for 2-3 minutes. Continue adding the stock as before, until the rice is tender but with a firm bite (you may not need to add all the stock). The rice should hold together in a creamy mass.

4 Stir in the lemon rind, tomato paste and tarragon. Season with salt and pepper to taste and leave to stand for a few minutes before serving.

NOTE Arborio rice is the classic Italian risotto rice and produces a delicious creamy texture. Ready-prepared mixed seafood is sold in packets from most supermarkets.

VARIATION If preferred, make the risotto with one type of seafood only, such as prawns or mussels. You can also vary the herbs used.

SEAFOOD RISOTTO

PREPARATION TIME 10 minutes
COOKING TIME 30 minutes
FREEZING Not suitable

SERVES 4   **420 CALS/SERVING**

- *60 ml (4 tbsp) sunflower oil*
- *1 onion, peeled and finely chopped*
- *2 garlic cloves, peeled and crushed*
- *225 g (8 oz) Arborio rice*
- *100 ml (3½ fl oz) dry white wine*
- *1.5-1.6 litres (2¼-2½ pints) hot fish stock*

- *300 g (10 oz) prepared mixed seafood*
- *grated rind of 1 small lemon*
- *30 ml (2 tbsp) sun-dried tomato paste*
- *15 ml (1 tbsp) chopped fresh tarragon*
- *salt and pepper*

1 Heat the oil in a heavy-based pan, add the onion and garlic and cook until softened. Add the rice and cook, stirring, for about 1 minute.
2 Add the wine and stir until it is absorbed. Add

MUSSELS IN TOMATO SAUCE

PREPARATION TIME 5 minutes
COOKING TIME About 10 minutes
FREEZING Not suitable
COLOUR INDEX Page 18
♡ ⏱

SERVES 4   **260 CALS/SERVING**

- *45 ml (3 tbsp) olive oil*
- *1 onion, peeled and finely chopped*
- *2 garlic cloves, peeled and crushed*
- *700g (1½ lb) plum tomatoes, peeled, deseeded and chopped*

- *5 ml (1 tsp) sugar*
- *45 ml (3 tbsp) chopped fresh oregano*
- *salt and pepper*
- *15 ml (1 tbsp) tomato purée*
- *450 g (1 lb) shelled cooked mussels*

1 Heat the oil in a saucepan, add the onion and cook for 5 minutes until softened. Stir in the garlic, tomatoes, sugar and half the oregano. Season with salt and pepper to taste and simmer gently for 2-3 minutes until the tomatoes soften.
2 Stir in the tomato purée, add the mussels and simmer for 1-2 minutes until heated through. Scatter the remaining oregano over and serve hot.

CHARRED SCALLOPS WITH FENNEL AND PERNOD

PREPARATION TIME 10 minutes
COOKING TIME 10-15 minutes
FREEZING Not suitable

SERVES 4

- *1 large fennel bulb, about 225 g (8 oz)*
- *50 g (2 oz) butter*
- *4 shallots, peeled and chopped*
- *2 garlic cloves, peeled and crushed*

415 CALS/SERVING

- *30 ml (2 tbsp) Pernod*
- *90 ml (3 fl oz) double cream*
- *oil for frying*
- *salt and pepper*
- *12-16 shelled scallops*

1 Trim the green feathery tops from the fennel. Reserve a few tops for garnishing and chop the remainder – you need 15 ml (1 tbsp) chopped tops. Slice the fennel bulb.
2 Heat the butter in a small saucepan, add the shallots and garlic and cook for 3 minutes until soft. Add the Pernod and cream and cook gently for 2-3 minutes. Stir in the chopped fennel tops.
3 Heat a heavy-based ridged frying pan or griddle pan with a little oil until very hot and just smoking. Turn down the heat a little, then place the fennel slices on the frying pan or griddle and cook for a few minutes on each side until slightly charred. Transfer to a warmed serving plate and keep warm.
4 Gently reheat the sauce and season with salt and pepper to taste.
5 Meanwhile, place the scallops on the frying pan or griddle and cook for 1-2 minutes on each side until slightly charred. Transfer to the serving plate of cooked fennel, garnish with the reserved fennel tops and serve at once with the hot sauce.

> ### TIP
> Serve the cooked scallops and fennel in scrubbed scallop shells for an attractive presentation.

CHICKEN AND APPLE CASSEROLE

PREPARATION TIME 20 minutes
COOKING TIME 1 hour 10 minutes
FREEZING Not suitable

SERVES 4

440 CALS/SERVING

- *30 ml (2 tbsp) olive oil*
- *4 chicken quarters, about 900 g (2 lb) total weight*
- *900 g (2 lb) mixed seasonal root vegetables, peeled and sliced*
- *350 g (12 oz) onion, peeled and roughly chopped*
- *125 g (4 oz) green lentils*
- *2 small eating apples, peeled, cored and sliced*
- *200 ml (7 fl oz) apple juice*
- *300 ml (10 fl oz) chicken stock*
- *salt and pepper*

1 Heat the oil in a large flameproof casserole, add the chicken quarters and brown well. Remove from the pan with a slotted spoon and drain on absorbent kitchen paper.

2 Add all the vegetables to the pan and sauté for 4-5 minutes or until beginning to colour. Add the lentils, sliced apples, apple juice and chicken stock and bring to the boil. Season well and replace the chicken quarters.

3 Cover and cook at 190ºC (375ºF) mark 5 for about 50 minutes or until the chicken and lentils are tender and cooked through. Adjust the seasoning before serving.

VARIATIONS You can add any of your favourite seasonal root vegetables to this casserole – just keep the total weight the same. If you prefer a casserole with thicker juices, simply purée some of the vegetables and stir back in.

TIP
If you want to prepare the apples slightly in advance, place the slices in cold water mixed with lemon juice as you cut them up. This will stop the flesh from discolouring.

SPICY COCONUT CHICKEN

PREPARATION TIME 10 minutes
COOKING TIME 35 minutes
FREEZING Not suitable
COLOUR INDEX Page 20
♡

SERVES 6   270 CALS/SERVING

- 6 chicken breast
  fillets with skin,
  about 700 g (1½ lb)
  total weight
- 45 ml (3 tbsp)
  vegetable oil
- 225 g (8 oz) onion,
  peeled and finely
  chopped
- 1 garlic clove, peeled
  and crushed
- 1 cm (½ inch) piece
  fresh root ginger,
  peeled and finely
  chopped
- 2.5 ml (½ tsp)
  ground turmeric
- 5 ml (1 tsp) each
  ground cumin,
  ground coriander and
  mild curry powder

- pinch hot chilli
  powder (optional)
- 225 g (8 oz) can
  chopped tomatoes
- 75 g (3 oz) creamed
  coconut, coarsely
  grated
- 30 ml (2 tbsp) poppy
  seeds
- 300 ml (10 fl oz)
  chicken stock
- salt and pepper
- 30 ml (2 tbsp) Greek
  natural yogurt
- chopped fresh
  coriander, to garnish

1 Tuck the ends of the chicken breasts under to
shape into neat rounds; tie with string.
2 Heat the oil in a pan and sauté the chicken
fillets until golden. Remove with a slotted spoon
and drain on absorbent kitchen paper.
3 Add the onion, garlic and ginger and cook,
stirring, for 1-2 minutes. Add the spices. Cook for
a further minute, then add the tomatoes, coconut
and poppy seeds. Cook for a further minute, add
the stock, then bring to the boil and simmer for
2-3 minutes.
4 Replace the chicken, cover and simmer for
about 20 minutes or until the chicken is cooked
through.
5 Skim off any excess oil and adjust the seasoning.
Off the heat, stir in the yogurt. Serve garnished
with fresh coriander.

ORIENTAL CHICKEN PARCELS

PREPARATION TIME 20 minutes, plus marinating
COOKING TIME 35 minutes
FREEZING Not suitable
COLOUR INDEX Page 20
♡

SERVES 4   215 CALS/SERVING

- 3 oranges
- juice of 1 lemon
- 30 ml (2 tbsp) dark
  soy sauce
- 30 ml (2 tbsp) yellow
  bean sauce
- 15 ml (1 tbsp) dry
  sherry
- 15 ml (1 tbsp)
  vegetable oil
- salt and pepper
- four 125 g (4 oz)
  skinless chicken
  breast fillets

- 50 g (2 oz) stem
  ginger or 2.5 cm (1
  inch) piece fresh root
  ginger, peeled and
  thinly sliced
- 1 bunch spring
  onions, trimmed and
  shredded
- 125 g (4 oz) carrots,
  peeled and shredded

1 In a bowl mix together the finely grated rind of
one orange with 60 ml (4 tbsp) orange juice, the
lemon juice, soy sauce, yellow bean sauce, sherry
and oil. Season well with salt and pepper.
2 Lightly slash the chicken breasts all over and stir
into the marinade with the ginger, spring onions
and carrot. Refrigerate overnight.
3 The next day, segment the remaining oranges.
Cut four 30 cm (12 inch) squares of foil and pull
up the edges to make open purses. Divide the
chicken and marinade among the foil pieces and
top with orange segments. Pinch the corners of the
foil together. Place the parcels in a roasting tin.
4 Cook at 180°C (350°F) mark 4 for about 35
minutes or until the chicken is tender. Open the
parcels into soup bowls to serve as there is quite a
lot of juice.

SOUTHERN FRIED CHICKEN
WITH CORN FRITTERS

PREPARATION TIME 15 minutes
COOKING TIME 20 minutes
FREEZING Not suitable
COLOUR INDEX Page 20

SERVES 4-6

- *6 allspice berries*
- *10 black peppercorns*
- *40 g (1½ oz) white plain flour*
- *1 garlic clove, peeled and finely chopped*
- *2.5 ml (½ tsp) dried thyme*
- *salt and pepper*
- *8-12 chicken drumsticks, skinned*
- *1 egg, beaten*
- *125-175 g (4-6 oz) dried breadcrumbs*
- *vegetable oil for frying*

CORN FRITTERS
- *75 g (3 oz) white plain flour*
- *1 egg*
- *75 ml (3 fl oz) milk*

660-440 CALS/SERVING

- *200 g (7 oz) can sweetcorn, drained*
- *2 spring onions, trimmed and finely chopped*

TOMATO SALSA
- *6 ripe tomatoes, cored and finely chopped*
- *1 red onion, peeled and finely chopped*
- *1 spring onion, trimmed and finely chopped*
- *¼ cucumber, finely chopped*
- *a little olive oil*
- *dash of wine vinegar*
- *chopped fresh chives, basil or coriander*

1 First make the tomato salsa. Mix the tomatoes with the chopped onions and cucumber, moistening with a little olive oil and vinegar. Season liberally with salt and pepper. Add chopped herbs to taste.
2 For the chicken, crush the allspice berries and peppercorns together, using a pestle and mortar. Mix the flour with the allspice mixture, garlic, thyme and plenty of salt. Toss the chicken in the flour mixture to coat evenly.
3 Dip each chicken portion first in the beaten egg, and then in the breadcrumbs to coat. Arrange in a single layer on a plate and chill while making the corn fritters.
4 To make the corn fritters, put the flour and a large pinch of salt into a bowl and make a well in the centre. Add the egg and milk and beat thoroughly to make a smooth thick batter. Fold the sweetcorn and spring onion into the batter.
5 Heat a little oil in a frying pan and fry a few large spoonfuls of the sweetcorn batter mixture for 2-3 minutes each side until golden brown and

crisp. Drain on absorbent kitchen paper and keep warm in a hot oven while you cook the remainder. (There should be sufficient to make 12 fritters.)
6 Meanwhile heat the oil for deep frying in a deep-fat fryer to 170°C (325°F). Fry the chicken, in batches, for about 10 minutes until crisp and golden and cooked right through. Keep warm with the corn fritters.
7 Serve the chicken and corn fritters as soon as they are all cooked, with the salsa.

CHICKEN BREASTS WITH
APPLE AND THYME

PREPARATION TIME 15 minutes
COOKING TIME 1 hour
FREEZING Not suitable
COLOUR INDEX Page 19
♡

SERVES 4

- *50 g (2 oz) butter*
- *175 g (6 oz) onion, peeled and chopped*
- *2 crisp dessert apples*
- *50 g (2 oz) mature Cheddar cheese*
- *40 g (1½ oz) fresh breadcrumbs*
- *30 ml (2 tbsp) chopped fresh thyme or 5 ml (1 tsp) dried*
- *salt and pepper*

330 CALS/SERVING

- *4 chicken breast fillets with skin, about 700 g (1½ lb) total weight*
- *75 ml (3 fl oz) apple juice*
- *20 ml (4 tsp) cornflour*
- *300 ml (10 fl oz) chicken stock*
- *15 ml (1 tbsp) wholegrain mustard*

1 Heat 25 g (1 oz) butter in a frying pan and sauté the onion until softened. Leave to cool. Grate the apples and cheese into the onion. Add the breadcrumbs, thyme and seasoning.
2 Loosen the skin of the chicken and push the stuffing underneath, pressing into place. Place in a roasting tin, dot with the remaining butter and season. Pour the apple juice over.
3 Cook at 190°C (375°F) mark 5 for about 50 minutes or until cooked through. Remove the chicken from the pan and keep warm.
4 Blend the cornflour with 30 ml (2 tbsp) cold water, add to the pan with the stock and mustard, bring to the boil, stirring, and cook for 2-3 minutes. Season and spoon over the chicken.

GARLIC CHICKEN WITH
ROAST PEPPER PUREE

PREPARATION TIME 20 minutes, plus marinating
COOKING TIME 1 hour and 5 minutes
FREEZING Not suitable

SERVES 6

- 6 *skinless chicken breast fillets*
- 4 *garlic cloves, peeled and crushed*
- 15 *ml (1 tbsp) chopped fresh thyme*
- 105 *ml (7 tbsp) olive oil*
- 15 *ml (1 tbsp) clear honey*
- 15 *ml (1 tbsp) white wine vinegar*
- *salt and pepper*
- 4 *red peppers, deseeded*

420 CALS/SERVING

- 2 *yellow peppers, deseeded*
- 2 *onions, peeled and sliced*
- 225 *g (8 oz) plum tomatoes, skinned and halved*
- 10 *ml (2 tsp) paprika*
- 15 *ml (1 tbsp) tomato purée*
- *thyme sprigs, to garnish*

1 Cut several deep slits across each chicken breast and lay them in a large shallow dish. Scatter the garlic over the chicken with the chopped thyme. Mix 30 ml (2 tbsp) oil with the honey and wine vinegar. Season and pour over the chicken. Leave to marinate for several hours.

2 Drain the chicken, reserving the marinade juices. Heat 30 ml (2 tbsp) olive oil in a frying pan. Add the chicken, slit sides down, and fry quickly to sear. Turn the chicken and cook for a further minute. Transfer to a shallow baking dish with a slotted spoon.

3 Cut each pepper into 8 chunks. Place the onions, peppers and tomatoes in a large shallow ovenproof dish. Sprinkle with the paprika and pour over the remaining oil.

4 Bake the vegetables at 200°C (400°F) mark 6, near the top of the oven, for 1 hour, until lightly charred. Halfway through cooking, place the chicken on a lower shelf and bake for 30 minutes until cooked through.

5 Reserve 6 pieces of red pepper and 6 pieces of yellow pepper for garnish – cut into strips and keep warm. Place the remaining vegetable mixture in a food processor or blender and blend until almost smooth. Place in a saucepan and heat through, adding the tomato purée and seasoning to taste.

6 Spoon the pepper purée onto warmed serving plates and top with the chicken breasts and reserved peppers. Garnish with thyme sprigs and serve.

a little at a time, until melted. Simmer, stirring constantly, until the sauce has reduced and thickened. Taste and adjust the seasoning, adding more sugar if the sauce seems too tart.

3 Heat the butter and oil in a large frying pan and pan-fry the steaks for 3-4 minutes on each side. Stir in the sauce with the reserved blueberries and heat through. Serve garnished with orange slices and coriander sprigs.

COUNTRY-STYLE RABBIT CASSEROLE

PREPARATION TIME 10 minutes
COOKING TIME 1¾ hours
FREEZING Suitable
COLOUR INDEX Page 24

♡ ❄

SERVES 6

335 CALS/SERVING

- 45 ml (3 tbsp) olive oil
- 1.1 kg (2½ lb) rabbit pieces
- 1 large onion, peeled and sliced
- 2 garlic cloves, peeled and crushed
- 125 g (4 oz) lean smoked bacon, diced
- 30 ml (2 tbsp) brandy
- 200 ml (7 fl oz) white wine

- 400 g (14 oz) can chopped tomatoes
- 2.5 ml (½ tsp) dried thyme
- 15 ml (1 tbsp) chopped fresh parsley
- salt and pepper
- 50 g (2 oz) brown cap mushrooms, sliced
- chopped flat-leaf parsley, to garnish

1 Heat the oil in a heavy-based flameproof casserole. Add the rabbit pieces and brown well on all sides. Remove with a slotted spoon.

2 Add the onion, garlic and bacon to the casserole. Gently fry until the onion has softened. Return the rabbit to the casserole.

3 Warm the brandy gently in a small pan or ladle. Remove the casserole from the heat, pour the brandy over the rabbit and set it alight.

4 When the flames have died down, return the casserole to the heat and add the wine, tomatoes, thyme and parsley. Season with salt and pepper. Cover and simmer over a low heat for about 1½ hours, adding the mushrooms 10 minutes before the end of the cooking time. Serve garnished with chopped parsley.

PAN-FRIED VENISON WITH BLUEBERRY SAUCE

PREPARATION TIME 15 minutes
COOKING TIME About 15 minutes
FREEZING Sauce only (stage 1)

♡ ⏲ ❄

SERVES 6

250 CALS/SERVING

- 15 g (½ oz) butter
- 15 ml (1 tbsp) vegetable oil
- 6 venison steaks, each weighing 125-175 g (4-6 oz)
- orange slices and sprigs of coriander, to garnish

BLUEBERRY SAUCE
- 225 g (8 oz) blueberries

- 150 ml (5 fl oz) dry white wine
- 10 ml (2 tsp) caster sugar, or to taste
- 60 ml (4 tbsp) freshly squeezed orange juice
- 15 ml (1 tbsp) wine vinegar
- salt and pepper
- 25 g (1 oz) unsalted butter

1 To make the blueberry sauce, reserve about one quarter of the blueberries and put the remainder in a heavy saucepan with the white wine and sugar. Bring to the boil, stirring, then cover and simmer for 10 minutes until the berries are soft, stirring occasionally. Remove from the heat and work through a sieve into a jug.

2 Return the puréed blueberries to the pan and add the orange juice, vinegar and salt and pepper to taste. Bring to the boil, then whisk in the butter,

RAISED GAME PIE

PREPARATION TIME 1¼ hours, plus resting and chilling
COOKING TIME 1 hour 55 minutes
FREEZING Suitable (stage 9)

✳

SERVES 8-10

HOT WATER CRUST
PASTRY
- 300 g (10 oz) white
  plain flour
- 1.25 ml (¼ tsp) salt
- 65 g (2½ oz) white
  vegetable fat

PIE FILLING
- 225 g (8 oz) rabbit
  joints, skinned
- 225 g (8 oz) shoulder
  venison
- 1.1 litres (2 pints)
  brown stock
- 225 g (8 oz) pork
  sausagemeat
- ½ onion, peeled and
  finely chopped
- 2 garlic cloves,
  peeled and crushed

440-355 CALS/SERVING
- 60 ml (4 tbsp)
  Madeira
- 2.5 ml (½ tsp)
  ground mace
- salt and pepper
- 125 g (4 oz) no-soak
  dried apricots
- 4 no-soak prunes
- 2 pheasant or
  chicken breasts,
  boned and skinned,
  about 225 g (8 oz)
  total weight
- 8 large sage leaves
  or 5 ml (1 tsp) dried
  sage
- beaten egg, to glaze
- 5 ml (1 tsp)
  powdered gelatine

1 For the filling, remove the flesh from the rabbit joints. Cut the rabbit and venison into small pieces. Place in a saucepan and cover with the stock. Bring to the boil, cover and simmer for 25 minutes, or until tender; drain and cool. Reduce the stock by boiling to 150 ml (5 fl oz).

2 Base-line a 25 x 7.5 cm (10 x 3 inch) loose-sided pie mould with non-stick baking parchment. Mix the cooled meats, sausagemeat, onion, garlic, Madeira, mace and seasoning. Cover and chill.

3 To prepare the hot water crust pastry, sift the flour and salt into a bowl and make a well in the centre. Heat the fat and 125-150 ml (4-5 fl oz) water gently together until the fat melts, then bring to the boil and pour into the well.

4 Gradually lap the flour into the liquid, then beat together. Lightly knead against the side of the bowl until smooth. Immediately wrap the pastry in a tea towel. (If exposed to the air, it will become dry and impossible to use.) Leave for up to 30 minutes; no longer. Use warm.

5 On a lightly floured surface, roll out three quarters of the pastry to an oblong 20 x 35 cm (8 x 14 inches), turning to keep an even shape and thickness.

Use the rolling pin to help lift pastry over the tin. (Keep the remaining pastry covered on a plate placed over warm water.)

6 Ease the pastry into the corners and press evenly up the sides of the tin. Trim off excess pastry. Line with baking parchment and beans and bake blind at 200°C (400°F) mark 6 for 15-20 minutes, until golden brown and set. Remove paper and beans. Allow to cool.

7 Spoon half the meat mixture into the pastry case. Scissor-snip half the apricots and 2 prunes into the tin. Place the pheasant or chicken breasts end to end over the fruit. Place the sage leaves on top. Repeat the fruit and meat layers.

8 Roll out the remaining pastry to a 28 x 10 cm (11 x 4 inch) oblong and use to top the pie. Seal well, then trim and flute the edges. Make a small hole in the centre of the pie, and two more near the edge. Shape the pastry trimmings into leaf and berry shapes. Arrange on top of the pie, half covering the holes.

9 Place the pie on a baking tray and glaze with egg. Bake at 200°C (400°F) mark 6 for 20 minutes, then reduce the temperature to 180°C (350°F) mark 4 and cook for a further 1¼ hours, covering the top lightly with foil if necessary. Ease away the sides of the tin and bake the pie for a further 20 minutes to brown the sides. Cool.

10 Soak the gelatine in 20 ml (4 tsp) water, then dissolve in the stock. Chill until beginning to set. Place the pie on a large edged plate, easing off the base gently. Gradually pour in the stock through the holes. Cover loosely, then refrigerate overnight.

CASSEROLE OF GROUSE WITH RED WINE

PREPARATION TIME 10 minutes
COOKING TIME 1¼ hours
FREEZING Suitable
COLOUR INDEX Page 24
♡ ✳

SERVES 4
- 2 brace of grouse
- about 45 ml (3 tbsp) vegetable oil
- 450 g (1 lb) shallots or button onions, peeled
- 4 large celery sticks, sliced
- 200 ml (7 fl oz) red wine

300 CALS/SERVING
- 2 bay leaves
- salt and pepper
- 200 ml (7 fl oz) stock
- 15 ml (1 tbsp) arrowroot
- 15 ml (1 tbsp) lemon juice
- chopped parsley, to garnish

1 Wipe the grouse, trim the feet and remove any feather ends. Heat the oil in a flameproof casserole and brown the birds well, in batches if necessary. Lift out of the casserole using a slotted spoon.
2 Add the shallots and celery to the casserole with a little extra oil, if necessary, and brown lightly.
3 Pour in the wine and bring to the boil. Add the bay leaves and seasoning and return the grouse to the casserole.
4 Cover tightly and cook at 170°C (325°F) mark 3 for about 50 minutes or until the grouse are just tender. Lift the birds out of the casserole, cover and keep warm.
5 Add the stock to the casserole and warm slightly. Mix the arrowroot to a smooth paste with a little water and stir into the casserole. Bring to the boil, stirring, and cook until slightly thickened. Stir in the lemon juice, adjust the seasoning and spoon over the birds. Garnish with parsley to serve.

FRENCH ROAST PHEASANT WITH GRAPES AND NUTS

PREPARATION TIME 25 minutes
COOKING TIME 1 hour
FREEZING Not suitable
COLOUR INDEX Page 24

SERVES 6
- 6 clementines
- 700 g (1½ lb) white or red grapes
- 15 ml (1 tbsp) green tea (Gunpowder or Darjeeling)
- 200 ml (7 fl oz) Madeira or sweet sherry
- 2 young oven-ready pheasants

635 CALS/SERVING
- softened butter, for basting
- salt and pepper
- 10 ml (2 tsp) balsamic or sherry vinegar
- 15 ml (1 tbsp) dark soy sauce
- 225 g (8 oz) walnut halves
- grapes, to garnish

1 Grate the rind from 2 clementines and squeeze the juice from all six; place in a bowl. Reserve the ungrated squeezed halves. Chop the grapes roughly in a food processor and pour into the clementine juice. Pour 300 ml (10 fl oz) boiling water over the green tea, leave to steep for 5 minutes, then strain and reserve.
2 Pour half the clementine and grape juice into a roasting tin, adding the Madeira and any giblets (except the liver). Place the reserved clementine halves inside the pheasant cavities. Smear the pheasants with butter and season with salt and pepper.
3 Place the birds in the roasting tin on one side. Roast at 200°C (400°F) mark 6 for 45 minutes, turning and basting every 15 minutes until cooked. Test by pushing a skewer into the meatiest part of the thigh; the juices should run clear. Transfer the pheasants to a warmed serving platter and keep warm.
4 Pour the reserved clementine and grape juice into the roasting tin. Stir in the tea, balsamic vinegar and soy sauce. Bring to the boil, scraping up any sediment from the bottom of the pan. Boil for 1-2 minutes, then strain into a saucepan. Stir in the walnuts, bring to the boil and reduce to 450 ml (15 fl oz). Adjust the seasoning. The sauce should be slightly syrupy; if not, reduce a little more. Spoon the walnuts around the pheasant and pour the sauce into a warmed sauceboat. Garnish with extra grapes.

NOTE If your butcher is preparing the birds, ask him to keep the giblets. Or use chicken or turkey giblets.

POT-ROASTED PHEASANT WITH RED CABBAGE

PREPARATION TIME 20 minutes
COOKING TIME 40 minutes
FREEZING Not suitable

SERVES 4   **505 CALS/SERVING**

- 25 g (1 oz) butter
- 15 ml (1 tbsp) vegetable oil
- 2 oven-ready pheasants, halved
- 2 onions, peeled and sliced
- 450 g (1 lb) red cabbage, finely shredded
- 5 ml (1 tsp) cornflour
- 250 ml (8 fl oz) red wine
- 30 ml (2 tbsp) redcurrant jelly
- 15 ml (1 tbsp) balsamic vinegar
- salt and pepper
- 4 rashers smoked streaky bacon, halved
- flat-leaf parsley and bay leaves, to garnish

1 Melt the butter with the oil in a large flameproof casserole. Add the pheasant halves, and brown on all sides. Remove the pheasant and add the onions and red cabbage to the casserole. Fry for 5 minutes until softened.

2 Blend the cornflour with a little water. Add to the pan with the red wine, redcurrant jelly, vinegar and seasoning. Bring to the boil, stirring.

3 Arrange the pheasant halves, skin-side up, on top of the cabbage. Place the halved bacon rashers on top of the pheasant. Cover with a lid and bake at 200°C (400°F) mark 6 for 30 minutes until tender. Lift out the pheasant halves and keep warm. Using a slotted spoon, divide the cabbage between warmed serving plates. Arrange the pheasant on top and garnish with parsley and bay leaves. Serve any juices in a sauceboat.

VARIATION Pigeon can also be cooked in this way. Use 4 oven-ready pigeons and place a quarter of an onion inside each bird before browning for extra flavour. Tuck the parsley and bay leaf garnish into the cavities for an attractive finish.

BEEF RENDANG

PREPARATION TIME 15 minutes
COOKING TIME About 2 hours 10 minutes
FREEZING Suitable
COLOUR INDEX Page 25

❄

SERVES 6

- *1 large onion, peeled and quartered*
- *6 garlic cloves, peeled*
- *5 cm (2 inch) piece fresh root ginger, peeled*
- *1 red pepper, deseeded and chopped*
- *4 dried hot chillies*
- *10 ml (2 tsp) ground coriander*
- *10 ml (2 tsp) ground cinnamon*
- *5 ml (1 tsp) ground cloves*

955 CALS/SERVING

- *5 ml (1 tsp) turmeric*
- *45 ml (3 tbsp) vegetable oil*
- *1.1 kg (2½ lb) stewing or braising beef, cut into large cubes*
- *1.7 litres (3 pints) coconut milk*
- *1 lemon grass stalk, bruised*
- *salt*
- *finely shredded lime leaves, to garnish (optional)*

1 Put the first nine ingredients in a food processor or blender with 15 ml (1 tbsp) water. Process until smooth.
2 Heat the oil in a large, wide flameproof casserole dish or a saucepan. Add the spice paste and cook over a moderate heat for 3-5 minutes, stirring all the time.
3 Add the meat and cook for 2-3 minutes, stirring to coat in the spice mixture.
4 Add the coconut milk and bring to the boil, stirring all the time. Add the lemon grass and about 5 ml (1 tsp) salt. Reduce the heat and simmer very gently, uncovered, for about 2 hours, stirring from time to time. The beef is ready when it is really tender and almost falling apart; the sauce should be well reduced and quite thick.
5 If the sauce is too thin, transfer the meat to a warmed serving dish, using a slotted spoon; keep warm. Bring the sauce to the boil and boil vigorously, stirring frequently, until sufficiently reduced. Pour over the meat. Check the seasoning before serving, garnished with shredded lime leaves, if available.

GRILLED STEAKS WITH SHALLOTS AND WINE

PREPARATION TIME 10 minutes
COOKING TIME 15–25 minutes
FREEZING Not suitable
COLOUR INDEX Page 25

🕐

SERVES 4

- *50 g (2 oz) chilled butter*
- *225 g (8 oz) shallots, peeled and chopped*
- *350 ml (12 fl oz) red Bordeaux wine*
- *4 sirloin steaks, each weighing about 175-200 g (6-7 oz)*
- *30 ml (2 tbsp) vegetable oil*

555 CALS/SERVING

- *salt and pepper*
- *8 slices French bread*
- *10-15 ml (2-3 tsp) Dijon mustard*
- *30 ml (2 tbsp) chopped fresh parsley*
- *parsley sprigs, to garnish*

1 Melt 15 g (½ oz) of the butter in a saucepan. Add the shallots and sauté for a few minutes until slightly softened. Add the wine and bring to the boil. Simmer, uncovered, until the wine is reduced by half and the shallots are soft.
2 Smear the steaks on both sides with the oil and arrange on the grill rack. Cook, as close to the heat as possible, turning the steaks every 2 minutes. Allow 4 minutes (one turn) for very rare steaks; 8 minutes (three turns) for medium. For well-done steaks allow 12 minutes, increasing the time between turns to 3 minutes. Season the steaks with salt and pepper as you make the final turn.
3 Meanwhile, cut the remaining butter into 6 cubes and beat one at a time into the shallot sauce.
4 Transfer the steaks to warmed serving plates and keep warm. Press the bread slices onto the grill pan to soak up the juices, then spread each lightly with Dijon mustard. Put 2 slices beside each steak. Pour the sauce over the steaks, sprinkle with chopped parsley and serve garnished with sprigs of parsley.

VARIATIONS Use rump rather than sirloin steaks. Use a hot griddle pan to cook the steaks, rather than grill them.

COUNTRY BEEF WITH BARLEY

PREPARATION TIME 15 minutes
COOKING TIME About 2¼ hours
FREEZING Suitable

♡ ✽

SERVES 4

- *450 g (1 lb) braising steak, cubed*
- *salt and pepper*
- *25 g (1 oz) plain flour*
- *15 ml (1 tbsp) vegetable oil*
- *350 g (12 oz) carrots, peeled and chopped*
- *575 g (1¼ lb) swede, peeled and chopped*
- *4 sticks celery, chopped*
- *225 g (8 oz) button onions, peeled*

330 CALS/SERVING

- *1 garlic clove, peeled and crushed*
- *50 g (2 oz) pearl barley*
- *pared rind and juice of 1 orange*
- *150 ml (5 fl oz) red wine*
- *2 large rosemary sprigs or 10 ml (2 tsp) dried*
- *450-600 ml (16-20 fl oz) beef stock*
- *fresh rosemary, to garnish*

1 Toss the beef in seasoned flour until evenly coated. Heat the oil in a 4.2 litre (7 pint) flameproof casserole and brown the beef in batches. Remove with a slotted spoon and drain on absorbent kitchen paper.

2 Lower the heat, add the carrots, swede, celery, onions and garlic, with a little more oil, if necessary. Sauté for 4-5 minutes, stirring occasionally. Return all the beef to the casserole with the pearl barley, orange rind and juice, wine, rosemary and enough stock to cover.

3 Bring to the boil, stir well, cover and cook in the oven at 170°C (325°F) mark 3 for about 2 hours or until the meat is tender. Adjust the seasoning. Serve garnished with fresh rosemary.

MOROCCAN LAMB PIE WITH
SPINACH AND SULTANAS

PREPARATION TIME 20 minutes
COOKING TIME 1¼ hours
FREEZING Suitable (stage 3)

❉

SERVES 4

- *15 ml (1 tbsp) oil*
- *175 g (6 oz) onion, peeled and finely chopped*
- *450 g (1 lb) minced lamb*
- *2 garlic cloves, peeled and crushed*
- *5 ml (1 tsp) ground cinnamon*
- *2.5 ml (½ tsp) ground cloves*
- *10 ml (2 tsp) ground cumin*
- *2.5 ml (½ tsp) mild curry powder*
- *45 ml (3 tbsp) Worcestershire sauce*
- *30 ml (2 tbsp) red wine*

580 CALS/SERVING

- *15 ml (1 tbsp) tomato purée*
- *50 g (2 oz) sultanas*
- *150 ml (5 fl oz) light stock*
- *225 g (8 oz) frozen leaf spinach, thawed, drained and finely chopped*
- *30 ml (2 tbsp) orange marmalade*
- *30 ml (2 tbsp) chopped fresh parsley*
- *salt and pepper*
- *50 g (2 oz) butter, melted*
- *275 g (10 oz) filo pastry*

1 Heat the oil in a heavy-based flameproof casserole. Sauté the onion, stirring, until it begins to soften and brown. Add the minced lamb and brown thoroughly over high heat, breaking up any lumps of meat.

2 Stir in the garlic with the next seven ingredients and cook for 5 minutes, stirring frequently. Add the sultanas and the stock and bring to the boil.

3 Cover tightly and cook gently for about 20 minutes or until the lamb is tender. Stir once or twice during cooking.

4 Stir the spinach into the casserole with the marmalade and parsley. Adjust the seasoning and leave to cool.

5 Lightly grease a 1.4-1.7 litre (2½-3 pint) shallow ovenproof dish with melted butter. Line with the pastry, buttering between the layers, leaving the edges hanging over the dish. Reserve three or four sheets of pastry. Add the mince mixture. Top with the remaining pastry, brushing with butter, and bring the pastry edges over the top, arranging them randomly. Brush over the remaining butter.

6 Bake at 200ºC (400ºF) mark 6 for 25 minutes or until golden brown. Cover loosely with foil and cook for a further 15 minutes or until the filling is piping hot.

LAMB CHOPS WITH LEEKS AND LENTILS

PREPARATION TIME 20 minutes, plus marinating
COOKING TIME 30 minutes
FREEZING Not suitable
COLOUR INDEX Page 27

SERVES 4   **420 CALS/SERVING**

- *4 loin lamb chops, each weighing about 125 g (4 oz)*
- *1 small onion, peeled and finely chopped*
- *125 ml (4 fl oz) fresh orange juice*
- *salt and pepper*
- *15 ml (1 tbsp) vegetable oil*
- *450 g (1 lb) leeks, washed, trimmed and cut into 1 cm (½ inch) slices*

- *125 g (4 oz) split red lentils, boiled rapidly for 10 minutes, then drained*
- *5 ml (1 tsp) paprika*
- *300 ml (10 fl oz) lamb stock*
- *fresh coriander, to garnish*

1 Trim the chops of fat and place in a non-metallic dish. Sprinkle onion and orange juice over the lamb and season with pepper. Cover and refrigerate for at least 12 hours, turning once.
2 Lift the chops out of the marinade and pat dry on absorbent kitchen paper. Heat the oil in a medium-sized frying pan and brown the chops on both sides. Drain on absorbent kitchen paper.
3 Add the leeks, lentils and paprika to the pan and stir over a moderate heat for 1 minute. Place the chops on the lentils. Pour in the marinade and stock and bring to the boil.
4 Cover and simmer for 20 minutes or until the chops are cooked. Adjust the seasoning. Serve garnished with coriander.

> *TIP*
> Fast-boiling pulses for 10 minutes before cooking ensures that any harmful toxins present are destroyed.

SPICED LAMB HOT POT

PREPARATION TIME 30 minutes
COOKING TIME 2½ hours
FREEZING Suitable
❄

SERVES 6   **560 CALS/SERVING**

- *about 45 ml (3 tbsp) vegetable oil*
- *900 g (2 lb) boned leg of lamb, trimmed and cut into 5 cm (2 inch) cubes*
- *350 g (12 oz) onion, peeled and roughly chopped*
- *4 garlic cloves, peeled and sliced*
- *2 red peppers, deseeded and roughly chopped*
- *700 g (1½ lb) potatoes, peeled and cut into large chunks*

- *10 ml (2 tsp) ground ginger*
- *1 cinnamon stick, broken in two halves*
- *50 g (2 oz) pearl barley*
- *600 ml (1 pint) beef stock*
- *30 ml (2 tbsp) Worcestershire sauce*
- *salt and pepper*
- *lemon wedges and marjoram sprigs, to garnish*

1 Heat 45 ml (3 tbsp) oil in a large flameproof casserole and brown the meat in batches, adding a little more oil if necessary. Drain on absorbent kitchen paper.
2 Sauté onions and garlic until well browned. Add the peppers, potatoes, ginger, cinnamon and pearl barley; sauté for 2 minutes. Stir in the stock, Worcestershire sauce and plenty of seasoning. Bring to the boil and replace the meat.
3 Cover and cook at 170°C (325°F) mark 3 for about 2 hours or until the lamb is tender. Adjust the seasoning and garnish with lemon wedges and marjoram sprigs to serve.

3 Add the mustards, Worcestershire sauce and anchovy paste to the pan. Cook over moderate heat, stirring, for 1-2 minutes. Stir in the cream and bring to the boil. Return the kidneys and mushrooms to the pan. Stir to coat with the sauce and simmer for 5 minutes. Season to taste and transfer to a warm serving dish. Sprinkle with plenty of chopped parsley.

VARIATION Brown cap or oyster mushrooms are equally delicious with these kidneys as chanterelles.

AUTUMN SPICED KIDNEYS

PREPARATION TIME 10 minutes
COOKING TIME About 20 minutes
FREEZING Not suitable

SERVES 4

595 CALS/SERVING

- *50 g (2 oz) unsalted butter*
- *700 g (1½ lb) lamb's kidneys, skinned, halved and cored*
- *225 g (8 oz) chanterelle mushrooms, thickly sliced*
- *30 ml (2 tbsp) green peppercorn mustard (Maille)*
- *15 ml (1 tbsp) wholegrain mustard*

- *dash of Worcester-shire sauce*
- *5 ml (1 tsp) anchovy paste or essence*
- *300 ml (10 fl oz) double cream*
- *salt and pepper*
- *plenty of roughly chopped fresh parsley, to garnish*

1 Heat the butter in a frying pan until foaming. Add the kidneys in batches and cook briskly until brown. Remove from the pan with a slotted spoon and transfer to a sieve to drain out the bitter juices.
2 Fry the mushrooms in the same pan, stirring occasionally until just tender, and remove to the sieve.

GRILLED PORK WITH
SPICED BUTTER

PREPARATION TIME 5 minutes
COOKING TIME 20 minutes
FREEZING Not suitable
COLOUR INDEX Page 29

SERVES 4

455 CALS/SERVING

- *300 ml (10 fl oz) cider*
- *30 ml (2 tbsp) mixed peppercorns, crushed*
- *60 ml (4 tbsp) brown sugar*
- *60 ml (4 tbsp) wholegrain mustard*

- *50 g (2 oz) butter*
- *salt and pepper*
- *4 pork chops, each weighing about 175 g (6 oz)*

1 Place the cider in a small saucepan and boil for 15 minutes.
2 Meanwhile, combine the peppercorns with the sugar, mustard and butter.
3 Season the chops and cook under a grill for 5 minutes on one side. Turn over, spread each chop with the butter, then cook for a further 5 minutes or until golden and cooked through.
4 Pour the grill pan juices into the cider and heat for 2-3 minutes. Pour over the pork chops and serve.

BRAISED PORK CHOPS
WITH PLUMS AND GINGER

PREPARATION TIME 15 minutes
COOKING TIME About 50 minutes
FREEZING Suitable
❋

SERVES 4

- *450 g (1 lb) plums*
- *2.5 cm (1 inch) piece fresh root ginger, peeled and shredded*
- *salt and pepper*
- *15 g (½ oz) butter*
- *15 ml (1 tbsp) oil*
- *4 pork chops, each weighing about 200 g (7 oz)*

415 CALS/SERVING

- *60 ml (4 tbsp) white wine*
- *175 ml (6 fl oz) vegetable stock*
- *30 ml (2 tbsp) Greek yogurt*
- *30 ml (2 tbsp) chopped fresh tarragon*

1 Halve the plums, remove the stones, and cut into slices. Mix together with the ginger, then spread evenly over the base of a lightly greased ovenproof dish. Season with salt and pepper. Bake in the oven at 200°C (400°F) mark 6 for 15 minutes.

2 Heat the butter and oil in a frying pan, add the pork chops and fry on both sides until browned. Remove the pork with a slotted spoon and arrange on top of the plums.

3 Add the wine to the frying pan and cook briskly to reduce by half. Add the stock and cook for a further minute, scraping up any sediment from the bottom of the pan. Pour over the pork.

4 Return the dish of plums and pork to the oven and cook for a further 20-25 minutes until the pork is tender.

5 Transfer the chops to a warmed serving dish or plates. Stir the yogurt and tarragon into the plums, adjust the seasoning, then spoon the plums around the pork. Serve at once.

PORK LOIN STUFFED WITH FIGS

PREPARATION TIME 30 minutes
COOKING TIME 1¼ hours
FREEZING Not suitable

SERVES 4   630 CALS/SERVING
- *45 ml (3 tbsp) olive oil*
- *1 onion, peeled and finely chopped*
- *2 garlic cloves, peeled and chopped*
- *75 g (3 oz) breadcrumbs*
- *4 no-soak dried figs, finely chopped*
- *8 pitted green olives, finely chopped*
- *25 g (1 oz) flaked almonds, toasted and chopped*

- *15 ml (1 tbsp) lemon juice*
- *15 ml (1 tbsp) chopped fresh parsley*
- *1 egg yolk*
- *salt and pepper*
- *900 g (2 lb) boned loin of pork*
- *sprigs of flat-leaf parsley, to garnish*

1 Heat 30 ml (2 tbsp) oil in a frying pan, add the onion and garlic, and fry gently until soft. Stir in the next seven ingredients and season.
2 Remove the string from the pork and unroll the flap away from the fillet in the centre, cutting away any excess fat or meat if necessary. Spread about half the stuffing over the flat piece. Roll up, starting from the thick side. Tie at intervals with string.
3 Pour the remaining oil into a small roasting tin and add the pork. Roast at 200°C (400°F) mark 6 for about 1¼ hours.
4 Shape the remaining stuffing into walnut-sized balls and add to the roasting tin 15-20 minutes before the end of the cooking time.
5 Allow the meat to rest for 10 minutes before slicing. Serve garnished with parsley sprigs.

SPANISH PORK AND BEAN CASSEROLE

PREPARATION TIME 15 minutes, plus soaking
COOKING TIME 2¼ hours
FREEZING Not suitable
COLOUR INDEX Page 30

SERVES 6-8   620-465 CALS/SERVING
- *900 g (2 lb) shoulder of ham or gammon joint*
- *125 g (4 oz) dried haricot beans*
- *125 g (4 oz) dried butter beans*
- *15 ml (1 tbsp) olive oil*
- *50 g (2 oz) streaky bacon, rinded and cut into thin strips*
- *2 garlic cloves, peeled and crushed*
- *2 Spanish onions, peeled and sliced*

- *225 g (8 oz) leeks, washed, trimmed and sliced*
- *1 carrot, peeled and chopped*
- *1 bay leaf*
- *5 ml (1 tsp) paprika*
- *salt and pepper*
- *125 g (4 oz) chorizo or other spicy sausage, cut into 2.5 cm (1 inch) lengths*
- *125 g (4 oz) black pudding, sliced*
- *bay leaves, to garnish*

1 Soak the ham overnight in enough cold water to cover. In a separate bowl, soak the haricot beans and butter beans in enough cold water to cover.
2 Drain the soaked ham. Drain the soaked beans and rinse thoroughly under cold running water. Place the beans in a saucepan of water and boil rapidly for 10 minutes, then drain.
3 Heat the oil in a large flameproof casserole, add the bacon and cook gently for 2-3 minutes, then stir in the garlic, onions, leeks and carrot and continue cooking for 10 minutes.
4 Stir in the drained beans with the bay leaf and paprika. Cover with cold water and season with salt and pepper to taste. Bring to the boil, then lower the heat, cover and simmer for 30 minutes. Add the ham or gammon and simmer for a further hour.
5 Add the chorizo sausage and black pudding and simmer gently for a further 20-25 minutes.
6 Allow to cool slightly, then remove the ham with a slotted spoon. Remove the fat and any string from the ham, then cut into bite-sized pieces and return to the casserole. Discard the bay leaf. Reheat gently and serve hot, garnished with fresh bay leaves.

HARVEST PORK CASSEROLE

PREPARATION TIME 20 minutes
COOKING TIME 2 hours
FREEZING Suitable

✳

SERVES 4-6
- *45 ml (3 tbsp) oil*
- *700 g (1½ lb) boneless leg of pork, cut into pieces*
- *225 g (8 oz) onion, peeled and chopped*
- *1 garlic clove, peeled and crushed*
- *450 g (1 lb) parsnips, peeled and sliced*
- *15 ml (1 tbsp) ground coriander*
- *5 ml (1 tsp) cumin seeds or 15 ml (1 tbsp) ground cumin*

530-355 CALS/SERVING
- *30 ml (2 tbsp) white plain flour*
- *300 ml (10 fl oz) beef stock*
- *300 ml (10 fl oz) apple juice or cider*
- *salt and pepper*
- *2 small, crisp, red eating apples, roughly chopped*
- *snipped chives, to garnish*

1 Heat the oil in a flameproof casserole, add the meat and brown well. Remove with a slotted spoon and drain on absorbent kitchen paper.

2 Add the onion and garlic to the casserole and sauté for 2-3 minutes. Add the parsnips, coriander and cumin and sauté for 2 minutes. Stir in the flour. Off the heat, gradually add the stock, apple juice and seasoning.

3 Bring to the boil and replace the meat. Cover and cook at 170°C (325°F) mark 3 for 1¼ hours or until the pork is almost tender.

4 Stir the apple into the pork, cover and cook for a further 15-20 minutes or until tender. Season to taste and garnish with snipped chives.

NOTE Do not peel the apples, as the red skin adds colour and texture to the dish.

STUFFED THAI OMELETTE

PREPARATION TIME 10 minutes
COOKING TIME About 15 minutes
FREEZING Not suitable
🕐

SERVES 2
- *3 eggs*
- *salt and pepper*
- *45 ml (3 tbsp)
  vegetable oil*
- *125 g (4 oz) minced
  pork*
- *1 large garlic clove,
  peeled and crushed*
- *2.5 cm (1 inch) piece
  fresh root ginger,
  peeled and grated*
- *1 carrot, peeled and
  grated*
- *1 small leek, trimmed
  and shredded*

460 CALS/SERVING
- *1 tomato, skinned
  and finely chopped*
- *5 ml (1 tsp) soft
  brown sugar*
- *15 ml (1 tbsp) nam
  pla (Thai fish sauce)
  (optional)*
- *10-15 ml (2-3 tsp)
  soy sauce*
- *5-15 ml (1-3 tsp)
  rice vinegar or cider
  vinegar*

1 In a bowl, beat the eggs together lightly, and
season with salt and pepper.
2 Heat half of the oil in a wok or frying pan. Add
the pork with the garlic and ginger and stir-fry
until the pork is cooked through.
3 Add the carrot and leek and stir-fry for 1
minute, then add the tomato, sugar, fish sauce if
using, soy sauce and vinegar. Season generously
with pepper and stir-fry for 2-3 minutes. Transfer
to a warmed dish and keep warm.
4 Wipe out the wok or frying pan, place over a
moderate heat and add the remaining oil; swirl to
distribute evenly. Pour in the beaten eggs.

5 When the omelette is just set but still moist, tip
the filling into the middle and fold the four sides
over the top to encase, like a parcel. Invert a
warmed plate over the wok or pan then turn out
the filled omelette. Serve immediately.

VARIATIONS Substitute minced beef for the pork.
For a vegetarian option, omit the meat altogether
and replace with another vegetable, such as
beansprouts.

CARAMELIZED ONION AND GRUYERE FRITTATA

PREPARATION TIME 10 minutes
COOKING TIME 40 minutes
FREEZING Not suitable
COLOUR INDEX Page 32
♡

SERVES 4
- *30 ml (2 tbsp)
  vegetable oil*
- *700 g (1½ lb)
  onions, peeled and
  sliced*
- *1 garlic clove, peeled
  and sliced*
- *4 eggs*
- *15 ml (1 tbsp) each
  chopped fresh chives
  and parsley*

330 CALS/SERVING
- *salt and pepper*
- *125 g (4 oz) fresh
  spinach, roughly
  chopped*
- *75 g (3 oz) each
  Gruyère and Edam
  cheese, cut into 1 cm
  (½ inch) cubes*

1 Heat the oil in a small 9 cm (7½ inch) non-stick
frying pan. Cook the onions and the garlic,
covered, for 25-30 minutes or until caramelized
and golden brown, stirring occasionally.
2 Beat together the eggs and herbs with plenty of
seasoning.
3 Remove the onions from the pan and add the
spinach. Stir over a low heat until wilted and all
the excess moisture has evaporated. Return the
onions to the pan with the cheese and stir until the
mixture is thoroughly combined.
4 Pour in the egg mixture and allow to run
through the onions. Cook over a medium heat,
loosening the edge with a spatula, for about 3-4
minutes or until the base and edge of the mixture
are set. Cover the pan handle with foil and place
under a hot grill for a further 3-4 minutes or until
the top is set and golden brown.

POACHED EGGS ON TOASTED BACON BAGUETTE

PREPARATION TIME 10 minutes
COOKING TIME 20 minutes
FREEZING Not suitable

⏱

SERVES 4

- *450 g (1 lb) cherry tomatoes, halved*
- *2 garlic cloves, peeled and crushed*
- *black pepper*
- *1 baguette*
- *60 ml (4 tbsp) mayonnaise*
- *15 ml (1 tbsp) olive oil*

520 CALS/SERVING

- *300 g (10 oz) thinly cut rindless streaky bacon*
- *30 ml (2 tbsp) chopped fresh parsley*
- *4 eggs*
- *1 small frisée lettuce*

1 Put the tomatoes in a bowl. Stir in the garlic and season well with black pepper.

2 Cut the bread into four lengths and slice each piece in half but not all the way through. Spread the inside of each piece with 15 ml (1 tbsp) mayonnaise, then toast the inside under a hot grill. Keep warm, covered, under a low grill.

3 Heat the oil in a non-stick frying pan and fry the bacon in two batches until crispy and golden brown. Keep warm. Quickly fry the tomatoes in the bacon fat for about 1 minute and stir in the parsley.

4 Lightly poach the eggs in an egg poacher or deep frying pan.

5 Top the baguette pieces with frisée, bacon, warm tomatoes and an egg. Grind over pepper to serve.

TIP

To poach eggs in a frying pan, fill to a depth of 7.5 cm (3 inches) with water, adding 30 ml (2 tbsp) vinegar. Bring to the boil, swirl the water, then slip the eggs in. Cook gently for about 4 minutes until lightly set.

277

CHICK-PEA AND PARSNIP SOUFFLES

PREPARATION TIME 20 minutes
COOKING TIME 2 hours
FREEZING Not suitable
COLOUR INDEX Page 32

♡

SERVES 4

- *175 g (6 oz) chick-peas, soaked overnight and drained*
- *450 g (1 lb) parsnips, peeled and cut into chunks*
- *salt and pepper*
- *50 g (2 oz) margarine*
- *45 ml (3 tbsp) white plain flour*

165 CALS/SERVING

- *300 ml (10 fl oz) semi-skimmed milk*
- *3 eggs, separated*
- *10 ml (2 tsp) mild curry powder*
- *50 g (2 oz) freshly grated Parmesan cheese*
- *fresh salad leaves, to garnish (optional)*

1 Boil the chick-peas in water to cover for 10 minutes, then drain and cover again with fresh water. Bring to the boil and simmer for 1½ hours or until tender, then drain.
2 Meanwhile, cook the parsnips in a saucepan of boiling salted water until just tender. Drain.
3 Melt the margarine in a saucepan, stir in the flour and cook, stirring, for 1-2 minutes. Gradually stir in the milk off the heat, then bring to the boil, stirring, and simmer for 2-3 minutes. Remove from the heat, cool slightly, then stir in the egg yolks, salt and pepper, curry powder and all but 45 ml (3 tbsp) of the cheese.
4 Purée the parsnips, chick-peas and sauce mixture together in a blender or food processor until almost smooth. Transfer to a bowl. Season.
5 Grease four deep 450 ml (15 fl oz) ovenproof dishes and coat with a little of the remaining cheese.
6 Whisk the egg whites until stiff but not dry, then fold into the mixture. Spoon into the prepared dishes and sprinkle over the remaining cheese.
7 Bake in the oven at 200°C (400°F) mark 6 for about 20 minutes or until the soufflés are well risen, golden brown and just set. Serve immediately, garnished with fresh salad leaves.

NOTE These delicious individual soufflés make a tasty starter or light lunch dish.

MELTING CHEESE AND HAM PARCEL

PREPARATION TIME 15 minutes, plus chilling
COOKING TIME 25 minutes
FREEZING Not suitable
COLOUR INDEX Page 31

SERVES 4

- *45 ml (3 tbsp) crème fraîche*
- *15 ml (1 tbsp) Dijon mustard*
- *370 g (13 oz) packet puff pastry*
- *350 g (12 oz) good-quality cooked ham, sliced*

685 CALS/SERVING

- *175 g (6 oz) Gruyère cheese, thinly sliced or grated*
- *1 egg yolk, beaten*
- *sea salt*

1 Mix together the crème fraîche and Dijon mustard.
2 Roll out a third of the puff pastry into a rectangle measuring 30 x 25 cm (12 x 10 inches) and place on a baking sheet.
3 Spread a third of the mustard mixture evenly over the pastry, leaving a 1 cm (½ inch) border. Top with a layer of ham, half the remaining mustard mixture, all the cheese and the remaining ham.
4 Spread the remaining mustard mixture over the ham and brush the pastry border with beaten egg yolk.
5 Roll out the remaining pastry into a rectangle about 2.5 cm (1 inch) larger than the base. Place the pastry over the filling and press the edges firmly together. Trim if necessary. Knock the edges up with a knife. Brush with beaten egg yolk and chill for 15 minutes.
6 Cook the parcel at 220°C (425°F) mark 7 for 25 minutes or until golden brown and the pastry base is cooked. If the pastry begins to burn around the edges, cover with foil and return to the oven to finish cooking. Season with sea salt.

NOTE Make sure the oven is preheated before cooking the parcel, otherwise the pastry could be disappointingly soggy.

AUBERGINE AND PEPPER PARMIGIANA

PREPARATION TIME 15 minutes
COOKING TIME 1¼ hours
FREEZING Suitable (stage 4)

✳

SERVES 6

- *two 400 g (14 oz) cans chopped tomatoes*
- *30 ml (2 tbsp) olive oil*
- *2 garlic cloves, peeled and crushed*
- *30 ml (2 tbsp) chopped fresh basil*
- *5 ml (1 tsp) grated lemon rind*
- *pinch of sugar*

360 CALS/SERVING

- *salt and pepper*
- *4 large red peppers, deseeded and quartered*
- *3 aubergines*
- *225 g (8 oz) Cheddar cheese, grated*
- *50 g (2 oz) freshly grated Parmesan cheese*

1 Start by making the tomato sauce. Place the chopped tomatoes in a saucepan and add half the oil, the garlic, basil, lemon rind, sugar and seasoning. Bring to the boil, cover and simmer gently for 30 minutes. Remove the lid and cook for a further 15 minutes. Allow to cool.

2 Meanwhile, place the pepper quarters on the grill pan, brush with a little oil and grill for 5-6 minutes on each side until charred and tender. Transfer to a plastic bag and leave to cool.

3 Cut the aubergines lengthways into thick slices, place on the grill pan and brush with oil. Grill for 6-8 minutes on each side, then leave to cool. Peel the cooled peppers.

4 Spoon a little sauce into the base of a large greased dish and top with a layer of aubergines and peppers. Sprinkle over a little of the Cheddar cheese. Continue to add layers of sauce, vegetables and cheese, finishing with a layer of Cheddar cheese. Sprinkle over the Parmesan.

5 Bake in the oven at 200°C (400°F) mark 6 for 30-40 minutes until bubbling and golden. Serve at once.

SEAFOOD SPAGHETTI WITH PEPPER AND ALMOND SAUCE

PREPARATION TIME 20 minutes
COOKING TIME 20 minutes
FREEZING Not suitable
COLOUR INDEX Page 33

♡

SERVES 4
- *1 small red pepper, about 150 g (5 oz)*
- *1 fresh red chilli*
- *50 g (2 oz) toasted, blanched almonds*
- *2-3 garlic cloves, peeled and crushed*
- *30 ml (2 tbsp) red wine vinegar*
- *350 ml (12 fl oz) tomato juice*
- *60 ml (4 tbsp) chopped fresh parsley*

305 CALS/SERVING
- *salt and pepper*
- *125 g (4 oz) dried spaghetti*
- *450 g (1 lb) cooked mixed seafood, such as prawns, mussels and squid*
- *chopped fresh chilli, to garnish*

1 Place the pepper and chilli under the grill and cook, turning occasionally, until the skins char and blacken. Cool slightly, then pull off the skins. Halve, discard the seeds, then put the flesh into a large food processor bowl.
2 Add the nuts, garlic, vinegar, tomato juice, half the parsley and seasoning. Blend until almost smooth. Transfer to a pan.
3 Cook the pasta in boiling salted water until just tender (*al dente*). Drain and toss in the rest of the fresh parsley. Season to taste and cover.
4 Meanwhile, gently heat the sauce until it simmers, then add the seafood. Simmer for 3-5 minutes or until heated through, stirring frequently. Adjust the seasoning and serve immediately over the spaghetti. Garnish with chopped fresh chilli.

NOODLES WITH MEATBALLS AND SHALLOTS

PREPARATION TIME 25 minutes
COOKING TIME 15 minutes
FREEZING Not suitable

♡

SERVES 4
- *300 g (10 oz) shallots, peeled*
- *30 ml (2 tbsp) olive oil*
- *225 g (8 oz) lean minced beef*
- *30 ml (2 tbsp) chopped fresh parsley*

335 CALS/SERVING
- *salt and pepper*
- *25 g (1 oz) pitted black olives*
- *30 ml (2 tbsp) chopped chives*
- *30 ml (2 tbsp) pesto sauce*
- *125 g (4 oz) dried noodles*

1 Chop 50 g (2 oz) shallots and sauté in 15 ml (1 tbsp) oil until golden. Cool, then mix with the beef mince, parsley and seasoning. Shape into 8 small patties. Fry in a non-stick pan for about 5-7 minutes each side or until cooked through.
2 Meanwhile, thinly slice the remaining shallots. Cook in the remaining oil in a covered pan for about 8-10 minutes until golden. Stir in the olives, chives and pesto, warm through and season.
3 Cook the noodles in boiling salted water until just tender, then drain well.
4 Toss the noodles with the shallot mixture and serve immediately accompanied by the meatballs.

TIPS
Remember to wear rubber gloves when handling chillies to prevent skin irritation. You can buy fresh or frozen mixed cooked seafood in supermarkets. If you can't find it, put together your own selection of prepared cooked seafood.

PASTITSIO

PREPARATION TIME 10 minutes, plus cooling
COOKING TIME 2 hours
FREEZING Suitable (stage 3)
❋

SERVES 4
- *45 ml (3 tbsp) olive oil*
- *125 g (4 oz) onion, peeled and finely chopped*
- *2 garlic cloves, peeled and crushed*
- *450 g (1 lb) lean minced lamb*
- *7.5 ml (1½ tsp) dried oregano*
- *5 ml (1 tsp) each dried thyme, ground cinnamon, ground cumin*
- *2.5 ml (½ tsp) each ground ginger and grated nutmeg*
- *1 bay leaf*

675 CALS/SERVING
- *150 ml (5 fl oz) dry white wine*
- *400 g (14 oz) can chopped tomatoes*
- *salt and pepper*
- *125 g (4 oz) pasta, such as macaroni*
- *45 ml (3 tbsp) chopped fresh coriander (optional)*
- *25 g (1 oz) butter*
- *25 g (1 oz) white plain flour*
- *450 ml (15 fl oz) milk*
- *50 g (2 oz) freshly grated Parmesan cheese*
- *2 eggs, beaten*

1 Heat the oil in a saucepan, add the onion and garlic and cook gently for about 10 minutes, stirring occasionally, until the onions are soft.
2 Add the lamb. Cook over a high heat for about 5 minutes, stirring, until evenly browned. Stir in the herbs, spices and bay leaf. Cook over a moderate heat for a further 5 minutes, stirring occasionally.
3 Mix in the wine, tomatoes and seasoning. Bring to the boil, lower the heat and simmer, covered, for 30 minutes. Uncover and cook for about 15 minutes, stirring occasionally, until the sauce is thickened and well reduced. Adjust the seasoning. Cool and skim off all the fat.
4 Cook the pasta in boiling, salted water until just tender (*al dente*). Drain. Stir into the lamb with the chopped coriander, if using. Spoon into a shallow ovenproof dish.
5 Melt the butter in a saucepan. Stir in the flour, seasoning and milk. Bring to the boil, stirring, then simmer for 3-4 minutes or until thickened. Cool slightly. Off the heat, beat in the Parmesan cheese and eggs. Pour over the lamb mixture.
6 Cook at 190°C (375°F) mark 5 for 35-40 minutes or until golden brown and piping hot. Serve at once with a green salad.

JAPANESE NOODLES WITH PAK CHOI AND MOOLI

PREPARATION TIME 15 minutes
COOKING TIME 30 minutes
FREEZING Not suitable

♡

SERVES 4

- *125 g (4 oz) flat rice or egg noodles*
- *30 ml (2 tbsp) sunflower oil*
- *1 garlic clove, peeled and sliced*
- *5 ml (1 tsp) freshly grated root ginger*
- *pinch of sugar*
- *3 pak choi, about 350 g (12 oz) total weight, roughly chopped*
- *1.1 litres (2 pints) vegetable stock*

215 CALS/SERVING

- *30 ml (2 tbsp) miso*
- *15 ml (1 tbsp) lemon juice*
- *15 ml (1 tbsp) light soy sauce*
- *125 g (4 oz) mooli, sliced*
- *1 packet mustard and cress, cut*
- *15 ml (1 tbsp) chopped fresh coriander*

1 Cook the noodles according to the packet instructions. Drain, refresh under cold water and drain again. Set aside.

2 Heat the oil in a saucepan and fry the garlic, ginger and sugar over a low heat for 2 minutes. Add the pak choi, in a single layer if possible, cover and cook over a low heat for 5 minutes. Add the stock, miso, lemon juice, soy sauce and mooli, bring to the boil, cover and simmer for 15 minutes.

3 Stir in the noodles, mustard and cress and coriander. Heat through for 1 minute and serve at once.

NOTE Miso is a thick paste made from fermented soya beans and is fermented together with either barley or rice. It is used to flavour soups, sauces, stews etc. Miso is available from good health food stores.

VARIATION Use another Chinese cabbage in place of pak choi. Mooli (related to the radish) is a popular Japanese ingredient and gives this dish a distinctive oriental flavour, but if it is unavailable use thinly sliced turnip instead.

PUMPKIN RAVIOLI WITH HERBS

PREPARATION TIME About 45 minutes
COOKING TIME 1¼ hours
FREEZING Suitable (stage 4)
COLOUR INDEX Page 34
❈

SERVES 4

- *200 g (7 oz) '00'
  pasta flour*
- *2 eggs (size 3)*
FILLING
- *450 g (1 lb) wedge
  pumpkin*
- *30 ml (2 tbsp) olive
  oil*
- *75 g (3 oz)
  prosciutto or Parma
  ham, finely chopped*
- *50 g (2 oz) Parmesan
  cheese, finely grated*

490 CALS/SERVING

- *20 ml (1½ tbsp)
  chopped fresh basil*
- *20 ml (1½ tbsp)
  chopped fresh
  parsley*
- *1 egg yolk*
- *freshly grated
  nutmeg, to taste*
- *30 ml (2 tbsp)
  double cream*
- *salt and pepper*
- *melted butter and
  chopped fresh herbs,
  to serve*

1 Brush the pumpkin flesh with the oil and bake in the oven at 190°C (375°F) mark 5 for about 1 hour until soft. Scrape out the flesh and mash until smooth. Add all the other filling ingredients.
2 To make the pasta, heap the flour on a work surface and make a well in the centre. Break the eggs into the well and work the flour into the eggs with your fingers to form a dough. Knead lightly for about 5 minutes. Wrap in clingfilm and leave to rest for 15 minutes.
3 Roll out the pasta dough as thinly as possible on an unfloured surface. Keep covered with clingfilm to prevent drying out.
4 Take a strip of pasta 10-12 cm (4-5 inches) wide. Spoon on heaped teaspoonfuls of stuffing at 6 cm (2½ inch) intervals. Brush the edges and between the stuffing with a little water. Cover with another sheet of pasta and press along the edges and between the stuffing to seal. Cut between the stuffing at 6 cm (2½ inch) intervals and cut neatly along the long edges. Repeat to use all of the pasta and stuffing, to make 20-24 ravioli.
5 Cook the ravioli in batches in boiling water for about 3 minutes until the sealed edges are just tender (*al dente*). Drain and serve tossed in melted butter and chopped herbs.

CALABRIAN PASTA

PREPARATION TIME 10 minutes
COOKING TIME 12-15 minutes
FREEZING Not suitable
COLOUR INDEX Page 35
🕐

SERVES 4-6

- *50 g (2 oz) sultanas*
- *150 g (5 oz)
  broccoli, cut into
  small florets*
- *300-350 g (10-12 oz)
  long fusilli or
  spaghetti*
- *salt and pepper*
- *125 ml (4 fl oz) olive
  oil*
- *75 g (3 oz) white
  breadcrumbs*

695-465 CALS/SERVING

- *2 garlic cloves,
  peeled and finely
  chopped*
- *25 g (1 oz) pine nuts*
- *10 ml (2 tsp)
  anchovy essence or
  anchovy paste*
- *45 ml (3 tbsp)
  chopped fresh
  parsley*
- *cayenne pepper, to
  taste*

1 Bring about 600 ml (1 pint) water to the boil. Put the sultanas in a bowl, pour on a little of the boiling water and leave to soak. Pour the rest of the boiling water over the broccoli in a pan and simmer for 30 seconds; drain.
2 Cook the pasta in a large pan of boiling salted water until just tender (*al dente*).
3 Meanwhile, heat the oil in a frying pan and add the breadcrumbs. Fry, stirring, until they begin to crisp, then add the garlic and pine nuts. Continue to fry, stirring until the pine nuts begin to colour, then add the broccoli to heat through.
4 Drain the pasta, setting it back on top of the saucepan to catch the last 15 ml (1 tbsp) cooking water. Stir the anchovy essence or paste and drained sultanas into this liquid, then return the pasta to the pan. Toss with a generous grinding of black pepper and half of the chopped parsley. Transfer to a heated serving bowl.
5 Mix the remaining parsley into the crumb mixture and sprinkle over the pasta. Sprinkle with cayenne pepper and toss at the table.

> *TIP*
> It's an Italian trick to toss the pasta with a little of its cooking water. This helps to keep the pasta hot, as well as preventing it from drying out before serving.

BAKED VEGETABLES WITH A SPICY SAUCE

PREPARATION TIME 30 minutes, plus standing
COOKING TIME 40 minutes
FREEZING Not suitable
COLOUR INDEX Page 38

SERVES 4-6

- 6-8 cherry tomatoes
- 2-3 rosemary sprigs
- 125 ml (4 fl oz) extra-virgin olive oil
- coarse sea salt and pepper
- 1 red and 1 yellow or orange pepper, deseeded and halved
- 6 shallots, peeled
- 1 aubergine, cut into thin slices
- 2-3 courgettes, thickly sliced on the diagonal
- 1 fennel bulb, quartered lengthwise
- 175 g (6 oz) parsnips, halved
- 125 g (4 oz) baby sweetcorn, halved lengthwise

425-285 CALS/SERVING

- 225 g (8 oz) mushrooms (large closed cup), left whole

SPICY SAUCE
- 15 ml (1 tbsp) sunflower oil
- 1 small onion, peeled and finely sliced
- 1 garlic clove, peeled and finely sliced
- 1 green chilli, deseeded and finely sliced
- 10 ml (2 tsp) capers
- 10 ml (2 tsp) soft brown sugar
- juice of ½ lemon
- 175 g (6 oz) passata

1 Cut a shallow cross in the base of each tomato, but leave them whole. Strip the leaves from one of the rosemary sprigs and chop finely. Pour the olive oil into a large bowl and add the chopped rosemary and whole sprigs with salt and pepper. Add the vegetables and turn to coat evenly with the oil. Leave to infuse for at least 1-2 hours.
2 Put all the vegetables, except the cherry tomatoes, into a large shallow baking tin with the rosemary sprigs and baste with the oil. Bake at 220°C (425°F) mark 7, turning and basting from time to time, for about 40 minutes until the vegetables are evenly browned and cooked through. Add the cherry tomatoes 10 minutes before the end of the cooking time.
3 To make the sauce, heat the oil in a small pan, add the onion, garlic and chilli and fry gently until tender.
4 Meanwhile put the capers, sugar, lemon juice and passata in a blender or food processor and

work until smooth. Season with salt and pepper and add to the chilli mixture. Cover and cook for 5-10 minutes, stirring occasionally, to make a thick sauce.
5 Transfer the baked vegetables to an oval serving platter and serve at once, accompanied by the sauce.

QUICK TOMATO AND GARLIC PIZZA

PREPARATION TIME 15 minutes
COOKING TIME 20 minutes
FREEZING Not suitable
COLOUR INDEX Page 36

SERVES 2

- 1 garlic bulb
- olive oil, for basting
- 4 tomatoes, about 400 g (14 oz) total weight, roughly chopped
- salt and pepper
- 145 g (5.1 oz) packet pizza-base mix

485 CALS/SERVING

- 15 ml (1 tbsp) chopped fresh rosemary or 10 ml (2 tsp) dried
- 75 g (3 oz) feta cheese
- about 8 black olives
- about 8 fresh basil leaves

1 Divide the garlic into cloves, discarding the outer, papery layers, but leaving the inner skins intact. Toss in a little oil. Put the tomatoes in a bowl with 5 ml (1 tsp) salt. Mix well.
2 Make up the pizza base mix according to the packet instructions. As you are kneading the dough, knead in the rosemary until it is evenly incorporated.
3 Roll out the dough thinly to a 25 cm (10 inch) round on a lightly floured surface. Transfer to a lightly greased and floured baking sheet.
4 Spoon the tomatoes over the pizza base to within 1 cm (½ inch) of the edge and crumble the feta cheese on top. Scatter the olives, garlic cloves and basil over the top. Season with pepper only.
5 Bake in the oven at 220°C (425°F) mark 7 for 20 minutes or until the base is crisp and golden. Serve, mashing the garlic as you eat.

VARIATION Replace the garlic, olives and feta cheese with a 350 g (12 oz) jar of pimientos, drained; 20 ml (4 tsp) capers; and 75 g (3 oz) smoked vegetarian cheese.

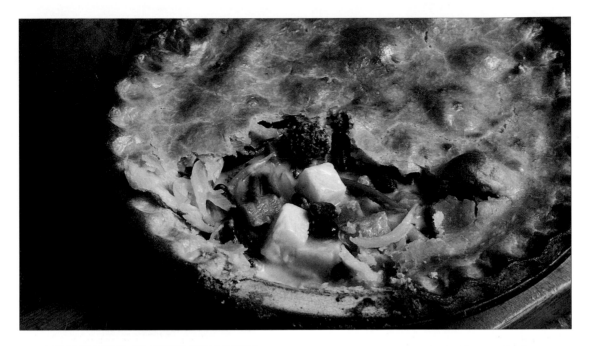

VEGETABLE CHEESE PIE WITH
POTATO CRUST

PREPARATION TIME 55 minutes, plus cooling
COOKING TIME 1 hour 10 minutes
FREEZING Suitable

✳

SERVES 4

- *225 g (8 oz) white plain flour*
- *salt and pepper*
- *100 g (3½ oz) butter, diced*
- *175 g (6 oz) mashed potato*

FILLING

- *25 g (1 oz) butter*
- *2 large onions, peeled and sliced*
- *4 garlic cloves, peeled and crushed*
- *350 g (12 oz) celeriac, peeled and cut into chunks*
- *50 g (2 oz) white plain flour*
- *300 ml (10 fl oz) vegetable stock*

645 CALS/SERVING

- *300 ml (10 fl oz) milk*
- *175 g (6 oz) broccoli, cut into small florets*
- *125 g (4 oz) French beans, trimmed and cut into 2.5 cm (1 inch) lengths*
- *2 large carrots, peeled and cut into chunks*
- *grated nutmeg*
- *400 g (14 oz) can pinto or red kidney beans, drained*
- *225 g (8 oz) Cheddar cheese, grated*
- *egg yolk, to glaze*

1 To make the pastry, sift the flour and salt into a bowl. Add the butter, and rub in with the fingertips. Add the mashed potato and about 20-25 ml (4-5 tsp) cold water. Mix to a firm dough and knead lightly. Chill while making the filling.
2 To make the filling, melt the butter in a large saucepan. Add the onions and garlic and fry gently for 5 minutes. Add the celeriac and fry for a further 10 minutes. Stir in the flour and cook for 1 minute. Gradually stir in the stock and milk and bring just to the boil, stirring.
3 Add the broccoli, French beans and carrots. Season with nutmeg and salt and pepper. Cover and cook gently for 15 minutes. Cool slightly, then stir in the canned beans and cheese. Turn the filling into a pie dish.
4 Roll out the pastry on a lightly floured surface until 5 cm (2 inches) larger than the diameter of the dish. Cut off a 2.5 cm (1 inch) strip of pastry from around the edges.
5 Moisten the rim of the pie dish with water and position the strip on the rim. Dampen the pastry strip and position the pastry lid, pressing the edges firmly together to seal. Flute the edge and make a hole in the top of the pie to allow the steam to escape. If wished, decorate with pastry trimmings.
6 Brush the pie with beaten egg to glaze and sprinkle with a little nutmeg. Bake at 200°C (400°F) mark 6 for 30-35 minutes until the pastry is golden.

and the mixture is quite dry (about 15 minutes). Add the drained wild mushrooms and cook for a further 5 minutes. Remove from the heat and set aside. Season.

4 Stir the nuts, wild rice and apricots into the mushroom mixture.

5 Butter one sheet of filo pastry with a little melted butter, fold in half and butter again – you should have a piece about 23 cm (9 inches) square. Place one-sixth of the mushroom mixture in the middle and gather up the sides to form a parcel. Press gently to seal. Continue with the remaining pastry and mushroom mixture. Brush with melted butter and sprinkle with sesame seeds.

6 Place the parcels on a heated baking sheet and cook at 190°C (375°F) mark 5 for 25-30 minutes.

7 Stir the chives into the crème fraîche; season. Arrange the parcels on plates with a spoonful of the sauce. Garnish with chives. Serve the remaining sauce separately.

MIXED MUSHROOM PARCELS

PREPARATION TIME 45 minutes
COOKING TIME 1¼ hours
FREEZING Not suitable

SERVES 6

- *50 g (2 oz) wild or brown rice*
- *salt and pepper*
- *about 125 g (4 oz) butter*
- *175 g (6 oz) onion, chopped*
- *2 garlic cloves, peeled and crushed*
- *175 g (6 oz) celery, chopped*
- *175 g (6 oz) carrot, peeled and chopped*
- *700 g (1½ lb) brown- and white-cap mushrooms, chopped*

450 CALS/SERVING

- *225 g (8 oz) jar mixed wild mushrooms in oil*
- *75 g (3 oz) toasted hazelnuts, chopped*
- *75 g (3 oz) no-soak dried apricots, chopped*
- *6 sheets filo pastry*
- *15 ml (1 tbsp) sesame seeds*
- *60 ml (4 tbsp) chopped fresh chives*
- *200 g (7 oz) crème fraîche*
- *snipped chives, to garnish*

1 Cook the rice in plenty of boiling salted water until tender. Drain and set aside.

2 Melt 25 g (1 oz) butter in a large frying pan and cook the onion and crushed garlic for about 10 minutes or until soft and brown. Add the celery and carrot and fry for 3-4 minutes.

3 Add a further 25 g (1 oz) butter and the fresh mushrooms to the vegetables. Cook uncovered, stirring, until all excess moisture has evaporated

GNOCCHI WITH RED PESTO

PREPARATION TIME 30 minutes
COOKING TIME 30-40 minutes,
FREEZING Not suitable
COLOUR INDEX Page 36

SERVES 4-6

- *900 g (2 lb) floury potatoes*
- *salt*
- *50 g (2 oz) butter*
- *1 egg beaten*
- *225-275 g (8-10 oz) white plain flour*
- *basil leaves, to garnish*

PESTO

- *1 large red pepper*
- *50 g (2 oz) fresh basil*
- *1 garlic clove, peeled and crushed*

980-655 CALS/SERVING

- *30 ml (2 tbsp) toasted pine nuts*
- *6 sun-dried tomatoes in oil, drained*
- *2 ripe tomatoes, skinned*
- *45 ml (3 tbsp) tomato purée*
- *2.5 ml (½ tsp) chilli powder*
- *50 g (2 oz) freshly grated Parmesan*
- *150 ml (5 fl oz) olive oil*

1 To make the pesto, grill the pepper, turning occasionally, until blackened all over. Cool, then peel off the skin. Remove the core and seeds. Place in a blender or food processor with all the remaining pesto ingredients, except the oil. Blend until smooth, then, with the machine running, slowly add the oil.

2 To make the gnocchi, cook the unpeeled potatoes

in boiling water for 20-30 minutes until very tender. Drain well, then halve and press through a potato ricer, or peel and press through a sieve into a bowl.

3 While the potato is still warm, add 5 ml (1 tsp) salt, the butter, beaten egg and half the flour. Lightly mix together, then turn out onto a floured board. Gradually knead in enough remaining flour to yield a soft, slightly sticky dough.

4 Roll the dough into thick sausages, 2.5 cm (1 inch) in diameter. Cut into 2 cm (¾ inch) pieces. Roll each piece over the back of a fork with your floured thumb to form ridges on one side and an indentation on the other. Lay on a floured tea towel.

5 Bring a large saucepan of salted water to the boil. Cook the gnocchi in batches. Drop them into the boiling water and cook for 2-3 minutes, until they float to the surface. Remove with a slotted spoon and keep hot while cooking the remainder. Toss with the red pesto and garnish with basil.

FILLED BAKED POTATOES

PREPARATION TIME 15 minutes
COOKING TIME 1-1½ hours
FREEZING Not suitable

SERVES 8

- *8 large potatoes, each weighing about 175 g (6 oz)*

CARROT, PEANUT AND ALFALFA FILLING

- *75 ml (5 tbsp) natural yogurt*
- *45 ml (3 tbsp) peanut butter*
- *45 ml (3 tbsp) mayonnaise*
- *4 large carrots, peeled and coarsely grated*
- *75 g (3 oz) roasted peanuts*
- *75 g (3 oz) alfalfa sprouts*
- *a squeeze of lemon juice*
- *black pepper*

335 CALS/SERVING

HOT CHILLI BEAN FILLING

- *400 g (14 oz) can chopped tomatoes*
- *10 ml (2 tsp) tomato purée*
- *2 garlic cloves, peeled and crushed*
- *2.5 ml (½ tsp) chilli powder*
- *2.5 ml (½ tsp) dried oregano*
- *425 g (15 oz) cooked red kidney beans or 400 g (14 oz) can red kidney beans, drained and rinsed*
- *30 ml (2 tbsp) chopped fresh coriander or parsley*
- *salt and pepper*

1 Wash and scrub the potatoes and prick all over with a fork.

2 Bake the potatoes in the oven at 230°C (450°F) mark 8 for about 1 hour or at 200°C (400°F) mark 6 for about 1½ hours or until the potatoes feel soft when gently squeezed, turning them over once during cooking.

3 Meanwhile, make the fillings. For the Carrot, Peanut and Alfalfa filling, beat the yogurt, peanut butter and mayonnaise together, then gradually fold in the carrots, peanuts and alfalfa. Season with lemon juice and black pepper.

4 For the Hot Chilli Bean filling, put all the ingredients into a saucepan, season with salt and pepper, and bring to the boil. Cook vigorously for 15-20 minutes or until reduced and thickened.

5 When the potatoes are cooked, cut them in half and mash the flesh lightly with a fork. Top eight potato halves with one filling and the remaining potato halves with the second filling.

VARIATION Keep the potatoes whole and offer one or other of the fillings.

MARROW WITH TOMATO AND ONION

PREPARATION TIME 20 minutes
COOKING TIME 30 minutes
FREEZING Not suitable
♡

SERVES 4-6   **100-65 CALS/SERVING**
- *1 marrow*
- *25 g (1 oz) butter or margarine*
- *2 onions, peeled and chopped*
- *1 garlic clove, peeled and crushed*
- *6 large tomatoes, skinned and chopped*

- *30 ml (2 tbsp) tomato purée*
- *30 ml (2 tbsp) chopped mixed herbs or 10 ml (2 tsp) dried*
- *salt and pepper*
- *parsley sprigs, to garnish*

1 Peel the marrow, cut in half lengthways and scoop out the seeds. Cut the flesh into 2.5 cm (1 inch) cubes.
2 Melt the butter in a large saucepan and gently fry the onions and garlic for 5 minutes, until soft. Add the marrow and cook for a further 5 minutes.
3 Stir in the tomatoes, tomato purée and herbs. Cover and simmer for 20 minutes, until the vegetables are tender. Season to taste. Serve at once, garnished with parsley.

MIXED ONION CASSEROLE WITH JUNIPER

PREPARATION TIME 15 minutes
COOKING TIME 1¾ hours
FREEZING Not suitable
COLOUR INDEX Page 40

SERVES 4   **460 CALS/SERVING**
- *6 onions*
- *1 bunch of spring onions*
- *8 juniper berries*
- *50 g (2 oz) butter*
- *5 garlic cloves, peeled and finely sliced*
- *approximately 600 ml (1 pint) vegetable stock*
- *coarse sea salt and pepper*

- *6-8 shallots, peeled*
- *6 slices French bread, 1 cm (½ inch) thick*
- *125 g (4 oz) coarsely grated vegetarian mature Cheddar cheese*
- *15 ml (1 tbsp) snipped chives, to garnish*

1 Peel four of the onions, taking care to trim the minimum from the tops and bases. Cut each one crosswise into quarters, leaving the root end intact to ensure the onions do not fall apart during cooking.
2 Peel, halve and slice the remaining two ordinary onions. Trim the spring onions, then slice both the white and green parts. Crush the juniper berries, using a pestle and mortar.
3 Melt the butter in a saucepan, add the sliced ordinary onions, garlic and juniper berries and fry gently until golden. Add 300 ml (10 fl oz) of the vegetable stock and bring to the boil. Season with salt and pepper.
4 Stand the quarter-cut onions upright in a 1.2 litre (2 pint) casserole and add the shallots and sliced spring onions. Spoon the sautéed onion and garlic mixture on top. Cook, uncovered, in the oven at 180°C (350°F) mark 4 for 1½ hours, checking occasionally that the liquid hasn't dried out. Top up with more stock as necessary. At the end of the cooking time the liquid should be thick and syrupy.
5 About 15 minutes before the end of the cooking time, butter the slices of French bread and arrange butter-side up on top of the onion mixture. Sprinkle with the grated cheese and return to the oven to crisp and brown. (If, by the end of the cooking time, the cheese has not browned, flash

the dish under a hot grill for 1-2 minutes.) Sprinkle with the snipped chives to garnish and serve immediately, directly from the casserole.

NOTE The temperature isn't crucial for this dish, so if you are cooking a main course at a higher temperature, simply position the casserole lower in the oven.

SPICED PUMPKIN FRITTERS

PREPARATION TIME 15 minutes
COOKING TIME About 15 minutes
FREEZING Not suitable

SERVES 4

- *700 g (1½ lb) pumpkin flesh, deseeded*
- *175 g (6 oz) wholemeal plain flour*
- *2.5-5 ml (½-1 tsp) salt*
- *1.25 ml (¼ tsp) baking powder*
- *5 ml (1 tsp) cumin seeds*
- *2.5 ml (½ tsp) ground cumin*
- *1 egg, separated*

355 CALS/SERVING

- *1 small onion, peeled and finely chopped*
- *1-2 garlic cloves, peeled and crushed*
- *7.5 ml (1½ tsp) chilli sauce*
- *30 ml (2 tbsp) chopped fresh coriander*
- *vegetable oil for frying*
- *coarse salt, to serve*

1 Cut the pumpkin flesh into thick slices about 10 cm (5 inches) long and 1 cm (½ inch) wide. Steam for 8-10 minutes or until only just tender. Remove from the steamer and cool.
2 Place the flour, salt, baking powder, cumin seeds and ground cumin in a bowl and mix well. Make a well in the centre, add the egg yolk and gradually stir in 175 ml (6 fl oz) water to form a smooth batter, adding a little extra if necessary. Stir in the onion, garlic, chilli sauce and chopped coriander. Stiffly whisk the egg white and fold lightly into the batter.
3 One-third fill a deep-fat fryer with oil and heat to 180°C (350°F) or until hot enough to brown a cube of bread in 30 seconds. Using two forks, dip a few slices of pumpkin into the batter to coat evenly and place in the hot oil. Fry for 1-1½ minutes, turning frequently, until the fritters are crisp, golden brown and cooked through.

4 Drain on crumpled absorbent kitchen paper and keep warm while cooking the remaining pumpkin in the same way. Serve hot, sprinkled with coarse salt.

VARIATION Button mushrooms are also extremely good cooked this way.

NOTE This is an excellent way of using up the flesh scooped out of a pumpkin lantern.

SQUASH WITH NUTTY GINGERED CRUMBS

PREPARATION TIME 15 minutes
COOKING TIME 15 minutes
FREEZING Not suitable

SERVES 4

550 CALS/SERVING

- *1.4 kg (3 lb) butternut squash, peeled and cut into large chunks*
- *125 g (4 oz) butter*
- *125 g (4 oz) fresh breadcrumbs*
- *5 cm (2 inch) piece fresh root ginger, peeled and chopped*
- *2 garlic cloves, peeled and crushed*
- *50 g (2 oz) pine nuts*
- *60 ml (4 tbsp) chopped fresh parsley*
- *salt and pepper*

1 Boil the squash pieces in water until just tender. Drain well and keep warm.
2 Meanwhile, heat the butter in a frying pan, add the breadcrumbs with the ginger, garlic and pine nuts and fry for about 5 minutes until golden. Add the parsley and season to taste. Stir the breadcrumb mixture into the squash and serve.

PARSNIP AND CARROT AU GRATIN

PREPARATION TIME 15 minutes
COOKING TIME 25 minutes
FREEZING Not suitable
COLOUR INDEX Page 40
♡

SERVES 4-6

195-130 CALS/SERVING

- *450 g (1 lb) parsnips, peeled and coarsely chopped*
- *450 g (1 lb) carrots, peeled and coarsely chopped*
- *600 ml (1 pint) chicken stock*
- *salt and pepper*
- *25 g (1 oz) butter*
- *50 g (2 oz) fresh breadcrumbs*
- *chopped fresh parsley, to garnish*

1 Put the parsnips and carrots in a saucepan with the stock and season with salt and pepper to taste. Bring to the boil, cover and simmer the vegetables gently for 15-20 minutes until they are well cooked. Drain and cool slightly.
2 Purée the vegetables in a blender or rub through a sieve. Add the butter and place in a flameproof dish. Sprinkle the breadcrumbs over the surface and cook under a hot grill until the top turns golden brown. Garnish with parsley.

CAULIFLOWER IN CURRY SAUCE

PREPARATION TIME 15 minutes
COOKING TIME About 20 minutes
FREEZING Not suitable
COLOUR INDEX Page 39

SERVES 4
- *1 large cauliflower*
- *90 ml (6 tbsp) ghee or vegetable oil*
- *5 ml (1 tsp) black mustard seeds*
- *5 ml (1 tsp) cumin seeds*
- *2.5 cm (1 inch) piece fresh root ginger, peeled and finely chopped*
- *1 small onion, peeled and finely chopped*
- *5 ml (1 tsp) salt*

260 CALS/SERVING
- *5 ml (1 tsp) ground turmeric*
- *3 tomatoes, skinned and finely chopped*
- *1 small green chilli, deseeded and finely chopped*
- *2.5 ml (½ tsp) sugar*
- *30 ml (2 tbsp) chopped fresh coriander*

1 Divide the cauliflower into small florets, discarding the green leaves and tough stalks. Wash well and dry on absorbent kitchen paper.
2 Heat the ghee or oil in a heavy-based saucepan or flameproof casserole. Add the mustard seeds and, when they begin to pop, stir in the cumin seeds, ginger, onion, salt and turmeric. Fry for 2-3 minutes, stirring constantly.
3 Add the cauliflower and mix well to coat with the spice mixture. Stir in the tomatoes, chopped green chilli, sugar and half of the chopped coriander. Cover the pan tightly with a lid and cook gently for 15 minutes or until the cauliflower is tender but not mushy.
4 Uncover the pan and boil rapidly for 1-2 minutes to thicken the sauce. Transfer to a warmed serving dish and sprinkle with the remaining chopped coriander. Serve immediately.

NOTE This spicy dish makes an excellent addition to an Indian meal. Alternatively serve on its own accompanied by chapatis, as a quick and tasty supper dish.

SWEDE AND ORANGE PUREE

PREPARATION TIME 15 minutes
COOKING TIME 30 minutes
FREEZING Suitable (stage 2)
♡ ❄

SERVES 4
- *1.1 kg (2½ lb) swede, peeled and sliced quite thinly*
- *salt and pepper*
- *25 g (1 oz) butter or margarine*
- *finely grated rind of 1 orange*

100 CALS/SERVING
- *30 ml (2 tbsp) orange juice*
- *45 ml (3 tbsp) soured cream*
- *parsley, to garnish*

1 Put the swede into a saucepan, cover with cold salted water and bring to the boil. Cook for about 20 minutes, until quite tender. Allow to drain thoroughly in a colander for several minutes.
2 Mash the swede, then add the butter, seasoning and grated orange rind. Stir over a moderate heat for several minutes until thoroughly hot and all excess moisture has been driven off.
3 Stir in the orange juice and the soured cream. Reheat gently, stirring all the time to prevent the purée sticking to the pan. Sprinkle with pepper and garnish with parsley.

WILD MUSHROOM AND LENTIL SALAD

PREPARATION TIME 15 minutes
COOKING TIME 5 minutes
FREEZING Not suitable
COLOUR INDEX Page 43
♡ ⏱

SERVES 4
- *5 ml (1 tsp) walnut oil*
- *50 g (2 oz) lean smoked back bacon, cut into strips*
- *350 g (12 oz) brown-cap or wild mushrooms, halved if necessary*
- *salt and pepper*
- *5 ml (1 tsp) fresh tarragon, chopped*
- *150 ml (5 fl oz) low-fat bio natural yogurt*

80 CALS/SERVING
- *5 ml (1 tsp) clear honey*
- *pinch of cayenne pepper*
- *selection of salad leaves, such as rocket, endive, lollo rosso*
- *50 g (2 oz) alfalfa sprouts*
- *125 g (4 oz) sprouting lentils*

1 Gently heat the walnut oil in a sauté pan and cook the bacon strips until crisp. Remove with a slotted spoon and drain on absorbent kitchen paper. Add the mushrooms to the pan, sauté until slightly softened and season to taste. Remove with a slotted spoon and drain on absorbent kitchen paper, reserving the pan juices to add to the dressing.
2 Combine the tarragon, yogurt, honey and pan juices. Season with salt and a pinch of cayenne pepper to taste.
3 Arrange the salad leaves, alfalfa sprouts, lentils, bacon and mushrooms on four plates. Spoon a little dressing on the side and serve the remainder separately.

SPICED COLESLAW WITH PECANS

PREPARATION TIME 15 minutes, plus standing
FREEZING Not suitable
COLOUR INDEX Page 43

SERVES 4
- *350 g (12 oz) white cabbage, finely sliced*
- *2 25 g (8 oz) carrots, peeled and coarsely grated*
- *2-3 celery sticks, finely sliced*
- *50 g (2 oz) pecans or walnuts (optional)*
- *paprika, for sprinkling*
- *chervil or parsley sprigs, to garnish*
DRESSING
- *75 ml (5 tbsp) mayonnaise*

340 CALS/SERVING
- *30 ml (2 tbsp) olive oil*
- *30 ml (2 tbsp) wine vinegar*
- *5 ml (1 tsp) chilli powder*
- *10 ml (2 tsp) mango chutney (optional)*
- *4 drops of Tabasco sauce*
- *coarse sea salt and pepper*

1 Combine the cabbage, carrots and celery in a large bowl.
2 To make the dressing, put all of the ingredients into a screw-topped jar and shake vigorously to combine.
3 Pour the dressing over the salad and toss well. Cover and leave to stand for several hours or overnight if possible, in a cool place.
4 Just before serving, toss the pecans into the salad. Sprinkle with a little paprika and garnish with chervil or parsley.

NOTE If possible make this salad the day before, or at least several hours ahead, to enable the flavours of the dressing to be absorbed.

VARIATION To make the dressing suitable for vegans, substitute 125 g (4 oz) tofu for the mayonnaise. Put all of the dressing ingredients into a blender or food processor and work until smooth, adding a little more oil to thin if necessary.

VEGETABLE AND APPLE STIR-FRY

PREPARATION TIME 15 minutes
COOKING TIME 15 minutes
FREEZING Not suitable

🕐

SERVES 4
- *60 ml (4 tbsp) vegetable oil*
- *1 garlic clove, peeled and crushed*
- *350 g (12 oz) small leeks, trimmed and sliced*
- *4 sticks green celery, sliced*
- *225 g (8 oz) courgettes, sliced*
- *1 red pepper, deseeded and chopped*

285 CALS/SERVING
- *30 ml (2 tbsp) medium curry paste*
- *5 ml (1 tsp) ground ginger*
- *15 ml (1 tbsp) clear honey*
- *2 crisp, green eating apples*
- *50 g (2 oz) unsalted cashew nuts*
- *salt and pepper*
- *juice of 1 lemon*
- *flat-leaf parsley, to garnish*

1 Heat the oil in a non-stick sauté pan and cook the garlic for a few seconds. Stir in the vegetables and cook over a high heat for 10 minutes, stirring occasionally.
2 Add the curry paste, ginger, honey and 45 ml (3 tbsp) water and stir until smooth.
3 Roughly chop the apples. Add to the pan with the cashew nuts and plenty of seasoning. Cook for a further 5 minutes or until the vegetables are just tender but retain some bite. Squeeze lemon juice over to serve. Garnish with flat-leaf parsley.

TIP
When stir-frying, always make sure that the oil is sizzling before you add the ingredients. Keep the food on the move to ensure even cooking.

293

APPLE AND FIG STRUDEL

PREPARATION TIME 25 minutes
COOKING TIME 30 minutes
FREEZING Suitable
COLOUR INDEX Page 46
♡ ❅

SERVES 6	160 CALS/SERVING
• *125 g (4 oz) no-soak dried figs, roughly chopped*	• *4 sheets filo pastry, about 125 g (4 oz) total weight*
• *grated rind and juice of 1 lemon*	• *25 g (1 oz) low-fat spread*
• *25 g (1 oz) fresh white breadcrumbs*	• *5 ml (1 tsp) caster sugar*
• *450 g (1 lb) cooking apples*	• *icing sugar, to dust*

1 Place the figs in a large bowl with the lemon rind and juice and the breadcrumbs.
2 Peel, quarter, core and thinly slice the apples. Mix the apples with the figs.
3 Lay two pieces of filo pastry side by side on a clean tea towel, overlapping the longest edges by about 5 cm (2 inches). Brush with a little melted low-fat spread. Top with the other two sheets of pastry and brush again.
4 Place the apple mixture along the longest edge and roll up, using the tea towel to help you. Roll onto a non-stick baking sheet, curling it slightly to fit the sheet. Brush with the remaining fat and sprinkle the sugar over.
5 Bake at 190°C (375°F) mark 5 for 30-35 minutes or until the pastry is golden brown and the apple is quite soft. Cover with foil if necessary. Serve hot, dusted lightly with icing sugar.

NOTE Using low-fat spread reduces the calorie content slightly, helping to make this delicious strudel a surprisingly healthy dessert.

VARIATION *Apple, Apricot and Almond Strudel*
Replace the figs with 125 g (4 oz) no-soak dried apricots. Add 30 ml (2 tbsp) ground almonds and 2.5 ml (½ tsp) ground cinnamon to the filling. Sprinkle 15 g (½ oz) flaked almonds over before baking.

BRAMLEY APPLES WITH GINGER

PREPARATION TIME 15 minutes, plus soaking
COOKING TIME 50 minutes
FREEZING Not suitable
COLOUR INDEX Page 45

SERVES 4	275 CALS/SERVING
• *175 g (6 oz) no-soak dried prunes*	• *grated rind and juice of 1 lemon*
• *150 ml (5 fl oz) apple juice*	• *about 150 g (5 oz) soft light brown sugar*
• *15 g (½ oz) stem ginger, finely chopped and 15 ml (1 tbsp) syrup from the stem ginger jar*	• *4 small Bramley apples, about 225 g (8 oz) each*

1 Snip the prunes into the apple juice and leave to soak for 30 minutes.
2 Mix the stem ginger with the ginger syrup, lemon rind and juice and 125 g (4 oz) sugar. Strain the prunes, reserving the juice, and add the prunes to the ginger mixture.
3 Wash and core the apples. Cut the skin at the centre of the apple to stop the fruit bursting in the oven. Place in an ovenproof dish.
4 Fill the centre of each apple with the prune mixture, sprinkling any extra over the top. Pour the reserved apple juice over and sprinkle with a little sugar. Cover loosely.
5 Bake at 200°C (400°F) mark 6 for about 50 minutes. Serve with the juices spooned over.

> *TIP*
> If you don't have stem ginger in your store-cupboard, use 2.5 ml (½ tsp) ground ginger and omit the ginger syrup.

ALMOND TARTE TATIN

PREPARATION TIME 15 minutes, plus chilling
COOKING TIME 35 minutes
FREEZING Not suitable

SERVES 6

- *125 g (4 oz) white plain flour*
- *pinch of salt*
- *25 g (1 oz) ground almonds*
- *50 g (2 oz) caster sugar*
- *125 g (4 oz) butter*
- *2 egg yolks*
- *few drops almond essence*

380 CALS/SERVING

- *125 g (4 oz) soft light brown sugar*
- *5 Cox's Orange Pippins, about 700 g (1½ lb) total weight*
- *50 g (2 oz) toasted flaked almonds*

1 Put the flour, salt, ground almonds, caster sugar and 50 g (2 oz) of the butter in a food processor and process until the mixture resembles fine breadcrumbs. Add the egg yolks and almond essence and process until the mixture just comes together. Knead to a smooth dough on a floured surface. Wrap and chill for about 1 hour.

2 Peel, quarter and core the apples. Melt the remaining butter in a non-stick frying pan, add the brown sugar and slowly dissolve. Increase the heat slightly and stir for about 1 minute or until the mixture becomes smooth and thick.

3 Add the apples and flaked almonds and cook over a medium heat, stirring occasionally, for 10 minutes or until the apples soften slightly and the sugar mixture caramelizes. Pour into a 2.5 cm (1 inch) deep, 20 cm (8 inch) round non-stick sandwich tin. Leave to cool.

4 Roll out the chilled dough to a round slightly larger than the sandwich tin. Place on top of the apples, tucking the edges down the sides of the tin.

5 Bake at 190°C (375°F) mark 5 for about 20 minutes or until the pastry is golden brown. Leave to cool for 10 minutes. Invert on to a serving plate and serve.

NOTE The cake tin must be non-stick or the metal may taint the apples.

firm to the touch. Cover the top with a double sheet of greaseproof paper after 40 minutes to prevent overbrowning.
4 Leave the pudding to cool in the tin for 5 minutes, then turn out and serve.

APPLE AND BLACKBERRY UPSIDE-DOWN PUDDING

PREPARATION TIME 20 minutes
COOKING TIME 1 hour
FREEZING Suitable

❄

SERVES 8 | 225 CALS/SERVING

TOPPING
- *90 ml (6 tbsp) raspberry jam*
- *350 g (12 oz) blackberries or loganberries*
- *1 large eating apple, peeled, cored and chopped*

CAKE
- *75 g (3 oz) white self-raising flour*
- *75 g (3 oz) wholemeal self-raising flour*

- *5 ml (1 tsp) baking powder*
- *large pinch of salt*
- *1 egg*
- *finely grated rind and juice of 1 large orange*
- *30 ml (2 tbsp) milk*
- *75 g (3 oz) butter or margarine*
- *75 g (3 oz) caster sugar*

1 To make the topping, gently heat the jam in a small saucepan and pour into a greased 23 cm (9 inch) round spring-release cake tin. Wash the blackberries and arrange with the apple evenly over the base of the cake tin.
2 To make the cake, put all the ingredients into a large bowl and beat until smooth and glossy. Carefully spread over the fruit
3 Bake in the oven at 190°C (375°F) mark 5 for about 1 hour until the pudding is well risen and

PLUM CUSTARD BAKE

PREPARATION TIME 10 minutes
COOKING TIME 40 minutes
FREEZING Not suitable
COLOUR INDEX Page 45

♡

SERVES 6 | 175 CALS/SERVING
- *450 g (1 lb) plums*
- *75 g (3 oz) caster sugar*
- *3 eggs*
- *300 ml (10 fl oz) milk*
- *grated zest of ½ lemon*

- *5 ml (1 tsp) ground ginger*
- *5 ml (1 tsp) vanilla essence*
- *45 ml (3 tbsp) clear honey*

1 Halve and stone the plums, then arrange, cut-side down, in a round, shallow 1.1 litre (2 pint) ovenproof dish. Sprinkle with 30 ml (2 tbsp) of the sugar.
2 Whisk the eggs with all the remaining ingredients except the honey to make a smooth custard. Pour over the fruit.
3 Place the dish in a roasting tin filled with enough hot water to reach halfway up the side of the dish. Cook at 150°C (300°F) mark 2 for 40 minutes or until just set. Serve immediately, drizzled with warmed clear honey.

VARIATION Use greengages instead of plums and replace the ginger with grated nutmeg to taste.

POACHED PEARS WITH APRICOTS

PREPARATION TIME 8 minutes
COOKING TIME 5-10 minutes
FREEZING Not suitable
COLOUR INDEX Page 44
♡ ⏱

SERVES 4   195 CALS/SERVING
- 25 g (1 oz) butter or margarine
- 25 g (1 oz) soft brown sugar
- 15 ml (1 tbsp) lemon juice
- 700 g (1½ lb) ripe but firm pears
- 50 g (2 oz) no-soak dried apricots
- 15 ml (1 tbsp) Grand Marnier or brandy
- chopped nuts, to decorate
- ice cream, to serve

1 Put the butter, sugar and lemon juice in a saucepan with 150 ml (5 fl oz) water and warm together.
2 Peel, quarter and core the pears. Halve each quarter again if large. Snip the apricots into shreds.
3 Add the pears and apricots to the syrup, cover and simmer for 5-10 minutes or until the pears are just tender. Stir in the Grand Marnier.
4 Serve hot, sprinkled with chopped nuts and topped with ice cream.

CRISPY PEAR CLAFOUTIS

PREPARATION TIME 15 minutes, plus standing
COOKING TIME 50 minutes
FREEZING Not suitable

SERVES 6   270 CALS/SERVING
- 3 eggs
- 50 g (2 oz) white self-raising flour
- 150 g (5 oz) white plain flour
- large pinch of salt
- 5 ml (1 tsp) ground cinnamon
- 200 ml (7 fl oz) milk
- 30 ml (2 tbsp) Armagnac
- 50 g (2 oz) butter
- 350 g (12 oz) ripe dessert pears
- caster and icing sugar, to serve

1 Whisk the eggs, flours, salt and cinnamon with 150 ml (5 fl oz) milk until smooth. Whisk in the remaining milk with the Armagnac. Cover and leave to stand for 2 hours.
2 Using half the butter, grease a 23 cm (9 inch) spring-release cake tin. Stand the tin on a baking sheet. Thinly slice the pears. Whisk the batter again and pour into the prepared tin. Lay the pear slices on top. Dot with the remaining butter.
3 Bake at 240°C (475°F) mark 9 for 15-20 minutes or until well risen, then lower the temperature to 220°C (425°F) mark 7 for a further 35 minutes or until risen and well browned. Dust with a mixture of caster and icing sugar to serve.

SAFFRON MERINGUES WITH BLUEBERRY SAUCE

PREPARATION TIME 25 minutes
COOKING TIME 2 hours
FREEZING Suitable
❉

SERVES 6   260 CALS/SERVING

MERINGUES
- small pinch of saffron strands (optional)
- 2 egg whites
- 125 g (4 oz) caster sugar
- 200 ml (7 fl oz) crème fraîche

BLUEBERRY SAUCE
- 450 g (1 lb) blueberries
- 40 g (1½ oz) caster sugar
- 30 ml (2 tbsp) chopped fresh mint

1 Line two baking sheets with non-stick baking parchment. Put the saffron (if using) in a small bowl and pour on 15 ml (1 tbsp) boiling water. Whisk the egg whites in a large bowl until holding soft peaks. Whisk in 30 ml (2 tbsp) of the sugar, then strain in the saffron liquid and whisk again until the meringue is stiff. Fold in the remaining sugar.
2 Using two large spoons, shape the meringue mixture into 12 oval mounds on the prepared baking sheets. Bake in the oven at 110°C (225°F) mark ¼ for about 2 hours until the meringues are well dried out. Carefully peel the meringues off the paper and leave to cool on a wire rack.
3 To make the sauce, place the blueberries in a saucepan with the sugar and 45 ml (3 tbsp) water and cook over a low heat for 5-7 minutes until they are just tender, but still holding their shape. Using a slotted spoon, remove about one quarter of the blueberries and press through a fine sieve into a large bowl. Stir in the rest of the blueberries with the chopped mint and leave to cool, stirring occasionally.
4 About 1 hour before serving, sandwich the meringues together with the crème fraîche. Pile on to one or two serving dishes, cover and chill until ready to serve. Pour the sauce into a jug and serve with the meringues.

VARIATION *Cinnamon Meringues with Red Sauce* Omit the saffron, and add 5 ml (1 tsp) ground cinnamon to the egg whites with the sugar. Replace the blueberries with 450 g (1 lb) cherries, raspberries or strawberries.

CHOCOLATE TRUFFLE CAKE

PREPARATION TIME 25 minutes, plus setting
COOKING TIME 20 minutes
FREEZING Suitable
COLOUR INDEX Page 47
❉

SERVES 16   580 CALS/SERVING

- 150 g (5 oz) sugar
- 90 g (3½ oz) blanched whole almonds, toasted
- 23 cm (9 inch) round chocolate sponge
- 90 ml (6 tbsp) Tia Maria

- 600 g (1 lb 6 oz) plain chocolate
- 600 ml (1 pint) double cream
- 3 egg yolks
- 40 g (1½ oz) caster sugar

1 Melt the sugar in a heavy-based saucepan over a gentle heat. Add the almonds and cook until dark golden. Carefully pour onto an oiled baking sheet – the pan and caramel will be very hot. Set aside to cool.
2 Line the sides of a 23 cm (9 inch) spring-release cake tin with non-stick baking parchment. Carefully slice a thin circle of chocolate sponge, about 5 mm (¼ inch) deep. Place cut side up in

the base of the tin. Push down firmly and use pieces of sponge to patch up any holes (any remaining sponge can be frozen). Drizzle 30 ml (2 tbsp) Tia Maria over and set aside.

3 Break the chocolate into a heatproof bowl and add 150 ml (5 fl oz) cream. Melt the chocolate over a pan of gently simmering water. Do not stir.

4 Meanwhile, using an electric whisk, whisk together the egg yolks and caster sugar in a bowl for 10 minutes or until pale, thick and creamy.

5 Break the almond caramel into small pieces. Process in a blender or food processor until it resembles coarse breadcrumbs.

6 With a metal spoon, fold the melted chocolate into the egg mixture and mix well. Fold in the almond caramel and the remaining Tia Maria.

7 Lightly whip the remaining double cream until it just holds its shape, then fold it into the chocolate mixture. Pour into the cake tin. Set in the refrigerator overnight.

8 To serve, remove from the tin, discarding the lining paper, and cut with a sharp, hot knife.

NOTE For an autumnal decoration, melt 50 g (2 oz) dark, milk and white chocolate in separate bowls. Coat about 10 opened cape gooseberries in chocolate. Heat 50 g (2 oz) sugar and melt until golden brown. Coat about 5 cape gooseberries in the caramel. Decorate the cake with coated and fresh cape gooseberries. Fix greaseproof paper around the base, then tie raffia over it.

HONEY-TOASTED RICE

PREPARATION TIME 10 minutes
COOKING TIME 3 hours
FREEZING Not suitable

SERVES 4

435 CALS/SERVING

- *600 ml (1 pint) milk*
- *300 ml (10 fl oz) single cream*
- *75 g (3 oz) pudding rice*
- *knob of butter*
- *30 ml (2 tbsp) caster sugar*
- *1.25 ml (¼ tsp) vanilla essence*
- *large pinch of grated nutmeg*
- *50 g (2 oz) flaked or shredded almonds, roughly chopped or cut into thin shreds*
- *45 ml (3 tbsp) clear honey*
- *15 ml (1 tbsp) lemon juice*

1 Mix together the first seven ingredients. Pour into a 5 cm (2 inch) deep 1.4 litre (2½ pint) ovenproof dish. Place in a roasting tin with enough warm water to come halfway up the side of the dish.

2 Cook at 150°C (300°F) mark 2 for about 2½-3 hours or until lightly set and golden. Turn off the oven and leave the pudding inside for about 20 minutes.

3 Scatter the almonds over the pudding. Mix together the honey and lemon juice and drizzle over the nuts. Place under a hot grill until a golden brown colour. Serve hot or cold.

TIP
Keep a whole nutmeg for grating in your store-cupboard, rather than a tub of ready-grated nutmeg. The flavour is fresh and cleaner and a single nutmeg will last for years.

CINNAMON COFFEE CAKE

PREPARATION TIME 20 minutes
COOKING TIME 35-40 minutes
FREEZING Suitable
COLOUR INDEX Page 49

❄

MAKES 8 SLICES **420 CALS/SLICE**

- *125 g (4 oz) butter*
- *200 g (7 oz) granulated sugar*
- *2 eggs*
- *150 ml (5 fl oz) soured cream*
- *10 ml (2 tsp) vanilla essence*
- *125 g (4 oz) white plain flour*

- *10 ml (2 tsp) baking powder*
- *pinch of salt*
- *150 g (5 oz) walnuts or pecan nuts, chopped*
- *10 ml (2 tsp) ground cinnamon*

1 Grease and base-line a deep 20 cm (8 inch) round cake tin. Lightly dust with flour.
2 Cream together the butter with 175 g (6 oz) sugar. Beat in the eggs, soured cream and vanilla essence. Fold in the flour, the baking powder and salt. Do not overbeat. Mix together the remaining sugar, nuts and cinnamon.
3 Spoon half the cake mixture into the prepared tin. Sprinkle over half the nut mixture. Add the remaining cake mixture and top with the rest of the nuts and sugar.
4 Bake at 180°C (350°F) mark 4 for about 35-40 minutes. Serve warm or cold.

CRUMBLY APPLE AND CHEESE CAKE

PREPARATION TIME 20 minutes
COOKING TIME 50 minutes-1 hour
FREEZING Suitable

❄

MAKES 10 SLICES **A345 CALS/SLICE**

- *175 g (6 oz) white self-raising flour*
- *5 ml (1 tsp) baking powder*
- *75 g (3 oz) light muscovado sugar*
- *50 g (2 oz) raisins*
- *50 g (2 oz) sultanas*
- *50 g (2 oz) brazil nuts, chopped*

- *575 g (1¼ lb) dessert apples, peeled, cored and thinly sliced*
- *2 eggs*
- *90 ml (3 fl oz) sunflower oil*
- *225 g (8 oz) Caerphilly cheese*
- *icing sugar*

1 Grease a 5 cm (2 inch) deep, 23 cm (9 inch) round loose-based flan tin.
2 Sift the flour and baking powder into a bowl. Stir in the sugar, raisins, sultanas, nuts and apples. Beat the eggs with the oil and add to the dry ingredients. Mix well together.
3 Turn half the mixture into the prepared tin and level the surface. Crumble the cheese over, then cover with the remaining cake mixture. Roughly spread the mixture to the edges of the tin.
4 Bake at 180°C (350°F) mark 4 for 50 minutes to 1 hour until golden and just firm. Leave to cool in the tin for 10 minutes, then transfer to a wire rack. Serve warm, sprinkled with icing sugar.

ALMOND, CHOCOLATE AND SWEET POTATO LOAF

PREPARATION TIME 20 minutes
COOKING TIME 1-1¼ hours
FREEZING Suitable
COLOUR INDEX Page 49

❋

MAKES 8-10 SLICES

- *225 g (8 oz) sweet potatoes, peeled and cut into chunks*
- *125 g (4 oz) soft margarine*
- *125 g (4 oz) light muscovado sugar*
- *5 ml (1 tsp) vanilla essence*
- *2 eggs*
- *160 g (5½ oz) white self-raising flour*
- *15 g (½ oz) cocoa powder*

435-350 CALS/SLICE

- *5 ml (1 tsp) ground mixed spice*
- *2.5 ml (½ tsp) bicarbonate of soda*
- *30 ml (2 tbsp) milk*
- *125 g (4 oz) milk chocolate, roughly chopped*
- *75 g (3 oz) flaked almonds, lightly toasted*
- *icing sugar, for dusting*

1 Add the sweet potatoes to a pan of cold water, bring to the boil and cook for 15 minutes or until softened. Drain well, then mash with a potato masher.
2 Grease a 900 g (2 lb) loaf tin and line the base and long sides with a strip of greaseproof paper.
3 Put the margarine, sugar, vanilla essence and eggs in a bowl. Sift the flour, cocoa, mixed spice and bicarbonate of soda into the bowl. Add the milk and beat well until smooth and creamy.
4 Stir in the mashed sweet potato, chopped chocolate and 50 g (2 oz) of the toasted almonds. Turn the mixture into the prepared tin and level the surface. Sprinkle with the remaining almonds.
5 Bake at 170°C (325°F) mark 3 for about 1-1¼ hours until well risen and just firm to the touch. Leave in the tin for 10 minutes, then transfer to a wire rack to cool. Serve dusted with icing sugar.

NOTE Cook this cake as soon as you have mixed it, as the bicarbonate of soda is activated on blending.

VARIATION *Chocolate, Orange and Parsnip Loaf* Replace the sweet potatoes with parsnips. Substitute 2.5 ml (½ tsp) ground coriander for the mixed spice, and add the finely grated rind of 1 orange.

GINGER CAKE

PREPARATION TIME 15 minutes
COOKING TIME 1 hour
FREEZING Suitable

♡ ❋

MAKES ABOUT 25 SLICES

- *225 g (8 oz) white plain flour*
- *pinch of salt*
- *2.5 ml (½ tsp) bicarbonate of soda*
- *15 ml (1 tbsp) ground ginger*
- *5 ml (1 tsp) ground allspice*
- *25 g (1 oz) medium oatmeal*
- *125 g (4 oz) black treacle*

140 CALS/SLICE

- *150 g (5 oz) golden syrup*
- *175 g (6 oz) butter*
- *50 g (2 oz) soft dark brown sugar*
- *150 ml (5 fl oz) milk*
- *2 eggs, beaten*
- *125 g (4 oz) stem ginger, drained and finely chopped*

1 Grease and line the base of a 5 cm (2 inch) deep, 20 cm (8 inch) square cake tin.
2 Sift the flour, salt, bicarbonate of soda, ground ginger and allspice into a bowl. Add the oatmeal.
3 Put the treacle, syrup, butter, sugar and milk in a saucepan and heat gently, stirring until melted.
4 Make a well in the centre of the dry ingredients. Add the eggs and stem ginger with the treacle mixture. Beat until smooth. Pour into the prepared tin.
5 Bake at 180°C (350°F) mark 4 for about 1 hour. Cool in the tin for 5 minutes, then cool on a wire rack. Store for up to one week.

HONEY AND YOGURT MUFFINS

PREPARATION TIME 15 minutes
COOKING TIME 17-20 minutes
FREEZING Suitable
COLOUR INDEX Page 51
♡ ◷ ❄

MAKES 12
- *225 g (8 oz) white plain flour*
- *7.5 ml (1½ tsp) baking powder*
- *5 ml (1 tsp) bicarbonate of soda*
- *pinch of salt*
- *2.5 ml (½ tsp) ground mixed spice*
- *1.25 ml (¼ tsp) ground nutmeg*
- *50 g (2 oz) medium oatmeal*

180 CALS/MUFFIN
- *50 g (2 oz) light muscovado sugar*
- *50 g (2 oz) butter*
- *225 g (8 oz) Greek yogurt*
- *125 ml (4 fl oz) milk*
- *1 egg*
- *60 ml (4 tbsp) clear honey*
- *oatmeal, for dusting*

1 Line 12 deep bun tins or muffin tins with paper muffin cases. Sift the flour, baking powder, bicarbonate of soda, salt, mixed spice and nutmeg into a bowl. Stir in the oatmeal and sugar.
2 Melt the butter and leave to cool slightly. Mix the yogurt and milk together in a bowl, then beat in the egg, butter and honey.
3 Pour over the dry ingredients and stir in quickly until only just blended; do not over-mix.
4 Divide the mixture equally between the paper cases. Sprinkle with oatmeal and bake at 200°C (400°F) mark 6 for 17-20 minutes until well risen and just firm to the touch. Remove from the oven and leave in the tins for 5 minutes, then transfer to a wire rack. Serve warm or cold, with a little butter if desired.

VARIATION *Chocolate Banana Muffins* Omit the honey. Mash 1 small ripe banana and mix with 125 g (4 oz) melted plain chocolate. Add to the muffin mixture after the liquids, blending until rippled with colour.

BERRY SCONES

PREPARATION TIME 20 minutes
COOKING TIME 10 minutes
FREEZING Suitable
COLOUR INDEX Page 51
♡ ◷ ❄

MAKES ABOUT 16
- *450 g (1 lb) white self-raising flour*
- *2.5 ml (½ tsp) salt*
- *10 ml (2 tsp) baking powder*
- *75 g (3 oz) butter, diced*
- *75 g (3 oz) caster sugar*

160 CALS/SERVING
- *225 g (8 oz) blackberries*
- *about 200 ml (7 fl oz) semi-skimmed milk*
- *1 egg, beaten*

1 Sift the dry ingredients together in a large bowl. Rub in the butter until the mixture resembles breadcrumbs. Stir in the sugar and the berries.
2 Stir in enough milk to form a firm dough. Knead very lightly and roll out on a floured surface until about 2.5 cm (1 inch) thick. Using a 6 cm (2½ inch) plain cutter, stamp out rounds, taking care to avoid cutting through the berries. Knead and carefully re-roll as necessary.
3 Place the scones on a greased baking tray and brush the tops with beaten egg. Bake at 220°C (425°F) mark 7 for about 10 minutes until well risen and golden.

NOTE Frozen blackberries also work very successfully in this recipe – just add them straight from the freezer.

VARIATION For traditional fruit scones, use 125g (4 oz) currants, sultanas, or raisins instead of the blackberries. Omit the sugar.

STICKY ORANGE FLAPJACKS

PREPARATION TIME 10 minutes
COOKING TIME 25-30 minutes
FREEZING Suitable

✳

MAKES 18

- *2 small oranges*
- *250 g (9 oz) unsalted butter, diced*
- *250 g (9 oz) caster sugar*
- *175 g (6 oz) golden syrup*

300 CALS/FLAPJACK

- *425 g (15 oz) porridge oats*
- *30 ml (2 tbsp) sunflower seeds*
- *45 ml (3 tbsp) fine-shred orange marmalade*

1 Grease a baking tin measuring about 22 x 9 cm (8½ x 11½ inches) across the top and 19 x 27 cm (7½ x 10½ inches) across the base.
2 Using a citrus zester, finely pare the rind from the oranges in strips. Place in a heavy-based saucepan. Add the butter with the sugar and syrup. Cook over a moderate heat, stirring until the butter has melted. Remove from the heat and stir in the oats, until evenly coated in syrup.
3 Turn the mixture into the prepared tin and level the surface. Sprinkle with the sunflower seeds. Bake at 180°C (350°F) mark 4 for 25-30 minutes until turning deep golden around the edges; the

mixture will still be very soft in the centre. Leave in the tin until almost cold.
4 Heat the marmalade in a small saucepan with 15 ml (1 tbsp) water until syrupy. Brush evenly over the flapjack. Turn out onto a board and cut into 18 bars. Store in an airtight container for up to 1 week.

NOTE To weigh syrup, first measure out the sugar quantity and leave it in the scales' bowl, making a small well in the centre. Add additional weights for the required quantity of syrup and spoon the syrup into the well. Both sugar and syrup will then slide cleanly into the saucepan.

VARIATION *Fruit and Nut Flapjacks* Omit the orange rind, sunflower seeds and marmalade. Add 125 g (4 oz) luxury mixed dried fruit and 75 g (3 oz) chopped and toasted mixed nuts with the oats.
Pear and Cinnamon Flapjacks Omit the orange rind, sunflower seeds and marmalade. Add 5 ml (1 tsp) ground cinnamon with the sugar, and 150 g (5 oz) roughly chopped dried pears with the oats.

baking sheets, spacing them well.
4 Bake at 180°C (350°F) mark 4 for 12-15 minutes or until golden and cooked through. Cool on wire racks.

COTTAGE CHEESE AND BRAZIL NUT TEABREAD

PREPARATION TIME 10 minutes
COOKING TIME 50-60 minutes
FREEZING Suitable
COLOUR INDEX Page 52
♡ ❋

MAKES ABOUT 12 SLICES

- 225 g (8 oz) cottage cheese
- 75 g (3 oz) light muscovado sugar
- 125 g (4 oz) wholemeal self-raising flour
- 125 g (4 oz) white self-raising flour
- finely grated rind and juice of 1 lemon
- 2 eggs, beaten
- 75 ml (5 tbsp) milk

190 CALS/SLICE

- 75 g (3 oz) stoned dates, rinsed and roughly chopped
- 75 g (3 oz) brazil nuts, chopped
- 6 whole brazil nuts, to decorate
- 15 ml (1 tbsp) clear honey, to glaze

1 Grease and line a 1.1 litre (2 pint) loaf tin.
2 Put all the ingredients, except the whole brazil nuts and honey, in a bowl and beat well until the mixture has a soft dropping consistency.
3 Spoon into the prepared loaf tin and level the surface. Lightly press the whole brazil nuts in a line down the centre of the mixture to decorate.
4 Bake at 180°C (350°F) mark 4 for 50-60 minutes until risen and golden. Cover with foil if the teabread browns too quickly. Turn out and brush with the honey while still warm. Cool on a wire rack. Serve sliced, spread with butter.

OAT AND SESAME BISCUITS

PREPARATION TIME 30 minutes
COOKING TIME 12-15 minutes
FREEZING Suitable
❋

MAKES 50

- 125 g (4 oz) wholemeal self-raising flour
- 125 g (4 oz) white self-raising flour
- 2.5 ml (½ tsp) salt
- 5 ml (1 tsp) mustard powder
- 150 g (5 oz) butter, diced

60 CALS/BISCUIT

- 5 ml (1 tsp) caster sugar
- 225 g (8 oz) medium oatmeal
- 50 g (2 oz) sesame seeds
- 50 ml (2 fl oz) milk
- oil for greasing

1 Place the first five ingredients in a bowl. Rub the butter into the flour until the mixture resembles fine breadcrumbs.
2 Stir in the sugar, oatmeal and sesame seeds. Add the milk with 25 ml (1 fl oz) water. Knead the mixture together to form a dough. Turn out onto a lightly floured surface.
3 Thinly roll out half the dough and cut into small biscuits, about 4 x 6.5 cm (1½ x 2½ inches) each. Repeat with the remaining dough to make about 50 biscuits. Place the biscuits on lightly oiled

TIP
Oat and Sesame Biscuits are delicious served with rich blue cheeses. Try dolcelatte, a quite mild Italian Gorgonzola-type cheese with a soft, creamy texture, or Cambazola, a blue-Brie type German cheese that is creamy white with blue-green veining.

OLIVE AND WALNUT BREAD

PREPARATION TIME 20 minutes, plus rising
COOKING TIME 37 minutes
FREEZING Suitable

♡ ❄

MAKES TWO LOAVES
(12 SLICES EACH)
- *125 g (4 oz) pitted black olives, roughly chopped*
- *75 g (3 oz) walnuts, finely chopped*
- *600 g (1 lb 5 oz) white strong plain flour*

125 CALS/SLICE
- *10 ml (2 tsp) salt*
- *7 g (¼ oz) sachet fast-action dried yeast*
- *75 ml (5 tbsp) chopped fresh parsley*
- *45 ml (3 tbsp) olive oil*

1 Mix the olives and walnuts together with the flour, salt, yeast and parsley.
2 Make a well in the centre of the dry ingredients and add 375 ml (12 fl oz) tepid water mixed with 45 ml (3 tbsp) oil. Stir together to form a soft dough, adding a little more water if necessary.
3 Turn the dough onto a well-floured surface and knead well for about 10 minutes, or until it is smooth and elastic.
4 Divide the dough in half and shape each piece into a roll 18-20 cm (7-8 inches) long. Place rolls of dough on separate oiled baking sheets and cover loosely with lightly oiled clingfilm.
5 Leave the dough in a warm place for 30-40 minutes or until doubled in size. Lightly slash the top of each loaf.
6 Bake at 220°C (425°F) mark 7 for 12 minutes. Lower the temperature to 180°C (350°F) mark 4 for a further 25 minutes or until well browned and sounding hollow when tapped. Leave to cool for a few minutes on wire racks.
7 Serve warm, thickly sliced.

APPLE AND MINT JELLY

PREPARATION TIME 30 minutes, plus standing
COOKING TIME About 1¼ hours
FREEZING Not suitable
COLOUR INDEX Page 53

- *2.3 kg (5 lb) cooking apples, such as Bramleys*
- *few large mint sprigs*
- *1.1 litres (2 pints) distilled white vinegar*
- *sugar (see method)*

35-40 CALS/15 ML (1 TBSP)
- *90-120 ml (6-8 tbsp) chopped mint*
- *few drops of green food colouring (optional)*

1 Remove any bruised parts from the apples, then roughly chop into chunks without peeling or coring. Put the apples in a preserving pan with 1.1 litres (2 pints) water and the mint sprigs.
2 Bring to the boil, then simmer gently for about 45 minutes or until soft and pulpy, stirring from time to time to prevent sticking. Add the vinegar and boil for a further 5 minutes.
3 Spoon the apple pulp into a jelly bag suspended over a large bowl and leave to drip through for at least 12 hours.
4 Discard any pulp remaining in the jelly bag. Measure the extract and return to the preserving pan with 450 g (1 lb) sugar for each 600 ml (1 pint) extract.
5 Heat gently, stirring, until the sugar has dissolved, then boil rapidly for about 10 minutes or until setting point is reached. Remove any scum with a slotted spoon.
6 Stir in the chopped mint and colouring, if using. Cool slightly, stir well to distribute the mint, then pot and cover in the usual way (see page 385).

NOTE It is not practicable to state the exact yield in jelly recipes because the ripeness of the fruit and the time allowed for dripping both affect the quantity of juice obtained. As a rough guide, for each 450 g (1 lb) sugar added, a yield of about 700 g (1½ lb) will result.

MARROW AND APRICOT JAM

PREPARATION TIME 10 minutes, plus soaking
COOKING TIME About 1 hour
FREEZING Not suitable
COLOUR INDEX Page 53

MAKES ABOUT 2.3 KG (5 LB)
- *900 g (2 lb) marrow, peeled, deseeded and cut into squares (prepared weight)*
- *225 g (8 oz) dried apricots, soaked overnight and drained*

40 CALS/15 ML (1 TBSP)
- *grated rind and juice of 2 lemons*
- *1.4 kg (3 lb) sugar*

1 Steam the marrow for about 15 minutes or until tender, then mash.
2 Put the apricots in a preserving pan with 900 ml (1½ pints) water and cook for about 30 minutes or until soft.
3 Add the marrow pulp to the apricots with the lemon rind, lemon juice and sugar. Heat gently until the sugar has dissolved, stirring to prevent sticking. Bring to the boil and boil rapidly for 15-20 minutes or until setting point is reached.
4 Remove any scum with a slotted spoon, then pot and cover in the usual way (see page 385).

NOTE For guidance on testing for setting point, see page 385.

SWEETCORN RELISH

PREPARATION TIME 15 minutes
COOKING TIME About 35 minutes
FREEZING Not suitable
COLOUR INDEX Page 53

MAKES ABOUT
2.3 KG (5 LB)
15 CALS/15 ML (1 TBSP)

- 6 corn cobs, trimmed, leaves and silk removed
- ½ a small white cabbage, roughly chopped
- 2 onions, peeled and halved
- 1½ red peppers, deseeded and quartered
- 10 ml (2 tsp) salt
- 30 ml (2 tbsp) white plain flour
- 2.5 ml (½ tsp) ground turmeric
- 175 g (6 oz) sugar
- 10 ml (2 tsp) mustard powder
- 600 ml (1 pint) distilled vinegar

1 Cook the corn cobs in boiling salted water for 3 minutes, then drain. Using a sharp knife, cut the corn from the cobs. Coarsely mince the cabbage, onions and red peppers and combine with the corn.
2 Blend the salt, flour, turmeric, sugar and mustard together in a saucepan, then gradually stir in the vinegar. Heat gently, stirring, until the sugar has dissolved, then bring to the boil. Reduce the heat, add the vegetables and simmer for 25-30 minutes, stirring occasionally.
3 Pot and cover in the usual way (see page 385).

DAMSON CHUTNEY

PREPARATION TIME 30 minutes
COOKING TIME 1½-2 hours
FREEZING Not suitable

MAKES ABOUT
1.8 KG (4 LB)
35 CALS/15 ML (1 TBSP)

- 1.6 kg (3½ lb) damsons, washed
- 2 onions, peeled and chopped
- 1 garlic clove, peeled and crushed
- 225 g (8 oz) seedless raisins, chopped
- 125 g (4 oz) stoned dates, chopped
- 700 g (1½ lb) dark soft brown sugar
- 1.4 litres (2½ pints) malt vinegar
- 15 g (½ oz) salt
- 25 g (1 oz) ground ginger
- 1.25 ml (¼ tsp) ground allspice

1 Mix all the ingredients together in a large saucepan. Heat gently, stirring, until the sugar has dissolved, then bring to the boil. Reduce the heat and simmer, uncovered, for 1½-2 hours, stirring occasionally, until no excess liquid remains and the mixture is thick. Scoop out the damson stones with a slotted spoon.
2 Pot and cover in the usual way (see page 385).

VARIATION If preferred, plums can be used instead of damsons.

Winter

With the arrival of the first frosts of winter, the cook naturally turns to comforting and sustaining dishes to help keep out the chill. Hearty casseroles, packed with seasonal root vegetables, and warming hot puddings are the order of the day. As Christmas approaches, the festive spirit takes over - now's the time to make exciting party food and Christmas treats. This creativity in the kitchen culminates in the grand turkey feast - one of the highlights of a busy season for the cook.

SOUPS AND STARTERS

FISH AND SHELLFISH

POULTRY AND GAME

Mustard-roasted Turkey
(page 334)

Oriental Turkey
(page 334)

Turkey, Apricot and Hazelnut
Pilaff
(page 335)

Roasted Pecan Chicken
(page 336)

Chicken Hotpot with Leeks
(page 337)

Chicken in Smoky Bacon Sauce
(page 337)

Sweet Gingered Chicken
(page 338)

Winter Chicken
(page 338)

Marinated Chicken with Prunes
(page 339)

Goose with Prune Stuffing
(page 340)

Duckling Breasts with Armagnac
(page 341)

Roast Duckling with Sherry
Vinegar
(page 341)

Crispy Chinese Duck with
Oriental Vegetables
(page 342)

Christmas Pheasant
(page 342)

Quails on Gnocchi with Cream
Sauce
(page 343)

MEAT

Spiced Rib of Beef
(page 344)

Beef Medallions with Stilton
Mousse
(page 345)

Festive Beef Casserole
(page 345)

Steak and Kidney Pudding
(page 346)

Classic Oxtail Casserole
(page 346)

Babotee
(page 347)

Fruity Lamb Casserole with
Spices
(page 348)

Honeyed Leg of Lamb with
Winter Vegetables
(page 348)

Lamb and Lentil Bake
(page 349)

Sautéed Liver with Orange and
Sage
(page 350)

Braised Ham with Madeira
(page 350)

Herby Rack of Pork with Roast
Vegetables
(page 351)

CHEESE AND EGGS

Golden Cheese and Spinach
Pudding
(page 352)

Stilton, Walnut and Bacon Flan
(page 352)

Sweet Potato and Leek Tortilla
(page 353)

PASTA AND NOODLES

Pasta with Tuna and Olive Sauce
(page 354)

Spaghetti with Clams
(page 354)

Linguine with Parma Ham and
Sun-dried Tomatoes
(page 355)

Creamy Pasta Bake
(page 356)

Roasted Vegetable and Pasta
Gratin
(page 356)

Pad Thai Noodles
(page 357)

VEGETARIAN DISHES

VEGETABLES AND SALADS

DESSERTS

BAKING

PRESERVES

To compensate for the cold and unfriendly weather outside, this is the time for warming, hearty food - dishes to comfort you through the chilly days and to bring a touch of warmth to the long, dark evenings.

Winter is also the season of giving and generosity, a time when family and friends get together to share food and drink in celebration of Christmas and the arrival of the New Year. So party food is definitely on the menu, too!

WINTER VEGETABLES

The seasonal vegetables are filling and nourishing, ideal for hearty bakes, roasts and casseroles.

Cabbages

Cabbages are at their best - Savoy cabbage is enjoyed for its bright colour and clean earthy flavour, while red cabbage adds texture and colour to satisfying casseroles. Curly kale, long neglected, is quite wonderful in thick soups or served as a vegetable dish, cooked lightly and tossed with lots of butter and black pepper.

Brussels Sprouts

Brussels sprouts are at their peak and provide the traditional accompaniment to the Christmas turkey. Take care not to overcook them - boil in salted water for 8-10 minutes until tender but still retaining their bite; or steam for about 15 minutes.
• For a tasty side dish, try tossing the hot, cooked sprouts in a dressing made with lemon juice and olive oil, flavoured with grated lemon rind, mustard and chopped parsley. Serve at once.
• For a nutty butter to serve with 1.4 kg (3 lb) Brussels sprouts, beat 75 g (3 oz) chopped toasted hazelnuts into 75 g (3 oz) softened unsalted butter, together with salt, pepper, nutmeg, 1 clove crushed garlic and the grated rind of 1 lemon.
• Top cooked sprouts with pieces of crisply-grilled streaky bacon and pared Parmesan cheese.

Root Vegetables

Traditional root vegetables, such as carrots, swedes, turnips, parsnips, Jerusalem artichokes and celeriac, are also at their prime at this time of year. They are delicious roughly mashed or finely puréed with butter or cream and plenty of salt, pepper, nutmeg or mace. Chopped fresh herbs add colour and flavour.

Sweet potatoes, especially the orange variety, make a great addition to stews, and are delicious roasted with sweet root vegetables such as parsnips

and carrots. They add a sweet nuttiness to mashed potato and are excellent puréed with fresh cooked chestnuts.

Try these easy ideas for seasonal root vegetables to give winter meals a lift.
• For extra-crunchy roast potatoes, parboil as usual, then toss in dried white breadrumbs and ground paprika before roasting. You will need 25 g (1 oz) breadcrumbs and a large pinch of paprika per 900 g (2 lb) potatoes.
• For glazed carrots with a difference, cook carrot sticks in boiling salted water for 5 minutes, then add halved kumquats (minus their pips). Cook for a further 5 minutes, then drain and toss in butter and pepper.
• Toss 700 g (1½ lb) cooked carrots or turnips in 15 ml (1 tbsp) clear honey with 15 ml (1 tbsp) lemon juice and sauté for 1 minute. Stir in 15 ml (1 tbsp) chopped fresh chives and plenty of seasoning.
• For creamed potato with celeriac, peel and slice 900 g (2 lb) potato and 450 g (1 lb) celeriac. Simmer in salted water with the juice of 1 lemon, for 25-30 minutes until tender, thcn mash. Return to a non-stick pan with 50 g (2 oz) butter, 30 ml (2 tbsp) milk and 30 ml (2 tbsp) roughly chopped watercress. Reheat, stirring all the time. Season and serve. This is delicious as a base for roast white fish fillets.
• Stir small cubes of Blue Brie into mashed potato a few minutes before serving.
• Slice root vegetables thinly and layer in a gratin dish, adding dots of butter between each layer. Pour in enough double cream and milk to cover, then season and bake at 180°C (350°F) mark 4 for about 1 hour until tender.

CHESTNUTS

Fresh chestnuts taste wonderful, but are time consuming to prepare. Try buying dried chestnuts from a good health-food shop or Italian delicatessen well before the festive season. These dried nuts are a great discovery - no boiling and peeling required, just cover with cold water and soak overnight, then use as described in a recipe.

Look out too for vacuum-packed ready-prepared chestnuts which come in tins and jars. These are expensive but handy if you are short of time.

Fresh Chestnuts

Fresh chestnuts only have a shelf life of one week, so buy near the day they are required, or prepare in advance, cook and freeze.

To peel chestnuts, make a tiny slit in the skin

A traditional meal of succulent roast turkey with all the trimmings is, for many, the high spot of Christmas Day.

near the pointed end, then cover with boiling water and leave for 5 minutes. Remove from the water, one at a time, and peel off the thick outer skin and thin inner skin while still warm.

To cook chestnuts, simmer the peeled nuts in unsalted water for 30-40 minutes. Alternatively, bake the nuts in their skins in the oven at 200°C (400°F) mark 6 for 20 minutes, then peel.

CITRUS FRUIT

Citrus fruits are abundant during the winter season, ranging from easy-peel and seedless varieties to new cross-varieties. They make a refreshing finish to a hearty winter meal.

January is the month for making marmalade with Seville oranges (see recipe page 381). Seville oranges make the clearest, sharpest marmalade and are in season in January and February. If you are pressed for time, freeze the oranges for making marmalade at a later date.

CHRISTMAS PLANNING

Christmas is the main festivity of this season. If you are entertaining, remember that you will need to make the Christmas cake (see page 376) and the pudding (see page 368) ahead of time. To make life easier, you can also make some of the accompaniments well in advance. For instance, Bread Sauce (see page 240), one of the traditional accompaniments to turkey, freezes well. Here are two more ideas for advance preparation.

Cranberry and apple relish This relish is an excellent accompaniment to roast turkey and can be made a week in advance. Peel, core and slice 350 g (12 oz) cooking apples. Place in a large saucepan with 225 g (8 oz) cranberries, 30 ml (2 tbsp) cider vinegar, 225 g (8 oz) demerara sugar, 2.5 ml (½ tsp) ground mixed spice and the grated rind of 1 orange. Simmer for 20 minutes or until the fruit is pulpy, stirring occasionally. Cool, cover and refrigerate for up to 1 week.

Whisky butter Whisky butter makes a delicious alternative to the traditional brandy butter for serving with Christmas pudding. Cream 125 g (4 oz) softened unsalted butter with 125 g (4 oz) light muscovado sugar until light and fluffy. Gradually beat in the grated rind and juice of 1 small orange, 1.25 ml (^{1}/$_{4}$ tsp) mixed spice, a pinch of ground green cardamom and 45 ml (3 tbsp) whisky. Spoon into a container, cover tightly and freeze or store in the refrigerator.

ROAST TURKEY

The main course of a traditional Christmas meal is turkey. Buy free-frange if possible, but if a frozen bird is your only option, make sure that the bird is thoroughly thawed before cooking. Leave the frozen turkey in the bag and thaw at cool room temperature, not in the refrigerator. Remove the giblets as soon as they are loose to make stock for the gravy. To ensure that the bird is completely thawed, check that there are no ice crystals in the cavity and that the legs are quite flexible. Cook as soon as possible, once thawed. For the general cooking method and timing see page 62.

Stuffing

Roast turkey is not complete without a good stuffing. As a general rule, allow about 225 g (8 oz) stuffing for each 2.3 kg (5 lb) dressed weight of bird and stuff just before cooking.

Classic chestnut stuffing For a 4.5-5.4 kg (9-12 lb) turkey. Mix 225 g (8 oz) pork sausagement with 225 g (8 oz) fresh brown breadcrumbs, 5 ml (1 tsp) fresh or dried thyme and salt and pepper. Roughly chop 440 g (15^{1}/$_{2}$ oz) can drained chestnuts, or 450 g (1 lb) peeled and cooked fresh chestnuts. Stir into the meat mixture. Place in a freezerproof container and freeze. To use, thaw and loosely stuff the neck end of the turkey only. Sew up the neck skin or use skewers to secure in place.

Gravy

Turkey gravy is all important. With so many trimmings you need a really tasty gravy to moisten the meat. If possible, make turkey stock from the giblets. Otherwise, make chicken stock in advance and reduce by half to increase the flavour.

• To make perfect gravy, lift the cooked turkey onto a warmed serving dish. Pour any liquid from the foil back into the tin. Tilt the tin to run the liquid into one corner. Spoon off all but 30 ml (2 tbsp) of the liquid fat, leaving the turkey juices behind. Place the tin over a low heat and add 30 ml (2 tbsp) flour. Stir in with a wooden spoon and cook for 1-2 minutes. Do not worry if it is lumpy at this stage. Slowly stir in 600 ml (1 pint) chicken or turkey stock. Bring to the boil, then simmer for 3-4

minutes or until the gravy is smooth and thin; whisk if necessary to make it quite smooth. Off the heat, add 30 ml (2 tbsp) dry sherry and season to taste. Strain into a warmed gravy boat and serve at once with the roast turkey.

CHRISTMAS GIFTS

Homemade food gifts will be much more appreciated than shop-bought presents, especially if they are gift-wrapped in pretty boxes or presented in glamorous twists of brightly coloured cellophane.

Chocolate Truffles

Chocolate truffles are rich and indulgent. Grate 225 g (8 oz) bitter, plain or milk chocolate into a small saucepan and add 75 ml (3 fl oz) double cream. Melt over a gentle heat, stir well, remove from the heat and cool to room temperature to thicken. Beat in 45 ml (3 tbsp) brandy, rum, orange liqueur, coffee liqueur, coconut liqueur or vanilla essence, then beat for about 5 minutes with an electric mixer until the mixture is light and fluffy and paler in colour. The mixture should stand in peaks when ready. Cover and chill until quite firm.

Sprinkle a tray with cocoa powder and place even-sized teaspoonfuls of truffle mixture on the tray. Dust your hands with a little cocoa powder and quickly roll the mixture into balls – make sure your hands are cool. Alternatively, roll in chopped nuts, chocolate vermicelli or grated chocolate. Place on waxed paper and refrigerate. The truffles can also be dipped in melted white or dark chocolate – freeze overnight before dipping.

These truffles will keep for about 4 days in the refrigerator. If giving them as a gift, don't forget to enclose a card with the 'eat by' details clearly marked!

Scented Sugars

Useful for adding delicate flavour to baked goods and desserts, scented sugars make excellent Christmas gifts. Simply choose from the flavourings given below and pack into attractive glass jars. Decorate with colourful ribbons.

• For vanilla sugar, split a half vanilla pod and bury in 225 g (8 oz) caster or granulated sugar.

• For spiced sugar, add 1 cinnamon stick, 2 cloves and 1 blade of mace to the sugar.

• For lavender sugar, use 5 ml (1 tsp) dried lavender heads in the sugar.

• For citrus sugar, dry the pared rind of 1 orange and 1 lemon in the lowest oven for about 40 minutes. Cool and add to the sugar.

Candied Peel

Candied peel is easy to make but the standing time is spread over 4-5 days. It is infinitely superior to bought peel and is much cheaper!

Scrub clean 2 oranges and 2 lemons and pat dry. Cut into quarters and remove the peel, then cut into strips, if wished. Simmer the peel in enough water to cover for 1½-2 hours until tender, topping up with boiling water. Add 50 g (2 oz) sugar per fruit, stir to dissolve and bring to the boil. Leave uncovered for 24 hours. Re-boil and simmer for 4 minutes and leave uncovered for another 24 hours. Bring to the boil again and simmer until almost all the syrup is absorbed. Drain and lay on a wire rack placed over greaseproof paper.

Dry in an airing cupboard for 2-3 days until no longer sticky. You can speed up this process by placing in a 110°C (225°F) mark ¼ oven for 12 hours, turning occasionally.

Pack between waxed paper in a cardboard box – do not use an airtight container otherwise the fruit may turn mouldy. Candied peel will keep for about 6 months.

Lovely gifts for Christmas – scented sugars, candied peel and rich Bûche de Noël (see page 378).

Chocolate Fudge

Easy to make and quite irresistible, fudge is a perfect Christmas gift. Place 450 g (1 lb) sugar in a large heavy-based saucepan with 150 ml (5 fl oz) milk, 150 g (5 oz) butter, 150 g (5 oz) plain chocolate and 50 g (2 oz) honey. Heat gently, stirring, until the sugar has dissolved. Bring to the boil without stirring, then continue boiling until a temperature of 115°C (240°F) is reached on a sugar thermometer, stirring occasionally. Stand on a cool surface for 5 minutes, then beat until thick and beginning to 'grain'. Pour into a lightly oiled 18 cm (7 inch) shallow square tin; mark into squares when almost set. Cut when cold.

• For vanilla fudge, reduce the butter to 75 g (3 oz) and use 175 g (6 oz) can evaporated milk instead of the chocolate and honey. Boil as above, then remove from the heat, add 2.5 ml (½ tsp) vanilla essence and beat until thick. Pour into the tin and mark into squares.

GINGERBREAD CASKET

A little treasure chest made of gingerbread is a novel twist on a traditional gingerbread house. It also makes an original way of serving biscuits, sweets or nuts.

For a shiny finish, brush the dough with egg white before baking. The casket is held together with royal icing. Either use chocolate icing or tint white icing with brown food colouring.

Gingerbread is traditionally decorated with cloves. Painted with edible gold paint after baking, they give the chest a realistic studded look.

You will need:
1 quantity of Craft Gingerbread dough (see below)
Thin card for templates
Large sharp knife
Non-stick baking parchment
Baking sheets
Cloves and star anise
Brown royal icing
Icing bag
Gold tassel and wooden stick

CRAFT GINGERBREAD
Place 175 g (6 oz) soft brown sugar in a sauccpan with 60 ml (4 tbsp) golden syrup, 30 ml (2 tbsp) black treacle, 30 ml (2 tbsp) water, 5 ml (1 tsp) grated nutmeg and 10 ml (2 tsp) each ground cinnamon and ginger. Heat gently until sugar has melted. Remove from the heat, add 200 g (7 oz) butter and 5 ml (1 tsp) bicarbonate of soda, then stir in 450 g (1 lb) plain flour to make a stiff dough. Turn out and knead into a ball and leave to cool for 1 hour. Roll out.

1 Cut templates for two sides 11 x 8 cm (4$^{1}/_{2}$ x 3$^{1}/_{4}$ inches), a front and back 16 x 8 cm (6$^{1}/_{2}$ x 3$^{1}/_{4}$ inches), a base 16 x 12 cm (6$^{1}/_{2}$ x 4$^{3}/_{4}$ inches) and a lid 16 x 14 cm (6$^{1}/_{2}$ x 5$^{1}/_{2}$ inches). Also cut two arched sides pieces for lid. Lay on the rolled-out dough and cut around.
2 Transfer the dough pieces to lined baking sheets. Allow room for spreading. Decorate with cloves and star anise. Bake at 180°C (350°F) mark 4 until just cooked and lightly browned.

3 Trim the edges while still warm, using the templates as a guide. Immediately place the lid on a curved surface to dry.
4 When the pieces are cold, assemble the casket – pipe royal icing along the edges and stick together, supporting the pieces until set. Attach a gold tassel to the lid with icing. Prop the lid open on a wooden stick.

GIFT-WRAPPED SWEETS

Fancy wrappings make the simplest gift look outstanding. Here inexpensive sweets and chocolates are wrapped up in stylish cellophane and presented in pretty boxes.

Look out for transparent cellophane in iridescent colours to bundle up sugared almonds, marshmallows or Turkish Delight. Tie up the little parcels with dainty ribbons to complement the colour theme. Save a collection of small boxes that can be re-lined or covered with giftwrap or handmade paper to hold sweets or chocolates.

You will need:
Small boxes, covered or
  uncovered
Giftwrap or handmade papers
  for covering boxes
Shallow basket
Shredded tissue paper
Metallic foil paper
White paper
Selection of sweets, such as
  Turkish Delight, marshmallow
  twists, sugared almonds in
  silver, white, turquoise and
  pink
Cellophane
White chocolate truffles
Soft, gauzy ribbon
Leaf-print labels

• Cover and line small boxes with giftwrap or handmade papers.
• To line a small round box, cut a band of thin white paper, twice as long as its circumference and slightly deeper than the sides, fold it concertina fashion and fit it round the inside of the box. Trim the collar into zigzag points to make a decorative edging.
• Cut circles or squares of cellophane and pile a few sugared almonds into the centre.

Tie the bundles up tightly at the top with ribbon and arrange them in a pretty box or shallow basket to give as a present.
• Line a basket with shredded tissue paper, then arrange chocolate truffles on top. Tie a big ribbon bow on the handle or around the rim.
• Wind a wide ribbon around a box with a lid and tie it off in a large bow.
• Attach labels to perishable sweets and chocolates, such as fresh cream truffles, giving an eat-by date.

CHRISTMAS MARZIPAN TREE

A little Christmas tree decorated with marzipan fruits and colourful baubles forms a cheerful centrepiece for a Christmas dinner table or on a window sill. The tree lasts particularly well when it is made from sprigs of blue spruce.

The fruits are modelled from either bought or homemade coloured marzipan and are so easy to make that children can have great fun helping to make them. You can choose a colour scheme that fits in with the other decorations in the room.

You will need:
Pink, green, white and yellow
    marzipan
Cloves
Wooden kebab sticks
Pot to stand the tree in
Green florist's foam
Plastic-coated wire netting
Paper for template
Secateurs or wire cutters
Stiff florist's wires
1 wooden houseplant stake
Branch of blue spruce
Christmas tree baubles

1 Mould the marzipan into fruit. Press cloves into the fruit as stems and calyces. Leave to dry, then spear onto sticks.

3 Pack the pot with foam and push in the pyramid stake. Cut sprigs of spruce and stick into pyramid to make a conical tree.

2 Cut pieces of foam to stack into a pyramid. Using a template, trim wire netting into a cone. Wrap around the foam and push in central stake.

4 When the tree is complete, push the sticks of fruits into the foam. Then tie the baubles onto the tree, spacing them evenly among the fruit.

PLAITED BREAD RING

A circular bread plait, baked until a rich golden brown, makes a lovely base for a ring of candles. The invitingly edible looking plait makes a particularly good dinner-table decoration, adding soft lines and golden tones to the table setting. The candles, with their defined shape, stand out strikingly against the natural curves of the plait, while the flickering flames enhance the mellow colouring of the bread crust.

Bread dough is excellent for modelling, being very flexible when raw and easy to carve into once baked. It's also surprisingly simple to make - just follow the bread recipe on page 384, up to stage 3.

You will need:
3 quantity Wholemeal Bread dough (see page 384)
Small pointed knife
Pastry brush
Apple corer
Beaten egg for glazing
8-10 white candles

1 Cut off one quarter of the kneaded dough and reserve for the decoration. Divide the remaining dough into three and shape into long rolls, making sure they are the same length.
2 Pinch the rolls together at one end and plait loosely. Shape into a ring and pinch the ends together.
3 Make the 'bunch of grapes' decoration using the reserved

dough. Roll small balls to represent the grapes and cut out simple, flat leaf shapes. Arrange the decorations in groups on the dough, sticking them in place by brushing the dough with water.
4 Cut holes for the candles with an apple corer. Brush the ring with beaten egg to glaze.
5 Bake the ring at 220° C (425° F) mark 7 for 20 minutes. Reduce the temperature to 180° C (350° F) mark 4 and bake for a further 15 minutes.
6 While still warm, trim the holes to fit the candles. When cold, slot the candles in place.
7 Remember to watch out that the candles do not burn down too far.

JERUSALEM ARTICHOKE AND PARMESAN SOUP

PREPARATION TIME 15 minutes
COOKING TIME 25 minutes
FREEZING Suitable

♡ ✳

SERVES 6

- *50 g (2 oz) butter*
- *2 shallots, peeled and diced*
- *5 ml (1 tsp) mild curry paste*
- *450 g (1 lb) Jerusalem artichokes, scrubbed clean and thinly sliced*
- *900 ml (1½ pints) chicken or vegetable stock*
- *150 ml (5 fl oz) single cream (or milk for a less rich soup)*
- *freshly grated nutmeg, to taste*

190 CALS/SERVING

- *pinch of cayenne pepper*
- *60 ml (4 tbsp) freshly grated Parmesan cheese*
- *salt and pepper*
  PARMESAN TOAST
- *3-4 slices day-old softgrain white bread*
- *a little freshly grated Parmesan cheese, for sprinkling*
- *1.25 ml (¼ tsp) paprika*

1 Melt the butter in a large saucepan and add the shallots. Cook gently for 5 minutes until soft and golden. Stir in the curry paste and cook for 1 minute. Add the sliced artichokes and stock; stir well. Bring to the boil, cover and simmer for about 15 minutes or until the artichokes are tender.

2 Meanwhile, make the Parmesan toast. Toast the bread lightly on both sides. Quickly cut off the crusts and split each slice in two. Scrape off any doughy bits, then sprinkle with Parmesan and paprika. Place on a baking sheet and bake in the oven at 180°C (350°F) mark 4 for 10-15 minutes or until uniformly golden.

3 Add the cream, nutmeg and cayenne to the soup. Transfer to a blender or food processor and work until smooth, then pass through a sieve into a clean saucepan. Reheat the soup and stir in the Parmesan cheese. Taste and adjust the seasoning. Serve at once, with the hot toast.

VARIATION Replace the Jerusalem artichokes with 1 large cauliflower. Cut away the leaves and core, and discard. Divide the cauliflower into florets. Add to the shallots with the stock and bring to the boil. Simmer for about 10 minutes or until very soft, then continue as in stage 3.

CREAMY CARROT AND CELERIAC SOUP

PREPARATION TIME 15 minutes
COOKING TIME 45 minutes
FREEZING Suitable (stage 3)
COLOUR INDEX Page 8
♡ ✳

SERVES 6
- *30 ml (2 tbsp) vegetable oil*
- *225 g (8 oz) onions, peeled and roughly chopped*
- *900 g (2 lb) carrots, peeled and roughly chopped*
- *900 g (2 lb) celeriac, peeled and roughly chopped*
- *1.7 litres (3 pints) chicken stock*

200 CALS/SERVING
- *5 ml (1 tsp) soy sauce*
- *finely grated rind and juice of 1 orange*
- *300 ml (10 fl oz) single cream*
- *salt and pepper*
- *croûtons and flat-leaf parsley, to garnish*

1 Heat the oil in a large saucepan and add the vegetables. Sauté for 5 minutes, stirring frequently. Add the chicken stock and bring to the boil. Cover and then leave to simmer gently for 20 minutes.
2 Stir in the soy sauce, orange rind and 60 ml (4 tbsp) orange juice. Cover and simmer for 20 minutes.
3 Cool slightly, then blend in a food processor until smooth. For an extra-velvety texture, push through a sieve.
4 Stir in the cream and warm gently. Season to taste and serve garnished with croûtons and parsley.

SPICED DAL SOUP

PREPARATION TIME 10 minutes, plus soaking
COOKING TIME 1½ hours
FREEZING Suitable
COLOUR INDEX Page 9
♡ ✳

SERVES 4-6
- *125 g (4 oz) yellow split peas*
- *5 ml (1 tsp) cumin seeds*
- *10 ml (2 tsp) coriander seeds*
- *3 dried red chillies*
- *15 ml (1 tbsp) desiccated unsweetened coconut*
- *30 ml (2 tbsp) ghee or vegetable oil*

200-130 CALS/SERVING
- *225 g (8 oz) tomatoes, skinned and roughly chopped*
- *2.5 ml (½ tsp) ground turmeric*
- *5 ml (1 tsp) treacle*
- *5 ml (1 tsp) salt*
- *coriander sprigs and lemon slices, to garnish*

1 Put the split peas into a sieve and wash thoroughly under cold running water. Drain well, then transfer to a bowl, cover with cold water and soak for 8 hours. Drain, place in a large saucepan, cover with 600 ml (1 pint) water and boil rapidly for 10 minutes. Cover and simmer for at least 1 hour, or until tender.
2 Finely grind the cumin, coriander, chillies and coconut in a small electric mill or with a pestle and mortar. Heat the ghee or oil in a heavy-based frying pan, add the spice mixture and fry, stirring, for 30 seconds. Set aside.
3 Mash the split peas and transfer to a large saucepan. Stir in the tomatoes, fried spices, turmeric, treacle, salt and 300 ml (10 fl oz) water.
4 Bring to the boil, then lower the heat, cover and simmer for about 20 minutes. Taste and adjust the seasoning and turn into a warmed serving dish. Garnish with coriander sprigs and lemon slices.

> ### TIP
> Poppadoms make an excellent accompaniment to this soup. To cook poppadoms, either fry for a few seconds in vegetable oil or brush with oil and grill for a few seconds on each side.

NAN BREAD WITH SPICY PRAWNS

PREPARATION TIME 20 minutes
COOKING TIME About 15 minutes
FREEZING Not suitable
COLOUR INDEX Page 10

MAKES ABOUT 60

- *15 ml (1 tbsp) vegetable oil*
- *1 garlic clove, peeled and crushed*
- *10 ml (2 tsp) mild curry powder*
- *4 spring onions, finely chopped*
- *350 g (12 oz) cooked peeled prawns, roughly chopped*

25 CALS/SQUARE

- *20 ml (4 tsp) mango chutney*
- *20 ml (4 tsp) natural yogurt*
- *salt and pepper*
- *2 large nan bread, about 300 g (10 oz) total weight*

1 Heat the oil in a frying pan and add the garlic, curry powder and onions. Cook for 1 minute, stirring, then add the prawns. Cook gently for a further 2-3 minutes. Off the heat, stir in the chutney and yogurt. Season to taste and set aside.
2 Heat the nan bread in the oven according to packet instructions, then cut into small squares and top with a little of the prawn mixture. Serve warm or cold.

LITTLE SPANISH SAVOURIES

PREPARATION TIME 30 minutes, plus pastry
COOKING TIME 10 minutes
FREEZING Suitable (stage 2)

❋

MAKES ABOUT 24

- *225 g (8 oz) Puff Pastry (see page 383)*
- *butter for greasing*
- *125 g (4 oz) firm goats' cheese or mozzarella, diced*
- *50 g (2 oz) sun-dried tomatoes in oil, drained and roughly chopped*

65 CALS/SAVOURY

- *50 g (2 oz) capers, chopped*
- *50 g (2 oz) can anchovy fillets, chopped*
- *50 g (2 oz) pitted olives, quartered*
- *50 g (2 oz) pesto sauce*
- *salt and pepper*

1 Roll out the pastry to 3 mm (⅛ inch) thick. Stamp out 24 circles with a 5 cm (2 inch) cutter and place on a greased baking sheet.
2 Top with the cheese, sun-dried tomatoes, capers, anchovies and olives. Spoon pesto sauce over and season with salt and pepper.
3 Cook at 200°C (400°F) mark 6 for 10-15 minutes or until crisp. Serve hot.

SMOKED SALMON ROULADE

PREPARATION TIME 30 minutes, plus chilling
FREEZING Not suitable

MAKES 70 ROUNDS
- *1 large bunch watercress*
- *225 g (8 oz) full-fat soft cheese with garlic and herbs*
- *10 ml (2 tsp) lemon juice*

20 CALS/ROUND
- *black pepper*
- *225 g (8 oz) smoked salmon*
- *lemon wedges, to garnish*

1 Finely chop the watercress, discarding any coarse stalks. Using an electric whisk, mix the watercress into the soft cheese with the lemon juice and plenty of black pepper.
2 Cut out a piece of greaseproof paper measuring 30 x 33 cm (12 x 13 inches). Lay the pieces of smoked salmon on top, overlapping each piece slightly to form a rectangle of about 30 x 28 cm (12 x 11 inches). Cut in half widthways to make two rectangles.
3 Spread the soft-cheese mixture over both rectangles, then carefully roll each one into a thin sausage, using the paper to help you. Cover and refrigerate overnight.
4 Cut each roll into 5 mm (¼ inch) slices and serve immediately, garnished with wedges of lemon.

NUTTY CHICKEN BITES

PREPARATION TIME 40 minutes, plus marinating
COOKING TIME About 15 minutes
FREEZING Not suitable

MAKES ABOUT 70
- *900 g (2 lb) skinless chicken breast fillets*
- *125 g (4 oz) onion, peeled and finely chopped*
- *90 ml (6 tbsp) dark soy sauce*
- *50 ml (10 tsp) dark muscovado sugar*
DIP
- *15 ml (1 tbsp) vegetable oil*

115 CALS/ BITE WITH DIP
- *2 garlic cloves, peeled and crushed*
- *5 ml (1 tsp) mild curry powder*
- *10-15 ml (2-3 tsp) mild chilli powder*
- *450 g (1 lb) crunchy peanut butter*
- *pinch of salt*
- *½ cucumber*

1 Beat out the chicken breasts between sheets of greaseproof paper. Cut into 2.5 cm (1 inch) pieces.
2 Mix the onion with the soy sauce and 20 ml (4 tsp) sugar. Pour over the chicken and toss well. Cover and refrigerate overnight.
3 Meanwhile, make the dip. Heat the oil in a pan and add the garlic, curry and chilli powders. Cook for 1-2 minutes, then add the peanut butter, salt and remaining sugar with 450 ml (15 fl oz) water. Simmer for 5 minutes, stirring, until thick.
4 Thread the chicken onto cocktail sticks. Cook at 220°C (425°F) mark 7 for 10 minutes until cooked through. Cut the cucumber into 1 cm (½ inch) pieces and thread onto the sticks. Serve with the cold dip.

VEGETABLE SAMOSAS

PREPARATION TIME 45 minutes, plus cooling
COOKING TIME About 35 minutes
FREEZING Suitable
❄

MAKES 24

- *450 g (1 lb) potatoes, peeled and halved*
- *salt and pepper*
- *15 ml (1 tbsp) vegetable oil*
- *1 onion, peeled and finely chopped*
- *1 garlic clove, peeled and crushed*
- *1-2 hot green chillies, deseeded and chopped*
- *10 ml (2 tsp) ground coriander*
- *10 ml (2 tsp) cumin seeds*
- *5 ml (1 tsp) ground fenugreek*
- *1 large ripe tomato, chopped*

150 CALS/SAMOSA

- *50 g (2 oz) frozen peas*
- *30 ml (2 tbsp) chopped fresh coriander*
- *15 ml (1 tbsp) chopped fresh mint*
- *oil for deep-frying*
- *mint sprigs and lime halves, to garnish*

PASTRY
- *450 g (1 lb) white plain flour*
- *5 ml (1 tsp) salt*
- *45 ml (3 tbsp) chopped fresh coriander (optional)*
- *60 ml (4 tbsp) vegetable oil, melted ghee or butter*

1 Cook the potatoes in boiling salted water until just tender. Drain and chop into fairly small pieces.
2 Heat the oil in a frying pan, add the onion and garlic and cook for about 5 minutes until softened. Add the spices and cook for 2 minutes, stirring continuously.

3 Add the tomato to the pan and simmer until softened. Add the potatoes and stir to coat in the spice mixture. Add the peas and cook for 1-2 minutes until thawed. Add the herbs and plenty of seasoning, then allow to cool.
4 To make the pastry, mix the flour with the salt and herbs, if using, in a bowl. Add the oil or melted fat and enough warm water to make a soft dough - about 200 ml (7 fl oz). Turn onto a lightly floured surface and knead for about 5 minutes.
5 Divide the dough into 12 pieces; keep covered with a damp cloth to prevent drying out. Roll one piece out to a 15 cm (6 inch) round and cut in half to make two semi-circles. Place a heaped teaspoon of filling on each semi-circle. Dampen the edges, fold over the filling and press together to seal. Repeat with the remaining pastry and filling.
6 Heat the oil in a deep-fat fryer to 180°C (350°F). Test the temperature by dropping a small piece of pastry into the oil - the pastry should sizzle immediately on contact and rise to the surface.
7 Deep-fry the samosas, about three at a time, for 3-5 minutes or until pale golden brown. Drain on crumpled absorbent kitchen paper. Serve warm, garnished with mint and lime halves.

VARIATION *Meat samosas* Omit the potato. After frying the spices, add 175 g (6 oz) minced lamb or beef and fry until browned. Add 5-10 ml (1-2 tsp) curry paste and a few spoonfuls of water, and cook for about 20 minutes or until the meat is tender. Add the peas and cook for 2 minutes. Cool and complete as above.

TIP
Make a quick chutney to accompany the samosas. Peel and finely slice a few spring onions, mix with a little crushed garlic, then toss with freshly torn mint and coriander leaves, a splash of lemon juice, a dash of oil and plenty of seasoning.

CARPACCIO OF SALMON

PREPARATION TIME 20 minutes
FREEZING Not suitable
COLOUR INDEX Page 11
♡ ⏲

SERVES 10

- *575 g (1¼ lb) salmon fillet, skinned*
- *125 ml (4 fl oz) olive oil*
- *225 g (8 oz) tomatoes, skinned, deseeded and finely chopped*
- *1 bunch fresh chives or spring onions, cut into long pieces*

200 CALS/SERVING

- *juice of 2 limes*
- *salt and pepper*
- *lime wedges, to garnish*
- *slices of brown bread and butter, to serve*

1 Cut the salmon into 20 slices. Bat out thinly between sheets of oiled clingfilm. It should be the thickness of sliced smoked salmon.
2 Mix the tomatoes and chives or spring onions with the lime juice, olive oil and seasoning.
3 Just before serving, arrange the salmon on individual serving plates and spoon the dressing over. Garnish with lime wedges and serve with slices of brown bread and butter.

VARIATION If the idea of eating raw salmon doesn't really appeal to you, serve the same quantity of sliced smoked salmon instead. Alternatively, place the thin salmon slices in single layers in ovenproof dishes and cook in the oven at 220°C (425°F) mark 7 for about 5 minutes or until the salmon just turns opaque. Serve warm, garnished with lime.

GRILLED PEPPER AND AUBERGINE SALAD

PREPARATION TIME 20 minutes
COOKING TIME 10 minutes
FREEZING Not suitable
♡ ⏲

SERVES 4

- *30 ml (2 tbsp) French dressing*
- *15 ml (1 tbsp) extra-virgin olive oil*
- *2 small, fat aubergines, cut into slices*
- *2 large, long red peppers*

120 CALS/SERVING

- *10 ml (2 tsp) lemon juice*
- *30 ml (2 tbsp) chopped fresh basil*
- *1 garlic clove, peeled and thinly sliced*
- *salt and pepper*
- *fresh basil leaves, to garnish*

1 Mix together the French dressing and olive oil. Brush the aubergine slices with the dressing mixture and then grill with the whole peppers until blackened all over, turning the aubergine slices and brushing with more dressing. Put them in a bowl and immediately cover with a damp tea towel. Leave until cool enough to handle.
2 Remove the charred skins from the peppers and cut lengthways into quarters, removing the core and seeds and reserving any juices in a bowl. Stir the remaining cooking juices from the grill pan into the bowl, then add the lemon juice, basil and garlic. Season with salt and pepper. Drizzle the mixture over the vegetables. Serve at room temperature, garnished with basil leaves.

FISH PLAKI WITH ROOT VEGETABLES

PREPARATION TIME 15 minutes, plus cooling
COOKING TIME 35-45 minutes
FREEZING Suitable
COLOUR INDEX Page 13
♡ ❄

SERVES 4

- *45 ml (3 tbsp) olive oil*
- *2 onions, peeled and sliced*
- *2 garlic cloves, peeled and crushed*
- *2 carrots, peeled, halved lengthways and sliced*
- *225 g (8 oz) celeriac, peeled and diced*
- *salt and pepper*
- *3 plum tomatoes, skinned, deseeded and diced*

290 CALS/SERVING

- *1 lemon, sliced*
- *15 ml (1 tbsp) chopped fresh thyme*
- *75 ml (3 fl oz) dry white wine*
- *4 cod or tuna fish steaks, each weighing about 150 g (5 oz)*
- *45 ml (3 tbsp) chopped fresh parsley, to garnish*

1 Heat the oil in a large shallow saucepan, add the onions and cook over moderate heat for 5 minutes until softened and beginning to brown. Add the garlic, carrots and celeriac and cook for 8 minutes, stirring occasionally.

2 Stir in 150 ml (5 fl oz) water and season with salt and pepper to taste. Cover and simmer for 10-15 minutes, until the carrot and celeriac are very tender. Add the tomatoes, sliced lemon and thyme and simmer for 2-3 minutes. Add the wine.

3 Place the fish steaks in the sauce, cover and cook over a low heat for 10-15 minutes until the fish is cooked and flakes easily. Leave to cool for about 15 minutes, then sprinkle with the parsley to garnish and serve warm.

COD IN ORANGE AND CIDER SAUCE

PREPARATION TIME 15 minutes
COOKING TIME 25-30 minutes
FREEZING Suitable
COLOUR INDEX Page 13
♡ ❄

SERVES 4

- *4 cod fillets, skinned, each weighing about 175 g (6 oz)*
- *1 orange*
- *175 g (6 oz) onion, peeled and chopped*
- *black pepper*
- *150 ml (5 fl oz) medium-dry cider*

160 CALS/SERVING

- *125 ml (4 fl oz) fish stock*
- *10 ml (2 tsp) chopped fresh coriander*
- *coriander sprigs and orange slices, to garnish*

1 Place the fish in a 1.1 litre (2 pint) ovenproof dish. Pare the rind from the orange and cut into 7.5 cm (3 inch) long thin strips. Place on top of the fish with the onion and season with black pepper.

2 Mix 30 ml (2 tbsp) orange juice with the cider and fish stock. Pour over the fish, cover and bake in the oven at 190°C (375°F) mark 5 for 20-25 minutes or until the fish is cooked through.

3 Carefully place the onion, orange strips and fish in a serving dish and keep them warm.

4 Strain the cooking liquid into a small saucepan and boil rapidly for about 5 minutes or until the liquid is reduced by half. Pour over the fish and sprinkle with the coriander. Garnish with coriander sprigs and orange slices and serve immediately.

KEDGEREE WITH LENTILS

PREPARATION TIME 15 minutes
COOKING TIME About 45 minutes
FREEZING Not suitable

♡

SERVES 6

- 75 g (3 oz) green
  lentils, rinsed in cold
  water and drained
- 450 g (1 lb) smoked
  haddock fillets
- 300 ml (10 fl oz)
  milk
- 1 onion, peeled and
  sliced
- 175 g (6 oz) basmati
  or long-grain rice
- 10 ml (2 tsp)
  coriander seeds

305 CALS/SERVING

- 2 cloves
- 2 cardamom pods
- 15 ml (1 tbsp)
  vegetable oil
- finely grated rind
  and juice of 1 lime
- 2 eggs, hard-boiled
  and cut into wedges
- chopped fresh
  coriander or parsley
  and lime slices, to
  garnish

1 Put the lentils in a pan with enough cold water
to cover generously. Bring to the boil and boil
vigorously for 10 minutes, then simmer for about
15 minutes or until tender. Set on one side.

2 Meanwhile, put the smoked haddock into a
wide saucepan, pour the milk over and add the
onion. Bring to the boil and cook, covered, for 20-
25 minutes, depending on the thickness of the fish,
until the flesh flakes easily. Set on one side.

3 Rinse the rice several times in cold water to
remove the starch.

4 Crush the coriander seeds, cloves and cardamom
pods. Heat the oil in a large saucepan, and add
the spices. Cook for 1 minute, then add the rice.
Stir until the grains are coated in oil, then add
600 ml (1 pint) water. Bring to the boil and
simmer gently, covered, for about 20 minutes,
until the rice is tender.

5 Remove the fish skin and flake the flesh.

6 Add the lime juice and rind to the rice. Stir in
the eggs. Drain the lentils and add to the rice with
the fish. Reheat briefly, stirring. To serve, sprinkle
with coriander or parsley and garnish with lime.

blended. Add the remaining spinach and blend. Season to taste. Arrange the fish on plates, spoon over the sauce and garnish with lime

FISH WITH LEMON AND GINGER

PREPARATION TIME 20 minutes, plus marinating
COOKING TIME 20-25 minutes
FREEZING Not suitable
COLOUR INDEX Page 14
♡

LEMON SOLE WITH SPINACH AND LIME HOLLANDAISE

PREPARATION TIME 15 minutes
COOKING TIME 20 minutes
FREEZING Not suitable

SERVES 4   **680 CALS/SERVING**
- oil for brushing
- 4 lemon sole, each weighing 225 g (8 oz)
- 45 ml (3 tbsp) wine vinegar
- 4 black peppercorns
- 4 egg yolks
- 250 g (9 oz) unsalted butter, melted
- 10 ml (2 tsp) lime juice
- grated rind of ½ lime
- 50 g (2 oz) young spinach leaves
- salt and pepper
- lime wedges, to garnish

1 Lightly oil a baking tray. Place the fish on the tray in a single layer, with the brown sides uppermost. Brush with oil.
2 Place the fish under a hot grill, about 10-15 cm (4-6 inches) from the heat source, and cook for 15-20 minutes, without turning.
3 Meanwhile, boil the vinegar and peppercorns in a heavy-based saucepan until reduced to 22 ml (1½ tbsp). Remove from the heat, then lift out and discard the peppercorns. Place the egg yolks in a blender and process for 1-2 minutes. Keeping the machine running, add the reduced vinegar, then very slowly add the hot melted butter, adding at intervals the lime juice, lime rind and 30 ml (2 tbsp) hot water.
4 Add half the spinach and process until well

SERVES 6   **295 CALS/SERVING**
- 5 ml (1 tsp) garam masala or curry powder
- 5 cm (2 inch) piece fresh root ginger, peeled and finely chopped
- 2 garlic cloves, peeled and crushed
- 12 sole fillets, skinned, about 1.1 kg (2½ lb) total weight
- 175 g (6 oz) spring onions, chopped
- 45 ml (3 tbsp) chopped fresh coriander
- finely grated rind and juice of 1 lemon
- salt and pepper
- 50 g (2 oz) creamed coconut
- 2.5 ml (½ tsp) saffron strands
- 25 g (1 oz) salted cashew nuts
- 15 ml (1 tbsp) vegetable oil
- 150 ml (5 fl oz) single cream
- fresh coriander, spring onions and lime slices, to garnish

1 Mix together the garam masala, ginger and garlic. Place the sole fillets in a flat, non-metallic dish and rub over with the spice mixture. Cover tightly and marinate in the refrigerator overnight.
2 Mix half the spring onions with the coriander, lemon rind, 45 ml (3 tbsp) lemon juice and seasoning. Place the fillets, skinned-sides up, on a plate and spoon a little of the onion mixture into the centre of each one. Roll up and secure with a cocktail stick.
3 In a food processor, blend the coconut, saffron and cashew nuts with 200 ml (7 fl oz) water.
4 Heat the oil in a large shallow flameproof casserole and fry the remaining spring onions for 2-3 minutes. Add the coconut liquid and fish with any remaining marinade. Bring to the boil, cover and simmer very gently for 15-20 minutes or until the fish is cooked but still tender.
5 Add the cream and heat gently without boiling for 2-3 minutes. Season, garnish and serve hot.

NORMANDY SKATE WITH CAPER SAUCE

PREPARATION TIME 5 minutes
COOKING TIME 15-20 minutes
FREEZING Not suitable

♡ ⏲

SERVES 4

- *4 pieces of skate wing, each weighing about 200 g (7 oz)*
- *1 celery stick*
- *2 shallots, peeled and roughly chopped*
- *2 bay leaves*
- *5 ml (1 tsp) black peppercorns*
- *75 ml (5 tbsp) cider vinegar*

330 CALS/SERVING

- *10 ml (2 tsp) capers, chopped*
- *150 ml (5 fl oz) double cream*
- *30 ml (2 tbsp) chopped fresh parsley*
- *salt and pepper*
- *parsley sprigs, to garnish*

1 Ask your fishmonger to skin the skate wings if necessary, and cut to the right portion size.
2 Break the celery stick into 3 or 4 pieces. Put them into a large saucepan with the shallots, bay leaves, peppercorns and 60 ml (4 tbsp) of the cider vinegar. Add 1.1 litres (2 pints) cold water, slide in the skate and slowly bring to just below the boil.
3 Cover the pan, lower the heat and cook for 7-10 minutes, until the skate flesh just parts from the central cartilaginous layer.
4 While the fish is cooking, put the capers into a small pan with the cream. Stir in the parsley and season with salt and pepper. Bring to the boil, lower the heat and simmer for 1 minute. Take off the heat and stir in the remaining vinegar. Check the seasoning.
5 Lift the skate from the poaching liquor onto warmed serving plates. Spoon on the cream sauce and garnish with parsley sprigs. Serve immediately.

NOTE Drain the skate scrupulously as you lift it from the poaching liquor and flick off any flavouring debris adhering to the fish.

SALMON PIE WITH PARMESAN CRUST

PREPARATION TIME 30 minutes, plus chilling
COOKING TIME About 55 minutes
FREEZING Suitable

❄

SERVES 8

- *225 g (8 oz) butter*
- *50 g (2 oz) onion, peeled and finely chopped*
- *400 g (14 oz) white plain flour*
- *450 ml (15 fl oz) fish stock*
- *150 ml (5 fl oz) dry white wine*
- *900 g (2 lb) salmon fillet, skinned and cut into chunks*

720 CALS/SERVING

- *225 g (8 oz) queen scallops (optional)*
- *125 g (4 oz) Gruyère cheese*
- *salt and pepper*
- *75 g (3 oz) freshly grated Parmesan cheese*
- *1 egg, beaten*
- *beaten egg, to glaze*
- *chopped fresh herbs, to garnish (optional)*

1 Melt 50 g (2 oz) butter in a medium saucepan. Sauté the onion, stirring, for 5-6 minutes or until softened but not coloured.
2 Off the heat, stir in 50 g (2 oz) flour, the stock and wine. Bring to the boil, stirring, then simmer for 3-4 minutes until thickened. Remove from the heat, and allow to cool slightly.
3 Add the salmon, the scallops (if using) and the Gruyère cheese. Season to taste, then turn into a 1.7 litre (3 pint) shallow, ovenproof dish and leave to cool.

4 Rub the remaining butter into the rest of the flour, then stir in the Parmesan. Add the beaten egg and 45-60 ml (3-4 tbsp) cold water. Bind the pastry together with your hands, adding extra water, if necessary.
5 Turn out onto a floured surface and knead lightly until smooth. Cover and chill for about 15 minutes.
6 Roll out the pastry and cover the filling, pressing the edges down well. Trim any excess pastry and re-roll.
7 Cut out holly leaves from the trimmings. Brush the pie with beaten egg and cover with the leaves. Brush with egg again, then chill for 15-20 minutes.
8 Bake at 190°C (375°F) mark 5 for 45-50 minutes or until crisp, covering loosely with foil if necessary. Serve immediately, sprinkling herbs over each serving, if wished.

ROAST SALMON IN MUSTARD BUTTER

PREPARATION TIME 10 minutes
COOKING TIME 20 minutes
FREEZING Not suitable
COLOUR INDEX Page 15

🕐

SERVES 6

- *1.1 kg (2½ lb) piece of boned middle cut of salmon*
- *175 g (6 oz) butter, melted*
- *45 ml (3 tbsp) wholegrain mustard*

560 CALS/SERVING

- *20 ml (4 tsp) dried dill*
- *salt and pepper*
- *300 g (10 oz) fresh spinach, rocket or mixed salad leaves*

1 Open out the salmon like a book until almost flat by pressing along the backbone area. Place skin-side up in a shallow ovenproof dish just large enough to hold it.
2 Mix together the butter, mustard, dill and seasoning. Pour over the salmon. Cook at 230°C (450°F) mark 8 for about 20 minutes or until just tender.
3 Toss the salad leaves and season well. Place on large plates.
4 Cut the salmon into thick slices and serve on top of the salad leaves with the mustard butter spooned over the top.

SMOKED SALMON FISHCAKES

PREPARATION TIME 45 minutes, plus chilling
COOKING TIME About 45 minutes
FREEZING Suitable (stage 4)

❄

SERVES 12
- *1.1 kg (2½ lb) old potatoes*
- *salt and pepper*
- *450 g (1 lb) salmon fillet, skinned*
- *150 ml (5 fl oz) white wine*
- *juice of 1 lemon*
- *450 g (1 lb) smoked salmon pieces*
- *10 ml (2 tsp) anchovy essence*
- *30 ml (2 tbsp) chopped fresh dill or 10 ml (2 tsp) dried dill*

380 CALS/SERVING
- *1 spring onion, finely chopped*
- *flour for coating*
- *3 eggs, beaten*
- *350 g (12 oz) fresh white breadcrumbs*
- *oil for frying*
- *lemon wedges and fresh dill, to garnish*

1 Boil the potatoes until tender, then drain, mash and season with salt and pepper. Keep warm.
2 Meanwhile, poach the salmon fillet in a covered saucepan with wine and lemon juice for about 15 minutes or until just cooked. Cool the salmon in the liquid, then coarsely flake the fish. (The liquid can be frozen for stock.)
3 Roughly chop the smoked salmon, then mix it with the fresh salmon, anchovy essence, dill and spring onion. Beat half the fish mixture into the warm potatoes. Fold in the remaining fish and season to taste. Spread the mixture on a baking sheet lined with greaseproof paper to a depth of 4 cm (1½ inches). Cover and chill for about 2 hours.
4 Shape the mixture into 24 fishcakes. Dip them in the flour, beaten egg and breadcrumbs to coat.
5 Shallow fry the fishcakes a batch at a time in 5 mm (¼ inch) of hot oil for about 4 minutes on each side or until golden and crisp. Drain on absorbent kitchen paper and keep warm while cooking the remainder. Garnish with lemon wedges and fresh dill to serve.

NOTE When coating any food in egg and breadcrumbs, it is best to have plates of flour, beaten egg and breadcrumbs lined up on the work surface. Use one hand for dipping and coating the food into the dry ingredients and the other hand for dipping into the egg.

The fishcakes can be cooked in the oven if preferred – place on a lightly greased baking sheet, brush lightly with melted butter and cook at 220°C (425°F) mark 7 for about 25 minutes.

TIPS

Smoked salmon trimmings can be bought from fishmongers more cheaply than slices. Quality varies, so check before buying.

These fishcakes freeze well, making an excellent standby for instant meals over the Christmas holiday period.

WINTER FISH STEW

PREPARATION TIME 15 minutes, plus soaking
COOKING TIME 45-50 minutes
FREEZING Not suitable

SERVES 8

- good pinch of saffron strands
- about 1.8 kg (4 lb) mixed fish fillets, such as red mullet, plaice or cod, skinned
- 90 ml (6 tbsp) olive oil
- 2 large onions, peeled and finely chopped
- 4 garlic cloves, peeled and crushed
- 1 red pepper, deseeded and sliced
- 900 g (2 lb) tomatoes, skinned, deseeded and chopped

420 CALS/SERVING

- 4 anchovy fillets, drained
- 300 ml (10 fl oz) dry white wine
- 4 bay leaves
- 90 ml (6 tbsp) chopped fresh basil
- salt and pepper
- 20-24 cooked peeled prawns
- 150 g (5 oz) cooked shelled mussels
- 8 slices of toast
- chopped fresh parsley, to garnish

1 Soak the saffron strands in a little boiling water for 30 minutes.

2 Meanwhile, cut the fish into chunky pieces.

3 Heat the oil in a saucepan, add the onions, garlic and pepper, and fry gently for 5 minutes.

4 Add the tomatoes and anchovies and stir to break them up. Add the wine and 300 ml (10 fl oz) water, bring to the boil, then lower the heat and add the bay leaves and half the basil. Simmer, uncovered, for 20 minutes.

5 Add the firm-textured fish to the tomato mixture, strain in the saffron water and season to taste. Cook for 10 minutes, then add the delicate-textured fish and cook for 5 minutes more.

6 Add the prawns and mussels, cover and cook for 3-5 minutes until warm. Remove the bay leaves and discard.

7 Put one slice of toast in each of eight soup bowls and spoon over the stew. Serve garnished with chopped parsley.

MUSSELS WITH GINGER, CHILLI AND CORIANDER

PREPARATION TIME 20 minutes
COOKING TIME 10 minutes
FREEZING Not suitable
COLOUR INDEX Page 18

♡ ⏱

SERVES 2

- *1 kg (2¼ lb) mussels in their shells*
- *15 g (½ oz) fresh coriander sprigs*
- *1 bunch spring onions, trimmed and shredded*
- *2 garlic cloves, peeled and finely chopped*
- *2.5 cm (1 inch) piece fresh root ginger, peeled and finely chopped*

348 CALS/SERVING

- *1 small red chilli, deseeded and cut into slivers*
- *150 ml (5 fl oz) white wine*
- *40 g (1½ oz) butter*
- *coriander sprigs, to garnish*

1 Discard any mussels with damaged shells, or any that remain open when tapped smartly on the shell. Scrub the mussels thoroughly under cold running water, pulling away the coarse threads (beards) from the side of the shells.
2 Strip the leaves from the coriander and set aside; reserve the coriander stalks.
3 Put the spring onions, garlic, ginger, chilli and coriander stalks in a saucepan which is large enough to hold the mussels. Add the wine and 150 ml (5 fl oz) water. Bring to the boil and simmer for 2 minutes.
4 Add the mussels to the pan, cover with a tight-fitting lid and cook for 4-5 minutes over a moderate heat, shaking the pan occasionally, until the shells open. Turn the mussels into a colander set over a bowl. Discard the coriander stalks and any unopened mussels.
5 Pour the liquid from the bowl back into the pan. Place over a low heat and whisk in the butter, a piece at a time, then add the coriander leaves.
6 Transfer the mussels to individual serving dishes and pour over the sauce. Serve at once, garnished with coriander sprigs.

VARIATION Replace the wine with 150 ml (5 fl oz) coconut milk for an exotic sauce.

OYSTERS AU GRATIN

PREPARATION TIME 20 minutes
COOKING TIME 10 minutes
FREEZING Not suitable

♡ ⏱

SERVES 4-6

- *50 g (2 oz) streaky bacon, finely chopped*
- *75 g (3 oz) celery, finely chopped*
- *200 g (7 oz) can artichoke hearts, drained and finely chopped*

220-150 CALS/SERVING

- *12 large oysters*
- *200 g (7 oz) mozzarella cheese, thinly sliced*

1 In a small frying pan, fry the bacon until the fat begins to run. Add the celery and artichokes. Cook, stirring, for 2 minutes. Cool.
2 Scrub the oyster shells well. Open the oysters by inserting an oyster knife into the hinge linking the shells and cutting through the muscle. Prise the shells apart and discard the flatter ones.
3 Spoon a little of the bacon and artichoke mixture over each oyster. Top with cheese.
4 Cook under a medium grill for 10 minutes.

MUSTARD-ROASTED TURKEY

PREPARATION TIME 30 minutes, plus standing
COOKING TIME 3¾-4 hours
FREEZING Not suitable

SERVES 8

- *oven-ready turkey, about 4.5 kg (10 lb)*
- *45 ml (3 tbsp) wholegrain or Dijon mustard*
- *butter or margarine*
- *salt and pepper*
- *about 450 ml (15 fl oz) turkey or chicken stock*
- *60 ml (4 tbsp) sherry (optional)*
- *grated rind and juice of 1 orange*
- *cornflour*
- *fresh rosemary and sage, to garnish*

650 CALS/SERVING
STUFFING

- *450 g (1 lb) onions, peeled and finely chopped*
- *50 g (2 oz) butter*
- *45 ml (3 tbsp) chopped fresh sage, or 10 ml (2 tsp) dried sage*
- *225 g (8 oz) fresh breadcrumbs*
- *125 g (4 oz) medium oatmeal*
- *grated rind and juice of 1 orange*
- *salt and pepper*
- *1 egg, beaten*

1 To make the stuffing, sauté the onions in the butter for 6-7 minutes or until beginning to soften. Mix with the sage and breadcrumbs.
2 Toast the oatmeal under the grill and stir into the breadcrumb mixture with the grated orange rind and 30 ml (2 tbsp) orange juice. Season well and bind with beaten egg. Cool.
3 Spoon the stuffing into the neck end of the turkey only. Shape into a neat rounded end, then tuck the neck skin under the bird and secure firmly with a small skewer or wooden cocktail

stick. Place any remaining stuffing in a buttered ovenproof dish, dot with butter and cover with foil. Weigh the turkey and calculate the cooking time (see page 62).
4 Place the turkey on a large, strong sheet of foil, in a large roasting tin. Spread the breast and legs thinly with the mustard. Dot the turkey generously with butter and grind over some pepper. Fold the foil around the turkey to enclose it.
5 Cook at 180°C (350°F) mark 4 for about 3 hours. Fold the foil back, baste well and return to the oven for a further 45 minutes-1 hour. Put the stuffing in the oven to bake for about 1 hour. The turkey will be a rich golden brown.
6 Lift the turkey onto a warmed serving dish, cover with foil and leave to rest for 30 minutes to make carving easier.
7 Pour the cooking liquor into a saucepan and skim. Add the stock, sherry, grated orange rind and juice. Boil for 4-5 minutes to reduce slightly.
8 Mix about 60 ml (4 tbsp) cornflour to a smooth paste with a little water. Stir into the pan juices and bring to the boil. Simmer for 1-2 minutes or until slightly thickened. Adjust the seasoning. Garnish the turkey with sprigs of fresh rosemary and sage, and serve with the gravy.

ORIENTAL TURKEY

PREPARATION TIME 20 minutes, plus standing
COOKING TIME 1 hour
FREEZING Ginger butter (stage 1)
COLOUR INDEX Page 22

✳

SERVES 6

- *1.8 kg (4 lb) oven-ready turkey saddle or breast, bone in*
- *lychees and limes, to decorate*
- *apple and plum sauce, to serve (see Note)*
GINGER BUTTER
- *5 cm (2 inch) piece fresh root ginger, peeled and finely grated*
- *125 g (4 oz) butter, softened*

765 CALS/SERVING

- *salt and pepper*
GLAZE
- *5 cm (2 inch) piece fresh root ginger, peeled and finely grated*
- *30 ml (2 tbsp) each light soy sauce and rice or distilled malt vinegar*
- *90 ml (6 tbsp) clear honey*
- *salt and pepper*

1 To make the ginger butter, beat the ginger with the butter and season well.
2 To make the glaze, mix all the ingedients together and season to taste.
3 Carefully loosen the turkey skin and push the soft ginger butter evenly underneath.
4 Place the turkey in a roasting tin and brush with the ginger glaze. Cover with foil and cook at 190°C (375°F) mark 5 for 15 minutes per 450 g (1 lb). Baste frequently with the glaze.
5 Uncover the turkey for the last 15 minutes to brown the skin. At this stage baste the breast again with any remaining glaze.
6 Rest the turkey for 15 minutes before carving. Serve with apple and plum sauce (see Note).

NOTE To make the accompanying apple and plum sauce, peel, core and chop 900 g (2 lb) apples and cook over a low heat with 30 ml (2 tbsp) caster sugar and 150 ml (5 fl oz) water until soft. Add the grated rind and juice of 1 lime and 50 ml (2 fl oz) oriental plum sauce. Work in a blender until smooth. Season. Reheat gently to serve hot or serve cold. Garnish with chopped chillies.

TURKEY, APRICOT AND HAZELNUT PILAFF

PREPARATION TIME 20 minutes
COOKING TIME 45 minutes
FREEZING Not suitable

SERVES 4

- 30 ml (2 tbsp) hazelnut or olive oil
- 8 baby onions, peeled and halved
- 2 garlic cloves, peeled and crushed
- 15 ml (1 tbsp) medium curry powder
- 10 ml (2 tsp) ground coriander
- 5 ml (1 tsp) ground mixed spice
- 2 celery sticks, thickly sliced
- 125 g (4 oz) dried apricots, halved

540 CALS/SERVING

- 225 g (8 oz) easy-cook brown rice
- 750 ml (1¼ pints) chicken stock
- 350 g (12 oz) cold cooked turkey, shredded
- 125 g (4 oz) French beans, trimmed and halved
- 50 g (2 oz) hazelnuts, toasted
- 30 ml (2 tbsp) chopped fresh parsley
- salt and pepper

1 Heat the oil in a heavy-based saucepan, add the onions, garlic, spices and celery and fry for 10 minutes until browned. Add the apricots and rice and stir-fry for 1 minute until all the grains are glossy
2 Pour in the stock, stir well and bring to the boil. Cover and simmer gently for 20 minutes. Stir in all the remaining ingredients, and cook for a further 10 minutes. Remove from the heat and leave undisturbed for 5 minutes. Season to taste and serve at once.

VARIATION This dish can be adapted to serve cold as part of a salad spread. Chop an onion and fry in the oil with the garlic and spices for 5 minutes. Leave until cold and fold into 150 ml (5 fl oz) bought mayonnaise. In a large bowl, combine the turkey with 350 g (12 oz) cooked brown rice and the sliced raw celery, French beans, chopped dried apricots, toasted hazelnuts and parsley. Toss in the mayonnaise and serve.

ROASTED PECAN CHICKEN

PREPARATION TIME 25 minutes
COOKING TIME 1½ hours
FREEZING Not suitable

SERVES 4

- *50 g (2 oz) creamy goats' cheese*
- *7.5 ml (1½ tsp) lemon juice*
- *75 g (3 oz) pecan nuts*
- *1 small garlic clove, peeled*
- *30 ml (2 tbsp) olive oil*
- *salt and pepper*

430 CALS/SERVING

- *1.6 kg (3½ lb) oven-ready chicken*
- *lemon and onion slices*
- *150 ml (5 fl oz) dry white wine*
- *300 ml (10 fl oz) chicken stock*
- *about 10-15 ml (2-3 tsp) cornflour*

1 Place the first five ingredients in a food processor and season with black pepper only. Blend until the mixture forms a paste.
2 Loosen the skin around the chicken breast and spread the mixture underneath the skin to form an even layer. Try not to pierce or break the skin. Secure the skin with a cocktail stick and tie the chicken legs together.
3 Place the chicken in a roasting tin with the lemon and onion slices, wine and 150 ml (5 fl oz) stock. Cook at 200°C (400°F) mark 6 for about 1½ hours, basting occasionally. If necessary, cover with foil towards the end of the cooking time. Test the thickest part of the thigh with a fine skewer – when cooked, the juices run clear.
4 Keep the chicken warm. Discard the lemon and onion slices. Skim the fat from the juices and stir in the remaining 150 ml (5 fl oz) stock. Bring to the boil, scraping any sediment off the base of the pan. Mix the cornflour to a smooth paste with a little water. Off the heat, stir it into the pan juices. Return to the heat and bring to the boil, stirring all the time. Bubble for 2-3 minutes. Adjust the seasoning and serve with the chicken.

VARIATIONS Beat together 50 g (2 oz) butter with 30 ml (2 tbsp) pesto sauce. Spread this under the chicken-breast skin and over the legs and cook as above. Stir 45 ml (3 tbsp) fromage frais into the gravy just before serving.
• Beat together 45 ml (3 tbsp) olive oil with 30 ml (2 tbsp) sun-dried tomato paste. Spread underneath the chicken-breast skin. Cook as above. If

you can't find the paste, use 75 g (3 oz) sun-dried tomatoes in oil. Purée with a little olive oil.
• Beat together 50 g (2 oz) softened butter with 5 ml (1 tsp) dried tarragon and the grated rind of 1 lemon. Spread underneath the chicken-breast skin and over the legs and cook as before, using dry vermouth instead of the wine.
• Beat together 50 g (2 oz) softened butter with 5 ml (1 tsp) each of ground cumin, ground coriander and ground turmeric, 1.25 ml (¼ tsp) mild chilli powder and 1 crushed garlic clove. Spread underneath the chicken-breast skin and over the legs, and cook as before.

CHICKEN HOTPOT WITH LEEKS

PREPARATION TIME 15 minutes
COOKING TIME 1 hour 35 minutes
FREEZING Not suitable
COLOUR INDEX Page 21
♡

SERVES 4

• 15 ml (1 tbsp) olive oil	• 175 ml (6 fl oz) chicken stock
• 1 large garlic clove, peeled and crushed	• 10 ml (2 tsp) cornflour
• 700 g (1½ lb) trimmed leeks, thickly sliced	• 8 skinless, boneless chicken thighs, about 350 g (12 oz) total weight
• 200 g (7 oz) reduced-fat soft cheese with garlic and herbs	• salt and pepper
• 125 ml (4 fl oz) white wine	• 300 g (10 oz) potatoes, unpeeled and thinly sliced

350 CALS/SERVING

1 Heat the oil in a flameproof casserole. Add the garlic and leeks and cook for about 5 minutes or until beginning to soften.
2 Meanwhile, place the cheese, wine, stock and cornflour in a food processor and blend for about 30 seconds or until smooth.
3 Arrange the chicken thighs on top of the leeks, pour the cheese mixture over and season to taste. Layer the potatoes on top of the chicken. Place a lightly oiled sheet of greaseproof paper on top of the potatoes, then cover with a lid or foil.
4 Cook at 180°C (350°F) mark 4 for 1½ hours or until the potatoes are quite tender. Brown the potatoes under a hot grill before serving.

CHICKEN IN SMOKY BACON SAUCE

PREPARATION TIME 10 minutes
COOKING TIME 20 minutes
FREEZING Not suitable
COLOUR INDEX Page 19
♡ ⏱

SERVES 4

• 30 ml (2 tbsp) vegetable oil	• salt and pepper
• 125 g (4 oz) chopped bacon pieces	• 1 bunch spring onions, trimmed and roughly chopped
• 4 skinless chicken breast fillets, each weighing about 150 g (5 oz)	• 225 g (8 oz) crisp red apples, thickly sliced
• 200 ml (7 fl oz) apple juice	• 60 ml (4 tbsp) crème fraîche
• 15 ml (1 tbsp) chopped fresh thyme or 5 ml (1 tsp) dried thyme	

350 CALS/SERVING

1 Heat the oil in a large deep frying pan or sauté pan. Add the chopped bacon and chicken pieces and fry for a few minutes until golden, stirring and turning occasionally.
2 Stir in the apple juice and thyme, and season to taste. Bring to the boil, cover and simmer for 10 minutes.
3 Uncover, then add the spring onions. Tip the apples into the pan and cook over a high heat for about 5 minutes or until the liquid has reduced by half and the chicken is tender.
4 Reduce the heat to low and stir in the crème fraîche. Adjust the seasoning and serve.

NOTE Chopped bacon pieces are sold in most supermarkets, but if unavailable, simply buy thin-cut, smoked, streaky bacon and chop roughly yourself.

SWEET GINGERED CHICKEN

PREPARATION TIME 10 minutes
COOKING TIME About 30 minutes
FREEZING Not suitable

SERVES 6

- *120 ml (8 tbsp) apricot jam*
- *75 ml (5 tbsp) light soy sauce*
- *120 ml (8 tbsp) dry sherry*
- *juice of 1 lemon*
- *2 garlic cloves, peeled and crushed*
- *2.5 cm (1 inch) piece fresh root ginger, peeled and finely grated*

435 CALS/SERVING

- *350 g (12 oz) aubergine, thinly sliced*
- *6 chicken breast fillets with skin, each weighing about 150 g (5 oz)*

1 Mix together the first four ingredients. Add the garlic and the ginger.
2 Line a large roasting tin with foil. Spread out the aubergine and chicken in the tin. Spoon the ginger mixture over the top.
3 Cook at 220°C (425°F) mark 7 for about 30-35 minutes, basting occasionally, until the chicken and aubergine are well browned and glazed. Add a little water, if necessary, towards the end of cooking.

WINTER CHICKEN

PREPARATION TIME 20 minutes
COOKING TIME 45 minutes
FREEZING Not suitable
COLOUR INDEX Page 21
♡

SERVES 4

- *4 chicken leg portions, about 700 g (1½ lb) total weight*
- *salt and pepper*
- *15 ml (1 tbsp) white plain flour*
- *15 ml (1 tbsp) olive oil*
- *225 g (8 oz) onion, peeled and cut into small wedges*
- *450 g (1 lb) carrots, peeled and cut into chunks*
- *450 g (1 lb) celery, cut into chunks*

350 CALS/SERVING

- *50 g (2 oz) rindless lean back bacon, roughly chopped*
- *200 ml (7 fl oz) apple juice*
- *400 g (14 oz) can butter beans (300 g/10 oz drained weight)*
- *1 bunch watercress, roughly chopped*
- *15-30 ml (1-2 tbsp) lemon juice*

1 Skin the chicken portions and divide them into thighs and drumsticks. Toss the chicken in seasoned flour.
2 Heat the oil in a medium-size, flameproof casserole. Add the onion, carrots, celery and bacon and fry for 2-3 minutes. Mix in the apple juice, drained butter beans and the chicken.
3 Bring to the boil on the hob, cover and cook in the oven at 180°C (350°F) mark 4 for about 45 minutes or until all the ingredients are tender.
4 Stir the watercress into the casserole with the lemon juice and seasoning to taste before serving.

MARINATED CHICKEN
WITH PRUNES

PREPARATION TIME 10 minutes, plus marinating
COOKING TIME 50 minutes
FREEZING Not suitable

SERVES 4

570 CALS/SERVING

- 4 chicken quarters (breast or leg), about 900 g (2 lb) total weight
- 4 garlic cloves, peeled and sliced
- 10 ml (2 tsp) dried mixed herbs
- 30 ml (2 tbsp) red wine vinegar
- 125 ml (4 fl oz) vegetable oil
- 225 g (8 oz) pitted no-soak prunes
- 30 ml (2 tbsp) capers, drained
- salt and pepper
- 300 ml (10 fl oz) dry white wine
- 25 g (1 oz) demerara sugar
- 5 ml (1 tsp) cornflour
- 150 ml (5 fl oz) chicken stock
- about 5 ml (1 tsp) lemon juice
- flat-leaf parsley, to garnish

1 Place the chicken in a large non-metallic bowl with the garlic. Add the next five ingredients with plenty of seasoning and mix well. Cover and marinate in the refrigerator overnight.

2 Remove the chicken from the marinade and reserve the marinade. With a little oil from the marinade, brown the chicken in a flameproof casserole large enough to hold the chicken in a single layer. Pour the remaining marinade, with the prunes and capers, over the chicken. Pour over the wine and sprinkle with the sugar. Bring to the boil.

3 Cover and bake at 180°C (350°F) mark 4 for 30 minutes, then uncover and baste. Return to the oven, uncovered, for a further 20 minutes, or until the chicken quarters are cooked through.

4 Using slotted spoons, lift the chicken into a serving dish. Cover the chicken and keep it warm. Skim the juices. Mix the cornflour to a smooth paste with 15 ml (1 tbsp) water. Add to the pan juices with the stock and bring to the boil, stirring all the time. Cook for 1-2 minutes. Adjust the seasoning, add about 5 ml (1 tsp) lemon juice to taste, spoon over the chicken and serve, garnished with flat-leaf parsley.

GOOSE WITH PRUNE STUFFING

PREPARATION TIME 30 minutes
COOKING TIME 1¾-2¼ hours
FREEZING Not suitable

SERVES 10

- *4-5 kg (9-11 lb) oven-ready goose, with giblets*
- *salt and pepper*
- *450 g (1 lb) prunes, soaked overnight*
- *300 ml (10 fl oz) dry white wine*
- *50 g (2 oz) butter*
- *1 small onion, peeled and finely chopped*

480-600 CALS/SERVING

- *30 ml (2 tbsp) port*
- *125 g (4 oz) fresh breadcrumbs*
- *5 ml (1 tsp) white plain flour*
- *caramelized clementines and roasted onion wedges, to garnish*

1 Pull the inside fat out of the goose and reserve. Prick the skin of the goose with a fork in several places. Rub salt over the skin.

2 Drain the prunes and put in a saucepan with the wine. Bring to the boil and simmer for about 10 minutes or until tender. Remove the prunes from the liquid, discard the stones, chop the flesh and put in a bowl. Reserve the cooking liquid.

3 Melt 40 g (1½ oz) of the butter in another pan, add the onion and cook gently until soft but not coloured. Separate the goose liver from the giblets and chop finely. Add to the onion and cook gently for 2-3 minutes, then mix with the prunes.

4 Add the port to the pan and bubble for 1 minute, scraping the pan to dislodge any sediment. Pour the liquid into the prune mixture, add the breadcrumbs and mix well. Allow to cool for 10 minutes.

5 Spoon the stuffing into the neck cavity of the goose. Skewer the neck skin to the back of the bird, then truss and tie up the goose with string. Weigh the bird and calculate the cooking time, allowing 15 minutes per 450 g (1 lb) plus 15 minutes.

6 Put the goose on a wire rack in a roasting tin. Cover the breast with the reserved fat and foil. Roast in the oven at 200°C (400°F) mark 6, basting frequently. Remove the foil for the last 30 minutes to brown.

7 When the goose is cooked, transfer to a serving dish and keep warm in a low oven. Pour off all but 30 ml (2 tbsp) fat from the juices in the roasting tin. Transfer to the top of the cooker and blend in the flour. Cook for 1 minute until just colouring, then slowly add the reserved prune liquid, stirring well. Bring to the boil and simmer for 2-3 minutes. Season to taste and whisk in the remaining butter. Serve the sauce with the garnished goose.

NOTE For the clementine garnish, make a butter and brown sugar syrup, add the peeled fruit and coat well.

DUCKLING BREASTS WITH ARMAGNAC

PREPARATION TIME 5 minutes, plus marinating
COOKING TIME 25 minutes
FREEZING Not suitable
COLOUR INDEX Page 23
♡

SERVES 6

240 CALS/SERVING

- *6 duckling breast fillets, each weighing about 175 g (6 oz)*
- *salt and pepper*
- *2 shallots or small onions, peeled and finely chopped*
- *2 garlic cloves, peeled and crushed*
- *75 ml (5 tbsp) Armagnac*
- *sprigs of fresh thyme*
- *bay leaves*
- *sprigs of fresh herbs, to garnish*

1 Score the duckling skin and rub with salt. Place the breasts side by side in a shallow non-metallic dish.
2 Mix the shallots or onions with the garlic and Armagnac and spoon over the duckling breasts. Add sprigs of fresh thyme, bay leaves and plenty of black pepper. Turn the duckling in the marinade, cover and marinate at room temperature for about 1 hour.
3 Place the duckling breasts on a wire rack standing over a roasting tin. Baste with marinade.
4 Roast at 230°C (450°F) mark 8 for 10 minutes, then lower the temperature to 200°C (400°F) mark 6 for a further 10-15 minutes.
5 Serve thickly sliced, garnished with sprigs of fresh herbs.

ROAST DUCKLING WITH SHERRY VINEGAR

PREPARATION TIME 15 minutes
COOKING TIME 50 minutes
FREEZING Not suitable
COLOUR INDEX Page 23

SERVES 6

390 CALS/SERVING

- *salt and pepper*
- *6 duckling breast fillets, each weighing about 175 g (6 oz)*
- *125 g (4 oz) sugar*
- *60 ml (4 tbsp) each dry sherry and white wine vinegar or 120 ml (8 tbsp) sherry vinegar*
- *900 ml (1½ pints) chicken stock*
- *350 g (12 oz) carrots, peeled and roughly chopped*
- *225 g (8 oz) turnips, peeled and roughly chopped*
- *40 g (1½ oz) butter*
- *125 g (4 oz) spring onions, trimmed and roughly chopped*
- *125 g (4 oz) mangetout, trimmed*
- *lemon juice*

1 Season the duckling breast fillets and place in a roasting tin. Cook at 230°C (450°F) mark 8 for 10 minutes, then reduce the temperature to 200°C (400°F) mark 6 for about a further 20 minutes.
2 Meanwhile, place the sugar, the dry sherry and white wine vinegar in a heavy-based pan and cook over a gentle heat until the sugar dissolves and caramelizes to a deep golden colour. Add the chicken stock and bring to the boil, stirring. Boil to reduce by half, then set aside.
3 Place the carrots and turnips in a saucepan with 150 ml (5 fl oz) water, 25 g (1 oz) butter and a pinch each of salt, pepper and sugar. Bring to the boil, then cover and simmer for about 15 minutes until the vegetables are just tender and the liquid has evaporated to leave the vegetables glazed and shiny. Boil off excess liquid if necessary.
4 Blanch the spring onions and mangetout in boiling salted water for 1-2 minutes. Drain.
5 To finish, leave the duckling to rest in a warm place for about 10 minutes, then carve into thick slices. Bring the sauce to a simmer, whisk in the remaining butter and sharpen with lemon juice. Adjust the seasoning.
6 Reheat the vegetables in the sauce. Arrange the duckling and vegetables on a large serving platter and serve.

CRISPY CHINESE DUCK WITH ORIENTAL VEGETABLES

PREPARATION TIME 10 minutes
COOKING TIME 20 minutes
FREEZING Not suitable
COLOUR INDEX Page 23

SERVES 6

410 CALS/SERVING

- 6 duckling breasts, each weighing about 175 g (6 oz)
- salt and pepper
- 45 ml (3 tbsp) vegetable oil
- 30 ml (2 tbsp) sesame oil
- 90 ml (6 tbsp) yellow bean sauce
- 45 ml (3 tbsp) caster sugar
- 2 garlic cloves, peeled and crushed
- 1 cm (¹/₂ inch) piece fresh root ginger, peeled and finely chopped
- 15 ml (1 tbsp) sesame seeds

- 125 g (4 oz) cabbage, cut into fine strips
- 125 g (4 oz) carrots, peeled and cut into fine strips
- 1 red pepper, deseeded and cut into fine strips
- 75 g (3 oz) baby corn, quartered
- 5 cm (2 inch) piece cucumber, cut into fine strips
- 6 spring onions, cut into fine strips

1 Prick the skin of the duck breasts well with a fork and rub with salt and pepper. Place on a baking sheet on the top shelf of the oven and cook at 230°C (450°F) mark 8 for about 15-20 minutes or until the duck is just cooked, but still pink.
2 Meanwhile, heat 15 ml (1 tbsp) of each oil in a frying pan, add the yellow bean sauce, sugar and 30 ml (2 tbsp) water, and cook for 1 minute. Remove and leave to cool.
3 Heat both remaining oils in the rinsed and dried frying pan. Add the garlic, ginger and sesame seeds and stir for about 1 minute or until golden brown. Add the cabbage, carrots, pepper and baby corn and stir-fry briskly for 2-3 minutes. Remove from the heat and stir in the cucumber and spring onions.
4 Carve the duck into slices and arrange on top of the vegetables. Serve immediately with the sauce.

VARIATION Use chicken breast pieces instead of duckling.

CHRISTMAS PHEASANT

PREPARATION TIME 30 minutes
COOKING TIME 2¼ hours
FREEZING Suitable (stage 4)
COLOUR INDEX Page 24

❄

SERVES 6

490 CALS/SERVING

- 2 oven-ready pheasants
- salt and pepper
- 30 ml (2 tbsp) vegetable oil
- 50 g (2 oz) butter
- 225 g (8 oz) shallots or small onions, peeled
- 225 g (8 oz) streaky bacon, chopped
- 2 garlic cloves, peeled and crushed
- 300 ml (10 fl oz) Madeira
- 600 ml (1 pint) beef stock

- sprig of fresh thyme or pinch of dried
- 2 bay leaves
- 6 juniper berries
- pared rind and juice of 1 orange
- 90 ml (6 tbsp) redcurrant jelly
- 225 g (8 oz) fresh cranberries
- 225 g (8 oz) cooked chestnuts
- fresh thyme, to garnish

1 Joint both pheasants into four, discarding backbone and knuckles. Season to taste.
2 Heat the oil and butter in a large, flameproof casserole and brown the shallots and bacon. Remove and set aside. Add the pheasant, half at a time, and fry for 5-6 minutes or until golden. Remove the pheasant from the casserole.
3 Stir in the garlic, half the Madeira, the stock, thyme, bay leaves, juniper berries and pared orange rind. Bring to the boil and add the pheasant. Cover and cook at 170°C (325°F) mark 3 for 1 hour.
4 Add the shallots, bacon and redcurrant jelly. Re-cover and return to the oven for 45 minutes or until the pheasant is quite tender.
5 Meanwhile, marinate the cranberries and chestnuts in the remaining Madeira and the orange juice for 30 minutes.
6 Remove the pheasant, vegetables and bacon from the liquid, cover and keep warm. Bubble the sauce for about 5 minutes to reduce to a syrupy consistency. Add the cranberry and chestnut mixture and simmer for a further 5 minutes. Adjust the seasoning and spoon the sauce over the pheasant. Serve garnished with fresh thyme.

QUAILS ON GNOCCHI WITH
CREAM SAUCE

PREPARATION TIME 25 minutes, plus cooling
COOKING TIME About I hour
FREEZING Not suitable

SERVES 6

550 CALS/SERVING

- 6 oven-ready quails
- salt and pepper
- 6 thin rashers pancetta or smoked streaky bacon
- 25 g (1 oz) butter
- 50 g (2 oz) pine nuts
- 75 ml (5 tbsp) white wine
- 25 g (1 oz) raisins
- 75 ml (5 tbsp) double cream
- 15 ml (1 tbsp) chopped fresh tarragon
- sprigs of tarragon and parsley, to garnish

GNOCCHI
- 450 g (1 lb) floury potatoes, peeled and cut into small chunks
- salt
- 25 g (1 oz) butter
- 1 egg yolk
- 125 g (4 oz) white plain flour
- 15 ml (1 tbsp) chopped fresh tarragon or 5 ml (1 tsp) dried
- 15 ml (1 tbsp) chopped fresh parsley

1 To make the gnocchi, cook the potatoes in boiling salted water for 15 minutes until tender. Drain and leave to cool slightly.

2 Beat in the butter and egg yolk. Add the flour and herbs and stir until the mixture forms a firm dough. Turn out onto a lightly floured surface and divide into six portions. Shape each into a flat cake, about 1 cm (½ inch) thick.

3 Bring a saucepan of water to the boil. Add 3 of the gnocchi cakes and simmer gently for 2-3 minutes or until they rise to the surface. Turn the gnocchi and cook for a further 2 minutes. Remove with a slotted spoon and place in a lightly greased dish. Cook the remainder in the same way.

4 Season the quails and wrap a piece of bacon around each, tucking the ends underneath. Place in a small roasting tin and dot with half the butter.

5 Bake the quails at 190°C (375°F) mark 5 for 25 minutes until turning golden. Remove from the oven and place a quail on each piece of gnocchi. Return to the oven while making the sauce.

6 To make the sauce, melt the remaining butter in the roasting tin and add the pine nuts. Fry for 2-3 minutes until coloured, then add the wine. Cook briskly for 2 minutes. Lower the heat, add the raisins and cream, and cook gently to combine, adding a little water if too thick. Season and stir in the tarragon.

7 To serve, transfer the quails to warmed serving plates, spoon the sauce over and garnish.

SPICED RIB OF BEEF

PREPARATION TIME 15 minutes, plus resting
COOKING TIME 2 hours
FREEZING Not suitable

SERVES 6

- 2.3 kg (5 lb) rib of beef or 1.8 kg (4 lb) boned and rolled rib of beef
- 75 g (3 oz) softened butter
- salt and pepper
- 30 ml (2 tbsp) soft brown sugar
- 5 ml (1 tsp) ground allspice
- 2.5 ml (½ tsp) each ground mace and ground cloves

725 CALS/SERVING

- 30 ml (2 tbsp) wholegrain mustard
- 45 ml (3 tbsp) chopped fresh parsley
- 2 garlic cloves, peeled and crushed
GRAVY
- 45 ml (3 tbsp) white plain flour
- 750 ml (1½ pints) beef stock or vegetable water

1 Wipe the rib of beef and place fat side up in a roasting tin that is just large enough to hold it. Spread 25 g (1 oz) butter over the surface of the beef and season well.

2 Roast at 230°C (450°F) mark 8 for 30 minutes, then baste well. Lower the oven to 200°C (400°F) mark 6 and return the meat for a further 1 hour, basting the beef occasionally.

3 Mix together the remaining 50 g (2 oz) butter with the sugar, spices, mustard, parsley, garlic and plenty of seasoning.

4 Remove most of the fat from the roasting tin. Spread the spiced mixture evenly over the meat fat and return to the oven for a further 30 minutes, basting occasionally. Cover loosely with foil if the meat begins to overbrown.

5 Place the meat on a carving dish, loosely cover with foil and leave to rest for 15 minutes.

6 Meanwhile, prepare the gravy. Skim off the excess fat to leave 60 ml (4 tbsp) in the tin. Sprinkle in the flour and whisk over a low heat until the mixture begins to brown and is a smooth paste.

7 Gradually whisk in the stock, scraping all the sediment off the bottom of the pan. Bring to the boil, then simmer gently for 2-3 minutes, adjust the seasoning and serve with the beef.

BEEF MEDALLIONS WITH STILTON MOUSSE

PREPARATION TIME 15 minutes
COOKING TIME 15 minutes
FREEZING Not suitable
COLOUR INDEX Page 25

SERVES 6

- *225 g (8 oz) skinless chicken breast fillets, chilled*
- *300 ml (10 fl oz) double cream, chilled*
- *225 g (8 oz) crumbled Stilton cheese*
- *salt and pepper*
- *25 g (1 oz) butter*
- *300 g (10 oz) celery, cut into matchsticks*

630 CALS/SERVING

- *six 150 g (5 oz) fillet steaks*
- *15 ml (1 tbsp) chopped fresh parsley*
- *squeeze of lemon juice*
- *extra Stilton, to crumble (optional)*

1 Blend the chicken in a food processor until smooth. Add the cream and pulse for 2-3 seconds or until the cream is just combined. Add the Stilton cheese to the chicken in the same way. Season and refrigerate for 10 minutes.
2 Meanwhile, melt the butter in a medium saucepan, add the celery and cook gently, covered, for about 5 minutes or until just tender. Keep warm.
3 Heat a non-stick frying pan. Fry the steaks on both sides for about 3 minutes for rare (5 minutes for medium; 6-7 minutes for well done). Be careful to time your steaks accurately. Place on a hot baking sheet.
4 Divide the chilled Stilton mixture among the medallions and spread evenly over the top of each one. Grill for about 6 minutes or until the mousse turns golden brown and is firm and cooked through.
5 Add the chopped parsley and lemon juice to the celery and serve alongside the beef medallions. Crumble a little extra Stilton over the steaks, if wished.

FESTIVE BEEF CASSEROLE

PREPARATION TIME 30 minutes, plus soaking
COOKING TIME 2 hours 25 minutes
FREEZING Suitable (stage 3)
COLOUR INDEX Page 25

♡ ✳

SERVES 8

- *150 g (5 oz) each no-soak pitted prunes and apricots*
- *125 g (4 oz) raisins*
- *finely grated rind and juice of 1 orange*
- *200 ml (7 fl oz) orange juice*
- *150 ml (5 fl oz) dry sherry*
- *450 g (1 lb) stewing beef, cut into 4 cm (1½ inch) cubes*
- *450 g (1 lb) venison, cut into 4 cm (1½ inch) cubes*
- *5 ml (1 tsp) salt*
- *30 ml (2 tbsp) vegetable oil*

275 CALS/SERVING

- *450 g (1 lb) onions, peeled and finely sliced*
- *2.5 ml (½ tsp) each ground mace and ground cinnamon*
- *5 ml (1 tsp) black peppercorns, crushed*
- *pinch of allspice*
- *10 ml (2 tsp) coriander seeds, crushed*
- *15 ml (1 tbsp) white plain flour*
- *450 ml (15 fl oz) beef stock*
- *30 ml (2 tbsp) balsamic vinegar*

1 Soak the dried fruit in the combined orange juices and the sherry. Cover and leave for 1 hour or overnight. Season the meat with salt.
2 Heat the oil in a large, flameproof casserole and brown the meat in small batches. Ensure it is well browned so that the casserole juices will have a rich, dark colour. Add a little more oil if necessary and fry the onions until they are golden. Return all the meat to the pan with the spices, orange rind and flour. Cook, stirring, for 3 minutes. Add the beef stock and bring to the boil. Add the vinegar. Cover and cook at 150°C (300°F) mark 2 for 1 hour.
3 Remove the casserole from the oven. Strain the fruit and reserve. Add the soaking liquid to the casserole, re-cover and cook for a further 1 hour 10 minutes or until the meat is very tender. Stir in the reserved fruits and return to the oven for 5 minutes to heat through before serving.

STEAK AND KIDNEY PUDDING

PREPARATION TIME 20 minutes, plus cooling
COOKING TIME 3½-4 hours
FREEZING Suitable (stage 3)
COLOUR INDEX Page 25

✳

SERVES 6

- *45-60 ml (3-4 tbsp) vegetable oil*
- *700 g (1½ lb) stewing steak, cut into chunks*
- *225 g (8 oz) ox kidney, cut into chunks*
- *225 g (8 oz) onion, peeled and chopped*
- *45 ml (3 tbsp) white plain flour*
- *600 ml (1 pint) beef stock*
- *15 ml (1 tbsp) wholegrain mustard*

610 CALS/SERVING

- *salt and pepper*
- *60 ml (4 tbsp) chopped fresh parsley*
- *300 g (10 oz) white self-raising flour*
- *150 g (5 oz) shredded suet*
- *grated rind of 1 lemon*
- *butter for greasing*
- *flat-leaf parsley, to garnish*

1 Heat 45 ml (3 tbsp) oil in a flameproof casserole and brown the steak and kidney in batches, adding more oil if necessary. Remove the meat and drain on absorbent kitchen paper.

2 Add the onion to the casserole and lightly brown. Off the heat, stir in the plain flour, stock, mustard and seasoning. Bring to the boil and replace the steak and kidney.

3 Cover the casserole and cook at 170°C (325°F) mark 3 for 2 hours or until the meat is tender. Adjust the seasoning, stir in the parsley and leave to cool.

4 Mix together the self-raising flour, suet, grated lemon rind and seasoning. Bind to a soft dough with about 175-200 ml (6-7 fl oz) water. Knead lightly until just smooth.

5 Roll out the dough to a 33 cm (13 inch) round. Cut out one quarter and reserve. Line a 1.7 litre (3 pint) greased pudding basin with the large piece of dough, damping and overlapping the join to seal as securely as possible.

6 Spoon in the meat and juices. Roll out the reserved dough and use to top the pudding, damping the pastry edges to seal. Trim to neaten.

7 Cover the basin with greased and pleated greaseproof paper and foil. Tie it securely with string.

8 Place in a pan, standing the basin on a heat-proof saucer. Pour boiling water around basin to come halfway up the sides. Cover tightly. Boil for 1½-2 hours, topping up as necessary. Garnish with flat-leaf parsley to serve.

CLASSIC OXTAIL CASSEROLE

PREPARATION TIME 20 minutes
COOKING TIME 3-3½ hours
FREEZING Suitable (stage 4)
COLOUR INDEX Page 26

✳

SERVES 6

- *1.8 kg (4 lb) oxtail, in 5 cm (2 inch) pieces, trimmed*
- *450 g (1 lb) onions, peeled and chopped*
- *450 g (1 lb) carrots, peeled and roughly chopped*
- *225 g (8 oz) turnips, peeled and roughly chopped*
- *30 ml (2 tbsp) vegetable oil*

635 CALS/SERVING

- *2 garlic cloves, peeled and crushed*
- *30 ml (2 tbsp) white plain flour*
- *600 ml (1 pint) beef stock*
- *150 ml (5 fl oz) red wine*
- *15 ml (1 tbsp) tomato purée*
- *1 bay leaf*
- *salt and pepper*

1 Place the oxtail and vegetables in a large roasting tin with the oil. Roast them at 230°C (450°F) mark 8 for 30 minutes or until they are lightly browned, turning once.

2 Drain about 60 ml (4 tbsp) fat from the tin and heat in large flameproof casserole. Add the garlic and fry for 1 minute.

3 Off the heat, stir in the flour, stock, wine, tomato purée and bay leaf. Season well. Bring to the boil, add the oxtail mixture and cover.

4 Cook at 150°C (300°F) mark 2 for 2½-3 hours or until the oxtail begins to fall away from the bone. Skim well.

5 Adjust the seasoning and serve.

TIP
For extra-rich flavour, add a 105 g (4 oz) can smoked mussels at stage 6. The mussels break up during cooking, leaving a smoky gravy.

BABOTEE

PREPARATION TIME 20 minutes, plus soaking
COOKING TIME 1 hour
FREEZING Not suitable

SERVES 4

695 CALS/SERVING

- *2 slices of bread*
- *450 ml (15 fl oz) milk and single cream, mixed*
- *30 ml (2 tbsp) vegetable oil*
- *225 g (8 oz) onion, peeled and chopped*
- *2 eating apples, peeled and grated*
- *5 ml (1 tsp) chilli seasoning*
- *5 ml (1 tsp) ground coriander*
- *2 garlic cloves, peeled and crushed*
- *450 g (1 lb) lean minced beef*
- *salt and pepper*
- *30 ml (2 tbsp) white plain flour*
- *25 g (1 oz) flaked almonds*
- *25 g (1 oz) no-soak dried apricots, roughly chopped*
- *15 ml (1 tbsp) tomato purée*
- *10 ml (2 tsp) balsamic vinegar*
- *3 eggs*
- *5 ml (1 tsp) ground turmeric*
- *about 125 g (4 oz) grated Cheddar cheese*

1 Break up the bread and leave to soak in the milk and cream for 30 minutes.

2 Heat the oil in a saucepan and stir in the onion and apples. Add the chilli seasoning, coriander and garlic. Cook, stirring, for 2 minutes. Add the meat and seasoning and fry until it changes colour and is lump-free, stirring occasionally. Mix in the flour, almonds, apricots, tomato purée and balsamic vinegar.

3 Squeeze the milk out of the bread, reserving the milk. Beat the bread into the meat mixture and season well. Whisk the eggs and turmeric with the reserved milk and seasoning.

4 Spread the meat into a 2.8 litre (5 pint) shallow ovenproof dish. Pour over the milk and egg mixture and sprinkle over 75 g (3 oz) Cheddar cheese.

5 Cook at 180°C (350°F) mark 4 for about 50 minutes or until light golden and piping hot. To serve, sprinkle with more grated cheese if wished.

1 Place the diced lamb in a bowl, add the next 5 ingredients and stir well. Pour the orange juice and 45 ml (3 tbsp) olive oil over. Stir. Cover the bowl and leave the lamb to marinate in the refrigerator for 3-8 hours.

2 Mix the dried apricots and raisins with the saffron, sherry and vinegar. Cover and leave to marinate at room temperature for at least 3 hours or overnight, stirring the mixture occasionally.

3 Heat the remaining olive oil in a large, flameproof casserole. Lift the meat from the marinade and brown in batches on a high heat. Lower the heat and return all the meat to the casserole dish. Add the flour and stir well. Add the marinade, soaked fruit and its liquid and lamb stock. Season, stir well and bring to the boil.

4 Cover the casserole with a tight-fitting lid and cook at 180°C (350°F) mark 4 for about 1¼ hours or until the meat is very tender. Serve the lamb with saffron rice.

FRUITY LAMB CASSEROLE WITH SPICES

PREPARATION TIME 30 minutes, plus marinating
COOKING TIME 1½ hours
FREEZING Suitable (stage 4)

❄

SERVES 8

- 1.4 kg (3 lb) diced shoulder of lamb
- 10 ml (2 tsp) ground cumin
- 2.5 ml (½ tsp) ground cloves
- 10 ml (2 tsp) dried coriander
- 10 ml (2 tsp) dried thyme
- 4 garlic cloves, peeled and crushed
- 175 ml (6 fl oz) fresh orange juice
- 60 ml (4 tbsp) olive oil
- 175 g (6 oz) no-soak dried apricots

540 CALS/SERVING

- 75 g (3 oz) raisins
- 5 ml (1 tsp) saffron strands
- 300 ml (10 fl oz) sherry
- 75 ml (3 fl oz) vinegar, preferably sherry vinegar
- 60 ml (4 tbsp) white plain flour
- 600 ml (1 pint) stock, preferably lamb stock
- salt and pepper
- saffron rice, to serve

HONEYED LEG OF LAMB WITH WINTER VEGETABLES

PREPARATION TIME 20 minutes
COOKING TIME 1½ hours
FREEZING Not suitable
COLOUR INDEX Page 27

SERVES 4

- 1 orange
- four 10 cm (4 inch) sprigs rosemary
- 1 small half leg of lamb, weighing about 1.1 kg (2½ lb)
- 30-60 ml (2-4 tbsp) vegetable oil
- 225 g (8 oz) carrots, peeled and cut into large chunks
- 225 g (8 oz) parsnips, peeled and cut into large chunks

600 CALS/SERVING

- 450 g (1 lb) potatoes, peeled and cut into large chunks
- 75 g (3 oz) turnip, peeled and cut into large chunks
- 6 shallots, peeled
- 300 ml (10 fl oz) white wine
- 15 ml (1 tbsp) honey
- salt and pepper

1 Pare the rind from half the orange and cut into strips about 5 mm (¼ inch) wide and 2.5 cm (1 inch) long. Squeeze the juice from the orange and reserve. Divide the rosemary into 2.5 cm (1 inch) pieces.

2 Place the lamb and 30 ml (2 tbsp) oil in a large

roasting tin and, over a high heat, brown the lamb all over. Remove from the tin using slotted spoons. Add the vegetables to the pan, adding more oil if necessary, and sauté for 4-5 minutes or until golden, stirring occasionally.

3 Meanwhile, make 10-12 incisions in the lamb and insert a piece of rosemary and orange rind in each.

4 Sprinkle the extra pieces of orange rind and rosemary over the vegetables. Top with the lamb. Mix together the white wine, juice of the orange, the honey and seasoning. Pour over the lamb.

5 Roast at 200°C (400°F) mark 6 for about 1¼ hours; for well done meat, roast for about 30 minutes longer. Serve the lamb accompanied by the vegetables with any juices spooned over.

LAMB AND LENTIL BAKE

PREPARATION TIME 20 minutes, plus cooling
COOKING TIME 1¼ hours
FREEZING Suitable (stage 4)

❦

SERVES 4

- *30 ml (2 tbsp) vegetable oil*
- *125 g (4 oz) onion, peeled and finely chopped*
- *2.5 cm (1 inch) piece fresh root ginger, peeled and finely chopped*
- *1 garlic clove, peeled and crushed*
- *2.5 ml (½ tsp) chilli seasoning*
- *2.5 ml (½ tsp) paprika*
- *2.5 ml (½ tsp) dried marjoram*

520 CALS/SERVING

- *225 g (8 oz) minced lamb*
- *175 g (6 oz) red lentils*
- *30 ml (2 tbsp) tomato purée*
- *30 ml (2 tbsp) lemon juice*
- *50 g (2 oz) raisins*
- *600 ml (1 pint) chicken stock*
- *salt and pepper*
- *50 g (2 oz) butter*
- *about 125 g (4 oz) filo pastry*
- *poppy seeds*

1 Heat the oil in a saucepan. Fry the onions until translucent, about 4-5 minutes. Stir in the ginger, garlic, chilli seasoning, paprika and marjoram. Cook, stirring, for 1 minute. Add the mince and stir until it changes colour and is free of lumps.

2 Mix in the lentils, tomato purée, lemon juice, raisins and stock. Cover and cook over a low heat for 20-25 minutes or until the lentils and mince are tender and most of the liquid is absorbed.

Uncover and bubble off any excess liquid, stirring occasionally. Adjust the seasoning then turn into a bowl and allow to cool completely.

3 Melt the butter and lightly grease a 23 cm (9 inch) base measurement, 3 cm (1¼ inch) deep, loose-based fluted flan tin. Line with sheets of filo pastry, brushing with butter between the layers and overlapping them in a random manner. There should be no gaps in the pastry and the excess pastry should hang over the sides of the tin.

4 Spoon the cold filling into the flan case. Wrap over the pastry to enclose the filling. Brush with butter and garnish with crumpled up pastry trimmings. Brush with butter again, and sprinkle with poppy seeds.

5 Cook at 190°C (375°F) mark 5 for about 50-55 minutes, covering lightly with foil after about 30-35 minutes. Cool for 10 minutes before serving.

TIP

Filo pastry sheets come in all sizes. You'll need about 125 g (4 oz) pastry sheets to line and cover the flan. Cut or trim the sheets as required so that they easily fit into the tin; use a little extra pastry if necessary. Whilst lining the tin, always keep the pastry covered with clingfilm or a tea towel as once it's exposed to air it quickly dries and becomes impossible to handle as it often breaks into pieces.

SAUTEED LIVER WITH ORANGE AND SAGE

PREPARATION TIME 10 minutes
COOKING TIME 10-15 minutes
FREEZING Not suitable

♡ ⏲

SERVES 4

310 CALS/SERVING

- 450 g (1 lb) lamb's liver, cut into 5 cm (2 inch) strips
- 25 g (1 oz) seasoned flour
- 10 ml (2 tsp) chopped fresh sage or 5 ml (1 tsp) dried

- 3 large oranges
- 15 ml (1 tbsp) vegetable oil
- 225 g (8 oz) onion, peeled and roughly chopped
- chopped fresh sage or parsley, to garnish

1 Toss the liver in the seasoned flour and sage mixed together. Using a serrated knife, peel, halve and thickly slice one orange.
2 Heat the oil in a frying pan, add the onion and cook, stirring, for about 3-4 minutes. Add the liver and toss over a high heat for a further 5-7 minutes until browned and just cooked.
3 Reduce the heat, stir in the grated rind and juice of the remaining 2 oranges and allow to heat through. Garnish with the orange slices and herbs.

BRAISED HAM WITH MADEIRA

PREPARATION TIME 30 minutes, plus soaking
COOKING TIME 3¼-3½ hours
FREEZING Suitable: Sauce only
COLOUR INDEX Page 30

❄

SERVES 12-16

625-515 CALS/SERVING

- 2.7 kg (6 lb) piece of gammon
- ½ bottle medium white wine
- 6 cloves
- 8 peppercorns
- ½ bottle Madeira
SAUCE
- 300 ml (10 fl oz) dry white wine
- about 300 ml (10 fl oz) chicken or vegetable stock
- 75 g (3 oz) butter
- 40 g (1½ oz) white plain flour

- 6 juniper berries, crushed
- 8 shallots, peeled and chopped
- 6 dried green peppercorns, crushed
- 125 ml (4 fl oz) white wine vinegar
- 30 ml (2 tbsp) Dijon mustard
- 125 ml (4 fl oz) crème fraîche or soured cream
- salt and pepper

1 Cover the gammon with cold water and leave to soak overnight. Scrub the skin and drain and dry well. Calculate the poaching time, allowing 25 minutes per 450 g (1 lb).
2 Place the gammon in a large saucepan and cover with cold water. Bring slowly to the boil, then drain. Pour the wine into the pan and add the cloves and peppercorns and enough hot water to cover. Cover and simmer very gently for the calculated time. Allow the gammon to cool in the liquid, then drain.
3 Strip the rind off the gammon and score the fat into a diamond pattern. Place the gammon in a roasting tin and pour over the Madeira. Braise in the oven at 180°C (350°F) mark 4 for 45 minutes to 1 hour, basting frequently until golden brown, then transfer to a platter, cover loosely and keep warm while making the sauce.
4 Pour off the juices from the roasting tin into a measuring jug and wait for the fat to rise to the surface. Skim off the fat and reserve 30 ml (2 tbsp). Make the braising liquid up to 1.1 litres (2 pints) with the wine and stock.
5 Melt the butter and reserved ham fat in a saucepan. Add the flour and cook, stirring, for 3-4 minutes until foaming. Whisk in the wine and stock mixture. Add the juniper berries and half the

shallots. Bring to the boil and simmer for 10 minutes, stirring constantly.

6 Meanwhile, put the green peppercorns, remaining shallots and vinegar in a saucepan and reduce to 10 ml (2 tsp). Dip the base of the pan into cold water to stop the reduction. Stir the Madeira sauce into the reduced vinegar with the mustard and simmer for at least 15 minutes. Stir in the crème fraîche or cream and bring to the boil. Check the seasoning. Pour into a warmed sauceboat.

7 Slice the ham and serve with the sauce and seasonal vegetables.

HERBY RACK OF PORK WITH ROAST VEGETABLES

PREPARATION TIME 15 minutes, plus marinating
COOKING TIME 1 hour 40 minutes
FREEZING Not suitable

SERVES 6

645 CALS/SERVING

- 10 ml (2 tsp) each finely chopped fresh sage, oregano and rosemary or 5 ml (1 tsp) each dried
- 15 ml (1 tbsp) chopped fresh parsley
- 1.4 kg (3 lb) rack of pork, chined
- 5 ml (1 tsp) each salt and coarse ground black pepper
- 1.1 kg (2½ lb) mixed vegetables, cut into large chunks
- 275 g (10 oz) sweet potatoes or baking potatoes, cut into large chunks
- 200 ml (7 fl oz) olive oil
- 45 ml (3 tbsp) redcurrant jelly
- juice of 1 small lemon
- 2 garlic cloves, peeled and crushed

1 Mix all of the herbs together. Score the fat of the pork in narrow vertical lines with a sharp knife. Rub the joint with 30 ml (2 tbsp) herbs and half the salt and pepper. Cover and refrigerate for at least 1 hour or overnight.

2 Toss the vegetables and potatoes with the remaining seasoning and 50 ml (2 fl oz) olive oil.

3 Place the vegetables in a large roasting tin, lay a wire rack over the top and place the pork on it. Cook at 220°C (425°F) mark 7 for 1 hour 25 minutes, turning the vegetables frequently.

4 Heat the redcurrant jelly with 30 ml (2 tbsp) water. Bring to the boil then take off the heat.

Remove the pork from the oven and brush the redcurrant glaze over the rind of the pork. Cook the pork for a further 15 minutes.

5 To serve, carve the rack into chops. Toss the vegetables with the lemon juice, garlic, the remaining olive oil and herbs. Serve immediately with the pork.

> **TIP**
> If the rack of pork is quite a loose shape, tie securely at intervals with fine string.

buttered 2 litre (3½ pint) ovenproof dish. Cover with half of the bread and sprinkle over two-thirds of the Gruyère. Add the remaining spinach, then top with the remaining bread. Pour over the egg and milk mixture. Press the bread gently into the milk.

4 Sprinkle over the remaining Gruyère and Parmesan and allow to stand for at least 30 minutes to absorb most of the liquid.

5 Place the dish in a roasting tin and pour in enough boiling water to come halfway up the sides of the dish. Bake at 220°C (425°F) mark 7 for about 30 minutes or until puffed, lightly set and well browned, covering loosely with foil if necessary.

GOLDEN CHEESE AND SPINACH PUDDING

PREPARATION TIME 20 minutes, plus standing
COOKING TIME 35 minutes
FREEZING Not suitable

STILTON, WALNUT AND BACON FLAN

PREPARATION TIME 10 minutes, plus pastry and chilling
COOKING TIME 50 minutes
FREEZING Suitable
COLOUR INDEX Page 31

❋

SERVES 4 — 625 CALS/SERVING

- *450 g (1 lb) spinach leaves*
- *600 ml (1 pint) milk*
- *3 eggs*
- *60 ml (4 tbsp) freshly grated Parmesan cheese*
- *2.5 ml (½ tsp) chilli seasoning (not powder)*
- *freshly grated nutmeg*
- *salt and pepper*
- *5 large thick slices white crusty bread, about 225 g (8 oz) total weight*
- *butter for greasing*
- *225 g (8 oz) Gruyère cheese, grated*

1 Cook the spinach with just the water clinging to the leaves after washing, for about 4-5 minutes or until wilted. Drain thoroughly, squeezing out as much of the liquid as possible. Chop the spinach.

2 Whisk together the milk, eggs, 45 ml (3 tbsp) Parmesan, the chilli seasoning and nutmeg. Season with salt and pepper. Halve the bread slices if large.

3 Place half the spinach in the base of a well

SERVES 4-6 — 610-405 CALS/SERVING

- *Walnut Shortcrust Pastry, made with 175 g (6 oz) white plain flour (see page 383)*

FILLING
- *125 g (4 oz) rindless back bacon, diced*
- *10 ml (2 tsp) olive oil*
- *2 sticks of celery, chopped*
- *75 g (3 oz) Stilton cheese, crumbled*
- *1 egg*
- *1 egg yolk*
- *150 ml (5 fl oz) single cream*
- *salt and pepper*

1 Roll out the pastry on a lightly floured surface and use to line a 20 cm (8 inch) flan tin. Prick the bottom with a fork and chill for 20 minutes.

2 Bake the flan blind (see page 383) at 200°C (400°F) mark 6 until pale golden.

3 Dry fry the bacon for 5 minutes to release the fat. Add the oil to the pan with the celery and fry for 2 minutes. Scatter the bacon, celery and Stilton over the base of the flan.

4 Beat the egg and egg yolk into the cream, and season with salt and pepper. Pour the cream mixture into the pastry case, and bake the flan for 30 minutes, until just set and golden. Serve warm or cold.

SWEET POTATO AND LEEK TORTILLA

PREPARATION TIME 10 minutes
COOKING TIME About 20 minutes
FREEZING Not suitable

🕐

SERVES 4

525 CALS/SERVING

- *450 g (1 lb) sweet potato*
- *salt and pepper*
- *60 ml (4 tbsp) olive oil*
- *3 leeks, trimmed, washed and thinly sliced*
- *4 eggs*
- *125 ml (4 fl oz) single cream or milk*
- *125 g (4 oz) Gruyère or mature Cheddar cheese, grated*
- *30 ml (2 tbsp) chopped fresh parsley*

1 Peel the sweet potato, and cut into 2.5 cm (1 inch) chunks. Cook in boiling salted water for about 5-8 minutes, until just tender. Drain.
2 Heat the oil in a large frying pan, add the leeks and cook until softened. Add the sweet potato, and cook, stirring occasionally, until the potato is just beginning to colour.
3 Meanwhile, beat the eggs with the cream. Season with salt and pepper, then pour into the frying pan. Add the grated cheese, and stir a little until the cheese is evenly distributed. Cook gently until set on the bottom.
4 Place the omelette under the grill, and cook until puffed up and golden. Serve straight from the pan, sprinkled with the parsley.

VARIATION Use carrots instead of sweet potato.

TIP
This variation of a Spanish tortilla can be served as a tapas-style snack with drinks – allow to cool and cut into neat chunks.

PASTA WITH TUNA AND OLIVE SAUCE

PREPARATION TIME 10 minutes, plus soaking
COOKING TIME About 25 minutes
FREEZING Not suitable
COLOUR INDEX Page 33

SERVES 4 490 CALS/SERVING

- *50 g (2 oz) can anchovy fillets*
- *milk, for soaking*
- *15 ml (1 tbsp) olive oil*
- *1 onion, peeled and chopped*
- *1 garlic clove, peeled and crushed*
- *5 ml (1 tsp) dried marjoram*
- *400 g (14 oz) can chopped tomatoes*
- *350 g (12 oz) dried pasta shapes*
- *salt and pepper*
- *225 g (8 oz) can tuna steaks in brine, well drained and flaked*
- *50 g (2 oz) black or green olives*
- *30 ml (2 tbsp) dry white wine*
- *fresh marjoram, to garnish (optional)*
- *coarsely grated Parmesan cheese, to serve*

1 To remove the salt from the anchovies, drain well and place in a bowl. Cover with milk and soak for 20 minutes. Drain, pat dry and chop.
2 To make the sauce, heat the oil in a saucepan and gently cook the onion for 5 minutes. Add the garlic, marjoram and tomatoes with their juices. Bring to the boil and simmer for 15 minutes, stirring occasionally, until slightly thickened.
3 Meanwhile, cook the pasta in boiling salted water for 10-12 minutes, or until just tender *(al dente)*.
4 Add the tuna fish, anchovies and olives to the sauce. Return to the boil, stirring, then simmer for 2-3 minutes. Stir in the wine and pepper. Drain the pasta and serve hot with the sauce spooned over. Garnish with fresh marjoram, if wished, and top with coarsely grated Parmesan.

SPAGHETTI WITH CLAMS

PREPARATION TIME 15 minutes
COOKING TIME About 8 minutes
FREEZING Not suitable
COLOUR INDEX Page 33

SERVES 4-6 685-460 CALS/SERVING

- *700 g (1½ lb) venus or baby clams in shells*
- *75 ml (5 tbsp) extra-virgin olive oil*
- *3 garlic cloves, peeled and finely chopped*
- *2.5 ml (½ tsp) dried chilli flakes, crushed*
- *350 g (12 oz) tomatoes, skinned, deseeded and chopped*
- *100 ml (3½ fl oz) dry white wine*
- *salt and pepper*
- *400 g (14 oz) dried spaghetti*
- *30 ml (2 tbsp) chopped fresh parsley*
- *40 g (1½ oz) butter*

1 Wash the clams in plenty of cold water and scrub the shells with a small brush. Leave to soak in a bowl of fresh cold water for 10 minutes, then rinse again and drain well. Discard any clams which do not close if their shells are tapped firmly.
2 Heat the olive oil in a large frying pan (large enough to hold and toss the spaghetti later). Add the garlic and chilli and cook over a medium-high heat for 2 minutes; do not let the garlic brown. Stir in the chopped tomatoes and wine.
3 Add the clams in their shells to the pan. Season with salt and pepper, stir well and bring to the boil. Cover with a tight-fitting lid and cook for 2-3 minutes to steam open the clams. Remove from the heat; discard any clams which have not opened.
4 Meanwhile, cook the spaghetti until just tender *(al dente)*. Drain thoroughly.
5 Return the clam sauce to the heat and stir in the parsley. Add the drained spaghetti and cook for 1 minute. Add the butter, toss lightly and serve.

VARIATIONS When fresh clams are not available, use jars or cans of clams in their shells, available from Italian delicatessens and larger supermarkets. Drain thoroughly before use, and include a few chopped anchovy fillets to taste.

Alternatively, replace the clams with 1 kg (2 lb) fresh mussels in their shells.

LINGUINE WITH PARMA HAM AND SUN-DRIED TOMATOES

PREPARATION TIME 5 minutes
COOKING TIME 11 minutes
FREEZING Not suitable

SERVES 4

- *400 g (14 oz) dried linguine (or fettucini)*
- *salt and pepper*
- *30 ml (2 tbsp) olive oil*
- *125 g (4 oz) Parma ham (about 6 thin slices), cut into thin strips*
- *65 g (2½ oz) butter*
- *1 large onion, peeled and chopped*
- *2 garlic cloves, peeled and crushed*
- *50 g (2 oz) sun-dried tomatoes, drained and cut into strips*

1020 CALS/SERVING

- *150 ml (5 fl oz) double cream*
- *150 g (5 oz) mascarpone cheese*
- *small bunch of marjoram or oregano sprigs, leaves pulled from stalks*
- *30-45 ml (2-3 tbsp) toasted pine nuts (optional)*

1 Cook the pasta in a large saucepan of boiling, salted water for 10 minutes or until almost tender *(al dente)*.

2 Meanwhile, heat the oil in a frying pan, add the strips of Parma ham and fry quickly for about 1 minute or until frazzled. Using a slotted spoon, remove the ham from the pan and reserve.

3 Add the butter to the frying pan and gently fry the onion, garlic and sun-dried tomatoes for 2 minutes. Drain the pasta, and while still hot, add to the frying pan. With a fork in each hand, lift the pasta strands a few times, so the buttery mixture coats and separates them.

4 In a saucepan, gently heat the cream with the mascarpone, stirring until smooth. Season with salt and pepper, add to the pasta mixture and toss with half the Parma ham and half the marjoram or oregano leaves.

5 Transfer the mixture to a warm serving bowl and scatter with the remaining Parma ham, herbs and toasted pine nuts, if using. Serve at once.

VARIATIONS Use strips of pancetta or smoked streaky bacon instead of Parma ham and cook in the same way. Sautéed sliced mushrooms or asparagus tips also make tasty additions.

CREAMY PASTA BAKE

PREPARATION TIME 15 minutes
COOKING TIME 45 minutes
FREEZING Not suitable

SERVES 4   **550 CALS/SERVING**

- *175 g (6 oz) dried pasta shapes, such as penne*
- *salt and pepper*
- *olive oil*
- *125 g (4 oz) onion, peeled and finely chopped*
- *1 garlic clove, peeled and crushed*
- *300 ml (10 fl oz) single cream*
- *2 eggs*
- *175 g (6 oz) Gruyère cheese, coarsely grated*

1 Cook the pasta in boiling, salted water until just tender *(al dente)*. Drain well and toss in a little oil.
2 Meanwhile, heat 15 ml (1 tbsp) oil in a small frying pan and add the onion and garlic. Fry for a few minutes until the mixture is beginning to soften.
3 In a large bowl, whisk together the single cream and the eggs; then season generously. Stir in the cheese, the onion mixture and the cooked pasta.
4 Spoon into a 1.1 litre (2 pint) ovenproof dish. Stand the dish on a baking sheet and bake at 190°C (375 °F) mark 5 for 35-40 minutes or until the top is golden brown.

ROASTED VEGETABLE AND PASTA GRATIN

PREPARATION TIME 35 minutes
COOKING TIME 1½ hours
FREEZING Suitable (stage 4)
COLOUR INDEX Page 34

✳

SERVES 8   **585 CALS/SERVING**

- *450 g (1 lb) aubergines, cut into bite-sized pieces*
- *700 g (1½ lb) mixed peppers, deseeded and cut into bite-sized pieces*
- *450 g (1 lb) squash, such as butternut or pumpkin, peeled and cut into bite-sized pieces*
- *90 ml (6 tbsp) olive oil*
- *225 g (8 oz) dried pasta shapes*
- *50 g (2 oz) butter*
- *50 g (2 oz) white plain flour*
- *900 ml (1½ pints) milk*
- *30 ml (2 tbsp) wholegrain mustard*
- *150 g (5 oz) soft cheese with garlic and herbs*
- *225 g (8 oz) mature Cheddar cheese, grated*
- *salt and pepper*
- *450 g (1 lb) frozen leaf spinach, thawed and drained*

1 Put the aubergines, mixed peppers and squash into two roasting tins with the oil. Roast at 220°C (425°F) mark 7 for 45 minutes or until tender and charred.

2 Meanwhile, cook the pasta shapes in boiling salted water until just tender *(al dente)*. Drain them thoroughly.

3 Melt the butter in a pan and then stir in the flour. Cook, stirring, for 1 minute before adding the milk. Bring to the boil, stirring all the time. Simmer for 2-3 minutes or until the sauce thickens. Off the heat, add the mustard, soft cheese and all but 50 g (2 oz) of the Cheddar. Stir thoroughly until smooth. Season well.

4 Mix the pasta, spinach and roasted vegetables with the sauce. Spoon the vegetable and pasta gratin into a large, shallow ovenproof dish and sprinkle over the remaining Cheddar cheese.

5 Stand the dish on a baking sheet and cook at 200°C (400°F) mark 6 for about 40 minutes or until hot and golden brown, covering with foil, if necessary, to prevent over browning.

VARIATIONS This dish is a great way of using up leftovers. You can add cooked ham, chicken or spicy sausage. Any variety of cheese can be used; for a special vegetarian meal, add goats' cheese or Stilton.

PAD THAI NOODLES

PREPARATION TIME 15 minutes
COOKING TIME 5 minutes
FREEZING Not suitable

🕐

SERVES 4   **615 CALS/SERVING**

- 250 g (9 oz) flat, thin rice or egg noodles
- 30 ml (2 tbsp) sesame oil
- 125 g (4 oz) turnip, diced
- 2 garlic cloves, peeled and crushed
- 2.5 ml (½ tsp) hot paprika
- 60-75 ml (4-5 tbsp) fish sauce
- juice of 1 lime
- 15 ml (1 tbsp) tomato purée

- 125 g (4 oz) tofu, diced
- 50 g (2 oz) roasted peanuts, finely chopped
- 125 g (4 oz) cooked, peeled prawns
- 175 g (6 oz) beansprouts
- 2 eggs, beaten
- chopped peanuts, to serve
- whole cooked prawns and basil, to garnish

1 Cook the noodles according to the packet instructions. Heat the oil in a wok or large non-stick sauté pan. Add the noodles, turnip, garlic and paprika and sauté for 1-2 minutes, stirring to prevent the noodles from sticking. Add the fish sauce, lime juice and tomato purée and cook for a further 1 minute, stirring continuously.

2 Stir in the tofu, peanuts, prawns and bean-sprouts. Lower the heat, add the eggs and stir for about 1 minute or until the noodles are coated in lightly cooked egg. Serve sprinkled with chopped peanuts and garnished with prawns and basil.

TIP
Work quickly and merely toss the ingredients in the pan to heat them through and lightly cook the egg.

1 To make the rouille, place the pepper, garlic and chilli in a food processor or blender with the oil and breadcrumbs and blend to a smooth paste. Transfer to a small serving dish.

2 To make the stew, heat the oil in a large saucepan. Add the leeks, ginger, orange rind and bay leaves and fry for 3 minutes. Add the stock and potatoes and bring to the boil. Reduce the heat and simmer gently for 10 minutes or until the potatoes are almost tender.

3 Add the red pepper, courgettes, mushrooms, kidney beans and saffron. Cover and simmer gently for 10-15 minutes until all the vegetables are tender but not pulpy. Add the cream and season to taste.

4 Spoon into large bowls or onto plates and serve with the rouille handed separately.

VEGETABLE STEW WITH ROUILLE

PREPARATION TIME 30 minutes
COOKING TIME 28 minutes
FREEZING Not suitable

SERVES 4

- 45 ml (3 tbsp) olive oil
- 2 large leeks, trimmed and sliced
- 2.5 cm (1 inch) piece fresh root ginger, peeled and grated
- piece of pared orange rind
- 2 bay leaves
- 900 ml (1½ pints) vegetable stock
- 450 g (1 lb) small whole potatoes, scrubbed and halved, if necessary
- 1 red pepper, deseeded and chopped
- 225 g (8 oz) courgettes or green beans, sliced
- 225 g (8 oz) brown mushrooms, halved
- 400 g (14 oz) can red kidney beans, drained and rinsed

600 CALS/SERVING

- generous pinch (½ sachet) saffron strands (optional)
- 60 ml (4 tbsp) double cream
- salt and pepper
ROUILLE
- 1 red pepper, deseeded and roughly chopped
- 4 garlic cloves, peeled and chopped
- 1 fresh chilli, deseeded and chopped, or 2.5 ml (½ tsp) crushed dried chillies
- 75 ml (5 tbsp) olive oil
- 25 g (1 oz) fresh breadcrumbs

MIXED VEGETABLES AND TOFU IN COCONUT SAUCE

PREPARATION TIME 20 minutes
COOKING TIME About 30 minutes
FREEZING Not suitable
COLOUR INDEX Page 38

SERVES 4

- 75 g (3 oz) creamed coconut, cut into small pieces
- 225 g (8 oz) tofu, cut into cubes
- sunflower oil, for deep-frying, plus 15 ml (1 tbsp)
- 6 spring onions, finely chopped
- 2.5 cm (1 inch) piece fresh root ginger, peeled and finely chopped
- 1 garlic clove, peeled and crushed
- 2.5 ml (½ tsp) ground turmeric

365 CALS/SERVING

- 2.5 ml (½ tsp) chilli powder
- 30 ml (2 tbsp) soy sauce
- 4 carrots, cut into matchstick strips
- 225 g (8 oz) cauliflower florets, separated into small sprigs
- 175 g (6 oz) French beans
- 175 g (6 oz) beansprouts
- salt and pepper

1 Place the coconut in a measuring jug. Pour in boiling water to the 900 ml (1½ pint) mark. Stir until dissolved, then strain through a muslin-lined sieve. Set the milk aside.

2 Pat the tofu dry with absorbent kitchen paper.

Heat the oil to 190°C (375°F) in a wok or deep-fat fryer, and deep-fry the tofu until golden, turning frequently. Remove and drain on absorbent kitchen paper.

3 Heat the 15 ml (1 tbsp) oil in a saucepan or flameproof casserole and gently fry the spring onions, ginger and garlic for about 5 minutes until soft.

4 Add the turmeric and chilli powder. Stir-fry for 1-2 minutes. Pour in the coconut milk and soy sauce and bring to the boil, stirring. Add the carrots and cauliflower and simmer, uncovered, for 10 minutes.

5 Add the French beans and simmer for a further 5 minutes before adding the tofu and beansprouts. Heat through and adjust the seasoning, then turn into a warmed serving dish. Serve immediately.

CRUSTY MEDITERRANEAN PARCELS

PREPARATION TIME 30 minutes, plus pastry
COOKING TIME I hour 10 minutes
FREEZING Suitable (stage 5)

❋

SERVES 8
- 700 g (1½ lb) mixed vegetables, such as carrots, leeks, courgettes, red peppers, aubergines, sweet potatoes, cut into 2.5 cm (1 inch) chunks
- 30 ml (2 tbsp) olive oil
- salt and pepper
- 225 g (8 oz) onions, peeled and roughly chopped
- 2 garlic cloves, peeled and crushed
- 400 g (14 oz) can chopped tomatoes

480 CALS/SERVING
- 15 ml (1 tbsp) sun-dried tomato paste
- 125 g (4 oz) Gruyère cheese, grated
- 200 g (7 oz) mascarpone cheese
- 50 ml (2 fl oz) single cream
- 30 ml (2 tbsp) finely chopped fresh chives
- 50 g (2 oz) pine nuts, toasted
- 450 g (1 lb) Puff Pastry (see page 383)
- 1 egg
- chopped fresh chives, to garnish

1 Place the vegetables in a small roasting tin with 15 ml (1 tbsp) olive oil and seasoning. Cook at 200°C (400°F) mark 6 for 40-45 minutes or until just tender, stirring occasionally. Remove from the oven and leave to cool.

2 Heat the remaining olive oil in a frying pan. Add the onions and garlic and fry for 5 minutes or until lightly coloured. Add the tomatoes and tomato paste and simmer, uncovered, for 15-20 minutes or until thick and pulpy. Set aside.

3 Mix 75 g (3 oz) Gruyère cheese with the mascarpone cheese, single cream and chives. Mix the vegetables with the tomato sauce, 25 g (1 oz) pine nuts and seasoning. Roll out the pastry quite thinly to 2 rectangles measuring about 35 x 30 cm (14 x 12 inches).

4 Beat the egg with a pinch of salt. Place half the vegetables down the centre of each oblong, about 10 cm (4 inches) wide. Top the vegetables with the cheese mixture. Brush the pastry with the egg glaze.

5 With a sharp knife, make diagonal incisions about 2.5 cm (1 inch) apart, down each side of the filling to within 2.5 cm (1 inch) of the filling. Plait from the top by overlapping alternate strips from either side across the filling. Make sure that the strips cross over or the pastry might burst in cooking. Tuck any loose pastry under the base. Brush liberally with the egg glaze and sprinkle with pepper, salt, the remaining grated cheese and pine nuts.

6 Place the plaits on a baking sheet. Cook at 220°C (425°F) mark 7 for 25 minutes or until golden brown. Cover loosely with foil if they begin to brown too quickly.

7 Serve cut into slices and sprinkled with chopped chives.

BAKED CABBAGE WITH FRUITED BULGHUR WHEAT STUFFING

PREPARATION TIME 30 minutes
COOKING TIME 40-45 minutes
FREEZING Not suitable

SERVES 4

355 CALS/SERVING

- 8 large green cabbage leaves
- 125 g (4 oz) bulghur wheat
- 30 ml (2 tbsp) olive oil
- 2 large onions, peeled and sliced
- 50 g (2 oz) hazelnuts, roughly chopped
- 1 garlic clove, peeled and crushed
- 175 g (6 oz) carrots, peeled and diced
- 50 g (2 oz) no-soak dried apricots, roughly chopped
- 10 ml (2 tsp) coriander seeds, lightly crushed
- 45 ml (3 tbsp) chopped fresh parsley
- 25 g (1 oz) raisins
- salt and pepper
- 10 ml (2 tsp) white plain flour
- 450 ml (15 fl oz) vegetable stock
- coriander or parsley, to garnish

1 Cut the stalks away from the cabbage leaves. Bring a large pan of water to the boil and cook the leaves for 1-2 minutes until softened. Drain.
2 Put the bulghur wheat in a bowl and cover with boiling water. Leave for 10 minutes until softened, then drain.

3 Heat the oil in a large frying pan. Add the onions and fry for about 8-10 minutes until turning golden brown, adding the hazelnuts after 5 minutes of cooking. Drain and reserve three-quarters of the mixture.
4 Add the garlic, carrots, apricots, bulghur wheat, coriander, parsley and raisins to the pan. Stir well and season to taste.
5 Spoon the stuffing onto the cabbage leaves. Fold two sides of the leaves over the filling and then roll up to enclose completely. (If they start to unroll, secure with cocktail sticks.)
6 Place the reserved onion mixture in a flame-proof casserole over moderate heat. Blend in the flour, then the stock. Bring to the boil and season lightly. Place the cabbage parcels in the casserole in a single layer.
7 Cover with a lid and bake at 200°C (400°F) mark 6 for 30 minutes. Carefully remove the parcels. Using a slotted spoon, transfer the onions and nuts to warmed serving plates. Top with the parcels and pour over the pan juices. Serve scattered with coriander or parsley.

VARIATIONS Use prunes in place of the apricots. Any other nuts, such as brazil nuts, almonds or walnuts can be used instead of hazelnuts.

VEGETABLE BIRYANI

PREPARATION TIME 20 minutes
COOKING TIME 45 minutes
FREEZING Not suitable
COLOUR INDEX Page 37

SERVES 4

485 CALS/SERVING

- 350 g (12 oz) basmati rice
- salt and pepper
- 50 g (2 oz) ghee or clarified butter
- 1 large onion, peeled and chopped
- 2.5 cm (1 inch) piece fresh root ginger, peeled and grated
- 1-2 garlic cloves, peeled and crushed
- 5 ml (1 tsp) ground coriander
- 10 ml (2 tsp) ground cumin
- 5 ml (1 tsp) ground turmeric
- 2.5 ml (½ tsp) chilli powder
- 3 carrots, peeled and thinly sliced
- 225 g (8 oz) French beans, halved
- 225 g (8 oz) small cauliflower florets
- 5 ml (1 tsp) garam masala
- juice of 1 lemon
- hard-boiled egg slices and coriander

1 Put the rice in a sieve and rinse under cold running water until the water runs clear.

2 Put the rice in a saucepan with 600 ml (1 pint) water and 5 ml (1 tsp) salt. Bring to the boil, then reduce the heat and simmer for 10 minutes or until only just tender.

3 Meanwhile, melt the ghee or butter in a large heavy-based saucepan, add the onion, ginger and garlic and fry gently for 5 minutes or until soft but not coloured. Add the coriander, cumin, turmeric and chilli powder and fry for 2 minutes more, stirring constantly to prevent the spices burning.

4 Remove the rice from the heat and drain. Add 900 ml (1½ pints) water to the onion and spice mixture and season with salt and pepper. Stir well and bring to the boil. Add the carrots and beans and simmer for 15 minutes, then add the cauliflower and simmer for a further 10 minutes. Lastly, add the rice. Mix gently and heat through.

5 Stir the garam masala and lemon juice into the biryani and simmer for a few minutes. Taste and adjust the seasoning, then turn into a warmed dish. Garnish with egg and coriander and serve.

SPICED VEGETABLE TAGINE

PREPARATION TIME 15 minutes
COOKING TIME 10 minutes
FREEZING Suitable (stage 4) without couscous

❋

SERVES 4
- *225 g (8 oz) couscous*
- *60 ml (4 tbsp) olive oil*
- *2 garlic cloves, peeled and crushed*
- *2.5 ml (½ tsp) chilli flakes*
- *1 onion, peeled and chopped*
- *10 ml (2 tsp) ground coriander*
- *10 ml (2 tsp) paprika*
- *5 ml (1 tsp) each ground cumin, turmeric and cinnamon*
- *2 medium potatoes, peeled and cubed*

560 CALS/SERVING
- *2 large carrots, peeled and sliced*
- *225 g (8 oz) celeriac, peeled and cubed*
- *400 g (14 oz) can chick-peas*
- *300 ml (10 fl oz) tomato juice*
- *30 ml (2 tbsp) tomato purée*
- *15 ml (1 tbsp) chilli sauce*
- *125 g (4 oz) sultanas*
- *salt and pepper*
- *45 ml (3 tbsp) chopped fresh coriander*

1 Place the couscous in a sieve and wash under cold running water to moisten all the grains, turn out onto a baking sheet and spread out to the sides. Leave until required.

2 Heat the oil in a saucepan and fry the garlic, chilli flakes, onion and spices for 10 minutes. Add the potatoes, carrots and celeriac and continue to fry gently for a further 5 minutes.

3 Stir in the chick-peas with their liquid, together with the tomato juice, tomato purée and chilli sauce. Bring to the boil. Cover, reduce the heat slightly and simmer for 20 minutes.

4 Stir in the sultanas and cook, covered, for a further 10 minutes.

5 Meanwhile, cook the couscous according to the packet instructions. Season the stew to taste, stir in the chopped coriander and serve with the couscous and extra chilli sauce, if wished.

VARIATION For meat eaters, lamb makes a delicious addition to this stew. Cube 450 g (1 lb) lean lamb, seal the meat in hot fat until well browned, then add the garlic, onions and spices and continue as above.

> ### TIP
> If you possess a double boiler, steam the couscous over the stew which will impart a lovely flavour to the couscous as it cooks.

RED CABBAGE WITH PINE NUTS

PREPARATION TIME 10 minutes
COOKING TIME About 25 minutes
FREEZING Not suitable

♡

SERVES 8

- *25 ml (1 fl oz) olive oil*
- *900 g (2 lb) red cabbage, finely shredded*
- *2.5 cm (1 inch) piece fresh root ginger, peeled and grated (optional)*
- *150 ml (5 fl oz) light stock*

135 CALS/SERVING

- *salt and pepper*
- *40 g (1½ oz) butter*
- *30 ml (2 tbsp) balsamic vinegar or red wine vinegar plus 10 ml (2 tsp) muscovado sugar*
- *50 g (2 oz) toasted pine nuts*

1 Heat the oil in a large saucepan and sauté the cabbage with the ginger, if using, over a high heat for 3-4 minutes or until reduced in bulk, stirring occasionally.
2 Add the stock and seasoning, bring to the boil, then cover and cook over a low heat for about 20 minutes. Stir occasionally.
3 When the cabbage is just tender, uncover and bubble down any excess liquid. Off the heat, stir in the butter, balsamic vinegar and pine nuts. Adjust the seasoning and serve.

CITRUS LEEKS WITH SUGAR SNAP PEAS

PREPARATION TIME 15 minutes
COOKING TIME 10-15 minutes
FREEZING Not suitable
COLOUR INDEX Page 39
♡ ⏲

SERVES 6

- *20-30 ml (1½-2 tbsp) olive oil*
- *700 g (1½ lb) trimmed leeks, cut into 1 cm (½ inch) slices*
- *450 g (1 lb) sugar snap peas or mangetouts, topped and tailed*
- *salt and pepper*
  DRESSING
- *45 ml (3 tbsp) olive oil*

150 CALS/SERVING

- *15 ml (1 tbsp) balsamic vinegar*
- *2.5 ml (½ tsp) soft light brown sugar*
- *10-15 ml (2-3 tsp) lemon juice*
- *2.5 ml (½ tsp) Dijon mustard*
- *grated rind and juice of ½ orange*

1 Heat the oil in a large sauté pan. Add the leeks and sauté gently for 5-6 minutes or until just tender. Cook the sugar snap peas in boiling salted water for 5 minutes. Drain, then mix with the leeks.
2 Mix together all the dressing ingredients and season with salt and pepper to taste. Stir into the hot vegetables and serve at once.

> **TIP**
> This dish can also be served cold as a tangy salad accompaniment to cold turkey.

CHESTNUT AND SPROUT SAUTE

PREPARATION TIME 15 25 minutes
COOKING TIME 15-45 minutes
FREEZING Not suitable

SERVES 8

- *900 g (2 lb) fresh chestnuts or 875 g (1 lb 15 oz) can whole chestnuts*
- *600 ml (1 pint) chicken stock*
- *900 g (2 lb) Brussels sprouts, trimmed*
- *salt and pepper*

350 CALS/SERVING

- *450 g (1 lb) onions*
- *125 g (4 oz) butter*
- *225 g (8 oz) celery, cut into 2.5 cm (1 inch) pieces*
- *grated rind of 1 lemon*
- *chopped fresh parsley, to garnish*

1 If using fresh chestnuts, nick the brown outer skins with a sharp knife. Cook in boiling water for 10 minutes. Drain, cool and peel off the shells and inner skins. Cover with the stock and simmer for 20 minutes or until tender. Drain the chestnuts well.
2 Cook the sprouts in boiling, salted water for 3-4 minutes only, then drain well. Peel the onions, then quarter them and separate the layers.
3 Melt the butter in a large sauté or frying pan. Sauté the celery and onions with the lemon rind until beginning to soften.
4 Add the cooked chestnuts, Brussels sprouts and seasoning. Sauté over a high heat for a further 2-3 minutes or until piping hot, stirring frequently. Cover and keep warm until ready to serve, then sprinkle with chopped parsley to garnish.

PARSNIPS IN A LIME GLAZE

PREPARATION TIME 5 minutes
COOKING TIME 17 minutes
FREEZING Not suitable

🕐

SERVES 4
- *700 g (1½ lb) parsnips, peeled*
- *salt and pepper*
- *1 lime*
- *50 g (2 oz) butter*

225 CALS/SERVING
- *25 g (1 oz) light muscovado sugar*
- *thyme sprigs, to garnish*

1 Cut the parsnips in half lengthways. (If using older, tougher parsnips, cut into quarters and remove the woody cores.) Add to a pan of boiling salted water and cook for 5 minutes.
2 Meanwhile, using a vegetable peeler, pare thin slivers of rind from the lime, then set aside for the garnish. Halve the lime and squeeze out the juice.
3 Melt the butter in a large saucepan together with the sugar. Add the lime juice and heat gently,

stirring, to dissolve the sugar.
4 Drain the parsnips, then add to the lime mixture in the pan. Toss in the buttery lime mixture and cook over a moderate heat, shaking the pan frequently, for about 10 minutes until golden brown.
5 Transfer to a warmed serving dish and garnish with the slivers of lime rind and thyme sprigs.

VARIATIONS The sharp glaze can be used with any sweet root vegetable to excellent effect – try it with sweet potatoes or carrots. A handful of walnuts tossed in towards the end of the cooking time adds a delicious crunch.

AROMATIC SWEDE AND CARROTS

PREPARATION TIME 20 minutes
COOKING TIME 15 minutes
FREEZING Not suitable
COLOUR INDEX Page 40

♡

SERVES 4

- *450 g (1 lb) swede, peeled and diced*
- *450 g (1 lb) carrots, peeled and thinly sliced*
- *salt and pepper*
- *25 g (1 oz) butter*

105 CALS/SERVING

- *5 ml (1 tsp) black mustard seeds*
- *2 pieces preserved stem ginger in syrup, drained*
- *parsley or chervil sprigs, to garnish*

1 Cook the vegetables separately in boiling salted water until tender.
2 Meanwhile, melt the butter in a small heavy-based saucepan. Add the mustard seeds and heat gently until the seeds begin to pop. Add the chopped ginger and cook for 1 minute over a low heat.
3 Drain the cooked swede and carrots thoroughly, then mash together using a potato masher or vegetable mill. Season generously with pepper and stir in half of the mustard and ginger mixture.
4 Transfer the mashed swede and carrots to a warmed serving dish and drizzle the remaining mustard and ginger mixture over the top. Garnish with parsley or chervil and serve at once.

POTATO AND CELERIAC GALETTE

PREPARATION TIME 25 minutes
COOKING TIME 1¼ hours
FREEZING Not suitable
COLOUR INDEX Page 41

♡

SERVES 4

- *450 g (1 lb) old potatoes, peeled*
- *450 g (1 lb) celeriac, peeled*
- *1 garlic clove, peeled and crushed*
- *freshly grated nutmeg*

150 CALS/SERVING

- *salt and pepper*
- *25 g (1 oz) butter, melted*
- *chopped fresh parsley, to garnish*

1 Grease and base-line a 20 cm (8 inch) sandwich tin with non-stick baking parchment.
2 Very thinly slice the potatoes and celeriac, preferably in a food processor.
3 Layer up the vegetables with the garlic, nutmeg and seasoning, pressing down firmly as you go. Pour the melted butter over the vegetables.
4 Cover with foil and bake at 230°C (450°F) mark 8 for 1¼ hours or until the vegetables are quite tender. Test with a skewer.
5 Turn the galette out onto a serving plate and garnish with parsley.

GOLDEN POTATOES

PREPARATION TIME 5 minutes
COOKING TIME 1½ hours
FREEZING Not suitable
COLOUR INDEX Page 41

SERVES 6

- *1.1 kg (2½ lb) old potatoes*
- *salt and pepper*
- *2 sprigs rosemary*

230 CALS/SERVING

- *6 garlic cloves (optional)*
- *45 ml (3 tbsp) olive oil*

1 Wash the potatoes and cut into large chunks, but do not peel. Place in cold, salted water, bring to the boil and simmer for 3 minutes. Drain the potatoes well. Strip the spiky rosemary leaves off the sprigs.
2 Place the potatoes in a roasting tin with the unpeeled garlic cloves, if using, rosemary and olive oil.
3 Roast at 200°C (400°F) mark 6 for 1½ hours, basting and turning a few times.

SWEET AND HOT GREEN BEANS WITH PEANUTS

PREPARATION TIME 15 minutes
COOKING TIME About 10 minutes
FREEZING Not suitable
♡ ⏲

SERVES 4-6
- 450 g (1 lb) French beans, topped
- 30 ml (2 tbsp) vegetable oil
- 1 onion, peeled, halved and cut into thin slivers
- 6 dried red chillies, finely chopped

200-135 CALS/SERVING
- 2 garlic cloves, peeled and crushed
- 15 ml (1 tbsp) dark soy sauce
- 30 ml (2 tbsp) clear honey
- 50 g (2 oz) unsalted roasted peanuts

1 Blanch the beans in a pan of boiling water for 2 minutes. Drain and refresh the beans under cold water, then drain well again.
2 Heat the oil in a wok or large frying pan, add the beans, onion, chillies and garlic and stir-fry for 2 minutes. Add the soy sauce and the honey, reduce the heat, cover and cook for 3 minutes.
3 Uncover and cook until the liquid thickens, turning the beans to coat them in the honey and soy mixture. Sprinkle with the nuts and serve.

SPICY MUSHROOMS

PREPARATION TIME 10 minutes
COOKING TIME 45 minutes
FREEZING Not suitable
COLOUR INDEX Page 39
♡

SERVES 6
- oil for frying
- 1 large aubergine, about 350 g (12 oz), cut into chunks
- 3 garlic cloves, peeled and crushed
- 2 large onions, about 450 g (1 lb), peeled and finely sliced
- 5 cm (2 inch) piece fresh root ginger, peeled and coarsely grated
- 10 ml (2 tsp) hot chilli powder

180 CALS/SERVING
- 5 ml (1 tsp) turmeric
- 5 ml (1 tsp) garam masala
- 5 ml (1 tsp) cumin
- two 400 g (14 oz) cans chopped tomatoes
- salt and pepper
- 350 g (12 oz) button mushrooms, halved
- 225 g (8 oz) frozen peas

1 Heat about 60 ml (4 tbsp) oil in a large, non-stick frying pan. Fry the aubergine pieces until golden brown, adding more oil if necessary. Remove the aubergine from the pan and drain on absorbent kitchen paper. Add a little more oil to the pan if necessary then add the garlic, onions and ginger. Cook until golden, stirring occasionally. Mix in the spices and cook for 1 minute, stirring all the time.
2 Return the aubergine to the pan with the tomatoes. Adjust the seasoning then bring to the boil, cover and simmer for about 20 minutes or until the aubergines are tender.
3 Stir in the mushrooms and frozen peas and cook for about a further 10 minutes, adding a little water if necessary to thin down slightly. Transfer to a heated serving dish.

TIP
Hot chilli powder is a blend of chilli, cumin, salt, garlic and oregano. It can be found on the spice racks in supermarkets. Don't be tempted to use pure ground chillies as they are too hot for this recipe.

BUCKWHEAT AND LENTIL PILAFF

PREPARATION TIME 10 minutes, plus soaking
COOKING TIME 30 minutes
FREEZING Not suitable
COLOUR INDEX Page 42

SERVES 8

- *250 g (9 oz) green lentils*
- *250 g (9 oz) buckwheat*
- *10 ml (2 tsp) ground cinnamon*
- *10 ml (2 tsp) ground coriander*
- *5 ml (1 tsp) salt*
- *12 rashers streaky bacon, cut into 2.5 cm (1 inch) strips*
- *450 g (1 lb) onions, peeled and finely sliced*

335 CALS/SERVING

- *3 garlic cloves, peeled and crushed*
- *olive oil*
- *60 ml (4 tbsp) chopped fresh parsley*
- *60 ml (4 tbsp) chopped fresh coriander*
- *black pepper*
- *150 ml (5 fl oz) soured cream and ground cinnamon, to serve*

1 Soak the lentils and the buckwheat separately in bowls of cold water for 1 hour.
2 Drain the lentils and the buckwheat and place the lentils in a saucepan with 900 ml (1½ pints) water, the spices and salt and bring to the boil. Cook, uncovered, for about 20 minutes or until all the liquid has been absorbed and the lentils are tender. Boil the buckwheat for about 15 minutes, then drain. Mix the lentils and buckwheat together.
3 In a non-stick frying pan, fry the bacon until crispy and drain on absorbent kitchen paper. Add the onion and garlic to the pan and fry until golden brown, adding a little oil if necessary.
4 Add the bacon and the onion mixture to the lentils and buckwheat. Stir in the parsley and coriander, then mix in 30 ml (2 tbsp) oil. Season to taste. Serve warm or cold, topped with soured cream and sprinkled with cinnamon.

WINTER SALAD

PREPARATION TIME 20 minutes
FREEZING Not suitable

SERVES 4

- *1 lemon*
- *30 ml (2 tbsp) olive oil*
- *150 ml (5 fl oz) natural yogurt*
- *salt and pepper*
- *2 eating apples*
- *225 g (8 oz) red cabbage, thinly sliced*
- *1 small onion, peeled and thinly sliced*

340 CALS/SERVING

- *4 celery sticks, trimmed and thinly sliced*
- *125 g (4 oz) Cheddar cheese, cut into cubes*
- *50 g (2 oz) unsalted peanuts in skins*
- *celery leaves, to garnish (optional)*

1 In a large bowl whisk together the grated rind of half the lemon, 45 ml (3 tbsp) lemon juice, the olive oil and yogurt. Season well.
2 Core and roughly chop the apples, then toss in the dressing.
3 Toss all the ingredients, except the peanuts and celery leaves, with the apples, mixing well. Sprinkle with peanuts and garnish with celery leaves, if liked.

LIGHT CHRISTMAS PUDDINGS

PREPARATION TIME 40 minutes, plus steeping and drying
COOKING TIME 2½ hours
FREEZING Suitable (stage 5)
❄

SERVES 8
- *225 g (8 oz) sultanas, roughly chopped*
- *150 g (5 oz) raisins, roughly chopped*
- *50 g (2 oz) stoned dates, chopped*
- *50 g (2 oz) currants, roughly chopped*
- *25 g (1 oz) no-soak dried apricots, roughly chopped*
- *1 small eating apple (preferably Granny Smith), peeled and coarsely grated*
- *grated rind of 1 lemon*
- *50 ml (2 fl oz) brandy*

445 CALS/PUDDING
- *125 g (4 oz) butter, softened*
- *125 g (4 oz) soft dark brown sugar*
- *2 small eggs, beaten*
- *125 g (4 oz) fresh white breadcrumbs*
- *40 g (1½ oz) white plain flour*
- *1.25 ml (¼ tsp) each of ground nutmeg and ground cinnamon*
- *2.5 ml (½ tsp) bicarbonate of soda*
- *frosted holly leaves, to decorate*
- *brandy sauce, to serve*

1 Mix the dried fruit with the apple, lemon rind and brandy. Cover and leave in a cool place for two days.
2 Beat the butter and sugar until light and fluffy, then gradually beat in the eggs. Add the fruit mixture with the remaining ingredients and mix.
3 Divide the mixture among eight 25 cm (10 inch) squares of well-floured muslin. Draw up the edges

of muslin and tie with string, allowing room for expansion.
4 Tie the puddings onto skewers and hang them over a large pan of boiling water. Tightly cover the pan with foil and steam for about 1½ hours, topping the pan up with more boiling water, if necessary.
5 While the puddings are warm, mould into neat rounds. Hang in a cool place until quite dry. Overwrap in foil and refrigerate for up to a week.
6 To serve, remove the foil and steam, as above, for about 1 hour. Decorate with frosted holly leaves and serve with brandy sauce.

BREAD AND BUTTER PUDDING WITH PRUNES

PREPARATION TIME 10 minutes, plus soaking
COOKING TIME 1-1¼ hours
FREEZING Not suitable
COLOUR INDEX Page 46

SERVES 6
- *25 g (1 oz) butter*
- *4 slices brown bread, about 150 g (5 oz)*
- *3 eggs*
- *25 g (1 oz) caster sugar*
- *150 ml (5 fl oz) single cream*
- *450 ml (15 fl oz) skimmed milk*

285 CALS/SERVING
- *15 ml (1 tbsp) brandy*
- *125 g (4 oz) pitted no-soak prunes, finely chopped*
- *1.25 ml (¼ tsp) ground cinnamon*
- *25 g (1 oz) demerara sugar*

1 Lightly butter a 7.5 cm (3 inches) deep 1.1 litre (2 pint) ovenproof dish. Spread one side of the bread with the remaining butter. Cut into 2.5 cm (1 inch) squares. Whisk together the eggs, sugar, cream, milk and brandy.
2 Scatter the bread and prunes into the prepared dish. Pour the egg mixture over. Leave to soak for about 20 minutes, lightly pressing the bread into the egg mixture. Sprinkle with the cinnamon and demerara sugar.
3 Place the dish in a roasting tin with enough warm water to come about 2.5 cm (1 inch) up the side of the dish. Cook at 170°C (325°F) mark 3 for about 1 hour-1¼ hours or until the pudding is lightly set. Serve immediately.

STICKY FUDGE AND WALNUT PUDDING

PREPARATION TIME 15 minutes
COOKING TIME 50 minutes
FREEZING Not suitable

SERVES 6   660 CALS/SERVING

- 150 g (5 oz) butter, plus extra for greasing
- 175 g (6 oz) soft light brown sugar
- 300 ml (10 fl oz) double cream
- 125 g (4 oz) chopped dates
- 2.5 ml (½ tsp) bicarbonate of soda
- 1 egg, beaten
- 125 g (4 oz) white self-raising flour
- 50 g (2 oz) chopped walnuts

1 Butter a 1.1 litre (2 pint) deep, ovenproof dish. In a saucepan gently warm 75 g (3 oz) butter, 125 g (4 oz) soft light brown sugar and the double cream. Bring the mixture up to a vigorous boil and bubble for about 3 minutes. Pour a little of the fudge sauce into the prepared dish just to cover the base.

2 Put the dates in a small bowl and pour over 125 ml (4 fl oz) boiling water, add the bicarbonate of soda and leave to stand for 10 minutes.

3 In a bowl, beat the remaining sugar with 50 g (2 oz) butter until light and fluffy. Beat in the egg with the date mixture – it will look slightly curdled. Stir in the flour and nuts. Pour into the dish.

4 Bake at 180°C (350°F) mark 4 for about 50 minutes or until firm to the touch. Cool for 5 minutes, run a palette knife around the edge of the dish, then turn out. Warm the remaining fudge sauce and pour over the pudding.

GOOEY CHOCOLATE PUDDING

PREPARATION TIME 15 minutes
COOKING TIME 1 hour 10 minutes
FREEZING Not suitable

SERVES 4

570 CALS/SERVING

- *200 g (7 oz) milk chocolate*
- *200 ml (7 fl oz) milk*
- *50 g (2 oz) butter, softened*
- *75 g (3 oz) caster sugar*
- *2 eggs, separated*
- *50 g (2 oz) white self-raising flour*
- *25 g (1 oz) cocoa powder*
- *extra cocoa powder, to decorate*
- *vanilla ice cream, to serve*

1 Break the chocolate into small pieces, place in a saucepan with the milk and heat very slowly until all the chocolate has melted. Stir until smooth.
2 Cream together the butter and sugar until light and fluffy. Keep beating and gradually add the egg yolks, chocolate mixture, flour and cocoa powder.
3 In a separate bowl, whisk the egg whites until they hold their shape. Gently fold into the chocolate with a metal spoon.

TIP
The egg whites should stand in soft peaks so that the tips of the peaks flop over gently when held up by the whisk. Overbeaten egg whites will be difficult to fold in evenly.

4 Pour into a deep 1.1 litre (2 pint) ovenproof dish. Place in a roasting tin filled with hot water and bake at 180°C (350°F) mark 4 for about 1 hour or until the pudding is very firm to the touch, but still slightly runny underneath. Cover loosely with foil after about 40 minutes to prevent overbrowning, if necessary. Dust with cocoa powder to decorate and serve with ice cream.

APPLE AND WALNUT FILO PIE

PREPARATION TIME 25 minutes
COOKING TIME 50 minutes
FREEZING Not suitable
COLOUR INDEX Page 47

SERVES 6

425 CALS/SERVING

- *50 g (2 oz) walnut pieces*
- *125 g (4 oz) butter, softened*
- *50 g (2 oz) caster sugar, plus 30 ml (2 tbsp)*
- *finely grated rind and juice of 1 lemon*
- *1 egg*
- *25 g (1 oz) white self-raising flour*
- *2.5 ml (½ tsp) ground cinnamon*
- *700 g (1½ lb) crisp eating apples, peeled and sliced*
- *300 g (10 oz) packet filo pastry*
- *icing sugar, to dust*

1 Toast the walnuts. Allow to cool, then finely chop in a food processor.
2 Beat half the butter with 50 g (2 oz) caster sugar, the lemon rind, egg, flour, half the cinnamon and the chopped walnuts.
3 Mix the apples together with 30 ml (2 tbsp) caster sugar, 15 ml (1 tbsp) lemon juice and the remaining cinnamon.
4 Melt the remaining butter and grease a 25 cm (10 inch) loose-based, fluted flan tin. Use about three-quarters of the pastry to line the tin, buttering well after each piece of pastry and allowing about 7.5 cm (3 inches) of pastry to hang over the sides of the tin.
5 Spread the nut mixture over the pastry base and top with the apples. Fold the pastry edges over the filling and top with a little more pastry to cover the filling completely. Butter between the pastry layers as before. Crumple up any remaining pastry and scatter over the pie. Drizzle with butter.
6 Stand the tin on a baking sheet and bake at 190°C (375°F) mark 5 for about 50 minutes, covering loosely with foil when well browned.
7 Serve warm, dusted with icing sugar.

RAISIN AND ORANGE
CUSTARD TART

PREPARATION TIME 25 minutes, plus chilling
COOKING TIME 1 hour
FREEZING Not suitable

SERVES 8

- *finely grated rind and juice of 1 orange*
- *about 250 ml (8 fl oz) fresh orange juice*
- *325 g (11 oz) raisins, preferably the large Lexia variety*
- *225 g (8 oz) white plain flour*

450 CALS/SERVING

- *150 g (5 oz) butter*
- *75 g (3 oz) icing sugar*
- *2 egg yolks plus 3 whole eggs*
- *450 ml (15 fl oz) milk or double cream, or milk and cream mixed*

1 Strain the juice from the orange and make up to 300 ml (10 fl oz) with the fresh orange juice. Place in a saucepan with the raisins and simmer until all the liquid has evaporated.

2 Meanwhile, place the flour, butter, icing sugar, egg yolks and 15 ml (1 tbsp) water in a food processor and blend until the mixture resembles a crumble topping. Press into the base and up the sides of a 23 cm (9 inch) round 4 cm (1½ inch) deep, loose-based, fluted flan tin. Chill for 45 minutes.

3 Bake blind (see page 383) at 200°C (400°F) mark 6 for 15 minutes or until the edges have turned golden brown. Remove the beans and paper. Reduce the oven temperature to 180°C (350°F) mark 4 and cook for a further 7-10 minutes.

4 Whisk the whole eggs and milk together until they are evenly mixed. Spoon the raisins into the flan and pour in the egg mixture.

5 Bake for 35 minutes or until the custard is just set. Set aside for about 15 minutes before serving warm, or leave to cool completely.

TIP
To test the custard, gently shake the flan: the surface should not wobble. Or press gently on the surface of the custard – if set, it will be quite firm to the touch.

WHITE CHOCOLATE TORTE

PREPARATION TIME 20 minutes, plus chilling
COOKING TIME 10 minutes
FREEZING Suitable

❄

SERVES 12
- *75 g (3 oz) butter*
- *225 g (8 oz) ginger biscuits, finely crushed*
- *700 g (1½ lb) white chocolate*
- *600 ml (1 pint) double cream*

785 CALS/SERVING
- *icing sugar and cocoa powder, to decorate*

CHOCOLATE STARS
- *225 g (8 oz) white, plain or milk chocolate*
- *25 g (1 oz) butter*

1 To make the chocolate stars, roughly chop the chocolate and melt with the butter in a bowl set over a pan of simmering water. Spread thinly on two baking sheets lined with non-stick baking parchment and refrigerate to set. Soften at room temperature for a few seconds and stamp out star shapes. Place the star shapes in the refrigerator as you make them. When the chocolate gets too soft to handle, chill again. Freeze the complete batch interleaved with non-stick baking parchment.
2 Line the base of a 23 cm (9 inch) round, 6.5 cm (2½ inches) deep, spring-release tin with non-stick baking parchment or greaseproof paper.
3 Melt the butter and stir into the biscuit crumbs. Press into the prepared tin and chill for 15 minutes.
4 Break up the chocolate and put it in a medium-size saucepan with half the cream. Heat very gently, stirring occasionally, until almost smooth. Pour into a bowl and cool for 15 minutes or until just beginning to thicken. Stir occasionally.
5 Whip the remainder of the cream until it forms soft peaks. Fold into the cool chocolate mixture. Pour over the biscuit base and chill for at least 3 hours, preferably overnight.
6 Serve chilled. Remove from the tin, decorate with the frozen chocolate stars and dust with icing sugar and cocoa.

NOTE Chocolate should be barely warm but still liquid before adding the whipped cream at stage 5. If the chocolate is allowed to reach too high a temperature it becomes a solid mass, but if it's too cold it won't combine with the cream.

CHOCOLATE CHESTNUT MERINGUES

PREPARATION TIME 30 minutes, plus standing
COOKING TIME 2 hours
FREEZING Suitable (stage 2)
COLOUR INDEX Page 48

❄

SERVES 6

- *325 g (11 oz) milk or plain chocolate*
- *4 egg whites*
- *225 g (8 oz) caster sugar*
- *250 g (9 oz) can or tube sweetened chestnut purée (or chestnut spread)*

725 CALS/SERVING

- *finely grated rind of 1 orange*
- *300 ml (10 fl oz) double cream*

1 Finely grate 125 g (4 oz) of the chocolate. Line 2 baking sheets with non-stick baking parchment. Whisk the egg whites until stiff but not dry. Whisk in half the sugar, about a heaped tablespoonful at a time. Continue whisking until stiff and shiny. Fold in the remaining sugar and the grated chocolate. Using spoons, shape the mixture into about 30 meringues on the baking sheets.
2 Bake at 100°C (200°F) mark low for about 2 hours or until well dried out. (Meringues cooked in gas ovens sometimes take a little longer.) Switch the baking sheets round during baking if necessary. Cool on wire racks and store in airtight containers until required (up to 3 weeks).
3 Beat together the chestnut purée and the orange rind until smooth. Reserve 45 ml (3 tbsp) cream. Whisk the remainder until it just holds its shape. Stir a large spoonful into the chestnut mixture, then fold in the remaining whisked cream.
4 Sandwich the meringues together with the cream and refrigerate until required – about 2 hours. Leave to stand at room temperature for 10-15 minutes.
5 Meanwhile, make the sauce. Break up the remaining chocolate and place in a saucepan with the reserved cream. Pour in 50 ml (2 fl oz) water and warm very gently until the chocolate melts, stirring occasionally. Simmer gently for about 1-2 minutes, stirring, until the sauce thickens slightly. Serve warm with the meringues.

PASSION FRUIT AND MANGO SOUFFLE

PREPARATION TIME 40 minutes, plus chilling
COOKING TIME 3 minutes
FREEZING Suitable (stage 6)
COLOUR INDEX Page 45

❄

SERVES 10

- *three 400 g (14 oz) cans mangoes, drained*
- *3 large passion fruit*
- *50 ml (2 fl oz) fresh orange juice*
- *30 ml (2 tbsp) powdered gelatine*

320 CALS/SERVING

- *4 eggs, separated*
- *125 g (4 oz) caster sugar*
- *300 ml (10 fl oz) double cream*
- *mango slices and star fruit, to decorate*

1 Place the mangoes in a large saucepan with the pulp of the passion fruit and the orange juice. Heat gently, stirring continuously, for 3-4 minutes or until pulpy. Purée and rub through a nylon sieve. Leave to cool. There should be 450-600 ml (¾-1 pint) purée.
2 In a small bowl, sprinkle the gelatine over 90 ml (6 tbsp) water and leave to soak for 5 minutes.
3 Whisk together the egg yolks and sugar until very thick and pale. Gradually whisk in the fruit purée.
4 Place the bowl of gelatine over a pan of gently simmering water for 2-3 minutes, until the gelatine has completely dissolved. Whisk into the fruit mixture.
5 Whip the cream until it just begins to hold its shape. Fold into the mixture. Whisk the egg whites until stiff but not dry and fold in.
6 Pour the mixture into a 2.3 litre (4 pint) serving dish. Refrigerate to set for about 5 hours.
7 Arrange the mango slices and the star fruit over the surface of the soufflé. Serve immediately.

the syrup and pour over the fruit in the bowl.
Cover and chill for 1 hour.
4 Spoon the fruit salad into a serving dish or
individual glass bowls and scatter the kumquats
on top. Serve with whipped cream.

NOTE Kumquats are readily available at
Christmas and have a sharp perfumed flavour.
Some stores sell crystallized kumquats which are
ideal for decorating desserts and cakes.

VARIATION Substitute 4 ripe pears for the
pineapple and cook the kumquats in a syrup
flavoured with jasmine tea rather than Earl Grey.

PINEAPPLE AND DATE SALAD WITH KUMQUATS

PREPARATION TIME 35 minutes, plus chilling
COOKING TIME 15 minutes
FREEZING Not suitable

SERVES 6   330 CALS/SERVING
- *75 ml (5 tbsp) acacia*
  honey
- *50 g (2 oz) soft*
  brown sugar
- *300 ml (10 fl oz)*
  Earl Grey tea,
  strained
- *225 g (8 oz)*
  kumquats, halved

- *2 oranges, peeled*
- *1 medium pineapple*
- *12 fresh or dried*
  dates, halved and
  stoned
- *125 g (4 oz) walnut*
  halves

1 First make the syrup. Place the honey, sugar and
tea in a saucepan and bring to the boil. Boil for 1
minute. Place the kumquats in the syrup. Simmer,
uncovered, for about 10 minutes until the
kumquats are tender. Leave to cool in the syrup.
2 Slice the oranges crosswise and place in a bowl.
Using a sharp knife, cut the top and bottom off
the pineapple and cut away the skin. Quarter the
pineapple lengthways and cut out the core. Cut
the flesh into large chunks. Carefully mix with the
oranges.
3 Stir the dates into the fruit mixture with the
walnuts. Drain the kumquats and set aside; strain

CLEMENTINES IN BRANDY

PREPARATION TIME 10-15 minutes
FREEZING Not suitable
COLOUR INDEX Page 45
♡ ⏱

SERVES 6   140 CALS/SERVING
- *10 clementines or*
  other seedless 'easy
  peelers'
- *12 pitted dates or no-*
  soak prunes
- *juice of 1 lemon*

- *30 ml (2 tbsp) caster*
  sugar
- *60 ml (4 tbsp)*
  brandy

1 Peel the clementines. Remove as much pith as
possible then thickly slice into a bowl. Roughly
slice the dates or prunes and stir into the
clementines.
2 Stir the lemon juice, sugar and brandy into the
fruit. Cover and chill until required.

LIME AND CRANBERRY ICE

PREPARATION TIME 15 minutes, plus freezing
COOKING TIME 5-10 minutes
FREEZING Suitable
COLOUR INDEX Page 48
❄

SERVES 8
- *550 g (1¼ lb) cranberries*
- *8 egg yolks*
- *225 g (8 oz) caster sugar*
- *450 ml (15 fl oz) milk*

270 CALS/SERVING
- *2 limes*
- *500 g (1 lb 2 oz) carton bio natural yogurt*
- *juice of 1 orange*

1 Place the cranberries in a saucepan with a little water and heat gently until slightly softened. Drain well.
2 Whisk together the egg yolks and 175 g (6 oz) sugar until thick and pale. Bring the milk to just below boiling point, then pour it onto the egg mixture, whisking continuously. Rinse out the saucepan.
3 Return the mixture to the pan and heat gently, stirring, until the custard thickens slightly and just coats the spoon. Do not boil or the custard will curdle. Strain into a large bowl. Leave to cool.
4 Finely grate the rind of both limes and squeeze out 30 ml (2 tbsp) lime juice. Add the yogurt to the custard with 350 g (12 oz) cranberries and the lime rind and juice. Blend in batches in a food processor until almost smooth.
5 Pour into a freezer container to a depth of about 5 cm (2 inches). Freeze for about 4 hours until mushy, then beat well to break down the ice crystals. Freeze again until firm, for at least 8 hours. (If using an ice-cream maker, churn the mixture in the usual way.)
6 Place the remaining cranberries in a pan with the remaining sugar and the orange juice. Place over a gentle heat until the sugar dissolves and the cranberries are heated through. Pour into a bowl and leave to cool. Cover and chill.
7 About 1½ hours before serving, transfer the ice cream to the refrigerator to soften. Serve scoops with the cranberries in syrup.

VANILLA ICE WITH ESPRESSO

PREPARATION TIME 5 minutes
FREEZING Not suitable
🌀

SERVES 6
- *espresso coffee*
- *vanilla or a 'nutty' luxury ice cream*

260 CALS/SERVING
- *chocolate-covered coffee beans or tiny chocolates, to serve*

1 Make up the espresso coffee according to the instructions on your machine.
2 Scoop the ice cream into glasses and pour about 45-60 ml (3-4 tbsp) hot espresso over each serving.
3 Serve with some chocolate-covered coffee beans or tiny chocolates.

TIP
If you don't have an espresso machine, use very strong black coffee or the sachets or jars of instant espresso coffee that can be found in most supermarkets.

RICH CHRISTMAS CAKE

PREPARATION TIME 30 minutes, plus storing and icing
COOKING TIME 2½-3 hours
FREEZING Not suitable

SERVES 12-16

- *150 g (5 oz) each glacé cherries, dried figs, apricots, dates, raisins, sultanas*
- *50 g (2 oz) mixed peel*
- *175 ml (6 fl oz) dark rum*
- *175 g (6 oz) skinned, roasted hazelnuts*
- *225 g (8 oz) butter, softened*
- *grated rind of 1 lemon*
- *225 g (8 oz) soft dark brown sugar*
- *4 eggs, beaten*

610-460 CALS/SERVING

- *30 ml (2 tbsp) black treacle*
- *225 g (8 oz) white plain flour*
- *10 ml (2 tsp) ground mixed spice*

TO COVER

- *60-90 ml (4-6 tbsp) honey or apricot jam*
- *350 g (12 oz) white marzipan*
- *450 g (1 lb) ready-to-roll fondant icing*

TO DECORATE

- *gold ribbon*
- *red and gold berries*
- *gold fir cones*

1 Line a 20 cm (8 inch) round deep cake tin with a double thickness of greaseproof paper.
2 Rinse the glacé cherries to remove all the syrup.

Drain and dry on absorbent kitchen paper. Very roughly chop the cherries, figs, apricots and dates. Mix all the fruit and the mixed peel with 125 ml (4 fl oz) rum and soak for 3-4 hours.
3 Place 50 g (2 oz) hazelnuts in a blender or food processor and blend until finely chopped. Roughly chop the remainder.
4 Beat the butter with the lemon rind until soft and pale in colour. Gradually beat in the sugar until well mixed. Beat in the eggs a little at a time. Beat in the treacle until evenly blended.
5 Sift the flour and spice together and fold half into the creamed ingredients. Stir in all the hazelnuts. Gently fold in all the fruit, followed by the remaining flour. Spoon into the prepared cake tin, then level off the surface. Tie a band of brown paper around the outside of the tin.
6 Bake at 150°C (300°F) mark 2 for 2½-3 hours or until a fine skewer inserted into the centre comes out clean.
7 Pierce the surface with a fine skewer and spoon over the remaining rum. Leave the cake in the tin for 1 hour, then turn out. Cool on a wire rack. Remove all the lining paper and wrap tightly in fresh greaseproof paper and foil. Store in a cool, dry place for at least a week and up to 2 months.
8 To marzipan the cake, warm half the honey or apricot jam with 15 ml (1 tbsp) water in a pan

and brush over the cake. On a surface lightly dusted with icing sugar, roll out the marzipan in a circle, large enough to cover the top and sides of the cake – about 10 cm (4 inches) bigger than the cake top. Place over the cake, press gently around the sides, then trim the edges. Dry for 2 days.

9 To fondant-ice, warm the remaining honey or sieved apricot jam with 15 ml (1 tbsp) water in a pan. Lightly brush over the cake. Sprinkle a work surface and rolling pin with cornflour. Roll out the fondant icing until it is about 10 cm (4 inches) larger than the cake top. Cover the cake. Leave to dry in a cool place for 2 days, covered, then decorate with ribbon, berries and cones.

an oiled bowl. Cover with oiled clingfilm and leave in a warm place for 1½-2 hours until doubled in size.

3 Using floured hands, knock down the dough, then place on a lightly floured work surface and knead for 1-2 minutes only. Roll out the dough to a 25 cm (10 inch) square. Brush lightly with melted butter. Knead and roll out the almond paste to a strip about 23 x 10 cm (9 x 4 inches) and place down the centre of the dough. Fold the dough over the almond paste and seal well.

4 Pinch the ends together to enclose the almond paste. Place, seam-side down, on a buttered baking sheet. Make a few slits across the top. Cover and leave in a warm place for 30-45 minutes until doubled in size.

5 Bake at 190°C (375°F) mark 5 for 40 minutes or until sounding hollow when tapped. Cool on a wire rack. Dust with icing sugar.

STOLLEN

PREPARATION TIME 40 minutes, plus rising
COOKING TIME About 40 minutes
FREEZING Suitable
COLOUR INDEX Page 50

❄

SERVES 10
- 15 g (½ oz) fresh yeast or 7 g (¼ oz) sachet fast-action dried yeast
- about 175 ml (6 fl oz) tepid milk
- 350 g (12 oz) strong white plain flour
- 5 ml (1 tsp) salt
- 3.75 ml (¾ tsp) ground mixed spice
- 50 g (2 oz) butter
- finely grated rind of 1 lemon
- 25 g (1 oz) caster sugar

325 CALS/SERVING
- 50 g (2 oz) currants
- 75 g (3 oz) raisins or sultanas
- 25 g (1 oz) chopped mixed peel
- 40 g (1½ oz) flaked almonds
- 1 egg, beaten
- melted butter, for brushing
- 175 g (6 oz) almond paste or white marzipan
- icing sugar for dusting

1 If using fresh yeast, blend with the milk. Sift the flour, salt and spice into a bowl and rub in the butter. Stir in the lemon rind, sugar, currants, raisins, mixed peel, almonds and fast-action dried yeast, if using. Make a well in the centre of the dry ingredients and add the yeast liquid or milk and egg. Beat to form a soft dough, adding a little more milk if necessary.

2 Turn out the dough onto a floured surface and, with floured hands, knead for 8-10 minutes until the dough is elastic and almost smooth. Place in

MINCE PIES

PREPARATION TIME 1 hour
COOKING TIME About 25 minutes
FREEZING Suitable
COLOUR INDEX Page 51

❄

MAKES ABOUT 24
- Shortcrust Pastry, made with 225 g (8 oz) flour (see page 383)
- about 225 g (8 oz) Apricot Mincemeat (see page 380)

105 CALS/MINCE PIE
- 1 egg white, lightly beaten
- caster sugar
- cream, to serve

1 Roll out the pastry thinly and cut out about 48 5.5 cm (2¼ inch) rounds, re-rolling as necessary.

2 Place half the rounds on baking sheets and spoon mincemeat onto the centre of each. Moisten the pastry edges. Cover with the remaining pastry rounds, sealing the edges well; flute, if wished. Make a hole in the top to allow steam to escape.

3 Bake at 200°C (400°F) mark 6 for about 15 minutes or until just set but not browned.

4 Take out of the oven and brush with lightly beaten egg white and dredge with caster sugar. Return to the oven for a further 8-10 minutes or until well browned. Serve the mince pies warm with cream.

BUCHE DE NOEL

PREPARATION TIME 1 hour
COOKING TIME About 10 minutes
FREEZING Suitable (stage 7)

❄

SERVES 8-10
- *3 eggs*
- *125 g (4 oz) caster sugar*
- *75 g (3 oz) white plain flour*
- *30 ml (2 tbsp) cocoa powder*
- *440 g (15½ oz) can sweetened chestnut purée*
- *icing sugar for dusting*

720-575 CALS/SERVING
- *holly sprigs, to decorate*
  BUTTER CREAM
- *225 g (8 oz) unsalted butter*
- *50 g (2 oz) plain chocolate*
- *450 g (1 lb) icing sugar*

1 To make the cake, grease a 33 x 23 cm (13 x 9 inch) Swiss roll tin. Line with greaseproof paper and grease the paper. Dredge with a little caster sugar, then with a little flour, knocking out any excess.

2 Put the eggs and sugar in a deep heatproof bowl and stand it over a saucepan of simmering water. Whisk until thick enough to leave a trail on the surface when the whisk is lifted.

TIP
For an attractive additional decoration, make meringue mushrooms; bake 'caps' and 'stalks' separately and stick together with butter cream.

---

3 Take the bowl off the saucepan and continue whisking the mixture for 5 minutes or until cool. Sift in the flour and cocoa and gently fold into the mixture. Fold in 15 ml (1 tbsp) hot water.

4 Pour the mixture gently into the prepared tin and lightly level the surface. Bake in the oven at 200°C (400°F) mark 6 for about 10 minutes or until slightly shrunk away from the sides of the tin.

5 Meanwhile, place a sheet of greaseproof paper on top of a tea towel. Dredge the paper with caster sugar and turn the cake out onto it. Trim off the crusty edges with a sharp knife. Roll up the cake with the paper inside. Transfer to a wire rack, seam side down, and leave to cool for 20 minutes.

6 To make the butter cream, beat the butter until soft. Put the chocolate with 15 ml (1 tbsp) water in a heatproof bowl over hot water. Melt, then leave to cool slightly. Gradually sift and beat the icing sugar into the softened butter, then add the melted chocolate.

7 Unroll the cold Swiss roll. Remove the paper and spread the chestnut purée over the cake. Roll up again and place on a cake board or plate.

8 Cut a thick diagonal slice off one end of the Swiss roll and attach with butter cream to the side of the roll.

9 Using a piping bag and a large star nozzle, pipe thin lines of butter cream over the log. Pipe one or two swirls of butter cream to represent knots in the wood. Decorate the log with sprigs of holly and dust lightly with icing sugar.

FLORENTINES

PREPARATION TIME 20 minutes, plus cooling
COOKING TIME About 15 minutes
FREEZING Not suitable
COLOUR INDEX Page 52

MAKES ABOUT 30
- *100 g (3½ oz) butter*
- *125 g (4 oz) caster sugar*
- *125 g (4 oz) flaked almonds, roughly chopped*
- *25 g (1 oz) sultanas*
- *5 glacé cherries, chopped*

120 CALS/SERVING
- *25 g (1 oz) chopped mixed peel*
- *15 ml (1 tbsp) single cream or milk*
- *300 g (10 oz) plain chocolate*

1 Line 4 baking sheets with non-stick baking parchment. Melt the butter in a saucepan over a low heat, add the sugar and boil the mixture for 1 minute.

2 Remove the pan from the heat and add all the remaining ingredients, except the chocolate, stirring well to mix.

3 Drop the mixture into small heaps onto the prepared baking sheets, allowing space between each for the mixture to spread.

4 Bake in the oven at 180°C (350°F) mark 4 for 10-15 minutes or until golden brown.

5 Remove from the oven and press around the edges of the biscuits with the blade of a knife to neaten the shape. Leave on the baking sheets for 5 minutes or until beginning to firm, then cool on a wire rack.

6 When the biscuits are cool, melt the chocolate and leave it to cool for about 10-15 minutes or until it coats the back of a spoon and is just beginning to set.

7 Spread the chocolate over the backs of the biscuits. Mark wavy lines in the chocolate with a fork and leave to set.

VARIATION To make more elaborate florentines, for serving as petits fours, make them slightly smaller than here. Coat half with plain and half with milk chocolate, then pipe with contrasting lines of chocolate to decorate.

SHORTBREAD

PREPARATION TIME 20 minutes, plus chilling
COOKING TIME 20 minutes
FREEZING Not suitable

MAKES 24-36   270-180 CALS/BISCUIT
- 450 g (1 lb) butter
- 225 g (8 oz) caster sugar
- 450 g (1 lb) white plain flour
- 225 g (8 oz) rice flour or ground rice
- *pinch of salt*
- *golden or coloured granulated sugar, for coating*
- *caster sugar, for sprinkling*

1 Line 2 baking sheets with greaseproof paper. Cream the butter and sugar together in a bowl until pale and fluffy. Sift the flour, rice flour and salt together and stir into the creamed mixture until it resembles breadcrumbs.

2 Gather the dough together with your hand and

turn onto a clean work surface. Knead lightly until it forms a ball, then lightly roll into a sausage, about 5-7.5 cm (2-3 inches) thick. Wrap in clingfilm and chill until firm.

3 Unwrap the roll and slice into discs, about 7-10 mm (⅓-½ inch) thick. Pour golden or coloured granulated sugar onto a plate and roll the edge of each disc in the sugar. Place the biscuits, cut-side up, on the baking sheets.

4 Bake at 190°C (375°F) mark 5 for about 15-25 minutes, until very pale golden. Remove from the oven and sprinkle with caster sugar. Allow to cool on the baking sheet for 10 minutes, then transfer to a wire rack to cool.

VARIATIONS *Spiced Shortbread:* Sift 15 ml (1 tbsp) ground mixed spice with the flours.
Ginger Shortbread: Sift 5 ml (1 tsp) ground ginger with the flours. Add 50 g (2 oz) chopped crystallized ginger to the dough.
Chocolate Chip Shortbread: Knead 50 g (2 oz) chocolate chips into the dough.

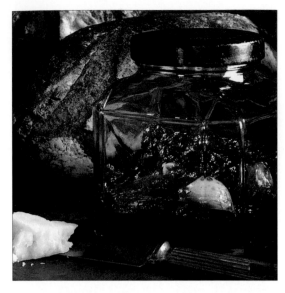

any discoloured ones. Place in a heavy-based saucepan with the ginger, remaining sugar, mustard seeds, red wine and vinegar. Bring slowly to the boil and simmer for 10-15 minutes until the cranberries burst and the mixture thickens. Remove from the heat.

4 Stir in the shallots. Deglaze the roasting tin with the liqueur and reduce until syrupy, then pour into the cranberry mixture. Return to the heat and simmer very gently, stirring occasionally, for 10-15 minutes or until the chutney is thick. Pot and cover in the usual way (see page 385).

APRICOT MINCEMEAT

PREPARATION TIME 10 minutes, plus standing
FREEZING Not suitable
COLOUR INDEX Page 54

MAKES 1.8 KG (4 LB)
- *225 g (8 oz) no-soak dried apricots*
- *finely grated rind and juice of 1 orange*
- *900 g (2 lb) mixed currants, sultanas and raisins*
- *60 ml (4 tbsp) orange marmalade*

45 CALS/15 ML (1 TBSP)
- *450 g (1 lb) demerara sugar*
- *7.5 ml (1½ tsp) ground mixed spice*
- *1.25 ml (¼ tsp) freshly grated nutmeg*
- *300 ml (10 fl oz) brandy*

1 Snip the apricots into small pieces, and mix with the orange rind, 45 ml (3 tbsp) orange juice and all the remaining ingredients.
2 Cover and leave for 48 hours, stirring occasionally.
3 Pot and cover in the usual way (see page 385) and store in a cool place for up to 2 months.

TIP
Make the mincemeat at least a week ahead. Always stir the mincemeat before using as ingredients at the top can become dry.

CRANBERRY AND ROAST SHALLOT CHUTNEY

PREPARATION TIME 25 minutes
COOKING TIME About 40 minutes
FREEZING Not suitable

MAKES 900 G (2 LB)
- *450 g (1 lb) shallots*
- *45 ml (3 tbsp) olive oil*
- *225 g (8 oz) soft brown sugar*
- *salt and pepper*
- *450 g (1 lb) cranberries*
- *2.5 cm (1 inch) piece fresh root ginger, peeled and finely grated*

45 CALS/25 G (1 OZ)
- *15 ml (1 tbsp) mustard seeds*
- *150 ml (5 fl oz) red wine*
- *200 ml (7 fl oz) red wine vinegar*
- *45 ml (3 tbsp) crème de cassis liqueur*

1 Plunge the shallots into a pan of boiling water for 5 minutes to loosen the skins, then remove. When cool enough to handle, carefully peel, leaving on a little root end to hold them intact.
2 Halve the shallots lengthwise and place in a roasting tin with the olive oil and 45 ml (3 tbsp) of the sugar. Roast at 200°C (400°F) mark 6 for at least 30 minutes, turning twice until softened and caramelized, but not burnt. Season generously with salt and pepper.
3 Meanwhile, pick over the cranberries, discarding

TANGERINE JELLY MARMALADE

PREPARATION TIME 40 minutes
COOKING TIME About 2¼ hours
FREEZING Not suitable
COLOUR INDEX Page 54

**MAKES ABOUT 2.3 KG
(5 LB)**
- *900 g (2 lb)
  tangerines, washed*
- *1 large grapefruit,
  washed*

35 CALS/15 ML (1 TBSP)
- *1 lemon, washed*
- *5 ml (1 tsp) citric
  acid*
- *1.4 kg (3 lb) sugar*

1 Peel the tangerines and cut the peel into fine
shreds. Tie the shreds in a piece of muslin.
2 Peel the grapefruit and lemon and cut the peel
up finely. Roughly chop the flesh of all the fruit,
reserving the juice, and put the flesh, juice and
peel in a preserving pan with the muslin bag.
3 Add the citric acid and 2.8 litres (5 pints) water
to the pan and simmer for about 2 hours or until
the fruit is soft. Remove the muslin bag after 30
minutes, squeezing it well and allowing the juice
to run back into the pan.
4 Untie the muslin bag, place the tangerine peel in
a sieve, wash under cold water, then drain and
reserve.
5 Spoon the pulped fruit into a jelly bag or cloth
attached to the legs of an upturned stool, and
leave to strain into a large bowl for about 2
hours.
6 Discard the pulp remaining in the jelly bag.
Pour the extract into a clean preserving pan and
add the sugar. Heat gently, stirring, until the sugar
has dissolved. Bring to the boil, stir in the
reserved tangerine peel and boil rapidly for 10
minutes or until setting point is reached (see page
385).
7 Remove any scum with a slotted spoon, leave
the marmalade to stand for 15 minutes, then stir
to distribute the shreds. Pot and cover in the usual
way (see page 385).

NOTE All together, the unprepared fruit should
weigh about 1.3 kg (2¾ lb).

SEVILLE ORANGE MARMALADE

PREPARATION TIME 30 minutes
COOKING TIME About 2½ hours
FREEZING Not suitable

**MAKES ABOUT 4.5 KG
(10 LB)**
- *1.4 kg (3 lb) Seville
  oranges*

35 CALS/15 ML (1 TBSP)
- *juice of 2 lemons*
- *2.7 kg (6 lb) sugar*

1 Halve the oranges and squeeze out the juice and
pips. Tie the pips, and any membrane that has
come away during squeezing, in a piece of muslin.
Slice the orange peel thinly or thickly, as preferred,
and put it in a preserving pan with the fruit juices,
muslin bag and 3.4 litres (6 pints) water.
2 Simmer gently for about 2 hours or until the
peel is really soft and the liquid reduced by about
half. Remove the muslin bag, squeezing it well and
allowing the juice to run back into the pan. Add
the sugar. Heat gently, stirring until the sugar has
dissolved.
3 Bring to the boil and boil rapidly for 15 minutes
until setting point is reached (see page 385).
4 Remove any scum with a slotted spoon. Leave
to stand for 15 minutes, then stir to distribute the
peel. Pot and cover in the usual way (see page 385).

BASIC RECIPES

Making your own stocks and pastry will give recipes that extra depth of flavour, while homemade mayonnaise and bread will give everyday meals a culinary lift.

VEGETABLE STOCK

PREPARATION TIME 15 minutes
COOKING TIME 1¾ hours
FREEZING Suitable

MAKES 1.1 LITRES (2 PINTS)
- *30 ml (2 tbsp) vegetable oil*
- *1 onion, peeled and finely chopped*
- *1 carrot, peeled and diced*
- *50 g (2 oz) turnip, peeled and diced*
- *50 g (2 oz) parsnip, peeled and diced*
- *4 celery sticks, chopped*
- *vegetable trimmings, such as celery tops, cabbage leaves, mushroom peelings, tomato skins*
- *1 bouquet garni*
- *6 black peppercorns*
- *a little salt*

1 Heat the oil in a saucepan, add the onion and fry gently for about 5 minutes until lightly coloured.
2 Add the other vegetables to the pan with the trimmings and 1.7 litres (3 pints) water. Add the bouquet garni and peppercorns. Season with salt.
3 Bring to the boil, partially cover and simmer for 1½ hours, skimming occasionally.
4 Strain the stock and leave to cool. Cover and store in the refrigerator. Use within 1-2 days.

BEEF STOCK

PREPARATION TIME 15 minutes,
COOKING TIME 4½-5½ hours
FREEZING Suitable

MAKES 900 ML (1½ PINTS)
- *450 g (1 lb) shin of beef, cut into pieces*
- *450 g (1 lb) marrow bones or knuckle of veal, chopped*
- *1 bouquet garni*
- *1 onion, peeled and sliced*
- *1 carrot, peeled and sliced*
- *1 celery stick, sliced*
- *2.5 ml (½ tsp) salt*

1 To give a good flavour and colour, brown the meat and bones in the oven before using them. Place in a roasting tin and cook at 220°C (425°F)

mark 7 for 30-40 minutes until well browned.
2 Put the bones and meat in a saucepan with 1.7 litres (3 pints) water, the bouquet garni, vegetables and salt. Bring to the boil and remove any scum.
3 Partially cover and simmer for 4-5 hours.
4 Strain and, when cold, remove all traces of fat.

CHICKEN STOCK

PREPARATION TIME 15 minutes
COOKING TIME 2-3 hours
FREEZING Suitable

MAKES 1.1 LITRES (2 PINTS)
- *1 chicken carcass, bones and trimmings from a roast chicken*
- *1 onion, peeled and sliced*
- *1 carrot, peeled and sliced*
- *1 celery stick, sliced*
- *1 bouquet garni*
- *1 bay leaf*
- *salt*

1 Break up the chicken carcass and put in a large saucepan with any skin and meat attached, plus other bones and trimmings.
2 Add 1.7 litres (3 pints) water, the onion, carrot, celery, bouquet garni, bay leaf and a little salt. Bring to the boil, then skim.
3 Partially cover and simmer for 2-3 hours.
4 Strain and, when cold, remove all traces of fat.

FISH STOCK

PREPARATION TIME 10 minutes
COOKING TIME 20 minutes
FREEZING Suitable

MAKES 900 ML (1½ PINTS)
- *450-750 g (1-1½ lb) fish bones and trimmings*
- *salt*
- *1 bouquet garni*
- *1 onion, peeled and sliced*

1 Put the fish bones and trimmings into a saucepan, cover with 900 ml (1½ pints) water and add a little salt. Bring to the boil, then skim.
2 Reduce the heat and add the bouquet garni and

onion. Cover and simmer for 20 minutes.
3 Strain and leave to cool. Use on the same day, or store in the refrigerator for not more than 2 days.

SHORTCRUST PASTRY

PREPARATION TIME 10 minutes, plus resting
FREEZING Suitable

For shortcrust pastry, the proportion of flour to fat is 2:1, or twice the quantity. Therefore, for a recipe using quantities of shortcrust pastry other than 225 g (8 oz), simply use half the quantity of fat to the flour weight specified.

MAKES 225 G (8 OZ)
- *225 g (8 oz) white plain flour*
- *pinch of salt*

175 CALS/25 G (1 OZ)
- *125 g (4 oz) butter or margarine, chilled and diced*

1 Mix flour and salt together in a bowl. Add the fat to the flour. Using your fingertips, rub the fat lightly into the flour until the mixture resembles fine breadcrumbs.
2 Add 45-60 ml (3-4 tbsp) chilled water, sprinkling it evenly over the surface.
3 Stir in with a round bladed knife until the mixture begins to stick together in large lumps. Collect the dough mixture together to form a ball.
4 Knead lightly for a few seconds to give a firm, smooth dough; do not overhandle the dough. Wrap in clingfilm or greaseproof paper and rest in the refrigerator for about 30 minutes.
5 To roll out the pastry, sprinkle a very little flour on a work surface and the rolling pin (not on the pastry) and roll out the dough evenly in one direction only, turning it occasionally. The usual thickness is 3 mm (⅛ inch). Do not pull or stretch the pastry.

VARIATION *Walnut Shortcrust Pastry* Follow the recipe for Shortcrust Pastry, stirring in 40 g (1½ oz) very finely chopped, shelled walnuts before adding the water.

BAKING BLIND
If a recipe for a flan or tart instructs you to bake blind, it means that you should partially or completely bake the pastry case before filling. To bake blind, first prick the pastry base with a fork, then line with a large piece of greaseproof paper

or foil. Fill with ceramic baking beans or dried pulses. Small cases don't need lining – just prick with a fork.

For partially baked cases, bake at 200°C (400°F) mark 6 for 10-15 minutes until the case looks 'set'. Carefully remove the paper or foil and the beans and bake for a further 5 minutes until the base is firm to the touch and lightly coloured.

For completely baked cases, return to the oven for about 15 minutes until firm and golden brown.

PUFF PASTRY

PREPARATION TIME 40 minutes, plus resting
FREEZING Suitable

The richest of all the pastries, puff requires patience, practice and very light handling. Whenever possible it should be made the day before use. It is not practical to make in a quantity with less than 450 g (1 lb) flour weight. This quantity is equivalent to two 375 g (13 oz) packets.

MAKES 450 G (1 LB)
- *450 g (1 lb) strong plain flour*
- *pinch of salt*
- *450 g (1 lb) butter or margarine, chilled*

270 CALS/25 G (1 OZ)
- *15 ml (1 tbsp) lemon juice*

1 Mix the flour and salt together. Cut off 50 g (2 oz) of the butter and flatten the remaining butter with a rolling pin to a slab 2 cm (¾ inch) thick.
2 Cut the 50 g (2 oz) butter into small pieces, add to the flour and rub in. Using a round-bladed knife, stir in the lemon juice and about 300 ml (10 fl oz) chilled water to make a soft, elastic dough.
3 Quickly knead the dough until smooth and shape into a round. Cut through half the depth in the shape of a cross. Open out to form a star.
4 Roll out, keeping the centre four times as thick as the flaps. Place the slab of butter in the centre.
5 Fold the flaps envelope-style and press gently with a rolling pin. Roll out to a rectangle measuring about 40 x 20 cm (16 x 8 inches).
6 Fold bottom third up and top third down, keeping the edges straight. Seal edges. Wrap in greaseproof paper and rest in the refrigerator for 30 minutes.
7 Put the pastry on a lightly floured work surface with the folded edges to the sides, then repeat the rolling, folding and resting sequence 5 times.

PATE SUCREE

PREPARATION TIME 10 minutes, plus resting
FREEZING Suitable

Pâte Sucrée is the classic French rich short pastry used for sweet flans.

MAKES 125 G (4 OZ)
- 125 g (4 oz) white plain flour
- pinch of salt
- 50 g (2 oz) butter (at room temperature)

255 CALS/25 G (1 OZ)
- 2 egg yolks
- 50 g (2 oz) caster sugar

1 Sift the flour and salt onto a work surface. Make a well in the centre and add the butter, egg yolks and sugar.
2 Using the fingertips of one hand, pinch and work the sugar, butter and egg yolks together until well blended.
3 Gradually work in all the flour to bind the mixture together. Knead lightly until smooth, then wrap the pastry in clingfilm and leave to rest in a cool place for at least 30 minutes. Roll out as for Shortcrust Pastry (see page 383).

SWEET FLAN PASTRY

PREPARATION TIME 10 minutes, plus resting
FREEZING Suitable

This is made by the same method as shortcrust pastry, but beaten egg is used instead of water.

MAKES 125 G (4 OZ)
- 125 g (4 oz) white plain flour
- pinch of salt
- 75g (3 oz) butter or margarine, chilled and diced

250 CALS/25 G (1 OZ)
- 5 ml (1 tsp) caster sugar
- 1 egg, beaten

1 Sift the flour and salt into a bowl. Rub in the fat until the mixture resembles fine breadcrumbs. Stir in the sugar.
2 Add the egg, stirring with a round-bladed knife until the ingredients begin to stick together.
3 With one hand, form into a firm, smooth dough. Wrap the pastry in clingfilm and rest in a cool place for at least 30 minutes. Roll out as for Shortcrust Pastry (see page 383).

WHOLEMEAL BREAD

PREPARATION TIME 30 minutes, plus rising
COOKING TIME 35 minutes
FREEZING Suitable

MAKES 1 LOAF
- 15 g (1/2 oz) fresh yeast or 7 g sachet (1 1/2 tsp) fast-action dried yeast
- 150 ml (5 fl oz) tepid milk
- 450 g (1 lb) wholemeal plain flour

1700 CALS/LOAF
- 5 ml (1 tsp) salt
- 5 ml (1 tsp) caster sugar
- 25 g (1 oz) butter or margarine
- beaten egg, water or milk for glazing

1 If using fresh yeast, blend with the milk. Mix the flour, salt and sugar in a bowl, and stir in the fast-action dried yeast if using. Rub in the butter. Make a well in centre and pour in the yeast liquid or milk and about 175 ml (6 fl oz) tepid water. Mix to a soft dough.
2 Turn out the dough onto a lightly floured surface and knead for about 10 minutes until smooth and elastic. If using fresh yeast, place in an oiled bowl and cover with oiled clingfilm. Leave to rise until doubled in size and sponge-like.
3 Knock the risen dough down, then knead again on a lightly floured surface for 3-4 minutes until smooth. Flatten the dough to an oblong the length of a 900 g (2 lb) loaf tin but three times as wide. Fold in three, turn over, then place in the lightly greased tin.
4 Cover the dough with oiled clingfilm and leave to rise in a warm place for about 45 minutes, or until the dough has risen to the rim of the tin.
5 Brush with beaten egg, water or milk to glaze. Bake at 220° C (425° F) mark 7 for 20 minutes. Reduce the temperature to 180° C (350° F) mark 4 and remove the bread from the tin. Bake for a further 15 minutes. To test, tap the bottom crust; the bread should sound hollow. Cool on wire rack.

NOTE Dough made with fast-action dried yeast only requires one rising. Glazing with beaten egg produces a deep golden shiny finish; brushing with water gives a crisp crust; milk produces a soft, golden crust.

VARIATION *Soft White Bread:* Use strong white plain flour with 200 ml (7 fl oz) tepid milk and 75 ml (3 fl oz) tepid water.

MAYONNAISE

PREPARATION TIME 10-15 minutes
FREEZING Not suitable

MAKES 150 ML (5 FL OZ)
- *1 egg yolk*
- *2.5 ml (½ tsp) mustard powder or 5 ml (1 tsp) Dijon mustard*
- *2.5 ml (½ tsp) salt*
- *1.25 ml (¼ tsp) pepper*

140 CALS/15 ML (1 TBSP)
- *15 ml (1 tbsp) white wine vinegar or lemon juice*
- *about 150 ml (5 fl oz) oil*

1 Put the egg yolk in a bowl with the mustard, seasoning and 5 ml (1 tsp) of the vinegar or lemon juice. Mix thoroughly.

2 Add the oil drop by drop to begin with, then in a steady stream, whisking constantly, until the sauce is thick and smooth. If it becomes too thick, add a little more vinegar or lemon juice.

3 When all the oil has been added, add the remaining vinegar or lemon juice gradually and mix thoroughly. Store for up to 3 days in the refrigerator.

NOTE Never use eggs straight from the refrigerator as this may result in curdling.

PRESERVING TIPS

Making your own jams, jellies, chutneys and other preserves is one of the most satisfying ways of storing abundant seasonal fruit and vegetables. To achieve the best results, there are certain points about the process you should bear in mind.

PRESERVING EQUIPMENT

If you make a lot of preserves, it's worth investing in a proper preserving pan; the sloping sides help maintain a fast boil and reduce the chances of everything boiling over. Choose a pan made from stainless steel, tin-lined copper or lined aluminium. Don't use unlined aluminium.

If you don't have a preserving pan use a large heavy-based saucepan instead. Note that if you are using a saucepan rather than a preserving pan the preserve will take much longer to reach the setting point owing to the reduced surface area.

For jelly making, you will need a jelly bag for straining the juice from the cooked fruit. Although you can improvise with a large piece of muslin, a jelly bag is a worthwhile investment because it makes things easier. Whatever you use, it should be scalded with boiling water before use. If the jelly bag doesn't have a stand, suspend it from the legs of an upturned chair or stool.

TESTING FOR A SET

Jams, jellies, marmalades and conserves are cooked sufficiently when setting point is reached. There are various tests to determine this. Remove the pan from the heat while you are testing, to prevent overcooking.

Temperature test: The preserve is ready when the temperature registers 105°C (221°F) on a sugar thermometer.

Saucer test: Drop a spoonful of the preserve onto a chilled saucer and leave to cool. Push your finger through the jam; if the surface wrinkles, the preserve is ready.

Flake test: Using a wooden spoon, lift a little of the preserve out of the pan. Let it cool slightly then tip the spoon so that the preserve drops back into the pan; if the drips run together and fall from the spoon in a 'flake' rather than as drips, it is ready.

There is no accurate test for chutneys and pickles, because they are not cooked to a setting point. Instead, be guided by the consistency and cooking time specified in the recipe; they are ready when the mixture is very thick.

POTTING PRESERVES

All preserves should be potted into scrupulously clean containers. Wash jars or bottles in really hot soapy water, rinse thoroughly, then dry in a warm oven. Stand them upside down on a clean tea towel until the preserve is ready. Aim to pour hot jam or marmalade into the jars while they are still warm, to reduce the chances of the glass cracking, and fill them almost to the top. If potting jam, jelly, marmalade or conserve, cover with a waxed disc while the preserve is piping hot or else completely cold, then seal with a dampened clear disc secured with an elastic band. If you seal while the preserve is warm, mould will grow on the surface. Chutneys and pickles are covered in the same way. For long-term storage, cover the jar with a screw top as well.

EATING FOR HEALTH

During the last 20 years or so we have all become more aware that 'we are what we eat', and that a healthy, balanced diet is the cornerstone of a healthy lifestyle – one which will help ensure that we remain fit in later life.

There is no longer any doubt that the food we eat can have an important effect on our health. Conditions such as arthritis, heart disease, and even cancer are now all known to be linked to diet, so the importance of making sure we are getting enough vitamins, minerals, trace elements, essential fatty acids and fibre from the food we eat cannot be stressed enough.

FIVE STEPS TO A HEALTHY DIET
Recent research on healthy eating suggests that following these guidelines would improve our health.
1 Eat at least five portions of fruit and vegetables (in addition to potatoes) a day
2 Reduce total fat intake
3 Increase fibre intake
4 Reduce salt intake
5 Aim to get almost half the daily intake of calories from complex carbohydrates found in starchy foods such as bread, potatoes, rice, pasta and breakfast cereals.

This doesn't mean being condemned to a life of eating lettuce leaves and cottage cheese. It simply means that we need to eat more of some foods – such as fruit and vegetables – and less of others, such as those which contain large amounts of fat and sugar.

Eating a wide variety of foods is very important to ensure that all the nutrients necessary for good health are included in the diet. Foods can be divided into four main groups, and you should try to eat food from each group each day. The key to a healthy diet is to get the balance right.

FRUIT AND VEGETABLES
Basically, the more you eat from this group the better. Most people in the UK need to double the amount they already eat in order to reach the recommended level. Fruit and vegetables are low in fat and calories (the only notable exceptions being avocados and olives). They contain useful amounts of fibre, particularly soluble fibre – a good intake of which can help reduce high blood cholesterol levels. Most fruit and vegetables contain vitamin C,

the richest sources being citrus fruits, kiwi fruit, strawberries and peppers.

The highly coloured fruit and vegetables such as apricots, pumpkin, spinach, red peppers and carrots are a good source of beta carotene, which the body converts into vitamin A. Beta carotene and vitamin C are antioxidant vitamins – a good intake of these will help protect against heart disease and certain types of cancer.

Getting the most from vegetables
Many of the vitamins in fruit and vegetables can easily be destroyed during storage, preparation and cooking. To get the highest nutritional value from fruit and vegetables always try to:
• Buy little and often rather than in huge quantities. Look for firm, shiny-skinned produce, avoid limp wilting greens. Buy from a shop that you know has a quick turnover.
• Store vegetables in a cool dark place, ideally for no more than 3 days.
• Never leave vegetables standing in water before cooking.
• Do not add bicarbonate of soda to the water when cooking vegetables.
• The best way to cook vegetables in order to preserve their vitamins is to use cooking methods that require little or no water as boiling vegetables in large quantities of water can destroy up to 70% of the vitamin C. If you do boil vegetables, keep the water to an absolute minimum, do not add the vegetables until it is boiling and then, once the vegetables are cooked, use the remaining water to make gravy, sauce, soup or stock.
• Cut vegetables into large chunks so less surface area is exposed (vitamin C is lost when cut surfaces come into contact with the air). Keep peeling to a minimum, since the highest concentration of vitamins is found directly under the skin.
• Eat vegetables as soon as you can after they are cooked. Keeping food warm results in more vitamins being lost.

CARBOHYDRATE FOODS
Bread, grains, rice, breakfast cereals, pasta and potatoes come under this heading. They provide fibre, protein, vitamins, (particularly those from the B group) and minerals such as calcium and iron. They are foods to fill up on – and should provide the bulk of our calories. To meet current

healthy eating targets most people need to double their present intake. Many people mistakenly believe that foods from this group are fattening – in fact they're low in fat and those which contain appreciable amouts of fibre will help satisfy the appetite. However, it is worth remembering that if foods from this group are combined with large amounts of fat they will become extremely calorific – 125g (4 oz) boiled potatoes contain only 80 calories compared with the same weight of chipped potatoes which contain 250 calories!

MILK AND DAIRY PRODUCTS

Foods from this group (including cheese, yogurt, fromage frais) are a major source of calcium – essential for strong bones. They also provide protein, vitamins A, D, B1, B2, B6 and B12. Most dairy products also contain large amounts of saturated fat and for this reason they should only be eaten in moderation. Using reduced-fat varieties such as skimmed milk, fromage frais and low-fat cheese can help to control fat intake.

PROTEIN FOODS

This group includes meat, poultry, fish, eggs, nuts and pulses (beans and lentils); foods which provide protein, fat, vitamins and minerals.

Fish is an excellent source of protein and vitamins A and D. Recent studies have shown that people who eat oily fish two or three times a week have a significantly lower rate of heart disease.

Beans and pulses are naturally low in fat and an excellent source of protein, soluble fibre, and vitamins, particularly those from the B group.

Meat provides protein, vitamins and minerals, particularly iron and zinc. It is certainly not necessary to avoid red meat completely in a healthy diet but neither is it necessary to eat meat every day. Always choose the leaner cuts of meat and trim away any visible fat before cooking. Use smaller quantities of meat in stews and casseroles and bulk them out with vegetables or pulses.

Eggs provide protein, vitamin A, vitamin B1, B2, B12 and folic acid. Egg yolks are known to be a rich source of cholesterol; however, it is the amount and type of fat in the diet rather than the level of cholesterol in individual foods which will effect blood cholesterol levels. Because of the risk of salmonella poisoning the Department of Health recommends that dishes containing raw or lightly cooked eggs should be avoided, particularly by young children, the elderly, pregnant women and anyone with an immune deficiency disease.

FATS AND OILS

Small amounts of fat are necessary in our diet to provide essential fatty acids and to allow the absorption of fat-soluble vitamins. Fat also helps to make our food palatable – it gives texture and flavour to foods. However, most people in the UK eat far too much fat. For good health we should aim for a balance between the three different types of fat saturated, monounsaturated and polyunsaturated. Olive oil, peanuts and peanut oil, avocado pears and rape seed oil all contain high levels of monounsaturated fats. Vegetable and seed oils and oily fish provide mainly polyunsaturated fatty acids.

Saturated fatty acids are found predominantly in animal products such as the fat in meat and dairy produce. Diets which contain high levels of saturated fat are known to increase the risks of heart disease and certain types of cancer. However, this does not mean that these foods need to be avoided completely – simply that they should be eaten in moderation.

SUGAR

Like fat, sugar helps to make food palatable and, also like fat, most people eat more of it than is recommended for good health. Sugar provides calories but nothing else in the way of protein, fibre, vitamins or minerals. Contrary to popular belief brown sugar and honey have no nutritional advantage over white sugar although some people prefer the taste. Like fat it's not necessary to avoid sugar completely but it makes good sense to think about the amount of sugar that we eat – it provides 'empty calories' – calories which most people could do without.

SALT

Although sodium is an essential part of all body cells, the average daily intake of salt is 12 times higher than the amount needed. In fact, if we didn't add salt to anything we cooked or ate, our needs would still be met from the small amounts which occur naturally in most foods. Much of the salt we eat is added to foods during cooking or at the table, so one of the easiest ways to reduce salt intake is to stop adding it at the table. An appetite for salty foods is a learned preference. Many people add salt to their food out of habit, often without even tasting the food first. By trying not to add salt to food at the table you can significantly reduce your intake and therefore continue to use small amounts in cooking.

FREEZING

Freezing is an easy and convenient way to preserve fresh food, allowing you to save and store for later use the wealth of seasonal delicacies that are available fresh for only a short time of the year. Whether you freeze ingredients in their basic state or made up into complete dishes, you will find a well-stocked freezer an invaluable help for producing nutritious meals with the minimum of fuss - especially if you also own a microwave for rapid thawing and reheating.

TIPS FOR EFFICIENT FREEZING

• Freeze only food of the best quality. Never freeze food that looks blemished or old.
• Handle the food as little as possible.
• Never put any foods that are still slightly warm into the freezer, as a rise in temperature causes frosting up and deterioration of other foods will result.
• Never freeze more than one tenth of your freezer's capacity in any 24 hours, as this will also cause the internal temperature to rise.
• When freezing large quantities, use the fast-freeze option.
• Pack and seal food with care. If moisture or cold air is allowed to come into contact with the food it will begin to deteriorate. Cross flavouring might also occur.
• Be sure to wrap non-packaged foods well before freezing. Solid foods must be packaged tightly, with as little air as possible. Wrap items in foil or freezer film; ordinary clingfilm is not suitable for the freezer. Freezer film can also be used as a lining for acidic foods which should then be over-wrapped in foil.
• Where possible use square containers to store food in the freezer; they stack better than round ones and therefore waste less space.
• Interleave any items of food that might otherwise stick together with pieces of greaseproof paper, polythene, foil or freezer film.
• When freezing liquids always leave room for expansion, as frozen liquid expands by about one-tenth of its volume and will push the lids off containers that have been overfilled.
• Freeze single and double portions for easy use.
• Keep you freezer as full as possible. If necessary add loaves of bread to fill up spaces. Empty spaces require more energy to keep cool.
• Make sure food is clearly labelled and dated.

Always use up old stocks first. To help you do this it is a good idea to keep a freezer log book, adding items (with the date) as you freeze them and deleting them as they are consumed.
• Do not re-freeze food once it has been thawed, unless it has been subsequently cooked.
• Check your freezer is operating correctly with a freezer thermometer. It should read -18°C (0°F).

FREEZER STORAGE CHART

This chart is a guide to approximate maximum storage times for certain types of food. Always follow the manufacturer's instructions.

VEGETABLES
blanched vegetables (most types) 10-12 months
mushrooms and tomatoes 6-8 months
vegetable purées 6-8 months

FRUIT
fruit in syrup 9-12 months
open frozen fruit 6-8 months
fruit purées 6-8 months
fruit juice 4-6 months

FISH
white fish 6-8 months
oily fish 3-4 months
fish portions 3-4 months
shellfish 2-3 months

MEAT AND POULTRY
beef and lamb 4-6 months
pork and veal 4-6 months
offal 3-4 months
sliced bacon/other cured meat 2-3 months
ham and bacon joints 3-4 months
chicken and turkey 4-6 months
duck and goose 4-6 months
venison 4-6 months
rabbit and game 4-6 months
sausages, sausagemeat 2-3 months
minced beef 3-4 months

PREPARED FOOD
soups and sauces 3 months
stock 6 months
prepared meals 4-6 months
　　if highly seasoned 2-3 months
bread 2-3 months

pastries 3-4 months
cakes 4-6 months

DAIRY PRODUCE
cream 6-8 months
butter (salted) 3-4 months
cheese (hard) 4-6 months
cheese (soft) 3-4 months
ice cream, mousses etc 3-4 months

FREEZER EMERGENCIES

The most common freezer emergency is loss of power. This can be as a result of a power cut or someone inadvertently turning the freezer off. If there is a power cut, don't panic; if you leave the freezer door closed the food should stay frozen for about 30 hours (48 hours in a chest freezer). If possible, wrap the freezer with a blanket to increase insulation.

If you have advance warning of a power cut, turn on the fast-freeze switch, making sure the freezer is full to capacity. Towels or rolled newspaper can be used to fill any gaps.

Do not re-freeze any food you suspect may have begun to thaw.

FREEZING FRESH VEGETABLES

Vegetables can be very successfully frozen, but only if they are really fresh - no more than 12 hours after they were picked. Blanching the vegetables before freezing will help to preserve their colour, flavour and texture.

To blanch vegetables, bring a large pan of water to the boil and immerse the vegetables up to 450 g (1 lb) at a time. Bring back to the boil and keep the vegetables immersed for the required time - delicately textured or leafy vegetables such as spinach, mangetout and sliced courgettes will only need about 10 seconds, while firmer varieties such as broccoli and cauliflower florets, green beans and peas will need to be blanched for 1 minute. Root vegetables like carrots should be sliced and blanched for 2-3 minutes, while whole dense vegetables like globe artichokes and small beetroot need 4-5 minutes.

Once blanched, immediately remove the vegetables and plunge into a bowl of iced water. The blanching water can be used 6-7 times and the iced water refreshed with more ice as necessary. The vegetables can be put into a blanching basket for this part of the operation, but if you do not have one a suitable strainer or a large piece of muslin will do.

FREEZING FRESH FRUIT

First, check that the fruit you wish to freeze is properly ripe and in peak condition, free from any blemishes. Any overripe fruit should be puréed before freezing. With fruits such as apples you will have to cook them first before puréeing, but fruits such as peaches and raspberries can be puréed in their fresh form.

Before freezing the fruit, consider how it will eventually be used. Small fruits which do not need peeling are best frozen as they are; remove any stalks if necessary, and open freeze by spreading them on trays lined with non-stick paper, then transfer to polythene bags. They will not stick together, enabling small quantities to be removed as needed.

Firm fruits and any which have a tendency to discolour should be frozen in a syrup made with 450 g (1 lb) sugar to 1 litre (1³/₄ pints) water and the juice of 1 lemon. The fruits can be left whole, halved or sliced into the cool syrup as appropriate. For fruits such as grapefruit and pineapple omit the lemon juice and substitute any juice from the fruit.

THAWING FROZEN FOOD

Thawing must be done thoroughly and efficiently to ensure food is safe to eat.
- Never leave food to thaw in a warm environment; this is the ideal breeding ground for harmful bacteria. Instead, let the food thaw gradually in the refrigerator or in a cool larder.
- Cover food loosely while thawing.
- Make sure large items such as joints of meat are thoroughly thawed before cooking. The legs of poultry should be able to move freely.
- Dispose of any liquid which seeps from thawing meat and poultry. Do not allow it to come into contact with other food.
- Cook food as soon as possible after it is thawed.
- If thawing frozen food in a microwave, follow the manufacturer's instructions.
- Only use the microwave if you plan to eat or cook the food immediately.

FOOD SAFETY

Everyone knows that eating well-prepared nutritious meals composed of lots of delicious fresh ingredients will keep us strong and healthy. However, food that is not hygienically dealt with – prepared on a dirty work surface, kept for too long or incorrectly stored – can also be our enemy, causing anything from mild stomach upset to chronic food poisoning.

FOOD POISONING

Although food poisoning is rarely life-threatening, it can be very unpleasant and may cause serious illness in vulnerable groups. People who are particularly at risk include:
• Children under 2 years old
• Pregnant women
• Elderly people
• Anyone who is already ill or convalescing
• Those with an impaired immune system
• Anyone taking drugs which suppress their body's natural defences, such as transplant patients, people receiving chemotherapy or taking large doses of steroids.

Correct food storage and hygienic preparation of ingredients is important for the prevention of food poisoning. Following a few simple guidelines will help make your kitchen a safer place for preparing and storing both raw and cooked ingredients.

KITCHEN HYGIENE

• Wash down work surfaces regularly with a mild detergent solution or multi-surface cleaner.
• Use rubber gloves for washing up, so that the water can be hotter than hands can bear. Leaving dishes to drain is more hygienic than drying them with a tea towel.
• Keep raw and cooked foods separate. If possible use different chopping boards and utensils for cooked and raw produce. Wash knives and kitchen utensils in between preparing raw and cooked foods. Never put cooked or ready-to-eat foods onto a surface which has just had raw food on it.
• Always wash your hands before handling food and again between handling different types of food (raw and cooked meat, for example). Cover any cuts with a waterproof plaster.
• Use absorbent kitchen paper to wipe up spills from meat or poultry juices, and dispose of it immediately.
• Keep pets away from work surfaces.

STORAGE

• Always check to see if the manufacturer has given any storage advice. This is important even with familiar foods. As manufacturers have started to remove some of the additives from foods and reduce sugar and salt, storage requirements may have changed.
• Never keep goods beyond their 'use-by' date.
• Keep your cupboards, refrigerator and freezer scrupulously clean.
• Once opened, canned foods should be treated as though fresh. Transfer the contents to a clean container, cover and keep in the refrigerator.
• Transfer dry goods such as sugar, rice and pasta into moisture-proof containers. Old supplies should be used up before new ones are started and containers washed out and dried thoroughly before refilling.

REFRIGERATOR STORAGE

• Use a refrigerator thermometer to check that your refrigerator is operating at the correct temperature, between 1-5°C (34-41°F).
• Always store cooked and raw foods on separate shelves in the refrigerator. Place raw foods at the bottom and cooked foods at the top.
• Never put hot food into the refrigerator as this will cause the internal temperature to rise.
• Avoid overfilling the refrigerator as this restricts the circulation of air and prevents it from working properly. Do not leave the door open longer than necessary. Defrost the refrigerator regularly.

COOKING AND RE-HEATING FOOD

• Remember that to kill any food poisoning bacteria present food needs to reach a temperature of 70°C (158°F) for at least 2 minutes.
• Never eat undercooked pork or poultry.
• Always reheat food until it is 'piping hot', 63°C (145°F) or over. Never re-heat food more than once.
• Cooked food should be cooled as quickly as possible before placing it in the refrigerator or freezer. Small quantities will cool quite quickly but larger quantities should be either divided into smaller portions, or transferred into a container with a large surface area. During warm weather place the container into a bowl of iced water. Do not cover the food while it is cooling. Ensure the food is cooled within 1½ hours.

GLOSSARY

A brief guide to cooking methods, terms and ingredients used in the recipes featured in this book.

Arrowroot Can be used as an alternative to cornflour as a thickening agent in liquids, such as sauces and glazes. Arrowroot gives a clear gloss, unlike cornflour which produces an opaque sauce.

Au gratin Describes a dish which has been coated with sauce, sprinkled with breadcrumbs or cheese and finished by browning under the grill or in the oven. Low-sided gratin dishes are used.

Baking blind The method used for cooking flans and tarts without their fillings.

Baking powder A raising agent consisting of an acid, usually cream of tartar and an alkali, such as bicarbonate of soda, which react to produce carbon dioxide. This expands during baking and makes cakes and breads rise.

Basting Spooning the juices and melted fat over meat, poultry or game during roasting to keep it moist. The term is also used to describe spooning over a marinade.

Beating A method of incorporating air into an ingredient or mixture by agitating it vigorously with a spoon, fork, whisk or electric mixer. Also used to soften ingredients.

Beurre manié Equal parts of flour and butter kneaded together to form a paste. Used for thickening soups, stews and casseroles. It is whisked into the hot liquid a little at a time at the end of cooking.

Blanching Immersing food briefly in boiling water to whiten it, as in sweetbreads, or to remove the skin, such as peaches and tomatoes. Vegetables which are to be frozen and kept for a certain length of time are blanched to destroy enzymes and preserve the colour, flavour and texture.

Bouquet garni Small bunch of herbs - usually a mixture of parsley stems, thyme and a bay leaf - tied in muslin and used to flavour stocks, soups and stews.

Braising A slow cooking method used for cuts of meat, poultry and game which are too tough to roast. It is also good for some vegetables. A pan or casserole with a tight-fitting lid should be used so that little liquid is lost through evaporation.

Brining A method of preserving by immersing food in a salt and water solution.

Brochette Food cooked on a skewer or spit.

Brûlée A French term, literally meaning 'burnt' used to refer to a dish with a crisp coating of caramelized sugar.

Calorie A scientific term used in dietetics to measure the heat and energy producing quality of food.

Canapé Small appetizers, usually served with drinks and often consisting of a topping on a bread or pastry base.

Caramel Substance obtained by heating sugar syrup very slowly to a rich brown colour.

Casserole Strictly speaking, a dish with a tight-fitting lid used for cooking meat and vegetables. Now applied to the food cooked in this way.

Chilling Cooling food without freezing.

Chining Applied to joints of meat, this means severing the rib bones from the backbone by sawing through the ribs close to the spine. This makes them easier to carve into chops or cutlets.

Chorizo A Spanish sausage made of smoked pork and pimiento. It is sold ready cooked.

Clarifying Process of removing sediment or impurities from a food. Butter and dripping may be clarified so that they can be used for frying at higher temperatures.

To clarify butter, heat until melted and all bubbling stops. Remove from the heat and stand until the salt and sediment have sunk to the bottom, then gently pour off the fat, straining it through muslin. Chill and use as required. Clarified butter is also known as ghee.

Clarifying also means to clear a liquid or jelly, such as consommé, usually by adding egg white.

Compote Mixture of fruit stewed in sugar syrup. Served hot or cold.

Couscous Processed semolina in tiny pellets. Staple food in North African countries.

Crackling The crisp skin on roasted pork.

Cream of tartar (tartaric acid) A raising agent which is an ingredient of baking powder and self-raising flour.

Creaming Beating together fat and sugar until the mixture is pale and fluffy and resembles whipped cream in texture and colour. Used in cakes and puddings which contain a high proportion of fat and require the incorporation of a lot of air.

Crêpe French term for a pancake.

Crimping Decorating the edges of a pie, tart or shortbread by pinching it at regular intervals to give a fluted effect.

Croûte A circle or rectangle of fried or toasted bread on which game and some main dishes and savouries are served. The term may also refer to a pastry crust, usually crescent shaped, served with savoury dishes.

Croûtons Small pieces of fried or toasted bread which are served with salads and soup.

Curdle Used to refer to creamed mixtures which have separated when the egg has been beaten in too quickly.

Deglaze To heat stock, wine or other liquid with the cooking juices left in the pan after roasting or sautéeing meat, stirring to dissolve the sediment.

Dredging Sprinkling food with flour, sugar or other powdered coating. Fish and meat are often dredged with flour before frying, while cakes, biscuits and pancakes may be sprinkled with caster or icing sugar after cooking.

Dropping consistency Term used to describe the correct texture of a cake or pudding mixture just before cooking. Test for it by taking a spoonful of the mixture and holding the spoon on its side above the bowl. The mixture should fall of its own accord within 5 seconds.

Dust To sprinkle lightly with flour, cornflour or icing sugar.

Escalope A thin slice of meat such as veal, turkey or pork, cut from the top of the leg.

Fillet A term used for the undercut of a loin of beef, veal, pork or game; boned breasts of birds; boned sides of fish.

Fines herbes Classic French mixture of chopped herbs, ie parsley, tarragon, chives and chervil.

Flambé Flavouring a dish with alcohol, usually brandy or rum, which is then ignited so that the actual alcohol content is burned off.

Folding in Method of combining a whisked or creamed mixture with other ingredients by cutting and folding so that it retains its lightness. Use a large metal spoon.

Frying Method of cooking food in hot fat or oil. There are various methods: shallow-frying in a little fat in a shallow pan; deep-frying where the food is totally immersed in oil; dry-frying in which fatty foods, such as bacon, are cooked in a non-stick pan without extra fat; see also Stir-frying.

Garnish A decoration, usually edible, such as parsley or lemon, which is added to a savoury dish to enhance its appearance.

Gelatine An animal-derived gelling agent sold in powdered form in sachets and as leaf gelatine.

Ghee Clarified butter widely used in Indian cookery.

Glaze A glossy coating given to sweet and savoury dishes to improve their appearance and sometimes flavour. Ingredients for glazes include beaten egg, egg white, milk and syrup.

Griddle A flat, heavy, metal plate used on top of the cooker for cooking scones or for searing savoury ingredients.

Grinding Reducing foods to small particles in a food mill, pestle and mortar, electric grinder or food processor. Foods ground include nuts and spices.

Gut To clean out the inside of a fish, removing all the entrails.

Hanging Leaving meat or game suspended in a cool, dry place to allow air to circulate around it to tenderize the flesh and develop the flavour.

Hulling Removing the calyx from soft fruits, such as strawberries.

Infusing Method of imparting flavour to a liquid. Flavourings, such as aromatic vegetables, herbs, spices etc are added to milk or water, sometimes brought to the boil, then left to soak.

Knead To work dough by pummelling with the heel of the hand.

Knock back To knead a yeast dough for a second time after rising, to ensure an even texture.

Marinate To soak meat, poultry or game in a mixture of oil, wine, vinegar and flavourings to tenderize it and add flavour. The mixture, which is known as a marinade, may also be used to baste the food during cooking.

Mocha A term which has come to mean a blend of chocolate and coffee.

Parboiling A term used to described boiling food for part of its cooking time before finishing it by another method.

Passata A purée of plum tomatoes, used in many Italian dishes. Available ready-made from supermarkets.

Pâte The French word for pastry, familiar in pâte sucrée, a sweet flan pastry.

Pâté A savoury mixture made from minced meat, flaked fish and/or vegetables, usually served as a starter with bread, toast or salad vegetables.

Pectin A naturally occuring substance found in most fruit and some vegetables which is necessary for setting jams and jellies.

Pesto A paste-like sauce made from puréed herbs and oil, used to add flavour to pasta, meat and fish. The classic Italian pesto sauce sold in shops is made from basil, pine nuts, garlic and olive oil.

Piping Forcing cream, icing and other smooth mixtures through a nozzle fitted into the end of a nylon or greaseproof paper piping bag to create a decorative finish.

Pith White lining under the rind of citrus fruit.

Plucking Removing feathers from poultry and game.

Poaching Cooking food gently in liquid at simmering point, so that the surface of the liquid is just trembling.

Prosciutto Italian raw smoked ham.

Purée Fruit, vegetable, meat or fish which has been pounded, sieved or liquidized to a smooth pulp. Purées often form the basis for soups and sauces.

Reducing Fast-boiling a liquid in an uncovered pan to evaporate water and produce a more concentrated flavour.

Rubbing in Method of incorporating fat into flour when a short texture is required. It is used for pastry, cakes, scones and biscuits.

Salsa A tangy sauce made with chopped raw vegetables and sometimes fruit, served with cooked meat and fish.

Sautéeing Cooking food in a small quantity of fat in a sauté pan (a frying pan with straight sides and a wide base), which browns the food quickly.

Scalding Pouring boiling water over food to clean it, loosen hairs or remove the skin. Also the term used for heating milk to just below boiling point, to retard souring or to infuse it with another flavour.

Scoring To cut narrow parallel lines in the surface of food to improve its appearance or help it cook more quickly.

Searing Browning meat quickly in a little hot fat before grilling or roasting.

Seasoned flour Flour mixed with a little salt and pepper for dusting meat and fish before frying.

Seasoning Adding salt, pepper, herbs and spices to a dish to enhance flavour.

Shredding Grating cheese or slicing raw vegetables into very fine pieces or strips.

Sieving Pushing food through a perforated sieve to get a soft, even texture.

Sifting Shaking dry ingredients through a sieve to remove lumps.

Simmering Keeping a liquid just below boiling point.

Skimming Removing froth, scum or fat from the surface of stock, gravy, stews and jam. Use either a skimmer, a spoon or absorbent kitchen paper.

Steaming Cooking food in the steam of rapidly boiling water.

Sterilizing Destroying bacteria in foods by heating.

Stewing Long, slow cooking method where food is placed in liquid which is kept at simmering point. Good for tenderizing tougher cuts of meat.

Stir-frying Quick method of frying in shallow fat. The food must be cut into small, even-sized pieces and moved around constantly until cooked. Stir-fried food is usually cooked in a wok.

Suet Hard fat found around the kidneys in beef or mutton. Sold in packets. Used in pastry and steamed puddings. A vegetarian alternative is available.

Tapenade A Mediterranean paste made from black olives, used for adding flavour to savoury dishes.

Tenderizing Beating raw meat with a spiked mallet or rolling pin to break down the fibres and make it more tender for grilling or frying.

Tepid The term used to describe temperature at approximately blood heat, ie 37°C (98.7°F).

Trussing Tying or skewering into shape before cooking. Applied mainly to poultry and game.

Whipping (whisking) Beating air rapidly into a mixture either with a manual or electric whisk.

Wok Chinese pan used for stir-frying. The food cooks on the sloping sides of the pan as well as in the rounded base.

Zest The coloured outer layer of citrus fruit which contains essential oil.

INDEX